The Way to a Great Country

Population is the most influential factor in social development and economic growth, especially in China. In this book, author Tian Xueyuan provides macro illustrations of the main issues confronting China's population and development in the 21st century and advises on facing population development challenges to sustainable future development. This book explores issues such as the relation between the change of population and consumption, how the age of the working population affects economic structure and transition when above or below the Lewis turning point, the impact of population aging on growth speed and the pension system, how to remove the urban–rural dual structure, how to reform exam-oriented education, and how to balance relations between population, resource, environment, and sustainable growth.

The discussions on population–consumption relations, labor–economy relations, urbanization and rural–urban relations, and beyond provide insightful judgment on and prospects for China's future development. This book is helpful for international audiences to better understand China's population and development challenges and strategies.

Tian Xueyuan is the former director of the Chinese Academy of Social Sciences (CASS) Institute of Population, a CASS research fellow, and a PhD supervisor.

China Perspectives

The China Perspectives series focuses on translating and publishing works by leading Chinese scholars, writing about both global topics and China-related themes. It covers humanities and social sciences, education, media, and psychology, as well as many interdisciplinary themes.

This is the first time any of these books have been published in English for international readers. The series aims to put forward a Chinese perspective, to give insights into cutting-edge academic thinking in China, and to inspire researchers globally.

Titles in sociology currently include:

Social Transformation and Chinese Experience
Peilin Li

China's Low Birth Rate and the Development of Population
Guo Zhigang, Wang Feng, Cai Yong

Petitions and Power
A Story of the Migrants of a Dam in China
Xing Ying

Living Conditions and Targeted Aiding Mechanisms of the Urban Underclass in China
Zhu Li, Mao Feifei

The Way to a Great Country
A Macroscopic View on Chinese Population in the 21st Century
Tian Xueyuan

For more information, please visit www.routledge.com/series/CPH

The Way to a Great Country

A Macroscopic View on Chinese Population in the 21st Century

Tian Xueyuan

Routledge
Taylor & Francis Group
LONDON AND NEW YORK

中国社会科学出版社
CHINA SOCIAL SCIENCES PRESS

This book is published with financial support from the Chinese Fund for the Humanities and Social Sciences.

First published in English 2019
by Routledge
2 Park Square, Milton Park, Abingdon, Oxon OX14 4RN

and by Routledge
605 Third Avenue, New York, NY 10017

First issued in paperback 2020

Routledge is an imprint of the Taylor & Francis Group, an informa business

British Library Cataloguing-in-Publication Data
A catalogue record for this book is available from the British Library

Library of Congress Cataloging-in-Publication Data
Names: Tian, Xueyuan, author.
Title: The way to a great country : a macroscopic view on
Chinese population in the 21st century / Tian Xueyuan.
Other titles: Da guo zhi lu. English
Description: Abingdon, Oxon ; New York, NY : Routledge, 2019. |
Series: China perspectives | Includes index.
Identifiers: LCCN 2018057060 (print) | LCCN 2019004015 (ebook) |
ISBN 9780429447792 (ebook) | ISBN 9781138330603 (hardcover)
Subjects: LCSH: China–Population. | China–Population policy.
Classification: LCC HB3654.A3 (ebook) |
LCC HB3654.A3 T495313 2019 (print) | DDC 304.60951–dc23
LC record available at https://lccn.loc.gov/2018057060

Typeset in Times New Roman
by Newgen Publishing UK

ISBN 13: 978-0-367-72788-8 (pbk)
ISBN 13: 978-1-138-33060-3 (hbk)

Contents

Figures

Tables

Introduction

Invigorating China through Science and Education, a 14-episode TV series made in a joint venture by the National Working Committee of the Young Pioneers of China and China Central Television (CCTV) in 1996, featured in the last episode an award ceremony in the China Hall of Science and Technology that honored the best 10 letters of a competition to write *A Letter to the Future* out of more than 600,000 entries by juveniles nationwide.

Also featured at the ceremony were comments and brief speeches by 10 scholars from the natural and social sciences whose fields were relevant to what the awarded letters touched on. The 10 awarded letters and the 10 speeches were all targeted at 2050, projecting potential changes, development trends, big pictures, and characteristics during the next half century in the fields of interest and how to strive for and contribute to the imagined future. The 10 letters and the speech drafts were then sealed and kept in CCTV's television tower, and will be reopened in 2050 to test the accuracy of the predictions.

I remember my brief speech started with the following:

> Up until now, China is still the biggest country by population in the world. However, as all predictions go, India will pass us in population by the mid-21st century, and when that happens, we will happily hand over the seat of the largest population to them.

Why did I say "happily"? It was based on the "three-step" population strategy: growth control, then zero growth, and finally negative growth to a degree. The strategy was aimed to solve comprehensively the population problems in China, the success of which will mark a vital point on the road to the great revival of the Chinese nation, and the "happily-handing-over-the-seat" will demonstrate that the strategy has been well carried out.

China is a big country, and that is a fact that cannot and should not be avoided. Actually, it is always by comparison to claim something is big or small, much or little, and tall or short, which are all relative and not absolute descriptions. Meanwhile, comparisons can be drawn only between similar objects; for example, the tiger can only be compared with animals such as the elephant, the horse, and the cow, but not with cars or ships. Then how do we compare countries as whole objects with no strings attached?

The answer is to look at each country's size and composition. Many factors make up a country, all of which can be grouped into the three categories of people, wealth, and things. People denotes the size, the health, and the structure of a population, and populations are usually compared by size; wealth, usually material wealth, is often compared with others' in terms of its quantity and value; and things are evaluated in terms of how rich the natural resources are within a country's borders and in territorial seas.

Measured by these standards, China had a population of 1.37462 billion in 2015 (excluding the special districts of Hong Kong and Macao, the region of Taiwan, and the overseas Chinese; the same below), accounting for 18.8% of the world's 7.30219 billion people and ranking first in the world. The land area of China is 9.60 million square kilometers (km^2), accounting for 7.2% of the world's 134.290 million km^2 of land and ranking fourth worldwide; on top of land, China also owns a vast area of water with around 4 million km^2 of seas.

China is rich in natural resources, ranking fourth or fifth worldwide in terms of the total quantity. For comparisons, the largest country by land area in the world is Russia with 17.098 million km^2 of land, which accounts for 12.7% of the world's land; in second place is Canada with 9.9985 million km^2 of land, or 7.4% of the world's land; and in third place is the United States, with 9.832 million km^2 of land, or 7.3% of the world's land.

Now let us take a look at the gross domestic product (GDP). In 2014, the world's total GDP was USD $77.8688 trillion, of which $17.4190 trillion, or 22.4%, was made by the United States, $10.3601 trillion, or 13.3%, by China, and $4.6015 trillion, or 5.9%, by Japan.[1] Compared to 2013, China's GDP share increased by one percentage point, having narrowed its gap with the world's number one, the United States, and further widened its gap with the world's number three, Japan.

Evidently, in terms of the current people, wealth, and things in the world, China ranks first, second, and fourth to fifth, respectively, all of which may position China as a big country, and we are indeed a large developing country. Faced with such a reality, we must take a perspective in accordance with a big country and draw strategies, tactics, directions, and policies comprehensively for the country's economy, politics, science and technology, culture, population, resources, environment, national defense, and foreign affairs.

I did not say all of this to flatter us Chinese, neither did I mean to foster blind arrogance. Quite contrarily, I meant to remind all of us that there is always something small in the bigness and that a big country has its own problems and responsibilities, the essence of which is also captured in a philosophical line in the famous novel *The Dream of Red Mansion* (*Hongloumeng*): "A tall tree catches the wind." Isn't that right? It is true that China is rich in natural resources, but there is a lack of arable lands, water, mineral resources of iron, bronze, and oil, and energy resources; in addition, despite the rapid economic development since the Reform and Opening Up, many problems hinder our further development, such as compromised product quality, extensive development mode, an industrial structure that is still behind, and, particularly prominently, a sharp shortage of resources and environmental pollution that is approaching the limit.

Furthermore, the unprecedented scale of economic growth will no longer be impressive when divided by China's 1.37462 billion people, and the per capita amounts of many resources, economic production, and GDP fall behind many countries and regions, although the total amounts are in top positions. Therefore, we must apprehend the development of a big country and the changes of its people, wealth, and things during development through a dynamic scope. After all, in the socioeconomic development of a country, the things evolve into natural resources, the wealth becomes output resources (production resources), and the people provide human resources, and we must be updated all the time to master all the resources in terms of the directions, speeds, results, and effects of their evolutions so that we may coordinate the people, wealth, and things for sustainable development.

It is well known that economies are not staged by what is produced, but by how products are made and with what means. By this standard, in my opinion, the human history of more than 4 million years so far may be roughly divided into three major stages of handmade tools, mechanical tools, and intelligent tools. The key to differentiating the stages is that the nature of the mainstream tools of production is totally different in different stages.

In the stage of handmade tools that covered primitive, slave, and feudal societies, socioeconomic development relied heavily on natural resources and the advantage of human resources was mostly embodied in the quantities of laborers. This is why the ancient and Middle Age civilizations were usually found in areas with fertile lands, abundant rainfall, moderate climates, and convenient land and water transport. The "Five Cradles of Civilization" – Mesopotamia by the Tigris and Euphrates Rivers, ancient Egypt by the Nile River, ancient India by the Ganges River, China by the Yellow River, and ancient Greece – are all typical examples in this stage. In addition, the Seljuk, Russian, and French empires in the Middle Ages all benefited from the rich natural resources in these areas. However, just as everything in the world keeps changing and developing, the pattern of big countries has never stopped changing either. Two major changes occurred in the world's pattern of big countries after the Industrial Revolution.

The first major change took place right after the Industrial Revolution, during which the industrialized countries leapt ahead of the big countries with ancient civilizations and even started to rob, oppress, and partition those countries, transforming them into colonized or half-colonized poor, weak countries. The Industrial Revolution started in the 1860s and was marked by the replacement of the hand-powered spinning wheel by spinning machinery and that of the hand-driven grinder by steam engines, after which socioeconomic development became dependent on output resources or production resources and those nations that had first industrialized became big countries. The United Kingdom, France, Spain, Portugal, and the Netherlands, as pioneers in industrialization, all occupied vast areas of colonies, and the United Kingdom even won the title of "the empire on which the sun never set." Not surprisingly, they were deemed big countries.

The second major change took place after World War II (WWII), which was backed by political, scientific, and technological factors. In the political background, as determined by the universal law in the natural and human worlds that "action and reaction [are] always equal," the anticolonial movement swept the globe and the peoples of the colonized and half-colonized countries all strived to break away from the colonists and claimed independence, which resulted in several developing countries of considerable sizes. Consequently, the "big countries" that had become big through colonizing other nations were overwhelmed and gradually went back to their original positions in the world; there was no longer "the empire on which the sun never set."

In science and technology, microelectronics pioneered the technological revolution, bringing new technologies in materials, energy, astronomy, and marine environment and biological engineering, and now life sciences, including genetic engineering and cloning technologies, are leading the way. All of these technological advancements have greatly changed people's modes of production, living, thinking, and behaviors.

Under these circumstances, the world's natural, production, human, and social resources have all been reshuffled, and a new pattern of the world's big countries has been laid out. On one hand, the traditional industrialized countries are now transitioning to the postindustrial phase, resulting in new, post-industrial countries and henceforth new developed economies; on the other hand, emerging economies in developing countries have thrived and quickly become countries of considerable impact. With these major changes, China, as the biggest developing country and a typical example of emerging economies, must adapt to these new trends and tides in its development and learn from both positive and negative experiences of world history.

Changes are bound by both external and internal factors. "The road of a big country" for China's development must be founded on the realities of China and approached from the real demands of changes in people, wealth, and things. It is widely known that the Chinese nation, made up of an industrious and brave people, has created a splendid and magnificent culture and is one of the widely acknowledged ancient civilizations. Around the time of the "Qianlong Period of Prosperity" during the Qing Dynasty (1636–1912), it was estimated that the total wealth in China accounted for one-third of the global wealth, leaving all other countries behind by a huge margin.

However, when the Opium War blasted open China's gate that had been closed tightly, China descended into a half-colonized, half-feudal society, falling down from the seat of a big country and staying down for more than a century as a poor country left behind and constantly bullied. During these 100 years, revolutionists never stopped struggling against oppression, with constant efforts to abolish the corrupted rule of the Qing Dynasty from the inside and to expel the imperialist invaders from the outside, which eventually culminated in the establishment of the People's Republic of China in 1949.

The emergence of the new China on the eastern horizon heralded the termination of the old China that was bullied and oppressed and the initiation of the new China's development. However, the road to development was full of bumps, especially during the first 30 years with a highly centralized command economy, when the social economy went through big rises and falls and reached the brink of collapse.

The subsequent 30 years and more after the Reform and Opening Up saw impressive achievements; China has now an image as one of the world's leading big countries and has won back the dignity lost during the period of more than 100 years after 1840. However, how to walk the future road of a big country is still a challenge in front of the 1.4 billion Chinese people, and it is a difficult question that can only be answered through collective wisdom of the whole nation, by absorbing all the essence of human advancement, and in practices.

It is a difficult question because, faced with the largest population in the world, a vast area of lands and seas, an immense economy, and a web of complicated relations including the forces and means of production, the superstructure and the economic base, and domestic and foreign affairs, the answer must provide a bundle of strategies, tactics, and plans that oversee the comprehensive development of a big country. The strategies, tactics, and plans must be decided scientifically and based on a clear recognition of, thorough analysis on, and explicit answers to the most fundamental, simplest questions that follow.

First, what do we want? That is also to ask what our objective and goal are. Our objective is to realize the common prosperity of all the people, and our goal is communism. However, what is communism? There has been no example of it in the world yet, and it is often twisted by impersonators. Despite this, there is no question that we want to establish a society that integrates the material, spiritual, and ecological civilizations. Therefore, "the three civilizations" are our concrete development goal.

Second, what do we have? The three civilizations cannot be bestowed by others, but only made based on the current development level, which thus necessitates the awareness of what we have so that we may employ our advantages and avoid our disadvantages. In addition, what we have is not restricted to material aspects such as people, wealth, and things, but should also include the superstructure and ideologies, which are reflected in various aspects of the population, the economy, the society, the resources, and the environment.

Third, what do we lack? Only when we are fully aware of what we lack can we take appropriate measures. Similarly, what we lack is not restricted to the shortage of people, wealth, and things, but also includes defects and shortages in aspects such as politics, science and technology, thoughts, awareness, ideologies, institutions, and ecological environment so that we may sort out a clear direction and focus for improvement and reforms.

Fourth, what do we use? We need to figure out strategies, tactics, guidelines, policies, and plans with which we may be able to employ our advantages and make up for our disadvantages. With such efforts and the Reform and Opening Up, we may shape our big country into a modern civilization that integrates the three civilizations.

In China's realities, the population is at the heart of the "four whats" listed earlier. With the people-oriented principle, "what we want" is essentially to satisfy the demands of the people for a wonderful life with their pursuits of the three civilizations. In terms of "what we have," as mentioned earlier, although China is rich in natural resources and has become the second biggest economy in the world, its greatest resource is still its population. Therefore, the population and the human resource are particularly important to China's development, which is echoed in the title of this book, *The Way to a Great Country*.

"What we lack" is reflected in the relative shortage of China's natural resources, some of which are in absolute shortage to a degree. As the globe's second largest economy, China is large, but not strong enough, with environmental pollution approaching the limit, and the strategic planning of the "Four-Pronged Comprehensive Strategy" is largely targeted at the disadvantages and shortages in China and how to make up for them.

Even with the advantageous population, there are still disadvantages in that the quantity, the quality, and the structure are not satisfactory, and there are contradictory demands between the population and the development of resources, the environment, the economy, and the society, which calls for a mode of development that is harmonious and sustainable.

"What we use" is essentially the systems and institutions we adopt and the strategies and tactics we employ to push for scientific and sustainable development. We need to be aware that there are both advantages and disadvantages in China's population. In the first half of the golden age of the population's age structure before 2010, the ever-increasing population profits and bonuses highlighted the advantages of the population; in the second half after the Lewis turning point, the population profits and bonuses started to decline and the disadvantages emerged. For the population changes and development, "what we use" is also relevant to the country's development strategies, policies, and plans, which cover all the people in all the social sectors. The key is the principle of people-oriented development so that we will walk a road of a big country that coordinates its population with its resources and the environment and that is in accordance with socioeconomic development.

Advancing with awareness of difficulties is the traditional secret of the Chinese nation that keeps its prolonged livelihood in the matrix of all the nations. As long as we walk in the right direction, persist with sustained efforts, and keep updating reforms, we will shape a road that leads to the great revival of the Chinese nation.

To this end, I made some novel attempts in my 1997 book, *Hardships of a Big Country – Problems in the Population of Current China*, which started from the population, then shifted to the association of the population and socio-economic development, and found unconventional explanations. The book was published by the China Today Publishing House, and the second edition was published a year later. In 2000, the book was translated into Japanese and published by the Shin-yo-sha Publishing House. Three years ago, the Beijing, Social Sciences Academic Press (China) included a new edition of the book in its Library of Academic Works of Social Sciences series, which would be the third edition of the book's Chinese version.

Why did the book, an academic effort, receive so much attention inside and outside China? I believe it was because the book locked up the factor of population – China has the world's largest population – among the three factors – people, wealth, and things – of a big country. Certainly I also provided several viewpoints from independent thinking, which could serve the readers with somewhat valuable analysis, verification, and study.

However, as the author of the book, I had long held something in mind that couldn't be put to rest. Although I published more than 100 papers and several books after *Hardships of a Big Country* was released, in which I further elaborated on the questions posed there, I always felt the studies were fragmented and not systematic. I always hoped for an opportunity to summarize the past 10 to 20 years to reexamine the population problems in China, especially the coordination between population and socioeconomic development, while taking into account international information, economic globalization, and China's comprehensive construction of common prosperity and its goal to become a developed country at a medium level by the mid-21st century, which might result in a new book that supported the development of a big country from a certain perspective. The opportunity finally came.

After we stepped into the 21st century, especially after 2010, when the population of working age passed the Lewis turning point, economic growth showed a sudden deceleration, with the growth rate of GDP decreasing from 10.4% in 2010 to 6.9% in 2015, which, all of a sudden, clarified many complex problems and made possible in-depth explorations in the development of the population and the economic society that had been in debate for years, such as the relationship between population changes in quantity and consumption, between changes in population of working age and employment, between population health and the strategy to reinvigorate China through science and education, between post-demographic transition and the mode of economic development, between urbanization and structural adjustments to industries, between population aging and reforms of old-age social security, between population migration and labor planning, and between population and sustainable development of resources and the environment.

If all these problems could be sufficiently discussed, decisions made based on facts, and answers found that fit the objective laws of development, we would be able to lay out a relatively unobstructed road to the great revival of the Chinese nation in the 21st century. This was the aim of this book as well as my biggest ambition in academic research.

Aside from the introduction, this book has eight chapters, which are briefly introduced in what follows.

The population trend: from increases to decreases

The total size of a population and its consumption are of the best macroscopic value to explore the association of the population and the economy and whether their changes and development are coordinated. The overall changes of the global population, from the 20th to the 21st century, were characterized by the deceleration of the population train that had been in full speed. During the 20th century, the world population increased from 1.65 to 6.115 billion, with an average annual growth rate of 1.32%.

In 2015, the world population reached 7.302 billion, with a decreased growth rate of 1.19% from 2000 to 2015. The average annual growth rate of the 21st century would be 0.44% if the world population were to reach 9.459 billion, as projected in the medium variant by the United Nations (UN), lower than that in the 20th century by 0.88 percentage points.[2] Compared to the world, China has similar changes in population as well as unique characteristics. From 1949 when the new China was founded, the national population increased from 541.67 million to 1.26743 billion in 2000, with an average annual growth rate of 1.68%.

In the 21st century, the national population reached 1.37462 billion in 2015, with the average annual growth rate decreased to 0.54%, a decrease of 1.14 percentage points compared to that in the second half of the 20th century. As projected by the UN's medium variant, China's population will reach 1.46544 billion in 2030, when zero growth will be realized, which leaves the average annual growth rate from 2000 to 2030 at only 0.29%.[3] Negative growth will take place after 2030 and the total population of China will decrease.

In accordance with the decelerated population growth, low consumer spending has been more or less prevalent in China and elsewhere in the world in the 21st century. From the Asian financial crisis at the end of the 20th century, to the U.S. subprime mortgage crisis from 2007 to 2008 and the European debt crisis, worldwide financial and economic crises have manifested their effects on consumption.

Some scholars and social activists tried to understand the crises with various approaches: some took the perspective of the traditional consumption function (consumption is a function of interest), some employed the Keynesian macroeconomic consumption function (demand for capital is dependent on the three factors of population changes, living conditions, and capital technologies), and Kuzenets and Friedman based their study on the theory of consumption demand, which covered consumption expectation and preferences, and concluded with a few factors leading to the crises including several society-intrinsic ones such as population aging. However, no consensus has been formed so far.

In China's attempt to correct the previous theoretical errors at the beginning of the Reform and Opening Up, some erroneous beliefs and their consequences, such as favoring production over consumption, were touched and corrected in practice. However, the corrections were not thorough, and the errors were always waiting for opportunities to come back. The declining consumption-to-GDP ratio since the start of the 21st century was one of the examples of this coming back.

According to statistical data, the ratio was at a normal, although slightly high, level, with an average annual ratio of 62.82% during the early years of the Reform and Opening Up (1978–2000), during which time the ratio was lower than 60.0% for only 6 years and was higher than 60.0% for the other 17, with a peak of 66.36% from 1981 to 1985. In the later years, especially after the turn of the 21st century, except for 2001 and 2002 when the ratios were 62.0% and 61.0%, respectively, the ratio of every year was below 60.0% and it even fell below 50.0% in 2008 and 2010, with an average annual ratio of 52.26% during the whole period. On the contrary, the ratio of investment to GDP during the same period was on the rise. From 2000 to 2014, the consumption-to-GDP ratio decreased from 63.7% to 51.4%, a decrease of 12.3 percentage points, while the investment-to-GDP ratio increased from 33.9% to 45.9%, an increase of 12.0 percentage points.[4] Why did the consumption ratio keep declining, and why was consumer spending always low? How to check the decline and how to reform? My suggestions are given in what follows.

First, reforms should target "the unaffordable." The low consumption was rooted in "the unaffordable," which directly resulted from low incomes and limited purchasing power. From 1979 to 2014, China's GDP increased, on average, by 9.7% annually, but the annual growth rates of the urban disposable income per capita and the rural net income per capita were 7.4% and 7.6%, respectively, lagging behind the growth rate of GDP by 2.3 and 2.1 percentage points, respectively.

In 2014, the GDP per capita reached 46,507 yuan or $7,594, which, according to the classification standards of the World Bank, marked China as a country with a medium-high level of incomes. An obvious boost to consumption would have accompanied the achievement; however, actual consumption declined instead. Apparently, many reasons were hiding behind "the unaffordable," which might include factors such as skewed distribution and a widened income gap. Put in other words, the growth in the urban and rural incomes was "averaged out," and the majority of the population who had low levels of income still saw "the unaffordable." Therefore, the direction and the focus of future reforms should be, one, to reasonably improve the income levels of all the residents as well as the proportion of the primary distribution of income, and, two, to adjust the distribution mechanism so that it tilts in favor of those with low incomes and to increase the progressive tax rates to embody social justice.

Second, reforms should target "the dare not." Many consumers have the desire and can afford to buy commodities, but "dare not" because they feel pressured to save for the future, i.e., medical and post-retirement expenses. To resolve these worries, reforms should be based on reality and build upon the existing system of social welfare and establish a comprehensive system that does not discriminate between urban and rural areas and a corresponding system of social insurance. Now the national health insurance system is going through accelerated reforms, social security for the elderly is trying to establish uniform rules for urban institutes and enterprises, and the new rural social endowment insurance system has been implemented and the implementation has been smoothly carried out toward full coverage in rural areas. Given the current situation, we should summarize lessons and push for a faster advancement to unity, justice, and sustainability.

Third, reforms should target the "nowhere to buy." Some commodities are in high demand among residents, but are hard to get from the market. It is widely known that market competitions and the average rate of profit usually negate shortages of commonly needed commodities on the market; however, when there is a shortage, it is mostly due to problems in the system, which is exactly what happens in the current situation of "nowhere to buy." For example, difficulties in seeking medical treatment (especially in top-level hospitals with good reputations domestically and internationally) and in going to good schools (especially the famous ones) are rooted in the monopolized resource allocation in the medical and education fields. Reforms, therefore, should be directed to break the monopolies and to restore the central role to the market of resource allocation.

Economic new normal meets post-demographic transition

All things change with time, place, and condition. Most studies on the association between population and economic development in the 20th century have been focused on the changes in the number of people. Now that the Chinese population has stepped into the post-demographic transition, especially after the Lewis turning point in 2010, more and more attention has been drawn to the impacts on socioeconomic development exerted by the changes in the working-age population. More theoretical and practical efforts are needed to straighten up the conventional theories of population transition and the course of the post-demographic transition so that demographic studies may accommodate the new normal of the economy.

Demographers, after having established the comprehensive, systematic theory of demographic transition, have continued to study the population pattern with low births, low mortalities, and low growth in recent years, and have performed phased in-depth analyses, which have already borne the characteristics of the post-demographic transition theory. Unfortunately, however, theories are always behind practices. Where will the population transition in the era of low fertility lead us? Experiences in China and internationally have provided us with sufficient room to explore for an answer.

The year 1991 marked the beginning of the post-demographic transition in China when the total fertility rate (TFR) fell below the replacement level of 2.1. I proposed that the post-demographic transition was a specific period between the time when a population's TFR fell below the replacement level and the beginning of the population's zero growth, and that it could be further divided into an early and a late phase. In the early phase, except for the common characteristics of natural changes in population, the golden age – especially the early years of it – of the changes in the structure of the working-age population is of particular importance to socioeconomic development.

Practices and projections have shown that China's post-demographic transition is from 1991 to 2030, and the divide for the early and late phases happens to fall in the middle, in that the early phase is between 1991 and 2010 and the late phase is between 2010 and 2030. In the early phase, the proportion of the working-age population increases, with those between 15 and 64 hitting the peak, 74.5% of the total population, in 2010; in the late phase, the proportion keeps declining, reaching 67.4% in 2030, when the population officially steps out of the "post-golden age."

The golden age is a time full of opportunities for socioeconomic development, and it is characterized by an abundant supply of the working-age population(laborers) and a low proportion of the supported population(the elderly and the young), and thus a low social burden. Put in other words, the golden age with changes in the structure of the working-age population provides "population profits" and "population bonuses." Divided by 2010, the early phase saw increases in the profits and the bonuses, and the late phase has seen and will continue to see decreases. However, decreases are not the same as disappearance, and a current opinion, which argues for the disappearance of China's "population bonuses," is not correct. In fact, there will eventually be disappearance, which won't happen until after 2030, and we are currently in the phase of decreases.

The post-golden age in China coincides with the new normal of the economy. On one hand, the continuously decreasing "population profits" and "population bonuses" are still present to offer opportunities for socioeconomic development; on the other hand, the "profits" and "bonuses" are diminishing and will disappear completely around 2030, when China will step into the age of "population deficit" and "population debt."

Since 2010, the Chinese economy has been in a new normal and economic growth is under huge pressure from downward development, which must be taken calmly. The biggest pressure from the downward economic growth comes from the changes in the working-age population. Analyses of the association between economic growth and employment since the Reform and Opening Up have shown that with every percentage point increase in GDP comes more than 1.3 million jobs and a decrease of 0.5 percentage points in the urban registered unemployment rate.

The GDP growth rate in 2014 was 7.4% and the urban registered unemployment rate was 4.09%. Therefore, if the unemployment rate is to be maintained within 4.5% in 2015, there may be one percentage point decrease in the growth rate of GDP. If 5.0% is set as the upper limit of the unemployment rate, the growth rate of GDP can decrease by two percentage points and it can stay at 5.4% or above safely. However, if the limit is broken, i.e., the unemployment rate rises above 5.0% and the GDP growth rate falls below 5.4%, the economy will run a high risk, threatening social stability, which must be avoided. These results agree with the recommended economic growth rate from the analysis aimed to transform the economic mode, adjust the economic structure, and avoid the middle-income trap. Therefore, the reasonable economic growth rate for the future should be between medium-high and medium, and a moderate and reasonable demand for economic growth is to keep the rate at least at medium and to aim for a medium-high level.

China's economy has been growing at a high speed for a long time, and people have become particularly fond of high speed. However, now that the economy is of an enormous scale with prominent problems of low quality and low efficiency, it is high time to study the economic growth rate and its association with quality and efficiency with more scientific methods and to eradicate the mind-set that values GDP only.

This is not to say that speed does not matter, or that a low speed is better than a high one. This is to say that all development must accommodate reality, and the reality in China now is such that China is already the second largest economy in the world and is closing its gap with the first while economic quality and efficiency, both not high, have become the principal aspect of the social contradiction, which, if not resolved, will hold back China's further healthy development.

Therefore, the biggest challenge now is how to construct healthy, harmonious, and sustainable development. The economic new normal is not just about slowing down the growth but also about continuous improvement in economic quality and efficiency as well. Growth in only speed and quantity can no longer meet the demands of further economic development, and sometimes even hinders it. Now that China's economy is in a new normal, new opportunities are available for comprehensively deepening the reform of the economic system, and an important turning point is ahead where quality and efficiency are improved at the cost of speed and the economy is upgraded and transitioned. A clear vision of how to trade speed for quality and efficiency is needed. Through improvement in quality and efficiency while sacrificing some speed, socioeconomic development will be healthy, harmonious, sustainable, and fine, which will drive the reform to transform the economic mode and structure and to benefit the people.

The acceleration trend in population aging

One of the direct consequences of the post-demographic transition is the deepening of population aging. The 21st century is one with population aging. The population aging in China is fast, profound, and uneven among urban and rural areas, and is distinguished among the aging world by its large scale and unique structure. As socioeconomic development usually lags behind population aging, the contradiction between China's aging population and its not-quite-rich society is prominent.

According to estimations based on the current measures to raise funds for old-age insurance and pension payments, the expenditure on old-age pensions will account for more than 10.0% of GDP in 2029 and more than 29.0% of total salaries, which may very well exceed the safety limit recognized by international society. The only way to solve the problem is to reform the current old-age security mechanism and to find a path on which the old-age insurance system is accommodated with China's conditions and unified across all the sectors.

In February 2014, the *Opinion by the State Council on Establishing a Unified Social Old-Age Endowment System for Urban and Rural Resident* (denoted as Opinion hereafter) was issued. The Opinion summarized the experience of the new rural endowment insurance system and the experience in the trial sites of the social endowment insurance system for urban residents (urban residential insurance) and integrated the two systems into one unified endowment insurance system for urban and rural residents nationwide.

The comprehensive implementation and continuous self-improvement of the new system sought full coverage, basic insurance, flexibility, and sustainability, and paid particular attention to increasing social justice, accommodating population migration, and ensuring sustainability. Now, the reform has already been fully in action to establish the nationwide endowment insurance system centered on individual contributions, supported by employer contributions, and accumulated and complemented in a national fund. However, there are still problems in practice and efforts are needed to raise consensus and to make breakthroughs on the following key aspects.

First, the top-down design of the endowment system must be perfected. The construction of the system for elderly care must be rooted in clear differentiation of the concepts of old-age security, old-age insurance, old-age system, old-age institution, and old-age mechanism, and to establish a reasonable structure with top, middle, and bottom layers.

The top layer is the layer of social security for elderly care, and is composed of three subsystems of social insurance, social welfare, and social support for the elderly (with health insurance and commercial insurance systems on the side and also included in the whole system). The three subsystems form a structure of one torso and two wings: the torso is the social insurance system for the elderly and it is located in the center, dominating and radiating toward the wings; the social welfare and support systems are supplementary to the center, which, although in a supporting role, are particularly important and indispensable to the disadvantaged elderly who are of a highly senior age, sick, or disabled.

The middle layer is the layer of the insurance system made up by families, communities, and care rotations and functioning through the government, employers (enterprises/units), families, and the elderly themselves. The majority of elderly care in this layer is family based, with support from the communities and care rotations.

The bottom layer is the layer that manifests how family-, community-, and care rotation-based elderly care is realized. The majority is composed of families of the elderly, parents, and children, or elderly complex. On the side are community-based care facilities such as nursing homes and elderly centers with medical support and care rotation-based facilities such as daycare centers for the elderly and care rotation plans, which, from the perspective of future development, are promising to some degree.

Second, the "double-dual system" of old-age security must be broken. As a measure to break the dual system in urban and rural areas, the new rural endowment insurance system has already achieved full coverage although many problems remain. More important, improvement must be continuously made to the system so that it truly covers basic needs, maintains full coverage in rural areas, and is sustainable. At the same time, there is another dual system in urban areas that have differential old-age mechanisms for enterprise and institutional employees. Reform has also been started to integrate the urban dual system and has collected valuable experiences in trial sites. The reform is immensely challenging as it has touched on the benefits of various sides, enterprises, institutes, government offices, and individuals, and it must ensure that the benefits of the elderly are truly protected and that at the same time it will not add to the burden of enterprises and institutes.

In my opinion, in order to carry out the reform to integrate the urban dual old-age system and to establish an insurance system with accumulation and complementation that has full coverage, basic insurance, flexibility, and sustainability and can improve social justice, accommodate population migration, and ensure sustainability, the primary task is to persist with the principle of individual contributions, which is the foundation of the new system. This is somewhat similar to as well as different from the current system of "social coordination plus individual accounts."

The new system, as the goal of the reform, emphasizes the importance of individual contributions, which are deposited in personal accounts and will eventually be linked directly to the annuities. In addition, the supporting role of the employer contribution cannot be overlooked, either. The current social endowment system in urban areas has laid a heavy burden on employers, which may be lessened, perhaps to a degree comparable to the employee contribution.

The government and the market must be motivated to play their roles. The government's dominance and function are in its role to write the rules for the endowment system, laws to implement the system, and regulations to supervise it, while the market may play a decisive role in allocating the resources of elderly care so that enterprises, social groups, and individuals are encouraged to invest in elderly care, various types of facilities and industries of elderly care are established, and a corresponding market mechanism is introduced and set up.

Third, the value preservation and increment of the endowment fund must be ensured. The financial market is not at rest all the time, and the social endowment fund is under huge pressures of value preservation and increment. The only way to solve the problem is to reform, and through reforms, the endowment system may be well supervised, embezzlement of the fund may be eliminated through law enforcement, and the system may run independently with clear top-down layers. The empty individual accounts should be filled to a degree, a plan to consolidate a proportion of individual accounts within a certain period of time should be made, and the proportion, the amount, the source of funds, and means of supervising the consolidated accounts must be specified so that the endowment fund may have increased resistance to risk.

The urbanization trend in the migrant agrarian population

In the 65 years after the establishment of the new China, urbanization went through many bumps. Based on my studies of the countries with high-level urbanization and China's unique conditions, I built upon the traditional theory of three-step urbanization of population and proposed a paradigm to stage urbanization and deliberated the standards of staging and how the standards were in agreement with urbanization's s-shaped changes.

The first stage is at the bottom of the s curve with an urbanization rate below 25.0%, the second stage is in the middle flat part of the s curve with an urbanization rate between 25.0% and 65.0%, and the third stage is on the top of the s curve with an urbanization rate over 65.0%. Urbanization is progressive, keeps upgrading, and evolves through the three stages, and is characterized by the following features.

In the first stage, urbanization is slowly made, mainly through small cities and towns; in the second stage, urbanization is on the fast track and population is urbanized mostly in big cities; and in the third stage, urbanization is once more slowed down and lingers around, with the population in the center of big cities intending to move out. The Chinese population, on the contrary, went through three periods of urbanization: the fast growth between 1949 and 1960, the lingering time between 1960 and 1980, and the acceleration phase since 1980. The three periods have crossovers with the three-stage paradigm. When evaluated with the three-stage s-shaped paradigm, China's urbanization was at the bottom of the s curve between 1949 and 1987, with the urbanization rate increased from 10.64% to 25.32%, an increase of 14.68 percentage points, with an average annual growth rate of 0.39 percentage points. It then moved to the middle flat part in 1987, and by 2015, the urbanization rate had increased to 56.10%, an increase of 30.78 percentage points with an average annual growth rate of 1.10 percentage points. The growth rate during this period was 2.82 times that in the first stage.[5]

There was certainty for China's urbanization to move to the fast track as it had accumulated for a long time and its occurrence must have been fast. However, just as violent torrents of waves leave sands behind, the fast-moving urbanization in the 21st century has so far left many problems unsolved. One problem is the prominent contradiction between large walled areas and their small cities that resulted from excessively fast urbanization. After China's urbanization entered the second stage, its average annual growth rate exceeded 1.10 percentage points, a result that was partially caused by human factors, which was particularly prominent when urbanization was used as a measure to boost economic growth. For example, in 2008, 4 trillion yuan was added to investment, and urbanization ranked number one in attracting investment and was the most important engine to drive economic growth. The consequence was the emergence of a series of empty cities and ghost cities, which was a huge waste and great pretension.

A second problem is that the urbanization of people is behind the excessive urbanization of land. From 1990 to 2012, the nationwide area of urban construction lands increased 2.9 fold, from 11,608 km^2 to 45,751 km^2, with an average annual growth rate of 6.4%.[6] In contrast, urban residents during the same period increased only by 1.36 fold, from 301.59 million to 711.82 million, with an average annual growth rate of 4.0%, lower than that of the land area by 2.4 percentage points. The production of steel and cement, which had been heavily overabundant, now found a way of external circulation and was thus absorbed by the excessive urbanization of land and blind expansion of cities.

A third problem is blind expansion of cities and towns, which has hindered the functions of the expanded cities and towns. Excessively fast urbanization with an extensive mode and advanced urbanization of land has directly resulted in expansion to the surrounding areas. The expansion is like making a pita, which is made bigger and bigger, thicker and thicker, heating up "vertical urbanization," and more and more Westernized. For example, after Beijing announced its plan to build a world city, as many as 70 or 80 cities followed suit, among which were quite a few medium-sized cities that did not even understand what a world city really meant. Such blind expansion that aims for bigger, higher, and more Westernized is only focused on the appearance of a city, and the urbanization easily becomes "image projects" to demonstrate officials' work, but it overlooks the real functions of urbanization: that the city should be the center of an area to radiate to and guide its surroundings.

A fourth problem is the bottleneck effect of urbanization resources that has compromised environmental quality. The urbanization that is after speed and scale usually favors speed over efficiency, scale over cost, and input over output, and the extensive, extended mode with habitual high input and high expense has become the norm. As a result, natural resources such as land, water, and energy, which are already scarce, become scarcer, environmental pollution worsens, and development proves unsustainable.

The direction of the reform to solve these problems is after coordinated development of urban and rural areas, which is fundamentally different from the mode of urbanization that is at the cost of rural areas and peasants, as well as the way to prevent reform and urbanization from falling into the "Latin American trap." Specifically, we must first hold on to the realities and face the problems during the current urbanization, and then eliminate the malpractice that builds big walled areas with small cities, more walled areas than cities, or even walled areas without cities.

After all, when stripped of the "urban" part, the concept of urbanization would be without a core and misleading. In terms of connotations of the concept, the lack of an "urban" core would lead cities and towns to be without size control or geographic boundaries and become something that people could arbitrarily decide. In practice, when stripped of the "urban" core, walled areas would stay walled areas, towns would stay towns, and cities would stay cities, and walled areas could exist without any "city" while "cities" could stay so without walled areas. There would be no boundary between natural urbanization and man-made wall building. Cities and towns may even emerge that are built just for the purpose of urbanization, resulting in a bizarre state of reversed urbanization with cities built first and urbanization second.

In addition, new problems in urbanization must be taken seriously, and the peasants who come to live in cities must be granted identities of urban citizens. This is a practical problem of urbanization that must be solved sooner or later, and better sooner than later because the sooner, the larger effect, and vice versa. In China's reality, the most important way to avoid the trap of urbanization seen in Latin America is to help the peasant workers to integrate into city lives, transforming them into new urban residents who are the same as everyone else in the city. Specifically, peasant workers who have come to cities should first be given the same rights and status as city residents.

Many of the barriers for peasant workers to start their own businesses have been recently removed; however, peasant workers still face barriers in many cities, especially big cities and metropolises, in employment, housing purchases, and child education, which may easily marginalize them.

Second, more opportunities in settling down and employment should be provided to peasant workers. After all, shelter and work are the first two demands of peasant workers in cities, and how they are met directly affects how well peasant workers are integrated into city lives. This is also the key to preventing China's urbanization from falling into the Latin American trap, as well as an essential cog in improving urbanization quality.

Currently, as many peasant workers are poorly educated and lack technical training, there is a "lack of peasant workers" in some cities that coexists with a lack of jobs, i.e., employers cannot find eligible workers while many workers cannot find jobs. Therefore, efforts to absorb peasant workers into urban job markets must be repositioned and efforts should be made to offer more jobs to them through ways such as professional training.

Third, a green light should be given to peasant workers to come to and leave cities. Urbanization should not compromise cultivated lands in rural areas and peasant workers who have entered cities to work should still keep in their possession the contracted lands back at their rural homes, at least for a reasonable period of time. Once they cannot survive in cities, they can always go back home and resume their agricultural work, which gives them a certain degree of freedom. For those who have lost their lands, reasonable compensation must be made to them and no expropriation with unequal exchange should be allowed; additionally, these peasants should be properly placed in jobs in cities and guaranteed stable positions and incomes.

Fourth, planning for urban development should include peasant workers. Coordinated development of rural and urban areas requires inclusion of peasant workers' employment, residential houses, child schooling, cultural lives, and community management in city planning. When implementing its plans, a city government should also favor peasant workers and their families in policies so they may share in the development of the city and have faith and desire to integrate into city life, politically, economically, and culturally, helping them to become standard city residents.

Fifth, new village construction must be strengthened in the rural areas where peasants have moved out. A distinguished character of China's urbanization is to bring the countryside on board, pushing for further development of agriculture and new villages, so that urbanization is coordinated in both urban and rural areas. Despite this, many problems have occurred that hinder coordinated development. One prominent problem is that a large population of peasants has entered cities, leaving behind them "an army of March 8, June 1, and September 9" – women, children, and the elderly – in the countryside where there is a sharply imbalanced population in terms of sex and age structures; in addition, with increasing numbers of peasants entering cities and towns, large areas of rural land are deserted or half-deserted with reserved or concentrated homestead lands, or, "hollowed-out lands." This poses a lot of problems such as what is a moderate size of rural land exchanges, how to make sure that land exchanges are all voluntary, and how to supervise the exchanges properly. These problems are closely associated with speedy urbanization, and they must be solved. This book has some proposals for policy making based on practices in some areas and suggestions to comprehensively solve them during the construction of new villages.

The slow-decrease trend in the sex ratio at birth

Ernest Miller Hemingway, an American writer, published a story collection in 1927, *Men without Women*. Almost 90 years have passed now, and some depictions in the title novel have come true: there are nearly 100 million more men than women in Asia! With the largest population in the world, China has attracted widespread attention for its growing sex ratio at birth for quite a while.

Sex ratio at birth is also called the secondary sex ratio by the international community as fetuses already have sexes in wombs and the ratio at this stage is called the primary sex ratio. Sex ratio at birth is based on live births, and the normal range of the ratio is 105±2, i.e., 103–107. China historically had a high, but still normal level of sex ratio at birth until the establishment of the new China. In the first 30 years after the establishment, the ratio decreased a little, even approaching the standard value of 105 in some years.

However, things started to change again after 1980 and the ratio started to climb, exceeded the upper limit of the normal range, kept climbing, and reached 121.21 in 2010, marking China as one of a handful of countries in the world with a high level of sex ratio at birth. The ratio in China declined slightly after 2010 and it was 115.88 in 2014.[7]

An increased sex ratio at birth leads to two problems. One is the imbalanced ratio of men and women and a surplus of men, which delivers a direct blow to marriage and families. Comparison of the two population censuses in 1990 and 2010 showed that the sex ratio of the age group under 19 years old increased from 107.61 to 114.84, an increase of 7.23 points; men exceeded women by 15,868,099 in 1990 and by 22,186,941 in 2010, an increase of 6,318,842 people.

Such an imbalance has already shown its effect on families: the divorce rate increased by 0.8 percentage points, from 0.6% in 1990 to 1.4% in 2010, the average number of family members decreased by 0.86, from 3.96 to 3.1, and the proportion of single-person families increased by 7.8 percentage points, from 6.7% to 14.5%. All these numbers demonstrate the effect of the "surplus men," accumulated due to the ever-increasing sex ratio at birth, on marriage and families.

The other problem is the indirect blow to economic, social, and cultural development by the increased ratio. The most prominent blow is to women's rights, which is especially manifested in the harms sexual offenders cause to women's physical and mental health; there are also blows to the social order, including violations of the laws pertaining to marriage, reproduction, employment, and education; the blow to cultural development is mostly manifested in the compromise of the principle of gender equity, and negative energies carried by crimes such as prostitution may also harm social and cultural development.

To check the increase in the sex ratio at birth, the root of the increases must first be identified, especially the aspect related to population and fertility policies, and effective measures can then be figured out. However, many conflicting views have arisen concerning the root, with some holding that the increases are positively associated with the policies, some partially associated, and others not associated at all. I believe that all views must be based on practices, and the first questions to answer are what concepts or motives dominated the increases, what underlay the formation of the concepts or motives, and what was the key or condition in the 1980s behind the increases then.

Only after we find answers to "the three whats" and their interactions can we have in-depth perception from the surface into the core and reach correct conclusions. In fact, the sharp increases in the ratio since the 1980s are man-made, dominated by people's preference for boys. This has been widely accepted by all scholars with different opinions. Then how was the preference for boys formed? The fundamental reason should be the cost–benefit ratio of raising children.

Boys bring far more benefits to parents than girls, especially in the aspects of continuing the family line and caring for aging parents. Why has the sex ratio at birth kept increasing since the 1980s? The policy advocating for one child per couple, with a particular regulation in rural regions that couples with one girl were allowed to have a second child, was, without question, the key. Another strong line of evidence to prove the conclusion was the sharply increased sex ratio of second-order births. Now we can prescribe the following measure to check the ever-increasing sex ratio: reforms on improving the equity of men and women must be continued from the economic, political, cultural, and social aspects, and it is the most important to eradicate the foundations of the preference for boys in terms of the cost–benefit ratio. Unfortunately, such a reform to tradition is extremely difficult and requires a long time, and it must be validated in practice.

However, although such a fundamental reform is by all means needed to tackle the problem of the high sex ratio at birth, it cannot be taken as the anchor of all the other measures to tackle the problem; after all, faced with the ever-increasing ratio, if it attracts the most attention while all the other measures are less used, we will miss the window to solve the problem, leading to disastrous consequences, no matter how "fundamental" the reform is claimed to be. In fact, what is needed to check the high ratio is to adjust fertility policies and to abolish the sex discriminative regulation that rural families may have a second child if their firstborn is a girl.

As it happened, right at the time when this book was drawing to a conclusion, the Central Committee of the Communist Party of China (CCCPC) announced in its *Planning* on the 13th Five-Year Plan that "all couples [were] allowed to have two children." Hopefully, the ratio will now start to approach the normal range since the barrier that blockaded the channel to decrease the ratio for many years has finally been removed.

Another important measure is to strengthen supervision of fetus sex determination tests for nonmedical reasons and of sex-selective abortion. Currently, there is difficulty in supervising these practices, and to make it worse, a trend has now emerged to do the sex test and abortion overseas, with the addition of "sex-customized" service for fertilization with biological engineering. Therefore, affirmative measures must be taken.

The experiences in fighting corruption may be borrowed in that typical cases can be publicized to educate people with the power of mass media in propaganda and supervision. Centralized investigations may be conducted on fetus sex identification tests for nonmedical reasons and sex-selective abortion, and the defendants, medical staff involved in the cases, and those in the corresponding government units responsible for the cases should be publicly investigated by law to form a strong sphere of shocking power for at least a while so that no one dares to follow suit. Meanwhile, detailed, in-depth efforts should also be made and those who violate the laws may be persuaded to make public speeches. The bottom line is to educate everyone in China that a normal sex ratio at birth is protected by law, and whoever breaks the law will be punished, and people should also be educated to understand fertility laws and to behave lawfully.

The comprehensive-improvement trend in the health of the population

More than 30 years ago, I proposed a population development strategy in the first paper of the research project *China in 2000, China's Population and Employment in 2000*, as the lead researcher and writer. In the paper, I elaborated on the three-in-one strategy, i.e., containing the total number of the population, improving its health, and adjusting its structure should be performed as a whole while the most important task at present was to contain the population size. I emphasized the importance then of containing the total number of the population because what was the most important changed with changes in population. Now the importance has turned to improving the overall health of the population and, especially, to the reasonable adjustment to the population structure.

What is population health? There has been no consensus among the academic field and other sectors in society. Many have chosen to use the word *quality* instead of *health*, and *quality* is usually meant for the original nature of something, but when that something is population, it becomes confusing if the new phrase is taken as the original nature of a population. In my opinion, population health may be comprehended as literacy and excellence combined to generate new denotations and connotations. Literacy is reflected in one's cultural accomplishments in daily life or in one's understanding and employment of knowledge and the resulting behavioral codes, which covers a wide range of aspects such as physical and mental health, virtue, education, culture, and civilization. Excellence measures the absolute mass of an object, which can be generalized to measure how good the object is. Therefore, population health can be interpreted as a combined value of three aspects: the physical value that measures the physical health of a population, the intellectual value that measures the educational, scientific, and technological levels of a population, and the civility value that measures the thoughts, virtues, and culture of a population.

As a matter of fact, all three aspects of population health in China were greatly improved during the more than 60 years since the establishment of the new China; however, where and how fast the improvement was made varied in different periods of time, with, unfortunately, historic regression during the 10 years of the Cultural Revolution. After the Reform and Opening Up, the improvement was accelerated, especially in the intellectual value, which was closely associated with the shift of the country's development to focus on economic advancement.

Now that China's socioeconomic development has entered a whole new historical era guided comprehensively by the "Four-Pronged Comprehensive Strategy" and the "Five Development Concepts," it is time to improve the overall population health. Population health is a whole made up of three parts, with physical health as the basis, intellectual health as the core, and civility as the safeguard. These three things are not separable, but rely on, support, and complement each other. The overall improvement of population health is a demand from the "Four-Pronged Comprehensive Strategy," an indispensable part to reach the goal of overall common prosperity, the deposit of talents for modernizing all of China by the mid-21st century, and the bridge to channel the shift of the strategic focus of population development. A plan should therefore be made at an appropriate time and implemented with effective reform measures so that population health may be improved overall.

The plan must be carried out based on reality and with differentiated focuses of its reform measures; after all, we need a road to reinvigorate China with science and education. The three aspects of population health belong to three different fields and should be taken care of by different government sectors, and the detailed reform directions, demands, and goals are also different, which necessitates individual reform plans and action guides.

From the macroscopic view, system reform should always be the starting point and the focus of all three plans, especially the reform to break the exam-oriented system. In fact, reinvigoration through science and education was proposed quite early after the beginning of the Reform and Opening Up, and this strategy was particularly important in the history of the development of the Chinese nation. To carry out this strategy, science and technology are the key, education is the basis, and it is therefore the primary task to disrupt the exam-oriented system.

It is true that the restoration of the college entrance examination after the "Gang of Four" was put down healed many wounds and corrected many wrongs. However, China has since hugged an education system that is exam-oriented although that was no one's intention. The problems with the system are that books are overemphasized, teachers preach by books, and students give what they've learned from books back to teachers through exams; meanwhile, independent thinking and efforts to employ what has been learned have been overlooked, and, unfortunately, what Qian Xuesen warned of is now happening: "Why haven't there been any outstanding talents? No university is run with a mode that can nurture innovative, creative talents in science and technology." Middle schools that are called "factories of the college entrance examination" and "military camps of the college entrance examination" sprout out continuously, and schools are ranked according to the proportion of the students who enter colleges, especially good ones.

Under such circumstances, nurturing students and the principle of all-around education in virtue, intelligence, health, and aesthetics have become vain words. Similar situations are also present in the research world. The current system of research requires that scholars be promoted to higher ranks only after they have participated in national or provincial research projects as lead or important members, and have published a certain number of papers in prestigious, first-line, or core journals. Numerous efforts are therefore invested in grant applications, projects, paper publishing, and evaluation, as well as applying for awards at various levels.

In contrast, scholars have neglected the topics that they are truly interested and specialized in, and very few efforts are directed there. That is why no outstanding talents have emerged. Similarly, physical education, as a very important aspect of a population's physical health, has been focused on gold medals and championships while the principle of "developing sports, improving health" is ignored. Although socialist values have been strengthened in education in recent years in order to improve the civility of the population, many efforts have not been rewarded well, and they have all been dwarfed by the exam-orientation reality. All of this demonstrates that the exam-oriented education system is to be disrupted not only in efforts to improve the population's intellectual abilities but also in attempts to increase physical strength and civility. The reform should accommodate the three aspects of population health and establish a system and mechanism to boost balanced development of the population in virtue, intelligence, health, and aesthetics and to improve population health overall.

The stepwise-loosening trend in fertility policies

As one of the ancient civilizations, China was not an exception in the prehistoric world where fertility worship was common. In China, fertility worship was passed down, accepted by Ruism, codified for behaviors, and, going through the feudal society for more than 2,000 years, eventually transformed into a reproduction concept and culture that equated children to fortune, both of which were the more, the better, as embodied in the doctrine "there are three ways to be unfilial, the worst of which is to have no heir."

The reproduction concept and culture have also manifested themselves in population and fertility policies, directly and indirectly. The indirect policies, taking over control with time, encourage reproduction through laws and regulations in land, taxation, marriage, families, occupation, household management, and statistics. On the other hand, anti-mainstream voices have always been present, from Han Fei in the Spring and Autumn and the Warring States Periods(770–221 B.C.), who promoted a "small country and population," through Hong Liangji and Wang Shiduo in the Qing Dynasty (A.D. 1636–1912), to the school of sociology that advocated population control in the early 20th century, but none of them was widely accepted in the long history of more than 2,000 years, and they only made ripples or swirls in the torrents of mainstream policies. In fact, the reformists and revolutionists who touched on population problems and policies only made some modifications to the traditional view of population, but failed to break out of the bondage of the tradition that equated children to fortune, and were therefore still under the influence of population pluralism.

The first 30 years after the establishment of the new China saw a mismatch of population and fertility policies with demographic theories. The demographic theories at the time followed the doctrine in economic textbooks in the Soviet Union, i.e., "continuously rapid growth of population is the socialist demographic law," which thus set a flag for policies. The policies, on the other hand, winding their way from ambiguity to explicitness, took steps to eventually specify a goal to control population growth with family planning. However, these 30 years were characteristically rich in political movements and under the influence of these movements, population theories and policies also underwent vigorous changes.

In terms of theories, the school of sociology for population control reemerged in the 1950s, marked by an important work by Mr. Ma Yinchu, *A New Demographic Theory*; however, these theories and propositions for controlling population growth and reproduction were all criticized as the orthodox demographic theory still held that more people brought more laborers and thus faster development. There were no clear population policies in the 1950s, anarchism was prevalent in the mid-late 1960s under the influence of the Cultural Revolution, and the policies aimed to control population growth and associated laws and regulations were finally issued one by one and then escalated in the 1970s.

Exactly under these conditions that the theories were in sharp contrast to the practices, the Third Plenary Session of the 11th CCCPC was held in 1978, during which the guideline to seek truth from facts was once more honored, melting the ice that had frozen scientific development, including the development of demography. Demographic theories were thus corrected and the policy that advocated for one child for each couple was born, setting forth the strict control of population growth.

The correction of demographic theories was aimed at the doctrine, i.e., "continuously rapid growth of population is the socialist demographic law," which was started by picking up the new demographic theory by Ma Yinchu. After all, without reexamining and acknowledging Ma's theory, studies on the relationship between population and socioeconomic development and the nature of population problems would be like a pond of muddy water, with the-more-people-the-better doctrine hiding safely inside, and correcting demographic theoretical errors would be in vain. I was particularly aware of the situation. On August 5, 1979, I published an article in *Guangming Daily*, "It's Time to Pay Respect to Mr. Ma Yinchu's New Demographic Theory," which was met with warm invitations to present my work from institutes in the central government, provinces, autonomous regions and municipalities, universities, research institutes, and some grassroots administrations, and a wave of studies was started on demographic theories and population problems. Right after that, the CCCPC held a discussion seminar on population problems, marking the entrance of China's population policies into a new historical phase.

From late March to early May 1980, the Secretariat of the Central Committee commissioned the General Office of the Central Committee to hold a series of five meetings on population issues. A total of 63 people participated in the meetings, among whom 25 were leaders in the central government including ministers and vice ministers of pertinent departments, 19 scientists in areas such as neuroscience and gynecology and obstetrics, and 19 scholars in social sciences such as demography, economics, and sociology. The meetings were first held in the west wing conference room in Zhongnanhai, then moved to the Great Hall of the People, and in the end, the meeting report was presented to the Secretariat in Qinzheng Hall of Zhongnanhai. Commissioned in the meetings, I was in charge of writing up the report, which was officially finished in early May. Titled *Report on the Demographic Meetings*, it included a theme and five appendices.

The *Report* had three sections. The first section focused on the key to solving China's current population problems: one child per couple. The *Report* summarized the discussions and opinions of those at the meetings, who all agreed that the current population problems in China must be taken seriously and who supported a policy of one child per couple.

The second section focused on the policy of one child per couple. This was the central piece of the *Report*, and elaborations were made with six aspects. The first was about laborers and the dependent population. Some worried that the policy would lead to population aging, a shortage of laborers and soldiers, and increases in the dependent population, which might be as bad as four aged people and two children supported by only two laborers, or the so-called 4:2:1 generational structure. The second aspect was population health. When one child per couple was advocated, it was thought that population health would be highly valued and efforts would be made to promote quality reproduction, nurturing, and education. The third aspect was social security insurance for the elderly. It must be well addressed and managed under the one child per couple policy so that issues such as retirement and elder care would be removed from the public. The fourth aspect was child education. The only child in a family tends to be indulged and spoiled, and attention should be directed to the problem as there would be an increase in the proportion of single children.

In addition, would there be an increase in crime rates? There was no sufficient evidence to answer that question then, but it was a question worth exploring. The fifth aspect was contraception. The *Report* proposed that more studies were needed on contraception to investigate pills and tools that were safer, more reliable, easier, and more effective than what was already available and that male sterilization surgeries should also be promoted. The sixth aspect was the sex ratio. Due to the tradition of continuing family lineages, after the policy was implemented, people might drown or desert newborn girls, which must be taken seriously and prohibited by law. The *Report* elaborated on all six aspects based on the discussions, investigations, and deliberations presented at the meetings, and then came to the final guidelines and conclusions as follows. It is important to effectively check population growth and to call for one child per couple; after issuance of the policy, there will be problems with laborers, population aging, generational relations, and sex ratio with different degrees of severity, and preventative measures should be taken as soon as possible; the policy should effectively control population growth with these problems also under control, i.e., policy making should weigh pros and cons and differentiate between acute and chronic, major and minor problems, and go down the way with more pros and fewer cons and acute and major problems.

One essential question was raised at the meetings, i.e., how long should the one child per couple policy last? If it was to be enforced in the short term, say, three to five years, the effect, if any, would quickly diminish with time; if it was to be enforced in the long term – some proposed 50, even 80 years at the meetings – shortage of laborers and population aging would become particularly prominent and the negative effects they would bring to socio-economic development would be too much for us to handle. Then how long was optimal?

Consensus was finally reached on the span of one generation, or 25 years, with 30 years as the upper limit. This way population growth would be effectively controlled as the fertility rate of one generation was to be contained as well as the number of parents of the next generations, which would effectively check population growth; meanwhile, shortage of laborers and population aging would not be severe and such negative impacts would also be controlled within an affordable range. What was to follow the 25 to 30 years after the one child per couple policy would be further adjustments to the policy and implementation of new ones with softened population control.

The third section was composed of several suggestions such as strengthening advocacy and education, pushing for a family planning law, establishing a population committee, implementing a social insurance system for the elderly, improving public health for women and child education, and landing a reward system for couples with one child.

The implementation and enforcement of the policy achieved the expected effects: the fertility rate in China decreased to below the replacement level in 1991, marking China as a low-fertility country, and population growth was effectively controlled. Meanwhile, the expected problems, such as shortage in labor supply, population aging, ill-structured family generational relations, and imbalanced sex ratio at birth, also emerged. However, we were not well equipped to face these problems, and the expected adjustments to the policy were also absent.

Under these circumstances, I published an article in 2009 in *People's Daily*, "China's Population Policies: Retrospect and Prospect," calling for adjustments to the population policy. In the article, I reminded the public that it was the promise at the time when the policy was being fermented that adjustments would be made, and it was therefore not an impulsive suggestion. I also proposed that adjustments could be made in one or more of the following ways: couples who are both single children may have two children, couples with either party being a single child may have two children, and all may have two but not three children.

Fortunately, the CCCPC stated in the *Decision to Comprehensively Deepen the Reform* that couples with either party being a single child could have two children in 2013, and in 2015, when drafting the 13th Five-Year Plan, allowed all couples to have two children, at which time the long-overdue adjustments to the population policy were finally landed. In my opinion, permitting two children for all couples was a fundamental adjustment to China's population policy. Since then, family planning with Chinese characteristics has embarked on a journey to conform to international practices.

The development trend in ecologic civilization

Where does this book lead readers? It leads readers to sustainable development of population. The human history of more than 4 million years is one with emergence, development, and continuous transformation and upgrades of civilizations. Economies are staged by the nature of the means of production, and when the "four civilizations" are combined with the "three means," handmade tools thus represent primitive and agricultural civilizations, mechanical tools symbolize industrial civilization, and intelligent tools signify modern ecologic civilization.

From the perspective of the rivalry between the two broad systems with humans in control and nature in control, primitive civilization was submissive and adaptive to the nature-controlled system, which dominated the human-controlled system. The underlying reason was primarily the small population in the world.

The first generation of *Homo sapiens* on the earth, who had successfully evolved from apes, was estimated to have approximately 50 million people, and they possessed very primitive tools such as stones and wood sticks. Humans were completely overwhelmed and dominated by nature. The emergence of agricultural civilization broke the monopoly of the nature-controlled system. The population multiplied and there were approximately 750 million people in the world on the eve of the Industrial Revolution in the mid-18th century. Iron tools were prevalent, and humans had leapt in improvement in physical strength, externalization, and materialization. However, handmade tools had their boundaries in advancement, and the human-controlled system was still no match for nature and had to be dominated by it to a large degree.

Then came industrial civilization with development in big machines and industries by leaps and bounds; the means of production and weapons, as the externalized and materialized crystals of human physical strength, grew magically in function. Rockets flew high up, submarines went deep down, and the immense energy generated by nuclear fusion was enough to destroy the earth several times. Proud mankind was finally able to shout out arrogant slogans such as "defeating nature" and "conquering nature," and, in attempts to keep the nature-controlled system under the dominance of the human-controlled one, committed many crimes against nature, which were not beneficial to humans, either. After all, "the action and the reaction are always equal," and this principle applies to both the natural and human worlds; therefore, when humans harmed nature, nature struck back.

Humans destroyed forests, grasslands, lakes, and swamps, transformed them into cultivated lands, ruptured the natural shield of the ecological system, cut down fauna and flora in great numbers, and broke the chain of biodiversity circulation. More alarming, industrialization advanced from all directions, quickly consuming and exhausting the material resources on land and underground, and air, water, and soil pollution exacerbated continuously, threatening mankind's health and survival and making all development unsustainable. Therefore, the call for sustainable development, first proposed at a UN environmental conference, attracted intense attention and won approval around the world, and it was followed by a series of international conferences during which decisions, policies, and propositions to save energy, reduce emission, and protect the environment were made, resulting in protocols, plans, and framework conventions one after another. Awareness has been raised to save resources and protect the environment and more and more countries and regions have started to make strategies for their own sustainable development.

China, with the largest population and the fastest development among developing countries, has also been troubled by resource exhaustion and environmental pollution that accompanied the continuous high-speed growth. Although China was among the first to take action on the promise made at the 1992 UN conference on environment and development and released *China's Agenda 21 – A White Paper of China's Population, Environment, and Development in the 21st Century* in 1994, the principles of which were carefully followed with evident effects in the following 20 years, two big challenges still face socioeconomic development: the resource consumption, albeit already enormous, has yet to reach its peak and the environment is nearing its limit to tolerate any more harms, both of which are caused by the long-term lack of an intensive mode of economic development, the ill-structured economy, and the omnipresent problems of high input, high consumption, high pollution, low output, and low benefits. People have now finally woken up from the indulgence in the high-speed economic development: the human-controlled system is not omnipotent, and only through cooperation with nature can mankind have a future.

Given China's population, resources, environment, economy, and society, how do we build the road to mutually survive, grow, and thrive with nature? In my opinion, the most important is to have confidence in and keep practicing with the belief that honors the ecologic system, values intelligent tools, and finds the moderate population from all perspectives.

The ecologic system must be always respected in practice. Ecologic civilization is the conclusion and consummation of primitive, agricultural, and, in particular, industrial civilizations, and at the same time sheds light on the direction, trend, and characteristics of future civilizations, hence bearing in itself the ultimate code that initiates the future in succession of the past. To respect the ecologic system in practice, we must first shift our value orientation from the single pursuit of development to the harmony of all developments. The value of mankind was originally oriented with survival in primitive civilization when humans took useful materials around them and used them directly as the means of production; in agricultural civilization, the value orientation shifted to development as humans no longer relied on ready-to-eat materials from nature for survival; then with industrial civilization came fundamental changes in production tools, machines and mass industries emerged, market rules were born and became prevalent, and the value orientation again shifted, this time to maximization of output and profit.

In summary, the value of the human world in primitive, agricultural, and industrial civilizations were all oriented with development since only "development" could help people realize their goals and expectations. However, such development assumed an unlimited supply of natural resources and thus completely, or almost completely, ignored the consequences and impacts. In modern ecologic civilization, development still has its seat, but it is the kind of development that is oriented with harmonious advancement of men and nature, men and societies, and men and men based on comprehensive evaluations of causes and consequences. Therefore, the pursuit of maximization of output and production must be stopped and the kind of development that comes at the cost of resources, the environment, the health of the current generation, and the future of the next must be abandoned. After all, when air is heavily polluted and the particulate matter 2.5 (PM 2.5) level rises to IV and V, ripping people's freedom of breathing fresh air, what is the need for GDP and a maximum profit? When our value orientation is changed, there will finally be hope for building ecologic civilization.

Intelligent tools must be valued. Intelligent tools correspond to modern ecologic civilization, the development of which relies on the transition and upgrade from conventional mechanical tools to modern intelligent tools. Machines in mass industries elongated humans' arms and legs and amplified their functions, making humans unprecedentedly powerful in front of nature, instilling in us the ambition to "defeat nature." The subsequent retaliation from nature forced mankind to hold the unlimited seizure from nature and to make an effort to find a development mode that expands from the core of saving on energy and protecting the environment. Expansion and reproduction from the core are based on the transition from output-driven development in the industrial age to capital-driven development in the modern age.

In China, practices to these ends should primarily focus on the following aspects: transition from increasing the amount of labor to improving the efficiency of production; from the extensive mode with high input, high consumption, high pollution, low output, and low benefits to the intensive mode with low input, low consumption, low pollution, high output, and high benefits; and from low- to medium-end to medium- to high-end quality and structures of products to drive further development.

In addition, the technology revolution after WWII pioneered by microelectronics has now progressed to a whole new stage centered on life sciences; accordingly, the Internet industry based on microelectronic technologies has now been outgrown by the new mode of "Internet plus," transforming the intelligent tools to a whole new level. New technologies and ideas have empowered the means of production and strengthened the human-controlled system while at the same time providing scientific ideas and technological means for humans to respect, accommodate, and cooperate with nature; we are now better equipped to learn the way nature runs, possess more scientific methodologies and applicable technologies, and boost further development that is in accordance with, coordinated with, and adaptive to nature. Finally, valuing intelligent tools and accelerating the transition from mechanical to intelligent tools are indispensable if we are to push the population down the path of sustainable development.

A moderate population should be decided in a comprehensive way. For a population to develop in a sustainable manner, strategies, tactics, and policies should be based on the population itself as well as its resources, environment, economy, and society. A proper population strategy is particularly important to China, which will have a large population for a long time. I have always persisted with a three-step strategy.

The first step is to control the size of the population, improve its health, and adjust its structure, with size control being the most important. The destination of this step is to bring the fertility rate below the replacement level so that the population will complete the transition from high births, low mortalities, and high growth to low births, low mortalities, and low growth.

The second step is to combine control, improvement, and adjustment to stepwise shift the population policy from size control to health improvement and particularly structural adjustment after the fertility rate is below the replacement level and the population has zero growth, which is also known as the "post-demographic transition." During this phase, population changes should be in concert with socioeconomic development, resources, and the environment to facilitate the enforcement of sustainable development.

The third step is to make a decision on what is a moderate population for China in a comprehensive way since the population will have decreased somewhat by this time due to momentum after it has reached zero growth, and the decision should be made based on the economic, social, resource, and environmental conditions at the time. An all-around moderate population does not only have a moderate number of people, but is also of high quality with a reasonable structure of age, sex, and urban–rural and regional distributions and in accordance with resource, environment, economic, and social development, and it is thus an essential component of the strategy that supports the sustainable development of China. China's fertility rate fell below the replacement level in 1991, marking the population strategy finishing the first step and starting the second. The second step will continue until 2030, when the population is estimated to reach zero growth, after which the third step will be started and will take an even longer time to complete.

We are now taking the second step of the population strategy, and the central piece is always improving population health and adjusting the distribution by age, sex, urban or rural area, and region. There is currently controversy, or we may even call it fundamental disagreement, on whether size control is still needed at the current step. With the shift of fertility policies and strategic focus becoming clearer and clearer, a voice has been raised, not only in China but also elsewhere in the world, that opposes the shift, vowing to safeguard the laurel of the "largest population" and calling for total abandonment of family planning, with some even going so far as to revile and insult those in favor of population control in the name of "speaking out for the people."

In this book, theories and practices are combined, and so are senses and sensibilities, and in-depth analysis is performed to describe whether the population is too big or too small for China, whether populism or Puritanism should be practiced, and whether the basic state policy of family planning should be totally abandoned. The theoretical explanations in this book restore the population as laborers and, in accordance with consumption, the reality of China's current 1.375 billion people and future prospects, makes the following illustrations: China's population density (number of people per square kilometer) in 2014 was 145, 258.9% of the world average; the per capita area of arable lands was 33.5% of the world average, the per capita area of forest 13.0%, the per capita area of grassland 50.0%, the per capita storage of fresh water 31.9%, the per capita area of territorial water 10.0%, and GDP per capita (in USD) 70.3%.

As for fossil fuels such as oil and natural gas and important mineral resources such as iron, manganese, and copper, the total and per capita amounts have all decreased greatly, leading to a sharp shortage of resources, and we are now heavily dependent on imports. In addition, air, water, soil, and noise pollution is still on the rise, approaching the limit of the environment.[8] In fact, it has long been difficult for the economy to transition and the economic structure to be adjusted; although the difficulty has mostly been caused by the economic system itself, the large population has also been responsible in that the large population and its large number of laborers have pressured the forces of production.

For example, "to ensure growth is to ensure employment," which is also to say that to ensure employment, it is necessary to have a high speed of growth, which in turn hinders the economic transition, structural adjustment, and reform to better people's lives. Therefore, it is still necessary and even a *sine qua non* to reasonably control population growth in the current, second phase, which is focused on the transition from size control to health improvement of the population no matter whether it is from the perspective of satisfying people's expectations for happy lives and improving the happiness index of the people or from the perspective of accommodating the current need of economic transition, structural adjustment, and health improvement at the cost of quantity and benefits.

In fact, to reasonably control the size of the population is a demand not only from the population development strategy but also from the strategy to reinvigorate China with science, education, and sustainable development. However, we must not forget that the control needs to be at a reasonable pace so that decreases in the birth and growth rates will be in concert with improvement in the quality and, particularly, with the structural adjustment to the population age and sex compositions. Eventually, it will facilitate but not hinder the sustainable development of the population, the resources, the environment, the economy, and the society.

Notes

1 *China Statistical Yearbook 2015*, Beijing, China Statistics Press, 2015, p. 964.
2 United Nations, *World Population Prospects: The 2008 Revision*, New York, United Nations, 2009, p. 48.
3 Tian, Xueyuan, et al., *Study on the Development Strategy of China's Population in the 21st Century*, Social Sciences Academic Press, 2007, pp. 443–444.
4 *China Statistical Yearbook 2015*, p. 77.
5 *Statistical Communiqué of National Economy and Social Development in 2015 of People's Republic of China*, Huaxia Jingwei web, www.huaxia.com/xw/dlxw/2016/03/4745100.html.
6 *China Statistical Yearbook 2013*, China Economic Publishing House, 2013, p. 421.
7 "Consecutive 6 Declines in China's Sex Ratio at Birth," *Daily Report*, February 4, 2015.
8 *China Statistical Yearbook 2015*, pp. 961–966; Zhang, Weiqing, Sun, Wensheng, and Xie, Zhenhua, eds., *Selected Works for Cadres on Population, Resources, Environment and Sustainable Development*, Zhejiang People's Publishing House, 2004, pp. 171–187.

1 The population trend – from increases to decreases

Exploring the path of moderate growth with green consumption

Material production is the foundation of the survival and development of human society. With advancement in technologies and societies come changes in the means of production, but not in production itself. Material production is composed of four stages: production, exchange, distribution, and consumption. Production is the starting point that determines and dominates the rest; exchange and distribution stand in between production and consumption to bridge them; and consumption is the destination of the whole sequence, consummating production and creating new demands to drive further development.

Population, as a reproduction process of generational continuity, comprises the three levels of quantity, quality, and structure. Quantity is the most representative of the whole population and attracts the most attention. Therefore, the total population and consumption are the most informative on the macro level in studies on the relation between population and economies and whether their changes and development are coordinated.

The general trend in the population in the 21st century

Twenty years ago, when I looked at the population changes back in the 20th century and into the 21st after finishing the book *Hardships of a Big Country*, I sighed at the extreme contrast of the two centuries: the 100 years of the 20th century saw population explosion while the 21st century would witness population aging. Why did population experience growth and then decline? After all, the world population has not recently been subjected to dramatic events of Earth itself or to social catastrophes such as wars and plagues. On the contrary, it has followed its own path of changes and development, which cannot be countered or altered as it is a law of nature. To study population changes and development, we must look at a span of time that is long enough, and comparing the two centuries certainly meets this demand.

The deceleration trend in the world population

My previous book, *Hardships of a Big Country: A Macroscopic View on the Chinese Population in the 20th Century*, describes the population change from the dawn of time to the end of the 20th century as “a train of population slowly setting off” and gradually “accelerating to a high speed.” “The train set off slowly” because the world population grew extremely slowly in the first 4 million years of human history and reached 1 billion only in 1830, staying in a state of simple reproduction with no growth at all in many years. This was due to many reasons.

Naturally, Earth went through the Little Ice Age for 500 years starting from the 13th century, and the resulting cold and detrimental climate led to reduction in agricultural production in many regions, especially in Europe, while natural disasters caused many people to die in famine. Socially and in public health, wars and epidemic diseases such as tuberculosis, cholera, malaria, and smallpox all led to large-scale deaths around the world, and the Black Death alone, for example, raged across Europe and killed more than 20.0% of its population. The most fundamental of all, however, lay in the low level of the productive forces in agrarian and other preceding societies: heavy exploitation and repression were prevalent in slave and feudal societies in which the populations were in a primitive or semi-primitive state with high births, high mortalities, and low growth, thus a turn to high births, low mortalities, and high growth was impossible.

After the Industrial Revolution in the mid-18th century, the productive forces of human society exploded unprecedentedly, capital became substantially capable to absorb laborers, and the production of population entered a brand-new historical era. The train of population growth now started to speed, which brought the world population to a record high of 1 billion in 1830.

After that, the population growth further accelerated, doubling in 100 years to reach 2 billion in 1930, with an average annual growth rate of 0.7%. The production of the next 1 billion people took only 30 years, and the world population reached 3 billion in 1960 at an average annual growth rate of 1.4%. The fourth billion took 15 years, and there were more than 4 billion people in 1975 at an average annual growth rate of 1.9%. The fifth billion took only 12 years, bringing the population to 5 billion in 1987 at an annual growth rate of nearly 1.9%. The sixth billion also took 12 years, with 6 billion people in 1999 but at a decreased annual growth rate of 1.5%. The seventh billion likewise took 12 years with 7 billion in 2011 at a further decreased growth rate of 1.3%. According to the UN medium projection for the world population, it will take a slightly longer time, 14 years, to make the increase of the eighth billion, and the world population will reach 8 billion in 2025 at an even lower annual growth rate of 1.0%, while the ninth billion will take as long as 21 years, with the population reaching 9 billion in 2046 at a still lower annual rate of 0.6%. According to some institutions and scholars, the world will have to wait as long as more than half a century for the tenth billion to arrive when the population reaches 10 billion at the end of the 21st century, while during the second half of the century, the average annual growth rate will be as low as 0.2%, bringing the population very close to zero growth.[1]

In summary, from 1830, when the world population reached 1 billion, until the end of the 21st century, the elapsed time to achieve every additional billion people experienced decreased and then increased, or the process accelerated and then decelerated. The interval began with 100 years and narrowed to 30, then to 15 and finally to 12 years; after the turn of the 21st century, the interval began to widen, from 12 years to 14, 21, then 54, and the population will possibly reach or get very close to zero growth.

It is widely known that a population resembles a savings account with principal and interest: the amount of money in a savings account increases exponentially according to the interest rate, and so does a population (at a growth rate). Therefore, the potential energy of a population at a specific time with a specific situation is particularly important. The deceleration of population growth in the 21st century is actually rooted in the continuous decline in fertility and birth rates.

According to the UN Population Division in the Department of Economic and Social Affairs, the world fertility and birth rates started to decline in the mid-20th century. From 1950 to 2000, the world's TFR decreased by 42.7%, from 4.92 to 2.82; the birth rate fell by 147 basis points, from 37.2‰ to 22.5‰; and the population growth rate lowered by 41 basis points, from 1.77% to 1.36%. In addition, the changes in the world fertility, birth, and growth rates, be they increases or decreases, were all mostly due to changes in developing countries.

In the years when the aforementioned decreases were observed, the three rates in developing countries all considerably decreased, with the TFR decreasing by 48.3%, from 6.00 to 3.10, a reduction that was larger than the world level by 5.6 percentage points; the birth rate falling by 186 basis points, from 44.0‰ to 25.4‰, 39 basis points over the world level; and the growth rate declining by 41 basis points, from 2.03% to 1.62%, which was the same as the world level.

Furthermore, developing countries account for a large proportion of the world population, and it has been on the rise. In 1950, 1.71732 billion people lived in developing countries, which was 67.9% of the world population of 2.52935 billion. In 2000, the former number grew to 4.92040 billion, accounting for 80.5% of the world's 6.11537 billion people, an increase of 12.6 percentage points.

During the same time, the population proportion of developed countries decreased from 32.1% to 19.5%, a reduction of 12.6 percentage points. In other words, the rapid growth of the world population in the 20th century was driven by the explosive growth of the population in developing countries, while the population growth in developed countries showed a trend of continuous decline with rapid decreases in the proportion. Stepping into the 21st century, the world has seen continuous changes in population and, again, the major changes were and will be decided by the birth, death, and growth rates in developing countries while the contribution by developed countries will be further weakened (Figures 1.1 and 1.2).[2]

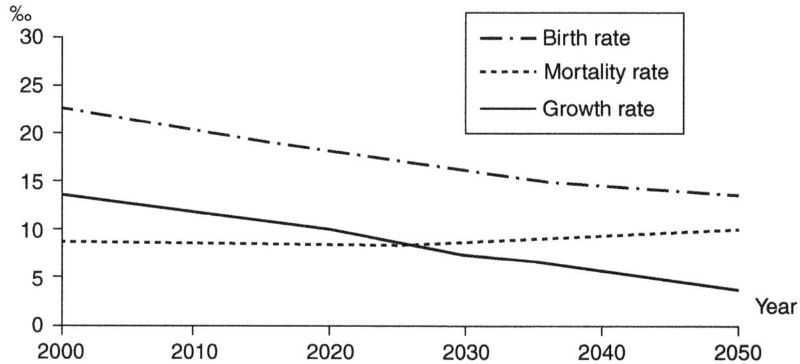

Figure 1.1 Projected natural changes of the world population, 2000–2050.

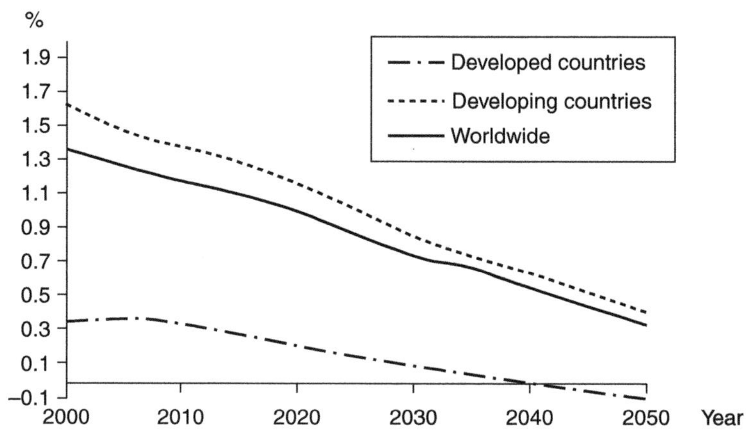

Figure 1.2 Projected growth rates of the world population, 2000–2050.

Figure 1.2 shows the population trends in developed and developing countries as well as the whole world in the first half of the 21st century. As depicted in the figure, the imbalance between the populations in developed and developing countries will further worsen, and the world population will have a new pattern of distribution. In 2015, there were 7.30219 billion people worldwide, with 1.25485 billion, or 17.18%, in developed countries and 6.04734 billion, or 82.82%, in developing countries.

In 2050, the world will have 9.14998 billion people, with 1.27524 billion, or 13.94%, in developed countries and 7.87474 billion, or 86.06%, in developing countries. That is also to say that among the newly increased 1.84779 billion people in the next 35 years, only 20.39 million will be in developed countries, accounting for just 1.10% of the total increase; meanwhile, developing countries will have an increase of 1.82740 billion people, 98.90% of the total increase. Developed countries all together will reach zero population growth between 2035 and 2040, after which time their population will grow negatively with a net reduction of 7.04 million people in 2050 compared to 2040 and 7.77 million compared to 2035. The zero growth and the subsequent negative growth starting in the late 2030s, with a growth rate of −0.07% in 2050, is only the tip of the iceberg of the population decline in developed countries.

The more rapidly the population in developed countries declines, the lower its proportion of the world population; as a result, its impact on the world's growing population will decrease and can be neglected. In contrast, what is really important is the fertility, birth, and growth rates in developing countries, which, when decreasing, will also lead the world population growth to decelerate. From 2010 to 2015, for example, the growth rate in developing countries declined to 1.28%, and it will rapidly decline to 0.41% in 2050. The former brought the world growth rate to 1.11% and the latter will bring it to 0.34%.

According to several international institutions, at the end of the 21st century, the world population will reach nearly 10 billion, i.e., another 2.7 billion to be added to the current population, and possibly zero growth with the same numbers of addition and reduction. It is undoubtful that, with developed countries reaching zero growth and negative growth in the late 2030s, the addition of 2.7 billion people, together with those needed to compensate for the loss due to the negative growth of developed countries, will be fulfilled by developing countries.

The decrease trend in China's population

The Industrial Revolution empowered the population growth that brought the world population from 770 million in 1750 to 1.241 billion in 1850, an increase of 471 million people, or 61.17%, in 100 years, with an average annual growth rate of 0.48%. However, such impressive growth was dwarfed by that of China during the same period. The population growth in China was not empowered by the Industrial Revolution; as a matter of fact, Chinese history had never been dominated by the Industrial Revolution or anything like it. Yet the Chinese population nonetheless departed in advance (before the Industrial Revolution): it doubled twice in number during the 100 years from 1750 to 1850, with a net increase of more than 300 million, an unprecedented growth rate.

Why did the Chinese population "depart in advance"? Economists, sociologists, demographers, statisticians, nutritionists, and historians all provided their own answers. Some argued that food abundance, due to the enlarged areas of rice cultivation during that time, had led to the large-scale population growth. Some favored the national conditions of peace and prosperity in that there were basically no wars during the reigns of Emperors Kangxi, Yongzheng, and Qianlong, which ensured a peaceful and stable environment in which the population could procreate. Some believed that the policy adjustments were the reason in that the replacement of the poll tax with the bill of *Tanding Rumu* (that the total amount of taxes due in each county is divided to all the lands in the county to be collected as land taxes) during the reign of Emperor Kangxi stimulated the population growth greatly. Some found that improvement to the statistical data was the answer since there had been severe underreporting of births before the abolishment of poll taxes, which became much better after the abolishment, leading to increases in the reported population data. Others credited medical advancements at the time in that treatment of many diseases, primarily through traditional Chinese medicine and medical means, advanced greatly, leading to improvement in people's health and life expectancy, despite inability to effectively prevent and cure some epidemic diseases.[3]

Interestingly, history always presents astonishing similarities. Just like the advance departure of the Chinese population, fundamental changes happened to the Chinese population in the 1980s. The fertility, birth, and growth rates in China have kept declining since the 1980s, leading to fundamental structural transitions of the population; meanwhile, the anticipation of timely adjustment to the one-child fertility policy after 25 years of implementation was not met and the belated adjustments, when they finally came, were not strong enough, both of which led to an accelerated decrease in China's population growth in the 21st century.

Projections have shown that the Chinese population will reach 1.465 billion around 2030, at which time zero growth of the population will be achieved. This is 5 to 10 years earlier than the predicted time point when developed countries will reach zero growth, and more than half a century earlier than the whole world, which is predicted to reach zero growth by the end of the 21st century. Now it seems possible that China has a dual role to play in leading population changes: the role of departing in advance from the mid-18th to the mid-19th century, and the role of first reaching zero growth and negative growth in the 21st century through declining in advance (Figure 1.3).

Many attempts from Chinese and international scholars have projected possible changes of the Chinese population in the 21st century, and they all show similar trends despite differences in certain details. My projections, including high, medium, and low variants, have the following tracks and results.

In the high variant, China's fertility rate rises gradually and becomes relatively stable after reaching the replacement level. The TFR is projected to be 1.90 on average from 2000 to 2005, 2.00 from 2005 to 2010, 2.13 from 2010 to 2020, and 2.15 from 2020 to 2050, which puts the national population (excluding the region of Taiwan and the special districts of Hong Kong and Macau, as is the case in what follows) at 1.375 billion in 2010, 1.490 billion in 2020, 1.548 billion in 2030, 1.585 billion in 2040, and 1.605 billion in 2050.

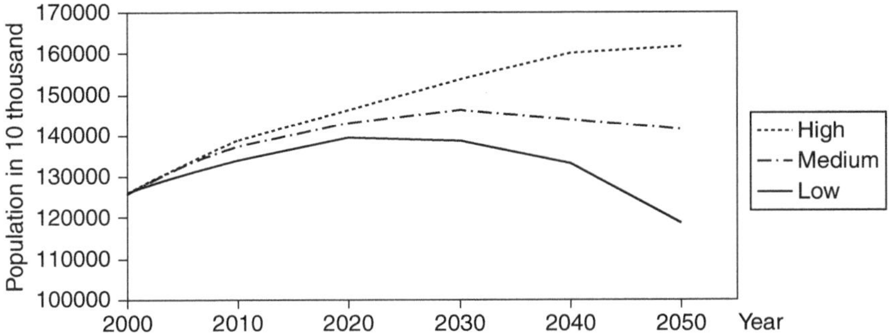

Figure 1.3 High, medium, and low projections of the Chinese population, 2000–2050.

By this time, the population growth will not have come to a complete stop, but will have stabilized with some characteristics of a stationary population.

In the medium variant, the fertility rate is relatively stable and is maintained at a level that is slightly higher than the current value after increasing for a short time. The projected TFR is, on average, 1.75 from 2000 to 2005, 1.80 from 2005 to 2010, 1.83 from 2010 to 2020, and 1.80 from 2020 to 2050, while the national population is 1.360 billion in 2010 and 1.444 billion in 2020, and reaches its peak of 1.465 billion in 2030, after which the population will decrease slowly, to 1.451 billion in 2040 and 1.402 billion in 2050. If the TFR is to be kept at 1.80, the national population will decrease to 1.024 billion in 2100.

In the low variant, the fertility rate is slightly lower than the current level and the projected TFR is, on average, 1.65 from 2000 to 2005, 1.56 from 2005 to 2010, 1.44 from 2010 to 2020, and 1.32 from 2020 to 2050, with the national population at 1.343 billion in 2010 and 1.386 billion in 2020, reaching its peak of 1.378 billion in 2021, after which the population will decrease gradually, to 1.367 billion in 2030, 1.302 billion in 2040, and 1.192 billion in 2050. If the TFR is to be kept at 1.32, the national population will decrease to 556 million in 2100.[4]

These projections are similar to the UN's estimation of China's population changes, the high, medium, and low variants of which are shown in Table 1.1.

For example, the medium variants of both my and the UN's projections have shown that zero growth of the Chinese population will be in 2030 although the UN's variant projected the total population at the time to be 30 million fewer than mine, but 15 million more in 2050, which are both small differences. In terms of other indicators such as the populations and the proportions of the young, the working age, and the elderly, birth, death, and natural growth rates are all similar. In fact, most projections made in China concluded with a trend similar to mine and the UN's, with a certain degree of variance here and there. The most important message is that, after the past 30

Table 1.1 Projected populations in China by the United Nations, 2000–2050 (in ten thousands)

Year	*2000*	*2010*	*2020*	*2030*	*2040*	*2050*
High projection	126,695	135,415	146,348	153,741	160,205	161,754
Medium projection	126,695	135,415	143,116	146,247	144,029	141,705
Low projection	126,695	135,415	139,683	138,780	133,387	123,696

Source: United Nations, *World Population Prospect: The 2008 Revision*, New York, United Nations, 2009, pp. 184–185.

to 40 years of population control, we can now more or less see the day when zero growth of the population is reached, a day that will come to China earlier than it will to developed countries and even more than half a century earlier than it will across the world and other developing countries.

The sluggish trend in consumption after the turn of the 21st century

The population growth around the world has slowed down and the trend is even more prominent in China, with the Chinese population approaching zero growth; accompanying the low growth of the population is sluggish consumption. In fact, population changes are slow and progressive, and their impact on socioeconomic development is usually barely detectable in the short term; however, when observation is made in a period of time that is long enough, the impact, including the fermented effect that has been progressively exerted on consumption, becomes increasingly evident.

The worldwide sluggish consumption

Financial crises exploded like rolling balls

Low consumer spending is closely associated with macroeconomic situations. The world economy started to shake violently toward the end of the 20th century. First came the 1997 Asian financial crisis that unveiled its disastrous effect in Thailand, and the Thai government announced its intention to replace the fixed exchange rate with a floating one on July 2, when the Thai baht immediately devalued by 17.0% relative to the U.S. dollar.

Subsequently, Malaysia, Singapore, Japan, South Korea, Indonesia, and the Philippines consecutively announced the devaluation of their respective currencies, which kept dropping in value relative to the U.S. dollar, and the "four tigers" of Asia were also trapped in the crisis one by one, all of which struck the world heavily. Under these circumstances, China made a high-profile announcement that the renminbi would not devalue in attempts to stabilize the market in front of the threatening challenge brought by the crisis, which was a prominent contribution to handling and resolving the crisis. The

Asian financial crisis nonetheless had a profound effect, which later affected a much wider range of areas and has restricted consumption until now.

Then came the subprime mortgage crisis in the United States from 2007 to 2008. It was generally considered the consequence of neoliberal policies of the U.S. government in the past 20 to 30 years that aimed to reduce the interference of the government in the financial and labor markets and to boost growth by high consumption, and it was therefore inevitable after long terms of stagflation. The crisis, as a concentrated explosion of stagflation contradictions, trapped finance, economies, and consumption in long-term recession, has lasted until today with many uncertainties.

Affected by the U.S. subprime mortgage crisis, Europe saw waves of sovereign debt crises. As early as October 2008, a tip of the debt iceberg was shown in Iceland in Northern Europe; luckily, the crisis was quickly crushed and did not cause much harm partly because Iceland had a small population, area, and economic scale and partly because the international community was quick to respond. One year later, Greece was struck by a debt crisis, to everyone's surprise, and it spread to Portugal, Italy, Ireland, and Spain, causing a wide-ranging and long-lasting crisis of European debts. To exacerbate the situation, the European Central Bank (ECB), the International Monetary Fund (IMF), and the members of the Euro zone could not reach a consensus over the crisis and failed to coordinate with each other, and the crisis was thus deepened continuously.

These crises, from Asia to America and then to Europe, taking turns to explode like rolling balls, led the world, especially developed economies, to prolonged economic crises and consumption has also been in recession, illustrated in the recent economic growth rates of global economies and changes in the consumer price index in Tables 1.2 and 1.3, according to the data provided by the IMF and consensus forecasts in the United Kingdom.

Explanations from the perspective of population consumption

The aforementioned financial crises that consecutively broke out like rolling balls all had different causes since the affected countries varied in economic structures, development levels, technological compositions, and development engines; however, from the perspective of consumption, they all had one direct cause, i.e., long-term, sluggish consumption, which made the crises consequences of overproduction and over-fluidity and resulted in a chain of reactions: insufficient effective demands – consumption recession – financial crisis – economic crisis. Between production and consumption, although production and the means of production primarily decide what can be consumed, how much is consumed, and even by which means consumption is made, consumption is by no means entirely submissive; as a matter of fact, it is the ultimate goal and completion of social production and reproduction, the destination of the cycle of reproduction, and the origin of the next cycle of reproduction. Therefore, if problems arise in consumption, products will not be consumed, which will

Table 1.2 Worldwide economic growth rates, 2012–2015 (%)

Year	*2012*	*2013*	*2014*	*2015*
IMF data				
Worldwide	3.4	3.3	3.4	3.5
Developed countries	1.2	1.3	1.8	2.4
United States	2.3	2.2	2.4	3.1
Euro zone	−0.5	−0.5	0.9	1.2
Japan	1.5	1.6	0.0	1.0
Developing countries	5.1	5.0	4.6	4.3
India	4.5	5.0	7.4	7.5
Russia	3.4	1.3	0.6	−3.8
Brazil	1.0	2.7	0.1	−1.0
CF data				
Worldwide	2.4	2.4	2.7	3.1
United States	2.3	2.2	2.4	2.5
Euro zone	−0.7	−0.5	0.9	1.5
Japan	1.5	1.6	0.0	0.9
India	4.5	6.9	7.4	7.8

Note: The growth rate of each year was based on the previous year as reference.

Table 1.3 Ratios of rises and falls of consumer prices, 2012–2015 (%)

Year	*2012*	*2013*	*2014*	*2015*
IMF data				
Developed countries	2.0	1.4	1.4	0.4
Developing countries	6.1	5.9	5.1	5.4
CF data				
Worldwide	1.0	2.8	3.0	2.6
United States	2.1	1.5	1.6	0.2
Euro zone	2.5	1.4	0.4	0.1
Japan	0.0	0.4	2.7	0.6
India	10.2	9.5	6.7	5.1

Sources: The 2012 data were from *Major Indices of World Economies* by the Information Center of World Statistics, National Bureau of Statistics, in *Globalization*, 2015, vol. 2; the rest of the data were from *Globalization*, 2015, vol. 6, p. 123.

Note: The growth rate of each year was based on the previous year as reference.

definitely affect the operation of the next cycle of reproduction; the flow of economic development will be obstructed, and economic risks induced.

In the traditional consumption function, consumption is a function of interest: raising interest rates leads to increased savings and decreased consumption and lowering interest rates leads to decreased savings and increased consumption. Obviously, this is a microscopic consumption theory centered on families in a natural or command economy, and it cannot explain consumer behaviors in a market economy although the reciprocal relationship described in the function is present, thus the function offers a theoretical foothold for using interest rates as a leverage to adjust savings and consumption. The modern consumption function, introduced by John Maynard Keynes in his 1936 work *The General Theory of Employment, Interest, and Money*, broke away from the bounds of the traditional function and linked consumption to income, which established the macroeconomic theory of consumption function. The basic model of the function is as follows.

$$C_t = a + bY_t$$

In this equation, C is total consumption, Y is total income, and a and b are both constants – a is a consumption coefficient ($a > 0$) and b is the coefficient of marginal propensity to consumption ($0 < b < 1$), which equates to MPC = $\Delta C / \Delta Y$, and t is time. When employment is introduced to the function, the variables of consumption C, employment n, and income Y are connected and the relationship and the dynamics of the three, income – employment – consumption are revealed, which is in fact one of the objectives of this book.

To this end, demands for capital can be summarized to come from the following aspects: population, specifically the size of the consumer population; living standard, i.e., the level of consumption per capita; and capital technologies, or the average amount of time needed for production.

During the half-century between 1860 and 1913, the demand for capital increased by 1.7 times, the population 50.0%, the living standard 60.0%, and the capital coefficient 10.0%. Obviously, the increase in the demand for capital was mostly caused by the increases in the population and consumption per capita. Therefore, decreases in birth and population growth rates will lead to insufficient effective demands, the total consumption is a function of the total income, and the marginal propensity to consumption tends to decrease as income increases. However, the Keynesian function was rather simple, and several scholars, including Simon Smith Kuznets and Milton Friedman, further modified and developed it. Based on the acknowledgment that consumption was decided by income, they argued that current consumption was not entirely decided by current income, but also partly by expected income; in addition, income was a factor to decide consumption, but not the only one since other non-income factors, especially consumer preferences, also affected consumption.

In fact, people with the same income differ in their consuming demands, sometimes to a large degree, due to their different preferences for consumption. The following factors that affect the preferences deserve particular attention: age, sex, occupation, level of education, social status, and position in the family. The population of any country or region can always be roughly divided into the three categories of juveniles, adults, and the elderly, among whom juveniles are current consumers and most of them are potential future laborers, adults are both laborers and consumers, and the elderly, as a population, have already exited from labor and are thus only consumers.

These three population categories are fundamentally different in their employment status and thus have a distinctively upside-down U-shaped pattern of income that increases and then decreases with age. Since consumption is a function of income, the pattern of consumption should also have an upside-down U shape, while the pattern of savings, which highly correlates with income and consumption, presents an even more typical shape of an upside-down U with particularly obvious decreases in the saving rate of the elderly. Therefore, aging of a population has apparent influences on income, savings, and consumption, which becomes increasingly stronger with the aging of the population. This is how demographic economics explains consumption recession as population aging profoundly impacts anticipated consumption.

When the differential consumption levels of the three age groups of a population are used to explain consumption preferences, it is clear that the economic crises in developed economies were directly caused by insufficient consumption underlain by population aging. From such a perspective, the world economic growth rates and the consumer price index changes in Tables 1.2 and 1.3 now offer us a clear map of the dynamics of the world economy. Specifically, the following observations can be made on the aging trend in developed countries' populations, combined as well as individually in Japan, France, and the United States, the UN's projections of which are illustrated in Figures 1.4 through 1.7.[5]

As shown in Figures 1.4 through 1.7, developed countries as a whole are fast in population aging and have reached a high level. Specifically, the proportion of juveniles below 14 years of age is expected to decline slowly from 18.3% in 2000 to 16.5% in 2015, 15.5% in 2030, and 15.4% in 2050. Among these countries, Japan is the fastest in aging and has the lowest proportion of those under 14, with the proportion expected to decline from 14.6% in 2000 to 12.4% in 2015 and 10.8% in 2030, and to increase a little to 11.2% in 2050.

In contrast, the United States is the slowest in aging and has a high proportion of those under 14 as its juvenile proportion has been projected to

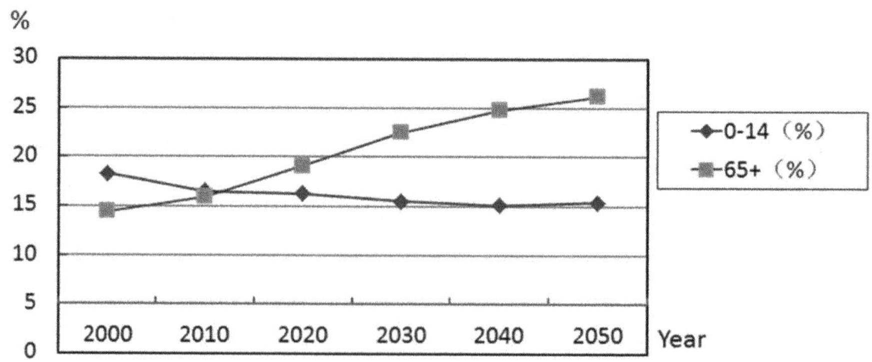

Figure 1.4 Projected proportions of juveniles (0–14) and the elderly (65 and above) in developed countries, 2000–2050.

decrease from 21.5% in 2000 to 19.8% in 2015, 18.0% in 2030, and 17.0% in 2050. The situation in France, as shown in Figure 1.6, is similar to that of all developed countries with a slow progress of population aging as the proportion of those under 14 has been projected to decrease slowly, from 18.8% in 2000 to 18.1% in 2015, 16.4% in 2030, and 16.2% in 2050, reductions totaling only 2.6 percentage points in 50 years.

The proportions of the elderly showed exactly the opposite trends to those of the young. Developed countries as a whole are projected to have increased

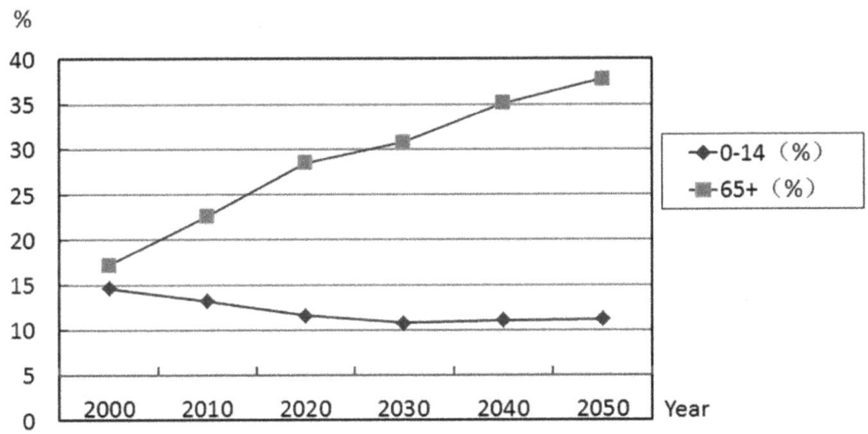

Figure 1.5 Projected proportions of juveniles (0–14) and the elderly (65 and above) in Japan, 2000–2050.

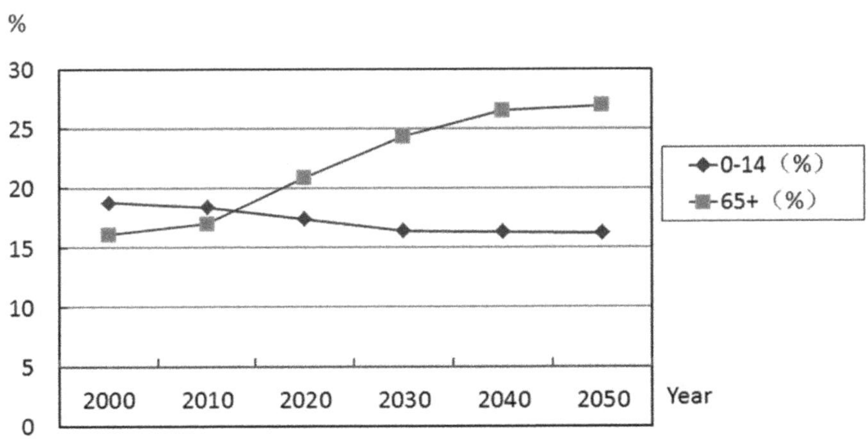

Figure 1.6 Projected proportions of juveniles (0–14) and the elderly (65 and above) in France, 2000–2050.

proportions of those above 65 years of age, from 14.4% in 2000 to 17.4% in 2015, 22.5% in 2030, and 26.25% in 2050. The projected 11.8 percentage point increase over the 50 years corresponds to an average annual increase of 0.24 percentage points. Specifically, in Japan, the proportion of those over 60 is projected to increase from 17.2% in 2000 to 37.8% in 2050, an increase of 20.6 percentage points with an average increase of 0.41 percentage points. The expected total increase in Japan is 170.8% of that in all developed countries combined, from 2.8 percentage points more in 2000 all the way up to 11.6 percentage points more in 2050, reinforcing Japan's image as "a country of the elderly."

In the United States, the proportion of those over 65 is projected to increase from 12.4% in 2000 to 14.3% in 2015, 19.8% in 2030, and 21.6% in 2050, a total increase of 9.2 percentage points over the first half of the 21st century with an average annual increase of 0.18 percentage points. The projected increase in the United States is 75.0% of that in all developed countries combined, 43.9% of that in Japan, and 81.8% of that in France. Apparently, the United States has a much slower pace of aging among developed countries and will reach a lower level of aging as well, which will have much less influence on consumption, as well as a smaller adverse effect on socioeconomic development and income.

In fact, studies on the changes and impacts of population aging cannot afford to overlook the ratio of the elderly to the young since the young generation will eventually become laborers, in complete contrast to the elderly, who are only consumers. The ratio of the elderly to the young in all developed countries was already 1.00 in 2010, i.e., there were equal numbers and proportions of the elderly and the young. The ratio was already 1.00 in Japan in 1996 and in France in 2012, and will be 1.00 in the United States around 2028. As shown in Figures 1.4 and 1.7, once the ratio is over 1.00, the proportion of the

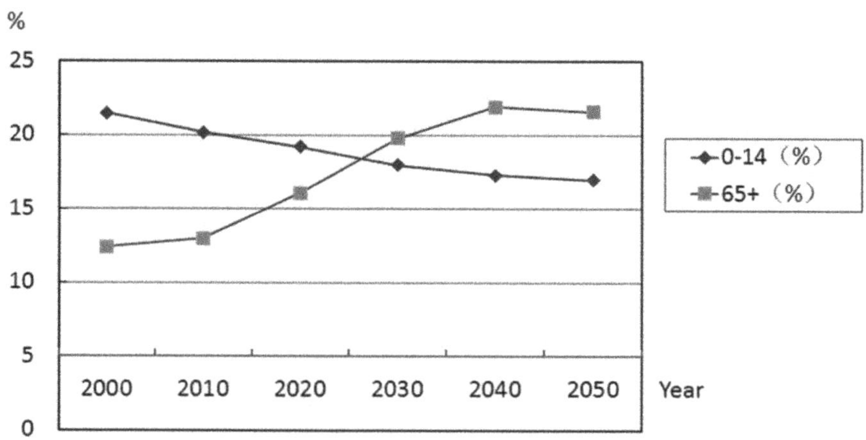

Figure 1.7 Projected proportions of juveniles (0–14) and the elderly (65 and above) in the United States, 2000–2050.

elderly keeps growing and that of the young falls due to momentum until it rests stable, leading the ratio to increase progressively.

By 2050, the ratio in all developed countries combined will be as large as around 1.70, 3.38 in Japan, 1.66 in France, and 1.27 in the United States. What will Japan be like in 2050 when the ratio of the elderly to the young reaches 3.38? It's hard to describe the characteristics of such "a country of the elderly," and only time will provide us with an answer. However, one thing is for sure, i.e., efforts to further socioeconomic development, income, and consumption will become difficult to make and the effect of an over-aged population on consumption will be fully revealed. Nevertheless, let us keep in mind that population aging is not the main cause of consumption recession or economic stagflation; the main cause is still to be found in the economic system, institutions, and policies that have led to the surplus of production and fluidity.

Sluggish consumption in China

China was an agrarian country with a self-sufficient natural economy in dominance, underdeveloped consumption, and, consequently, barely existent consumer awareness before 1949, when the People's Republic of China was established. After the establishment of the new China, consumption still did not receive immediate attention partly because the previous supply economy in the revolution bases was still influential such that production was intensified, through which consumption could be boosted, and partly because the experiences of the Soviet Union's industrialization and command economy were valued and production was favored over consumption to such a degree that consumer cities vowed to transform into production cities.

Setting aside the first 30 years after the establishment of the Republic, the first 35 years after the Reform and Opening Up saw continuous high-speed growth of the Chinese economy as well as a recent downward trend in consumption, especially after the turn of the 21st century, when the world was troubled by financial crises, economic crises, and consumption recession.

A peek into the dynamics of sluggish consumption

Changes in the consumption expenditure (% GDP) since the Reform and Opening Up may be divided by the turn of the 21st century into two stages. In the early stage (1978–2000) of 23 years, the consumption expenditure stayed at a normal, relatively high level, with an average annual rate of 62.82%. During these years, the consumption expenditure was lower than 60.0% for only 6 years and it was above 60.0% for the remaining 17 years.

The peak came between 1981 and 1985, with an average annual expenditure of 66.3%. In the late stage after 2000, except for the two years of 2001 and 2002, when the consumption expenditures were at a normal level of more than 60.0%, the expenditures of all the years fell below 60.0%, and the numbers

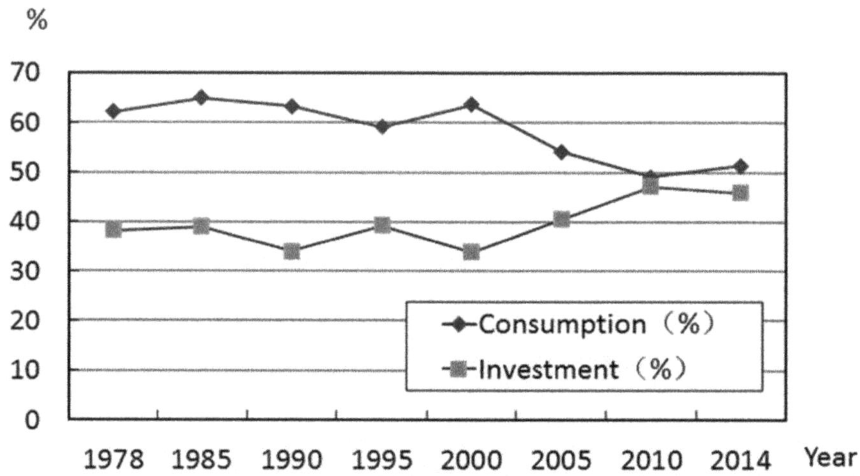

Figure 1.8 Changes in consumption and investment, 1978–2014.

even slid down to around 50.0% after 2007, when the U.S. subprime mortgage crisis broke out, resulting in an average annual consumption expenditure as low as 50.4%. In contrast, total investment (% GDP) started to increase, reaching 42.4% in 2004, after which it continued to climb with some fluctuation and evidently took up the room of consumption (Figure 1.8).

This sluggish trend in consumption is also manifested in the contributions to GDP and to GDP growth by the demands of consumption, capital, and net exports since the turn of the 21st century (Table 1.4).

As shown in Table 1.4, the contributions of consumer spending to GDP and GDP growth had an apparent overall declining trend after 2000. Compared to 2000, the consumption contribution to GDP decreased from 78.9% to 51.6% in 2014, a total reduction of 27.3 percentage points with an annual decline of 1.95 percentage points on average, the speed and scale of which had been rare before. Similarly, the decline of its contribution to GDP growth, from 6.6 percentage points down to 3.8 percentage points, was also rare as the reduction was as large as 42.4%.

In terms of net exports of goods and services, their contributions to GDP and GDP growth also slid several times, with negative growth from time to time, which was also a rare phenomenon. The only exception was capital, calculated by the total investment in fixed assets, and it had a stable growth in contributing to GDP and GDP growth, having successfully prevented the economic growth from falling rapidly.

In fact, the obstructed growth in net exports of goods and services was anticipated among the worldwide financial and economic crises as many countries resorted to trade protectionism for self-rescue. However, the sluggish

Table 1.4 Contributions to GDP and GDP growth by three types of demands (%)

Year	*Consumption contribution*	*Contributed growth*	*Capital contribution*	*Contributed growth*	*Net export contribution*	*Contributed growth*
1978	39.4	4.6	66.0	7.7	−5.4	−0.6
1990	81.0	3.1	−54.2	−2.1	73.3	2.9
2000	78.9	6.6	21.6	1.8	−0.5	0.0
2010	46.3	4.9	65.2	6.9	−11.5	−1.2
2011	62.8	6.0	45.4	4.2	−8.2	−0.8
2012	56.5	4.3	41.8	3.2	1.7	0.1
2013	48.2	3.7	54.2	4.2	−2.4	−0.2
2014	51.6	3.8	46.7	3.4	1.7	0.1

Source: *China Statistical Yearbook 2015*, p. 83.

Table 1.5 Proportions of resident and government expenditures, 1978–2013 (%)

Year	*Residents*	*Government*	*Rural residents*	*Urban residents*
1978	78.6	21.4	62.1	37.9
1990	78.3	31.8	49.6	50.4
2000	74.5	25.5	33.0	67.0
2010	72.5	27.5	22.7	77.3
2011	72.8	27.2	23.1	76.9
2012	72.7	27.3	22.6	77.4
2013	72.6	27.4	22.2	77.8

Source: *China Statistical Yearbook 2014*, p. 68.

consumption and its declining contributions to GDP and GDP growth were not only consequences of the crises but were also interlocked with changes in the proportions of consumer spending, government expenditure, rural spending, and urban spending (Table 1.5).

As shown in Table 1.5, the overall structural changes in consumption are that the proportion of resident expenditure has been declining while that of the government has been increasing. Except for a few years, the decreases in spending by residents and the increases in spending by government were slowly made, but they were persistent and have amounted to an apparent effect.

Compared to 1978, the resident expenditure in 2013 decreased by 6.0 percentage points, or 7.6%, in proportion, while the increase in government expenditure was 6.0 percentage points, or 7.6%. Between rural and urban areas, the spending of rural residents decreased by a larger scale and at a faster speed than that of urban residents, with a decrease in the rural proportion of 39.9 percentage points, or 64.3%, from 1978 to 2013 while the proportion of urban spending increased by 39.0 percentage points, or 64.3%, accordingly.

The changes in the rural and urban expenditures may be easily explained with the rapid progress of urbanization and they can be accepted as normal changes, but the reciprocal changes between the resident and government expenditures cannot be so easily interpreted and deserve attention and study. In fact, the government expenditure in China, although not as high, in terms of its proportion, as some developed countries, requires sober recognition and optimal solutions as on one hand, we have a large government, which has grown bigger and bigger despite efforts to downsize it, and on the other hand, the government expenditure has been slowly but continuously growing, which delivers a stable and immense progressive impact.

Tracking back to the origin of the sluggish consumption

As analyzed earlier, the sluggish consumption came from resident expenditure, and the discussions in this section are thus targeted at resident consumption. Since the Reform and Opening Up, especially in recent years, economic growth has been boosted primarily by investment in fixed assets as the contributions made by consumer spending and exports of goods and services have been declining. The causes can be found in both the economic system in China and the international financial and economic crises, which even led to negative growth in net exports of goods and services in several years after 2011.

Things have somewhat picked up in the recent one to two years. According to the *Statistical Communiqué* issued by the National Bureau of Statistics in February 2016, the society-wide investment in fixed assets in 2015 increased by 9.8% compared to 2014, the total retail sales increased by 10.7%, and the sum of imports and exports of goods decreased by 7.0%, showing consumption's increased contribution to economic growth.[6] Given the circumstances, if the return on investment had been improved or maintained at the same level as before, the economy would not have taken a downward turn, or, if it did, the turn would have negligible effects; unfortunately, however, with the increasingly large-scale growth in investment in fixed assets, the marginal revenue of investment had an apparent declining trend and the contribution by investment to economic growth was thus lost to a large degree.

Many domestic and international studies have explored China's sluggish consumption and concluded with various interpretations. These interpretations cover everything relevant, and there would be tens of causes of the sluggish consumption if all were to be listed here. However, exactly because of these many scholarly interpretations for the sluggish consumption, people get easily confused and find it difficult to identify the leading causes from all that are available.

To identify the leading causes, one must combine consumption theories with the current situations in China, especially the most fundamental fact that the Chinese economy is now in a new normal with the reform being comprehensively deepened, and then may reach reasonable and reliable conclusions.

As consumption is expressed as a function of income in the modern theoretical model of consumption, income is without question the decisive factor of consumption; therefore, let us start from it to track back to the origin of the sluggish consumption in China.

One leading cause is that the increases in the income per capita have lagged behind. According to statistical data, the national income and GDP grew at the same pace, with an average annual growth rate of 9.8% from 1979 to 2013. However, the increases in the income per capita of urban and rural residents have been much slower. The disposable income per capita of urban residents increased from 343.4 yuan in 1978 to 26,955.1 yuan in 2013, and that was an average annual growth rate of 7.4% calculated with constant prices, lower than the increase rate of the national income by 2.4 percentage points; the net income per capita of rural residents increased from 133.6 yuan to 8,895.9 yuan, and that was an average growth rate of 7.6% calculated with constant prices, lower than the increase rate of the national income by 2.2 percentage points.

In fact, the increase rate of the per capita income was slower than that of the national income by approximately one-fourth partly because the population also grew during the same period, from 962.59 million to 1.36072 billion, an increase of 41.4% with an average annual growth rate of 1.0%, which thus pulled down GDP per capita and income per capita. Yet between GDP per capita and income per capita, the increase in the latter bears more information since it has a closer relationship with consumption than the former; after all, consumption is a function of income.

In China, however, the increases in the per capita income of urban and rural residents could not be directly translated into increases in consumption because a large part of the increases were not spent, but went into people's savings accounts that had been growing at a high speed. The international community has long been talking about how Chinese prefer to deposit money in banks; but only talking about the "preference" is not enough, and its economic foundation must be found. The total savings deposits for urban and rural residents increased from 21.1 billion yuan to 44.7602 trillion yuan during the aforementioned period, and that was an increase of 2,120.3 times with an average annual growth rate of 24.5%.[7] How has the increase influenced consumption? A look at the changes in the proportion of deposits of national income can tell us the answer (Table 1.6).

Another leading cause is the economic system. Very few studies, domestic or international, on China's sluggish consumption have touched on problems of the system, and those that did only comprised superficial discussions and thus lacked depth. In my opinion, the system is exactly the most characteristic and fundamental factor that shapes China's consumption. Therefore, studies should be led into the core from the surface, and at the core is the economic system where the ultimate answer lies.

First, systematic problems underlie "the unaffordable." Why has consumption been sluggish as described earlier? The direct answer is that people have limited incomes and therefore consumption is "unaffordable." However,

Table 1.6 Proportions of savings deposits of national incomes, 1978–2013

Year	*1978*	*1990*	*2000*	*2012*	*2013*	*2014*
Total deposits, hundred million	211	7,120	64,332	399,551	447,602	506,890
National income, hundred million	3,645.2	18,718.3	98,000.5	518,214.7	566,130.2	636,463
Deposit/income, %	5.8	38.0	65.6	77.1	79.1	79.6

Sources: All calculations were made based on the data on pages 4 and 5 in *China Statistical Yearbook 2014*. The 2014 data were from the statistical communiqué released by the National Bureau of Statistics on February 16, 2015. The data of national income were GDP values, which were close to the national income.

according to the latest statistics of resident incomes, the GDP in 2014 was 63.6463 trillion yuan; given that the population was 1.36782 billion, the GDP per capita was 46,531 yuan. Based on the 2014 ratio of RMB to USD, 6.1152:1.0000, the GDP per capita was $7,609.

According to the standards of the World Bank – i.e., low-income regions are those with per capita GDP under $3,000; medium income is $3,000–11,000, among which the range of $3,000–5,000 is considered medium low and $5,000–11,000 medium high; and high-income regions are those with per capita income over $11,000 – China became a medium low-income country in 2008, when the GDP per capita reached $3,314 and a medium high-income country four years later in 2012, when the GDP per capita reached $6,093.

It's been nearly five more years now, and the income level in China must have further improved. In fact, the average GDP per capita of the whole world has exceeded $10,000, but most developing countries are way below the average with many under $3,000; in contrast, China's GDP per capita has undoubtedly exceeded the level of developing countries by a large margin although it is not much higher than the lower limit of the medium high range and is still lower than the world average.

In the current situation, China has evidently leapt in the consumption level, eradicated the problem of the most basic needs for clothing and food, realized preliminary common prosperity, and is now not far away from complete common prosperity on one hand, yet on the other hand, income composition, unfair distribution of wealth, and enlarged gaps of incomes have all negatively affected consumption. The impact on consumption is manifested in the amount, quality, and structure of consumer spending, and it needs comprehensive analysis and evaluation. As there has always been controversy among Chinese and international studies on problems of consumption in China and some views are actually far away from reality, it is necessary to have some discussions here.

A widening gap between high and low incomes is now a global issue. In the current era of information and economic globalization, advanced economies have been relocating their traditional industries to developing countries, leaving to themselves a modern industrial structure dominated by high-end manufacturing industries and financial services and leading to reductions in jobs of conventional labor, employment rate, and income, as well as increased demands for human resources in high-end manufacturing industries and financial services. As a result, incomes of the latter have risen, leaving behind a widened gap with the incomes of average laborers and thus worsened inequality between the rich and the poor.

Meanwhile, in developing countries, huge differences in natural resources such as geographical locations, transportation facilities, and natural features, output resources such as level of industrialization, and human resources such as age and education level of laborers have all resulted in huge differences in the cost of receiving the industries transferred from advanced economies, leading to an imbalance between high grounds and low swamps of development and, accordingly, high grounds and low swamps of salaries.

Fortunately, since the world has been under relatively stable development since WWII, the wage rates of all laborers have risen no matter whether in a high ground or low swamp of incomes, and thus laborers have been tolerant of the imbalance. The imbalance only becomes intolerable and presents as a grave social problem that requires intensive attention when a society has reached a certain degree of economic development, industrialization has been overall completed, and the industrial structure has stepped into a pattern dominated by modern services and characterized by the transition of laborers from being in surplus to shortage. However, differences in national conditions, socioeconomic development, population, and the quantity, quality, and structure of laborers usually lead different countries to give varying degrees of attention and to seek different solutions to the problem of income imbalance.

When it comes to China, the differences between the high grounds and the low swamps of income and consumption are particularly prominent as well as complex compared to other countries. Some attach great importance to the income imbalance and describe it as "reciprocal 20–80" or "reciprocal 30–70," i.e., 20.0% or 30.0% of the population receive a total income that is 80.0% or 70.0% of the entire amount of incomes society-wide. Some even call it "reciprocal 10–90," which is far from reality and is more confusing than alerting.

What the truth really is has something to do with the accuracy of data and information that people have talked about frequently. Some question the accuracy and the transparency of the data and statistics officially provided and accuse the government of downsizing or greatly downsizing the income inequality and the Gini coefficient in China. For example, China Household Finance Survey and Research Center at Southwestern University of Finance and Economics published the *Report on Inequalities among Household Incomes in China* in 2012 and reported that the Gini coefficient of household incomes in China in 2010 was 0.61; the Institute of Social Science Survey at Peking University concluded in its publication *China Family Panel Studies 2014* that the Gini coefficient of the net incomes among Chinese families in 2012 was 0.73

and that the top 1.0% of families possessed more than one-third of the national wealth; and the University of Michigan in the United States also wrote in one of its research projects that the gap between the rich and the poor in China had already exceeded that in the United States and that China was among the countries with the biggest gap, with a Gini coefficient of 0.55 in 2010.[8]

While it is not completely unreasonable that some questioned that the officially released Gini coefficient in China was too low to be true, most questioning, such as those just cited, have insufficient data or evidently small samples in their surveys, or problems with their sampling methods, and thus are not reliable themselves.

On one hand, people have an intuitive impression that the income gap is usually large, which has been fostered by reports now and then, domestically and internationally, on wealthy Chinese magnates, such as a Chinese conquering the seat of the richest person in Asia and the appearances of Chinese enterprises or individuals among the top 50 or 20 on world fortune lists; on the other hand, however, the number of wealthy magnates, the size and scale of their wealth, and particularly the proportion of society-wide wealth they possess are all rumors, and as alerting as they are, those reports cannot describe the entire China.

Therefore, although the officially released data may be questioned, the nongovernment studies and reports are not reliable, either. However, the officially provided data related to China's Gini coefficient are overall more thorough and reliable than the nongovernment data. After all, the government statistical institutes have made numerous efforts and great advancement.

Meanwhile, the questioning is not without ground as the accuracy and the transparency of some data, including those on incomes and consumption, need further improvement. Objectively speaking, it is very difficult to acquire nationwide data on incomes and consumption, especially now that people have a variety of sources of income, making it difficult to collect data on incomes in grey areas. However, one thing is certain, i.e., survey data must be representative of the whole, they should either come from nationwide population or economic censuses or from sampling surveys in areas that are representative of the entire country so that the surveys are scientifically sound in both sample size and sampling method. I took special care to write this down because some survey data were too arbitrary and were released to the public without having been carefully validated or studied, which was not scientifically sound and only caused confusion.

Table 1.7 lists the changes in incomes per capita by quintile among urban and rural residents in 2000, 2006, and 2013 based on *China Statistical Yearbook 2014*.

In Table 1.7, the incomes of urban and rural residents are both grouped by per capita income quintile; approximately speaking, the urban and rural populations are divided into five groups with each having one quintile of per capita incomes. Comparison of the data in 2000 and 2013 may lead to the following conclusions.

Table 1.7 Proportions of urban and rural residents in quintiles of per capita income (%)

	Low	*Medium low*	*Medium*	*Medium high*	*High*
Urban areas					
2000	9.7	14.3	18.2	23.1	34.8
2006	7.4	12.7	16.4	22.7	41.1
2013	8.0	12.9	17.1	22.6	39.2
Rural areas					
2000	6.6	11.8	16.4	22.7	42.6
2006	6.1	11.4	16.2	22.0	43.5
2013	5.3	11.3	16.3	23.4	43.7

Source: Calculations were made based on the data on pages 161 and 167 in *China Statistical Yearbook 2014*.

First, the proportions of those with low incomes and of those with high incomes have changed in opposite directions. The former shows apparent decreases: urban low-income residents accounted for 9.7% of all urban residents in 2000, and the proportion decreased by 1.7 percentage points to 8.0% in 2013; in rural areas, the proportion decreased from 6.6% to 5.3%, or 1.3 percentage points. The proportion of those with a medium-low income decreased by 1.4 percentage points from 14.3% to 12.9% in urban areas and 0.5 percentage points from 11.8% to 11.3% in rural areas. Evidently, the decreases are on larger scales in urban than in rural areas.

Similarly, the proportions of those with medium incomes also decreased, but by smaller scales with 1.1 percentage points in urban areas and 0.1 percentage points in rural areas. The changes in the other two higher-income quintiles are irregular: the proportion of those with a medium-high income decreased by 0.5 percentage points from 23.1% to 22.6% in urban areas, but increased by 0.7 percentage points in rural areas from 22.7% to 23.4%, both small-scale changes. The most prominent changes occurred to the proportions of those with high incomes, which increased by large scales, with 4.8 percentage points from 34.8% to 39.2% in cities and towns and 1.1 percentage points from 42.6% to 43.7% in rural areas. The increase in the urban proportion of high-income residents is higher by 2.8 times than the rural one.

All the numbers show that both rural and urban residents have seen continuously increasing incomes with socioeconomic development, and the proportions of low-income residents have shrunk in size in both urban and rural areas while those of high-income residents have grown. Decreases or increases, the scales are always higher in urban than rural areas, suggesting that cities and towns have progressed faster in bringing higher incomes to residents.

Second, the changes in the populations by income quintile have abnormal shapes. In fact, after China joined the group of countries with medium-high incomes, the distribution of residents by income quintile should have transitioned to a pattern shaped like an olive. However, this did not happen in China. The decrease in the proportions of those with low or medium-low incomes is not surprising as it followed the normal changes of development; the surprise is in the unusually high increase in the proportion of those with high incomes, which is against regular changes, and the distribution by income quintile thus stopped to transition to an olive-shaped pattern. Such abnormal changes of an antinomy have a profound impact on consumption.

Finally, the gap between high and low incomes first widened and then narrowed slightly. In urban areas, the average amount of per capita disposable incomes among the low-income residents was 3,132.0 yuan in 2000 and that of the high-income residents was 11,299.0 yuan; the latter was higher by 2.6 times than the former. In 2008, the average income of low-income residents was 6,074.9 yuan and that of the high-income residents was 34,667.8 yuan; the latter was 5.7 times as much as the former.

Apparently, the gap between the high and low incomes had been much widened. In 2013, the average income of the low-income residents increased to 11,433.7 yuan, while that of the high-income residents grew to 56,389.5 yuan, and the latter was 4.9 times as much as the former, showing that the gap had been closed to some degree. In rural areas, the average amount of per capita net incomes of the low-income residents was 802.0 yuan in 2000 while that of the high-income residents was 5,190.0 yuan, and the latter was 6.5 times as much as the former. In 2008, the gap was 7.5 times with the low-income residents making on average 1,499.8 yuan and the high-income residents making on average 11,290.2 yuan, and the gap was much larger than that of urban areas. In 2013, the average income of low-income residents was 2,583.2 yuan while that of high-income residents was 21,272.7 yuan, and the latter was 8.2 times the former, showing a further widened gap in incomes.

A clearer observation may be made when the rural and urban incomes are comprehensively evaluated from the perspective of the Gini coefficient. The Gini coefficient of resident incomes is an indicator to evaluate the equality of incomes, and it was proposed and deliberated by Italian economist Corrado Gini based on the Lorenz curve. It's generally accepted that when the Gini coefficient of a country is below 0.2, the country has an absolutely equal distribution of incomes, between 0.2 and 0.3 relatively equal, between 0.3 and 0.4 relatively reasonable, between 0.4 and 0.5 a relatively wide gap, between 0.5 and 0.6 a wide gap, and above 0.6 a great disparity.

On January 18, 2013, the State Council Information Office of China held a press conference on which the Gini coefficients of the resident incomes in China from 2003 to 2012 were released, and it also promised that the Gini coefficient would be included as an indicator of national social and economic development so that it would have more applications and be more transparent. I collected all the Gini coefficients released most recently by the National Bureau of Statistics and other pertinent government branches over the years and abridged the data of several years since the Reform and Opening Up to reveal the changes: it was 0.288 in 1981, 0.2656 in 1985, 0.343 in 1990, 0.445 in 1995, 0.412 in 2000, 0.485 in 2005, 0.491 in 2008 (which was the highest number released by the government), 0.481 in 2010, 0.477 in 2011, 0.474 in 2012, 0.473 in 2013, and 0.469 in 2014.[9] The changes in these Gini coefficients, in my opinion, have two prominent features.

One is that the Gini coefficients are all relatively high. After it became relatively high in 1994, when it was 0.436, China's Gini coefficient has been staying at a high level between 0.4 and 0.5 and was at an even higher level between 0.473 and 4.491 from 2003 to 2013, with the only exception being 1999, when the coefficient decreased to 0.397. It decreased to 0.469 in 2014, which, although falling below 0.47 as a record low for the previous 10 years, was still at a medium-high level that attested a relatively wide gap of incomes, 0.4 to 0.5, and China was still in the position with a relatively wide gap of incomes.

Another feature is that the Gini coefficients took a turn from increases to decreases. After it exceeded 0.4 in 1994, which marked China as a country with a relatively wide gap of incomes, the Gini coefficient showed a pattern of increases followed by decreases. Specifically, it increased from 0.436 in 1994 to 0.491 in 2008, which was a period of widening the gap with the increases as high as 12.6%.

The only exception was 1999, when the coefficient fell below 0.4, but it went right back to 0.412 in the next year and continued to climb until the peak of 0.491 in 2008. After 2008, the coefficient declined stepwise and slowly, to 0.469 in 2014, a decrease of 4.8%, which was not even 40.0% of the increases in the previous period. In fact, whether the 2008 value, 0.491, will remain the peak forever remains to be tested, and it is only the peak up until now. Of course, if the coefficient continues to decline, the value will become the peak of the past, the present, and the future.

An overall restricted level of incomes and a wide gap between high and low incomes have greatly impaired the level and structure of residential consumption, which is an important cause of the "unaffordable" kind of sluggish consumption. For example, everyone feels that houses are expensive. Inside the Second Ring Road in Beijing by the old city, the real estate price is now as high as 50,000 yuan per square meter (m^2); a 60 m^2 apartment costs 3 million yuan, 80 m^2 4 million, and 100 m^2 5 million. Based on the numbers in 2013, the disposable income per capita of urban residents was 11,433.7 yuan, and a family of three would have a total annual income of 34,301.1 yuan; even if all that money was saved up to purchase a 60 m^2 apartment, it would take the family 87 years.

How could one possibly realize the goal of owning his own living unit? And it would not be enough to save up for 100 years if one was to buy an apartment of 80 m^2 or 100 m^2. Similarly, for a family of three with a medium income of 24,518.3 yuan each and 73,554.9 yuan in total, it would take them 41 years to buy a 60 m^2 apartment, 54 years for an 80 m^2 one, and 68 years for a 100 m^2 one, a reality in which one can barely afford his own apartment. Only those with high incomes, especially those with very high incomes, can easily realize their dreams of purchasing apartments or houses of their own. Under such a circumstance, the government implemented a policy of economical housing to provide affordable living units for low-income families to rent or purchase. However, I do not think that the policy of economical housing is worthy of praise because it violates the rules of a market economy and leaves room for corruption; yet the policy is nonetheless useful to a degree as a remedy for "the unaffordable" so that those with low incomes can afford housing under the current condition of a wide gap of incomes.

Another example of "the unaffordable" is that education and medical resources are in high demand and severely monopolized, which, together with fraud crimes, forces those with low incomes to stop before prestigious schools and hospitals and give up their right as equal consumers; on the other hand, the rich have the liberty to walk around the market and boost high prices of anything as they like, leaving behind all the others to watch, which is the only thing they can do. This is a "deformed product" of the market economy, and it is rooted in resource monopolization to a degree in the system of education and medicine.

Second, systematic problems underlie "the dare not." Consumers have demands and can afford spending, but they dare not spend money because they have concerns, which, if tracked back, originate in the system, or the absence or lack of it in social welfare.

Individuals and families have to plan for their lives after retirement as the social welfare system for elderly care is overall not sufficient, although it has been continuously reformed with the end of breaking the "dual-double structure," i.e., different systems in urban and rural areas as well as in urban enterprises and urban government agencies. The way to save up for retirement is to buy commercial insurance products or to deposit money in banks, which has led to a fast-growing amount of total deposits.

In fact, the total balance of individual deposits of RMB in rural and urban areas increased from 21.1 billion yuan in 1978 to 712.0 billion in 1990, 6.4332 trillion in 2000, and 44.7602 trillion in 2013. The total deposits in 2013 were 2,121 times those of 1978, and the increase was at an annual rate of 24.5%, way faster than the growth rates of GDP, investment, and consumption. The immensely increased deposits have partially been transformed into investment through financial channels, facilitating economic growth, but they have stood away from consumption and thus hindered its growth. Fortunately, the reforms of the social security and insurance systems for elderly care have recently been accelerated, aiming to break the systematic hurdle caused by the dual-double structure by unifying the systems in urban enterprises and government agencies and pushing for the new rural social endowment system. Obviously, it is not easy to establish such a social endowment system that is unified in the entire country, and people will still be worried for their retirement plans for a short time, so measures to stimulate consumption will need time to exert their positive impacts. These aspects are further discussed later in this book.

Similar situations are also seen in the field of health insurance. The reform of the health insurance system in earlier years was a complete failure, which was a consensus among all sectors of the society. It was a complete failure because very few changes had occurred to the medical system, the imbalanced distribution of medical resources, and the burdens of people seeking medical treatment, which were more worsened than lightened, and the difficulties and the high costs associated with medical treatment were fundamentally the same.

A new reform has been pushed for in recent years; it alleviates the difficulties and the high costs of medical treatment by increasing the premiums paid by the public and decreasing individual costs. However, the medical system was not reformed on the whole, the imbalance in resource distribution was not bettered much, and individuals and families are thus still bound by concerns of medical costs and have to save up and restrict consumption.

Meanwhile, systematic reforms of other types of insurance, such as casualty and employment, have progressed and achieved a lot, facilitating the social security web and consumption growth. However, these two types of insurance are only related to some residents, most of whom are of working age, and they are not closely associated with consumption, so they have very limited impact on consumption growth. What really decides consumer spending from the perspective of social security is still the two types of insurance, old age and health. After all, it is a natural law that people are born, grow old, get sick, and die, and no one can escape the cycle; thus health and old-age insurance are either being used or will be used, and they cover one's entire life cycle until death. Therefore, a satisfactory solution to the reforms of the old-age and health insurance systems will be essential to release people of their concerns that make them "dare not buy," and should be worked on with great efforts.

Third, systematic problems underlie "the nowhere to buy." "The nowhere to buy" describes the situation that some common consumer goods cannot be easily obtained on the market. It is widely known that market competition and the average rate of profit usually negate shortage of commonly needed commodities on the market; however, when there is a shortage, it is mostly due to problems in the system, which is exactly what happens in the current situation of "nowhere to buy."

For example, the difficulties in and the high costs of seeking medical treatment is first manifested in registering for outpatient visits, especially when patients want to see a specialist. In Peking Union Medical College Hospital, a registration number to see a specialist can be scalped for 100, even several hundred yuan, and to contain the scalpers is like reaping Chinese chives: the crops quickly grow high after getting reaped. After all, "getting up for benefits" and that "there is always one to be bought if the price is high enough" are more powerful than "punishing one to intimidate others," and the efforts to eradicate touting have been ineffective.

Why are the registration numbers for specialists so hard to get? In my opinion, it is rooted in the medical system. Most of the prestigious specialists and scholars are concentrated in tertiary, grade A hospitals like the Union Hospital, Beijing Hospital, Beijing Tongren Hospital, Peking University Hospital, and 301 Hospital, just to name a few. Now that the Chinese have raised incomes overall, they are most willing to spend money on health, so their instinct, when sick, is to go to one of the tertiary hospitals to see a specialist, leading to a sharpened contradiction between supply and demand in health care, and thus the difficulty to register for specialists has only exacerbated itself. This is caused by the system, the system with highly imbalanced distribution of resources –facilities, resources, and talents – that has never been really touched in the previous reforms. In my opinion, the problem of "national leader institutes" is the biggest in the medical field among all fields and that of "Beijing leader institutes" among "national leaders" is even more prominent, and they are good places for reforms of the medical service system to start with.

The distribution of urban and rural residents by per capita income quintile as shown in Table 1.7 also illustrates that, although the middle class in China has not formed the backbone of consumers to decide the growth of society-wide consumption, the proportions of those in the first income quintile have obvious increases in both urban and rural areas, with an urban increase of 4.4 percentage points from 2000 to 2013 and a rural increase of 1.1 percentage points. Behind the large increases of high-income residents is a fast-growing demand for high-end consumption, which, not met by production and market supply, has led to the fashion of sweeping purchases among Chinese *dama* (aunties) when traveling abroad.

Another example of the contradiction between demand and supply of high-end goods and services is in elderly care. With the population aging and a weakened role of families in supporting the elderly, there has risen a high demand for nursing homes and hospice care institutes from the senior groups with high incomes in cities, especially big cities, and a growing shortage of the kind of elderly care institutes that cost 5,000 to 6,000 yuan per month, resulting in waiting time to get a spot of as long as six months and sometimes even more than a year, just like the difficulty to register for a specialist in Union Hospital. There is actually a current contradiction that there is insufficient supply of elder care institutes nationwide while there is also a low occupancy rate in the institutes. It is exactly a structural asymmetry between demand and supply since the high-end institutes of elderly care are overall in shortage. Apparently, the industry of institutionalized elderly care needs to come into concert with not only the progress of population aging but also the structures of income and consumption of the elderly so that high-quality services may be customized to the market.

The third leading cause of the sluggish consumption in China is China's traditional culture. From my experiences in the United States, Canada, the United Kingdom, France, Australia, and Japan, the Chinese in these places only have comparable incomes with the local people in general, and many cannot even make it to the medium-income level; however, quite a few of the Chinese drive extravagant cars and live in expensive houses, sometimes even in rich communities.

In contrast, many local people with similar incomes and social status live average lives, with average cars and average houses. The reasons why the overseas Chinese spend much money to make themselves look richer than they really are include wanting to gain respect from others, which is especially important for the overseas Chinese seeking equality and dignity, and being influenced by the traditional Chinese doctrine that one should endure difficulties, work hard, live economically, and save up for the future so that they rather save money on food and goods and spend the saved money on their images. This has also reminded me of some landowners and rich men I saw when I was a little boy, who always saved up to buy houses and lands while living a quite moderate life, typical actions of Grandets.

In summary, on one hand, history progresses, times develop, and the Chinese traditional cultures, including the consumption culture, also change; on the other hand, the traditional ideologies, concepts, and values have precipitated for thousands of years to mix with the traditional culture that was born with small-scale agrarian production, human-powered labor, and disperse operation to have shaped a value that honors diligence, bravery, economy, and independence and a consumer habit that is powerful in coding people's consumption behaviors through history, which has ultimately become a culture that values economy and inhibits consumption. This traditional consumer culture has obviously oriented people toward inhibiting their consuming impulses and investing in lands and houses, which is still felt today.

For example, both in rural and in urban areas, people quickly got rich after the Reform and Opening Up, yet those in urban areas usually saved money to buy an apartment and those in rural areas first spent money on building new houses or renovating old ones rather than rewarding themselves with better material consumption or investing in agricultural or agriculture-related production for further development; all of them insisted on "getting a house first, pursuing further development in career second." Some even wanted to buy lands, and they only stopped trying because it was not allowed by policies. Some real estate merchants in cities and towns made use of exactly this kind of consumer behavior and quickly drove high house prices by labeling houses as a "rigid demand" and some started to sell the concept, which altogether has resulted in the abnormal situation that house prices grow exponentially, especially in big cities.

Exploring the path of moderate growth with green consumption

The worldwide sluggish consumption has troubled the economic development of many countries, including China, and how to make consumption take off again is an essential problem of stimulating further economic growth. Under such a circumstance, many countries have relied on quantitative easing to boost consumption and investment in the hope of driving the economies out of stagflation; these countries also have all encouraged exports and restricted imports to boost consumption overseas, hoping for external trades to play their due role in bringing economic growth. However, is it really true that faster-growing consumption brings faster economic development? Are high consumption and in-advance consumption to be advocated for in order to shift the focus of economic development to consumption? The answers are negative from the perspective of sustainable development of material, spiritual, and ecologic civilizations. Instead, what should be advocated for is a path of green consumption and moderate growth.

Growing demands for consumption

In fact, consumption always grows continuously with production development unless in economic crises. It's decided by the status and the function of consumption in the chain of social reproduction as well as by people's desire to pursue high-quality lives and to satisfy their unlimited lust.

Status and function of consumption during social reproduction

As stated earlier, among the four nodes of production, exchange, distribution, and consumption, consumption is the last stop, which completes a cycle of production when it is realized. For production to run continuously, the next cycle of production is usually made on a larger scale than the previous one, which also relies on a moderate increase in consumption. After all, if the products of one cycle of production cannot be totally consumed, the cycle is not complete; if the consumption level is not improved compared to the previous cycle, the next cycle cannot be of a larger scale. These statements are exactly what the socioeconomic development progress since the establishment of the new China has told us.

Under the command economy from the establishment of the People's Republic of China until the start of the Reform and Opening Up, China's economy was mostly in a state of shortage as there were always insufficient products for the residents to consume and a communist kind of rationing had to be introduced as if China were still at war. Ration stamps for grains were distributed per capita so that the consumption of grains was under control, cotton cloth stamps were issued to ration the per capita consumption of cloth, and industrial consumer goods were rationed through industrial stamps and goods-specific coupons distributed according to the income and the size of a family. At the time, the products that could be easily produced could not be consumed, goods were like "emperor's daughters who could always be married," and sales were made "so fast as to become radishes that were quickly processed with mud on."

Overall, this was a typical yet unique supply market. After the Reform and Opening Up, there first developed a socialist commercial economy, regulated by planning in combination with the market, and finally it was specified that a socialist market economy should be established, which was a stepwise transition to a market economy that was common worldwide.

Meanwhile, the major contradiction in China took a fundamental turn, from the previous contradiction between insufficient production and excessive consumption (i.e., consumption demands were not met) to the contradiction between overproduction and insufficient consumption, and consumption has become an essential cog that decides whether a cycle of production can be completed. The actual process of production is a nonstop circulation among the four nodes, and when there are problems in the node of consumption, the next cycle of production must be affected as well as further production and development of society.

Therefore, consumption deserves attention and study since it is a key problem that decides the current and future socioeconomic development. However, consumption cannot be dealt with without production; nor can any abnormal measure in violation of reproduction principles be taken to handle the contradiction between production and consumption.

In fact, China has been a hotspot of construction since the Reform and Opening Up, and many foreigners are impressed when they visit China at how many construction sites there are, which is in sharp contrast to the West, where large-scale construction of infrastructure is no longer seen. The impression has its reasons. For quite a period of time, the production of steel and cement has been in extreme excess, and the consumption of these products has been mostly in production: steel is used to produce trains, automobiles, ships, machines, production tools, roads, and architectures, and cement is used to build roads, bridges, and houses. Such production-oriented consumption needs to be transformed to consumer-oriented consumption eventually. However, under specific circumstances, such production consumption may be independent of resident consumption, and the current aggressive urbanization projects present one of these.

In a nutshell, the aggressive urbanization goes as follows: the government buys land from peasants and calls for bids, real estate developers bid, and whoever wins starts construction and sells the units after the construction is over; residents buy the units usually for their own residence, although some buy them as investments. Such a process of urbanization seemingly illustrates how the government, real estate developers, and peasants all benefit, but it essentially illustrates how the chains of industries and profits have been formed that combine the land finance and commercial gains while the benefits on the sides of the government and developers are immense with the peasants gaining very little, a sharply imbalanced distribution of benefits.

Furthermore, a large proportion of the construction never enters the consumption sphere of the residents, but is constantly bought and sold, which I call "an external circulation" that is independent of the consumer market. The existence of such "an external circulation" is said by some to be caused by "rigid needs," which happens to have boosted house prices, and the boosted prices encourage businessmen to make more buying and selling.

As a result, many "ghost cities" have emerged where there are many unsold living units that can be afforded by neither the residents nor the peasants who have entered the cities. Meanwhile, the ever-growing housing prices boost the demands for more steel and cement, and the overproduction of steel and cement is thus sustained and even more is produced. In fact, there has been a wide range of discussions on "ghost cities," which have a society-wide impact, so extended expounding is needed here.

There is no consensus about how many "ghost cities" there are and how big they are due to lack of authoritative statistics and uniform standards; however, it is widely recognized that they are growing in number and size.

FAST-PROGRESSING URBANIZATION STIMULATES REAL ESTATE ACTIVITIES

The urbanization rate increased from 10.64% in 1949 to 17.92% in 1978, which was a total increase of 7.28 percentage points at an average annual rate of 0.19 percentage points; in contrast, urbanization reached 54.77% in 2014, which was an increase of 36.85 percentage points at an average annual rate of 1.02 percentage points after the Reform and Opening Up. Now China has leapt in urbanization, from a level lower than the world average and developing countries before the Reform to a level higher than the world by 2.0 percentage points and developing countries by 6.0 percentage points.[10] The fast progress of urbanization has stimulated real estate activities, and blind expansion like this always derails urbanization from the market track and traps it in "ghost cities."

ADVANCED PROGRESS OF LANDS AND THE REAL ESTATE INDUSTRY HAS IMPACTS

The total number of urban residents grew 59.26% from 2000 to 2013, from 459.06 million to 731.11 million. Meanwhile, the area of land approved for real estate enterprises to use but still waiting to be used increased 1.87 times, from 147.5477 million m^2 to 422.8047 million m^2, and the fees paid by real estate enterprises to obtain the use of land increased 17.39 times, from 73.399 billion yuan to 135.0173 billion yuan.[11]

Such immense increases were unprecedented even after the impact of increases in the price index during the same period was accounted for. In fact, when 2000 constant prices were used, the fees real estate enterprises paid to obtain land use increased 12.91, 6.39, and 10.30 times, respectively. Apparently, the increases of both the area of the undeveloped lands owned by real estate enterprises and the actual fees they paid were at much larger scales than the increase of urban population, actually by margins of 10 and even 20 times. Not surprisingly, the urbanization of lands and real estate activities in advance of the urbanization of population has provided abundant room for "ghost cities."

SCALE EXPANSIONS OF CITIES AND TOWNS BECOME ENGINES OF FURTHER URBANIZATION

On one hand, there is the horizontal expansion of cities and towns like spreading dough to make a pita. According to statistics, the constructed area of cities and towns increased by 25,416 km^2, or 113.27%, from 2000 to 2013, from 22,439 to 47,855 km^2, and the area of urban land for construction increased by 24,995 km^2, or 113.06%, from 22,114 to 47,109 km^2, an increase in scale similar to that of the constructed area.

These numbers illustrate a surprisingly fast pace in the horizontal expansion of cities and towns after the turn of the 21st century since the nationwide area of urban lands for construction and the area of constructed lands in cities and towns were both enlarged by more than 1.3 times.

On the other hand, there is the upright, vertical expansion that accompanies the blind expansion to the surroundings and the "pita" becomes thicker and thicker with nonstop heating up of "vertical urbanization." Skyscrapers rise up one after another, competing with each other for which one is higher and which keeps setting new records. Beijing announced its ambition to build a world city, and as many as tens of cities followed suit. With real estate activities aiming for bigger, higher, and more Westernized, it is not a surprise at all that "ghost cities" have emerged and grown.

Unlimited lust for high-quality lives

Consumption always increases, and increased demands are not only for the common consumer goods, but also in pursuit of quality and structure of consumption; after all, as the old saying goes, "men walk up, water flows down." When it comes to consumption, the upward changes are manifested in the upgrade of quality and structure, which also leads to increases in the amount of consumer spending. In fact, humans have unlimited lust for high-quality lives, and lust is the engine to drive development of production as it always poses new demands for production. When lust is scientifically recognized, accommodated, and harnessed, it can be used to guide the economy toward a healthy and vigorous future. Otherwise, consumption may be overemphasized and investment in enlarging reproduction is overlooked, the operation of the cycle of production will be affected, and further increase in consumption will also be harmed; alternatively, investment may be favored over consumption, and expanded reproduction will be derailed from the track of normal consumption and not aligned with people's growing demands in materials and in culture, which will eventually harm reproduction because consumption is compromised. The textbooks of political economics that were commonly used in the past often described the basic economic law of socialism as to keep satisfying the growing demands of people for material and cultural pursuits. Although it does not have full coverage, such a description is clear and positive as the principle of social reproduction.

Pursuit of high-quality lives is based on the development of the means of production in society, and it is also influenced by consumer habits and mental processes. At the establishment of the new China, the consumer behaviors were transitioning to aiming for getting warm and full, which was the most fundamental and essential need.

Unfortunately, later socioeconomic development had many bumps with big rises and falls that struck the economy hard and as a result, the high-quality lives were represented by the possession of "three turnings and one sound," a watch, a bicycle, a sewing machine, and a radio, during the 1950s through 1980s. With development and advancement in the economy, science and technology, culture, and society after the Reform and Opening Up, people's pursuit of high-quality lives also shifted to targeting "three machines plus a house and a car," i.e., a television, a computer, a cell phone, a house, and a car. In fact, the "three machines plus a house and a car" were not the same all the time, and they kept upgrading in quality, function, and level of automation, showing the unlimited lust of people for high-quality lives.

If the increases in consumption brought by the pursuit of high-quality lives are taken as the upgrade of consumer goods, the upgrade never stops and it always happens and goes forward at the same pace with the same periodic characteristics with production and consumption. Many factors affect the upgrade or replacement of consumer goods, and they differ in how they function and how much their functions are in different stages. From the perspective of the forces of production, the factors that have the most prominent influence on the upgrade or replacement of consumer goods at the current stage are the following four.

First, advancement in science and technology provides new production support for the upgrade or replacement of consumer goods. The upgrade in people's pursuit of consumer goods after the establishment of the new China, as described earlier, was essentially the consequence of scientific and technological advancement. A new technological revolution took place after WWII, pioneered by microelectronic technologies; innovative microelectronic products alone, one generation after another, were enough to change the consumer goods and consumption structure. From means of transportation of people and of goods, at sea, on land, and in air, to computers, televisions, phones, fax machines, cell phones, and video cameras to meet the demands of work, study, social lives, and cultural activities, everything with no exception was a product of technological advancement, and they have all accelerated the replacement of consumer goods.

The first technological revolution pushed human society to leave the age of handmade tools and to enter the age of machines, which was marked by conventional industrialization; the next technological revolution after WWII was pioneered by microelectronic technologies, and now we are in a technological revolution dominated by life sciences, including genetic and cloning technologies, marking the step mankind has taken to enter the age of intelligent tools, and a new round of replacement of consumer goods has followed.

Supercomputers, for example, have certain traits of human brains, and artificial intelligence has already been widely applied not only to production but also to family lives as it can replace housewives in some aspects, which is a revolutionary replacement of consumer goods.

Second, overall income increases make replacing consumer goods affordable. As described earlier, sluggish consumption is not uniquely Chinese, but is quite common around the world. Despite this, replacement of consumer goods is also everywhere, which is seemingly contradictory to the sluggish consumption. However, consumption is sluggish compared to actual consumer spending, and income increases have been there through history, and exactly due to the continuous increases in consumption at various historical stages and various types of loans for consumption, people are able to afford sustained replacement of consumer goods.

Third, people like to compare with others, which accelerates the replacement of consumer goods. In fact, consumption is not only decided by hardware such as income but also by software such as the mental activities of consumers, which are sometimes quite powerful. The mental activities of consumers include consumers' emotional state, expectation, and mental responses when choosing, buying, using, appraising, and transferring goods or services, and are usually divided into practical, conforming, novelty-seeking, and competing types, which have various functions in leading consumer behaviors at various historical stages.

When the force of production in a society is at a low level and so is consumption, people tend to be practical and conform to the majority when spending money; consumers favor the goods and services that are of good quality for a low price, last long, and are thus worth the money while they also like to copy the behaviors of those surrounding them who have similar tastes and incomes, i.e., conforming to the majority and unwilling to show uniqueness. When the economy reaches the level of prosperity and people have medium incomes, the consumers become less practical and conforming and more selective of goods and services; in their minds, "they want things that others own as well as things that others do not," and such a mental response is reinforced in consumption and the impact of pursuing high-quality lives and unlimited lust on consumption is manifested in these behaviors.

In fact, the behaviors of competing and seeking novelty are epidemic. Some feel insulted when left behind the consumption choices of others or fashions and make every effort to catch up. If others move into an independent house, they want a luxurious one; when others drive a Benz or BMW, they want a Lincoln or Bentley, or at least an Audi; when others travel to Singapore, Malaysia, Thailand, or the Gold Coast in Australia, they want to go to Las Vegas, Hawaii, etc. In fact, consumption choices are essentially material behaviors at present, and the influence of the mental activities of consumers on their behaviors is immense and cannot be overlooked when people have increased incomes, convenient transportation, and rich knowledge and value cultural activities and individualism.

Fourth, the revolution in circulation greatly shortens the time and narrows the space needed for the replacement of consumer goods. The revolution in circulation is the birth of the modern industry of logistics management that transmits information and transports goods in the modern information age, and it is pushing forward the replacement of consumer goods with great power. In the current era during which "time is money and efficiency is life," modern information transmissions such as "Internet plus" and the industry of logistics management are marching forward so fast as to have become a revolution that bridges producers and consumers and substantially shortens the interval between production and consumption as if there were express buses between the two, one after another. The conventional mode of business has been changing, many intermediate steps are no longer needed, the cost of consumption has been cut down, and more and more consumers have emerged. Now consumers only need to put orders and make payments online, with phones, cell phones, or e-mails, and they can make purchases easily and conveniently without having to step out of their doors. In addition, the "Internet plus" style of purchases keeps consumers instantly updated with the newest information on goods and is at the very front line of the trend of consumer goods replacement, thus it runs first to meet people's demands for new tastes and high-quality lives.

Implementing the strategy of green, moderate consumption

Conventional and modern theories of consumption alike have been challenged by the current reality as they both are contradictory to the aims of future development. Conventional theories of consumption value the decisive role of production and describe consumption from the perspective of production, which is therefore not well oriented with people, or with the goal of consumption to satisfy people's demands for all-around development. In contrast, modern theories of high consumption and high waste mistakenly place consumption and are therefore in violation of the ecological principles to save on resources and protect the environment and are harmful to sustainable development. As problems and measures to solve them always appear simultaneously, the problems of the two types of consumption theories await a solution. In my opinion, the solution is green, moderate growth of consumption. In fact, it is high time to advertise the concept of green consumption and to implement the strategy of green consumption with moderate growth.

Green consumption

What is green consumption? Green is the color born with forests, grasslands, and crops in nature. Chlorophylls in green plants consume water and carbon dioxide and synthesize organic compounds and oxygen with the help of sunlight through a process called photosynthesis. Therefore, green reflects the metabolic state of green plants. Decreases in the shade of green signal decreases in green plants, which leads to weakened photosynthesis, oxygen release, and ecologic balance; increases in the shade of green, on the other hand, signal increases in green plants, which leads to strengthened photosynthesis, oxygen release, and ecologic balance.

With socioeconomic development comes increases in environmental damage, and people have become more and more concerned with environmental issues and more and more expectant of green, which bears the terms of *green agriculture*, *green food*, *green production*, *green factories*, *green interior design*, and *green services* and, at a subordinate level, *green rice*, *green teas*, *green drinks*, *green flowers*, *green clothes*, *green paints*, *green appliances*, *green hotels*, *green cups*, and *green glasses*, where green embodies an attitude that is ecologically friendly and repulsive to pollution.

To further generalize this attitude, green is also deemed safe, clear, and elegant, and the terms of *green travel*, *green Internet*, *green countries*, *green cities*, and *green cultures* have thus been born. Green consumption is certainly in line with this, and comprises both aspects. From the perspective of being ecologically friendly and repulsive to pollution, consumer goods should of course come from green production with pollution contained in an acceptable range; and from the perspective of being safe, clear, and elegant, green consumption is at a high level that should become a goal of consumers so that consumption is transitioned and upgraded.

To this end, green consumption is the consumption that stands by the harmony between mankind and nature to facilitate the sustainable development of populations, resources, environments, economies, and societies. Facilitation of the sustainable development of consumption and resources necessitates recognition of and respect for the scarcity of resources: oil and minerals are scarce and get only more so because they are not renewable, and land and fresh water, although reproducible and renewable, may become scarce and worsened when reproduction and renewal are not fast enough to meet the demands of people. Therefore, to save and protect resources requires that social production and reproduction use resources for as long as possible, improve the efficiency of the use, and slow down the progress of exhaustion on one hand, and on the other hand, that green, reasonable consumption be called for, unreasonably high consumption and high waste be eliminated, and everything be consumed to the end to realize the value of resources.

The sustainable development of consumption and the environment requires the inclusion of consumption in the scope of the ecological environment so that consumer behaviors are curbed and directed to the harmony between mankind and nature. In fact, since the concept of sustainable development was first proposed, environmental protection has received exceptional attention in that a series of international conferences issued widely influential statements, protocols, and plans to protect the environment, which later included consumption.

Surveys and statistics in the 1980s and 1990s showed that in postindustrial countries in Europe and America such as Germany, the United Kingdom, and the United States, more than 80.0% of the consumers considered environmental friendliness the most important factor in their consumption choices and thus were willing to pay higher prices for environmentally friendly goods in order to show their attitude to refuse polluting and harming the environment. Consumers International (CI) has held annual events on "sustainable development and green consumption" consecutively since 1997 to promote the concept of green consumption. In China, departments of environmental protection started in 1999 a "triple-green project" aiming to call for and implement green passages, green markets, and green consumption, and the concept of green consumption has been accepted by people.

In fact, it is clear that acceptance of green consumption helps consumers choose green products that are not polluted or the pollution is contained within a limited, acceptable level, protection of green consumption raises consumers' awareness of garbage disposal to avoid added pollution, and elevation of green consumption places the concept at a higher level of sensible consumption that values environmental protection, resource and energy saving, and practices to sustain development.

Green consumption is thus not only a node of the cycle of production but also a way to transform consumer mind-sets and nurture new values. In fact, I have found through my conversations with the respondents of my field trip surveys that behind details of daily lives hide people's awareness of environmental protection and values: when one drives through a downtown road with pedestrians crossing the road, does he honk his car or wait quietly for the pedestrians to pass? After one peels fruit or unpacks a package of clothes, does he toss the peels or the package around or into a garbage bin, and if the latter, any garbage bin or those sorted according to recycle guidelines? After all, honking adds to a city's noise pollution and disposal of garbage arbitrarily adds to a city's mess and to the workload of environmental sanitation workers. There is always something big behind something small, and in this sense, green consumption is truly an ideological revolution.

The sustainable development of consumption and economies requires that economic development be included in the strategy of sustainable development and be landed on green consumption with moderate growth. The conventional concept of economic development values maximization of profits that is brought by maximization of production value, which has directly led to heated competitions of GDP.

In contrast, the concept of sustainable development oriented toward people aims to satisfy the demands of all-around development of people, which is not entirely aligned with profit maximization, and thus new ideas of economic development that include green consumption are needed. One idea is the concept that quality and efficiency must be unified.

As described earlier, green consumption is not only about ecological friendliness and elimination of pollution, but also about safety, clearness, and elegance, which certainly challenges the quality of consumption. Therefore, the conventional mode of economic development that is after production only must be put aside and what is now pursued should include product quality. Similarly, the mode of expanded reproduction that does not consider the cost with blind investment in fixed assets that does not calculate the return can no longer be used, and improvement in economic benefits must be valued and the output–input ratio carefully calculated.

Another idea is the concept of macroscopic benefits of development. Macroscopic benefits do not include only the common economic benefits based on output–input ratios but also the benefits to society with which a ratio of social output to input should be valued. Accordingly, systematically evaluating indicators should also be established through reforms; the example of the World Bank may be useful here in that GDP per capita, the average annual inflation rate, and the life expectancy at birth are used as indicators to evaluate the development of a society.

A third idea is the concept of long-term benefits. Of course, economic development pays attention to the current benefits; however, social reproduction is a continuous cycle and some benefits need time to show up. In fact, both the macroscopic spatial and temporal benefits need time, and so do the benefits of consumption. For example, it takes at least three years for a large jet plane that is improved in speed, noise, oil consumption, comfort, and safety to be designed, produced, and finally operated, and such consumer goods cannot be evaluated objectively in a short time.

The sustainable development of consumption and society relies on the society-wide comprehension and establishment of a system to accommodate green consumption with moderate growth and the needed reforms. There are always institutions in every society that are not compatible with green consumption. For example, some countries levy heavy taxes on residents, who under the pressure of taxation cannot afford to spend much money, and the resulting lack of effective consumption eventually hinders socioeconomic development; some countries over-stimulate consumption through financial policies that encourage financial institutions to use various leverages to boost consumption, which eventually leads consumers to be in high debt, and economic development is also troubled.

In China, the aforementioned consumption-hindering factors, "the unaffordable," "the dare not," and "the nowhere to buy," all have causes in the economic system. Overall, there are causes of low incomes, which is the basis of consumption; but more importantly, the gap between high and low incomes and the lack of an all-around social security system are the root of why some consumers with relatively low incomes dare not and cannot afford to spend money. As for the case of consumer goods that cannot be obtained easily on the market, it is also related to the system to some degree as there is a lack of policies that deal with the goods in shortage as well as an absence or lack of insurance of goods from policies.

Decision-making of green consumption with moderate growth

Green consumption with moderate growth has a twofold meaning: it is green consumption that should grow moderately, and the moderate growth of green consumption should coincide with socioeconomic development. As analyzed earlier, it is a demand of China's current economic development stage for green consumption with moderate growth, as well as the only choice to comprehend, accommodate, and develop the economy of the new normal. Given the current situation that China's population growth is slowing down and the residents are not enthusiastic about consumption, the path of green consumption with moderate growth needs reforms to be initiated and pushed for from the following aspects.

First, a complete set of policies that cover the whole cycle from production to consumption needs to be constructed to support green consumption. Although it has been promoted around the world and become a trend in socioeconomic development, technological advancement, and transition of cultural concepts, green consumption, as a new model of consumption, still needs policy support. China has been called by the international community an organized society with a powerful government; then the power of the government should be invested in promoting and facilitating green consumption as with anything new, and social organization should guide all the residents to participate in and practice it.

It is widely known that the conventional mode of development since WWII with high input, high output, high consumption, high waste, and high pollution was negated at the UN Conference Environment and Development in Rio De Janeiro, Brazil in 1992 by several files such as the *Rio Declaration on Environment and Development* and *Agenda 21*, and all countries were called on to pass their own *Agenda 21* to establish a new mode of production and consumption to reduce pollution and maintain ecological balance.

China particularly valued the *Rio Declaration* and *Agenda 21*, kept its promises, and was among the first to take action with the 1994 publication of *Agenda 21 in China – A White Paper of China's Population, Environment and Development in the 21st Century*. As stated in the *White Paper*,

> China's economic development still follows the conventional mode that consumes a large amount of resources and is characterized by extensive operation, which greatly harms not only the environment, but also the sustainable economic development. Therefore, a transition of the development strategy to a sustainable path through technological advances is the only right choice for speeding up economic development.[12]

This was one of the earlier proposals for China to talk about "transition of the development strategy," which was in line with the later proposals such as "transition of the mode of economic growth" and "transition of the mode of economic development."

The transition from an extensive, external mode of economic development to an intensive, endogenous mode is certainly based on production; however, production is not only restricted in the node of production within the cycle of production, exchange, distribution, and consumption. In fact, the complete sense of production comprises the whole cycle of social production and the transition of production mode is thus part of the cycle. After all, it is hard to imagine a way of green consumption when the production mode is still extensive, which only leads to extensive consumption, at least the production consumption; similarly, it is also hard to imagine that consumption is still at a conventional stage that harms the environment when the mode of economic development is intensive and endogenous.

In 2013, the Third Plenary Session of the 18th Central Committee of the CCCPC passed the *Decision by CCCPC on Several Important Issues of Comprehensively Deepening the Reform*, which marked a new stage of the Reform. The *Decision* specified that a systematic and complete mechanism must be established to develop ecological civilization, the strictest protection laws must be enforced to protect the environment from the origin and to hold accountable those responsible for environmental damages, and regulations must be perfected for environmental management and recovery, so that the ecological environment could be protected by laws and institutions.

Green consumption is also part of the development of ecological civilization, and it also needs regulations and policies to guide and manage. Two lights are needed when drafting the policies and regulations, i.e., specification of what is promoted and what is objected to, or what is the red light and what is the green light. In fact, the Chinese government has already made a lot of efforts.

For example, to encourage new-energy vehicles, various rewards for their production and sales have been issued and have substantially lowered the cost, many conventional vehicles have been eliminated before their expiration dates in order to reduce pollution with compensations paid to the owners, many enterprises that discharged excessive pollution have been fined and punished according to environmental laws, administrative, criminal, and economic punishments are in effect for pernicious environmental accidents, and cadres are now evaluated for quality of the natural resources when leaving office and held accountable for life for environmental damages.

All these measures have been effective in environmental management as well as consumption management, and should be acknowledged. However, they overall have limited effect and mostly cover the production side with a lack of consumption-related regulations. Therefore, the following efforts are still needed.

First, a comprehensive system of polices needs to be established and be practical to support green consumption and the policies need to combine guidance on one side and punishment on the other.

Second, reward polices may be issued toward several particular consumption areas. The aforementioned policy to encourage new-energy vehicles with rewards is a good example, except that the rewards vary in various places with various effects and thus need to be unified. In fact, aside from vehicles, economical consumption of other types of resources, such as electricity, gas, and fresh water, may be rewarded, say, those who consume less than the national average may get a prize to encourage economical consumption. The idea of rewards can also be applied on the production fields as each product may have a standard level of energy consumption and resource consumption in production, and those that consume less without compromising quality are rewarded. Such measures may not only lower consumption and cost but also facilitate the elimination of the underdeveloped, high-consuming industries and benefit mode transition and the structural adjustment of the economy as well.

Third, punishment policies may also be issued toward several particular consumption areas. For example, those who produce, operate, and sell harmful, fake, false, shoddy, or low-quality goods should be punished with economic and administrative measures, and their legal responsibilities should be impartially determined by the procuratorial and judicial institutions. After all, policies guide and bind people's behaviors while laws draw a red line and sanction those who cross the line.

Second, residents' incomes should be improved overall with reasonable preferential distribution to laborers. The current incomes in both urban and rural areas are not very high yet, which essentially holds back the moderate growth of consumption, including green consumption, and it is of prime importance to improve them. Given the actual incomes of the people, it is first necessary to understand that the key to income increases is increases in labor efficiency.

To this end, a balance needs to be kept: on one hand, the increases in salary rates and incomes should not lag behind the increases in labor efficiency because, if they do, consumption will have no basis to further increase; on the other hand, the increases in salary rates and incomes should not exceed the increases in labor efficiency because, if they do, inflation will result, which will not benefit consumers or their pursuit of a better life. Under the current situation, the former, lagging increases in salary rates and incomes behind increases in labor efficiency, is more common, and efforts should be primarily made to accelerate increases in the salary rates and incomes of laborers, the key of which is to improve the weight of labor in the primary distribution.

Fortunately, the decreases in the proportion and in the absolute number of the working-age population facilitate improvement in labor efficiency, which has created beneficial conditions for distribution that favors laborers. In the secondary distribution, in addition, the class of low incomes should be favored so that the gap between the rich and the poor may be narrowed. Now that much has been devoted to the gap in the foregoing analyses, it is clear that distribution policies should be oriented toward this issue in that not only the gap between high and low incomes should be narrowed, but policies in social welfare and social support systems should specifically favor the underprivileged as well.

Third, reforms of the social security system should be continued, which should reasonably favor the underprivileged. Behind "the unaffordable" and "the dare not" are not only restricted incomes but also limited functions of social support, which leaves much concern to consumers when spending money. The social support system is primarily to support the underprivileged, and it is therefore reasonable to favor them.

However, the current system of social support has many defects, and the underprivileged are not always taken care of. Problems in the institutions have led to these defects, but there are also problems in the managerial team in that some executive personnel are bound by interpersonal relationships and cannot always help the underprivileged. After all, institutions are fixed, but executives are humans who, when having their own preferences, cannot always benefit the underprivileged. It is therefore necessary to reassure society that the managerial teams at various levels are impartial in their actions to embody social justice.

Fourth, reforms are needed on consumption taxes and progressive taxes should be levied. When I visited academic institutions in Finland, Sweden, and Norway in Northern Europe, scholars showed me their research and data and told me proudly that there were no super-rich or super-poor residents in their countries, although they were all considered capitalist; therefore, they were really socialist countries as there was only a narrow gap between the rich and the poor; in contrast, they called some nominally socialist countries capitalist where there was a huge gap between the rich and the poor. No matter right or wrong, what they said was their view, but what is really inspirational is why there is a narrow gap there. It is due to progressive taxes in that those with high incomes have to pay their taxes at progressively higher rates, or the higher the income, the higher the tax rate and the taxes.

In the end, the amounts of money left to those with high, medium, and low incomes are not much different, actually a lot less different than what they are in many other countries. It is fair to say that the personal income taxation system in China has absorbed some experiences of progressive taxes, and those with higher incomes in China do pay higher taxes at a higher rate compared to others. However, the progressive tax rate in China is not progressive enough, and the intended effect is not evident. In addition, some of the rich try every effort to avoid paying taxes, which further increases the gap between the rich and the poor. Therefore, it is important to completely land the principles in the *Decision* to comprehensively deepen the Reform by the CCCPC, i.e.,

> the redistribution system must be perfected to adjust for the income imbalance with measures of taxation, social welfare, and mobile payment while at the same time the taxation system should play a larger role in adjusting for the income imbalance.[13]

Notes

1 United Nations, *World Population Prospects: The 2008 Revision*, New York, United Nations, 2009, p. 48.

2 Ibid., pp. 48–52.

3 Tian, Xueyuan, *Hardships of a Big Country: A Macroscopic View of the Chinese Population in the 20th Century*, Beijing, Social Sciences Academic Press (China), 2013, pp. 14–16.

4 Tian, Xueyuan, *Research on the Development Strategy of China's Population in the 21st Century*, Beijing, Social Sciences Academic Press (China), 2007, pp. 439–454.
5 United Nations, *World Population Prospects, 2008 Revision*, pp. 55, 236, 292, 484.
6 National Bureau of Statistics, *Statistical Communiqué of the People's Republic of China on the 2015 National Economic and Social Development*, February 29, 2016.
7 National Bureau of Statistics, *China Statistical Yearbook 2014*, Beijing, China Statistics Press, 2014, pp. 4–5, 158.
8 "The Middle Class Pays the Highest Interest in Arguments on China's Gini Coefficient," *Global Times* (huanqiu.com), January 21, 2014.
9 Wang, Zhiping, "Release of the Gini Coefficient: An Act Worth Embracing," *Wenhui*, January 21, 2013; and *Assembly of China's Gini Coefficients 1981–2014*, newest edition, Baidu Library, professional materials, http://wenku.baidu.com.
10 United Nations, *The World Population Prospects 1988*, pp. 200, 204. *Population Studies*, No. 106, New York, 1989; *China Statistical Yearbook 2014*, p. 25; National Bureau of Statistics, *Statistical Communiqué of the People's Republic of China on the 2014 National Economic and Social Development*, February 26, 2015.
11 *China Statistical Yearbook 2014*, p. 471.
12 *Agenda 21 in China – A White Paper of China's Population, Environment and Development in the 21st Century*, Beijing, China Environmental Science Press, 2013, p. 21.
13 *The Decision on Several Important Issues of Comprehensively Deepening the Reform*, Beijing, People's Publishing House, 2013, p. 66.

Bibliography

Agenda 21 in China – A White Paper of China's Population, Environment and Development in the 21st Century, Beijing, China Environmental Science Press, 2014.

Brown, Lester R., *Plan B: Rescuing a Planet under Stress and a Civilization in Trouble*, translated by Lin, Zixin and Bao, Yongning, Beijing, Oriental Press, 2003.

The Decision on Several Important Issues of Comprehensively Deepening the Reform, Beijing, People's Publishing House, 2013.

Keynes, John Maynard, *The General Theory of Employment, Interest and Money*, translated by Lu, Menglong, Beijing, Commercial Press, 1997.

Li, Jingneng, ed., Wu, Cunguo, vice ed., *Current Western Demography*, Taiyuan, Shanxi People's Publishing House, 1992.

Ouyang, Song and Gao, Yongzhong, eds., *Oral History of the Reform and Opening-Up*, Beijing, China Renming University Press, 2014.

Tian, Xueyuan, *New Opportunity of Reforms for Post-Population Transition*, Beijing, Social Sciences Academic Press (China), 2014.

Tian, Xueyuan et al., *Research on the Strategy of China's Population Development in the 21st Century*, Beijing, Social Sciences Academic Press (China), 2007.

United Nations, *Long-Range World Population Projections: Two Centuries of Population Growth 1950–2150*, New York, United Nations, 1992.

United Nations, *World Population Prospects: The 2008 Revision*, New York, United Nations, 2009.

2 Economic new normal meets post-demographic transition

Exploring the path of development driven by pursuit of quality and benefits instead of speed

Everything changes with time, place, and condition. Studies on the association between population and economic growth in the 20th century have mostly been concerned with changes in the number of people. However, the impact of the changes in the working-age population on socioeconomic development should also be carefully studied now that it has been more and more manifested in the current post-demographic transition, especially after the Lewis turning point was reached.

China, with the largest population in the world, should also accommodate the changes and take a new perspective on its own population. With theories and practices combined, the new perspective should help clarify how the population went from the traditional to the post-demographic transition, interpret the trend in the new normal of the economy that has met the post-demographic transition, and employ the positive energy of the residual population benefits and bonuses in the post-golden age while at the same time helping accommodate the declines of benefits and bonuses, find a path of development driven by pursuit of quality and economic benefits instead of speed, and push for reform to transform the economic mode, adjust the structure, and benefit the people.

Theories of demographic transition

Birth, death, and migration rates are three essential factors that shape the natural changes of a population, and changes in the working-age population and the total population are also attributable to these three rates. In any given country or region, population changes are usually not affected by internal migration, and when immigration and emigration are similar in scale and thus cancel each other out, population changes are primarily decided by birth and death rates.

Birth and death rates are influenced by many factors, including demographic, economic, technological, and social ones, and therefore usually show regular changes with historical stages. Theories of demographic transition resulted from the studies to summarize and extract the regular changes of populations, and have served as the golden key to unlocking the secret of population changes, including those in the working-age population.

In fact, comprehension and analysis of things always go from the surface to the core and from the concrete to the abstract while descriptions and summaries of changes and development go from the core to the surface and from the abstract to the concrete; these means help elucidate matters. Analysis in this section is thus organized from the abstract to the concrete, starting from theories of demographic transition.

The traditional theory of demographic transition

A scan of the formation

Demographic transition is a rather mature theory in demography, and it was formed through studies of regular changes in birth and death rates and continuously developed with practices. The Industrial Revolution initiated in the mid-18th century continuously brought new spurs to economic growth with advances in science and technology; as a result, production efficiency climbed to historically high levels and industrial and agricultural products were quickly accumulated; with all these changes also came marked increases in birth rates and decreases in death rates, leading to new records of natural growth rates one after another while the world population grew like magic. Things started to change in the 19th century, when France was the first to see the spell of population growth wear off. The birth rate in France from 1801 to 1810 was 32.0‰, the death rate 27.8‰, and the growth rate 4.2‰, while the birth rate declined to 22.1‰ from 1891 to 1900, the death rate 21.4‰, and the growth rate 0.7‰, marking a state of low population growth.[1]

Other countries in Western Europe such as the United Kingdom and Germany followed and showed evident decreases in birth and growth rates, although they were not as low as those in France, marking a transition in population growth in Western European countries with high levels of industrialization.

Arsene Dumont, a French socialist and demographer, noticed this phenomenon and tried to explain it with his theory of "social capillary." Dumont argued that one's drive for reproduction was reciprocal of his desire to move up the social ladder like a capillary effect: the larger the force that pushed him to move up the ladder, the lower the drive to procreate. Meanwhile, neoclassical economists led by Alfred Marshall were more interested in analyzing microeconomic behaviors and tried to interpret the population growth transition from new perspectives by introducing the concept of marginal utility.

Nevertheless, these efforts were still preliminary and did not explore the causes, phenomena, or characteristics of the transition. A further step was finally made by French demographer Aldophe Landry. Landry first proposed three stages in population change and development, i.e., the initial, middle, and modern stages, and provided theoretical interpretations in his paper "Three Theories of Population." He then associated the three stages with socioeconomic development in his subsequent book, *The Demographic Revolution*, to argue that the three stages were part of socioeconomic development and that different development stages had different problems, with a warning that Athens and Rome both declined due to depopulation.

Meanwhile, American demographer and socialist Warren S. Thompson reached a similar conclusion to Landry's when he compared demographic patterns in several places with various economic and social development levels and summarized these patterns into three stages of population development. These studies, already at the door of a demographic transition theory, eventually amounted to the achievement by American demographer Frank W. Notestein, who developed a formal, systematic, and comprehensive theory of demographic transition after WWII and made comprehensive descriptions of its preconditions, foundations, formats, contents, and consequences.

Concept outlines

As described earlier, the theory of demographic transition was formed gradually and matured stepwise. Notestein formalized the theory based on previous works by others, and his work is now the most cited to describe demographic transition; however, like everything else, the theory of demographic transition did not stay unchanged and has constantly been enriched and perfected, so it is a concept that develops with practices. In a nutshell, the theory is the theoretical abstraction of the nature of population changes and deals mainly with the foundations, images, characteristics, consequences, and impacts of the regular changes of birth, death, and growth rates. This summary is comprised of two layers of meanings.

The first layer is the theoretical abstraction of the nature of natural population changes. Natural population changes are the changes in the scale and the number of people of a population determined by births, mortalities, and migration. Births increase both the scale and the number of a population, deaths do the opposite, and migration does both with immigration increasing and emigration decreasing the scale and the number.

In fact, the word "population" originally denoted entirety, and then evolved to mean the entire people if not otherwise annotated. A population is not an individual, and all the individuals in a population are bound by economic, social, ideological, and family factors, including births, mortalities, and migration. For example, births are preconditioned by conception, which is preconditioned by sexual relations between men and women, which involves marriage, families, reproduction concepts, and the socioeconomic status of each family. In fact, ever since human beings became a species independent of other animals, human reproduction has been much more than a biological behavior with continuous improvement in the forces of production and human intelligence, and individual behaviors have been more and more confined by family and social relations.

The theory of demographic transition reveals the demographic, economic, technological, and social factors in fertility changes, thus the nature of the regular changes of fertility rates is also revealed; it aims to find how population corresponds with various levels of social development and how to deal with demographic issues by understanding the regular changes in birth, death, and growth rates.

The second layer is a scientific description of the factors in demographic transition. This is the major part of the theory that describes the foundations, images, characteristics, consequences, and impacts of the changes in birth, death, and growth rates in order to make scientific analysis and draw conclusions in accordance with natural laws. Although there had been studies on birth, death, and growth rates and a considerable number of conclusions had been reached before the theory of demographic transition, exploration of the patterns of the changes and development of the three rates only started with the efforts to establish the theory. This is also why demographic transition was established and developed as an independent theory, the points of which are further elaborated in what follows.

Major theoretical points

Based on these outlines, the following five aspects summarize the theory of demographic transition.

BACKGROUND OF THE BIRTH OF DEMOGRAPHIC TRANSITION

Fundamental changes in population reproduction as well as new patterns of social economies after about a century of the Industrial Revolution gave birth to the theory of demographic transition. As mentioned earlier, sustained declines in the death and birth rates were observed in Western European countries such as France, the United Kingdom, and Germany in the 19th century, which was exactly what demographic transition tried to explain with reasonable abstraction of theories from the changes.

What is a scientific, abstract theory? It is the summary and conclusion of studies to find the pattern of phenomena that is in accordance with the nature of the phenomena, and it comes from and can be applied in practice. The theory of demographic transition is still valued today and widely accepted by different schools of demography because it provides scientific abstraction and reasonable conclusion of practices.

TRANSITION OF POPULATION REPRODUCTION TYPES

Demographic transition is associated with changing types of population reproduction, although the two are not exactly the same. Both study the changes in births, deaths, and natural growth of population, but they differ in their aims. Population reproduction is divided into three types according to commonly accepted standards: the type of high births, high deaths, and low growth; the type of high births, low deaths, and high growth; and the type of low births, low deaths, and low growth.

Demographic transition, in contrast, is aimed to understand the transition of these three types, including the causes, images, characteristics, consequences, and impacts of the transition and involving several areas of demography, economics, science and technology, and sociology. The three, or sometimes more than three, types of population reproduction are considered three, or more than three, platforms of population development where the move from one platform to another may have regularities, and that is the focus of demographic transition so as to reveal its causes and countermeasures. From this perspective, the picture of demographic transition is comprehensive and covers a wide range, with the three types of population reproduction included as the three platforms for transitions to occur (Figure 2.1).

As shown in Figure 2.1, the range between points 1 and 3 on the x-axis is the type of population reproduction with high births, high deaths, and low growth; from 3 to 6 is the area of population expansion; from 6 to 9 population shrinkage; and from 9 to 11 the type with low births, low deaths, and low growth. The ranges of 1–3 and 9–11 are characterized by simple population reproduction, with 1–3 having low growth due to high births and deaths and 9–11 having low growth due to low births and deaths. The middle part of 3–9 features vigorous demographic transitional activities with violent changes in birth, death, and growth rates, showing an overall pattern of transitions from high births, high deaths, and low growth through high births, low deaths, and

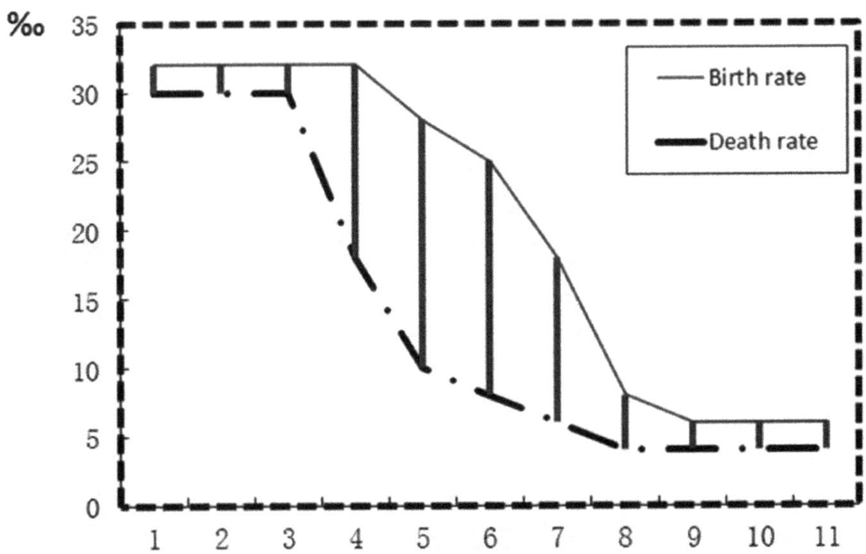

Figure 2.1 Three types of population reproduction and demographic transition.

high growth to low births, low deaths, and low growth; the range of 3–6 is the transition to population increases, and 6–9 is the transition to population decreases, and the result of these transitions is a population with low births, low deaths, and low growth.

BASIC CHARACTERISTICS OF DEMOGRAPHIC TRANSITION

Behind the stages of demographic transition hide many economic, demographic, technological, and social factors that all together push the population to transition. With reference to the three types of population reproduction and demographic transition shown in Figure 2.1, the basic characteristics of demographic transition are as follows.

First, demographic transition starts with decreases in death rates. In Figure 2.1, the curve of death rates starts to go down at point 3 of the x-axis and the downward part stops at point 8. Any population with a considerable size always starts its transition when its death rates decrease. This is because an overall decrease in the death rates results from development of the forces of production and improvement in the efficiency of production, which satisfies the demand of the population for food; in addition, advances in science and technology, especially breakthroughs in medical technologies, may also decrease death rates significantly by curing previously lethal diseases. Science and technology, together with human intelligence, are always marching forward, which brings labor efficiency and medical technologies to advance but not to turn back, and therefore, decreases in death rates are usually progressive.

Second, during the transition from the first type of population reproduction to the second and that from the second to the third, population increases first grow and then decline, and the turning point from the growth to the decline is crucial to the overall pattern of demographic transition. When the turning point shows up varies across countries and regions with different population age structures, but it is always after fertility rates drop to the replacement level and before the proportions of the working-age population reach their peaks, i.e., the region corresponding to point 6 on the x-axis in Figure 2.1. Once demographic transition reaches this point, the transition in the traditional sense is almost over, and the timing of the point must be watched intensively because after this point, the population will start to progress to the type with low births, low deaths, and low growth.

Third, decreases in birth rates last for a long time, with relatively strong momentum that continues the decreases even after the population reaches the state of "three low rates," which is the case in many countries and regions where the birth rates are very close to the death rates. However, it's been noticed recently that the type of "three low rates" may not be the terminal state of a population as there have been rebounds in birth and growth rates in some countries in Western and Northern Europe. Still, any conclusion is premature now, and patience and observation are needed for final conclusions reached in practice.

Consequences of demographic transition

One consequence of demographic transition is for the population to have low birth, death, and growth rates, as typified by Western and Northern Europe and Japan, which completed the transition a long time ago, and the consequence is also emerging in some countries going through the transition. However, it is not yet known whether it is the only consequence, and more practices are needed to tell us whether birth and growth rates will no longer take another turn for increases. Nevertheless, it is possible and has been seen that the total size of a population and its working-age group will decelerate in growth after the transition, even getting to or approaching zero growth.

Impacts of demographic transition

The theory of demographic transition has won consensus among academics and all social sectors and has become a mature demographic theory, which is of great importance and has profound impact. From the perspective of population changes, the theory has revealed the pattern of the changes, from high births, high deaths, and low growth through high births, low deaths, and high growth to low births, low deaths, and low growth; pointed to a direction of further changes for populations of considerable sizes; and provided scientific references for policy making concerning population changes.

From the perspective of economic development, the theory has revealed not only the changes in the total number of people in a society to provide data support for social reproduction but also the characteristics of the changes in each stage and how they affect the speed and structure of economic development. Particularly during the transition from high births, low deaths, and high growth to low births, low deaths, and low growth, there are usually increases in the proportion of the working-age population and decreases in the proportion of the supported elderly and young population, and it is thus the golden age of a population's age structure that benefits economic development.

The population benefits and bonuses in the golden age significantly boost economic development, yet after it, the proportion of the working-age population decreases and that of the supported population increases, which provides growing population deficits and liabilities for society that negatively impact economic development, holding back the speed and the rhythm of economic development to a large degree.

The progression and deepening of population aging actually has both pros and cons, but overall, there are more cons than pros and the cons will worsen with the progression of population aging. Therefore, a society must get ready for the challenges brought by an aged population in advance, and what is the most important is to raise consensus to establish a social security system of the elderly that covers the whole society and is fair and sustainable with sufficient endowment funds for elderly care.

The theory of post-demographic transition

After the term *post-industrialization* was coined, it suddenly became fashionable and popular to add *post-* to existing terms, topics, and concepts to give them a new meaning, such as post-urbanization, post-modernization, and post-financial crisis age. Similar ideas were also applied in noneconomic fields such as "the eighties" (those born between 1980 and 1989, which in Chinese is called 80th after), "the nineties," and "postdoctoral" researchers.

Just like all these newly coined terms, *post-demographic transition* is also a new term attached to the preexisting one with additions of new meanings. Therefore, to understand the new terms with the addition of *post-*, it is necessary to first understand the original, base terms, their denotations, and their connotations, so that the original terms and the new ones with *post-* can be associated as well as differentiated, which then may lead to accurate understanding of the terms with their backgrounds and evolution. The original, traditionally used term of *demographic transition*, the one without the addition of *post-*, has been described in terms of its background, points, and impacts on socioeconomic development, and needs not be repeated here.

Meanwhile, the traditional theory of demographic transition left something unanswered: where does a population go after it reaches the stage of "three low rates"? Will the transition stop or continue, and, if the latter, where does it go? In attempts to answer these questions, American demographer Harvey Leibenstein proposed that after a society was industrialized and modernized, the birth and death rates of its population would both decline to very low levels with the death rate being stably low and the birth rate fluctuating to the replacement level and that the population growth rate might decrease to a very low level, even as low as below zero. His view broke the bounds of the traditional model of demographic transition with three stages and three types.

In addition, other scholars of demographic and social transition proposed that demographic transition could be studied not only in the scope of economics but also in sociology; others questioned the decreases in death rates that were believed to happen first in demographic transition and argued that birth rates might decrease simultaneously with and sometimes even before death rates. Among these scholars, studies by C. P. Blacker, Ansley Coale, and Edgar M. Hoover deserve particular attention as they touched the peripherals of post-demographic transition.

In 1947, British demographer C. P. Blacker published a paper, "Stages in Population Growth," in which he divided demographic transition into five phases.

> Phase one is high stationary, marked by a balance of birth rates and death rates that are both very high while the population growth is stationary.
>
> Phase two is early expanding, characterized by falling death rates that get farther and farther away from birth rates, resulting in accelerated growth of population.

Phase three is late expanding, marked by continuous decreases in death rates and the onset of decreases in birth rates wherein the difference in the two rates is the largest and hence the population growth, the fastest; when the birth rates further decline, the population growth starts slowing down.

Phase four is low stationary, characterized by a new balance between death rates and birth rates when the two rates take turns to reach a low level; however, this balance is one at a low level, different from the balance in the high stationary phase.

Phase five is diminishing, marked by the momentum of decreasing birth rates that have started the decreases later than death rates, driving the birth rates to continue to decline after reaching the same level of the death rates, and the population starts to transition to negative growth.

American demographer Ansley Coale also divided demographic transition into five phases in his work in 1973, *The Demographic Transition Reconsidered*, but his phases were not the same as Blacker's. Coale came up with quantitative standards of birth, death, and natural growth rates for each phase through observations for long terms, which was meant to facilitate staging of population development (Table 2.1).

Needless to say, Coale's standards were not golden rules, neither were they entirely scientific or applicable, but his quantification showed that demographic transition was caused by constant changes of the three rates and could be calculated and measured. In contrast, Blacker specifically proposed that demographic transition would eventually arrive at the diminishing phase, leaving space for negative population growth.

In China, when the fertility rate fell low, discussions on post-demographic transition became heated. A literature review showed that Luo Chun coined the term and expounded it, and he was so proud as to call it "the most dashing" of his academic works.[2] In 1992, Zhu Guohong published "The Pattern in Southern Jiangsu: The Phase of Post-Demographic Transition" in *Population*, with the term in the title of the paper, and made a demographic analysis of the post-demographic transition. After the turn of the 21st century, a growing body of studies focused on the post-demographic transition, some of which questioned the concept.

Table 2.1 Coale's standards of five phases of a population (%)

	Preliminary stationary	*Premodern*	*Transitioning*	*Modern*	*Modern stationary*
Birth rates	5.0	4.37	4.57	2.04	1.29
Death rates	5.0	3.37	1.57	1.04	1.29
Natural growth rates	0.0	1.0	3.0	1.0	0.0

Overall, the post-demographic transition is relative to the previous, or common, conventional, demographic concept of population changes, and describes a new transition of a population after it has completed the traditional demographic transition, which is marked by a fertility rate that is below the replacement level while the "three-low-rate" population reproduction is further transitioning. Obviously, post-demographic transition can also be divided into early and late phases.

Population changes have three possibilities when a population has arrived at the stage of "three low rates" with its TFR under the replacement level: fluctuation, rebound, and further decline. If the TFR fluctuates with increases and decreases, it will take the population a long time to reach or approach zero growth, leaving a fairly long intermediate period; if the TFR bounces back from the bottom, due either to policies or to any other reason, to exceed the replacement level, zero growth will be far away for the population since it needs to first go through the traditional demographic transition all over again to approach the post-demographic transition. If the TFR continues to decrease, the population will fast-forward to zero growth and arrive at the late phase of post-demographic transition at an earlier time. Generally, a population fluctuates with more decreases than increases in its TFR; however, no matter what population changes occur, there will always be a certain degree of fluctuation in the early phase of the post-demographic transition.

How long does the fluctuation last? In my opinion, it may last for at least the period of one cycle of population reproduction, or 25 years. This is because after a population has arrived at the stage of "three low rates," the new generation born when the TFR is below the replacement level will take as long as a cycle of population reproduction to go through marriage and reproduction and gradually pass its peak of reproduction, which lays firm foundations for the post-demographic transition to continue; consequently, the population will advance to zero growth and transition to the subsequent negative growth to a degree.

Practices of post-demographic transition

As outlined earlier, China entered the age of post-demographic transition in the early 1990s, when its TFR and net reproduction rate (NRR) both fell below the replacement level. The post-demographic transition was based on the traditional demographic transition and continued and developed the latter, and therefore had profound impacts on the future changes and development of a population as well as the working-age and the elderly of the population.

Stepping into the age of post-demographic transition

The winding path of China's demographic transition

Before any detailed discussion of the post-demographic transition in China, it is necessary to clarify the types of population reproduction to give reasonable classification ranges that fit China's situations. Coale's standards are somewhat far away from China's reality as the high birth and growth rates in Coale's standards are rarely seen in modern populations. It is thus necessary to find new standards for classification based on real situations and horizontal and vertical analyses.

It is widely known that birth, death, and growth rates are all crude rates and that they vary greatly with various age structures, and any comparison based on them must first normalize the age structure. Comparison of crude rates without normalization generates errors, but crude rates cannot simply be denied for they have their own value in applications.

Given China's situations, I proposed the following standards to classify the population types: the high, high, low type has birth rates above 30.0‰, death rates above 20.0‰, and natural growth rates below 10.0‰; the high, low, high type has birth rates above 20.0‰, death rates below 10.0‰, and natural growth rates above 10.0‰; and the low, low, low type has birth rates below 20.0‰, death rates below 10.0‰, and natural growth rates below 10.0‰. These standards should be reasonable given the situations of the Chinese population. Of course, these numbers were not intended to be strictly binding since they were only intended to be used for staging the population changes in the past 65 years in China.

In addition, the three rates may not always change in ways consistent with the standards and they vary in different historical periods. For example, the birth rates in some years were above 30.0‰ while the death rates were below 20.0‰ and even 10.0‰, suggesting that the population was marching from the high, high, low to the high, low, high type, or might have already entered the high, low, high type. The actual staging of population changes is usually more accurate, swift, and convenient with TFR and NRR after the population has arrived at the high, low, high stage. That is to say, when the TFR is equal to or below 2.1 and the NRR is equal to or below 1.0, a population has a fertility rate below the replacement level, which, if lasting, will bring the population to zero and negative growth, and these two numbers can thus be used as the markers for the population to have transitioned to the low, low, low type. In fact, demographic transition is slow and progressive, and is usually unconvertible; it is therefore necessary and useful in practice to master the markers of each transitional phase.

China has one of the ancient civilizations in the world, and created an advanced agricultural civilization at a very early time. The agricultural production based on cultivating by males and weaving by females, handmade tools, and craftsman techniques needed an endless supply of laborers. Families, as the basic units of population reproduction, were able to produce children at a very low cost in the agrarian society, with a declining marginal cost when producing more children; meanwhile, the benefits children brought to their parents in labor, economy, elderly care, safety, and life satisfaction were rather high. The naturally occurring low ratio of costs to benefits laid the economic foundation for the social culture that equated children with fortune, both of which were the more, the better, and encouraged reproduction.

Meanwhile, national policies concerning population or population-related land and tax policies usually encouraged reproduction and thus created an external environment that was reproduction friendly. Therefore, birth rates were always high, often between 30.0‰ and 40.0‰ and even higher. However, due to high mortalities, the natural growth rates remained low. The concept that more children brought better fortune and that reproduction was always good was rooted deeply in people's minds, and high birth rates were the core and the bond of what maintained population reproduction.

Side by side with the high birth rates were high death rates. On one hand, the forces of production in the agrarian society were at a low level since labor efficiency with handmade tools was always low, and the demands of population reproduction were not met, leading to unsatisfactory health conditions; on the other hand, the peasants who were the majority of the society were exploited by the class of landowners, and had to always struggle to get warm and fed, to survive, and to support families. Diseases, especially epidemics, and natural disasters such as floods and droughts were devastating, preventing the death rates from falling. In recent history, China was invaded by imperialists while wars, diseases, and famine came one after another, depriving many people of their homes and trapping them in great hardships; thus the death rates were as high as above 30.0‰, giving the population the typical characteristics of the high, high, low type.

Eventually, the Chinese people ended the long-term wars and unbearable lives with a comprehensive victory against foreign invaders in 1945 when Japan surrendered, the first such victory in the past 100 years. The people finally had a moment to breathe and rest, although a civil war soon broke out, which was fought domestically and thus totally different from wars against foreign invaders. Population reproduction also bore marks of the victory with some decreases in the death rates and increases in the growth rates.

By the time when the People's Republic of China was established in 1949, the birth rate had reached 36.0‰, the death rate 20.0‰, and the natural growth rate 16.0‰, suggesting that the population reproduction was transitioning from the high, high, low to the high, low, high type, reaching the edge of the latter. In 1952, the birth rate increased slightly to 37.0‰ and the death rate decreased slightly to 17.0‰, with a natural growth rate at 20.0‰, marking the official entrance to the high, low, high type.

However, the population soon made an aberrant transition to low birth rates, high death rates, and low growth rates from 1958 to 1961 due to China's unique political, economic, and social institutions and mechanisms, especially to the three years of hardships after the Great Leap Forward movement in 1958. During these three years, the birth rates fell below 30.0‰, and the rate in 1961 was even at an extremely low level, under 18.0‰; the death rates increased to above 12.0‰, and the rate in 1960 was extremely high, above 25.4‰. The natural growth rates also decreased to below 17.2‰, and the rate in 1960 was as low as −4.6‰, the first negative rate since 1949. It was apparently an aberrant behavior of population reproduction, caused by accidents in socioeconomic development.

Once the aberrant accident was over, the birth and growth rates both showed compensatory increases while the death rates sped to decrease. In 1962, the birth rate came back to the previous peak, and in 1963, it created a new record, 43.4‰, marking the peak of birth rates in the 65 years since the establishment of the new China. Similarly, the natural growth rates also made a new record, 33.3‰, in 1963, marking the year as the Everest of population growth in the new China. Therefore, observations of the history of the demographic transition in the new China should treat the period of 1958–1961 as aberrant and exclude it when trying to find the patterns in the history.

When the aberrant period is excluded, the birth rates from 1962 to 1971 remain above 30.0‰, and above 20.0‰ from 1971 to 1990; the death rates remain above 10.0‰ before 1964 and then quickly decrease and stay between 7.5 and 6.2 ‰; the natural growth rate stays above 20.0‰ from 1962 to 1973, between 10.0 and 20.0‰ from 1974 and 1997, and consistently declines after 1998, getting below 5.0‰. Apparently, the changes in the birth, death, and growth rates were not synchronized.

For example, the population changes may be divided into early and late phases according to the natural growth rates; in the early phase, the average annual growth rate was 26.0‰ from 1962 to 1973, which was a peak of reproduction that lasted the longest and had the highest growth rate since the establishment of the new China, typical of the high, low, high type; after 1974, the growth rates decreased to below 20.0‰, below 10.0‰ since 1998, and below 5.0‰ since 2005, but it increased slightly to 5.21‰ in 2014. Therefore, the later phase of the high, low, high stage of the demographic transition should be after 1998. However, the birth rates had declined to 19.68‰ by 1991, not a match to the growth rate, 12.98‰, in the same year.

Which year was more appropriate as the transition point then? As described earlier, the key to ending the high, low, high type is fertility, or when the TFR is equal to or lower than 2.1 and the NRR is equal to or lower than 1.0. By this standard, 1991 was the year when the population reproduction entered the low, low, low type when the TFR was 1.98 and the NRR below 1.0, marking the end of the traditional demographic transition and the start of the post-demographic transition.

As shown in Table 2.2, the demographic transition in the new China started with decline in the death rates, which was followed by decreases in the birth rates, while the growth rates increased and then decreased. This was in accordance with the general pattern of transitions from the high, high, low through the high, low, high to the low, low, low type.

The only exception was the aberrant period with low, high, low rates from 1958 to 1961. The aberrant period broke the normal progression of demographic transition in China and impacted not only the abnormal population changes during the four years, but also the demographic transition in the

Table 2.2 Natural population changes in China, 1949–2015 (‰)

Year	*Birth rate*	*Death rate*	*Natural growth rate*
1949	36.00	20.00	16.00
1950	37.00	18.00	19.00
1951	37.80	17.80	20.00
1952	37.00	17.00	20.00
1953	37.00	14.00	23.00
1958	29.22	11.98	17.24
1959	24.78	14.59	10.19
1960	20.86	25.43	−4.57
1961	18.02	14.24	3.78
1962	37.01	10.02	26.99
1963	43.37	10.04	33.33
1964	39.14	11.50	27.64
1965	37.88	9.50	28.38
1966	35.05	8.83	26.22
1967	33.96	8.43	25.53
1968	35.59	8.21	27.38
1969	34.11	8.03	26.08
1970	33.43	7.69	25.83
1971	30.65	7.65	23.33
1972	29.77	7.61	22.16
1973	27.93	7.04	20.89
1974	24.82	7.34	17.48
1975	23.01	7.32	15.69
1976	19.91	7.25	12.66
1977	18.93	6.87	12.06
1978	18.25	6.25	12.00
1979	17.82	6.21	11.61
1980	18.21	6.34	11.87
1981	20.91	6.36	14.55
1982	22.28	6.60	15.68
1983	20.19	6.90	13.29
1984	19.90	6.82	13.08
1985	21.04	6.78	14.26
1986	22.43	6.86	15.57
1987	23.33	6.72	16.61
1988	22.37	6.64	15.73
1989	21.58	6.54	15.04
1990	21.06	6.87	14.39
1991	19.68	6.70	12.98
1992	18.24	6.64	11.60
1993	18.09	6.64	11.45
1994	17.70	6.49	11.21
1995	17.12	6.57	10.55
1996	16.98	6.56	10.42
1997	16.57	6.51	10.06
1998	15.64	6.50	9.14
1999	14.64	6.46	8.18
2000	14.03	6.45	7.58
2001	13.38	6.43	6.95

Table 2.2 (Cont.)

Year	*Birth rate*	*Death rate*	*Natural growth rate*
2002	12.86	6.41	6.45
2003	12.41	6.40	6.01
2004	12.29	6.42	5.87
2005	12.40	6.51	5.89
2006	12.09	6.81	5.28
2007	12.10	6.93	5.17
2008	12.14	7.06	5.08
2009	11.95	7.08	4.87
2010	11.98	7.11	4.79
2011	11.93	7.14	4.79
2012	12.10	7.15	4.95
2013	12.08	7.16	4.92
2014	12.37	7.16	5.21
2015	12.07	7.11	4.96

Sources: *China Statistical Yearbook 1986*, China Statistics Press, 1986, p. 92; *China Statistical Yearbook 2014*, China Statistics Press, 2014, p. 26; National Bureau of Statistics, "Statistical Communiqué of the People's Republic of China on the 2014 National Economic and Social Development," published in *China Population Today*, vol. 2, pp. 19–35; National Bureau of Statistics, "Statistical Communiqué of the People's Republic of China on the 2015 National Economic and Social Development."

subsequent years. After the aberrant period, the birth rates showed compensatory rebounds immediately, setting the record at 43.37‰ with the record high growth rate of 33.33‰. Momentum of population increases was thus generated, and it led to the largest reproduction peak of 1962–1973. This population cohort makes up a considerable bulk in the population pyramid, which keeps climbing the pyramid with time, bringing population problems wherever it goes.

Practices of post-demographic transition

Analysis of the changes in China's birth, death, and growth rates showed that the Chinese population entered the stage of post-demographic transition in 1991 when the fertility rate fell below the replacement level. After the post-demographic transition, the population continued to change; now that it has been more than 20 years, some features have showed up that are different from those in the traditional demographic transition.

The birth rates have shown evident and rapid decreases. They decreased to 18.24‰ in 1992, 17.70‰ in 1994, 16.98‰ in 1996, 15.64‰ in 1998, 14.64‰ in 1999, 13.38‰ in 2001, 12.86‰ in 2002, and 11.95‰ in 2009. They then fluctuated between 11.98‰ and 12.86‰ from 2010 to 2015, showing a trend of stability. By 2015, the fertility policy had already been adjusted to allow couples with either party being an only child to have two children, and now that the policy has been implemented that all couples are allowed to have two children, the birth rates may continue to increase by small scales with fluctuations, and then it is impossible for the rates to take a downward turn after a short term.

Compared to the declining birth rates, the death rates have been stable. After they decreased to 6.70‰ in 1991, the death rates fluctuated within a narrow interval of 6.40–6.93‰ during the next 16 years, with a slightly downward trend from 1991 to 2003 and a slightly upward trend from 2003 to 2007, illustrating a somewhat U-shaped curve of changes. With the population continuing to age, the right end of the U-shaped curve is still climbing, illustrating a typical feature of the post-demographic transition, which is at the same time a lethal problem of the population. The elderly have a particularly high death rate and the older the group, the higher the rate, leading the death rates of the entire population to increase.

Changes in birth and growth rates are related as described earlier, so the growth rates of a population are overall positively associated with the birth rates. In China, the natural growth rates decreased to 11.60‰ in 1992, and they kept declining afterward, to 11.21‰ in 1994, below 11.0‰ in the next three years, and 10.06‰ in 1997; afterward, they went down one step every three years, arriving at 9.14‰ in 1998, 8.18‰ in 1999, and 7.58‰ in 2000.

After the turn of the 21st century, they rested at a platform that was slightly higher than 6.0‰ from 2001 to 2003, slightly higher than 5.0‰ from 2004 to 2008, and slightly higher than 4.0‰ from 2009 to 2013. They made novel changes in 2014 when they came back to the platform of 5.0‰, reaching 5.21‰; they then declined to 4.96‰ on the platform of 4.0‰ in 2015. In my opinion, as the fertility policy kept getting adjusted to the fullest, increases in the growth rates to some extent are predictable and it is also possible for the increases to last for quite a while.

These changes in the three rates showed that the post-demographic transition had progressed with low levels of the birth, death, and natural growth rates with no abnormal behaviors. Post-demographic transition has attracted more and more attention and studies in recent years, and many questions have been raised that require further discussions and practical solutions. In my opinion, the post-demographic transition is a long period for a population to transition while its birth, death, and natural growth rates all show new changes.

Based on the practices in China, the post-demographic transition may be divided into early and late phases: the early phase starts when fertility rates fall below the replacement level – bringing down together birth and death rates – and ends with zero population growth – birth, death, and growth rates are all zero – and it is a phase when birth rates and natural growth rates decrease stepwise to zero. The late phase is marked by a certain degree of continuous decreases in birth rates and natural growth rates, which eventually become negative, and it is a phase when birth rates may be lower than death rates, resulting in negative growth rates.

How will a population transition after it grows negatively? There is no experience in practice to facilitate any conclusion. However, one thing is certain, i.e., the birth, death, and natural growth rates will fluctuate for a long time until they reach a new balance, possibly bringing the population to a stable state with the three rates roughly the same.

Changes in the working-age population

Post-demographic transition has long-lasting, multilayered, and profound impacts on population and socioeconomic development. This section is devoted to the impacts on the working-age population and the association of the transition with transformation of the economic mode and structural adjustment to the economy, both of which are related to the changes in the working-age population. To illustrate these, the focus should be on trends, images, and characteristics of the changes of the working-age population, which are described in what follows.

Curve of changes in the working-age population

In the background of the post-demographic transition, the population of working age shows a trajectory with increases followed by decreases in number. The Chinese population officially entered the stage of post-demographic transition in 1991 when the TFR and the NRR both fell below the replacement levels. The subsequent changes in the working-age population, from 1992 to 2014, in terms of both the absolute quantity and proportion, are shown in Table 2.3 and Figure 2.2.

As shown in Table 2.3 and Figure 2.2, from 1992 to 2014, the working-age population, those aged from 15 to 64, first went through 21 years of increases with an overall scale of 21.0%, reaching 1.00582 billion in 2013 compared to 776.14 million in 1992, and then for the first time met decreases in 2014 of 1.13 million, reaching 1.00469 billion. Thus the absolute number of the working-age population reached its peak in 2013, standing on the top of its curve. The changes in the proportion of the working-age population are similar to those in the number except that the proportion reached the peak earlier than the number.

Specifically, the proportion was 66.2% in 1992, increased to its peak, 74.5%, in 2010, and showed decreases in 2011 and thereafter, reaching 73.5% in 2014, which was one percentage point lower than that of 2010. Apparently, the turning point, or the peak of the change trajectory of the proportion of the working-age population, was 2010, three years earlier than that of the absolute number.

Many public articles, books, online posts, reports of various sorts, and speeches labeled 2010 as the Lewis turning point in China and asserted that the working-age population and laborers had since consistently declined, leading directly to the downward trend of economic growth. It was actually

Table 2.3 Changes in the working-age (15–64 years old) population, 1992–2014

Year	*Population (10,000)*	*Proportion (%)*
1992	77,614	66.2
1993	79,051	66.7
1994	79,868	66.6
1995	81,393	67.2
1996	82,245	67.2
1997	83,448	67.5
1998	84,338	67.6
1999	85,157	67.7
2000	88,910	70.1
2001	89,849	70.4
2002	90,302	70.3
2003	90,976	70.4
2004	92,184	70.9
2005	94,197	72.0
2006	95,068	72.3
2007	95,833	72.5
2008	96,680	72.7
2009	97,484	73.0
2010	99,938	74.5
2011	100,283	74.4
2012	100,463	74.4
2013	100,582	73.9
2014	100,469	73.5

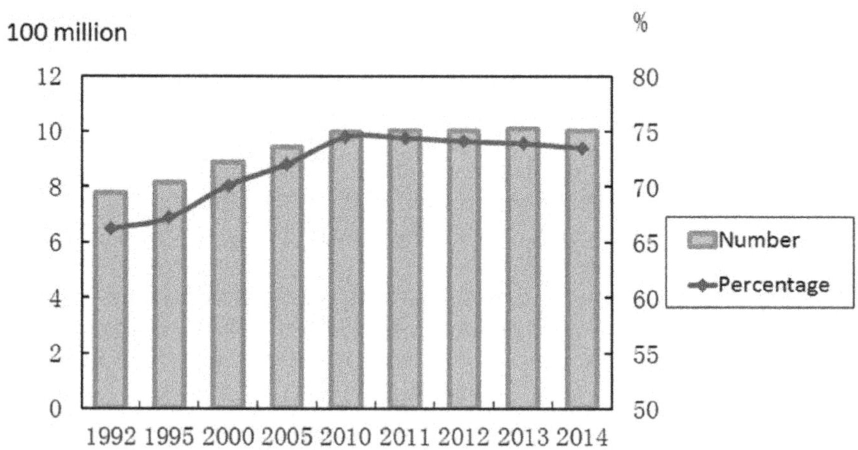

Figure 2.2 Changes in the working-age (15–64 years old) population, 1992–2014.

a misunderstanding of the data. The year 2010 was only the turning point of the proportion of the working-age population to change from increases to decreases, but that of the number of laborers was three years later. Although it is only a detail and does not really affect the overall trend, it is still not scientifically sound if the misleading information is used to explain various socioeconomic issues.

Stepping into the post-golden age

It is premature to summarize the changes in the working-age population under the post-demographic transition into a trajectory based on the data in the past 20 years or so; after all, the proportion of the working-age population only passed its peak five years ago, and the absolute number a bit more than two years ago, leaving a short track of the downward part at the right end of the curve, which might not be enough to illustrate a trend. Therefore, projections over a long term are needed to show the population changes, including the changes in the working-age group. The medium projections for China's population described in the last chapter from my previous work, *Research on the Development Strategy of China's Population in the 21st Century*, could be combined with the data of the past 20 years to show a clearer picture of the change trajectory (Figure 2.3).

Discussions on the changes in the working-age population after 2010 may be directed to the following two aspects.

First, changes in the proportion of the working-age population deserve careful study. The proportion reached its peak of 74.5% in 2010, which is widely accepted as the Lewis turning point. It then started

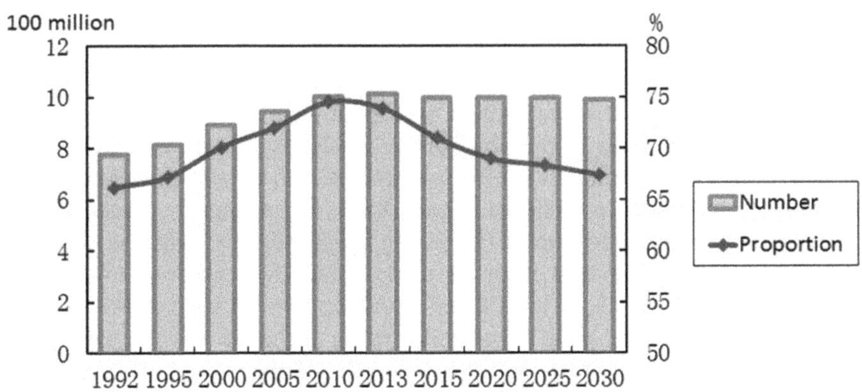

Figure 2.3 Changes and projected changes in the working-age (15–64 years old) population, 1992–2030.

to decline, reaching 71.0% in 2015, and was projected to be 69.0% in 2020, 68.3% in 2025, and 67.4% in 2030, a number comparable to the proportion at the time the Chinese population stepped into the post-demographic transition. These numbers illustrate a rather perfect trajectory of the working-age population in the early phase of the post-demographic transition: the trajectory starts at the point of 1992 as the origin of the post-demographic transition, goes up for 18 years until its peak, when it takes a turn to go down, and eventually comes back to the level of 1992 in 2030.

Second, changes in the absolute number of the working-age population also deserve study. From 1992 to 2013, the working-age population, or those aged from 15 to 64, steadily increased in number, from 776 million in 1992 through 889 million in 2000 to its peak, 1.01 billion, in 2013. A total of 234 million people were added to this age group, an average annual increase of 11 million people. After 2013, the number started to decrease, and it was projected to be 997 million in 2020 and 988 million in 2030, a total reduction of 102 million people over 17 years and an average annual decrease of 6 million. Between the increases and the decreases, the former had a larger scale of annual changes by 5 million than the latter. That is also to say that the total reduction of the working-age population in the 17 years of projected decreases is only 54.5% of the total increase in the years of increases. Since the scale and the speed by which the working-age population decreases are far less than those of the increases, the decreases will have a far smaller impact than that of the increases.

These changes in the number and the proportion of the working-age population have shown that China is still in the golden age of population structural changes; in fact, China is stepping into the late phase of the golden age, or, as some call it, the post-golden age.

The golden age of population structural changes describes a period during the demographic transition when a population has an age structure such that those of working age make up a high proportion while the elderly and the young make up a low proportion. Such a structure is beneficial to socioeconomic development as the population is rich in laborers while low in burdens. It is widely known that a population is often roughly classified into three age groups in demography, the young aged between 0 and 14, those of working age between 15 and 59 or 64, and the elderly at 60 or 65 and above. Each age group impacts socioeconomic development in its own way, and a society is most sensitive to the dependency ratio, or the ratio of the young and the elderly to those of working age. An increasing dependency ratio illustrates declines in the proportion of those of working age and increases in the proportion of the young and the elderly who need to be supported, and thus a heavy burden falls on society, which harms economic development by closing the population window that used to boost the economy.

In contrast, a decreasing ratio shows increases in the proportion of those of working age and decreases in that of the supported, lifting some of the burdens from society and opening the population window to facilitate economic development. The period from the opening to the closing of the population window is thus called the golden age of population structural changes, during which positive energy is transmitted to socioeconomic development.

I noticed the population window in 1980 when I was drafting the report on behalf of the central demographic meetings to the Secretariat. I later made specific points on it when I published a signed article in *People's Daily* on June 5, 1983, "Structural Changes of the Population to Boost Modernization," in which I argued that both the fertility and birthrates would show evident decreases during the 40 years after the basic state policy of family planning was implemented to control the population, which would lead the dependency ratio to consistently decline, bringing the population into the golden age. After all, decreases in the dependency ratio would alleviate the total burden of society as the total numbers of the dependent young and elderly were decreasing relative to those of working age, who were increasing in both number and proportion. If these changes were employed appropriately, it would greatly facilitate the modernization of China as well as realize the goal to quadruple the total industrial and agricultural production by 2000.

What was the population like in 1983? Everybody knows that in September 1980, *An Open Letter to All Members of the Communist Party and the Communist Youth League by the Central Committee of the Communist Party of China on Population Control* was published, which was followed by the decision of the 12th National Congress of the Communist Party of China (CPC) in September 1982 that family planning to control population growth was a basic state policy, when strict control of population growth started to heat up and public opinions started to overwhelmingly criticize surpluses of the population and laborers. With such a background, my article that argued for the beneficial effects of modernizing China and realizing the quadrupling goal by increases in the number and proportion of the working-age population had to elaborate on my points to avoid misunderstanding.

> On the one hand, efforts must be made to control increases in the population and those at ages of economic production, while on the other hand, efforts must be made to direct the laborer resources of those at ages of economic production to the right places. Modernization experiences in some countries, especially some Asian countries and areas, have shown that sufficient employment of domestic cheap laborers is the prime factor of high speed economic development, as is the case in Japan and Singapore. We should make every effort to improve the scientific and technological levels of the laborers, as best as conditions permit, to develop some specialized industries that are labor intensive to mine the potentials of the laborers. Apparently, this is not to say that more laborers bring better

> consequences, but it is always better to have more than fewer laborers when the total size of the population is already set.[3]

A literature review has shown that it was the first time in China when the idea of the golden age of population structural changes was proposed while it was also proposed that the golden age should be employed to boost the modernization of China and socioeconomic development. These views were in line with the concepts of population benefits, population bonuses, and population window, and they all emphasized that the apparent increases in the number and proportion of the working-age population could provide abundant human resources for socioeconomic development although they used different terms; in addition, decreases in the proportion of the dependent young and elderly lifted some of the social burden that holds back economic development, giving the economy a valuable opportunity to march forward. Based on this, further descriptions can be made of China's population, economy, and development.

On one hand, the dependency ratio kept and will keep declining. The proportion of the dependent elderly and young continued to decline, bringing decreases in the dependency ratio and social burden and offering opportunities to focus on economic construction. The total dependency ratio in China was around 50.0% in 1992, and the population age structure and changes in the ratio from then on to 2030 are listed in Table 2.4.

As shown in Table 2.4, the young dependency ratio consistently declined from 1992 to 2010 and saw a total decrease of 19.4 percentage points from 41.7% to 22.3%; in contrast, the aged dependency ratio kept climbing, from 9.3% to 11.9%, a total increase of 2.6 percentage points. Between the decreases in the young dependency ratio and the increases in the aged dependency ratio,

Table 2.4 Population age structure and total dependency ratio, 1992–2030 (%)

Year	*0–14*	*15–64*	*Over 65*	*Total dependency ratio*	*Young dependency ratio*	*Aged dependency ratio*
1992	27.6	66.2	6.2	51.0	41.7	9.3
1995	26.6	67.2	6.2	48.8	39.6	9.2
2000	22.9	70.1	7.0	42.6	32.6	9.9
2005	20.3	72.0	7.7	38.8	28.1	10.7
2010	16.6	74.5	8.9	34.2	22.3	11.9
2013	16.4	73.9	9.7	35.3	22.2	13.1
2015	19.4	70.8	9.9	41.4	27.4	14.0
2020	19.0	69.0	12.0	44.9	27.5	17.4
2025	18.0	68.3	13.7	46.5	26.4	20.1
2030	16.4	67.4	16.2	48.3	24.3	24.0

Sources: *China Statistical Yearbook 2014*, p. 27; *Research on the Development Strategy of China's Population in the 21st Century*, pp. 443–451.

the decreases were 16.8 percentage points more than the increases, leading the total dependency ratio to decline from 51.0% to 34.2%, the lowest ever; thus the population came to the early phase of the golden age with increasing population benefits and bonuses.

After 2010, the young dependency ratio fluctuated within a narrow range and will keep doing so until 2030, thus it has had and will have little impact on the total dependency ratio; in contrast, the aged dependency ratio departed quickly and will keep accelerating, from 11.9% in 2010 to 17.4% in 2020, and 24.0% in 2030, leading the total dependency ratio to climb as well, reaching 44.9% in 2020 and 48.3% in 2030. This period is the late phase of the golden age as the population benefits and bonuses will diminish gradually.

How is the golden age of a population age structure defined? It is without question whether the structure may provide population benefits and bonuses, which is decided by the total dependency ratio. In practice, if 50.0% is considered the value of a balanced ratio, a population is in deficit and in debt when its total dependency ratio is over 50.0% and it is in the golden age with population benefits and bonuses when the ratio is below 50.0%.

Based on this standard, the golden age of the age structure of the Chinese population may be divided into the early and late phases. The early phase lasted from 1992 to 2010, when the population benefits and bonuses kept increasing, until the peak in 2010, when the Lewis turning point showed up. During this phase, the demographic window opened and widened to its largest.

After 2010, the population benefits and bonuses diminished year by year until 2030, when the total dependency ratio will get very close to the value of balance, 50.0%. During this late phase, the demographic window started to narrow from the widest, and it will continue to narrow until it is completely closed. It is actually essential to differentiate between the two phases.

A wave of recent discussions in academic and other related fields asserts that the population bonuses in China have disappeared, which will further result in consumption recession, enterprise deficits, and a bear market for long terms. If one is to further inquire why the bonuses have disappeared so fast, those who asserted the disappearance will respond with excessively fast declines in birth rates by excessively large scales and the over-strict policy to control the population that has fast-forwarded the arrival and the departure of the bonuses, thus attributing everything to the over-strict population policy.

The response is seemingly logical, but even its logic cannot deny the contributions of the population policy to the population bonuses; at the same time, however, whether and when the bonuses have disappeared needs further study. In fact, whether the bonuses have disappeared has already been answered in Table 2.4: the population entered the late phase of the golden age of demographic structures after 2010, and the population bonuses decreased year by year; the bonuses have not disappeared and will not until around 2030.

In addition, the trajectory of the changes in the working-age population in Figure 2.3 clearly shows that the population benefits and bonuses provided during the golden age of the population structural changes, although diminishing now, will last for another 15 years until they are completely consumed. Diminishing is not disappearance, and that is common sense. It is therefore a misunderstanding and misleading when the diminishing bonuses are taken as disappearance to interpret various downward economic behaviors.

On the other hand, the absolute number and proportion of the working-age population kept increasing. The consistent increases in the number and the proportion of the working-age population offered abundant and relatively cheap laborers, which was beneficial to lowering the cost and elevating the competitiveness of products. As shown in Table 2.3, the number of those of working age, 15- to 64-year-olds, rocketed all the way up from 1992 to 2013, with an average annual addition of 10.93 million new laborers in those 21 years.

At the same time, the proportion of those of working age also increased steadily, leading to a consistent decrease in the total dependency ratio, which was and will be maintained below 50.0% from 1992 to 2030. The situation has contributed to economic growth from two aspects since the Reform and Opening Up: on one hand, abundant laborers were supplied to the large-scale economic development and the growing demand for laborers was met; and on the other hand, the abundance of laborers also kept low the price of laborers, including the 100 million peasants who migrated from rural to urban areas, which helped keep low the total cost of products and make them competitive on the international market. The low cost was essential to expand exports and immense amounts of foreign reserves, and its crucial role was a powerful engine to drive economic growth.

However, the recent international market slump resulting from the U.S. subprime mortgage crisis and the European debt crisis was also felt by China as the exports became restricted, which led the economy to slow down in growth. The international market started to recover in 2013, and so did China's exports soon after, which will resume their role in driving economic growth, at least to a degree.

Trading speed for quality and benefits

These descriptions of the shift from the traditional to the post-demographic transition and of the change trajectory of the working-age population have shown that a new pattern is facing us now that the proportion of the working-age population has reached its peak with the Lewis turning point having been passed; therefore, awareness must be raised of the declining population benefits and bonuses, although they are still present, so that their impact on economic development can be managed.

In fact, the current situation is one where the post-demographic transition meets the economic new normal, which demands a new perspective to consider the development of the population and the economy so that the post-demographic transition may be included in the scope of the new normal and a path may be found for the reform of replacing speed with quality and economic benefits.

The Chinese economy has a new normal

What is a new normal? New is opposite to old, and normal is a normal state. An economic new normal describes a newly emerged, sitting state of the economy relative to the normal state of the economy in another period, or the old normal of the economy. The economic new normal in China is characterized by the downward or decelerating growth of the economy compared to the old normal. However, it must be clarified that China's new normal is fundamentally different from the post-crisis new normal in the West, and the two cannot be used interchangeably or held together.

It is widely known that the world economy experienced about 20 years of extremely stable growth from the 1980s, which was taken as a normal state of development, and that was the background and reference for the new normal. In 1997, a financial crisis suddenly stormed Asia; 10 years later, a financial crisis broke out in the United States, followed by the European sovereign debt crisis that spread widely; all these evolved into a global financial and economic crisis by which only emerging economies such as China and India were little affected. The crisis, surprisingly, has lasted for a long time, spread over a wide range of areas, and impacted the world profoundly, and the world economy has yet to recover.

Under this circumstance, the term *new normal* was coined and the concept described in the 2004 book *The New Normal: Great Opportunities in a Time of Great Risk*, by Roger McNamee, in which it was asserted that the world economy had stepped into an unpredictable, new normal age and that it could never turn back to the past glorious age. In 2010, Mohammed El-Erian from PIMCO, a U.S. investment management company, described the new normal from multiple angles in his speech *The New Normal Has Sailed in the Industrialized Countries*, and the term became popularized and spread worldwide. Given the situations in recent years, the world economy still has many uncertainties and the new normal is still lasting, which is also reflected in the recent projection data by the IMF shown in Table 2.5.[4]

Other indicators, such as consumer price index (CPI), industrial production index (IPI), and purchasing managers' index (PMI), all showed sluggish trends, as manifested in the data of the World Bank and the British Consensus Forecast, which were only slightly different. Apparently, the advanced economies are still in the new normal of recession. According to the U.S. Department of Commerce, the U.S. economy in the first quarter of 2015 grew only 0.2%; the U.K. data showed that the United Kingdom's economic growth in the first quarter was 2.4% compared to the same period of the previous year, and only 0.3% compared to the last quarter,[5] much lower than the IMF data. The numbers showed that the advanced economies were still under

Table 2.5 World economic growth rates, 2012–2015 (%)

Year	*2012*	*2013*	*2014, predicted*	*2015, predicted*
World	3.4	3.3	3.3	3.5
Developed regions	1.2	1.3	1.8	2.4
United States	2.3	2.2	2.4	3.6
Euro zone	−0.7	−0.5	0.8	1.2
Japan	1.5	1.5	0.1	0.6
Developing regions	5.1	4.7	4.4	4.3
India	4.6	4.7	5.8	6.3
Russia	3.4	1.3	0.6	−3.0
Brazil	1.0	2.5	0.1	0.3

the spell of the economic crisis, and it is not clear yet when they can recover, a strong line of evidence for the new normal.

China did not fall into the trap of the new normal because of a unique system that was not entirely part of the global economy yet and was not heavily struck by the crises. However, the Chinese economy was still affected to some degree in terms of investment and exports. After 2011, the Chinese economy stepped on a track that went farther and farther away from the previous fast lane, and a new kind of economic growth at a medium-high speed emerged in that the economy continued to slow down with the GDP growth rate sliding from 10.4% in 2010 to 7.0% in the first half of 2015.

Meanwhile, problems such as an underdeveloped economic mode, unbalanced structure, insufficient drive of demands, and overproduction showed up. In May 2014, General Secretary Xi Jinping visited Henan Province on an inspection tour, during which he proposed the concept of the new normal of the Chinese economy, and he later expounded it at the Central Economic Work Conference, setting forth a new development stage with comprehension of, in theory and in practice, accommodation of, and development of the new normal.

Now, nearly five years after General Secretary Xi's speech, I propose, based on my understanding of Xi's speech and recent practices, that China's new normal is similar to as well as different from the new normal of advanced economies. They are similar on the surface, but different at the core. Therefore, we can neither deny the similarities nor mix up the two types of new normal since neither is supported by the reality.

The similarities have already been mentioned: different degrees of downward economies, deceleration in economic growth, sluggish consumption, decreased benefits, structural imbalance, overproduction, and constant frictions in commerce are all present in both types of new normal. In addition, in today's age of information and economic globalization, the two types of new normal also increasingly affect and permeate each other. It is therefore not a good idea to deny the similarities as denial neither helps the acknowledgment that China's new normal is somewhat associated with globalization nor facilitates efforts to learn from its positive and negative lessons. After all, as the old Chinese saying goes, "stones from other hills may help polish one's own jade," and we should not overlook international experiences.

However, the two types of new normal are different in essence. First, the new normal in regions represented by advanced economies is a theoretical summary of the long-term economic recession in the shade of the financial and economic crises, while China's new normal is a reflection of the demand to resolve the contradictions that built up during the high-speed economic growth, and is thus a new normal that moderately decelerates the growth and has nothing to do with the crises.

Second, the new normal in advanced economies often has economic growth rates near zero and sometimes even below zero, while the current 7.0% growth rate in China is a medium-high speed, which will not fall under the medium level even if it is to walk down several steps.

Third, advanced economies employed all economic leverage, including quantitative easing, in attempts to counter the critical new normal, thus planting threats for their own future economies; in China, in contrast, except for the investment of 4 trillion yuan to hold the economic slump during the 2008 global financial crisis, no extreme measures have been taken to boost the economy and efforts have been focused on mode transition, structural adjustment, and reforms while a certain degree of stable growth is guaranteed in order to resolve the contradictions from the previous high-speed growth.

Fourth, many countries with advanced economies have taken various protectionist measures to restrict imports, although they are in violation of World Trade Organization rules while China has followed the rules in practice and proactively advocated for free trade and objected to protectionism, pushing for economic globalization and safeguarding the international trade order with real actions. Therefore, the new normal in countries represented by advanced economies is one that is defensive, in recession, and under risk for a long time while China's, which only started about four or five years ago, is one with a limited degree of deceleration, retracting in order to advance later, and in search of innovative development with transition and upgrade. The difference between the two is captured vividly in the following description: the former is a slip down a slide with momentum and will arrive at an economic crisis due to stall caused by its high speed and long track; in contrast, China's new normal is a walk down a staircase and is still at a medium-high speed as it accommodates laws, keeps adjusting itself, deepens reforms, and advances in stability.

Propelling the reform to replace speed with quality and benefits

Economic growth decelerates in the new normal

It is important to differentiate between China's new normal and the new normal elsewhere, especially on the growth rate and the root since it shapes the whole picture of current and future economic development; however, at the same time, it is also important to acknowledge without hesitation that both kinds of new normal correspond to downward economies except that China's economy is still running at a medium-high speed and that the advanced economies have lost control over their slumping movement. It is essential to be aware of both aspects because only when the economic deceleration is acknowledged can we face and manage the new normal, and only when the timing and the rate of the deceleration in each window are mastered can we keep control of it so that the economy will walk but not slide down with moderate macro-regulation and deepened reforms. Then the question is how to apprehend the decelerating economic new normal and how to find scientific and reasonable steps for the economy to go down.

In my opinion, it is a universal law that the growth rate of an economy is inversely related to its increment in that when the increment is large enough, the growth rate will slow down. Then why did the universal law only show its impact after 2011 in China? The answer is in the exploration of both the direct cause and the deep root through theories combined with practices.

First, the direct cause of the downward economic growth needs to be specified. When talking about economic growth and development, people's first impression is always "the three carriages" that drive an economy, and when the economy is traveling on a downward track, the direct cause must be in the three carriages of consumption, investment, and exports, either in the vehicle itself or in the engine that may have failed.

As described in the first chapter, the sluggish consumption in China indeed contributed to the less robust economy, but the situation has picked up a little in recent years; the obstruction in exports of goods and services led to an abnormal row of negative growth after 2011, and the situation only became alleviated in 2014 and the first half of 2015; in contrast to these two, investment in fixed assets has been strong and remained the only carriage still carrying the economy forward. However, consistent declines have been observed in the marginal revenue of investment, which has offset much of the driving force by the carriage of investment. Overall, there has been a serious lack of energy from the three carriages, and they cannot play their role in driving economic growth to the fullest like before.

Second, the deep root of the downward economic growth needs to be specified as well. Many factors are in the root of the downward economic growth and they interplay to sometimes form persistent problems that are extremely difficult to solve or to reform. The factors are primarily manifested in the following five aspects.

The first aspect is the mode of economic development that is underdeveloped and unsustainable. In fact, it was noted as early as 20 years ago that the mode was not up to date and it was proposed to transform it, from the proposal to transform the way of economic growth in the beginning to the proposal to transform the way of economic development later, which covered somewhat wider connotations. It cannot be denied that the previous mode of economic growth and development had its functions and brought sustained high-speed growth of the economy. However, with the economy now reaching a completely new level, technologies advancing to an unprecedented degree, and structural adjustment touching deep down, problems that built up with the previous mode have become so evident as to harm further healthy development of the economy and can thus no longer be used. Specifically, the following two problems are why the previous mode has made development unsustainable.

One problem was pursuit of speed that ignored the principle of economic growth, i.e., to meet the demands of the all-around development of people. Therefore, the previous mode easily trapped production in a loop that the aim of production was more production and the goal of development was more development; thus GDP was valued above everything else and the concept of development was based on blind pursuit of production. Consequently, repeated construction, redundant production, surplus of production, and economic bubbles built up day by day, and development became unsustainable.

Another problem was the bulky extensive economy that made high-speed growth unsustainable. The previous rapidly growing economy relied mostly on investment in fixed assets. Then where did the investment go and which industries were boosted? The answer is the heavy chemical industry. Related fields in the industries grew at abnormal speeds and many are now facing uncontrollable cost and severe overproduction. Let us take cement as an example. In 1978, 65.24 million tons of cement was produced while production rocketed to 2.41614 billion in 2013, a total increase of 36.0 times and an annual increase of 10.9%. Another example is steel, and in this period, the production of steel grew from 22.08 million to 1.06762 billion tons, a total increase of 47.4 times and an annual increase of 11.2%.[6] It is now impossible to sustain further growth of such industries as the cost will rocket, the quality will decline, and the sales will be difficult.

The second aspect is imbalance of the economic structure with questionable economic benefits. The economic development that is evaluated by GDP and driven by investment often sets fire to competitions over projects, investment, and exports between departments, regions, and enterprises since in that background any project would be implemented immediately with construction and production mounted right away as long as it could bring jobs, investment, especially from overseas, and growth in exports. Long-term practices like this have fostered an economic culture that favors input over output, quantity over quality, and bringing in over absorbing and mastering technologies, leading to a structurally imbalanced economy with questionable quality. Structurally, the secondary sector of the industry centered on manufacturing accounts for a majority of the entire economy while the tertiary sector is underdeveloped; in addition, in the secondary sector, the heavy chemical industry is the majority, which has a severe level of overproduction still waiting resolution. With an imperfect market economy, monopolization of many fields, and persistent regional protectionism in some areas, the imbalance of the economic structure with disproportionate industries holds not only the speed but also the quality of economic development.

The third aspect is decreasing population bonuses, which boosts high the cost of labor. Much analysis has been devoted to this aspect, and it is unnecessary to elaborate here. However, one point needs to be emphasized: the age with almost an unlimited supply of laborers was over, and the end of that age was the start of increases in wage rates and the cost of labor. Since China has an extremely big population and reservoir of laborers, the pressure of the population was felt by the forces of production to the fullest in the age of high births, low deaths, and high growth; during that period, wage rates were kept from growing as there were more than 200 million peasant workers in the laborer reservoir and the labor market was long dominated by the buying party.

Things started to change when the proportion of the working-age population reached its peak in 2010 and its absolute number in 2013; the subsequent declines in the proportion as well as the number made it possible and laid firm foundations for rudimentarily transforming the labor market from one dominated by buyers to one dominated by sellers. The increases in the cost of labor have also been fostered by the labor shortage in recent years that kept spreading. In fact, we are now at a critical point to solve the population problems in China and to pave the way for improving labor efficiency and strengthening human resources; however, for a specific period, the changes in the population would definitely affect the economy in that the mode of development based on low labor cost will no longer work.

The fourth aspect is the bottleneck effect of resources with the ecological environment approaching its safety limit. The extensive mode of development relies on the factors of people, wealth, and things and is characterized by two highs and two lows: high input, high consumption, low benefits, and low output. In fact, the extensive mode has been there since the establishment of the new China; it was not obvious in the First Five-Year Plan, but it later became much worse during the Great Leap Forward under the impact of the desire to overtake leading countries; combined with the experience of boosting the economy with investment, the extensive mode of development interplayed with the two highs and two lows and lasted for a long time.

In such a mode of development, the energy consumption per unit of production and the consumption of resources were both way higher than those in developed countries, as well as below the world average; the excessive consumption of energy and resources eventually led to a bottleneck effect and further development had to rely heavily on imports. Let us take oil as an example. In 1990, China produced 138.306 million tons of oil and imported 7.556 million tons, with a ratio of imports to production at 1.0:18.3; in 2000, China produced 163.000 million tons and imported 97.485 million tons, with the ratio at 1.0:1.7; in 2012, 207.478 million tons of oil was produced and 330.888 million tons was imported, with the ratio at 1.0:0.6, which is also to say that China only produced 62.7% of the imported oil, showing a heavy reliance on imports. Imports of other resources such as iron, bronze, and nonmetal minerals are also enormous with striking increases; so are plant products such as wood. Even coal, which is abundant in China, also has net imports. Apparently, the shortage of resources has far exceeded people's expectations.

In fact, we have all come to feel deeply how severe the environmental problems are. My assessment of the situation is that measures to tackle the problems have shown some effects, but the environment has not been completely cured and the conventional forms of pollution of air, water, soil, and noise have not been fundamentally bettered while new forms of pollution such as PM 2.5 and pollution of ozone have stormed their way in with high levels and long periods; all of these challenge us in an unprecedented way.

There are also new features in the current environmental problems. First, the traditional forms of pollution have spread from cities and industrial and mining areas to a vast range of urban and rural areas and from industrial to residential pollution. Such a spreading trend, once combined with industrialization, urbanization, and agricultural modernization, will form a new pollution paradigm in the coming society of common prosperity, and new perspectives and strategies are needed to manage it. Second, the modern forms of pollution represented by PM 2.5 and ozone, including electronic radiation and light pollution, have not been fully recognized by people, and in-depth exploration is needed to reveal their harms and to handle them. Beijing, Tianjin, and Hebei Province are particularly affected by PM 2.5, and the people always sigh, when realizing they've lost the freedom to breathe fresh air, "what is the point to have high GDP?" People praise the APEC blue, but that was in exchange of stopping the smoking of chimneys, halting the dusting of construction sites, and alternating use of even- and odd-numbered vehicles in Beijing, Tianjin, Hebei Province, and some areas in the provinces of Shanxi, Shandong, and Henan, and was thus unsustainable. Now pollution of PM 2.5 has spread wide and areas from as far north as the Songhua River to as far south as the Zhujiang River and from the shore of the Eastern Sea to the Talimu Basin are all affected to a degree, yet the impact on the economy and people's health has not been fully revealed. The conventional forms of pollution are waiting to be managed and the new forms are knocking at the door; their grasp on the economy and the whole society has reached or approached the limit of what can be afforded, just as pointed out at the Central Economic Conference in 2014.

The fifth aspect is the obstruction in foreign trade due to the sluggish international market. In recent years, the exports kept declining, which negatively affected economic growth, as already described. Things only picked up a little in 2015 when the total amount of imports and exports in the first quarter increased by 6.0% compared to the same period in 2014, and the exports increased by 4.9%. However, the international economic crisis is still going on and there are many uncertainties. In addition, it will take some time to reform the mechanism of foreign trade in China to clear out the internal vicious competitions and to adjust the export structure. Therefore, the glorious days of exports that used to drive economic growth powerfully will not be seen any time soon.

What is the right speed of economic growth in the new normal?

The slowdown of economic growth in the new normal is a consequence of the interplay of economic laws, but it may have several degrees and rhythms, and it is important to find the degree and the rhythm that fits with our situation and facilitates the healthy development of our society and economy. In fact, a large body of domestic and international empirical experiences is available that explored the right speed for economic growth. Internationally, advanced economies will never go back to the super-stable growing age of the 1980s and 1990s, and they have all fallen to a super-low, near-zero-growth state; some are even negatively growing and are in danger of losing control of their economies. We must learn the lessons from them in order not to step down the same track. Meanwhile, we should also learn the lessons from some Latin American and Asian countries, which have been in the middle-income trap for a long time. Therefore, we should, on one hand, acknowledge and tolerate the decelerating, new normal economy as deceleration agrees with economic laws, while on the other hand, being fully aware that the economy may decelerate but we may not lose control of it so that it will not fall in the crisis-like stall state as in advanced economies or struggle in the middle-income trap as in some developing countries.

Domestically, the growth rate of the economy decreased by three percentage points in four years after it took a downward turn in 2011. Changes in various economic indicators are without question strong lines of evidence of the condition of the economy as well as the foundation for predictions of future growth. Based on the indicators, two points can be made. One, the downward growth did not harm the entire economy profoundly. In fact, the downward growth was only in the rate but not in the amount of increases. For example, the GDP growth rate was 0.3 percentage points lower in 2014 than in 2013, but the amount of GDP increment was 1.7 trillion yuan more; 13.22 million new jobs were offered in 2014, leading the employment rate to steadily grow; progress was made in transforming the economic mode and adjusting the structure, improving the sustainability of economic growth; and the quality of economic development was also improved with marked growth in the capacity of research and development.[7]

In the first quarter of 2015, the GDP growth rate declined to 7.0% and major indicators of the national economy showed stability: compared to the same period of the previous year, the total retail of consumer goods increased by 10.6%, the industrial value added of enterprises above a designated size increased by 6.4%, the urban disposable income per capita increased by 8.3%, and the cash income per capita of rural residents increased by 10.0%.[8] Information from various sectors has shown that the current economic growth rate of 7.0% is appropriate and meets the demand of a steadily developing economy. However, the problem now is that the 7% rate is still under pressure of further declines. Is there space for further decreased growth rates? What is the growth rate of the new normal in a longer frame of development? To answer the questions, in-depth studies are needed and tested in practice.

It is now the reality that the economic new normal has brought decelerated growth. If we do not want to lose control of the growth, we need to explore what is an economy out of control and how to prevent it. In my opinion, the growth rate at around 2.0% in advanced economies is where control has been lost, the direct consequence of which is that some countries and areas are now like an airplane in stall and destined to crash eventually. For example, the city of Detroit in the United States was in deep debt and had to announce bankruptcy, and Greece has been in a debt crisis for years and struggling in an economic crisis. Evidently, the stall speed that leads economies to crisis is absolutely disastrous and must be avoided in any situation.

Tolerance of a declining but not stalled growth rate necessitates the recognition of a development speed that is nowhere around a stall and how it is decided. What factors decide it? The answer involves many factors, including economic goals, foundations, structure, employment, investment, consumption, and exports.

In the past, the Chinese economy was primarily driven by the three carriages of investment, consumption, and exports. In the new normal, deep and wide transitions are crucial to the development speed that are based on mode transition, structural adjustment, life improvement, and reform boost so that the economy will be driven by innovations instead of factors.

However, a comprehensive perspective is needed for the transition: in the early phase, the previous factors are more powerful than innovation in driving the economy while with time and the reform constantly deepened, the factors will attenuate and innovation will be strengthened to become the major engine to drive further development of the economy. We need to be honest about the degree to which innovation may drive the economy while at the same time being realistic and making appropriate predictions for the future development speed based on the reform hotbed of mode transition, structural adjustment, skipping the middle-income trap, and realizing reasonably sufficient employment. The prediction should account for demands of the following three aspects.

First, the appropriate speed of economic growth needs to satisfy the demand to transition the mode of economic development and to adjust the structure. Whoever drives knows that, when making a turn, one needs to slow down, shift gears, step over the throttle slightly or not at all, and sometimes even brake slightly to control the speed of the car to drive through the turn safely. So does an economy when it is trying to turn from the extensive mode of high input, high consumption, low output, and low economic benefits to the intensive mode of low input, low consumption, high output, and high economic benefits, which cannot be completed through the previous high and super-high speed of development.

In fact, one of the key reasons why little was achieved during the 10 to 20 years after it was proposed to transform the economic mode was that the economic growth had not slowed down and efforts to transform the economic mode had been restricted by the pressure of keeping fast and stable growth. Now that the growth has finally slowed down since 2011, a good environment is created for the mode transition; however, the growth is still under pressure to continue to decelerate, suggesting that the current 7.0% growth rate is not low enough and clearly signaling that further deceleration from the current medium-high to a medium speed is moderate for the transition.

Things are similar for structural adjustment. Although the economy has slowed down in growth now, overproduction is still a problem, underdeveloped industries are hard to eliminate, and no change can be made to the structure if the current growth rate is to be maintained. Among the three sectors of the economy, although the tertiary industry has shown fast growth in recent years and tops the other two in proportion, the secondary industry is still powerful and the unreasonable structure of the economy is not going to be changed any time soon.

As for the internal structure of each of the three sectors, there are even more problems and the excessively high proportions of the heavy chemical industry, regular manufacturing and low-end services still need a long time to be transformed. Therefore, despite the importance to prevent a stall speed of economic growth so that we will not fall into the crisis that's been trapping advanced economies, the appropriate growth rate for structural adjustment has not been reached and it is probably both necessary and indispensable to shift from a medium-high to a medium speed.

Second, the appropriate speed of economic growth needs to satisfy the demand to skip the middle-income trap. The GDP of 2020 and 2025 may be projected to have low, medium, and high variants as shown in Table 2.6 when the baseline is set at 2014 when the GDP was 63.6 trillion yuan, the population was 1.368 billion, and the reference rate of the renminbi to the U.S. dollar was 6.12:1.00.

There are still controversies about where to draw the line between middle and high incomes, and GDPs per capita of $8,000, $10,000, and $11,000 are all used by people. It is perhaps more appropriate to take the World Bank standard of $11,000 given foreseeable increases in socioeconomic development and incomes. Therefore, the low projection with a growth rate of 4.0% puts China at the exit of the middle-income group and at the entrance of the high-income group in 2025, when the projected GDP per capita reaches $10,957.8; the medium projection with a 5.5% growth rate puts China in the group of high-income countries in 2023, when the projected GDP per capita reaches $11,556; and the high projection with a 7.0% growth rate sees China enter the high-income group in 2021, when the projected GDP per capita

Table 2.6 Projections of China's GDP in 2020 and 2025

Projections	*GDP (trillion RMB)*	*GDP per capita (trillion RMB)*	*GDP (trillion USD)*	*GDP per capita (trillion USD)*
2020				
Low (4.0%)	80.5	55,748	13.15	9,109.1
Medium (5.5%)	87.7	60,730	14.33	9,923.9
High (7.0%)	95.5	66,099	15.60	10,806.5
2025				
Low (4.0%)	97.91	67,062	16.00	10,957.8
Medium (5.5%)	114.61	78,502	18.73	12,826.8
High (7.0%)	133.87	91,691	21.87	14,982.3

Source: The baseline data of 2014 were from "Statistical Communiqué of the People's Republic of China on the 2014 National Economic and Social Development" by the National Bureau of Statistics.

reaches $11,516, four to five years earlier than the low projection and two years earlier than the medium.

Apparently, the next 10, especially six years are crucial to land an appropriate growth rate. Even with the steady growth in the low projection, China will be able to skip the middle-income trap after the 14th Five-Year Plan is completed, with the medium projection, in the middle of the 14th Five-Year Plan, and with the high projection, after the 13th Five-Year Plan. Therefore, as long as the economy maintains steady growth, it is entirely in our hands when to skip the middle-income trap. However, the time needed is quite different between the low and high projections, and the difference is as big as two times. It is thus a probable and realistic choice to aim for the 7.0% high projection and stay at or above the medium 5.5% projection.

Third, the appropriate speed of economic growth needs to satisfy the demand for sufficient employment. The association between economic growth and employment rate since the Reform and Opening Up has shown that the increase of every percentage point in GDP provides 1.3 million jobs and brings a decrease of 0.5 percentage points in the urban registered unemployment rate. Given that the urban registered unemployment rate in 2014 was 4.09% and that the rate was required to be contained within 4.5% in 2015 proposed in the report on the work of the government, the GDP growth rate still has space to decrease by one percentage point and as long as it is maintained above 6.4%, the unemployment rate will not exceed 4.5%. If 5.0% is set as the limit for the unemployment rate, the GDP growth rate may decrease by two percentage points and stay above 5.4%, which falls in the range of the medium projection. If the unemployment rate exceeds the limit, it will rise above 5.0% and the GDP growth rate will fall below 5.4%, bringing great risk to the economy and threatening social stability, which should therefore be avoided.

This analysis shows that economic growth in the next tens of years at medium-high to medium speeds is acceptable and reasonable, and a speed in such a range can satisfy the demands to skip the middle-income trap and to keep the unemployment rate in control while providing a comfortable and beneficial ecological environment for the economy to transition its mode and adjust its structure.

Therefore, we must not let the opportunity of the moderately slowing down economy to slip away and must seek a whole new leap of economic benefits, efficiency, quality, and structure by placing technological advancement and efficiency improvement at the front line so that the new leap may lead the new normal economy to healthfully develop. The most recent statistical data have shown that changes and new development are taking place. In the first quarter of 2015, investment in fixed assets increased by 14.5%, the primary sector of the economy 32.8%, the secondary 11.0%, and the tertiary 14.7%, based on constant prices, showing differential growth rates for the three sectors; in addition, compared to the same period of the previous year, the GDP in the first quarter of 2015 increased by 7.0%, the primary sector 3.2%, the secondary 6.4%, and the tertiary 7.9%, leading to expected structural changes that the tertiary sector increased by 1.8 percentage points and accounted for 51.6% of the economy, higher than the proportion of the secondary sector by 8.7 percentage points.

Meanwhile, the upgrade and innovations in industries have accelerated with the value added of high-technology industries increasing by 11.4% compared to the same period of the previous year, five percentage points higher than that of industrial enterprises above a designated size. In terms of employment, 3.20 million new jobs were created in the first quarter of 2015, with the unemployment rate well controlled below the limit. The income gap between urban and rural residents has also narrowed in that the disposable income per capita of rural residents increased at a rate that was 1.9 percentage points higher than that of urban residents and the gap was closed by 0.05 compared to the same period of the previous year. Furthermore, progress has been made in saving energy and lowering consumption in that the energy consumption per unit of GDP decreased by 5.6% compared to the same period of the previous year.[9]

On a side note, the relationship between the post-demographic transition and the economic new normal shapes the demographic environment for the economic growth in the new normal. As mentioned earlier, China entered the stage of post-demographic transition in the early 1990s, when the fertility rate fell below the replacement level; thus the day when decreases in the fertility rate bring zero growth to the population is no longer invisible.

In addition, the working-age population, or those aged between 15 and 64, passed the Lewis turning point in 2010 and started the post-golden age of the transition, during which the population benefits and bonuses began to diminish. With further decreases in the fertility rate and declines in the proportion of the working-age population, the pressure from the population and employment started to lessen, which opened up a new demographic window for the economy to transition its mode, adjust its structure, and improve its quality in reforms. We should acknowledge that the golden age of the population structural changes before 2010 offered immense population benefits and bonuses for the super-fast economic development that was labor intensive and made irreplaceable contributions to the development in the first 20 years after the Reform and Opening Up.

We should also recognize that the current post-golden age has provided a new demographic window for transitions in the economic engine, mode, and structure and a beneficial ecological environment for the healthy and benign development of the economic new normal, including the growth rate, and its impact is all around, profound, and sustained. Time is the best judge. Decades later, the opportunities created for and the contributions made to the economic new normal by the post-golden age will be written in history and remembered by generations.

The reform to pursue economic benefits and quality instead of speed

This is a topic with strategic denotation in a specific historical period, which is also to say that replacement of speed with economic benefits and quality will be a fundamental economic strategy and tactic now and in the foreseeable future that will steer the direction, goals, and policies of the mode transition and structural adjustment. Analysis can be made from the following three aspects.

First, a plan for replacing speed with economic benefits and quality must be specified. It's widely known that China has achieved remarkably high-speed growth in the economy since the Reform and Opening Up; however, questionable quality and benefits are also side by side with this remarkable growth, which have built up and formed a significant contradiction in the current socioeconomic activities. To push for the social economy to march forward healthfully and for the strategy of sustainability to be carried out, the contradiction between the high speed and the questionable quality and benefits must be resolved. As in all kinds of contradictions, speed and quality with benefits are the two sides of a contradiction and either grows at the cost of the other; thus a friendly environment is needed for corrections and changes. Pursuit of quality and economic benefits at the cost of speed shapes the direction, the path, and the methods for such a friendly environment.

China is now the biggest country in manufacturing, but we are only big, yet not strong enough, and produce a lot with unimpressive quality and economic benefits, which has resulted in uncoordinated and unsustainable socioeconomic development. For example, China produced 823 million tons of crude steel in 2014, accounting for 49.5% of the world's production of 1.662 billion tons and for 182.08% of the sum of the production by the 28 countries in the European Union, the United States, Japan, Canada, and Russia. However, restricted by the quality, only a small proportion of crude steel was exported and even questioned and deliberately obstructed by many countries while a large amount of money was spent on importing crude steel. Now that China's economy has a new normal, which opens up a new opportunity for comprehensively deepening the reform of the economic system and a new stage of economic transition to replace speed with quality and benefits, a strategy and tactics should be specified on how to pursue economic benefits and quality instead of speed. Through the transition from pursuit of speed to economic benefits and quality, the economy may be healthy, coordinated, and sustainable with high-quality development and deepened reforms to transform the economic mode, adjust the structure, and better people's lives.

Second, the economy should be freed so that its growth may slow down from a medium-high to a medium speed. The Chinese people were invaded, oppressed, and exploited throughout recent history and were dying for China to grow rich and strong; therefore, everyone loved to see a high growth speed and favored speed way over other aspects of economic growth.

After the new China was established, a wave of construction swept the country in the 1950s with slogans such as "Great Leap Forward," "Passing the U.K.," and "Catching up with the U.S." In the 1970s, when Lin Biao and the antirevolutionary group of the "Four Gangsters" was crushed, a new "Westernized Great Leap Forward" occurred to build tens of Daqings and tens of commercial food bases. Favor of speed always shows up in a new dress with the changing economic environment. Even after the Reform and Opening Up, there were rushes in speed from time to time except that the rushes were not large scale and were always corrected quickly. Now that the economy is in the new normal, will there be more rushes and will people make peace with speed in their minds?

Unfortunately, love for high speed and refusal to accept deceleration will stay with people to various degrees and sometimes become manifested prominently. People love high speed not just because they have loved it for so long that they have become attached to it, but there is also a realistic reason: the combination of the focus on economic development and a strong government has led to a pattern of economic development that is dominated by the government that directs its attention primarily to the economy. Although the reform to establish a market economy has more or less been completed, the domination by the government is still visible here and there. After all, evaluation of cadres, especially on their talents and achievements, is always linked to the economies in their terms, which is one of the most important factors to decide their future promotion. Therefore, awareness must first be raised of the deceleration of economic growth in the new normal in order to recognize and accommodate the new normal.

This multi-perspective analysis of what is the appropriate speed for China's economic growth in the new normal already concluded that a medium-high to medium speed was reasonable. It is therefore necessary to straighten up the relationship between growth speed and economic benefits and quality and to eliminate the negative effects of GDP-centered evaluation since the love for a high speed has been rooted in people's minds for a long time while the economy is of an immense size with not very high quality or economic benefits.

That is not to say that speed is not important at all, or that a lower speed is always better; that is actually to say that given the situation that China is already the second largest economy that is continuously closing its gap with the first while under pressure of further healthy development, it relies on improvement of economic benefits and quality and quality or economic benefits have become the "tiger hurdle" that obstructs China's healthy, coordinated, and sustainable development. The economic new normal needs a certain degree of speed, but it needs consistently improved quality and economic benefits more badly. After all, increases in only speed and amount cannot meet the demands for further economic growth and can sometimes even harm it.

For example, China produced 1.125572 billion tons of steel in 2014, which was more than the production in 2013 by 4.0%; however, not all of the steel could meet the market demands in quality and variety and China had to import 14.43 million tons, which was more than the imports in 2013 by 2.5%. Despite governmental measures to restrict, lower, transform, and stop steel production, the production is not lowered. Apparently, repeated construction of factories and repeated production are also counted as the total production and increases in production; such increases could only be overproduction and are in complete opposition to healthy and sustainable development.

Third, laborers will grow in quality and structure, but not in number. With decreases in the marginal revenue of investment and the working-age population having passed its peak, the economic mode that is characterized by immense investment and vast human resources has come to an end and will be replaced by the new mode that is driven by innovation and characterized by technological advancement and human capital.

Human capital is the value of the knowledge, techniques, experiences, and health of all laborers. For them, it is crucial to improve their quality and construct a good structure. To improve their quality is to improve their health and strength, which involves development in the medical, hygiene, and sports fields; their education level, knowledge, and techniques, which involves reforms of the systems of education, science, and technology, the key to the whole picture of labor growth in quality and structure but not in number; and their legal, moral, and value systems, which involves strengthening the construction of the modern civilization and implementation of rule of law.

In fact, structural adjustment of laborers is also the guarantee of innovations and moderate economic growth. To avoid excessive aging of the working-age population that will weaken economic vigor, timely adjustments are needed of fertility policies so that birth rates and the age structure of those of working age are kept in appropriate ranges, which is one of the firm foundations for reasonable and healthy economic development. In addition, the urban rural changes of laborers are closely associated with urbanization, and the transformation of rural laborers into non-rural ones, and their distribution between rural and urban regions must be reasonably controlled. It is a crucial cog to push for laborers to grow in structure but not in number and for the economic new normal to decelerate but not to stall, the functions and impacts of which cannot be replaced.

Notes

1 Weeks, John, R., *Population – An Introduction to Concepts and Issues*, San Diego, San Diego State State University Press, updated 5th edn., translated by Zhang, Kaimin, et al., Shanghai, Shanghai Translation Publishing House, 1985, p. 210.
2 http://blog.163.com/keke19870609.
3 Tian, Xueyuan, "Structural Changes of the Population to Boost Modernization," *People's Daily*, June 5, 1983.
4 *Globalization*, vol. 2, 2015, pp. 123–130. The data of 2014 and 2015 are predictions.
5 *People's Daily*, May 6, 2015; *Economic References*, April 30, 2015.
6 *Beijing, China Statistics Press, 2014*, pp. 6–7.
7 Calculated based on the data on pages 4, 5, and 12 in *Beijing, China Statistics Press, 2014*.
8 Zhang, Yi, "7%, A Steady Start with a New Engine," *Guangming Daily*, April 16, 2015.
9 National Bureau of Statistics, "GDP Increased by 7% in the First Quarter of 2015," People's Web, Politics Channel, www.people.com.cn/rmrbwb/html/2015-04/25/cmtnt, April 15, 2015.

Bibliography

Fan, Hongda, "China: Rising or Collapsing?" *Social Sciences Abroad*, vol. 2, 2015.
Lin, Yifu, "A Growth Rate of 7% Is Reasonable and Necessary," Guangming Daily, March 25, 2015.
Liu, Wei, and Su, Jian, "Options of Macroregulation Policies in the New Normal," *Economics*, vol. 4, 2014.
Proceedings of the 3rd Plenary Meeting of the 18th Central Committee of the Communist Party of China, Beijing, People's Publishing House, 2013.
Tian, Xueyuan, *Post Demographic Transition Meets New Reform Opportunities*, Beijing, Social Sciences Academic Press (China), 2013.
Xu, Xianchun, "Analysis on the Economic Pattern in 2014 and Projections for 2015," *Globalization*, vol. 3, 2015.

3 The acceleration trend in population aging

Exploring the path of reforms for unified old-age security

The aging trend in population in the 21st century

Post-demographic transition, characterized by low births, low deaths, and low growth, leads populations to progressively age, which, like a boat on rising water, cannot be stopped, giving population development in the 21st century a prominent mark. Developed countries were the first to start the post-demographic transition and for a long time, they have led the global trend of population aging; now that developing countries, one group after another, are and will be pushing into the wave of population aging with scales and speeds that developed countries have never seen, how are we going to withstand the unprecedented grey tide?

The aging trend in the world population

The 20th century saw explosive growth in population: the world population grew 2.83 times from 1.60 billion in 1900 to 6.12 billion in 2000, with an average annual growth rate of 1.35%, marking historically high population growth.[1] However, great disparities exist between developing and developed countries due to unbalanced development of economies, science and technology, cultures, and societies. Developing countries still have growing populations while developed countries have weakened growth, with some even reaching zero or negative growth, setting their feet in the age of "grey tides."

Western and Northern European nations such as France and Sweden were the first to transition to an aged population structure, and, by 1950, those at or above 60 years of age accounted for 11.7% in developed countries, and those at or above 65 accounted for 7.9%, marking developed countries as a whole with an elderly age structure. Developing countries, in contrast, have only 6.4% and 3.9% of these two age groups, typical of a young age structure. In 2000, those at 60 or above and those at 65 or above accounted for 19.5% and 14.4%, respectively, in developed countries, showing a grave degree of population aging, while in developing countries, the two percentages were only 7.5% and 5.0%, showing these countries to be either transitioning from young to adult populations or just entering the adult stage. When the world population is taken as a whole, those aged at 60 or above accounted for 9.9% in 2000, and those aged at 65 or above 6.8%, marking the completion of the transition from an adult to an elderly population, which, however, was still yet to be called an aged population officially.

Since the start of the 21st century, the world population has been aging at a progressive rate. Evaluation of the aging level of a population is usually based on the proportion of those at 60 and above or 65 and above, the median (or average) age of the population, and the ratio of the elderly to the young. The proportion of the elderly is the most frequently used because it is intuitive and explicit. According to the UN, those aged at 65 or above worldwide will increase from 6.8% in 2000 to 10.4% in 2025 and 16.2% in 2050, while the median age will grow from 26.6 to 32.8 and 38.8 years, respectively.

Specifically, in developed countries, the proportion of those at 65 or above will grow from 14.4% to 20.8% and 26.2%, respectively, and the median age from 37.3 to 43.0 and 45.6 years, respectively; in developing countries, the proportion of those at 65 or above will increase from 5.0% to 8.4% and 14.6%, respectively, while the median age will grow from 24.1 to 30.8 and 37.2 years, respectively. The aging trends from 2000 to 2050 in the world, in developed countries, and in developing countries are summarized in Figure 3.1.

As shown in Figure 3.1, the proportion of those at 65 or above grows rapidly in the first half of the 21st century; however, there is an apparent disparity between the first 25 years and the second 25 years in developed countries and developing countries. In developed countries, the proportion increases by 6.4 percentage points in the first 25 years, but only by 5.4 percentage points in the second; the reduction of 1.0 percentage point in growth in the second 25 years compared to the first shows a decelerating trend in population aging.

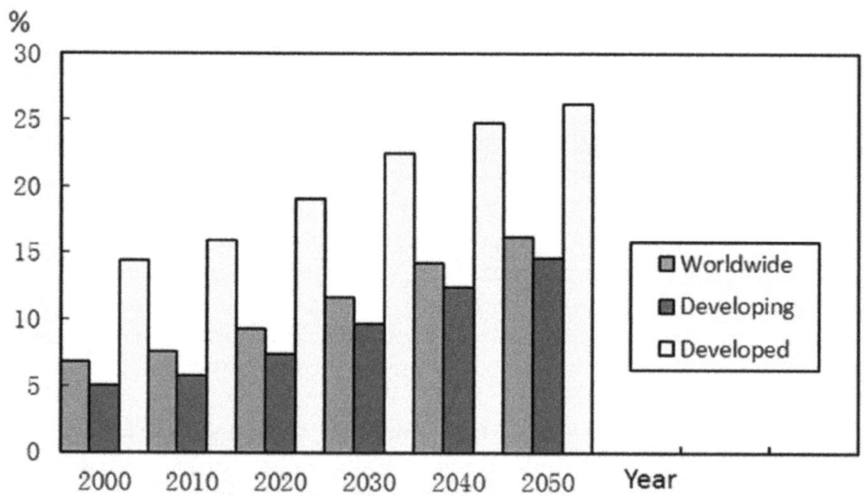

Figure 3.1 Changes in the proportion of those aged 65 or above, 2000–2050.

In contrast, in developing countries, the proportion increases by 3.4 percentage points in the first 25 years, but by 6.2 percentage points in the second, showing an accelerating aging trend with a total increase of 2.8 percentage points in the second 25 years compared to the first. Apparently, by the mid-21st century, developed countries will see an end to population aging and there will be very limited growth in their proportion of the elderly while developing countries will still have a long way to go and their proportion of the elderly will continue to rise.

Overall, the worldwide aging trend will be mostly decided by the aging progression in developing countries as developed countries are consumed by marked decreases in birth rates, births, and proportions of the world population, and the worldwide proportion of the elderly in the second 25 years is higher than the first by 2.2 percentage points. Therefore, the world will not see the peak of the proportion of those at 65 or above until 2050, when the proportion will be 16.2%, after which the population aging will slow down.

In the second half of the 21st century, the population aging in developed countries will be stable with some fluctuations and the increases in the proportion of the elderly, if any, will be very limited; the aging in developing countries will also slow down, but it will not stabilize until the proportion of those at 65 or above reaches 20.0%. These numbers show that in the first half of the 21st century, the first 25 years are a period with a slowly aging population while the second 25 years are a period with a quickly aging population; in the second half of the 21st century, the population will keep decelerating in aging until it reaches a stable stage. Therefore, the entrance of the world population into an elderly age structure until the stabilization of the structure has taken place and will be completed in the 21st century, and the 21st century is one of population aging.

The aging trend in China's population

2.1 The basic trend in population aging

The changes in the population aging vary greatly in different projections for the Chinese population, and discussion of the future trend in the population aging has to first specify a population projection. The projection used here is the one described in the previous chapter as it agrees with the demographic changes in the recent years and is in the middle range among all domestic and international projections. The projection is composed of three variants, high, medium, and low, as described in what follows.

In the high, "slow-landing" variant, the fertility rate takes steps to rebound from its current level until it reaches the replacement level where it stays stable. The projected TFRs are, on average, 1.90 between 2000 and 2005, 2.00 between 2005 and 2010, 2.13 between 2010 and 2020, and 2.15 between 2020 and 2050. With these TFRs, the national population would have been 1.375 billion in 2010 and will be 1.490 billion in 2020, 1.548 billion in 2030, 1.585

billion in 2040, and almost 1.605 billion in 2050, when the population hits its peak, after which it will be stable.

In the medium, "soft-landing" variant, the fertility rate is stable in that it stabilizes at a level that is slightly higher than the current level and fluctuates after it increases by a small scale. The projected TFRs are, on average, 1.75 between 2000 and 2005, 1.80 between 2005 and 2010, 1.83 between 2010 and 2020, and 1.80 between 2020 and 2050. With these TFRs, the national population would have been 1.360 billion in 2010, will reach 1.444 billion in 2020 and 1.465 billion in 2030, which is the peak of the population, and will then slowly decline to 1.451 billion in 2040 and 1.402 billion in 2050. If the TFR of 1.80 is to be maintained, China's population will downsize to 1.024 billion in 2100.

In the low, "hard-landing" variant, the fertility rate decreases slightly from the current level. The projected TFRs are, on average, 1.65 between 2000 and 2005, 1.56 between 2005 and 2010, 1.44 between 2010 and 2020, and 1.32 between 2020 and 2050. With these TFRs, the national population would have been 1.343 billion in 2010, will reach 1.386 billion in 2020 and 1.387 billion in 2021, which is the peak of the population, and will then stepwise decline to 1.367 billion in 2030, 1.302 billion in 2040, and 1.192 billion in 2050. If the TFR of 1.32 is to be maintained, China's population will downsize to 556 million in 2100.

The high, medium, and low variants of this population projection illustrate a low, medium, and high level of population aging, respectively. Why does population aging always change in an inverse direction to population changes? It is primarily decided by fertility and birth rates. The higher the fertility and birth rates are, the higher the growth rate of a population is and the lower the level of its aging is; on the contrary, the lower the fertility and birth rates are, the lower the population growth rate is and the higher the level of aging.

Therefore, the aging of China's population in the 21st century will likely follow one of the trends as projected by the high, medium, and low variants; of course, there are significant differences between the variants. The overall trend is that the population will grow old slowly with a low level of population aging if the high variant proves right, the population will grow old moderately with a moderate level of aging if the medium variant proves right, and the population will grow old fast with a high level of aging if the low variant proves right. The changes in the age structure of China's population in the 21st century are illustrated in Figure 3.2 according to the three projection variants.

Figure 3.2 shows the proportions of the elderly aged 65 or higher according to the high, medium, and low variants of the population projection. As shown in the figure, changes in the elderly population are always inversely related to those in the total population in that the aging is at a low level in the high variant and at a high level in the low variant. The specific changes are as follows.

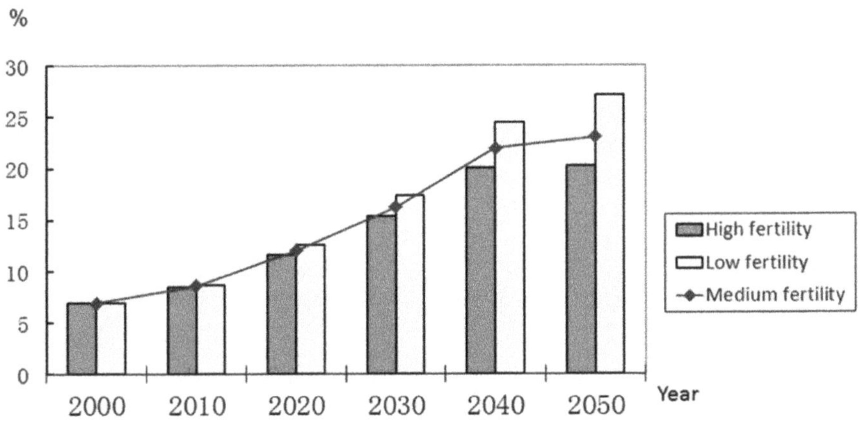

Figure 3.2 Projected proportions of the elderly aged 65 or higher in China, 2000–2050.

In the high variant, the proportion of the elderly at 65 or higher of the total population increases from 6.9% in 2000 to 8.5% in 2010, 11.7% in 2020, 15.4% in 2030, 20.1% in 2040, and 20.2% in 2050.

In the medium variant, the proportion increases from 6.9% in 2000 to 8.6% in 2010, 12.0% in 2020, 16.2% in 2030, 22.0% in 2040, and 23.1% in 2050.

In the low variant, the proportion increases from 6.9% in 2000 to 8.7% in 2010, 12.5% in 2020, 17.4% in 2030, 24.5% in 2040, and 27.1% in 2050.

Apparently, these high, medium, and low variants have given quite different pictures in terms of the speed at which and the level to which the population ages. All three variants start with the year 2000, when the proportion of the elderly at 65 or higher was 6.9%. The percentage came from a national population census and should be by all means reliable. Overall, there are relatively small differences between the three variants during the first 20 years of the projected period in that the proportion of those aged 65 or higher in 2020 is only 0.3 percentage points lower in the high than in the medium variant, 0.5 percentage points lower in the medium than in the low variant, and 0.8 percentage points lower in the high than in the low variant. By 2040, however, the difference in the proportion between the high and medium variants is as large as 1.9 percentage points, 2.5 percentage points between the medium and low variants, and 4.4 percentage points between the high and low variants; by 2050, the gaps between the three variants are further widened to be 2.9, 4.0, and 6.9 percentage points between the high and medium, medium and low, and high and low variants, respectively.

These three variants are somewhat different from projections given by various international organizations, but the differences are not great. For example, the medium variant of the UN's projection predicted that the proportion of those aged 65 or higher in China would grow from 6.8% in 2000 to 8.2% in 2010, 11.7% in 2020, 15.9% in 2030, 21.8% in 2040, and 23.3% in 2050.[2]

In fact, however, the proportion of those aged 65 or higher in China already reached 8.9% in 2010, 0.7 percentage points higher than the UN medium projection.[3] The UN had an underestimated projection of China's population aging for the first 20 years from 2000 to 2020; for the next 30 years from 2020 to 2050, in contrast, the UN's projection came to agree with the projection described in this book, with a difference of only 0.2 percentage points in the proportion of the elderly in 2050. However, population projections are prospects, but not forecasts, and whether they are accurate will be tested in practice.

Major characteristics of China's population aging

The age structure of a population including the elderly is the consequence of all the changes in the past brought by births, deaths, and migration that have been passed down to the present. Similarly, the aging and the overall age structure of a population in the future are the consequence of all past and present births, deaths, and migration that will be passed down to the future. That is also to say, the root of the changes in the present and future population aging and overall age structure is in the births, deaths, and migration in the past.

With the same logic, the current population age structure is clearly of crucial importance to the future, which itself results from all the demographic changes after the establishment of the new China, including the transition of population reproduction to the high, low, high type from 1949 to 1952, the first fertility boom from 1953 to 1957, the first aberrant fertility recession from 1958 to 1961, the second fertility boom from 1962 to 1973, and the second fertility recession since 1974. Among all the changes, the second fertility boom that lasted for 12 years with 320 million people born is most influential. This cohort makes up a particularly large bulk of the population pyramid, and it keeps moving up the pyramid with time, bringing demographic problems with it wherever it goes. When the bulk moved to working age and to marriage and reproduction age, there was increased pressure on employment and reproduction, and problems arose; when it moves to senior age, a critical time of population aging will come with it, resulting in China-specific characteristics of aging. The basic characteristics are as follows.

First, the population aging in China is fast and will reach a high level. The absolute number of those aged 65 or higher in 2050 is already known, i.e., the number of those aged between 28 and 64 in 2013 minus the annual age-specific mortalities in the subsequent years until 2050. However, factors that impact the level of population aging also include those such as birth rates and births, death rates, and life expectancy.

We can illustrate the speed and the degree of the population aging in China based on the changes in the proportion of those aged 65 or higher. According to the projection described earlier, how aged the population will be in 2050 may be represented by the proportion of those aged 65 or higher, which will be 20.23% as projected in the high variant, 23.07% in the medium, and 27.1% in the low.[4] Given the current fertility policy in China that each couple may have two children, it is most probable that the population aging will take the path of the medium variant. Along this path, the progression of the population aging in China may be summarized with two words, fast and high. It is fast because it will take China 23 years to progress from an elderly population at the turn of the 21st century to a severely aged population in 2023, when the elderly will account for 12.3% of the total population, while it will take the world more than 30 years and developing countries more than 40 years. It will take China 32 years for the proportion of the elderly to grow from 7.0% to 17.0% as it will be 17.5% in 2032 while all developed countries as a whole took twice as long to reach the same level of aging from the mid-20th century all the way up to 2015. Japan is the only exception as its proportion of those aged 65 or higher increased from 7.1% in 1970 to 17.2% in 2000, and the progression took 30 years, similar to China. It is high because the degree of the population aging will be high. In 2050, those aged 65 or higher in China will account for 23.07% of the total population, 6.87 percentage points higher than the world level, then 16.2%, 8.47 percentage points higher than the level of developing countries, 14.6%, and only 3.31 percentage points lower than the level of developed countries, 26.2%, marking China as a member of the global club of aged countries.[5]

Second, the population aging in China is phased and progressive. Such characteristics result from the past age structure of the population that was shaped by natural changes in births and deaths. The natural changes in China's population first experienced the transition of population reproduction from 1949 to 1952 after the People's Republic of China was founded in 1949, i.e., the transition from high births, high deaths, and low growth to high births, low deaths, and high growth. Then came the first reproduction peak between 1953 and 1957, during which the national population grew from 574.82 to 646.53 million, an increase of 71.71 million with an average annual growth rate of 2.4%, or an addition of 14.342 million people every year.

What followed the baby boom was the first reproduction recession from 1958 to 1961, during which the national population increased by only 12.06 million, from 646.53 to 658.59 million, at an average annual growth rate of just 0.5%, or an addition of 3.015 million people every year; in fact, negative growth was observed in 1960 and 1961, with 10 million fewer people in 1960 than 1959 and another reduction of 3.48 million people in 1961 compared to 1960.

After the reproduction recession came the second baby boom from 1962 to 1973, during which the national population increased by 233.52 million from 658.59 to 892.11 million, and that was an addition of 19.46 million people every year, or an average annual growth rate of 2.6%.

After that, the second reproduction recession has been residing in China since 1974 while the national population grew from 892.11 million to 1.36782 billion in 2014, an increase of 475.71 million people at an average annual growth rate of just 1.1%, or an addition of 11.893 million people every year.[6] Apparently, the rises and the falls of the birth, death, and natural growth rates of the population in these five periods have resulted in an uneven age structure, which decides that the future aging of the population will be irregular with rises and falls, phased, and progressive.

In the population pyramid representing China's population age structure, the most prominent bulk is the cohort born during the second baby boom from 1962 to 1973, who, after deaths through the years, still totals about 300 million, and it deserves particular attention in studies on China's population changes, including aging. This cohort of about 300 million people grew into adulthood over 15 from 1977 through 1988, and most of them became laborers from 1980 to 1991, bringing huge pressure on employment; at the same time, a golden age also started as the proportion of those of working age reached its peak while the total dependency ratio of the elderly and the young hit bottom, bringing "population benefits" and "population bonuses" that best facilitated economic development.

This cohort should also have brought another baby boom from 1986 to 1997 as the age-specific fertility peak of women in both rural and urban areas is 24 years of age; however, another baby boom that would have lasted for more than 10 years did not show up in practice due to the continuously strengthened population control and implementation of the basic state policy of family planning, and the cohort only made its impact on the birth rate slightly in the mid- to late 1980s. Nevertheless, this cohort will show its impact on the aging progression such that when these 300 million people are below age 65, there will be no severe aging of the population, but when this huge group grows old, the grave "rainy season" of the aging will come. Consequently, the aging progression has an s-shaped curve with several phases, just like the urbanization of the population.

The first phase is from 2000 to 2020 at the bottom of the s-curve when the population slowly ages. The proportion of those aged 65 or higher may increase by 5.08 percentage points, from 6.96% to 12.04%, at an average annual growth rate of 0.25 percentage points.

The second phase is from 2020 to 2040, which falls in the middle, rising part of the s-curve when the population accelerates to age. The proportion of those aged 65 or higher may increase by 9.92 percentage points, from 12.04% to 21.96%, at an average annual growth rate of 0.5 percentage points, twice as fast as the first phase.

The third phase is from 2040 to 2050, which is the top part of the s-curve when the population once again slowly ages and becomes stable. The proportion of those aged 65 or higher may increase by 1.11 percentage points, from 21.96% to 23.07%, at an average annual growth rate of 0.11 percentage points, making the third phase the slowest in aging among the three. After

2050, the proportion of the elderly may further increase, but the increase will be extremely limited and the aging progression will fluctuate at the top of the s-curve.

Third, the population aging in China is unevenly distributed between urban and rural areas and among different regions. The characteristics of aging in China described so far are based on the nationwide situation; however, China is a vast country with great varieties in geographic, economic, scientific, technological, and social levels, and what is more relevant and important here is that the natural changes in the population such as births and deaths in the past differed greatly in different regions, resulting in apparent variations in the aging progression between urban and rural areas and among different regions.

The aging differs greatly between urban and rural areas. In the beginning of the 1980s, the age structure of China's population turned to the adult type, as the proportion of those aged 65 or higher reached 4.91% according to the third national population census in 1982, and it subsequently began to transition to the old-age type. However, the transition showed different characteristics between urban and rural areas: the descending order of the proportions of those aged 65 or higher by region in this census was counties (the countryside) at 5.0%, cities at 4.68%, and towns at 4.21%; apparently, counties had a higher proportion of the elderly and would stride faster than the other two regions in the transition to the old-age type

Similar situations were observed in the fourth national population census in 1990, and the nationwide proportion of those aged 65 or higher grew to 5.57% while the proportion in counties grew to 5.64%, cities 5.53%, and towns 5.49%; the descending order of the proportions was still counties, cities, and towns, and the only difference was that the gaps between the three regions were smaller than before.

The subsequent fifth census in 2000 showed in its data that the proportion of those aged 65 or higher increased to 6.96% nationwide while the gaps between counties, cities, and towns were kept and widened somewhat: the proportion grew to 7.74% in counties, 7.0% in cities, and 6.25% in towns. Among the three censuses in 1982, 1990, and 2000, the ratio of the proportions of those aged 65 or higher between counties, cities, and towns was first 1.00:0.94:0.84 and then went down to 1.00:0.98:0.97, but then increased to 1.00:0.90:0.81, showing that the proportion of the elderly in counties became larger in counties than in cities and towns.

Such widening differences were consolidated in the sixth census in 2010, and a new feature showed up that towns passed cities in the proportion: the nationwide proportion of the elderly aged 65 or higher increased to 8.91% while the proportion in counties grew to 10.06%, towns 7.97%, and cities 7.69%, with the ratio of the proportions between counties, towns, and cities increasing to 1.00:0.79:0.76.[7]

Why did the ratio of the elderly proportions between urban and rural areas keep increasing? It was because of the increase in floating and migration, which was especially prominent after the turn of the 21st century. According to the fifth census in 2000, the migrant population of those residing at the current locations for more than half a year reached 144,390,748, and after excluding those who had migrated from other streets or towns in the same counties (town cities) and from other streets or towns in the same cities, 92,870,183 had migrated from other villages in the same cities or from villages in other provinces.

That is also to say that most of the more than 90 million migrants were actually residents who had moved from villages to cities and towns. The sixth population census in 2010 showed that the number of those who had separate locations of residence and house registration (*hukou*) reached 260.94 million, higher than that of the fifth census by a large margin.

The trend is still continuing; a statement by the National Bureau of Statistics showed that the nationwide number of those whose residential and *hukou* locations were not in the same streets of the same villages or towns and who had left their *hukou* locations for more than half a year (i.e., those with separate residential and *hukou* locations) was 289 million in 2013, among whom 245 million were migrants; the numbers continued to grow in 2014 and reached 298 million and 253 million, respectively.[8] As the migrants who had moved to cities and towns where they resided regularly for at least half a year were taken as urban residents in statistical analysis, the aging in urban areas, especially cities, was alleviated and the urban proportion of the elderly became distant from that in rural areas.

In fact, the total number of regular residents in cities and towns exceeded that in the countryside on June 28, 2011, for the first time based on the population natural growth rate, marking the initiation of the structural transition between urban and rural populations. It also directly impacted the distribution of population aging between rural and urban areas in that the elderly population progressively increased in rural areas and the uneven distribution of the elderly between urban and rural areas became worsened. It has been projected that in the 2020s, when the urban population accounts for 60.0% of the national population, the migration of rural to urban areas will slow down and shrink in size, which will set the condition for narrowing the gaps in population aging between counties, cities, and towns and accelerated aging will be observed in cities and towns, especially in metropolises.

The population aging is also uneven among geographic regions in China. The population migration described earlier did not only shape the aging progression in cities, towns, and counties but also impacted the aging and the deepening of aging among geographic regions, which cannot be ignored. A remarkable feature of the impact is that the proportions of the elderly that used to descend along the "three plates" of the eastern, middle, and western areas are now transitioning to a distribution of "two plates" with the middle and western areas fusing into one.

The transition began in 2005 when the nationwide proportion of the elderly aged 65 or higher was 9.07% while 13 provinces and municipalities had higher proportions with seven, or 53.8%, along the east coastline, three, or 23.1%, in the middle area, and three, or 23.1%, in the western area; the middle and western areas together claimed six provinces and municipalities, or 46.2%.

In contrast, 18 provinces and municipalities had lower proportions than the national level, with four, or 22.2%, along the east coastline, five, or 27.7%, in the middle area, and nine, or 50.0%, in the west; the middle and western areas together accounted for 77.8%, showing a low level of aging.[9] Things further developed as shown in the sixth population census in 2010: the nationwide proportion of those aged 65 or higher grew to 9.4% with the proportion in the middle and western areas further increasing. Although there was still a clear gap between the east and the middle areas and between the east and the west, the gap between the middle area and the west was closed, showing a clear trend that the aging had a "two plate" distribution between the east and the mid-west with the middle and western areas fusing into one plate.

Establishing an old-age social security system with complete coverage

During the 65 years after the establishment of the new China, the old-age social security system was started without any preexisting foundation. It grew from small to big, and a system with considerable mechanisms and institutions was established through endless explorations during the 35 years of the Reform and Opening Up. It is now on the way to perfection. Now that the reform is being comprehensively deepened, a top-down design is needed.

Evolution of the old-age social security system

A look back at history

In the old China that was half colonized and half feudal, the people lived in horrible conditions without enough clothes to cover or food to feed themselves, and there was nothing that was even close to a social security system; nor was elderly care related to the society in any way. However, elderly care was given some degree of attention in the Central Soviet Area and some special forms of old-age security were tested.

For example, in *Plans of Economic Wars*, passed in the Second National Labor Congress in 1925, it was proposed "to set up a social insurance system so that laborers [would] be compensated for if injured or killed at work and paid a relief pension when ill, unemployed, or old." It was subsequently proposed in the *Resolution on Economic Wars*, passed in the Fourth National Labor Congress in 1927, to "implement a social labor insurance system for diseases, deaths, unemployment, and aging that all must face to provide security for the lives of laborers."[10]

A labor law was later issued in the Central Soviet Area, which demanded that employers pay 10.0% to 15.0% of the total expense on salaries each month to compensate for childbirth, aging, diseases, death, and disabilities of employees. In 1948, the Sixth National Labor Congress was held in Ha'erbin and a resolution was passed that required that all workers be paid a monthly old-age pension that was 30.0% to 60.0% of their salaries according to length of service. The resolution, also called the Northeastern Regulations, once benefited 796 workers in 420 factories in the northeast.[11] However, these insurance plans of elderly care were restricted to the liberation areas, and not until the establishment of the People's Republic of China in 1949 did the nationwide insurance system made its first steps and develop.

The first law of the new China, the Common Program, sought to "stepwise implement a labor insurance system" in article 23. In 1951, *Labor Insurance Regulations of the People's Republic of China* was issued and implemented by the Government Administration Council, and it regulated that workers in state-owned industrial enterprises with more than 100 employees enjoyed insurance for injuries at work, diseases, and elderly care, which pioneered the insurance cause in the Republic. By 1956, 16 million workers had been covered by the regulations, accounting for 94.0% of all the employees in state-owned, mixed public and private, and privately owned enterprises, and all the cost was paid for by the enterprises.

In 1958, the State Council issued the *Temporary Regulations on Retirement of Workers and Other Employees*, which separated enterprise retirement from the coverage of the *Labor Insurance Regulations* and covered it, together with retirement of employees in institutes and units, in a much wider-coverage insurance system for elderly care that included enterprises, government units, and institutes. Unfortunately, however, the old-age insurance system set up in the 1950s was damaged after the Cultural Revolution and the labor insurance fund raised by the unions at various levels stopped being enriched in 1969.

In 1978, the *Temporary Regulations on the Retirement and Withdrawal from Work of Workers* and the *Temporary Regulations on Caring for the Elderly, Underprivileged, Ill, and Disabled Cadres* were passed at the Second Plenary Session of the Fifth National People's Congress (NPC) and issued by the State Council. The regulations demanded that the retirement pension be calculated based on the starting time of work and length of service, and be 60.0–90.0% of the monthly salary, but no lower than the minimum pension of 25 yuan per month. The two files of regulations officially distinguished workers from cadres in terms of retirement plans and gave them separate systems and mechanisms.

In 1991, the State Council issued the *Decision on Reforming the Old-Age Insurance System for Enterprise Employees*, which was aimed to establish an insurance system of elderly care that extended its coverage to the collective economic sector and the premiums were paid for collectively by the state, enterprises, and individuals, so that the insurance system would cover basic needs in elderly care and be based on the savings accounts of the employees combined with supplementary contributions by the enterprises.

In 1995, the *Notification by the State Council on Deepening the Reform on the Old-Age Insurance of Enterprise Employees* proposed that "the basic cost of elderly care should be paid for jointly by enterprises and employees so that the society-wide coordination and overall planning [might] be combined with individual contributions," and among the supplementary files of the *Notification*, there was the *Implementation Measures to Combine the Society-Wide Coordination and Individual Accounts of Elderly-Care Insurance for Enterprise Employees*.

Also in 1995, it was further demanded, with the issuance of the *Notification by the State Council on the Suggestions of the Ministry of Civil Affairs on Further Steps to Develop Old-Age Social Insurance in Rural Areas*, that practical measures should be taken to establish an old-age insurance system in the rural areas that were ready for it and peasants should be guided to participate in the social old-age security system.

In 1996, the *Law of the People's Republic of China on Protection of the Rights and Interests of the Elderly* was published, in which it was specified to "establish an old-age social security system by the state to ensure the basic needs of the elderly," and the right to pensions of the elderly, the amount of pensions, supervision of pensions, benefits of the elderly, and relief services of the elderly were all specified.

In 2000, the *Decision by the Central Committee of the Communist Party of China and the State Council on Strengthening the Work Related to the Elderly* was issued, in which cities and towns were required to "establish a relatively comprehensive old-age security system with basic old-age insurance, basic medical insurance, commercial insurance, social relief, social welfare, and support among the society" and to "stepwise establish a mechanism for old-age security based on a combination of contributions by the state, society, families, and individuals."

In 2005, the *Decision by the State Council on Perfecting the Old-Age Insurance System for Enterprise Employees* was released, in which it was reiterated that the basic pensions must be paid on time and in full amounts, the coverage of the old-age insurance system should be enlarged, individual pension accounts should be consolidated in steps, the collection of insurance contributions should be strengthened and so should its supervision, and the coordination of the accounts must speed to a higher level.[12] By now, the current social security system and insurance system for the elderly in cities and towns had its shape.

In September 2009, the State Council released guidelines for the new rural social old-age endowment insurance system (New Rural Insurance), which aimed to guarantee the basic needs of rural elderly residents by establishing an old-age social insurance system in coordination with family care, land support, and social relief services, and was meant to cover the basics and all areas with flexibility and sustainability and to be paid for jointly by individuals, collectives, and the government.

The New Rural Insurance broke the previous pattern of old-age insurance that was paid for only by individuals and distributed the cost among individuals (who could choose one of the five plans available with the cheapest plan costing 100 yuan per year and 100 yuan to upgrade to the next level from any plan), collectives (that offered allowance at amounts decided through democratic procedures by village congresses), the government (with the central government offering full subsidy to the middle and western areas and 50.0% to the eastern area based on the minimum pension set by the central government, which is now 55 yuan per month per person), and the regional government that helped pay the premiums of every insurant (for at least 30 yuan per year per insurant).

Pension payments of the New Rural Insurance are made up of a basic component and a personal account component, and the former is backed by the national treasury. According to the regulations of the system, peasants aged 60 or older who are not covered by the basic old-age insurance system for urban employees are entitled to a monthly pension at an amount set by the basic component, but their children must pay for their own pensions under the New Rural Insurance if eligible; those who are less than 15 years away from receiving pensions should pay for the premiums on an annual basis while late payments are acceptable, and collectively, they should pay for at least 15 years; those who are 15 or more years away from receiving pensions should also pay on an annual basis for at least 15 years.

The monthly payment of pensions from personal accounts is calculated by dividing the entire amount of each personal account by 139, a coefficient that is the same as that used to calculate the monthly pensions for urban employees concerning their personal old-age insurance plan. In case of death of an insurant, the remaining money in his/her personal account can be lawfully inherited, but not the component of government subsidy. The guidelines required to cover 10.0% of the nationwide counties (cities, districts, and Qis) as trial sites in 2009 and to achieve full coverage by 2020; but in fact, the progression of the New Rural Insurance was much faster than planned and it has now achieved full coverage.

On July 1, 2013, a new version of the *Law of the People's Republic of China on Protection of the Rights and Interests of the Elderly* (the new law of elderly protection) was officially enforced. The new law of elderly protection had nine chapters and 85 articles compared to the old version that had eight chapters and 50 articles; after all, things were quite different now as aging was furthered, families became smaller, and empty nests with old-age parents were more common, and the law thus emphasized respect for the wills and choices of the elderly and the protection of their lawful rights. The law is the "protective spell" of the current aging society, and it also reveals certain aspects of the current old-age insurance system. Specifically, four aspects deserve particular attention in the law.

First, children must fulfill their responsibilities to take care of their parents, including economic support, daily care, and emotional comfort; particularly, it was written into the new law of elderly protection that children should "go back home to visit the parents often" when time and money permit, which was met with society-wide heated discussions. In fact, "visits" should include various forms such as in-person visits, letters, and phone calls. Those who refuse to take care of their parents are to be reprimanded and educated by pertinent institutes. Family abuses are also covered in the law; those abused by their family members may seek mediation from village committees and community committees or administrative punishment on the abusers from the police, and file cases in courts if crimes are found.

Second, the government, together with social organizations, must take on further responsibilities to perfect the service system for the elderly. The government should keep improving the system of social services for the elderly that is based on family care in the first place, community care as the backup, and institutes as the support, while both the government and social organizations should push for community services for the elderly in villages and towns, establish a web of facilities and institutes that cater for the needs of the elderly, and to provide services such as daily care, medical care, and emergency help.

Third, the living conditions of the elderly are to be improved by building more houses and renovating existing ones. The law emphasized pushing for and offering help for house renovation with accessibility for the elderly based on the basic standards of elderly friendly housing, and supporting the development of housing for the elderly, and called for governments at all levels and all social organizations to take effective measures to build a safe, convenient, and comfortable environment for the elderly to live in.

Fourth, the new law of elderly protection emphasized that the wills of the elderly should be taken as priority in all issues related to them. As regulated by the law, when handling matters such as changing the ownership of houses and moving *hukou*, governments at all levels must ask the elderly involved for their opinions and take their wills as the priority. In addition, pertinent government departments have special responsibilities in handling important issues involving the rights of the elderly to help prevent unauthorized management that may harm the life and financial interest of the elderly.

On February 21, 2014, the *Opinion by the State Council on Establishing a Unified Social Old-Age Endowment System for Urban and Rural Residents* (Guofa [2014] No. 8, abbreviated as the Opinion hereafter) was issued. The Opinion combined the New Rural Insurance and the social old-age endowment insurance system for residents in cities and towns (the Urban Resident Insurance) based on the experiences in the trial sites of the two systems and designed a unified system of old-age insurance (urban-rural old-age insurance) for both urban and rural residents in the entire country.

The new unified insurance system aimed to have full coverage, basic security, flexibility, and sustainability and was committed to increasing justice, adapting to mobility, and ensuring sustainability; the insurance system of basic elderly care was to be comprehensively pushed for and continuously improved so that the impact of the social insurance system would be fully exerted on ensuring the basic needs of the people, adjusting the social distribution of incomes, and facilitating the coordinated development of the urban and rural economic societies.

The Opinion is composed of 12 parts of guidelines, objectives, range of coverage, funding, establishing personal accounts, old-age pensions and adjustments, eligibility for old-age pensions, transfer of accounts and regulations, management and operation of the funds, supervision of the funds, handling and management services and information management, and strengthening the leadership of the party and advocacy for the policy. There are specific guidelines for each part, among which the following deserve detailed description.

In terms of the range of coverage and how to establish personal old-age insurance accounts, urban and rural residents aged 16 or older (excluding students enrolled in school) who are not employees of government agencies or public institutes and are not covered by the basic employee old-age insurance system may enroll in the urban-rural old-age insurance plan of elderly care at locations associated with their *hukou*. The government sets up a lifelong personal account for every insurant, which tracks all the payments by the insurant, allowance to the insurant from the local people's government, allowance by the collective, and all other contributions by social economic organizations, charities, and other individuals. All personal accounts have interest based on the rates set by the government.

How to raise funds is crucial to the insurance system, and it was explicitly defined in the Opinion that the funds would consist of three components of individual contribution, collective allowance, and government subsidy. The individual contribution has 12 categories of annual payments of 100, 200, 300, 400, 500, 600, 700, 800, 900, 1,000, 1,500, and 2,000 yuan while the provincial (as well as district and city) people's government may add more categories according to the local situations.

The collective allowance may come from economic organizations in village collectives if they can afford it, and the amount of the allowance may be decided through democratic procedures in village congresses held by village committee members; eligible communities are also encouraged to include the collective allowance in fund-raising for community public services, and other social economic organizations, charities, and individuals are all encouraged to donate to personal accounts of the enrolled. The government subsidy is the basic component of old-age pensions that are paid in full amounts to those eligible to receive pensions from the insurance system; the subsidy in the middle and western areas is paid in full by the central government while only 50.0% of the subsidy in the east is paid for by the central government.

In fact, regional people's governments shall provide subsidy to the personal accounts of the enrolled, and the subsidy should be no less than 30 yuan per year per insurant to those who have chosen the lowest level of insurance while the amount should be increased moderately for those who have chosen a higher level so that those who pay 500 yuan or more every year shall receive a subsidy of at least 60 yuan per year per person, and the detailed standards and measures shall be decided by the provincial (or district, city) people's governments. The regional people's governments should also help pay the premiums, in part or in full, for the underprivileged who cannot afford the insurance such as those with severe disabilities.

In terms of pension payments and standards, all urban and rural residents may receive pensions that comprise the basic component and the personal account component until death. The minimal amount of the basic component is set by the central government based on a mechanism that decides how to adjust the nationwide minimal amount of basic pensions according to economic development and changes in prices; in addition, regional people's governments may add to the basic pensions according to local conditions and for those who have paid for the insurance for long terms, and the extra amounts of the basic pensions are entirely provided and managed by the regional governments. The monthly payment from one's personal account is decided by dividing the balance of the account by 139 (which is the same as the current standard to calculate the monthly pension payments from personal accounts for urban employees).

Those who have enrolled in the urban-rural old-age insurance system may start to receive monthly pensions after turning 60 years of age, having paid for the insurance for collectively 15 years, and having received no subsidy from the government for basic elderly care. Those aged 60 or older by the time the New Rural Insurance or the Urban Resident Insurance was implemented and who had not received any subsidy from the government for basic elderly care when the Opinion was issued are entitled to a monthly payment of pensions at the amount of the basic component of the urban-rural old-age insurance system; those who are less than 15 years away from the legal age at which one may receive pensions should pay for the insurance on an annual basis while payments to make up for earlier years are accepted until a total of payments for at the most 15 years are made; and those who are at least 15 years away from the legal age at which one may receive pensions should pay the annual premiums for at least 15 years.

In addition, the enrollees in the insurance system who need to transfer the geographical association of their insurance plans due to transfer of their *hukou* while still contributing to the insurance may apply for the transfer at the immigration sites with the balance from the personal accounts transferred all at once and continue to pay the premiums in accordance with the regulations at the immigration sites while the length of contribution payments is additive; those who have already started to receive monthly pensions may not transfer the geographic association of their insurance plans no matter whether there is need to transfer *hukou*.

The urban-rural old-age insurance system shall coordinate according to pertinent rules and regulations with various social security systems, such as the basic old-age security system for urban employees, the web of social relief for veterans and other entitled groups and their family members, the system to secure basic needs in urban and rural areas and the rural five-security system, and the subsidy system for one-child families in partial rural areas. There are also specific regulations on the fund supervision and management and informatization of the system to ensure standardized operation.

In fact, the issuance of the Opinion marked a milestone in the development of China's old-age security insurance system. First, it was the first decree to break the "double-dual system" of the urban and rural insurance systems with a unified system for elderly care. As a matter of fact, it had been called for to break the "double-dual system" for many years. Its harms were studied and explored in hundreds of published papers, and multiple measures were proposed in order to explore a practical approach to break it, but all the efforts were in vain in front of the solid iceberg of institutions as there was no way in.

The Opinion chose to break in with "the urban and rural residents who [were] not employees of government agencies or public service institutes and who [were] not covered by the basic old-age security insurance system for urban employees," and it thus inflicted minimal frictions with the preexisting insurance systems in social welfare and relief so that the political cost to establish "a unified system of old-age security for all urban and rural residents" was minimized.

Second, the Opinion covers residents in cities and towns who have not benefited from the basic old-age insurance system for employees and rural residents who had no social insurance until the New Rural Insurance, i.e., the underprivileged in the social web of old-age security. In fact, only after these groups are included in the social web of old-age security has the urban-rural old-age insurance system achieved full coverage and bridged seamlessly with the very bottom of the society. Therefore, it was an extraordinary effort to issue the Opinion, and every step must be made solidly.

It was hoped that by the end of the 12th Five-Year Plan, the New Rural Insurance system and the Urban Resident Insurance system would be integrated nationwide, which would also be compatible with the basic old-age insurance system for urban employees, and that by 2020 a fair, unified, and standardized old-age insurance system for all urban and rural residents would be well established and in concert with other social security systems such as social relief and welfare to ensure the basic needs of the elderly who enrolled in the system in urban and rural areas together with the positive impacts of the traditional, family-based efforts to care for the elderly.

Comparison of pension systems between China and other countries

The system of old-age insurance is the core of old-age security in a society, and the type of old-age security is also shaped by the nature of the insurance system. There are various classifications of global old-age insurance systems, but they can all more or less be categorized into the following five types and mechanisms.

The first type links one's insurance with income, which is also called the traditional type. It is characterized by the dependency of pensions on incomes and contributions, the latter of which are shared by employers and employees. This type of insurance system does not seek wide coverage and has moderate pension replacement rates and highly developed financial markets of pensions while the collection of contributions and payments of pensions are both in good shape. This type is typically seen in some countries with developed market economies such as the United States, Germany, and France.

The second type is centered on social welfare. It emphasizes "universal benefits" as the principle and offers basic pensions to cover all the nationals. The pensions come mostly from tax revenue. However, the pensions are almost minimal and people have to rely on other forms of insurance. This type is typical in some developed countries such as the United Kingdom, Australia, Canada, and Japan.

The third type is based on savings. Self-protection is the principle of this type of insurance plans and modes of fully cumulative funds are provided to offer old-age insurance based on various personal accounts and public reserve funds, the balance of which is the basis of how much one receives as pension. This type is typical in some countries with emerging economies such as Singapore and Chile.

The fourth type is a mixed one. Some countries originally possessing systems centered on social welfare had to reform their systems due to economic stagflation and shortage of funds, during which the type with shared payments of contributions between employers and employees was borrowed. The reform resulted in a mixed type of insurance system of the traditional type that linked pensions to incomes and the welfare type. This mixed type is typical in the United Kingdom and Canada.

The fifth type is a full-package insurance plan for elderly care in the previous command economies. In these countries, the employees who work in publicly or collectively owned enterprises do not have to contribute to the old-age insurance systems, but may receive monthly pensions from the government after retirement based on length of service and salary levels. In fact, this type is no long existent due to political dramas; however, remains of this type are still extant in some countries even after reforms.

Where does China stand among the five types? The system in China seems similar to while at the same time quite different from them. Of course, it is reasonable to summarize China's old-age system as one with "social coordination plus personal accounts," as has been widely referred to; however, it is hard to ascertain whether the summary is based on collection of contributions, pension payments, or operation. It seemingly includes all three aspects, but it also only targets urban employees and not those residing in vast rural areas. In fact, the positioning of the old-age insurance system must be clear because only clear placement may set a clear direction and goal for reforms and then effective reforms and institutional innovations may result. The reasoning can be revealed in analogy with marching more than 100 miles: only when the current position is specified can the distance to the destination be learned and the route planned.

In my opinion, the current old-age insurance system in China may be summarized as a mixed transitioning type. It is mixed because personal contributions are linked to incomes in that a proportion of one's income (usually 8.0%) is contributed to the personal pension account. It is quite similar to the aforementioned type that links pensions to incomes and type of savings; meanwhile, enterprises and units also contribute to employees' basic component accounts at a ratio of their incomes (usually 20.0%), full coverage is emphasized, social coordination is performed, and the government subsidizes the deficits of the pension fund to some degree, all of which bear marks of the aforementioned type centered on social welfare. It is transitioning because the insurance system has been transitioning since the establishment of the new China 65 years ago that grew with no preexisting foundation and from small to big in size and from narrow to wide in coverage.

As already described, the insurance regulations on elderly care were first included in the labor insurance regulations (1951); an old-age insurance system with relatively wide coverage was later established in 1958 after retirement of enterprise employees was isolated from labor insurance laws and fused with retirement of government agency employees. In 1978, two systems of retirement and old-age insurance were implemented for cadres and workers; the systems were then extended to cover employees in the collectively owned sector of the economy in 1991, and it was also proposed to establish a basic old-age insurance system that combined the supplementary insurance in enterprises and the insurance based on individual savings.

In 1995, it was proposed that the basic pensions should be jointly afforded by enterprises and individuals and a social system be implemented based on the mechanism of social coordination combined with personal accounts; also in 1995, it was first proposed to develop an old-age insurance system in rural areas that were ready for it and to guide peasants to join the system. In 2009, trial sites were selected for the New-Rural Social Old-Age Endowment system, which subsequently covered as many as 405 million peasants by mid-2012, among whom more than 40 million had already received pensions, and full coverage has already been achieved. On July 1, 2013, the *Law of the People's Republic of China on Protection of the Rights and Interests of the Elderly* was officially implemented, which marked that the old-age security stepped on the track of rule of law.

In 2014, the Opinion was issued, which included, for the first time, those who had not been covered by the old-age insurance system for urban employees in the social web of old-age insurance and was the ice-breaking initiative to demolish the double-dual system among urban and rural areas; however, the Opinion still needs time to be fully enforced and problems need to be studied and resolved. Looking back at the old-age insurance system through the 65 years after the establishment of the new China, it evolved step by step, forming a "double-dual system" and progressing under it; there were mixtures of old rules and reforms on prior mechanisms, as well as new mixed mechanisms after the reforms. Therefore, it is appropriate and acceptable to summarize China's old-age social endowment insurance system as a "mixed transitioning" type.

The top-down design of the old-age social security system

Faced with the accelerating population aging in the 21st century, many countries have redesigned and reorganized their own old-age security systems with reformations of their prior insurance systems in the hope to glide safely through the upcoming "rainy season" when the population aging peaks. China is no exception. The Chinese population is speeding to age and during the progression to a seriously aged society, economic development has also brought the people a medium level of income, which has resulted in a contradiction between an aged population and a not-so-rich people; on top of that, the social security system is not advanced and the dual-double structure between rural and urban areas and within urban areas is waiting anxiously for a resolution. All of this have pushed China to embark on an innovative path to shape its own old-age insurance system.

Innovations must be rooted in practices and come from preexisting foundations, and the foundations were built in the progression of the old-age security system with changes and reforms in the past 65 years, especially the recent 35 years after the Reform and Opening Up. The most important innovation is the innovation of the social security and insurance systems at the level of the top-down design. In fact, domestic and foreign studies on China's old-age security system have formed a consensus, i.e., lack or absence of a top-down design. However, it is first needed to have well-defined descriptions of the "materials" used to build a scientific top-down design, and this is messy with ambiguous concepts, obscure definitions, careless descriptions, and arbitrary explanations, all of which only leads to confusion while the authors themselves are confused too. Therefore, before any top-down design can be made, it is necessary to give clear and brief explanations and definitions of the following concepts: old-age security, old-age insurance, old-age system, old-age institutions, and old-age mechanisms.

Old-age security and *old-age insurance* are different. According to domestic and international studies that have involved the two terms and various professional dictionaries, I believe that *old-age security* denotes the institutions and procedures to enforce them that ensure the elderly can afford their lives without violation and thus involves all of the aspects of elderly care and its organization; in contrast, *old-age insurance* is to pool funds for elderly care from various sources and entrust the funds to designated insurance institutes for management so that periodic payments of pensions may be made available to the enrolled and other eligible old-age citizens. In fact, there is a clear difference between *security* and *insurance* in English; however, the difference is not as clear between the corresponding terms in Chinese, and people get easily confused between them. Particularly, some papers in Chinese do not differentiate between the two terms, resulting in confusion in their denotations and connotations, and this deserves attention.

Old-age system, *old-age institutions*, and *old-age mechanisms* also need clarification. An *old-age system* is an ensemble that comprises and binds all the organizations involving old-age care according to a specific structure and corresponds to old-age security. *Old-age institutions* are the standardized rules and laws of old-age care that involve the government, enterprises, units, and individuals. *Old-age mechanisms* describe the relations between the organizations, groups, and individuals involved in old-age institutions and how they interact and interplay with each other. Here we use *system* to denote the Chinese term of *tixi* and *institutions* to denote *tizhi* in order to differentiate between the two although they may both be translated into English as *system*. Thus the two concepts are not well differentiated in English, but their difference in Chinese is quite obvious in that *tixi* has a wider range of meanings than *tizhi*.

Based on these terms' definitions and descriptions, as well as their progression and evolution during the past 65 years in China, it is clear that, under the new historical situation in the 21st century and the current comprehensively deepened Reform, the top-down design of the old-age security web must first abolish the dual-double structure of the preexisting old-age insurance system.

The dual-double structure describes the divided system of elderly care between urban and rural areas, and the divided system within urban areas. On one hand, an old-age insurance system has been established in cities and towns although it has many defects; in contrast, there was no old-age insurance system in rural areas for a long time until 2009, when the New Rural Insurance was first tested in trial sites, which quickly achieved full coverage. However, the New Rural Insurance differs considerably from the system in cities and towns as it is jointly contributed by individuals, collectives, the central treasury, and regional governments, which can only raise limited amounts of funds, leading to low levels of pensions and, consequently, full coverage at a low level, much lower than what urban residents are entitled to.

On the other hand, there are two mechanisms within urban areas as well, which have covered cadres and workers separately since 1978. In government agencies and public service institutes, the mechanism inherited from the command economy is still in effect while in enterprises, the insurance is based on a combined mechanism of social coordination and personal accounts. This dual-double structure between urban and rural areas and within urban areas is the lethal defect of China's old-age insurance institutions, and it has

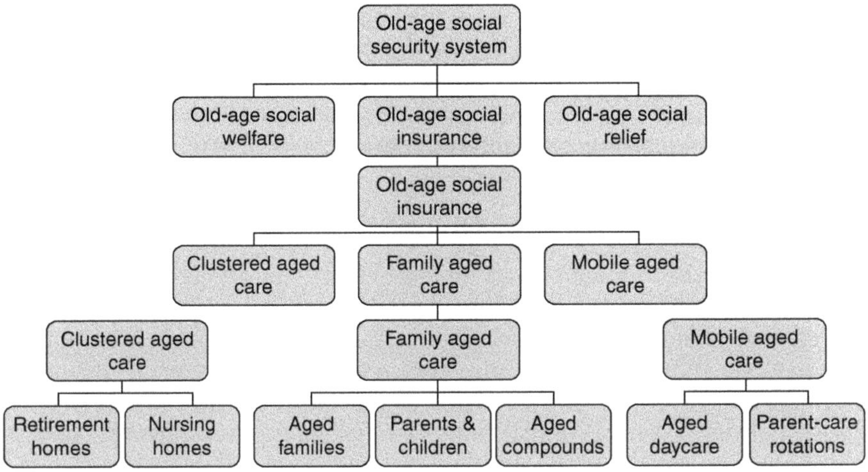

Figure 3.3 Structure of the old-age social security system.

resulted in divisions between urban and rural areas and among social sectors and geographic regions while the old-age insurance system is decentralized and fragmented with multiple mechanisms and channels. The top-down design of the system is to fuse the multiple mechanisms and channels as well as the fragments, and to establish a nationwide unified system and take steps to implement it in the entire country. A preliminary draft of such a design is illustrated in Figure 3.3.

As shown in Figure 3.3, a complete pyramid of a society's old-age security has three layers from the top to the bottom.

The first layer comprises the compositions of the old-age security system, which are primarily the three subsectors of insurance, welfare, and social relief for the elderly (while the supplementary mechanisms of medical insurance and commercial insurance are not listed). The three subsectors form a structure with one torso and two wings: the old-age insurance system is the torso and it sits at the heart of the layer to guide and influence the others, and the social welfare and relief for the elderly are supplementary although they are vital and indispensable to the underprivileged among the elderly such as those who are older, sick, and disabled.

The second layer is the layer of the old-age insurance institutions. It is primarily composed of families, clusters (public services), and mobile care, which together ensure the functions and impacts on the sides of the state, enterprises (institutes), families, and the elderly themselves. The torso of the layer is family care while the other two types of clustered and mobile care for the elderly are supplementary.

The third layer comprises the specific forms to realize the three types of elderly care, families, clusters (public services), and mobile care. At the heart of the layer are the three types of families that provide family care for the elderly, families of the elderly, families with parents and children, and compound families of the elderly. From a development perspective, it is necessary to have clustered care such as retirement and nursing homes and mobile care such as aged daycare centers and care rotations among children as supplementary forms, and they all have considerable potential.

Establishing unified institutions for old-age insurance

At the core of this pyramid of the old-age social security web is the old-age social insurance system, which is the spine that supports the existence and further development of the entire social security system. It is true that both the social welfare and relief mechanisms need reforms so that they can play their supplementary, yet indispensable roles in the social security system for the elderly, but they are only supplementary as, one, they cover only a particular, underprivileged group of the elderly, who are composed of a very limited number of people and account for a very low proportion of the elderly, and, two, they provide particular services like special-case security and thus cannot apply to the public. Therefore, the major reforms and innovations are made of the mechanisms and institutions of the old-age social insurance system, and the following two aspects are the most important: to position the institutions of the old-age insurance system accurately and to have a clear vision and direction for the reforms and innovations, and to ensure the value preservation and increment of pensions and the sustainability of the system once the supervision mechanisms are perfected.

The train of thought to reform the old-age insurance system

The global pension crisis

The entire international society is now in an unprecedented crisis of pension shortage, with problems in both supply and demand of pensions. On the supply side, the global economy is in stagflation, particularly after the subprime mortgage crisis broke out in the United States in 2008; financial and economic crises have since devoured advanced economies in Europe, North America, and Japan, which has brought profound and widespread impacts that have far exceeded anyone's expectation.

On top of continuous declines in economies, rises of financial crises one after another, and rapid growth of fiscal deficits, populations have progressively aged and continuously driven high the pensions. According to a survey by more than 30 countries of the Organization for Economic Co-operation and Development (OECD), the life expectancy of the retired elderly has grown from 13 to 19 years since 1958, and the increase of 6 years, or 46.15%, in life span has turned the prior pension promises made by governments years ago very shaky and unlikely to be kept. In addition, the continuous declines in birth rates and the proportion of taxpayers have also threatened the sustainability of pensions, which has actually cut down the supply of pensions.

Things are not much better in developing countries, which have their own unique problems. In developing countries, traditional big families have quickly dissolved and elderly care by children, a mode that has been prevalent in Asia, is faced with unprecedented challenges. Younger generations form their own core families, and the tide of the downsizing of traditional big ones will no longer turn back. As a result, more and more parents are now living out of the reach of their children and can only rely on care provided by society. Apparently, both developed and developing countries have seen considerable weakening in their abilities to provide elderly care, no matter whether from society in the former or from families in the latter, among the current financial and economic crises.

What about the demand for pensions? It has been on the rise continuously. As mentioned earlier, there was a global baby boom after WWII. Those born during the boom have gradually turned old to reach 60 and 65 years old and become pension receivers. For example, from 1950 to 1955, 98.321 million people were born every year on average, and these cohorts, excluding those who died, reached 60 years of age from 2010 to 2015, and will reach 65 from 2015 to 2020. In 1950, 13.3% of the world population, or 336.403 million people, were 14 or younger, and all of them, excluding those who died, reached 60 in 2010 and 65 in 2015, resulting in the proportion of those aged 60 or older to climb to 11.0% in 2010 and 12.2% in 2015. In addition, the proportion of the elderly aged 65 or older in 2015 was 8.2%, and the number will grow to 9.3% in 2020.[13] With such a fast-growing elderly population, the demands – physically for livelihood and population reproduction, emotionally for mental comfort, socially for interpersonal communication, and culturally for cognitive, literary, artistic, and spiritual satisfaction – are without question going to grow.

However, many advanced economies such as those in Europe and North America and Japan cut down expenses on social services, among which measures delaying and decreasing pension payments was the first priority, in attempts to fight financial and economic crises with Keynesian economic stimuli of increasing investment and quantitative easing policies. To comment on these measures, David McHugh, a journalist of the Associated Press, concluded in his report that was published on *World of Truth* on December 30, 2013, that the 2008 financial crisis made the global retirement problems even more difficult to deal with.

The crisis led to reduction in tax revenue in Europe and the United States while the governments had to bail out the banks in trouble, which forced them to cut down on pension expenses. According to Standard & Poor's, a credit-rating agency, rich countries will have government debts that are three times their year-end economic production in 2050 if they do not cut down on pension expenses, and their national bonds will be rated at a level essentially synonymous with garbage. In the United States, it is common for the retired elderly to loan money for various payments. According to the Federal Reserve Bank of New York, the family debts from 2003 to 2008 increased by $5.4 trillion, an increase of 75.0% within five years, while the savings rate declined from 13.0% of posttax incomes in the 1980s to 2.0% in 2005. If all the retirees in the United States are to enjoy a comfortable life, at least $6.8 trillion is needed to fill in the savings accounts, and that is more than $110,000 per family.[14]

China is not faced with a much more positive situation. On the bright side, the national pension account has a considerable balance and is sustainable at least to a degree, according to measures of mobile payments and at-counter payments, while personal accounts have progressively grown in savings, all of which points to a bright future of elderly care in China. However, there are still many problems and contradictions once detailed analysis is made. Specific descriptions are given in later sections and only conclusive points are stated here.

Based on the current measures to collect contributions and distribute pensions, the government expense on pensions in 2029 will account for 10.0% of the GDP and more than 29.0% of total salaries, which may exceed the internationally accepted alarm line of pensions; in addition, despite the huge amounts of and continuous increases in personal savings, the elderly do not have a large amount of savings and collectively account for a small proportion, which may not contribute much to pension accumulation. Therefore, the pension crisis is present globally as well as in China, except that it is not as severe in China as in some other countries. Therefore, reforms are demanded to have innovative institutions and mechanisms of pension collection and payments.

Demolishing the institutions of the dual-double structure

The issuance of the Opinion was an ice-breaking posture to launch efforts to demolish the institutional barriers that separated urban and rural old-age systems. However, it only covered "the employees in nongovernment agencies and nonpublic service institutes and the urban and rural residents not covered by the basic old-age insurance system for enterprise employees."

That is also to say, the old-age insurance systems that have covered employees in government agencies and public service institutes and some enterprise employees are not affected by the Opinion, and the proposed unified insurance system in it thus becomes a marginalized system that is irrelevant to the majority of the people. In addition, even the marginalized old-age insurance itself has many problems. The first and the foremost problem is its low-level coverage, which is not enough at all to support elderly lives. Let us take the plan with the lowest annual payment of 100 yuan as an example. With this plan, one pays 1,500 yuan cumulatively in 15 years and his/her personal pension account after 15 years of payments will be almost 2,500 yuan, including interest; he/she is then able to receive 73 yuan as his/

her monthly pension, which is the sum of 55 yuan of the basic pension component and 18 yuan of the personal account component calculated by dividing the 2,500 yuan by the coefficient 139. If one is to take the highest-level pension plan, i.e., 2,000 yuan per year, he/she is only going to receive 329 yuan as the monthly pension after 15 years of contributions. These monthly pensions are far away from enough for the elderly to live, with the former, 73 yuan, close to nothing and the latter, 329 yuan, as much as only 16.1% of the monthly disposable income of urban residents in 2012.[15]

In the countryside, 329 yuan is almost half of the net income of rural residents, which is enough to support basic needs; however, the annual contribution of 2,000 yuan is a heavy burden for these people who are at the very bottom of the social pyramid, and very few of them did or will choose this plan. Therefore, the Opinion did not really change the foundations of the dual-double structure of the urban-rural and urban systems of old-age insurance. It only offered a unified insurance system for those who did not have retirement pensions with very limited annuities.

The review of the evolution of the old-age social security system since the establishment of the new China, detailed in the previous section, showed that the current dual-double structure of old-age insurance institutions evolved into its current shape and is the cumulative result of stepwise transitions from a command to a market economy during the past 65 years. It cannot be denied that such a structured system once provided security for retired laborers and positively pushed for socioeconomic development. However, with history striding forward, society keeps developing and the population continues transitioning; the dual-double structure that differentiates between urban and rural areas as well as between urban government agencies and institutes and enterprises is far behind the social development and population transition, and it must be demolished through reforms that accommodate the current age.

To explain the underlying logics, we must track back to the very start of establishing a system to provide old-age security. Why is a social insurance system for elderly care needed at all? The fundamental reason is to help people to properly allocate their incomes and expenses within the expected life span of the population and to save up and set aside in advance some money for various demands of survival, leisure, and development after retirement by establishing a somewhat mandatory social endowment system for old-age security so that people may live a secure life in the last phase of their lives. Once free from worries for post-retirement lives, laborers may devote themselves to the innovative work they are currently involved in. At the same time, people differ in how much money they make and have different concepts of consumption, and it is therefore necessary and indispensable for the government to intervene and adjust individual and market behaviors, provide moderate subsidy, and establish a legally binding system to provide old-age security.

China has a long history, as long as several thousand years, of feudal systems, which has enduring and profound impacts. It is fair to say that the economic, political, and cultural institutions of the feudal system were developed to the extremes while an agrarian society was deeply rooted in the land of China; the responsibilities of providing elderly care thus fell on families and children who were fully responsible and functional to care for their aged parents. Such an agrarian society characterized by natural economies had no form of social security or social insurance, and the traditional mode that children took care of their parents shone through epochs and was valued by every dynasty. As the old saying goes, "being filial ranks the first among all goodness," and the way that children took care of their elderly parents within families was integrated into the schools of Confucius, Mencius, the Cheng brothers, and Zhu Xi, leading to the formation of a unique Xiao culture in China. The culture has lived on since the establishment of the new China. After all, China had long been an immense, agrarian country and it needed time and a historical progression to transition to an industrial one; in addition, traditions have historical momentum, and it is also a historical progression to demolish one that has been practiced for thousands of years, which is why the tradition that children take care of their elderly parents has been largely intact in rural areas.

However, with progression in industrialization, the urban economy has become the majority and dominated the national economy while the urban-rural structure of the population made a historic transition in 2010, when the urban population exceeded the rural one for the first time, marking the conclusion of traditional industrialization and embarking on the postindustrial era.

Furthermore, since the Reform and Opening Up, institutions of a market economy have been set up by and large with the market mainstays being legal person units, factor flows following the market, macroeconomic regulations and controls turning indirect, and economic operation running by law, while the commercial economies with the rises in exchange values have shocked people's traditional concepts, including the tradition that children provide care for their aged parents, which is faced with unseen challenges.

In fact, the thrice industrial structure has experienced constant changes during the past 60 years and more, and the ratio of production between the primary, secondary, and tertiary industries in 2014 was 58,332:271,392:306,739, or 0.092:0.426:0.482, or 1.00:4.65:5.26.[16] Apparently, agriculture, villages, and peasants have become the underprivileged, in both the relative and absolute sense, in the national economic structure, and together with elderly care for peasants, all need powerful support from a social security system.

In addition, with population urbanization and the acceleration of the transition from rural to non-rural *hukou*, population aging in rural areas has sped up with continuous downsizing of rural families, and problems in elderly care for peasants have been sharper and sharper. Under these conditions, continuation of the dual-structural old-age insurance system and institutions between urban and rural areas is in utter opposition of the principle to provide fair security for the elderly.

Meanwhile, in cities and towns, the dual-structural old-age insurance system between government agencies and public service institutes on one side and enterprises on the other is still in effect and has been increasingly questioned as unfair and unreasonable. There is first inequality in the pension sources. Although many rounds of reforms have been made of the old-age insurance system and institutions since the Reform and Opening Up, as already mentioned, no real changes have been made to the old-age insurance system and institutions in government agencies and public service institutes as in each round of the reforms, there was always this convention to "apply new rules on new employees and keep old rules on the old," so the old institutions have been kept and neither employers nor employees have to contribute to the pension accounts, resulting in the preservation of the so-called steel bowl (a Chinese metaphor to describe positions or benefits that do not break).

However, things are completely different for enterprises. Employers need to pay for the basic component of pension accounts and supplementary contributions according to regulations, and employees must contribute to their personal accounts by law, and some need to pay for the supplementary contribution if they can afford it. The contributions by employers are often quite a lot, causing great burdens on many enterprises with some even behind their payments for long terms. Second, there are huge pension gaps between retirees. Aside from the difference in pensions between retirees in various regions due to different regional socioeconomic development, it is widely acknowledged that there is a big gap of pensions between retirees from government agencies and public service institutes and those from enterprises. For example, an employee who is a division head or equivalent in government agencies may receive a monthly pension of 5,000 to 6,000 yuan after retirement, while an enterprise employee at the same administrative level can only receive half that amount or less. In some regions, a retired university professor can only have a monthly pension as much as what a section head or equivalent in civil service is entitled to after retirement. No wonder a professor once wrote down the following couplet:

> With similar contributions
> Come contrasting pensions
> Hengpi:
> Hello, public sector employees!

Such unfair and unreasonable gaps in contributions to and payments of pensions between government agencies and public service institutes on one side and enterprises on the other have received more and more attention, driving demands for reforms, and they certainly deserve careful management. From another angle, the dual-structural system cannot last in terms of the safety and sustainability of the operation. Projections have shown that the government expense on pensions will account for more than 29.0% of total salaries and 10.0% of GDP, the internationally acknowledged danger zone on this matter, in 2029 if the current mechanisms of collection of contributions and payments of pensions are to be kept, and a pension crisis will arise. That is also to say, even if people are content with the current system and its institutions, such a system of side-by-side collection of contributions and payments of pensions with the former directly transformed into the latter cannot last, and reforms are mandatory.

Establishing unified old-age insurance institutions based on savings and supplementary contributions

Any reform must come from realities because reforms are needed to resolve contradictions and problems in real life. At the same time, reforms must be in concert with the time and be aligned with contemporary economic, political, technological, cultural, and social development to lead but not chase the time. In fact, from the angle of methodologies, the old saying is always true: theories shall apply to realities. Therefore, three problems must first be configured in explorations of how to reform the old-age insurance institutions: the current situation of old-age security, the direction of the reforms, and the blueprint of the reforms. These three aspects are detailed in what follows.

The first problem to clarify is the current situation of old-age security. Old-age security, or "support of the elderly" as often used in gerontology, is the foundation of all elderly demands, including health service and education for as well as pursuits and pleasure of the elderly. If they cannot even be supported to survive, how can the elderly be satisfied in terms of any of these demands? However, to support the elderly entails a wide range of connotations. Broadly speaking, old-age security should provide security for one's physical, mental, social, and cultural life after retirement so that the survival and development of the elderly, in the physical and spiritual senses, are guaranteed. In a narrower sense, old-age security meets the basic needs for survival and is dominated by providing material support while other kinds of necessary support are also offered. From the perspective of old-age security and insurance, it is without question that the first and foremost concern is to meet the needs for survival, or to ensure that the elderly have economic means. Only when their most basic need, i.e., economic security, is met with favorable packages can the elderly live through the last phase of their lives without worries. In practice, the elderly in China have more economic sources than just the pensions from the old-age social endowment insurance system; however, the proportion of pensions is evidently growing in both urban and rural areas (Table 3.1).

As shown in Table 3.1, among all the sources of economic support of the elderly, i.e., pensions, support by children, personal earnings, and others (which is composed of primarily personal savings, endowment from relatives, social welfare, and social relief), the first three sources that provide social, family, and self-support predominate. Among all the sources, the support by

Table 3.1 Changes in compositions of economic sources to support the elderly in China, 1987–2010 (%)

	Year	*Pensions*	*Children*	*Wages*	*Others*
Urban	1987	63.7	16.8	14.6	4.9
	2005	76.9	7.0	9.6	6.5
	2010	80.6	7.5	5.1	6.8
Rural	1987	4.7	38.1	50.7	6.5
	2005	9.8	37.1	39.8	13.3
	2010	20.1	42.5	31.3	6.1

Sources: The data of 1987 were from "Materials of the Sampling Survey on the Elderly at 60 or above in China in 1987," *Chinese Journal of Population Science*, Special Issue, 1988 (1), pp. 260–263. The data of 2005 were calculated based on the data from *Analysis on a Longitudinal Survey on the Elderly in Urban and Rural Areas in China in 2006*, China Social Publishing House, 2009, pp. 63–66. The data of 2010 were from *Materials of the Survey on the Population of 7 Provinces in 2010*, Institute of Population and Labor Economics, Chinese Academy of Social Sciences, 2010.

pensions has been on the rise as the proportion of pensions of all the sources increased by 16.9 percentage points, from 63.7% in 1987 to 80.6% in 2010 in urban areas, and by a larger scale in rural areas, 15.4 percentage points, from 4.7% to 20.1%. Support from children showed declines in urban areas, with a 9.3 percentage point decrease from 1987 to 2010 while a slight increase was observed in rural areas of 4.4 percentage points. Apparently, the care that children provide to their elderly parents had changes in opposite directions in urban and rural areas: its contribution further decreased in urban families but increased slightly in rural families.

In terms of self-support by the elderly through working, its proportion of all the economic sources declined in both urban and rural areas, with a decrease of 9.5 percentage points during the same period in urban areas, leading the already low percentage of self-support to a new low of 5.1%, and a decrease of 19.4 percentage points in rural areas, from 50.7% to 31.3%.

All these numbers show that Chinese society has overall been on track to transition from getting all warm and fed to common prosperity, and that the levels of the economy and livelihood, including that of the elderly, have improved significantly, which is also why quite a proportion of the elderly do not have to work to support themselves; these numbers also show that the social insurance system for elderly care has further developed in that the reduction in the proportion of self-support by the elderly has been made up for by the increase in the proportion of social old-age insurance, which mirrors the development of the cause of social old-age insurance.

The cause of social old-age insurance has indeed leapt in development, but the institutions and mechanisms are diversified, decentralized, and fragmented. There are primarily five types of social old-age insurance institutions and mechanisms in China now, which are described respectively next.

The first type applies to public sector workers in government agencies. The mechanisms in this type came from regulations made after the establishment of the new China, particularly the *Temporary Regulations on Withdrawal and Retirement of Workers* and the *Temporary Regulations on Arrangements of the Aged, Underprivileged, Ill, and Disabled Cadres* issued in 1978 by the State Council. Employees covered in this type may receive pensions that are 75.0% to 100.0% of their final salaries according to when they started to work and the length of service. In addition, the agencies and individuals do not need to contribute to any pension account, and this part, showing characteristics of all-in-one packages in the era of a command economy, has never been touched in all the previous rounds of reforms and is kept as "old rules to cover old employees."

The second type covers the cadres and workers in public service institutes. Public service institutes are not a group of unified institutes but include three types: those supported entirely by the national treasury, those supported partially by the national treasury, and those that operate on their own financially. The public service institutes in the public mind are usually represented by the first type, but in fact, the other two types, although on the borderline of the definition, are in great numbers and account for a large proportion. The institutes that are fully supported by the government usually are not responsible for pension contributions and the employees do not have personal pension accounts. The retirees are paid monthly pensions at a ratio based on their length of service and final positions and salaries.

The third type covers enterprise employees. The mechanisms came from the *Decision on Reforming the Old-Age Insurance System for Enterprise Employees* issued by the State Council in 1991, which extended the previous social insurance to cover other economic units while the pension contributions were shared between the government, enterprises, and employees. There then was established an old-age insurance system that covered basic needs and combined the supplementary contributions by enterprises and the individual contributions by employees to personal savings accounts, and the system bears typical marks of structural insurance for elderly care.

The fourth type applies to urban residents. The social old-age endowment insurance system for urban residents (Urban Resident Insurance) covers unemployed residents with urban *hukou*. The Urban Resident Insurance requires individual contributions, and the government also provides subsidies to enrollees. The more one contributes to it, the more subsidy amounts one gets from the government, both of which are deposited in a personal pension account. The Urban Resident Insurance is composed of a personal account component and a basic component with the former being contributed by individuals and government subsidy and the latter fully paid for by the government.

The fifth type provides old-age insurance for rural residents. In 2009, the New Rural Insurance terminated the previous situation of elderly care in rural areas that the elderly had to manage on their own and offered an insurance mode that the pensions for the rural elderly were to be contributed by the individual enrollees, supplemented by the collectives, subsidized by the central government, and received as allowance from regional governments. On February 21, 2014, the Opinion was issued. The Opinion combined the New Rural Insurance and the Urban Resident Insurance based on the experiences in the trial sites of the two systems and designed a unified system of old-age insurance for both urban and rural residents in the entire country. The Opinion also provided measures to bridge the New Rural Insurance and the newly unified insurance system so that rural residents have improved security in terms of their elderly lives.

The second problem to sort out is the direction of the reforms. The direction is toward the establishment of a unified system in China to provide old-age insurance for urban and rural areas. The unified system must first have a unified system across urban and rural areas and then within one area across government agencies, public service institutes, and enterprises. To this end, the Opinion has already set up a model although this model only involves employees who do not work in government agencies or public service institutes and the urban and rural residents who were not previously covered by the basic insurance system for enterprise employees and is therefore only peripheral.

The first and foremost principle to follow when establishing a unified basic old-age insurance system for urban and rural areas is to be fair. In fact, the biggest contradiction and problem of the current double-dual structural institutions of the old-age insurance system is its inequalities. The inequality between urban and rural areas has led to the rural old-age insurance falling much behind the urban in development, and the rural elderly are not well covered by insurance. The inequality between government agencies and public service institutes on one side and enterprises on the other within urban areas has led enterprise employees to be more poorly covered than those in the government and public sectors.

In order to ensure social justice and fairness and to provide security to all laborers after retirement, the old institutions must be broken and a unified basic old-age insurance system must be established. All cadres and workers must be held under the same standard and according to everyone's contributions in labor and final salaries; a unified rate for basic pension payments should be set so that there will be no huge gap of pensions. Of course, fairness does not equal egalitarianism in distribution and reasonable and necessary differential levels should be kept. It must be made clear to all that the most prominent contradictions and problems now are, one, the dual-double structure of pension contributions whereas some do not have to contribute to pension accounts while others rely on a system that combines social coordination and personal accounts, and two, excessively huge gaps in pension distribution, which is against the principle of fairness. It is therefore necessary to comprehensively push for and continuously perfect the basic old-age insurance system for all urban and rural residents following the guidance to have full coverage, basic insurance, flexibility, and sustainability with focuses on improving fairness, accommodating mobility, and ensuring sustainability so that the positive impacts of social insurance may be fully exerted to secure people's basic lives, adjust income distribution, and facilitate the coordinated development of urban and rural economies.

The third problem to clarify is the blueprint of the reforms. As stated in the *Decision* to comprehensively deepen reforms, which was passed by the Third Plenary Session of the 18th CCCPC:

> The basic old-age insurance system must be persisted with that combines social coordination and personal accounts, the regulations be perfected on the personal accounts, and a sound incentive mechanism be constructed to reward higher contributions with higher pension payments so that the rights of enrollees are guaranteed, the basic component of pensions nationally coordinated, and the principle of actuarial science and balance followed; in addition, the reform on the old-age insurance system in government agencies and public service institutes must be pushed for, and the institutions of the old-age insurance systems for urban and rural residents must be integrated.[17]

All these set a clear blueprint for reforms. Following this blueprint, I propose that the reform of the rural old-age insurance system may be steadily pushed for on the basis of the Opinion. That is also to say, the contributions and pension payments should be elevated now that the agrarian economy and peasants' incomes have both leapt in development so that social insurance will gradually assume a dominant role as the major economic support for the rural elderly and the support by children and the elderly themselves reduces annually in proportion, a prospect that the rural old-age insurance is similar to that of urban areas.

A key step in the process is to reform the old-age insurance systems in cities and towns. In the first place, the urban population has exceeded the rural population since 2010, as already mentioned, and it will continue to grow with the progression of urbanization and its proportion of the national population will keep climbing at a relatively fast speed.

Next, old-age insurance was first implemented in cities and towns and there are now various forms of insurance mechanisms; in fact, four of the aforementioned five major insurance types in China now are found in urban areas. Thus things are quite complicated there. In addition, the direction of the reform of the rural old-age insurance system is to converge with the urban systems to establish a unified system across the country to cover the basic needs of both the urban and the rural elderly, and the key to achieving the goal is the reform of the urban systems.

Based on practices and the experiences from the past tens of years, together with the experiences of successful pension systems around the world, I propose an old-age insurance system based on accruals and complementary contributions. Such a system is comprised of two components: one is the basic pension component that is financed jointly by government agencies, public service institutes, and enterprises at a set ratio (contributions to final salary) on a monthly basis and that serves as one's basic pension.

The other component comprises complementary contributions, which laborers make at a certain ratio (contributions to final salary) monthly and that becomes the personal complementary pension fund of laborers to be deposited in personal pension accounts. The two components of pensions together decide the pension replacement rate, which should also consider the current levels of pension contributions and payments so that a smooth transition can be made. The length of contribution years shall also borrow experiences of the current measures; for example, a temporary limit may be set at 15 years.

Following these lines of thought, the proposed new old-age insurance system may be summarized as one based on accruals and supplementary contributions. The basic ideas and major points are as follows.

First, the foundation of the new system is accrued personal contribution. The new system of accrued and supplementary old-age insurance that is the aim of reforms and that needs to be well constructed is built upon individual contributions that accumulate in personal accounts. It is just as related to as different from the current urban system that combines social coordination and personal accounts. They are related because the current personal accounts will be upgraded to personal accumulative accounts and serve as solid proofs of entitlement to pensions.

Meanwhile, they are different because the employees of government agencies and public service institutes do not have personal accounts yet and many enterprise employees have unreliable balances while the current measures of pension payments are based on direct transfer of collections to payments. The new system of accrued and supplementary old-age insurance aimed at by reforms is built upon the foundation of personal contributions that accumulate in personal accounts and aims to gradually build a channel between the accrued balances of personal accounts and the pension payments to the owners.

The following are proposals for specific reform measures. A worker may start to contribute to his own personal pension account on his first job for a minimal period of 20 years; he may continue to contribute to the account after 20 years, and the contributions between then and his retirement must be guaranteed to transfer to added pensions after retirement based on the principle that more contributions lead to higher pensions. At present, the balance of one's personal pension account does not translate into the amount of pensions one will receive after retirement, and measures should be taken, after first tested in trial sites, to gradually make the pension payments to an enrollee according to the balance of his personal account, plus the amount from the supplementary insurance.

In rural areas, transition to orienting pension payments with personal accumulative accounts may be made stepwise based on the current New Rural Insurance and the new system of urban-rural old-age insurance. In this way, the social old-age endowment insurance system will proceed step by step from the foothold of social coordination to that of personal accumulation.

Second, enterprises also make contributions in a supporting role. The current system that combines social coordination and personal accounts demands that enterprises (units) contribute to employees' pensions at an amount that is 20.0% of the employees' salaries, which is a burden too heavy to bear for those that are not in good shape or not negligible for those that are only achieving mediocre performance, and is not a problem at all only to those making good profits. Considering the current rises in production costs brought by increases in the labor price (wage rate) and the profits and development of enterprises, the contribution at 20.0% of salaries is indeed excessively high for enterprises (units).

It is therefore reasonable to lower the percentage for enterprises moderately, for example, to a percentage that is closer to the 8.0% personal contribution that is currently in effect while enterprises shall also contribute for 20 years, the same as employees. If employees decide to continue to contribute after 20 years, the enterprises shall also follow, at an amount that is equal to or slightly higher than the employees', until the employees retire. These reformative measures that aim for long terms to achieve big may, on one hand, effectively alleviate the excessively heavy burden of enterprises now and benefit their healthful and sustainable development, and, on the other hand, facilitate contribution collections from enterprises (units) as they will be willing to actually make the payments now that the amounts due are lowered; with reductions in overdue contributions by enterprises (units), the new, accrued, and supplementary old-age insurance system will be established and operate at a lower cost.

Third, the positive roles of the government and the market are to be enhanced. The implementation of the new system of accrued and supplementary old-age insurance must involve the government, which is to guide and coordinate the system by writing the laws, regulations, and rules by which the new old-age insurance system runs, by setting up a supervision mechanism from the top down, and by making concrete plans to implement the system in urban and rural areas.

In addition, special attention must be paid to the underprivileged in both urban and rural areas who are extremely old, injured, sick, disabled, childless, or spouseless, and a well-constructed web of social welfare and relief must be established to cover them with improved support so that they are not left far behind compared to the overall situation of elderly care. It is also necessary to increase the threshold of the subsistence allowances to support the basic needs of the elderly in poverty.

Aside from the guiding role of the government in reforming and innovating the system, appropriate market mechanisms should also be introduced. For example, enterprises, social organizations, and individuals may all be encouraged to invest in the business of elderly care to initiate various types of old-age insurance and to advance the industry of elderly care so that all sectors, the government, social organizations, and individuals are motivated.

As a matter of fact, the government has already taken measures to exert its impact to guide reform of the insurance system and to help the market to play its role in allocating resources, such as the proposals in the *Decision* by the CCCPC on comprehensively deepening the reform that "a system to provide moderate social security benefits to all social sectors with reasonable adjustment mechanisms is to be established and continuously improved" and that "the policy to progressively extend the retirement age is to be studied and made while the administrative mechanisms of social security and the service system to provide it are to be perfected at a faster speed."

In terms of extending the retirement age, I proposed the idea and wrote an article to elaborate on the necessity and possibility to extend it as early as 26 years ago, with discussions on how to avoid competition in the labor market between elder and average working-age laborers. However, my perspective at the time was from how to effectively employ the laborer resources to reach their potential. For example, a worker will be close to 30 if he receives education from primary school to PhD, which takes about 22 years, and can only work for a little more than 30 years if he retires at 60, at which age most people are still in good health and have no problem to continue working for quite a few years. In contrast, if he retires at 65, his working time is extended by 16.6%, or the utilization of human capital is increased by 16.6%.

Now that the population is accelerating to age, postponing retirement is also indispensable to helping to alleviate the pressure on pension payments. Of course, to extend the retirement age, the current statutory retirement age must first be the age at which most laborers retire, and this is not the case yet – the actual average retirement age of all the laborers is not quite 55 now. Therefore, it is only practical and meaningful to extend the statutory retirement age when everyone retires not before the current statutory age.

Some hotly discussed issues in reform

Recently, several reform-related issues have been hotly discussed and widespread with a seeming message that plans for reform are to be implemented soon. However, most discussions are no more than "oral literature" with more propaganda than solid data, and have misled people on these issues. Solid and clear discussions are therefore needed, especially on the topics of extending and postponing the retirement age, extending the length of pension contributions and the age to receive pension payments, and paying for elderly care with houses or rural homestead lands.

The first issue is extension of the statutory retirement age. As early as the 1980s, when I was in charge of a key state project, *A Survey on the Population of the Elderly in China and a Study on Reforming the Old-Age Social Security*, I proposed that extension of the retirement age would become a solution to meet the challenge of population aging in the final research report and the three books resulting from the research that were all edited by me: *The Elderly Population in China*, *The Economy of the Chinese Elderly*, and *The Elderly Society in China*.

I proposed the issue because it was in line with the prospects that the elderly were to have increased life expectancy and improved health, leading many to have strong desires to work, and it would effectively add to the economic incomes of the elderly, benefiting the advancement of the elderly as well as society. At the same time, I also argued that extension of the retirement age should consider the employment structure of the elderly and take measures to prevent competitions in the labor market between the elderly and other working-age laborers by diverting the elderly to the industries that were appropriate for their physical and intelligent levels as well as their interests so that the human resources of the elderly might be explored and employed properly.

I made references to some seriously aged countries such as Japan. In the late 1980s, the National Diet of Japan made a decision to extend the national statutory retirement age to 65; the Labor Ministry made a plan to implement it on October 1, Heisei era 2 (1990) and to progressively carry it out until Heisei era 5 (1993) when all the laborers at 60 would retire at 65. The measure sought to ensure employment opportunities for all laborers and to make up for the shortage of labor supplies due to reductions in the birth rates; at the same time, the elderly would have increased economic incomes and thus improved self-support and security.

Based on the experiences of Japan and other developed countries that also extended the retirement age, I further proposed that:

> The experiences of some developed countries that [had] gone through the transition from encouraging the elderly to retire to encouraging them to work longer [were] valuable for us to learn. In fact, reasonable support for the elderly to continue to work within their capabilities and advocacy for them to self-support economically should be a major pillar of the old-age security system with Chinese characteristics.[18]

Of course, the proposals I made at the time were targeted at the "future," which was projected to have a severely aging population and would necessitate learning from the experiences of developed countries. More than 20 years have passed now, with the "future" then having become "the present," and we are at a historical intersection where extension of the retirement age must be considered.

However, the message that the retirement age might be postponed by pertinent government agencies, once released, was met with strong responses. Numbers varied in different reports, but overall, there is no doubt that the majority of the responses were against the extension while only a few were in favor of it. When the numbers are broken down by social sector, those who opposed the idea were mostly blue-collar workers while those who were for it were mostly white-collar workers.

The underlying reason of the stratified stands was interest. The blue-collar workers were mostly enterprise employees with relatively low pension replacement rates and limited pensions after retirement; if they were to postpone retirement, they would not be able to receive much more in pensions, but they would have to contribute to the pensions for a few more years. After all, the blue-collar workers were usually physical laborers and always felt it was difficult to work until the retirement age, the extension of which, even for a few more years (five in some proposals), would make many begrudge the work.

In addition, some enterprises had tested a procedure for employees to retire before the statutory retirement age by "buying out their remaining work years," and these employees had already received a lump sum of the salaries for the work years that had been bought out; therefore, they not only would be unable to get their pensions as before if the retirement age was to be delayed, but would have to continue to contribute to the pensions as well. Of course they opposed the idea to extend the retirement age.

The white-collar workers, especially the public sector employees, in contrast, were almost all in favor of it. After all, neither they nor their employers needed to contribute to the pensions, and they would continue to enjoy the benefits at work if the retirement age was to be extended; of course it was good news to them.

Nevertheless, it is inevitable to extend the statutory retirement age, and it is both needed and possible now. In fact, it was already proposed in November 2013 when the *Decision by CCCPC on Several Important Issues of Comprehensively Deepening the Reform* was publicized to "establish a fairer and sustainable social security system" when "pushing for the innovative reforms on social public causes" and to "research and make a policy on progressively extending the statutory retirement age." In my opinion, extending the retirement age is a way to accommodate the aging trend in the population age structure.

In 2013, the proportion of those aged 60 and higher in China was as high as 14.9% and the proportion of those aged 65 and higher was 9.7%, driving China to approach a medium-to-high level of population aging at a fairly fast speed. Thus a reliable old-age security system is needed, yet it requires reforms in many aspects, and one of the basic tactics is to reform the retirement mechanisms, including the extension of the retirement age.

As mentioned earlier, the proportion and the absolute number of the working-age population at 15–64 have both passed their peaks, and the pressure on employment, although it will still be present for a long time, will be alleviated gradually, so postponing the retirement age will not add to the pressure on the labor market. Meanwhile, the current retirement situation in China is such that males usually retire at 60, female cadres at 55 and female workers at 50, all at ages when most are still healthy and totally capable to work for a few more years.

At the same time, the current age structure of China's population is going to reach the medium level of aging in that the life expectancy in 2012 was 74.83 years (males 72.38 years and females 77.37 years), the education levels of the population and civil behaviors have both improved significantly, the urbanization of the population reached 53.73% in 2013, and socioeconomic development has brought China into the group of countries with medium-high incomes. Faced with all these situations, it is certainly appropriate timing to make a decision to progressively extend the retirement age.

The progressive extension has been interpreted differently on different media. Some have proposed to extend the retirement age by a quarter, or three months, every year so that the retirement age would be extended by a full year after four years, which would take 20 years to extend the retirement age from 60 to 65; some have argued that the extension should be started in the industries with relatively early retirement ages so that the retirement age would first be set at 60 for all and further extension would be the next step.

I propose that three steps be taken on this reform. First, the retirement ages for men and women should be unified to extinguish the inequality of the sexes in the retirement mechanisms; this should be easy to achieve and it is also a real step forward toward the realization of gender equality.

Second, all industries and occupations should be inspected in terms of differences in retirement ages, and new regulations on the age should be made to resolve the problem of vastly differential retirement ages across industries that have built up through history; at the same time, strict implementation of the new regulations must be made and any form of retirement in advance should be prohibited.

Third, on the basis of the first two steps, a unified plan to extend the nationwide retirement age may be made. The plan cannot be hastened, neither can it be decentralized, fragmented, or dragged on for a long time. A possible timetable is as follows: starting from 2016, the retirement age is to be extended by half a year (six months) every year, and it will be 65 by 2026. The first two steps may be started in 2015 while the third step may be tested in some areas at the same time to gain experience, after which the reform to extend the retirement age may be officially implemented in 2016.

The second issue is to increase the minimum years of pension contributions. There are various cases internationally where the minimum years of pension contribution do not agree with the retirement age, and the solutions also vary in different countries. However, observation of the effects of pension plans clearly speaks for the agreement of the two, and it is exactly why many countries have adopted incentives to increase the minimum years of contribution so that most employees would not stop their contributions before retirement.

Almost all of the countries with measures to this end have relatively good security for the retired elderly and stable and peaceful societies.

In China, the minimum length of pension contributions is usually 15 years as regulated in the terms of pension collection. Although people may continue to contribute to their pension accounts after 15 years in return for higher monthly pensions, few choose to do so due to lack of strong incentives. Therefore, following the issue of extending the retirement age, the proposal to increase the minimum contribution years was also met with challenges and was questioned by many, just like the extension, or perhaps more questioned than the extension had been.

After all, increases in the minimum years of pension contribution would make enterprises contribute to the employees' basic pensions for longer terms, adding to the burden and cost and cutting down the profits of the enterprises; similarly, employees would also contribute to their personal accounts for longer terms with heavier burdens before retirement but limited increases in the pensions after retirement. The direction of the reform, therefore, is to establish an effective incentive mechanism so that those who contribute more will have higher future compensations with doubled pensions. To achieve this goal, the increment rate of the extra contributions may be elevated so that higher contributions may be rewarded with progressively increasing pensions.

The third issue is to extend the pension age. It is as related to the aforementioned two issues as different from them. On August 29, 2013, a report by Xiang Nan in *China Youths* described a proposal by Tsinghua University to "extend the pension age to 65" as part of the reform of the old-age security system, and it immediately triggered a new round of debates on whether to extend the retirement age while the proposal was criticized as a way to sneak it in: how would a worker support himself for the first five years after retirement until eligible for pensions?

A report by Wang Lin, on September 4 of the same year in *Securities Daily*, described a survey performed by the Sohu news app commissioned by the social survey center of *China Youths* that asked 25,311 respondents, "What is your attitude on extending the retirement age?" As shown in the survey, 94.5% of the respondents answered with explicit opposition while only 3.2% were in favor of it and 2.3% stayed neutral. In terms of the proposal to extend the pension age, despite the explanations by those behind it that it was not intended to postpone retirement, many would not accept it as the idea that there might be no pension for a while after retirement was unacceptable. After all, one would be like without a job if receiving no pension, actually even worse because it would make retirement like unemployment.

These two reports actually mirrored the attitude of the masses toward extending the pension age, which also implied disagreement on the separation of extending the retirement age and the pension age. The reasons of the disagreement need no further deliberation. Apparently, any promise would look like an "empty voucher" and be unacceptable to the majority if one is not eligible for the pension until five years after retirement, no matter what measures are taken to help get another job after retirement or provide economic incomes through "wonderful ideas."

The fourth issue is whether a worker may support himself after retirement with his own apartment. After the turn of the 21st century, I cooperated with two professors for multiple times while in charge of a key project of the Chinese Social Sciences Academy, *Impacts of Population Aging on the Economic and Social Development*, and we had many discussions on how to reform the old-age insurance system, which resulted in a coauthored book, *Population Aging: From Population Profits to Population Deficits.*[19] In this book, aside from arguments on the systematic reform from the ordinary perspectives, particular attention was given to mobilizing the assets owned by the elderly and transforming them into old-age insurance funds as a way to make up for the shortage of pension funds as well as to improve the security of the old-age insurance. One of the measures to do so was to bid one's house for elderly care.

In fact, the practice to bid one's house in exchange for elderly care has been on the rise in some areas recently, but there are no clear rules, standard operations, or reasonable payments in return for the house. Such a practice must be carried out positively yet cautiously after the concepts are clarified, trials made, and experiences gained. The practice usually targets the elderly in cities and towns who have no regular incomes or who have regular, but extremely low incomes. The procedure should be as follows: the apartments owned by the elderly who wish to enroll in the program must first be evaluated and reasonably appraised and then offered to professional insurance companies as investment based on the appraisal; the investors, i.e., the elderly who have invested their apartments, shall then receive their investment interest and their part of their investment apartments from the professional insurance companies, by year or by month. In this procedure, there are three key aspects.

First, the mechanisms of house appraisal and pension management for the elderly are crucial. The appraisal of the apartments owned by the elderly shall be fair and reasonable through professional procedures and made public. The mechanism and the form to run the practice may be chosen from one of the following three.

One, it may be made through sales, i.e., the apartments may be sold to professional insurance companies and the elderly will no longer own them; in return, the insurance companies pay periodic pensions to the former elderly owners as the installments of buying their apartments.

Two, it may be made through futures contracts, i.e., the apartments may be given to professional insurance companies, but the elderly owners keep their right to live in them for a period of time, e.g., until death, while the apartments are not really owned by the elderly, neither can anyone inherit them. In return, the insurance companies pay periodic pensions to the elderly as advance payments for the apartment futures. For the elderly, this is a way to sell their apartments by installments while still keeping the right to use them, and for the professional insurance companies, it is to buy them by installments while giving up the right of use in the near future.

Three, it may be made through pawning, i.e., the elderly pawn their apartments with professional insurance companies and receive periodic pensions, by year or by month, from the companies. After the elderly pass away, their heirs may redeem the apartments by paying the amounts agreed; otherwise, the apartments will go to the insurance companies.

Second, the operation principles of the professional old-age insurance companies involved must be clarified. As insurance companies, they must operate according to standard market rules. The apartment appraisal, price agreements, and insurance contracting for the elderly, together with the pension payments and the establishment and management of individual accounts, must all follow market rules. Individual wills are to be respected and procedures made public, while contracts must be executed. In addition, the professional old-age insurance companies also have their share in providing social welfare as they serve the elderly who are underprivileged in a way. Therefore, the government should provide some policy incentives and exemption of taxes and charges in the loaning, taxation, and investment of the apartments involved in old-age insurance. At the same time, the government should also guide and supervise these professional old-age insurance companies in terms of their establishment and operation so that they can do their job in old-age insurance well.

Third, there should be intercity adjustments. Many of the elderly who have their own apartments do not live with their children, some of whom live in other places within the same city and some of whom live in other cities. Considering the geographic locations, neighbor relations, and distances to their final workplace, there will be considerable demand for adjustments. In fact, when the elderly offer their apartments to professional old-age insurance companies in return for pensions based on the apartment values and through certain payment means, it is convenient for necessary adjustments to be made since all transactions are through individual accounts. The government and professional managing agencies should publicize the information of adjustments online and through other media to guide and help the elderly who need the adjustments. Such adjustments certainly follow market rules and are to be done on individual wills, through cooperative negotiations, and are governed by law so that the rights of all the parties are protected.

The fifth issue is the practice to use contracted lands in rural areas as a way to buy old-age insurance. To use the rural contracted lands as a way for the elderly to support themselves is for the elderly peasants to invest their own contracted lands and entrust them with corresponding rural old-age insurance agencies, such as rural old-age insurance bases or companies, and these agencies make periodic payments to the elderly as pensions, by year or by month, based on the sizes and qualities of the invested lands.

However, such insurance means with contracted lands may only gain limited pensions for the elderly as China has a large population but limited arable lands, and can be practiced in combination with investment in the healthy elderly by providing them with work and money to some degree so that the overall investment is increased and possibly so are the pensions. Currently a variety of old-age insurance plans of similar sorts are being practiced in rural areas, such as insurance by investing trees, domesticated animals, and woods. The ultimate goal of these insurance types is to mobilize the assets owned by the elderly to include them in various types of insurance so that all the elderly are supported in some way while the level of social security for the elderly is enhanced.

The value preservation and increment of pensions

For quite some time, there have been heated discussions on the issues of empty pension accounts and that the ends of the basic pensions for urban employees in half the provinces do not meet.[20] Pertinent government agencies have stepped up to refute the rumor: there was no problem with managing the pension fund and the balance of China's pension account accrued over the past 10 years was 1.9 trillion yuan.

Meanwhile, another agency was reported to make plans to extend the pension age, which some immediately took as evidence of difficulty in making pension payments. Officials from this agency also stepped up to refute rumors: extending the pension age was not meant for extending the retirement age, and it had nothing to do with pension pressure, but was conceptualized to accommodate the population aging and especially the resulting increased life expectancy.

What is the reality, then? There are indeed empty pension accounts, but these are all individual accounts of enrollees; there is also indeed positive pension balance, but it is calculated based on the current measure that contribution collections are directly transferred into pension payments. According to statistical data, from 1990 to 2011, the deposits to the basic pension fund for urban employees increased from 17.88 billion to 1.68947 trillion yuan, while the expense increased from 14.93 billion to 1.27649 trillion yuan; deduction of the expense from the deposits gives rise to the accrued balance over the 21 years, which is 1.94966 trillion yuan.[21]

The numbers show that there is no problem about whether the ends of the pension account meet based on the current measure that pension collection is directly transferred to payments; however, with accelerated population aging and the progressive increases in the retired elderly, together with an increasing number of enterprises that refuse to make their contributions to pensions, risk is rising and there will be a day when an overall deficit is seen in pension accounts within 20 years.

In addition, the peak of the proportion of the working age is already past, which has meant the end of unlimited supplies of laborers; the economy that is characterized by increases in numbers has grown fast for more than 30 years, which has resulted in considerable reduction in the self-supply of natural resources and a growing dependency on imports; overall, the national economy is in the final phase of traditional industrialization and the beginning of modernization, which sees increases in the cost of many factors such as laborers, energy, and raw materials, resulting in increases in the price index and decreases in the marginal investment return, and this prospect brings huge pressure on the value preservation and increment of pensions. The only way out is through reforms of the supervision system and mechanisms of pensions. Aside from establishing and perfecting the legal framework to ensure timely full collection of pensions, the following three aspects deserve careful deliberation in systematic reforms and innovations.

First, the supervision institutions and mechanisms must be perfected. For quite a while, there has been embezzlement of pensions from time to time, suggesting problems with the institutions. After all, breaches in the regulations, institutions, and management mechanisms may have caused the pensions to be used in other ways. In addition, supervision of pension management is not well constructed, lacking structured layers from the top to the bottom and institutions and mechanisms for it to run independently. Therefore, a complete and well-constructed system to manage and supervise the pension fund must be established with borrowed experiences from successes internationally and conforming to the principle of rule of law.

Second, the empty individual accounts should be moderately filled. Some do not think the empty individual accounts are a big problem, and thus see no need for reforms as long as the current measure of pension payment that is directly transferred from collections is to be kept with appropriate adjustment to and moderate increases in contributions in the future. Some, on the contrary, worry that a crisis is waiting not far ahead as they see the current pension accounts marching toward deficits.

In my own opinion, it is too hasty to conclude now that the pension funds are in trouble to make ends meet just because there are empty individual accounts. While we should not deny any potential risk to the pension fund, we should not sleep on it, either, just because there is considerable balance in the pension accounts accrued over the past decade or two. From the perspective of long-term development, the reform should fill the empty individual accounts moderately. To do so, appropriate regulations and rules shall be made and a plan drawn to fill some of the empty accounts within a certain period of time with specific goals of the percentage of the empty accounts to be filled, the amount of money to fill them with, the source of the money, and the rules of supervision, so that the pension fund will have effectively improved resistance to risks.

Third, market institutions and mechanisms should be introduced. Innovations in the institutions and mechanisms of the old-age insurance system cannot be made without a hand from the government or operation by law; however, the administrative means of the government are far from enough and the efficiency of reforms dependent on them only is also poor. Innovative measures to realize the value preservation and increment of the pension fund should include introduction and establishment of a necessary set of market institutions and mechanisms.

Since the 1980s, the Asian financial crisis, the U.S. subprime mortgage crisis, and the European debt crisis have taken turns trapping advanced economies in stagflation; however, the social pension systems in major countries have long been stable in the value preservation and increment. For example, the average return on investment (ROI) of the pensions in the United States, Germany, the United Kingdom, Canada, the Netherlands, and Switzerland reached 6.25% in this period, contrasting completely with the economic stagflation. Their major experiences are to include private agencies in pension management, to widen the investment channels vigorously for pensions, and to strengthen the supervision of pensions to avoid financial risks so that their pension funds continued to increase in value.[22] The financial market for pensions has just been installed in China, and it is inevitable and a *sine quo none* for us to borrow experiences from successful management around the world to push for reforms of and innovations in the institutions and mechanisms of the financial market.

Notes

1 United Nations, *World Population Prospects: The 2008 Revision*, New York, United Nations, p. 48.
2 Ibid., p. 184.
3 National Bureau of Statistics, *China Statistical Yearbook 2012*, Beijing, China Statistics Press, 2012, p. 102; the data were released by the State Council Information Office on January 18, 2012.
4 Tian, Xueyuan, et al., *Research on the Strategy of China's Population Development in the 21st Century*, Beijing, Social Sciences Academic Press (China), 2007, pp. 440–454.
5 The data of all countries excluding China came from United Nations, *World Population Prospects*, pp. 48–52.
6 Department of Population Statistics, National Bureau of Statistics, *China Population Statistical Yearbook 1988*, Beijing, Outlook in China Press, 1988, p. 198.
7 The calculations were based on the data in the following materials: *Tabulation on the 1982 Population Census of the People's Republic of China*, Beijing, China Statistics Press, 1985, pp. 272–313; *Tabulation on the 1990 Population Census of the People's Republic of China*, vol. 2, Beijing, China Statistics Press, 1993, pp. 2–17; *Tabulation on the 2000 Population Census of the People's Republic of China*, vol. 1, Beijing, China Statistics Press, 2002, pp. 570–581; *Tabulation on the 2010 Population Census of the People's Republic of China*, vol. 1, Beijing, China Statistics Press, 2012, pp. 270–276.
8 The Web page of the National Bureau of Statistics at www.360doc.com, January 20, 2014; *China Population Today*, vol. 2, 2015, p. 19.
9 *China Statistical Yearbook 2006*, Beijing, China Statistics Press, 2006, p. 109.
10 *A Compilation of Proceedings of All National Labor Congresses in China*, Beijing, China Workers Publishing House, 1957, p. 17.
11 Tian, Xueyuan, ed., *China's Elderly Population, Society*, Beijing, Social Sciences Academic Press (China), 2007, p. 313.
12 Sun, Lujun, ed., *A Compilation of Files Concerning the Elderly in China*, Beijing, China Social Publishing House, 2009, pp. 1–53.
13 United Nations, *World Population Prospects*, p. 48.
14 McHugh, David, "The World Braces for Retirement Crisis," edited and translated by Wu, Xueli, *Social Sciences Weekly*, February 20, 2014.

15 Calculated based on the data on page 20 in *China Statistical Yearbook 2013*.
16 "Statistical Communiqué of the Beijing, People's Republic of China on the 2014 National Economic and Social Development," *Contemporary Chinese Population*, no. 2, 2015, p. 19.
17 *An Assembly of Files of All the 3rd Plenary Sessions of All the Central Committees since the Reform and Opening-Up*, Beijing, People's Publishing House, 2013, p. 210.
18 Tian, Xueyuan, "The Population Aging and the Economic and Technologic Advancement in Japan," in *Works of Tian Xueyuan*, vol. 1, Beijing, Social Sciences Academic Press (China), 2011, p. 327; Tian, Xueyuan, "Establishing an Old-Age Security System with Chinese Characteristics," in *Works of Tian Xueyuan*, vol. 1, Beijing, Social Sciences Academic Press (China), 2011, p. 278.
19 Tian, Xueyuan, Wang, Jingying, and Zhou, Guangqing, *Population Aging: From Population Profits to Population Deficits*, Beijing, China Economic Publishing House, 2006.
20 Zheng, Bingwen, and Sun, Yongyong, "The Ends of Urban Basic Pensions Don't Meet in Half the Provinces," *Journal of Shanghai University*, vol. 3, 2012.
21 National Bureau of Statistics, *China Statistical Yearbook 2012*, p. 943.
22 Luo, Xi, "It Is Our Inevitable Choice to Manage the Pension Fund in the Financial Market," *Hongqi Essays*, vol. 20, 2012.

Bibliography

"The 12th Five-Year Plan for Economic and Social Development of the People's Republic of China," People's Daily, March 17, 2011.

McHugh, David, "The World Braces for Retirement Crisis," edited and translated by Wu, Xueli, *Social Sciences Weekly*, February 20, 2014.

Mesa-Lago, Carmelo, "Review: *Social Security in Latin America: Pension and Health Care Reforms in the Last Quarter Century*," *Latin American Research Review*, vol. 42, no. 2, 2007, pp. 181–201.

Sun, Lujun, ed.; Guo, Ping, and Ouyang, Zheng, vice eds., *A Compilation of Files Concerning the Elderly in China*, Beijing, China Social Publishing House, 2009.

Tian, Xueyuan, ed., *Population Aging and the Middle Income Trap*, Beijing, Social Sciences Academic Press (China), 2013.

Tian, Xueyuan, et al., *Research on the Strategy of China's Population Development in the 21st Century*, Beijing, Social Sciences Academic Press (China), 2007.

Tian, Xueyuan, Wang, Jingying, and Zhou, Guangqing, *Population Aging: From Population Profits to Population Deficits*, Beijing, China Economic Publishing House, 2006.

United Nations, *World Population Prospects, the 2008 Revision*, New York, United Nations, 2009.

U.S. Department of Commerce Economics and Statistics Administration, U.S. Census Bureau, *An Aging World 2001*, Washington, DC, Author, 2001.

Wang, Yiming, "Adjustment and Transition: China's Economic Development in the Post-Financial Crisis Era," *Macroeconomics*, vol. 12, 2009.

Zhang, Kaidi, ed., *The Social Activities of the Elderly and Study on Their Mental States in Urban and Rural China*, Beijing, China Social Publishing House, 2009.

Zheng, Bingwen, and Sun, Yongyong, "The Ends of Urban Basic Pensions Don't Meet in Half the Provinces," *Journal of Shanghai University*, vol. 3, 2012.

4 The urbanization trend in the migrant agrarian population

Exploring the path of coordinated development of rural and urban areas

The urbanization of the population in China has been acclaimed in the international community and held up by some as one of the two greatest achievements in the world in the 21st century together with the technological advancement made in the United States. The acclamation was received because the rapid progression of urbanization in China did not bring destitution to agriculture or to the countryside, but brought the rural areas along with industrialization on a path with Chinese characteristics that achieved coordinated development of both urban and rural areas.

Now that more than 50.0% of the population has been urbanized, marking the entrance of urbanization to the middle part of its s-shaped development curve and to the stage when urbanization is dominated by metropolises, China is challenged in terms of whether its urbanization will keep on the track of coordinated development and transmit positive energy to the whole society along the way, a question that can only be answered with updated studies and through practices.

The trend of population urbanization

The general trend of urbanization in the global population

Urbanization, as defined in the demographic dictionary of the UN, is the increase of the proportion of those residing in urban areas. Then how did urbanization start and spread? To answer this question, we must first differentiate between two types of urban development. One is the emergence and development of cities in the past. Looking back at the human history of more than 4 million years, we may conclude that the emergence of the first cities was the consequence of development of the forces of production, especially the social division of labor and exchange of goods.

According to studies, one of the earliest cities in the world, Jericho, emerged on the north shore of the Dead Sea around 9,000 years ago, and later more cities were built in Uruk in Mesopotamia and Cairo on the bank of Nile around 5,000 years ago. At the time of the Roman Empire, Rome had a population of approximately 100,000. In 1363, Venice had a population of

78,000.[1] In China, cities were born at a very early time. According to *Xici, volume 2* of *Yi*[2], markets were set up in the middle of the day and people dispersed when the market was over, suggesting that there were no full-day markets at the time.

With development of exchange of goods and further division of labor, fixed markets were formed with considerable numbers of people living around them. Walls were then built to protect the markets and the people, which gave rise to cities that provided space for crafts and commerce to be independent of agriculture. Cities were documented in China from ancient times, such as Anyi during the Xia Dynasty (approximately 21st–16th century B.C.), Chaoge during the Shang Dynasty (16th century–1046 B.C.); in the periods of the Spring and Autumn and the Warring States (770–221 B.C.), big cities emerged such as Linzi, which had a population of more than 70,000, and Xianyang, which had more than 100,000 people. However, these cities were still built upon self-sufficient economies, and they were more of a political, economic, military, and cultural center than an industrial center.

The other type of urban development was based on the emergence and development of modern cities. After the Industrial Revolution in the mid-18th century, the development of cities was also revolutionized. Cities were no longer a consequence of prosperity in agriculture and crafts, but headquarters for centralized industrialization and the frontline to lead industrialization and socioeconomic development. Urbanization advanced at an unprecedented rate and size, driven by the industries of textile and mechanical manufacturing, by coal and charcoal and steel, or by oil and chemical industries; traditional industrialization thus prospered with cities as the bases.

After WWII, a new technological revolution emerged piloted by microelectronics, bringing a new pattern of informatization and economic globalization and new trends and characteristics to the transition and upgrade of urbanization. Discussions and studies followed, resulting in several theories and models in attempts to interpret the phenomenon. However, urbanization involves a wide range of academic fields, and the resulting theories are complicated with various viewpoints, and this book could only describe certain issues related to urbanization from the perspective of multidisciplinary studies on population.

After the Industrial Revolution, urbanization in the modern sense began. The prime feature of modern urbanization is the flow and migration of rural population and laborers to cities, which has given rise to the theory of "push and pull" of population migration and urbanization. It is generally acknowledged that the pilot of the theory was British scholar Ernst Georg Ravenstein. He studied domestic population migration in more than 20 countries and found that the majority migrated to industrial and commercial centers, and those who were born in urban areas were generally less migratory than those born in rural areas.

Everett S. Lee made modifications to Ravenstein's theory in the 1960s and described the patterns of changes in and development of the migration flow, its size, and the counter-migration flow under various circumstances. Aside from analysis on the positive and negative factors that impacted the origin and the destination of migration, Lee also studied interfering factors such as the distance of migration and immigration laws and personal factors such as personal or family knowledge of the destination of migration, intelligence, and sensitivity. Based on these analyses, he proposed six laws of migration and counter-migration that explained how migration flows, given a specific region, varied according to the degree of differences, difficulties of migration, and development stage of a country. In fact, Lee constructed the theoretical framework of the spatial, temporal, and causal factors of migration.

However, it was Rudolf Herberle who officially proposed and elaborated on the "push and pull" theory. As early as the 1930s and 1940s, he proposed that migration was the consequence of two forces in opposite directions with one "pushing" from a place and the other "pulling" from another; the "pushing" and "pulling" forces might have resulted from multiple factors, and the net force was the vector sum of all the forces. Herberle gave several examples of "pushing" and "pulling" forces based on contemporary situations, some of which are still inspiring today. However, the "push and pull" theory was criticized by many at the time for its oversimplified analysis, yet no one could deny its impact and contribution.

Meanwhile, the "push and pull" theory can be applied to migration between urban and rural areas to explain the major engine that has driven the birth and development of modern urbanization because the countryside pushes and cities pull, which combined results in urbanization. Of course, in-depth understanding and interpretation of the progress of modern urbanization demand further equipment, the Lewis dual-sector model.

In 1954, British economist W. Arthur Lewis argued in his paper "Economic Development with Unlimited Supplies of Labor" on "the development model of a two-sector structure" that developing countries have both the traditional economic system of self-sufficient agriculture and the modern system of urban industries, which he termed the "dual-sector structure."

In Lewis's theory, the surplus labor that has zero marginal labor productivity (MLP) in the agricultural sector, when transformed into nonagricultural labor, will cause the dual-sector structure in developing countries to gradually diminish. As he pointed out, there is only a limited supply of arable lands in the traditional agricultural sector, thus the population and the laborers are always in surplus with unlimited supplies, and together with slow advancement in technologies, the output of production can no longer increase after having reached a certain level and the addition of one laborer can bring almost no addition in production, i.e., the MLP of the agriculture is close to zero and even negative sometimes.

The surplus laborers, also called the "zero-value laborer population," are the prime reason why developing countries have paused in economic development for long terms. Meanwhile, in the modern, urban industrial system, there is vast space for further development and the expansion of production size and economic growth can always exceed the growth of the population. This is due to the lower MLP and wages in the agricultural than the industrial sector. The industrial sector may absorb the surplus laborers from the agricultural sector since the former provides higher wages than the latter, which makes the zero-value laborers fairly easy to absorb, while the former, by paying less for wages, may invest the surplus capital in investment and attract more peasants into industry.

In this process, with the increase in the transition of agricultural laborers into industrial ones, population urbanization is expanded. Ten years after Lewis proposed his theory, John C. H. Fei and Gustav Ranis modified and extended the Lewis model, resulting in the classic Lewis–Fei–Ranis dual-sector economic model. In their theory, the surplus peasants are divided into the group that does not add to agricultural production, i.e., the zero-value labor population with zero MLP, and the group of "not entirely in excess" who cannot generate enough production to satisfy their own consumption despite their positive MLP.

Based on this classification, Lewis, Fei, and Ranis proposed a three-phase model of the transition of the agricultural population to industrial population. In the first phase, the "zero-value agricultural surplus population" transitions to the industrial sector, which will not impact overall agricultural production, and the transition will be completely made as long as there is demand for laborers in the industrial sector. The wages paid to peasant workers only need to equal their wages in the agricultural sector, and due to decreases in the number of peasants the transition has brought, the peasants still in the agricultural sector will have increases in their incomes.

In the second phase, the peasants who are not in entire excess, i.e., those who produce less than they consume despite positive MLP, transition to the industrial sector. After this transition, the total agricultural production and the per capita income of the peasants staying in the agricultural sector decrease, which inhibits further accumulation of capital and increase in investment in the industrial sector, looking less attractive to the peasants who have not transitioned. Thus the loss caused by the transition of the peasants "not in entire excess" can only be made up for by improving the efficiency of agricultural production.

In the third phase, after the loss is made up for and when there is no longer excess of agricultural population of working age, the flow of laborers between the two sectors is primarily decided by the competitive wage levels of the two. The flow of factors, including the population of working age, between the agricultural and industrial sectors follows the market rules of free competition and eventually traditional agriculture is transformed into commercial agriculture.

On a side note, the premise for these two theories to exist and to function, be it the "push and pull" theory by Herberle or the "dual-sector" model by Lewis, is the institution of a market economy with free competitions, i.e., the economy is immune to any exterior interference and runs solely according to market rules. However, such a pure market economy that is free of any sort of interference is rarely seen in the current world, and governments and organizations always find reasons to interfere through various means, which certainly affects the flow of laborers of working age between the agricultural and industrial sectors.

In China, a command economy was previously implemented that was highly centralized, and only after the Third Plenary Session of the 11th Central Committee of the CCCPC did reforms start to bring the economy on a path to a market economy step by step. However, the transition of rural laborers has not been satisfactory because, on one hand, the powerful old institution has left a strong impact that is hard to eradicate completely, and, on the other hand, the interference from the government and social organizations is everywhere. That is also to say that the "push and pull" and "dual-sector structure" theories still have their undeniable impacts on population migration and urbanization, but the restriction from institutions cannot be overlooked either, and proper interpretation from both the theoretical and practical perspectives is needed.

There is a trend of urbanization in the world. Setting aside the older ages, the trend since WWII and prospects for the future are clear according to the data provided by the UN (Figure 4.1).[3]

If the s-shaped development curve of population urbanization is divided into three phases, then the first phase should be at the bottom of the s curve and cover the period from the start of urbanization, which grows slowly, until the degree of 25.0%; the second phase is the middle rising part of the s-shaped curve with rapid urbanization when the urbanization degree is between 25.0% and 65.0%; and the third phase is the top part of the s-shaped curve when the urbanization degree is over 65.0% with slow growth, pausing, and lingering.

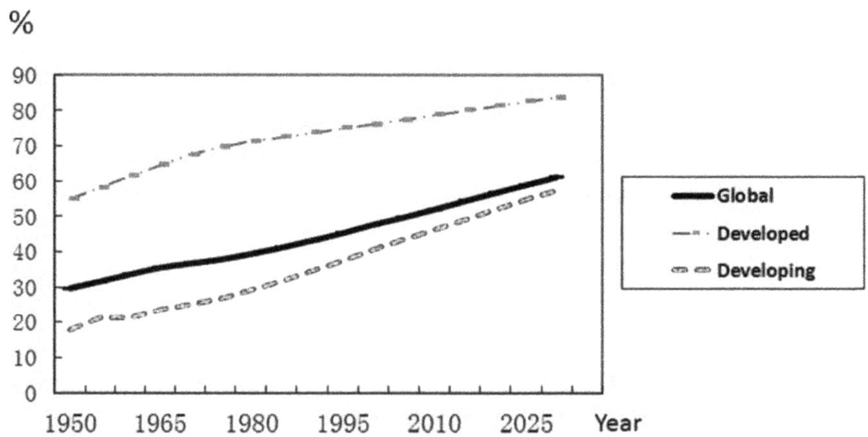

Figure 4.1 Global population urbanization from 1950 through projected 2025.

Based on this classification, the urbanization of the global population has been transitioning from the first to the second phase since WWII, i.e., marching from the bottom of the s curve to the middle part of fast growth. The world urbanization degree reached 53.0% in 2013, which increased by 23.3 percentage points compared to 1950 at an average annual rate of 0.39 percentage points. This was the period with the fastest urbanization in human history. Furthermore, the urbanization degree of developed countries already exceeded 65.0% in 1967, after which it came to the top part of the s curve with urbanization slowly growing, pausing, and lingering.

In contrast, developing countries are still catching up on urbanization despite a larger scale of increases. Overall, the urbanization degree of developing countries increased by 30.2 percentage points, from 17.8% to 48.0%, during this period, with an average annual increase of 0.48 percentage points. It has been projected that developing countries may further accelerate their urbanization rates in the future, closing their gap from developed countries from 30 percentage points in 2013 to 26.4 percentage points in 2030.

Urbanization in China on a fast track

Urbanization in China has progressed with many bumps and is therefore far more complex than that in developed countries and elsewhere. The complexity of China's urbanization progression is rooted in the first 30 years after the new China was established, during which a command economy was in effect and led population urbanization to go against its own laws of development. The new China, at establishment, borrowed experiences from the former Soviet Union and implemented step by step a highly centralized command economy. Meanwhile, China was also on track to transition from a previously backward agricultural society to industrialization, and the haste along the way brought urbanization to collide with industrialization, leading the transition to wind through its way. History is a mirror for the present. Only when what happened yesterday is understood can people interpret what is happening today, and only when people have in-depth understanding of yesterday and today can they make scientific projections for tomorrow and come up with ways to handle the future. Therefore, in order to feel the pulse of the current urbanization of the Chinese population, we need to look back at the history of urbanization in search for the historical origins and direction of future reforms. In my opinion, the history of China's population urbanization in the past 65 years may be summarized with the following three major historical turns.

At the first turn, urbanization went from fluctuations to a fast track

In 1949, when the People's Republic of China was established, China had little new or modern industry since it had been a backward agricultural country for a long time; in addition, for the previous nearly 100 years, China had been under the exploitation and oppression of imperialism, feudalism, and bureaucratic capitalism, which were also called "the three mountains," and had struggled through long-term wars; thus the national economy at the time was extremely weak, the people were destitute, and cities were torn and worn with a pathetic degree of urbanization in that only 10.0% of the population lived in cities.

Now that laborers became the master of history and the forces of social production were fully released, the wounds of the wars were quickly cured, and so was the economy. In merely three years, the major indicators of the national economy in 1952 were already at or exceeded the highest levels before the wars. From 1953 on, the first Five-Year Plan for the development of the national economy was implemented. China was in transition at the time, and the strategy then was "one industrialization and three transformations" (one industrialization: socialist industrialization; three transformations: socialist transformation of agriculture, handcrafts, and capitalist commerce), guided by which the masses were passionate and finished 156 important construction projections without bumps, leading the first Five-Year Plan to be concluded a year in advance; urbanization was also accelerated with the rapid development of economic constructions. Unfortunately, the subsequent "Great Leap Forward" in 1958 and the "Anti-Rightist Campaign" in 1959 were both grave mistakes economically and politically, yet they exerted an impact of "holding up the tail" on urbanization, which could not be overlooked, so the urbanization degree still increased quickly.

Such a phenomenon, different from the usually slow growth of urbanization at the beginning in most countries, was due to the unique situation of China in the 1950s. Particularly, the "tail-holding-up" kind of urbanization progression from 1958 to 1960 was in fact abnormal, and bubbles built up during it, which were to pop with improved economic patterns and resulted in fluctuations and pauses in urbanization in the following 20 years.

After 1961, urbanization first retrogressed, the percentage of the urban population dropping to the bottom of 17.1% in 1972, and then advanced for eight years as if compensation had been made for the retrogression, to the level of 19.4% in 1980, similar to that of 1960. Such long-term retrogression and pause of urbanization at the beginning of the progression is absolutely abnormal no matter where it happens, in China or elsewhere. Three reasons underlay the abnormal situation. One was the bubble created in the "holding-up-the-tail" kind of urbanization during 1958–1960 when the urban population, the total amount of all salaries, and the supply of grain commodities all set record highs, resulting in a fast blowing-up bubble of industrialization and urbanization that could not be supported by the agricultural economy.

Another reason was the strict control of the agricultural population to move to cities and towns under the command economy and household registration (*hukou*) system. In particular, the type of *hukou* was directly linked to the quantitative supply of grain commodities in the command economy, and adjustment to the rural and non-rural population would easily steer the urban-rural structure and the urbanization of the population.

The third reason was associated with the political and social changes at the time. The unprecedented "Cultural Revolution" interrupted political, economic, cultural, and social progression in China, and it brought such movements as sending down cadres to perform manual labor, following the route of the "Seven May Directive," and calling for intellectual youths to go to the mountainous and rural areas, all of which were counter-urbanization movements.

After the Third Plenary Session of the 11th CCCPC in 1978, the Reform and Opening Up brought new opportunities to society and the social economy kept leaping in development; at the same time, the command economy gave way to a market economy, and population migration and transformation of the rural population became active, bringing new vigor and vitality to population urbanization, which then shifted to a fast track. From 1980 to 2014, the proportion of the urban population in China increased by 35.37 percentage points, from 19.4% to 54.77%, at an average annual growth rate of 1.04 percentage points. This had never been seen in the history of population development in China; neither is it common around the world (Figure 4.2).[4]

According to the s-shaped three-phase theory of population urbanization, population urbanization in China entered its second phase in 1987, when the urban population accounted for 25.32% of the national population, which, now in the middle, upright part of the s-shaped curve, bore the characteristics of this phase of fast growth. In fact, compared to the nine years from 1978 to 1987, during which the urbanization degree increased by 5.4 percentage points from 19.92% to 25.32% at an average annual growth rate of 0.6 percentage points, the period from 1987 to 2014 saw an increase of 29.45 percentage points, from 25.32% to 54.77%, at an average annual growth rate of

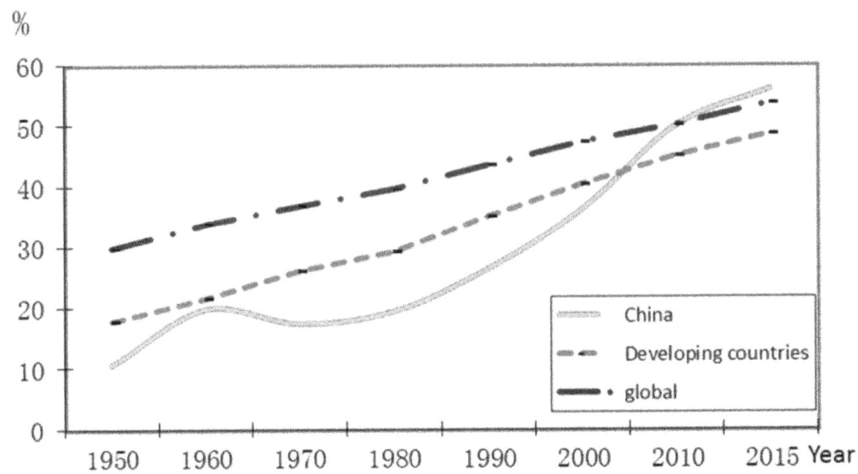

Figure 4.2 Population urbanization in China, developing countries, and around the world since 1950.

1.09 percentage points; this was 181.67% as fast as the former, marking the latter evidently a much faster progress of urbanization.

Ranked among urbanization progressions around the world, China was overall obviously behind the world and many developing countries before the Reform and Opening Up, but when on the fast track after the Reform and Opening Up, urbanization progression in China was much faster than in the world and developing countries, currently by 1.0 percentage point compared to the global rate and by 6.0 percentage points compared to developing countries. According to the UN, global urbanization would reach 53.7% in 2015 compared to 37.9% in 1975, an increase of 15.8 percentage points at an average annual growth rate of 0.4 percentage points; developing countries would see an increase of 21.8 percentage points, from 26.8% to 48.6% at an average annual growth rate of 0.55 percentage points. China saw an increase from 17.34% to 56.0%, or 38.66 percentage points, at an average annual growth rate of 0.97 percentage point, which was 0.57 percentage points higher than the global rate and 0.42 percentage points higher than, essentially doubling, that of developing countries.

There is no doubt that China's urbanization will continue at a fast rate after 2015 until it reaches the top part of the s-shaped curve and enters the third phase. The fundamental reason why China's urbanization has been kept on the fast track since the Reform and Opening Up is the sustained fast development of the economy; after all, it is common sense that urbanization must be firmly founded on economic development no matter which theory is involved. Based on comparative price levels, the average annual growth rate of China's GDP was 9.8% from 1979 to 2013, within which period it was 10.2% from 1991 to 2012.

This was more or less the same as the rate of population urbanization and it closed the gap, at least partially, between urbanization and socioeconomic development. In fact, the ratio of urban to rural population should have been 60:40 in China in 2005, according to the Chenery-Syrquin model, when the thrice industries in China had a ratio of 12.6:47.5:39.9 then and the ratio of employment in the thrice industries was 20:25:35.

After 2005, the economy kept growing at a fast speed and after the turn of the 21st century, the average annual growth rate was almost 10.0% while the thrice industry structure continued to transition to the modern pattern. In 2014, the ratio of the thrice industries reached 9.2:42.6:48.2, with the tertiary industries accounting for 5.6 percentage points more than the secondary, showing the dawn of a modern industrial structure and leaving spacious room for further urbanization of the population. The situations after the Reform and Opening Up are summarized in Figures 4.3, 4.4, and 4.5.[5]

At the second turn, urbanization started a structural transition to be centered on bigness

Global population urbanization may be roughly divided into three phases according to the structural changes. In the first phase, rural population

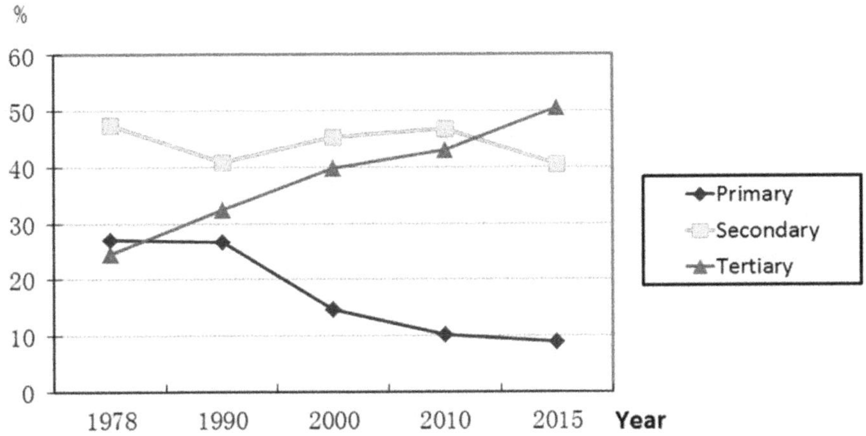

Figure 4.3 Proportions of the thrice industries, 1978–2015.

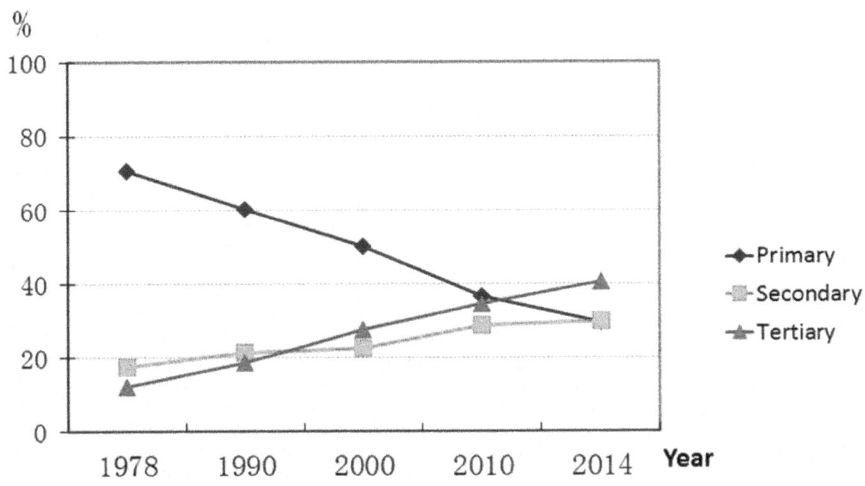

Figure 4.4 Proportions of employment in the thrice industries, 1978–2014.

poured into medium and small cities and towns, a phase of village urbanization; in the second phase, the population from villages and medium and small cities and towns moved and converged to big cities and metropolises, leading to population urbanization centered on and guided by big city circles; and in the third phase, the population from big cities, especially the central areas of metropolises, started to move to the suburbs and villages, resulting in counter-urbanization.

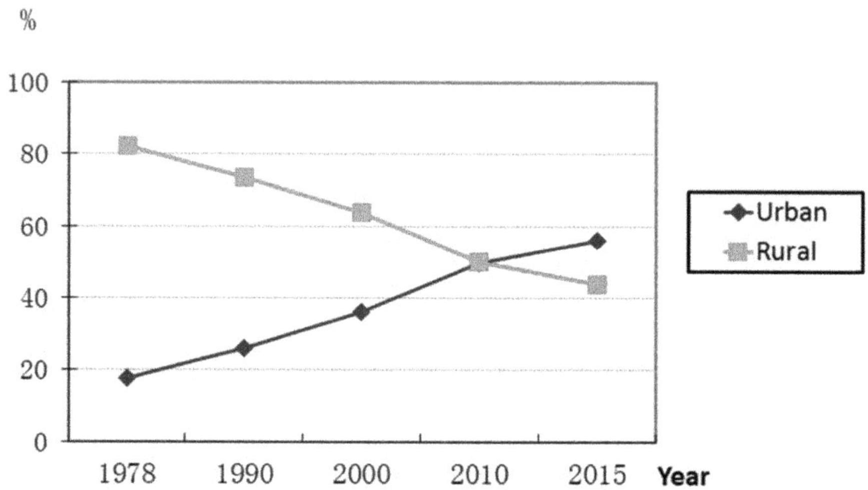

Figure 4.5 Proportions of urban and rural populations, 1978–2015.

These three phases, already witnessed by the urbanization progression of developed countries, more or less overlap with the three phases of the s-shaped urbanization curve that correspond to the bottom, middle, and top parts of the curve, representing the basic trends in population urbanization. In China, population urbanization had long employed the tactic of "valuing the small and ignoring the big" and had invested actively in small cities and towns and moderately in medium ones while strictly restricting the size of big cities; meanwhile, urban peasant workers had only left their soils, but not the cultural circles of their hometowns, which resulted in a situation of "small cities and towns, big issues," i.e., developing small cities and towns had solved the big issues of urban-rural development and the transformation of the agricultural surplus laborers. In fact, township and village enterprises prospered from nowhere in the 1980s, and village urbanization became the theme of population urbanization at the time, considerably facilitating and making significant contributions to socioeconomic development.

However, with the demographic transition came decreases in fertility and birth rates and in employment pressure, with the shift of economic development came the transition of the economic system and the economic growth mode from multiplying numbers to improving quality and benefits, and with the transition of society came preliminary effects and a promising future for the government to provide public services instead of dominating everything.

All these changes had made the urbanization of "valuing the small and ignoring the big" outdated in terms of meeting the demands of social development, and a historical turn finally came at the beginning of the 21st century, when population urbanization entered the second phase that big cities

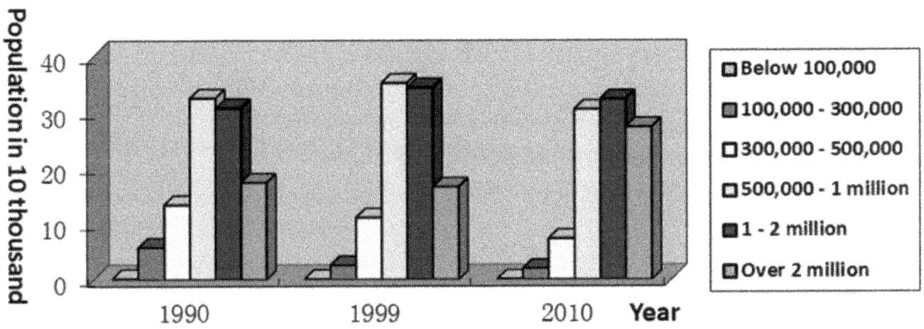

Figure 4.6 City distribution by size in 1990, 1999, and 2010.

and metropolises took the dominant role. According to statistical data, the proportion of medium-small cities with a population under 500,000 decreased by 5.54 percentage points from 1990 to 1999, from 19.41% to 13.87%, that of medium cities with a population between 500,000 and 1 million increased by 2.7 percentage points, from 32.49% to 35.19%, and that of big cities with a population more than 1 million increased by 2.84 percentage points, from 48.10% to 50.94%. The changes in the proportions of small, medium, and big cities showed that urbanization in China had already transitioned from centering on smallness to centering on bigness by the late 1990s, and it then further progressed (Figure 4.6).[6]

As shown in Figure 4.6, urbanization centered on bigness showed acceleration in progression after the turn of the 21st century. Comparison between the situations of 1999 and 2010 showed decreases not only in the proportion of the cities with less than 500,000 people, which declined by 4.38 percentage points from 13.87% to 9.49%, but also in the proportion of the cities with a population between 500,000 and 1 million, which reduced by 4.72 percentage points from 35.19% to 30.47%, and in the proportion of the cities with a population between 1 and 2 million, which reduced by 2.1 percentage points from 34.35% to 32.25%. Meanwhile, the proportion of the super big cities with a population over 2 million rocketed from 16.59% to 27.79%, an increase of 11.2 percentage points, and the proportion of the even bigger cities with a population over 4 million increased by 6.36 percentage points.

These changes were typically seen in the megalopolization of Beijing, Shanghai, and Guangzhou. In fact, as widely known, the theory of megalopolises originated with French and Italian geologists and economists in the 1970s, among which the megalopolis concept by Gottmann and that of "growth poles" by Perroux were the most definitive. These scholars described the growth of several big cities to the point that the GDP made by their metropolitan areas accounted for 65.0% to 80.0% of the total GDP of their respective countries and argued that megalopolization had become the most important growth pole of the economy. However, the theory was interpreted as a regional phenomenon during the economic development of developed countries and did not arouse much attention in China when China was only starting to urbanize its population with less than 25.0% urban residents.

Twenty years later, many problems emerged during China's urbanization that "valued the small and ignored the big"; it nonetheless transitioned to the second phase of urbanization that "centered on the bigness." The theory then became quickly widespread. The megalopolises of Beijing, Shanghai, and Guangzhou are still being formed and the proportion of their GDPs cannot yet match that of the New York, Tokyo, and London megalopolises; however, they are marching forward in megalopolization and have shown considerable sizes. Apparently, the urbanization progression in China is already halfway through the transition from being centered on the small to the big, and the status, functions, and dominance of megacities are growing day by day.

In fact, a mature theory exists to describe the relationship between the size of a city and the economic benefits it brings, i.e., they are positively correlated. However, since cities with various sizes differ in cost, various countries have made decisions according to their respective historical stages in terms of balancing the economic benefits and the cost relative to city sizes.

Meanwhile, an evaluation system, which takes into account economic, social, demographic, resource, and environmental benefits, has been established based on statistical analyses on the scale effects of cities and how to cross the limit of economic benefits, and a conclusion has been drawn that the comprehensive benefits a city brings increase with the size of a city in that small, medium, big, bigger, and megacities have growing benefits in ascending order, which has provided powerful theoretical support for the urbanization policy that is centered on big cities and coordinates urban and rural development.

Such a timely policy of big city-dominated urbanization is not only just a mirror of the fact that urbanization progression crossed the "turning point" of scale structures at the turn of the 21st century but is also in line with the strategy to change the mode of economic development and to make structural adjustment to the economy. In fact, big city-dominated urbanization, together with improving the quality of small cities and towns, is part of the transition of the development mode of the economy.

Up until now, the high growth of China's economy has primarily relied on investment: from 1989 to 2005, the GDP grew 9.7% on average annually while the society-wide investment in fixed assets grew 20.6%, showing evident marks of an extensive mode of expanded reproduction. In 2006, China's GDP accounted for 6.0% of the global GDP while its consumption of oil accounted for 8.0%, minerals 10.0%, electricity 13.0%, and coal and charcoal 30.0%; the consumption of energy and raw materials per unit of GDP was approximately 2.7 times that of the United States and 3.4 times that of Japan, illustrating the "big difficulty" of high consumption and low efficiency that had long bothered China.[7] In fact, the extensive mode of expanded reproduction was closely associated with the path and tactics of population urbanization.

As mentioned earlier, in the 1980s, when township and village enterprises prospered, due to the "short, flat, and fast" effect of these enterprises that did not require huge investment and had evident short-term benefits, GDP grew quickly, surplus rural laborers were largely transformed and employed, and population urbanization was hastened, leading to the solution of many big problems by the development of small cities and towns, as expressed by the term "small cities and towns, big problems."

However, by the end of the 20th century, when such development had lasted for more than a decade, the development mode that was backed by township and village enterprises with high consumption but low efficiency had come to a dead end as the waste of resources, the low level of efficiency, and the harm to the environment could no longer be tolerated and the interpretation of "small cities and towns, big problems" had held these cities and towns to be big problems themselves.

Now we must let go the conventional concept of development that values only GDP and construct a concept of scientific development that values all-around, coordinated, and sustainable development in order to realize the transition of the economic growth mode from expanding in numbers to improving in quality and benefits and to facilitate the structural upgrade of industries. To achieve these goals, the transition in the tactics and directions of population urbanization is one important foothold and plays irreplaceable roles.

At the third turn, urbanization broke through the limitation of cities' self-development

It is true that China's urbanization is now on a fast track and is centered on big cities, but it by no means equals the idea that faster urbanization and bigger cities are always better, and it is also possible that some big cities and megacities are oversized and need necessary control and adjustment. A reasonable strategy of urbanization is to search for a fast, yet moderate speed and a proper structure of big, medium, and small cities while following the principle of coordinated development of urban and rural populations with the economy, society, resources, and environment.

In fact, there are roughly four types of megalopolises, or metropolitan areas around big cities, in the history of global population urbanization.

The first is the European cultural type represented by Paris and Barcelona. The megalopolises of this type are deeply culturally rooted in the Renaissance and backed economically and technologically by the tradition of the Industrial Revolution in the mid-18th century so that these megalopolises are not only rich in European cultures such as democracy and equality, but also supported by advanced technologies and industries.

The second is the compact economical type represented by New York and Tokyo. The megalopolises of this type have strong impacts as centers that dominate their surroundings with manufacturing, financial, and commercial industries serving as pillars formed during technological advancement and industrial upgrade.

The third is the decentralized type represented by Los Angeles and by Salt Lake City in the Midwestern United States. These loosely connected megalopolises formed as the residents of eastern America migrated west.

These three types of megalopolises, either bonded by particular cultural ties or centered around modern industries and technologies, all walked a walk of urbanization that combined market economies and humanity ideals and coordinated urban and rural development as well as various sectors within the cities. During the urbanization of these areas, there were no substantial social contradictions, and their experiences are worth summarizing and learning.

There is a fourth type, the Latin American malfunction, which is represented by Mexico City, by Rio de Janeiro, by Buenos Aires, and by Mumbai and Delhi (Old Delhi) in India. The urbanization centered around these megalopolises fell into the trap of medium incomes by and large, bringing negative impacts to their societies. This point is elaborated on in a later section.

Which type does China's urbanization belong to? Probably none of these four types may enlist China because, from a certain perspective, China's urbanization is on a track with Chinese characteristics. The most prominent feature of the Chinese characteristics in urbanization is that the development of cities does not only cover the cities but must also benefit the countryside, agriculture, and peasants, so China's urbanization is on a track of coordinated development or urban and rural socioeconomic development. Specifically, urbanization with coordinated urban and rural development comprises the following concepts: the goal of urbanization is to meet the demands of urban and rural residents for comprehensive development, including physical, emotional, cultural, and social demands; urbanization is not only after the speed and the size of the cities; the engine that drives urbanization is primarily human capital.

In other words, urbanization in China is focused on strengthening the knowledge, techniques, experiences, and health of urban residents, including migrant peasants, and is driven by transition and upgrade, but not the kind of capital-driven expansion resembling pita-making by spreading the dough. Facilitation of urbanization shall first achieve coordinated development of the population, the resources, and the environment so that it is resource-efficient and environmentally friendly, which may end the old mode of urbanization that is at the cost of resources and the environmental quality. Despite multiple problems in these aspects, the urbanization tactic that persists with coordinated urban and rural development is still correct and is in line with the strategy of sustainable development. Further arguments on this point are provided in the later section of reforms on urbanization.

Preventing bloated urbanization cautiously

Despite the exceptional achievement in population urbanization since the establishment of the new China, which has been acclaimed across the world, problems have built up partially due to some events that were against the normal course of socioeconomic development in the first 30 years with a command economy, and partially due to the fast progression of urbanization since the Reform and Opening Up, and the problems have shown their effects on the relationship between "walled areas" and "cities/markets" while urbanization is at risk of losing cities.

Risk of losing the "city/market" during urbanization

All aspects of losing the "city/market" during urbanization

The most prominent contradiction and problem of the current urbanization is abstracting the "city" away from the progress, leading to situations in which there are more walled areas than cities, bigger walled areas than cities, and even walled areas without cities. Overall, the problem is primarily manifested in the following aspects: excessively fast progression of urbanization, advanced urbanization of land, blind expansion of urban sizes, and the bottleneck effect of resources.

One aspect of the risk in the current urbanization is that excessively fast progression has led to a contradiction between big walled areas and small cities. As described in the analysis of its progression along an s-shaped curve, urbanization is divided into three phases by the percentage of urban population, i.e., below 25.0%, 25.0–65.0%, and above 65.0%. The second phase corresponds to the middle part of the s-shaped curve and covers a long distance on the curve; therefore, it may be further divided into two periods of fast progression when the urban population accounts for 25.0% to 40.0% of the total population and accelerated progression between 40.0% and 65.0%. China's urbanization has had evident and marked characteristics of these two subphases in the middle, upright part of the s curve. In the first period of the second phase from 1987 to 2003, the proportion of urban population increased by 15.21 percentage points, from 25.32% to 40.53%, at an average annual growth rate of 0.95 percentage points. In the second period from 2003 to 2014, urbanization further increased by 14.24% in terms of the proportion of urban population, at an average annual growth rate of 1.29 percentage points, higher than that of the first period by 0.34 percentage points.[8]

The numbers showed accelerated progression of urbanization in the second phase of the s curve, which has been met with both acclaims and criticisms among the academic fields and all other sectors of society. Some were encouraged by the progression and called for further acceleration, with a few holding it up as the engine to drive economic growth and arguing for employing urbanization to push for further economic development; some, on the contrary, were not happy about it and called for an urgent stop to the progression because they believed that the "great leap forward" of urbanization had derailed from the track of normal economic development. Yet others acknowledged the achievement so far, but proposed to make appropriate adjustment as they argued that reforms were needed to shape healthy urbanization because the current problems must be taken seriously despite the achievements and the correct direction of the urbanization.

In my opinion, the urbanization in the first 30 years after the establishment of the new China went through too many bumps and was too slow for the economy, and after the Reform and Opening Up, which revitalized socioeconomic development as well as urbanization, it was in line with laws of nature for urbanization to shift on the fast track after it had been contained for so long that it had accumulated enormous energy for development. The problem is that during the accelerated progression on the fast track, new contradictions and problems emerged and built up, and they have not been taken seriously. To solve these contradictions, several basic questions must be properly answered based on theories and practices, as detailed in what follows.

First, was the accelerated urbanization progression in the past 35 years normal? How can we explain the aforementioned acceleration during the first period of the second phase from 1987 to 2003, when the proportion of urban population increased by, on average, 0.95 percentage points annually, and during the second period, when it increased by 1.29 percentage points annually? In my opinion, the first period of the second phase may be normal if the fast progression during that period was complementary growth of urbanization, but the acceleration in the second period was already mixed with certain arbitrary factors because urbanization was used to drive economic growth, and it was therefore not normal. For example, the investment of 4 trillion yuan in 2008, nicknamed "iron cocks" (the Chinese word for cock has the same pronunciation as "public infrastructure"), was mostly spent on urbanization construction and became the major leverage to lift the economy.

However, urbanization should have been the consequence of socioeconomic development, industrial upgrade, and structural changes in the urban and rural populations, yet it was now used to prevent and inhibit the economy from sliding down and to keep and stabilize economic growth, which utterly reversed the relationship between urbanization and the economy. As a result, the growth was stabilized and GDP reached the aimed growth rate while the urbanization was bloated and overproduction was worsened.

Second, how was the excessively high speed of urbanization achieved? Was it achieved through an intensive or an extensive mode of development? The answer is the latter, but not the former. As widely known, urbanization is the number one client of consumptive construction materials such as reinforced steel and cement. In fact, the demand for these construction materials grew rapidly after the Reform and Opening Up. From 1978 to 2013, steel had the highest growth in production output, 47.3 times, among all major raw material industrial products; cement came next, with an increase of 36.0 times in output; and crude steel was the last, with an increase of 23.5 times in output. Exactly due to the increases that kept doubling in the output of these three constructive products, the demands for constructing buildings and making roads and other infrastructure constructions such as supply of water,

Table 4.1 Output of major raw material industrial products, 1978–2012

Year	*1978*	*1990*	*2000*	*2013*	*2013/1978, %*
Crude coal (100 million tons)	6.18	10.80	13.84	36.80	595.5
Crude oil (10,000 tons)	10,405	13,831	16.300	20,947	201.3
Natural gas (100 m^2)	137	153	272	1,170	854.0
Cement (10,000 tons)	6,524	20,971	59,700	241,614	3,703.5
Crude steel (10,000 tons)	3,178	6,635	12,850	77,904	2,451.4
Steel products (10,000 tons)	2,208	5,153	13,146	106,762	4,835.2

Source: *China Statistical Yearbook 2014*, pp. 6–7.

electricity, coal, and gas during the fast urbanization were met. Also because of the unlimited supply of these "hosting materials" of rebar and cement, the extensive, "dough-spreading" urbanization was sustained (Table 4.1).

The biggest problem born with high-speed urbanization under an extensive mode of development is that walled areas are bigger than cities, that there are more walled areas than cities, or even that there are walled areas without cities, leading urbanization to lose the supporting industries it should have. The word "city" here denotes the level of economic development with a corresponding industrial structure. As mentioned earlier, urbanization is the consequence of socioeconomic development and structural changes in industries, which are the inherent engines to drive the emergence and development of urbanization. However, in China, for a long time, urbanization has derailed from this track of normal development to a large degree. For example, the secondary sector of the economy has occupied a prominent position with long-lived manufacturing industry dominated by heavy chemistry and led by an extensive mode of development, winning China the title of the "world's factory."

Meanwhile, the tertiary sector of the economy has been slowly ascending and its proportion in the national economy only approached that of the secondary in 2012 and took the lead with a margin of 2.2 percentage points when it reached 46.1% in 2013, bringing the economy of China across the threshold of the modern industrial structure.[9] However, it is not enough to look at only the proportions of the thrice sectors, and the industry distribution within the sectors is also important. In fact, the internal structure of the tertiary sector is, to some degree, indicative of the structure of the national economy. According to the National Bureau of Statistics, the tertiary sector comprises six industries, i.e., transport, storage and post, wholesale and retail trades, hotels and catering services, financial services, real estate, and others. Apparently, these are very rough classifications of industries, and there is also a lack of indicators of modern services, such as science and technology, education, culture, and logistics, while financial services are not further divided.

In addition, in the "explanation of major indicators" in the appendix of the *Statistical Yearbook*, there are total deposits, capital transfer, net financial investment, deposits, loans, securities, stock, stock shares, and insurance reserves, all of which are items on annual cash flow statements and annual balance sheets and cannot reflect the proportion of the tertiary sector. Therefore, we can only peek through the aforementioned six industries to learn the changes in the compositions of the tertiary sector.

In a nutshell, the composition of the value added of the tertiary industry has made a transition toward a modern structure. Specifically, from 1978 to 2013, the proportion of transport, storage, and post decreased by 10.5 percentage points, or 50.2%, from 20.9% to 10.4%, wholesale and retail trades decreased by 6.6 percentage points, or 23.7%, from 27.8% to 21.2%, and hotels and catering services decreased by 0.7 percentage points, or 13.7%, from 5.15% to 4.4%. In contrast, the proportion of financial services increased by 5.0 percentage points, or 64.1%, from 7.8% to 12.8%, real estate increased by 3.5 percentage points, or 38.0%, from 9.2% to 12.7%, and others increased by 9.0 percentage points, or 30.7%, from 29.3% to 38.3%.

The first three groups are mostly conventional industries and their proportions decreased; the last three groups, except for the category of others, which is unclear, are modern, emerging industries and their proportions climbed. The general trend shows a structural transition of the tertiary sector from a traditional, backward structure to a modern, advanced one. However, the transition was made slowly and sometimes turned back. Financial services, for example, once saw increases in their proportion to a fairly high level, above 17.0%, at the turn of the 1980s and the 1990s, after which its proportion took a step down and dropped to around 14.0% from 1991 to 1995 and almost 8.0% in the first five years of the 21st century. However, it started to climb again in 2006, reaching almost 13.0% currently.[10]

A review of the overall changes in the composition of the tertiary sector has shown that the backward tertiary industry is now marching toward an advanced, modern structure although the transition has been slow with steps backward and the proportion of the tertiary industry of the national economy is still four percentage points away from its historical best. In addition, the majority in the sector are low-end services, which became the primary challenge after the proportion of the tertiary sector topped the other two, as well as a new problem for the tertiary industry to transition and upgrade with an intensive mode of development.

A key problem is how urbanization "without cities" has survived and expanded. In fact, the foregoing analysis has already shown that it may operate independently of the normal cycle of production, exchange, distribution, and consumption by establishing a system of its own, which I term "the extracorporeal circuit." The extracorporeal circuit takes three steps to push urbanization to circulate.

First, the local government expropriates lands and sells them to interested developers, who may then apply for permission for construction projects;

at this step, the local government obtains revenue by selling lands and the peasants also get paid for giving up some of their lands. Second, the developers start constructions and pay the government certain fees and taxes levied on constructions such as buildings. Third, the constructions are done and enter the market for sale, and the developers engulf all the profits of the sales after paying the taxes levied on house sales. In this way, the local government receives revenue from land auctioning and taxes of construction and house sales, the peasants get paid for the lands they gave up, and the developers take all the other profits.

In fact, local governments have mastered such land finances while developers are certainly the biggest winner and peasants usually get the least. In addition, corruption is quite common in such extracorporeal circulation despite efforts to prevent it, and land financing is always lucrative for governments, leading real estate prices to skyrocket. Therefore, as long as the extracorporeal circuit is there, the real estate bubble will never pop, neither will house prices regress to normal levels.

Another aspect of the risk in the current urbanization is the coexistence of in-advance urbanization of land and laid-back urbanization of people. From 1990 to 2012, the nationwide urban built-up area (BUA) increased by 3.5 times, from 12,856 to 45,566 km^2, with an average annual growth rate of 5.9%; the urban construction land increased by 3.9 times, from 11,608 to 45,751 km^2, with an average annual growth rate of 6.4%.[11] Meanwhile, there was only a 1.36-fold increase in the urban population, from 301.59 million to 711.82 million, at an average annual growth rate of 4.0%.[12]

Apparently, the growth rate of the urban population was not only 1.9 percentage points lower than that of the urban BUA but also 2.4 percentage points lower than that of the urban construction land. It must be clarified that the urban population here covered the residents who had lived in urban areas for at least half a year, which actually included a large population who had migrated to cities and towns from rural areas. In 2012, a total of 279 million people nationwide lived in places that were different from their *hukou* sites and there were 236 million migrants, among whom nearly 200 million had migrated to urban areas and approximately 165 million had lived there for more than half a year and were listed as urban residents.[13]

Some have proposed to define urban population by those with non-rural *hukou*, and if this standard were adopted, the proportion of the urban population would dive by 18 percentage points and land at around 36.0%. I must say I do not agree with this definition; after all, in no countries (except for city-states) can all urban residents be nonagricultural, and there is always a certain proportion of agricultural population residing in cities. Based on experiences of the international community as well as the standards for cities and towns in China in the more than 60 years since the new China was established, it seems appropriate if 25.0% of urban residents are agricultural population. Based on this number, urbanization in China should be around 50.0%, four percentage points lower, or 35 million people fewer, than statistical data. Therefore, the real situation of in-advance urbanization of land and laid-back urbanization of people is worse than the statistics have shown.

In addition, it is also possible that there is underreporting of urban land areas in the statistical data because underreporting would help local governments avoid certain punishment such as the house vacancy tax and bring reduction in troubles and cost. Therefore, the real numbers of bloated land urbanization are larger than officially released.

Furthermore, the in-advance urbanization of land and the laid-back urbanization of people have also lowered the economic density of urbanization and tainted it with the bad smell of enclosure. Enclosure, especially seizing agricultural, arable lands, has intensified the already tense situation of the current use of arable lands, and it has already touched the bottom line ("red line" as in Chinese) of the 1.8 billion *mu* of arable lands. Some of the lands expropriated in in-advance urbanization are left vacant because construction was never started, was intermittent, or was deserted halfway through due to shortage of capital, materials, and labor, while the original value in agriculture of the lands is also lost. Thus a great deal of land resource has been idling and wasted. After all, a large population with limited arable lands is China's major character, and the bottom line of 1.8 billion *mu* of arable lands must not be crossed as they are the bottom line of food security for 1.3 billion people. Urbanization at the cost of land resources can no longer continue!

A third aspect of the risk in the current urbanization is that blind expansion of cities and towns has prevented their civil functions from playing roles. Blind expansion of cities and towns in size is an inevitable consequence of the excessively speedy urbanization, the extensive mode of development, and the in-advance urbanization of land, and it interferes with the civil functions, which sometimes are even reduced.

The "dough-spreading" kind of urbanization, as mentioned earlier, should be taken seriously while what is even more urgent is the expansion to the sky: the "dough" is spreading not only horizontally but also vertically, heating up vertical urbanization with skyscrapers shooting up one after another, which are built from similar materials and in similar structures and look similar too. Many cities now resemble each other while skyscrapers are still competing for the top, setting new records continuously. It's been revealed that an enterprise group is now preparing for its project of building the highest skyscraper, which will beat the 828-meter-high Burj Dubai by 10 meters.

After Beijing announced its intention to become a world city, similar proposals were made by as many as 70 to 80 cities, some of which were only medium-sized ones and did not even understand what a world city really meant. Maneuvers like these have spread the "dough" to become bigger and bigger, thicker and thicker, and more and more Westernized. Such blind expansion of urbanization values the outlook of a city, while the introduction of industries; infrastructure of water supply and sewers; supply of coal, gas, and electricity; and roads and service facilities like hospitals, schools, daycares, kindergartens, and nursing homes have all been ignored, leading some cities to eventually become "image projects," which do not have a city's due functions such as centralizing, radiating to, and guiding the surrounding areas, and the ultimate goal of urbanization is thus missed.

A fourth aspect of the risk in the current urbanization is the bottleneck effect of resources and daunting environmental challenges. The urbanization that has been after speed and size usually values speed over quality, size over cost, and input over output, which has led to a habitual extensive mode with high input and consumption to be the normal mode of development. Scarce natural resources such as land, fresh water, energy, wood, and minerals have thus turned even scarcer, and become the bottleneck that halts the healthy development of urbanization. The situation is clear from the rapid growth of and increasing dependency on the imports of crude oil and industrial raw materials such as iron ore (Table 4.2).

Not only has the bottom line of the 1.8 billion *mu* of arable lands been touched, but the water resource is far from safe as well; unfortunately, things may be even worse. China has never been a country with abundant fresh water: the total amount of water resource on land is 2.8124 trillion cubic meters per year, accounting for 6.9% of the global amount, and the per capita amount is only one-fourth of the world average. The urbanization that has been dominated by traditional industries has, on one hand, sharpened the contradiction between water supply and demand as the demand has been skyrocketing, and has, on the other hand, brought harms to the water resource, leading to marked increases in the proportion of used water of all usable water.

In fact, as early as the 1980s and the 1990s, the actual water consumption in China already reached the threshold of water security, 50.0% of the available water resource. However, that percentage kept climbing after the turn of the 21st century and has long passed the internationally recognized danger threshold. Among the 618 cities nationwide, more than half are running short of water and more than 100 are in grave shortage of water, among which the situation in megacities is particularly urgent.[14] As surface water sources keep decreasing, wells are dug to obtain water from underground, leading to an acute drop of the water table.

Table 4.2 Imports of crude oil and raw materials such as iron ore, 2000–2013

Year	*2000*	*2005*	*2010*	*2013*	*2013/2000, %*
Crude oil, 10,000 tons	2,027	12,682	23,931	28,174	13.9
Coal, 10,000 tons	201	2,617	16,478	32,702	162.7
Iron ore, 10,000 tons	6,997	27,526	61,863	81,910	11.7
Copper ore, 10,000 tons	181	406	647	1,007	5.6
Chrome ore, 10,000 tons	111	302	866	1,209	10.9

Source: *China Statistical Yearbooks*, 2001, 2006, 2011 and 2014, China Statistics Press, 2001, 2006, 2011 and 2014, p. 597, 747, 235, and 344, respectively.

Sixty years ago, digging for five meters was enough to find water in Beijing, but now it is 50 meters. At present, the sharp increases in water consumption and in the ratio of water consumption to available water and the acute drop of the water table show that water availability has become the bottleneck of further development, which has become so tight that no further development can be made. We have got a "yellow card." There are actually multiple bottlenecks, corresponding to various resources, and the bottleneck of the water resource is the most important, holding the top seat of all bottlenecks that prevent future urbanization and being the shortage plank of a barrel.

In addition, energy resources such as oil, natural gas and coal, and charcoal and mineral resources such as iron, copper, chromium, and gold are all becoming scarcer and scarcer. Now China has become a prominent country in terms of energy and mineral import, which has further narrowed the bottleneck of urbanization and faced us with increasing friction in international trade negotiations.

Together with the tightening bottleneck effect of natural resources, another bottleneck is being formed due to pollution caused by urbanization. If the former is the "bottleneck of imports" for development and production, the latter is the "bottleneck of exports," the two of which cap urbanization in China with bottlenecks on both ends. In fact, the freshwater crisis described earlier is also related to increased water pollution. The overall situation of the water resource now is that pollutant discharge has exceeded the capacity of the water bodies, which is further exacerbated by the over-discharge of nitrogen and phosphorous; unreasonable exploitation of water resources adds to the pollution of water bodies, and water conservation is compromised due to disruption of regional ecological systems, leading water pollution to spread upstream. Among all the streams in the seven river systems and 35 major lakes in China, more than half of the water bodies in each category have been polluted. The polluted water in rivers and lakes flows to the seas, leading more than one-third of the nearshore seawater to be qualified for only the fourth category of water quality.

In addition, ever since heavy smog first broke out in the Yangtze River delta in December 2013 and lasted for more than a week, large-area smog has frequented Beijing, Tianjin, Hebei Province, and Shandong Province. The smog crisis is closely related to the rapid progression of traditional industrialization and urbanization, during which nitrogen, phosphorous, and sulfur compounds from urban industries, auto emissions, and residuals from burning coal have all rocketed high and contributed to the formation of smog.

Unfortunately, environmental management has long been overlooked; at the same time, the high cost of environmental management during the transition from traditional industrialization to modernization has kept environmental management behind, performed side by side with, or completely ignored even after construction. As a result, various types of pollution, such as air, water, solid waste, noise, and light, have built up. We now must reflect on urbanization: what has urbanization brought us? What is the solution to the problems it brings? To answer these questions, we must track back to urbanization's very origin: resource allocation, the institutions, and the system.

Causes of "losing the city"

The various manifestations of "losing the city" during urbanization are actually the consequence of misunderstanding, in cognition and in theory, the relationship between walled areas (commonly called cities and towns) and real cities.

Urbanization is defined in the *Demographic Dictionary*, edited by Georges Tapinos, former secretary of the Population Committee of the United Nations, and published in 12 languages, including English, French, Chinese, German, and Spanish, as the process of the growth of the urban population.[15] I once discussed the term *urbanization* in person with Mr. Tapinos in 1982. As related by him, cities should be divided into big-, medium-, and small-sized categories, and the small-sized include towns. In addition, urbanization should be interpreted as to advance only cities, but not cities and towns, which is actually in line with China's traditional wisdom.

In Chinese, the word *city* (城市) is a compound of two characters, with the first denoting a walled area where the walls are built to defend against attacks from the outside and the second denoting a centralized market. In the ancient work *Xici, volume 2* of *Yi*, it is said, "a market is formed in the middle of the day," which will disperse after all trades are done. Apparently, there were no full-day markets at the time. Obviously, the Chinese version of a city is where markets are often formed, a product of a certain degree of economic development. Therefore, a walled area and a market are both indispensable for a city, with the former defining the geological borders and the latter setting the foundation and the core of the emergence and development of the city. The two rely on, improve, and develop with each other.

In the modern age, cities are the consequence of industrial expansion and upgrade and the major carrier of industrialization, informatization, and modernization of agriculture, except for a few cases with military and political agendas. From the theoretical perspective, when urbanization is abstracted as walled areas without the "market" inside so that cities and towns run on their own without the "market," the logic of the relationship between a walled area and a city is violated and reversed as the internal bond is severed.

After all, what is urbanization really? From the demographic perspective, it is the process of rural population moving to cities and towns, which changes the urban-rural distribution of the population. From the perspective of labor, it is the distribution of employment in the primary, secondary, and tertiary sectors of the economy and the structure of the thrice sectors. From the economic perspective, it is the structural change in the thrice industries of agriculture, manufacturing, and services. From the perspective of sociology, it is the replacement of the production and the way of life in an agrarian society by those of an industrial one and the advance of a society when an agricultural civilization is replaced by an industrial one and a traditional civilization by a modern one.

Of course, the economy is always the foundation, and modern urbanization usually results from industrialization and informatization and the core is the urbanization of the population as when rural population becomes urban and the demographic and employment structures are transformed and industries are upgraded while the society advances with the modern civilization replacing the traditional. Therefore, the "city" (or the "market" in the Chinese version of a city) that plays a central role in guiding and radiating to the surrounding areas economically, politically, and culturally is the most important economic foundation and pillar for the operation of the city. If the foundation and pillar is abstracted away, the walled area, now separated from the "city" (or "market"), becomes water without source and a tree without roots and departs from a reasonably denoted city in principle.

In terms of the connotations of a city, such independent walled areas are now free from the natural bondages a "city" should have in size and geological boundaries and become something that can be arbitrarily expanded, just like "spreading the dough to make a huge pita," leading to bloated urbanization.

It is widely known that since the Reform and Opening Up, especially since the 1990s, cities, even towns, regardless of size, have at least one special development zone set up to attract domestic and foreign investment. This has grown into a mode for regional governments to increase revenue, just like real estate.

According to the National Bureau of Statistics, the nationwide investment in real estate was 8.6013 trillion yuan in 2013, a nominal increase of 19.8% compared to 2012 and 19.4% when the price was adjusted for, among which investment in housing increased by 19.4%. The area of new construction nationwide was 2.01208 billion m^2, an increase of 13.5% compared to 2012, among which the area of housing increased by 11.6%; the nationwide area of commercially sold buildings was 1.30551 billion m^2, an increase of 17.3% compared to 2012, among which the area of residential constructions increased 17.5%; the national sales of commercial buildings totaled 8.1428 trillion yuan, an increase of 26.3% compared to 2012, among which the sales of residential constructions increased by 26.6%; the year-end area of the lands bought by real estate developers was 388.14 million m^2, an increase of 8.8% compared to 2012.

By the end of December, the nationwide area of unsold commercial buildings was 492.95 m^2, an increase of 35.2% compared to the same period of 2012; the year-end paid-in capital of real estate developers totaled 12.2122 trillion yuan, an increase of 26.5% compared to 2012; and domestic loans increased by 33.1%, self-raised funds by 21.3%, and foreign capital by 32.8%.[16]

In fact, the growth rate of the GDP in 2013 was 7.7%, while in contrast, the growth rate of investment in real estate development or housing and the area of new construction all exceeded the growth of GDP by at least a factor of two. Debates began years ago in academic fields and related sectors of society on whether there were real estate bubbles and whether housing prices had reached a point to fall; and now, several years later, we have seen progressive increases year by year in expropriated lands for real estate development, construction of residential houses, and sales of commercial buildings with record housing prices one after another while the real estate industry has become an important source of regional governments' revenue, leaving them more and more dependent on land finance. In fact, no matter whether political résumés are built by chasing GDP growth or rescuing regional governments from financial difficulties, expropriation and sale of lands and urbanization are the easiest and the most effective strategies. However, the more effective these measures are, the more addictive they are and the higher debts the regional governments are in, while urbanization with arbitrarily decided wall building keeps speeding up.

Watching for the "Latin American trap" of urbanization

A review of world urbanization now and throughout the second half of the 20th century would show that developed countries had urbanized more than 65.0% of their populations by as early as the end of the 1960s and have since entered the third phase of urbanization, slowly progressing while pausing and lingering at the top of the s-shaped urbanization curve. In contrast, developing countries, as a whole, will not enter the third phase until the end of the 2030s.[17]

This is only a macroscopic picture. When the number is broken down into specific countries, especially those in Latin America, things vary considerably. For example, Argentina had urbanized more than 65.0% of its population by the beginning of the 1950s, Chile by the end of the 1950s, Cuba by the mid-1970s, and Brazil and Mexico by the end of the 1970s, and they all entered the third phase of slow progression with pauses and lingering. The in-advance urbanization of these countries is best represented by the megacities of Mexico City, Rio de Janeiro, and Bueno Aires, which still bear the marks of colonization or half-colonization that may be summarized by three coexisting deformities.

The first deformity is the coexistence of the advanced and the underdeveloped; on one hand, these megacities possess advanced science and technology, modern industries, and luxurious houses and corresponding modern facilities while, on the other hand, there are also primitive manual production, communities for the poor lacking the most basic infrastructure, and large numbers of slums that have been marginalized to suburbs.

The second deformity is the coexistence of the rich and the poor. Entrepreneurs, bankers, and high-ranking clerks receive high incomes and are superbly rich while the poor, especially those in slums, are destitute and many have to beg to survive.

The third deformity is the coexistence of the civilized and the uncivilized; resources of education, health, and culture are monopolized by the rich, who account for a small proportion of the population and live a civilized life that is not much different from the lives of people in developed countries while the poor have no access to such resources and cannot afford school or health care. Therefore, urbanization in Latin American countries is a kind of polarized urbanization between the rich and the poor, with the rich 10.0% of the population possessing 60.0% of the social wealth and about 40.0% destitute, among whom more than 60.0% live in cities, especially megacities. This has resulted in a large population of the unemployed in cities, with unemployment rates exceeding 10.0%, topping the unemployment rates of all other continents. Consequently, social clashes are common, and safety has become an important factor impacting political stability; meanwhile, lack of revenue has forced the governments to rely on other countries for city management to a large degree, resulting in huge debts, urban public services are in severe shortage, transport and supply of water and gas are in trouble, the environment is increasingly polluted, the prices of urban lands keep climbing, and the unemployed and the peasants who moved to cities have to move to the suburbs, forming large communities of the poor that "surround cities like villages" in complete contrast to the central areas of cities.

Such deformed urbanization in Latin America failed to not only bring vigor to the development of cities but also to create new opportunities for the development of the countryside or agriculture; instead, urbanization has become a stumbling block to the overall development of the urban and rural economies, a drag on national finance, and an obstacle to social development.

Up until now, China has not fallen into the "Latin American trap" of urbanization, which is a remarkable achievement and has received international acclaim. However, the risk of falling into the trap has increased after urbanization adopted a mode centered on bigness at the turn of the 21st century, which has manifested itself in the following aspects to various degrees.

One aspect is the fashion to chase bigness and Western styles for cities, especially megacities, as already mentioned. Haste is observed in enclosing lands, making meadows, shaping squares, widening roads, and erecting original landmarks to highlight the achievements of the regions. At the same time, illegal expropriation of peasants' lands and forced demolishment of residential houses have also been on the rise, and those who have lost their lands or houses cannot get reasonable compensation and settlement, leading to sharpened social contradictions.

Another aspect is that peasant workers have contributed to the construction of cities, but cannot share what they have helped build; they have become a marginalized class living outside the urban circle. They do not have equal rights with other urban residents in politics, the economy, education, health care, and social security, and are virtually quasi-urban residents living in cities with compromised rights and benefits. This is a new dual-sector urban society.

The third aspect is the considerable size of many city and suburb villages mostly occupied by peasant workers. The buildings and infrastructure inside these villages are poorly made, posing new challenges for city management and healthy development. All these aspects show an increased risk of falling into the "Latin American trap" for China, and it must be taken seriously and a solution is imperative.

Promoting coordinated development of urban and rural areas

On April 30, 2015, General Secretary Xi Jinping remarked in his speech on the 22nd group learning of the Political Bureau of the CCCPC:

> Industry and agriculture, as well as urban and rural areas, shall be taken as a whole and coordinated plans made for their development. Urban and rural areas shall be promoted to integrate each other and develop side by side in terms of planning, factor allocation, industry development, public services, and ecological protection. Efforts should be directed to establishing institutions and systems to integrate urban and rural areas and shaping a new urban–rural and industrial–agricultural relationship whereas industry facilitates agriculture, cities help villages, and industry and agriculture benefit each other and cities and villages are fully integrated.[18]

In my opinion, these remarks clarified the direction and gave basic requirements for urbanization reforms and the coordinated development of urban and rural areas. Indeed, urbanization reforms cannot only take cities and towns into consideration and must plan for the integrated whole of urban and rural areas, treading a path of coordinated and mutual development of both. The path differs fundamentally from urbanization at the cost of rural areas and must be followed if the "Latin American trap" is to be avoided.

Then how are the reforms performed and what are the major points? The answer is to start from practices while, one, facing the current problems during urbanization and correcting the wrong that there are more and bigger walled areas than cities and even only walled areas without cities, and two, solving the new problems during the transition of rural to urban population and realizing the coordinated development of urban and rural areas by transforming the peasants living in cities into real urban residents.

Urbanization reforms to promote the "city"

The foregoing analysis has shown that the current urbanization has problems with the speed, the structure, the quality, and the coordination of development, all of which can be tracked to one problem, i.e., the loss of the "city" during urbanization to certain degree. Therefore, reforms must target the "city," and through promoting the "city," drive the urbanization to transition and upgrade as well as facilitate coordinated development of urban and rural areas.

In the first place, conceptual clarification of urbanization is demanded. To clarify the concept, we must track back to the origin of the term. As mentioned earlier, *urbanization* is defined as the process of the growth in the urban population in the *Demographic Dictionary*. In Chinese, the word *city* (城市) is a compound of two characters, with the first denoting a walled area where the walls are built to defend against attacks from the outside and the second denoting a centralized market, which always grows big and becomes fixed and regular through development. Therefore, a city is a place where trades are frequent and is formed when the market is combined with an economy that has developed to a certain degree. The walled area and the market are inseparable for a city as the former defines the geographical bounds and the latter is the economic foundation; therefore, the two are closely associated with each other as well as facilitate each other while developing side by side. In the current age, except for a few cases with political, cultural, and military goals, cities are the consequence of expanded and upgraded industrialization and of informatization and industrialization.

The next question is how the urbanization of building walled areas that has become prevalent originated. It was "made in China" or "created in China" and evolved with time. After the People's Republic of China was established in 1949, the focus of the government shifted from the countryside to cities and a great deal of attention was given to the management of the urban population. In 1951, approved by the Government Administration Council of the Central People's Government, the Ministry of Public Security published the *Temporary Regulations on the Management of Urban Household Registration*, which set up the rules for managing urban families and their migration, births, and deaths. The *Regulations* only covered cities and towns were not included in urban management at the time.

In June 1955, the *Instruction of the State Council on Establishing the Regular Household Registration System* made a small step forward; it mandated that "*hukou* should be registered in grassroots public security stations in cities and gather-towns and in people's committees in villages and the towns without a grassroots public security station."[19] It was only a small step forward because, one, the concept of gather-towns was mentioned for the first time and gather-towns were then officially recognized, and, two, gather-towns were divided into city-towns and rural-towns based on whether there was a grassroots public security station, and *hukou* was registered and managed in the former by the stations or by people's committees in the latter. In other words, gather-towns had dual identities and were not exactly towns yet.

In November of the same year, another small step was made in the *Regulations on the Classification of Urban and Rural Areas*, in which places were defined as cities or towns if, one, they were the location of people's committee of cities or of counties (or *qi*) or, two, they had more than 2,000 regular residents while at least 50.0% were non-rural. This was the first time cities and towns were listed together, a pioneering act to include towns as urban areas, which marked the official start of urbanization. However, under the highly centralized command economy at the time, migration between urban and rural areas was strictly inhibited while urbanization was often compromised by control of building new towns and downsizing suburbs, resulting in the lingering and hesitation of urbanization for long periods in the 1960s and 1970s.

Everything would sprout quickly if restricted while also saving up energy for a long time. Urbanization drove to a fast track rapidly after the Reform and Opening Up and instilled new vigor and vitality in society. I performed a literature review and found that the concept of building cities and towns was used as early as a 1984 book that resulted from a study the World Bank performed on China's economy, *Making Cities and Towns: International Experiences and Prospects for China*.[20] At the time, discussions were conducted on whether to translate the word *urbanization* into a Chinese phrase of making cities or making cities and towns, and the latter was chosen eventually due to the low urbanization degree then, merely 23.0% urban population, setting China at the beginning stage of urbanization, or the bottom of the s-shaped curve when the rural population migrated mostly to small cities and towns; meanwhile, the government was striving to develop small cities and towns vigorously and medium cities with moderate efforts but to inhibit big cities strictly, and the idea of making cities and towns seemed to fit in with the government's policy, thus the term then became widely used.

To be fair, the urbanization focused on developing small cities and towns for nearly 30 years played its due role, transmitted positive energy, and made undeniable contributions. However, making cities and towns is not a standard concept of urbanization because, as mentioned earlier, it equals making cities and small cities, with partial redundancy in connotations despite its original goal to focus urbanization efforts on small cities and towns.

Furthermore, even when the term of making cities and towns as the translation for *urbanization* was acceptable back then, it is no longer suitable now as the current urbanization is already in the second phase in the middle part of the s-shaped curve and is now focused on big cities. As mentioned earlier, in theory, the denotation of urbanization, when the "city/market" is abstracted away, means that cities and towns are only walled areas and may survive and develop independently of the "city/market," which severs the inseparable connection intrinsic to walled areas and the "city/market" and ultimately violates the reasonable denotation of cities and towns based on the "city/market." In terms of the connotations, the size and geographical boundaries of cities and towns are decided by the "city/market," and when that is lost, they become something that can be decided arbitrarily.

In practice, when the "city/market" is abstracted away from walled areas, walled areas are walled areas on their own and the "city/market" is the "city/market" on its own, neither of which relies on the other, blurring the line between normal urbanization and man-made city building; cities may even emerge built for the purpose of urbanization, a kind of reversed urbanization when cities and towns are built first and the "city/market" promoted next, laying various "theoretical foundations" for bloated urbanization. Therefore, the true meaning of *urbanization* must be clarified and the ambiguous concepts that only see walled areas but not the "city/market" extinguished.

In the second place, reforms must be advanced of city institutions and the relationship between the government and the market straightened. The bloated or low-quality urbanization mentioned earlier has its particular environment to develop, and the environment is the unreasonable allocation of urbanization resources, which is rooted in problems in the distribution mechanisms. The unreasonable allocation of resources is shown by the following three "mismatches."

The first mismatch is between land allocation and the market in that the market has not played its due role to decide the allocation. The "trilogy" of managing real estate development during urbanization, described earlier, puts the government between peasants on one end and real estate developers and customers on the other and plays the central and dominating role in allocating lands. With time, real estate finance has become an important source of revenue of regional governments and the latter become more and more dependent on the former. Such land finance does not only help obtain incomes by expropriating and then selling lands, which is of course the prominent as well as obvious goal, but also effectively boosts the credit of the regional governments through mortgaging the expropriated lands. However, negative effects have also come along as the deficits of the regional governments, including regional debts, have snowballed, bringing increasing risk to the governments. There is currently a total 20 trillion yuan of regional debts, and if it keeps growing, it is alarming and the risk must be watched although the debts have always been presented as "under control."

The second mismatch is between the allocation of human resources and urban-rural areas in that the former has long been restricted by the "dual-structured" urban-rural institutions. China's urbanization is currently located at the middle part of the s-shaped curve, and its main engine is still the migration of rural laborers and their dependents to cities and towns. According to statistical data, in 2000, 2005, 2010, and 2013, there were 144, 186, 261, and 279 million people, respectively, with separated residence and *hukou*, and 121, 147, 221, and 257 million migrants, respectively, showing stepwise increases over the years. Among these people, the majority migrated to cities and towns and were included as urban residents in various surveys. These numbers continued to grow in recent years despite a somewhat slowing trend in population migration and certain new patterns. Unfortunately, such large numbers of transformed agricultural population have been denied urban *hukou* due to the "dual-structured" institutions that separate urban and rural areas and cannot become true urban residents. This situation has long impacted the employment of human resources and their potentials negatively.

The third mismatch is between the allocation of resources and industries due to a twisted pattern of coexisting low-priced lands and high-priced housing. The acceleration of urbanization since the Reform and Opening Up has relied on two engines: one is the translocation of cheap, rural laborers to cities and towns, which has decreased the cost of labor, and the other is the continuous supply of cheap land resources, which has decreased the cost of land. The two "parents" (quoting William Petty, "labor is the Father and active principle of wealth, as lands are the Mother"), combined, have set forth the prosperity of their offspring, urbanization. Regional governments get profits by selling lands to real estate developers at fairly high prices that have been expropriated at much lower prices while the developers also get considerable profits by continuously pushing high the house prices; even the peasants who have given up on the right of operation of the lands get compensations although the compensations are much lower compared to what the governments and the developers get from the whole process.

The rapid progression of urbanization has boosted demands in real estate, and the continuously growing prices of houses have activated real estate transactions; as a result, the excessively high house prices have remained high and the mismatched resource allocation has been sustained as well. However, the "trilogy" of land expropriation, land auction, and marketing of commercial houses, based on the twisted pattern of cheap lands and expensive housing, has pushed the debts of the regional governments to climb by providing the lands as mortgages for their loans.

According to the National Audit Office (NAO), by the end of June 2013, the total debt of the central government with a direct responsibility for debt payment had reached 9.812948 trillion yuan, that with a guarantee responsibility 260.072 billion yuan, and that with a possible debt rescue responsibility 2.311084 trillion yuan, all of which totaled 12.384101 trillion yuan; meanwhile, the total debt of all regional governments with a direct responsibility for debt payment had reached 10.885917 trillion yuan, that with a guarantee responsibility 2.665577 trillion yuan, and that with a possible debt rescue responsibility 4.339372 trillion yuan, all of which totaled 17.890866 trillion yuan. With all things combined, the direct and indirect debts of the central and regional governments totaled 30.27497 trillion yuan.[21]

Apparently, such a huge amount of debt cannot be ignored. In particular, the total debt that regional governments were directly or indirectly responsible for exceeded 10 trillion yuan, already accounting for a considerable proportion of the regional financial revenue. The debt risk has emerged in that some regional governments had to loan more money in order to pay for the debts. The debts of regional governments were mostly born with and increased because of the real estate business, worsening the already mismatched wealth resource allocation. The root of the mismatch is the heavy reliance of regional governments on land, which, together with the excessive dominance of the governments and the weakened market, leads to the absence of the market in decisions of resource allocation.

These three mismatches of resources in urbanization are caused by, aside from mistakes in theories and people's understanding of urbanization, problems in the institutions and thus the solution can only be found in the institutions. In fact, it was already pointed out in the *Decision by CCCPC on Several Important Issues of Comprehensively Deepening the Reform* that

> the reform of the economic system [was] the key to comprehensively deepening the Reform and the central task [was] to straighten up the relationship between the government and the market so that the latter [might] decide the resource allocation and the former better [play] its due roles.[22]

Guided by this statement, further reforms need to reset the functions and roles of the government and the market during urbanization.

To reset the functions and roles of the government, conceptual transformations must be made first. The *Decision* by the CCCPC to comprehensively deepen the reform specified to "resolve the problems of an imperfect economic system, excessive interference of the government, and insufficient supervision"[23] while stressing that at the core of the reform of the economic system was the relationship between the government and the market waiting to be straightened up. Indeed, an overall review of various problems of urbanization may nail down the problematic relationship between the government and the market and defects of the institutions and the system. As stated earlier, urbanization is essentially the consequence of economic development, social advancement, and structural transition of populations. Although urban economies, once prospering, usually contribute immensely to the development of the entire society, it is still erroneous to reverse the relationship between cities and economies, i.e., urbanization cannot be taken as the origin of and engine for development; neither can it be used as a tool to push economic growth or prevent GDP from declining. Therefore, all parties involved in urbanization, including the government, must transform their concepts from valuing GDP to orienting toward people and hold urbanization as a way to coordinate development of urban and rural areas and to better the lives of both urban and rural residents.

Second, the government's roles must be transformed. In the past, the government was always at the front line of urbanization, taking care of everything from setting the tactics for the development of cities to planning and implementation of roads, transportation, housing, factories, mines, supplies of electricity and water, cultural development, education, sports, public health and hygiene, and garbage facilities, playing the triple role of designer, director, and actor. In fact, many things should have been left to the market, yet the government covered all, only to be blamed in the end. To transform the roles of the government is to make it take on the responsibility to set up and implement the strategy, plans, policies, and standards for a city and to provide supervision of the market and public services to the residents. In other words, the government should stop "acting," and assume a new triple role of designer, director, and supervisor.

Third, the government must withdraw from certain institutions and mechanisms, i.e., outdated, inappropriate regulations and rules such as improper approval and transactions. The government has made considerable progress to this end in the past year, and many approval procedures were eliminated from both the central and regional levels, the marked benefits of which may drive further deepening of reforms and reforms in other areas. After all, only when the government has withdrawn from inappropriate institutions and mechanisms can the market really exert its decisive role in allocating resources, and this is the unique situation of China.

To reset the functions and roles of the market is to allow the market to assume the "acting role" now that the government has taken on the triple role of designer, director, and supervisor, so that the market may set the rules for entrance and standards for selection, exerting its decisive role in resource allocation. In addition, the legal status of individuals and organizations during urbanization must be specified so that the eligible may become truly independent legal persons; the peasants in rural areas with contracted lands must be assured their rights to possess, use, benefit from, and transfer and mortgage the right to operate the lands as well as be allowed to buy in with their land rights to develop agricultural industries.

The transfer of contracting and operating rural contracted lands on open markets to professionals, family farms, rural cooperatives, and agricultural enterprises to reach diversity of scale should be encouraged. In fact, the green light to the marketing of the operation rights of rural contracted lands has not only extended the development of agriculture significantly but has also opened up a whole new world for healthy progression of urbanization. When resources are allocated by the market, the values of land and labor become well founded and the excessively low prices of land and labor and excessively high prices of housing may be corrected. Together corrected is the uneven distribution of benefits among peasants, developers, consumers, and the government.

In the third place, regional debts must be carefully controlled through reforms and appropriate institutions. For a while, government debt, especially the part owed by regional ones, has become a hotspot in the media and great controversies have arisen during discussions of the problems, risks, and countermeasures. Some hold that regional debts have amounted to an extremely high level with a growing risk of collapsing, and thus must be handled immediately so that regional governments may be free from heavy debt, while others believe that China's regional debts, although not negligible, are still in a normal range compared to the international community and are under control with an acceptable debt ratio. Then what is a reasonable perspective to evaluate the current risk of the regional debt, and how to pave a road for reforms that fit China's conditions? Further in-depth exploration is needed to find the answer.

First, the current regional debt and the risk it brings must be objectively evaluated. If we look back at the **New Year Messages** in the "two newspapers and one magazine" (*People's Daily*, *PLA Daily*, and *Hongqi* Magazine) from the past few years during the Cultural Revolution to the eve of the Reform and Opening Up, we may be impressed by the pride conveyed in the messages that "we [were] not in debt, foreign or domestic," despite the near-collapsed national economy at the time, which was always used as strong evidence that we were in a great era and the society was prosperous. It may seem absurd now, but it was a kind of self-praise at a time when things were all shut in and the economy was barely breathing, and it was quite persuasive and succeeded in encouraging people.

After the Reform and Opening Up, economic reforms took steps to eventually steer toward a market economy, and the bondage of "no foreign or domestic debt" was certainly broken while various financial leverages were employed to mobilize the economy in order to facilitate socioeconomic development. In the process, regional debt, in the forms of bonds issued by regional governments and other types of dominant and recessive debts, was not only inevitable but also beneficial to some degree. Of course, the "degree" must be specified reasonably and a higher degree is entirely harmful.

Changes in China's regional debt across the board have led to a growing debt ratio, especially in some prefecture-level cities, county-level cities, and towns where the local governments loaned huge amounts of money to build various "new districts," "industrial districts," and "cultural districts," leading to an excessively increasing debt of local finance; meanwhile, the debt has been extended to many aspects, with direct and indirect, dominant and recessive, and domestic and foreign types, covering a wide range of departments, regions, and enterprises; at the same time, supervision of debts has been loose in that there is lack of monitoring at the grassroots level of mortgaging, late payment of salaries and pensions, late payment of purchases, case-specific loans made by the local governments, and enterprise deficits, leading the debts to be long hidden, with some completely or partially out of control. Under these circumstances, regional governments have quickly piled up their ever-growing debts, which has now become a big challenge in economic activities.

As shown by the aforementioned data released by the NAO, the nationwide total of direct and indirect debts owed by the government had reached 30.27497 trillion yuan by the end of June 2013, among which the government was responsible to repay 68.4%, had a guarantee responsibility for 9.7%, and had a possible debt rescue responsibility for 21.9%.

Apparently, the amount directly owed by the government was immense and it would be extremely difficult to repay, which demands a reliable evaluation of the placement of the debt ratio. In my opinion, China's debt ratio, as implicated in the aforementioned data, is at an upper-medium level if compared to the world, lower than Europe, North America, and some Latin American countries, but higher than most developing countries. In fact, although China's debt is still distant from a crisis, or, as the second opinion cited earlier puts it, the debt is under control, the regional debt has been alarmingly high, and the risk it brings cannot be overlooked as it has already exerted its huge impact on overall socioeconomic development.

In some regions, the operation of the local governments has been compromised as high debt ratios have trapped the governments' finances and forced them to loan money from enterprises, some executives of which were even forced to hide from lenders. Meanwhile, normal government expenditure has also been affected under the pressure of immense debt, which drives the governments to get more loans from banks, taking on new debts to repay the old ones; thus the governments cannot function normally and their administrative abilities and efficiency are compromised; furthermore, the growing debts of some grassroots governments have already crossed the debt threshold observed internationally, with debt crises having already broken out to various degrees.

Second, international experiences, both of successes and of failures, are valuable in China's reforms. Here the bankruptcy of Detroit in the United States may give us many valuable lessons and inspirations. The city of Detroit once enjoyed international fame as "the world's automobile industrial city." Housing the biggest automobile manufacturing companies of the United States, Ford, General Motor, and Chrysler, and automobile-related industries such as steel, engines, electronics, meters, glass, plastics, and tires, Detroit had a high level of specialization, standardization, serialization, and centralization. At its peak, 40.0% of the employed in Detroit worked in automobile manufacturing companies, and the city population reached 1.80 million in the 1950s, winning Detroit the title of the "American Paris."

Unfortunately, however, since the 1970s, hit by oil crises, stagflation of the U.S. economy, and the rise of European and Japanese automobile companies, Detroit started to descend from its position in the automobile industry as well as in the entire economy. Struck by the U.S. subprime mortgage crisis in 2007 and 2008, factories in Detroit made large-scale layoffs, real estate collapsed, house prices plummeted, and the social order was completely messed up; meanwhile, the unemployment rate rocketed and stayed high for a long time, and the rich and middle classes moved out in herds, leaving Detroit only about 700,000 residents, which is not even 40.0% of its peak population. Consequently, the government revenue shrank acutely, and it became increasingly difficult for the local government to make ends meet. Eventually, in July 2013, the Detroit government was forced to file for bankruptcy. After long deliberation, the U.S. federal judges finally ruled that the application was in agreement with federal bankruptcy laws, marking Detroit as the biggest city approved for bankruptcy in U.S. history.

Note that city bankruptcies and enterprise bankruptcies in the United States are just as similar to as they are different from each other. They are similar in that both are governed by federal bankruptcy laws, and the assets of filers are counted before any arrangement to repay debts is made. They are different in that when a city files for bankruptcy, the assets to be counted, sold, and used to repay debts do not include all the assets the city owns, but only those in the government's financial revenue. In particular, after filing for bankruptcy, a city may use the protection time to adjust taxation to increase revenue, layoff government workers and cut down public expenditure, and reorganize debts to extend due dates in order to increase the government's tax revenue and to improve its capacity to repay debts and to survive the financial crisis safely.

The legal procedures after Detroit filed for bankruptcy are not complete yet, and it is not clear whether Detroit will eventually repay all of its debts, but we may learn many lessons from how Detroit got itself to the step of filing for bankruptcy and how it used the filing to handle the crisis. The following aspects are particularly important lessons.

First, regional debts must be carefully kept under control. Detroit did not fall into bankruptcy overnight. It was the outcome of long terms of unbalanced incomes and expenses and deficit accumulation by the city. It has been more than 200 years since Detroit was established. Located at the heart of the Great Lakes region, Detroit quickly prospered when the Industrial Revolution advanced to the stage dominated by automobiles. As a result, government finances also grew significantly with the growth of the automobile and related industries. Detroit reached its peak in the 1950s and the 1960s, becoming a dazzling pearl among all automobile cities in the United States and around the world. However, as the old saying goes, "successful due to Xiaohe, defamed due to Xiaohe." Detroit rose because of automobiles and declined because of automobiles.

When the Japanese and German automobile industries rose with competitive advantages in cost, price, quality, and practical use, the "Grandpa automobiles" made in Detroit suddenly lost a large chunk of their market share, bringing decreases to the city revenue as well. Then the 2007–2008 U.S. subprime mortgage crisis came, and hit by it, factories made immense layoffs, the unemployed increased in large numbers, and the rich and middle classes moved out of the city, all leading the government budget to lose balance and to have increasing difficulties to make ends meet.

By 2013, the debt owed by the city government of Detroit totaled $18 billion, leaving but one way for the city to go: filing for bankruptcy. In fact, there was at least more than a decade, maybe even tens of years, from the "old good days" to the days when the city was deep in debt, yet the government did nothing to avoid the latter, but kept loaning money until it could no longer survive. To be fair, it was rooted in the current financial system in the United States, and the city government of Detroit could do very little to save itself.

China has totally different administrative and financial systems from the United States, with different means and compositions to obtain and spend revenue. However, one lesson must be learned here: once the expense of a regional government exceeds its revenue by a certain scale, effective measures must be taken to increase revenue, such as taxation and cutting down public expense, to balance expense and revenue as soon as possible. In my opinion, some regional governments in China have already reached this scale as their debt ratios have exceeded the threshold, and thus decisive and effective measures must be taken to prevent the debt ratios from further climbing and to take a turn for a balanced sheet.

Second, urbanization must be oriented toward people. In the history of Detroit, the status in and the impact on its economy of the automobile industry is far more than just a pillar industry, but is indeed its "life industry." At its peak, more than 80.0% of Detroit's production was made by the automobile industry, marking the correlation between the city and automobiles such that the former prospered and declined with the rise and fall of the latter.

Under such a circumstance, the automobile industry became the key to the city's prosperity, and the development of the city was thus oriented toward automobiles while people gathered around the automobile industry when it developed and left when it declined. After all, most of the employed in Detroit worked in the automobile industry or those related to it, and the prosperity of the industry decided whether the majority of the residents would stay or leave.

The lesson here is that lack of diversity in the industries of a city leads to singular employment structures of the laborers and singular compositions of the scientific, educational, and cultural elements of the population, and the population is easily bonded to the singular industrial structure, leading to failures to orient city development toward people. Some cities in China have such a singular industrial structure, especially some cities based on resources.

For example, a group of resource cities was built after the new China was established to speed industrialization, among which the city of Fu Shun won the title of the "capital of coal," An Shan the title of "capital of steel," and Yi Chun the title of "city of forests," and all of these cities had glorious histories and contributed significantly to the industrialization of China.

However, when the resources, such as the coal in the coal city, the steel in the steel city, and the wood in the forest city, neared exhaustion, these cities became resource-exhausted and showed characteristics also seen in Detroit: the single industries could not support the cities' survival, economic growth slowed down, and the working-age population began to move out. Such cities are now more than sporadic cases, and there are more in the three provinces in the northeast than anywhere else, although some had already showed up in the Huabei area.

In fact, from the 1950s to the 1970s, these cities all prospered, with large scales of increases in production and in immigrant laborers and great achievements in construction. However, the immigrant laborers were mostly physical workers who did not receive high-level education and the majority were males. There were not very many enterprises that provided suitable positions for women, leading to a high sex ratio among the adults in these cities. Detroit's bankruptcy has taught us a dear lesson that a singular industrial structure and failure to orient urbanization toward people would not withstand oil, financial, or economic crises.

On the way to informatization, industrialization, and modernization, cities, especially big-sized ones, should have their own featured industries and unique characteristics while the featured industries and unique characteristics cannot be featured to the extent of the automobile industry in Detroit, and the development should always be oriented toward people.

Third, real estate bubbles must be watched carefully. Detroit used to have as many as 1.80 million people, but has only about 700,000 now, less than 40.0% of its peak. A large number of houses were vacated and house prices dove several times, but few residents have shown interest in purchase no matter how cheap the houses are now. It is said that a few thousand dollars is enough to buy a second-hand house, but due to the high property tax and that the buyer has certain responsibilities for repaying the loan that the previous owner obtained by mortgaging the house, few would actually purchase the house as the collective fees would be quite high. This directly impacted the government's tax revenue negatively and became one of the reasons for the government to file for bankruptcy.

Similarly in China, growing house prices combined with regional governments' land finance after the turn of the 21st century resulted in a large number of vacant houses and empty cities and "ghost cities" emerged, driving urbanization far away from the people-oriented principle. It's been a common practice in many places that urbanization is used to attract investment, build infrastructure, and stimulate economies, resulting in the urbanization of land in advance of the urbanization of people, planting the seed for urbanization bubbles. When there is potential danger, actions are to be taken to eliminate it. In particular, the cities on the list of "ghost cities" must be taken seriously and restored to urbanization oriented toward people and based on the "city/market."

Fourth, legal protection should be provided for cities seeking bankruptcy. When it filed for bankruptcy, Detroit was actually protected and offered an opportunity for reorganization so that the city government might replan its taxation, issue bonds, cut down public expenditure, and adjust various policies in the hope of getting itself back on its feet. The city was financially bankrupt, but the civil functions were still working. The aim of the city government was to adjust its policies and regulations in the protection time to pave the way for a new financial balance.

In comparison, there has not been a single law or code governing city bankruptcy in China yet, or any practical management measure. What a pity! What is available now is just to rely on temporary policies and to take appropriate actions. For example, issuance of municipal bonds is a way to alleviate debt pressure, but the quota is now entirely decided by the state and it cannot eradicate debt problems. What may eradicate the problems is to include regional debts in the nationwide frame of constructing the rule of law and to release a law on city bankruptcy.

Exploring the path of coordinated development of urban and rural areas

All of the problems described here, be it bloated urbanization such as walled areas built bigger than cities or the failure of urbanization to orient toward people such as land urbanization ahead of population urbanization, are highlighted as the discordance of rural and urban economic development and the asymmetry between the mechanisms and institutions that govern the emigration of rural population and those that govern the integration of immigration cities. Apparently, it is a *sine qua none* to choose a path of coordinated development of both urban and rural areas, and reforms to this end are imminent. However, what is the foothold of the reforms? Where do the reforms cut in? In my opinion, the key is transforming emigrant rural populations into real urban residents, and this is where the reforms should start.

First, the transformation is a practical problem that has to be solved. Since the Reform and Opening Up, the scale of those with separated residence and *hukou* sites has been on the rise, together with the rural population who has left their villages, which has been growing even faster, bringing ever-larger waves of "peasant workers." According to the National Bureau of Statistics, the nationwide number of people who resided in a different place from their *hukou* locations, or those with separate residence and *hukou* sites, reached 289 million in 2013, among whom 245 million were migrants and 170 million were taken into statistics as urban residents. All these people would either go back to villages or stay in cities and towns. We should offer the latter with justification of urban residency, i.e., acknowledgment of their urban identity and transformation officially into urban residents.

Next, transformation is a demand of further urbanization. Urbanization is indispensable to complete informatization, industrialization, and agricultural modernization, and at the core of the series is the people-oriented urbanization that relies on the integration of industries and urban development. As already shown by practical experiences, if the migrant rural population who are mostly agricultural laborers may stay in cities and towns and become equal residents as those born urban, urbanization will boost economic development through consumption; otherwise, if the migrant rural population keeps flowing between urban and rural areas, an "amphibian" sort of urbanization will only boost the economy through investment. In the latter scenario, large numbers of peasant workers build buildings, roads, and infrastructure such as water and electricity supply, and then move to another city to build more, playing a role of constructors but not participating in the development of the cities they built. This is the underlying reason why urbanization in the 21st century only boosted investment.

Last, mature experiences and measures are available for transformation. In the recent years, trials were made in several places such as Guangdong Province to transform migrant rural populations into true urban residents, and those tested in medium- and small-sized cities and village towns were particularly successful, and their measures would be easier for cities and towns with similar conditions to apply. The most important message of the experiences is that equal rights for all must be persisted with and methods to implement them must be carried out from the surface to the heart and from the near to the far and gradually perfected. In fact, clear tactics and policies were already given in the *Decision* by the CCCPC on comprehensively deepening the Reform, which has provided reliable reference for reforms to start from transformation.

Under the current conditions in China, the most effective prevention of falling into the Latin American trap of urbanization is to help the peasants working and doing business in cities and towns to truly integrate into the cities and towns and become new urban residents who are essentially the same as the original urban residents. To achieve this goal, the following suggestions may help.

In the first place, peasant workers should be allowed the same status and rights as urban residents. Some of the restrictions on the working conditions of peasant workers in cities and towns have been lifted now, but thresholds are still common in many cities, especially megacities. For example, some positions are only open to those holding the local urban *hukou*, and peasant workers are shut out. School enrollment relies on juniors' residential status in the neighborhood, and children of peasant workers are essentially denied the right to receive national education. However, shelter, employment, and schooling are the basic rights that everyone is entitled to; when denied these rights in the cities and towns they work in, peasant workers are easily marginalized.

In the second place, peasant workers should be given more opportunities of shelter and employment. Having a residence and working are the two most basic demands of urban peasant workers, as well as the basic conditions to sustain the reproduction of laborers. The most important lesson of the Latin American urbanization trap is that peasants, after moving into cities, cannot afford regular housing due to low incomes or long terms of unemployment and have to occupy vacant or public spaces and put up shabby living units with deserted bricks, forming closed or partially closed slums that lack clean water, public hygiene facilities, and necessary communication means and that are frequented by crimes; some slums even become headquarters for criminal gangs, greatly threatening social security.

To prevent the emergence of such Latin American slums in cities and towns, we must employ both the "invisible hand" and the "visible hand," i.e., the power and the mechanisms of the market and the government, to help peasant workers settle in cities and towns. In fact, housing is closely associated with employment, and if they are well employed, peasant workers will have less difficulty with dwelling and vice versa. A prominent problem now is the embarrassing situation that while a shortage of peasant workers has prevailed in some cities, there has also been a shortage of employment in the same cities such that many peasants cannot find jobs because most are not well educated and have not received specific technological training. Therefore, to avoid falling into the Latin American trap of population urbanization, absorption of peasant workers into the job market must be treated as one of the most important tasks and help with finding jobs may be delivered to them through professional training.

Third, a green light should be given to peasant workers for both staying in and leaving cities and towns. One of the underlying reasons for the emergence and expansion of the Latin American slums is that the peasants had completely lost their lands when they moved to cities and they have no way back. In China, the acute expansion of cities, especially big ones, has already resulted in a large number of peasants losing their lands, and they have to rely on cities to survive, becoming urban residents-to-be. Therefore, expropriation of arable lands must be minimized during urbanization, and peasant workers are to be allowed to freely flow between urban and rural areas in that those who have moved to cities should be allowed to keep their contracted lands for at least a while so that they can come back and pick up their agrarian lives if they cannot survive in the cities.

In addition, during the process of land expropriation, the peasants who lose their lands must be first reasonably compensated and any exploitation of them by unfair exchange must be strictly prohibited; next, arrangements should be made for the peasants to get jobs, with labor contracts properly signed so that the peasants who have lost their lands are guaranteed fairly stable jobs and incomes in cities.

In the fourth place, the livelihood of peasant workers should be included in urban development planning. To achieve coordinated development of both urban and rural areas, we must make long-term plans that include the employment, housing, schooling, cultural lives, and community management of peasant workers. When organizing for planning and implementation, the government should make as many efforts as possible to give peasant workers and their families favorable policies to share with them the benefits of urban development and to encourage them to fully integrate into the political, economic, and cultural lives of the cities by improving themselves to become qualified urban residents.

In the past, various thresholds and requirements barred peasant workers from integrating into city lives while they were also discriminated against to various degrees. Many of these problems have been and are being resolved. Those that have not been solved must be studied continuously until solved so that eligible peasant workers may enjoy equal rights with all urban residents. Meanwhile, strengthened management should be delivered where needed and in doing so, the government should be bold while basing its actions on solid facts and scientific measures.

On the other hand, there should be a certain threshold for peasant workers to become urban residents. After all, rural population still accounts for 45.0% of the total population in China, which is overall in the late phase of the demographic "golden age," and it is thus impossible to make any peasant, after moving into a city, an urban resident unconditionally and guarantee him a house, a job, and social security, which will cause disastrous social problems even if it is at all possible. The threshold should include three conditions, i.e., the peasant worker has moved into the city for a reasonable period of time, say, half a year; he has a relatively stable job, income, and a fixed abode; and he has no criminal record. If these three conditions are met, the peasant worker may acquire the rights and benefits of an urban resident and be counted in the city's residential population. In contrast, those who do not meet these three conditions after the allowed period of time are to be taken into shelters and managed so as to help them go back to their original rural residence. After all, if those who are unemployed for long terms, have no fixed abode, and may mess up the social order are allowed to stay in cities, they may very well gather and form communities similar to the Latin American slums, breaking the bond that coordinates the development of urban and rural development.

These measures are fair and just in that peasant workers have half a year to settle down with jobs, shelter, and incomes to integrate into city lives. They are also reasonable as management must be in place with those wandering from job to job and place to place for long terms, which has been practiced even in Western advanced countries. It is not meant to discriminate against peasant workers. It is meant to properly manage cities, especially big ones and megacities, which cannot keep large numbers of unemployed, homeless populations. Standardized management meets the demands not only for city construction and development but also for the construction and development of a new socialist countryside.

Helping the peasants who cannot stay in cities go back to their rural homes and resume their agricultural work ensures the labor supply for developing agriculture, which at the same time is also a responsible attitude toward those who moved to cities recklessly and blindly, and guiding and helping them work at the positions that best suit them is also a contribution to the coordinated development of urban and rural areas.

In the fifth place, the areas where peasant workers emigrate from must be constructed into the new socialist countryside. One prominent feature of China's urbanization is to develop agriculture and the countryside while cities are pushed to advance. Both urbanization with balanced urban and rural development previously advocated for and the new type of urbanization currently standardized aim to bring rural areas on board and to have a kind of urbanization with urban and rural areas facilitating and coordinating each other's development through advancing agricultural development and the new countryside.

Such urbanization is fundamentally different from the kind in Western countries that was advanced at the cost of the countryside. However, many problems disrupted synchronized and coordinated development, especially the structure of those left behind in the countryside, the "hollowing out" of land, and the transfer of land. These problems can only be tackled by reforms and after they are solved, coordinated development between urban and rural areas will continue to march forward.

One problem is the population structure of those left behind in rural areas. Large numbers of rural laborers moved to cities and towns, leaving behind them "the troop of March 8, June 1, and September 9" – women, children, and the elderly–leading to a sharply unbalanced structure of the rural population. Left-behind women are rural women whose husbands are not home for long terms and live in empty homes. They must take on the responsibilities that used to be on the shoulders of their husbands, such as farming, while taking care of children, the elderly, and the family social lives, and many feel weak from time to time. In addition, they are tested in the long-distance relationship and tortured by emotional distress. As a result, they are faced with many unforeseen difficulties and problems in economic activities, material lives, spiritual pursuits, and social participation.

In fact, for quite some time, the rural left-behind women have become inspiration for many writers and a number of novels have been published, some of which have enjoyed fame, and they depicted the women from multiple perspectives and levels in terms of their diligence, love for life, emotional entanglement, inner world, and abilities to manage complex environments, reflecting the changes after rural laborers left the countryside for work and inspiring in many ways.

Left-behind children are those who do not leave with one or both parents for long terms and are raised by grandparents or other relatives. There are many problems with these children. They have limited contacts, in person or through other ways, with their parents who moved to cities and towns, and can seldom feel the affection from them, living in a state like half orphans. In some provinces in western China that are the major sources of urban peasant workers, a class of "semi-orphans" has been formed with a considerable size, and these children are all negatively affected in their physical and emotional health such as growth, study, social behaviors, and especially mental health.

According to the *2015 White Paper on the Mental Condition of China's Left-Behind Children*, there are currently approximately 61.02 million left-behind children, among whom 29.4%, or 19.73 million, see their parents once or twice a year, and 15.1%, or 9.21 million, did not see their parents in the past year; in terms of other communication means such as talking on the phone, 10.4%, or 6.34 million, talk to their parents three to four times a year, 10.2%, or 6.22 million, talk to their parents once to twice a year, and 4.3%, or 2.62 million, have never talked to their parents on the phone. Seeing parents in person or talking to them on the phone directly affects children's mental health as well as academic performance and lives, and the impact on their mental health is particularly prominent. The overall association is that the less children see their parents or talk to them on the phone, the less possessed they are by joy and the more by nervousness, fear, and depression; in contrast, the more they see their parents or talk to them on the phone, the more often they feel joy and the less often they feel nervousness, fear, and depression.[24]

The left-behind elderly are the natural consequence of the migration of large numbers of rural laborers to cities and towns. As the old saying goes, "hometowns are hard to leave." Young laborers leave the countryside for cities and towns and older people stay put and become the guardians of the hometowns. On one hand, they still need to work to the level they are capable of to support themselves and, on the other hand, some of them assume the responsibility to take care of their grandchildren, which becomes a unique scene of "September 9 looking after June 1." The majority of the older people in rural areas are not entitled to pensions due to the previous restrictive dual-structured old-age insurance system in urban and rural areas, and have to work and rely on children's feed, social welfare, and the social rescue system to support themselves.

Now that the new rural old-age insurance scheme has been implemented nationwide and covered all the elderly, peasants have started to benefit from it. However, the new scheme offers only a small pension, which in some places is only 200 to 300 yuan a year, and sometimes even lower than 100 yuan, and is thus not enough to support the elderly. In addition, when it comes to caring for the extremely elderly, there are even more difficulties as children are out working and social institutes that provide elderly care are extremely limited in number and service, making these elderly the underprivileged among the elderly who are already underprivileged. This difficult situation has resulted from the loss of balance in the age and sex structures in rural areas during urbanization and demands immediate solutions.

These problems in the age and sex structures of the rural left-behind population cry for appropriate reforms as soon as possible. In my opinion, reforms should be conducted in the following three aspects. One, the dual-structured *hukou* system between urban and rural areas must be abolished and when a peasant worker lands his/her *hukou* in the city, his/her spouse, children, and parents should also be given *hukou* in the same city. It breaks one's heart to imagine that one peasant worker moves to a city to work and get the *hukou*, but his/her spouse, children, and parents will stay in the countryside forever, and there always has to be a way for a family to reunite. Family reunion is not just an emotional need. It is also demanded by practical lives and the solution to the needs of the young and the elderly.

Furthermore, from the perspective of socioeconomic development, it also lowers the cost of production and living, improves the health of the population, and facilitates economic, scientific, educational, cultural, and social development. Two, the old-age security benefits, social welfare, and the rescue service should be elevated by a large scale. The central piece is to improve the quality and the level of the new rural old-age insurance scheme based on the implementation of the unified old-age insurance system nationwide. The scheme should first cover the basic needs of all, including the left-behind elderly, so that their minimum needs are covered. Then the quality of the scheme should be improved to near the level of the urban old-age insurance system. Meanwhile, the social welfare and social rescue services should be expanded in rural areas with fair and reasonable mechanisms so that the left-behind who have no one to rely on will truly benefit from the services. Three, the reforms of the rural land transfer should be well constructed so that the left-behind, especially the women, may be freed from farming that they are barely capable of while at the same time the returns on the lands are elevated.

Another problem is the "hollowing out" of land. With rural laborers moving to cities and towns, large areas of arable lands have been deserted or partially deserted in rural areas; meanwhile, some of those with certain administrative power or powerful social networks have taken advantage and obtained new homestead lands in the name of newborns or with other justifications while keeping their old ones but leaving them uncultivated. Both conditions have led to large areas of uncultivated lands on the countryside and "hollowed out" the lands. In addition, with rapidly progressing urbanization, rural laborers are also at the peak of moving out, leading to significant reduction in the rural population, and some small-sized natural villages have disappeared.

In recent years, the media have repeatedly highlighted a speech by Mr. Feng Yicai at the Forum of Protecting Village Cultural Heritage in Northern China: in 2000, there were 3.60 million natural villages in China, but only 2.70 million in 2010; 900,000 natural villages disappeared in a decade. Mr. Feng is an expert on natural villages and his data are usually solidly based. According to his data, more than 200 natural villages disappeared every day, leaving behind a shocking number of empty lands. Of course, this was only estimated and not quite accurate as no authoritative data have been released from national statistical agencies.

Despite the uncertainty, a report from Shandong Province is probably quite typical, at least of the eastern part of China. On May 5, 2015, an article in *Economic Information Daily*, titled "Thirty Percent of Shandong's 90 Thousand Natural Villages Hollowed Out," reported that, during the development of countryside, peasants had applied for new homestead lands in the name of building new homes while still keeping their old ones, i.e., "occupying new lands but refusing to return the old"; many peasants had moved to cities and towns for a long time, and some had brought their wives and children, yet none had returned their homestead lands. People always took their homestead lands as private property and refused to see any reduction in their lands, even in cases of reduced family size caused by moving out or death of family members, passing down the lands through generations. All of these behaviors had resulted in an increase in the area of homestead lands by 1.0% every year while the proportion of the deserted lands had also grown, leading to the "hollowing out" of rural lands.[25]

It is one of China's most prominent characteristics that there is a large population but a limited area of arable lands. Currently, there are 1.826 billion *mu* of cultivated lands, nearing the bottom line of arable lands that must be kept, thus it is not acceptable and cannot be sustained for land to keep "hollowed out" like this. It is noteworthy that the lands expropriated by the "dough-spreading" urbanization are usually relatively flat, with convenient access to water, and of high quality, while the old homestead lands that are now idling and deserted are also located at superior sites, both of which have seriously compromised the quality of arable lands and threatened their security, and must be managed and rectified.

To do so, the current laws on land use must first be strictly enforced and expropriation of land, especially arable land, by urbanization must be controlled carefully in order to safeguard the 1.8 billion *mu* of arable lands. It is particularly important now to closely watch various construction projects of development districts, industrial parks, science and technology parks, and cultural parks by not only intense evaluation before approval, but also strengthened supervision and inspection as well as the legal right to take back the lands if the planned construction is delayed for a long term or fails to meet requirements.

Additionally, the rural homestead lands need management. On one hand, approval of new homestead lands must be given carefully and follow lawful procedures so that they will not grow out of control; on the other hand, policies and regulations concerning the lands should be issued to manage the old, extra, and transferred homestead lands in that those that may be kept by peasants are to be kept by them, those that should be taken back by the state are to be taken back, and those that should be delisted as homestead lands are to be delisted, with proper compensation to the peasants in some cases.

According to estimation made by pertinent agencies, management of the homestead lands that are occupied in surplus by peasants may result in recovery of more than 110 million *mu* of lands, and together with the lands taken back due to occupation by blind expansion of urbanization, a total of more than 200 million *mu* of lands can be recovered. The land recovery will benefit not only the development of agriculture and the new countryside but also the development of cities and the upgrade of urbanization from the "dough-spreading" expansion to intensive advancement.

A third problem is the transfer of land. This is in fact closely associated with the aforementioned two problems. On one hand, it should be acknowledged that land transfer is an important tactic and an effective measure for agricultural modernization and coordinating urban and rural development and should be advanced with great efforts; on the other hand, the current problems in land transfer must be taken seriously and understood as something that, if solved unsatisfactorily, will make the land transfer go wrong and harm not only agricultural development but also the healthy progression of urbanization. The problems in land transfer are mostly focused on the transfer principle, scale, and supervision.

First, the transfer must be made voluntarily. Since the policy was issued to allow transfer of the right of operation of rural contracted lands to encourage moderate development of scale operation in agriculture, a revolution has swept the countryside and some deserted arable lands have been restored to life. Many peasants and contractors of land transfer have benefited economically and the agricultural production improved. However, exactly because of these benefits, the land transfer is easily abused since many cannot wait to benefit from it, and sometimes, the transfer is not made voluntarily.

The history of agricultural modernization has told us that "scale operation" is immensely attractive. The "agricultural cooperative" that was started right after the establishment of the new China, for example, developed from the level of mutual help to the preliminary, from the preliminary to the advanced, and eventually escalated to people's communes, and the "scale operation" was widely propagandized as well as somewhat effective; the problem was excessive propaganda, leading people to believe that the bigger the scale, the better, and to attribute the success of the biggest people's commune at the time to "*yidaergong*" ("large in size, collective in nature"), only to see the exit of the communes from history due to their sizes, which exceeded the rural economic realities and the level of the forces of production.

The agricultural cooperative movement offers many lessons, one of which is that it violated the voluntary principle. After all, the new China, at its establishment, was dominated by individual peasants and had a self-sufficient economy. Peasants helped each other to face the challenges borne with such an economy, and there was also a need to expand the scale of production in order to have expanded reproduction in rural areas, which laid the foundations for the cooperatives of mutual help and of the preliminary level, which were voluntarily organized by peasants.

However, the trend of advanced cooperatives was more like a wave that engulfed many peasants rather than actions voluntarily taken by them; on top of the not-so-ready advanced cooperatives came the wave of people's communes under the slogan that "people's communes [were] good." Although this part of history is well known, it is still helpful to review it from time to time; as we always say, "history is a mirror of the present." The most important lesson from this part of history is that major moves related to the rights and benefits of all of the masses should be always taken after the masses reckon on their own based on the voluntary principle.

Similarly, the land transfer currently implemented in rural areas should also follow the voluntary principle. However, many lines of information already have said otherwise. Some grassroots organizations in rural areas have played soft and hard to centralize the contracted lands of the peasants and have attracted investment by "building phoenix-affinity nests" on a scale as big as possible and under a contract term as long as possible, leading the land transfer off the right track. As a result, contract violation and discard are frequent as many of those who obtained the lands and those who contracted their use broke their contracts, leading to losses such as discarded farming, withdrawal from farming, and wasted farming.

Rural grassroots organizations often favor a large scale of land transfer for several reasons. Some are conceptual: it is widely believed at the grassroots level that the bigger the size of land transfer, the lower the cost in farming the lands, and the higher the efficiency and thus the benefits. Therefore, many organizations propagandize the idea that scale operation of agriculture benefits the rural economy and improves the peasants' incomes, and based on this idea, perform organized transfer. Others are conventional and habitual: scale operation of land is a way to develop the collective economy, the path to the new countryside, and a contribution to perfecting socialism. How to evaluate cadres' work is also related: it seems that a large scale and a big number of land transfers in a county, township, or village translate into outstanding work of the organization and cadres there, who will be rated highly in terms of their work and political achievements.

Therefore, correcting and reforming the problems in land transfer need to start with changing people's minds, and together with lessons learned from history, the grassroots may finally discard the misconception that the scale of land transfer speaks for its quality. In addition, evaluation of rural grassroots organizations and cadres should exclude the rigid doctrine based on the scale and the proportion of transferred lands and be based on whether the transfer is moderate, has facilitated wise use of land, has benefited agricultural development and transformation of laborers, and has advanced the coordinated development of urban and rural areas.

In other words, the standard by which to evaluate the transfer of operation rights of rural lands is not set against the amount and proportion of transferred lands, but against the benefits of transfer; after all, benefit is the one and only practical standard to test all transfer.

Second, the scale of land transfer needs discussion. Competition for the scale of land transfer is currently the most prominent problem in the practice of rural land transfer. As described earlier, conceptual understanding as well as evaluation systems of grassroots organizations underlie the problem, with the latter as the definitive cause. In fact, land financing of local governments is also a reason that is related to the evaluation system. When the land transfer has reached a large scale in a region, the local government and organizations have much freedom to handle their financial problems. It is also beneficial to mobilize the land resource as well as revenue increases by land financing.

From the perspective of those who contract the use of transferred lands, like plantation owners, they cannot arbitrarily decide the size of their farms because it must accommodate the development level of industry and agriculture, the conditions of land resources, the amount and the quality of agricultural labor resources, the technologies of the agricultural production, and the characteristics of production means. In fact, global farms can be roughly divided into big-, medium- and small-sized ones.

The United States and Canada are typical of big-sized farms, which are usually located where it is rich in arable lands, low in population density, and advanced in large-sized agricultural machineries. Europe is typical of medium-sized farms, which are usually located where arable lands are of average quality, population density is high, and the major countries have a high level of post-industrialization with medium-sized agricultural machineries predominating. Japan is typical of small-sized farms, which are located where there is a shortage of arable lands, high density of population, and advanced small-sized agricultural machineries.

In China, there is a shortage of arable lands with a large population: China's arable land accounts for 7.0% of the arable land in the world while its population accounts for 19.4%, typical of a country with a large population but a small amount of land. Traditional industrialization has been completed in China while post-industrialization was started long ago, putting China in a transitional stage from traditional industrialization to post-industrialization overall and in possession of big-, medium- and small-sized agricultural machineries. Given that China is now at the middle part of the s-shaped urbanization curve and in transition from urbanization centered on small cities to that centered on big ones, the strategy for developing farms should accommodate each region instead of being unified across the whole country.

Similarly, rural land transfer should not chase scale as many places may not be able to afford a big scale. The incidences mentioned earlier of people violating, breaking, and discarding contracts and those of people deserting, withdrawing from, and wasting farming are mostly related to oversized land transfers and are results like "undercooked rice." Practices have shown that the land resource is usually scanty and the population dense in big cities and their immediate suburbs, and it is therefore suitable for transfers of small-sized farms. Medium- and small-sized cities have average land resources and population density and are suitable for medium-sized farms, and average counties and *qi*, especially those villages in the northeastern and northwestern areas, have large areas of arable lands and low-density population and are suitable for large-sized agricultural machineries to operate, and should therefore develop land transfers focused on large-sized farms to take advantage of the aggregated lands. To make region-specific strategies, the government must fully exert itself to plan for and guide the big play of rural land transfer.

Third, supervision mechanisms and institutions must be sorted out. In November 2013, the General Office of the CCCPC and the General Office of the State Council jointly issued the *Opinion on Guiding the Orderly Transfer of Operation Right of Rural Land and Developing Moderate Scale Operation of Agriculture*, which required that the principles of land transfer must be followed and land leasing and contracting by industrial and commercial enterprises strictly managed and supervised to ensure standardized progression of the transfer. The document offered directions, tactics, and policies for the problems of violating, breaking, and discarding contracts and provided a legal framework for rural land transfers.

In fact, transferring the right of operation of rural lands is brand-new, and reforms are to be carried out in big strides to land the opinion and to find institutions and mechanisms that fit the transfer.

The orderly progression of the current reform relies on signing pertinent agreements and contracts so that transfers are solidly grounded in law. First, the peasants who wish to transfer the right to use their lands must sign a standard authorization letter of land transfer with the village committee; next, the committee signs a land transfer contract with the party who wishes to obtain the right to use the lands. The current problems are that, on one hand, many land transfer cases are without the signed authorization letters or contracts, leading the transfers to lose legal protection and legal terms in case of controversies, and, on the other hand, the authorization letters and contracts, even though signed, are not standardized and usually favor the buying party, which is not fair, just, or impartial. Therefore, reforms are needed to strengthen education on the rule of law and to rewrite the authorization letter and contract in a unified, standardized form according to the requirement by the rule of law so that non-standardized forms are not legally binding and whoever produces and uses such forms is held accountable.

The orderly progression of the current reform also relies on strengthened management and supervision by establishing an appropriate system of institutions and mechanisms. With valid authorization letters and contracts do not automatically come behaviors. Rules and management must be strengthened together with effective supervision in the frame of systematic mechanisms and institutions. At present, loose management and supervision, as well as defective institutions or even lack of institutions of supervision, are all underlying the aforementioned violation, breaking, and discard of contracts and the associated desertion, withdrawal, and wasting of farming, which have frequented rural areas and stayed unresolved for long terms.

In my opinion, the government has a large part to play in these cases. After all, the transfer of rural land is essentially transferring the right to operate land and thus is an economic activity, which should follow market rules. The peasants, village committees, and land contractors are all independent legal persons who are responsible for their own behaviors and enjoy equal rights in transfers. Where does the government stand? The government is responsible for planning for, guiding, organizing, and supervising the transfer. The government is not any party involved in a transaction or an actor, and cannot make any assignment, allocate quotas, or seal a transaction regarding land transfers; instead, it is the director and supervisor such that the supervision of rural land transfer falls on its shoulders.

Specifically, after the peasant signs the agreement with the village committee and the village committee signs the contract with the party obtaining the right to operate the land, the government monitors all the parties to follow the items of the files they have signed and to punish those in violation of law. I suggest that an office be set up in the legal department of rural counties and urban suburbs to handle the legal issues of land transfer since many problems have arisen related to the transfer during urbanization, and in this way, legal disputes may be handled timely, rural land transfer pushed for and guided properly, and the healthy development of moderate-scale operation of agriculture facilitated.

Notes

1 Liu, Zheng, ed., Li, Jingneng, vice ed., *A Program of Demographic Theories*, Beijing, China Renmin University Press, 1985, p. 251.

2 *Xici* is traditionally attributed to Confucius as one of his seven essays to study *Yi*, which Emperor Wen (1153–1156 B.C.) of the Western Zhou Dynasty is traditionally believed to have compiled, and which summarized philosophical thought since prehistoric times.

3 United Nations, *World Urbanization Prospects: The 1996 Revision*, New York, 1998.

4 Population Division, Department of Economic and Social Affairs, United Nations, *World Urbanization Prospects: The 2001 Revision, Data Tables and Highlights*, 2002, p. 6; *China Statistical Yearbook 2014*, p. 25; the 2015 data were projections.

5 *China Statistical Yearbook 2011*, p. 12; *China Statistical Yearbook 2015*, p. 12; National Bureau of Statistics of the People's Republic of China, *Statistical Communiqué of the People's Republic of China on the 2015 National Economic and Social Development*, February 29, 2016.
6 The 1990 data came from *China Statistical Yearbook 1991*, p. 653; the 1999 data came from *China Population Statistical Yearbook 2000*, pp. 481–489; and the 2010 data were calculated based on *China Statistical Yearbook 2011*, pp. 93, 371.
7 Tian, Xueyuan, "Several Issues on Facilitating Harmony between Mankind and Nature," *People's Daily*, December 22, 2006.
8 *China Statistical Yearbook 2014*, p. 25.
9 Ibid., p. 51.
10 Ibid., p. 56.
11 *China Statistical Yearbook 2013*, p. 421.
12 Ibid., p. 95.
13 Ibid., p. 96.
14 Tian, Xueyuan, *Research on the Development Strategy of China's Population in the 21st Century*, Beijing, Social Sciences Academic Press (China), 2007, pp. 312–313.
15 Population Committee, United Nations, *Demographic Dictionary*, translated by Yang, Kuixin and Shao, Ningyi, Beijing, Commercial Press, 1992, p. 38.
16 National Bureau of Statistics, *Statistical Communiqué 2013*, the bureau's webpage, and www.360doc.com, January 20, 2014.
17 United Nations, *Prospects of the World Urbanization 1988*, New York, 1989, pp. 40–41.
18 *People's Daily*, May 2, 2015.
19 Tian, Xueyuan, ed., *China Population Yearbook 1986*, Beijing, China Social Sciences Press, pp. 79, 81.
20 Wang, Huijiong, and Yang, Guanghui, eds., *Making Cities and Towns: International Experiences and Prospects for China*, Beijing, China Meteorological Press, 1984.
21 National Audit Office, *Audit Results of Nationwide Governmental Debts, No. 32 of 2013*, www.audit.gov.cn, December 30, 2013.
22 *Decision by CCCPC on Several Important Issues of Comprehensively Deepening the Reform*, Beijing, People's Publishing House, 2013, p. 21.
23 Ibid.
24 Li, Yifei, "Dispersing the 'Misty Fog' inside Left-Behind Children," *Guangming Daily*, July 4, 2015.
25 *Economic Information Daily*, May 5, 2015.

Bibliography

Bai, Yanfeng, and Liu, Chang, "The Land Policies of the Central Government and Their Impact on Land Sales of Regional Governments," *Finance and Trade Economics*, vol. 7, 2013.

Chen, Jian, ed., *China Reform Report 2013*, Beijing, Law Press, 2013.

The Decision by CCCPC on Several Important Issues of Comprehensively Deepening the Reform, an Assembly of Files of All the 3rd Plenary Sessions of All the Central Committees since the Reform and Opening-Up, Beijing, The People's Publishing House, 2013.

Hertel, Thomas, and Fan, Zhai, "Labor Market Distortions, Rural–Urban Inequality and the Opening of China's Economy," *Economic Modeling*, vol. 23, 2006.

Li, Yifei, "Dispersing the 'Misty Fog' inside Left-Behind Children," *Guangming Daily*, July 4, 2015.

Liu, Ruiming, and Shi, Lei, "The Ownership Foundation of China's Lagging Urbanization: Theories and Empirical Evidence," *Economic Research Journal*, vol. 4, 2015.

Liu, Shilin, "China's Experience of City Clusters and Comparison between China and the West," *Wenhui Scholars*, October 22, 2012.

Maddison, Angus, *Chinese Economic Performance in the Long Run*, 2nd edn., 159, Development Center of the OECD, 2007.

Pan, Jiahua, and Wei, Houkai, eds., *Report on the City Development in China*, No. 6, Beijing, Social Sciences Academic Press (China), 2013.

Tian, Xueyuan, "Facilitating the Upgrade of Urbanization by Reforms," People's Daily, July 17, 2013.

Wang, Xiaolu, "China's Path of Urbanization and Economic Analysis of City Scales," *Economic Research Journal*, vol. 10, 2010.

Wei, Shouhua, Zhou, Shanren, and Qian, Huixiong, "Analysis on the Standard Deviation of the City Sizes in China," *China Industrial Economics*, vol. 4, 2015.

Xi, Jinping, "Xi Emphasized 'to Improve the Unified Institutions and Mechanisms of Urban and Rural Development and to Share Reform Benefits with All Peasants' at the 22nd Collective Study of the Political Bureau of the CCCPC," *People's Daily*, May 2, 2015.

Xu, Jinpeng, and Lou, Chen, "Thirty Percent of Shandong's Nearly 90 Thousand Natural Villages Hollowed Out," *Economic Information Daily*, May 5, 2015.

Zhang, Monan, "Actively Making the Strategy for High-Quality Urbanization in China," *Globalization*, vol. 2, 2014.

5 The slow-decrease trend in the sex ratio at birth

Exploring the path of modern equity of both sexes

Sex ratio at birth underlies all demographic sex ratios, including the age-specific sex ratio, the population sex ratio, and the related sex ratios of the school-age, the working-age, the elderly, and the urban and rural populations, and is therefore highly valued in demography, economics, sociology, and geography. The sex ratio at birth in China had long been high, always staying near the upper limit within the normal range before the new China was founded. After that, the ratio declined by a small scale during the 1950s and 1970s, but it increased in the 1980s and fluctuated around 120 at the turn of the 21st century, showing marked increases, until 2009, when it had small-scale decreases. The ratio shows a projectile that goes up first and then goes down, leaving many questions.

Risk of increases in the sex ratio at birth

Sex ratio at birth is the ratio of live boys born to girls and is expressed as the number of newborn boys per 100 newborn girls. The formula is as follows: live newborn boys/live newborn girls x 100. Increases in the sex ratio at birth do not only bring increases in the age-specific sex ratio and the population sex ratio but also impact the related demographic sex structure of schooling, employment, urban and rural distribution, and regional distribution, thus shaping the development of the population, the economy, and the society.

The trend in China's sex ratio at birth

Characteristics of changes in the sex ratio at birth

It is widely known that sex ratio at birth is usually quite stable under normal circumstances with rare dramatic changes. However, during the 30 years between 1980 and 2010, continuous increases in the sex ratio at birth were observed in China, showing a unique pattern. The trend in the ratio during the 30 years is analyzed here in order to identify some characteristics.

THE TREND IN THE SEX RATIO AT BIRTH

Sex ratio at birth is usually called the secondary sex ratio internationally because there is a primary sex ratio that describes the genders of fetuses living in wombs. Sex ratio at birth is calculated based on live births. Although only a very small proportion are stillbirths, the number varies in different countries and stillbirths cannot be included in the calculation of the sex ratio at birth. The normal value of the ratio is 105±2, i.e., ranging from 103 to 107. Why are there more boys than girls by three to seven percentage points? It is decided by biological laws. On average, boys have a higher risk of death than girls and the risk is evened out between the two genders as they grow up. This is a universal global phenomenon with very few exceptions where the sex ratios at birth are below 100.

Historically, China had a sex ratio at birth like everywhere else in the world, which stayed near the upper end within the normal range. After the new China was founded, the ratio decreased, reaching or getting close to the standard value, 105, in some years and staying at values only slightly higher than 105 in others. Things started to change after 1980, when the ratio continued to climb even after it exceeded the upper limit of the normal range, marking China as one of the few countries in the world with an exceptionally high sex ratio at birth. There is a low degree of disagreement between the data from pertinent government agencies, research institutes, and academic groups, and the most authoritative data should come from national population censuses. Therefore, the changes in the sex ratio at birth in the past few decades may be illustrated, as shown in Figure 5.1, based on the four censuses in 1982, 1990, 2000, and 2010 and the data released by the NHFPC.

Together with data from other sampling surveys and case-specific investigations, the trend in the sex ratio at birth since the establishment of the new China can be summarized in Figure 5.2.

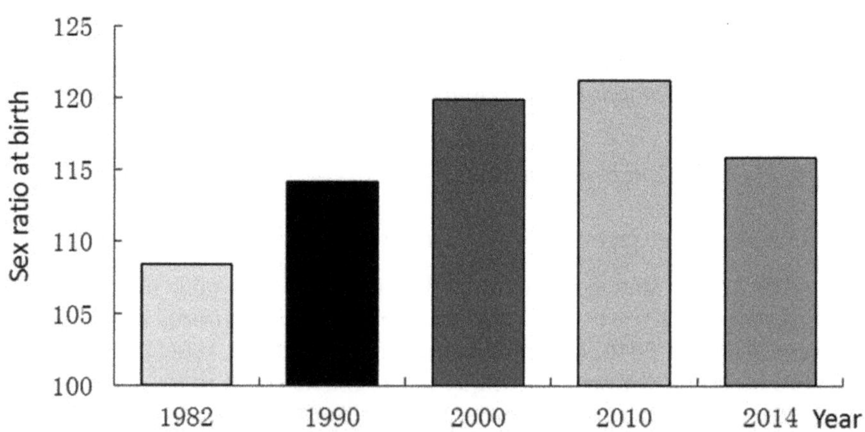

Figure 5.1 Sex ratios at birth in four population censuses and in 2014.

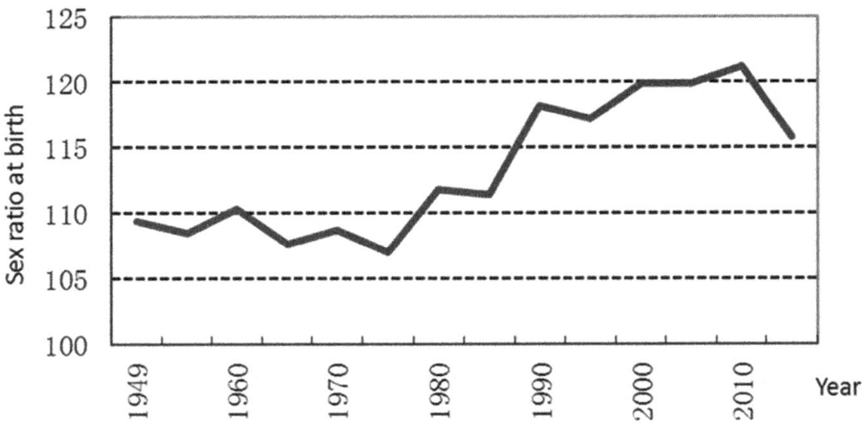

Figure 5.2 Trend in the sex ratio at birth, 1949–2014.

CHARACTERISTICS OF THE CHANGES IN THE SEX RATIO AT BIRTH

Sex ratio at birth does not usually change much and has quite mild fluctuations except in times of war and disasters such as plague. However, the changes in the sex ratio at birth in the past 65 years in China were not that mild and showed different features in various historical stages, at various birth orders, and between urban and rural areas. The features are mainly the following.

One feature is that the ratio changes with stage. The aforementioned changes in the sex ratio at birth in the past 65 years showed distinctive characteristics that can be roughly classified into four stages.

In the first stage (1949–1961), the ratio decreased with fluctuations. The national sex ratio at birth neared the upper limit of the normal range, 107, in 1961, decreased from 109 in 1949, with ups and downs during the period, showing a fluctuating downward trend throughout the 1950s. One of the underlying reasons was that gender equality was realized in the political, economic, legal, and social areas after the establishment of the new China and women's social and family status was elevated unprecedentedly. Women now had the same say in procreation as men, a certain degree of consensus was reached in society that "boys and girls [were] the same," and drowning and deserting newborn girls was basically eradicated.

A second reason was that the livelihood of the people was greatly improved while the population grew as if compensating for the severe loss of population, especially men, in the previous long term of wars. In the 1950s, the TFR reached 5.87, and in the 1960s, it reached 5.68, with no artificial interference in the number or sex of births.[1]

The third reason was that the government invested heavily in education and the people saw marked improvement in the level of education they received; meanwhile, the tradition that boys were valued more than girls was criticized and the idea that men and women were equal was gradually internalized by people with a new fashion that the rights and status of women were respected.

In the second stage (1962–1979), the sex ratio at birth fluctuated around the upper limit of the normal range. In 1962, the ratio declined below 107, the upper limit of the normal range, starting a 20-year window in which the ratio was confined within the normal range with fluctuations at the upper limit, which was similar to most times in history. It is widely known that the unprecedented Cultural Revolution took place from the mid-1960s to the mid-1970s, and it affected many political, economic, cultural, and social aspects, including reproduction, which was left in an archaic state. This was exactly why the highest fertility peak after the establishment of the new China was reached during the period from 1962 to 1973, with new records of birth and growth rates; during this time, the sex ratio at birth was in a natural state and stayed at levels slightly higher than the standard value.

In the third stage (1980–2010), the sex ratio at birth continued to climb. In 1980, the ratio exceeded the upper limit of the normal range, starting a period of 30 years of continuous increases, and this deserves special attention in studies on China's sex ratio at birth. It must first be figured out how the ratio changed and which path it took during the 30 years. As mentioned earlier, despite consensus about the increases in the ratio among all social sectors, there has been controversy over how high the ratio was, when the increases began, and the scale of fluctuations; and various parties had different data and conclusions, some with great disparities.

In my opinion, the best way to sort out the controversy is to rely on accurate annual data of the sex ratio at birth. Unfortunately, however, there are no such data, and the data presented by some have been questioned. Some quoted data in their research reports and papers from their own surveys or surveys by others, but the sample sizes of the surveys were not big enough to represent the whole and the studies sometimes further confused people instead of settling the controversy. Fortunately, four population censuses were performed during these 30 years, and the census data are more reliable sources for studies.

On a side note, the four censuses did not always reflect the sex ratios at birth of the years when they were performed. Dependent on the start time of each census, each ratio covered a different period of time. Specifically, the 1982 population census (third census) gave the sex ratio at birth of the year 1981; the 1990 (fourth) census from January 1, 1989, to June 30, 1990; the 2000 (fifth) census from November 1, 1999, to October 31, 2000; and the 2010 (sixth) census, from November 1, 2009, to October 31, 2010. Based on these timetables, the ratios in the four censuses were 108.47, 114.18, 119.92, and 121.21, respectively, showing continuous increases that made three consecutive steps up.

Since the beginning of the fourth stage (2011 until present), the sex ratio at birth has decreased slowly. The ratio showed consecutive declines after 2010. According to the report *Six Consecutive Decreases in Our Country's*

Sex Ratio at Birth, by the *Daily Post* of Xinhua Press on February 4, 2015, the national sex ratio at birth decreased in a row from 121.21 in 2010 to 117.78 in 2011, 117.70 in 2012, 117.60 in 2013, and 115.88 in 2014.[2] However, the "six consecutive decreases" described the continuous decreases in the sex ratio of those born during the six years between 2008 and 2014 while the ratio of 2010 was 117.94, 3.27 lower than that of the population census, which deserves further discussion. The report included a number that was 3.27 lower than the 2009 sex ratio at birth in the "six consecutively decreasing" ratios without specifying any problem with the 2010 ratio in the population census or providing any scientific foundation for the new data, a fairly confusing move.

A second feature is that the sex ratio at birth is remarkably high among births at second- or higher-order births. According to the fourth (the first half of 1989), fifth (November 1, 1999–October 31, 2000), and sixth (November 1, 2009–October 31, 2010) censuses, the sex ratio among first-order births of the fourth census was 105.27, similar to the standard value in the normal range; the ratio of the fifth census was 107.12, still in the normal range but close to the upper limit; and the ratio of the sixth census was 113.73, 6.73 higher than the upper limit of the normal range already, a phenomenon not seen before.

In addition, every census showed a remarkably higher sex ratio among second- and higher-order births than that of first-order births, so much higher as to climb a cliff. In fact, the sex ratios of second-order births in all the three censuses were higher than the respective sex ratios of first-order births by 15.43%, 41.8%, and 14.56%, respectively; those of third-order births by 17.99%, 49.65%, and 42.06%, respectively; those of fourth-order births by 24.40%, 50.69%, and 28.81%, respectively; and those of fifth-order births by 21.75%, 38.90%, and 26.31%, respectively, now showing marked declines in the increases.

Hidden behind the abrupt rises in the sex ratios of second- and higher-order births was the engine that drove the continuous increases in the ratio while at the same time, the high ratio of 113.73 in the sixth census made us wonder: have the moves that drove high the sex ratios of second- and higher-order births been applied to first births? The answer is positive based on various sources of information (Table 5.1).

A third feature is the distinct sex ratios at birth in urban and rural areas. The cost–benefit ratio of raising children in rural areas is different from urban areas due to the higher birth rates in rural areas than cities and towns, with towns having higher birth rates than cities, as well as different economic levels, education levels, and demands for labor on the job market. Such different cost–benefit ratios, together with different reproduction concepts, including sex choices, between rural and urban areas are ultimately manifested as different sex preferences between the two areas and consequently, distinct sex ratios at birth in cities, towns, and villages.

A section is devoted to this topic in the discussion of causes of increasing sex ratios at birth that follows, and no further description is provided here. Overall, all the population censuses and various sampling surveys have shown

Table 5.1 Sex ratios at birth by birth order in the fourth, fifth, and sixth population censuses

	Fourth census 1/1/1989–6/30/1990	*Fifth census 11/1/1999–10/31/2000*	*Sixth census 11/1/2009–10/31/2010*
Sex ratio at birth	114.18	119.92	121.24
First-order births	105.27	107.12	113.73
Second-order births	121.51	151.92	130.29
Third-order births	124.21	160.30	161.56
Fourth-order births	130.96	161.42	146.50
Fifth- and higher-order births	128.17	148.79	143.65

Source: *1990 Population Census of China*, pp. 536–538; *2000 Population Census of China*, pp. 1681–1683; *2010 Population Census of China*, pp. 2021–2026.

the distinct ratios. For example, the fifth census in 2000 revealed that the sex ratio at birth was the highest in the countryside, which was 121.67, 119.90 in towns, and the lowest in cities, which was 114.15. When broken down to birth orders, the sex ratio of first-order births was the lowest in the countryside, which was 105.65, as low as the standard value in the normal range, then in cities 108.88, and the highest in towns, which was 110.36.

The sex ratio of first-order births was overall lower than the total sex ratio at birth, and way lower than that of second- and higher-order births. The sex ratio of second- and higher-order births showed abrupt increases everywhere, be it cities, towns, villages, or nationally, while the peak in the ratio showed up at fourth-order births in cities and towns, with the former being 195.15 and the latter being 188.62, and at third-order births in villages, which was 158.20. Although the birth-order-specific sex ratio at birth reached its peak at fourth-order births in cities and towns and at third-order births in villages, the peak values did not impact the overall ratio to a large degree as the proportion of fourth-order births of all births in cities and towns was extremely low, 0.08% in cities and 0.62% in towns, and the proportion of third-order births of all births in villages was only 5.44% (Table 5.2).

Rises in the sex ratio at birth

In 1927, American novelist Ernest Miller Hemingway published a story collection, *Men without Women*. Now more than 90 years have passed, and some depictions in the title novel have come true: there are nearly 100 million more men than women in Asia! With the largest population in the world, China has attracted worldwide attention for its growing sex ratio at birth for quite a while.

The rises in China's sex ratio at birth have two aspects: in one aspect, the imbalanced ratio of men to women with men in surplus has a direct impact on marriages and families, and in the other aspect, the high sex ratio at birth

Table 5.2 Urban and rural sex ratios at birth in the fifth census (11/1/1999–10/31/2000)

	National	*Cities*	*Towns*	*Villages*
Sex ratio at birth	119.93	114.15	119.90	121.67
First-order births	107.12	108.88	110.36	105.65
Second-order births	151.92	147.63	154.59	152.14
Third-order births	160.30	164.92	180.53	158.20
Fourth-order births	161.42	195.15	188.62	157.65
Fifth- and higher-order births	148.79	164.22	163.28	148.98

Source: *2000 Population Census of China*, pp. 1684–1692.

has an indirect impact on economic, social, and cultural development. The impact of the first aspect is direct and requires immediate attention, while the impact of the second is the expansion and socialization of the first, and is indirect.

Direct impact on marriages and families

Continuous rises in the sex ratio at birth will result in an imbalanced sex ratio among those of marriageable age after 20 years. According to the marriage law in China, men are allowed to marry after the age of 22 and women after the age of 20. Therefore, the sex ratio of those of legal marriage age is the ratio of 22-year-old men to 20-year-old women. An imbalance of the ratio, sometimes referred to as the *marriage squeeze* or *marriage sex accumulation*, describes the imbalance between the numbers of men and women of marriageable age, which results in a considerable number of single men. The imbalance is even more evident when both sexes are grouped by marital status and age, and men are clearly accumulated as single. The imbalance of the sex ratio at marriage and by marital status and age group is the most direct and the gravest consequence of the rises in the sex ratio at birth.

As mentioned earlier, the sex ratio at birth in China started to climb in the beginning of the 1980s, and it has stayed high since the beginning of the 21st century, leading the number of men to pile up and the imbalance of the sex ratio of those of marriageable age to worsen. The media caught the problem and made it hotly discussed for a while with intensified coverage. For example, a news agency once did a report on the issue with a sensational title, *How to Do with the 40 Million Single Men in China?* The report drew public attention and pushed the discussion of the topic to a new high. In fact, I was asked about the report when I was invited by China net in November 2006 to discuss issues of population aging and old-age security with netizens. In response to the question, I gave my opinion in the following three points.

First, the "40 million single men" is still an assumptive proposition. Where are these 40 million single men? Who can find them? No one can answer these questions. If we track back to the origin of the assumption, it is said that it was deduced from the data of the fifth census. However, if we really get down to calculations, we can never obtain such a result.

The sex ratio at birth started to rise in the 1980s in China, and only 20 years had passed by the fifth census in 2000. The live males born during these 20 years should be aged from 0 to 19 at the census, the number of whom added up to 204,174,811, while the total number of females of the same age groups was 183,383,918.[3] There were 20,790,863 more males than females, 19.21 million less than the so-called 40 million single men, or 48.0% of the assumed single men. In addition, these males were all under age 20 and had not reached the legal marriageable age, and so were not qualified to be "single men." Only those who would survive would likely become future "single men."

Second, the number of females who reached the legal marriageable age in 2000 was 18,455,091, with 9,078,328 at 20 and 9,376,763 at 21. They were 88.8% of the 20,790,863 males aged between 0 and 19 who were in surplus compared to the number of females of the same age group.[4] That is also to say, the more than 20 million extra males were similar in number to the females who had just reached the legal marriageable ages of 20 and 21.

Therefore, as long as the legal marriageable age for men is two years older than that for women, the sex ratio of those of marriageable age will generally balance out. In fact, the contemporary marriage law indeed dictates that men are allowed to marry at 22 and women at 20 and that the difference between the two marriageable ages is exactly two. Therefore, the potential more than 20 million "single men" aged 0 to 19 at the fifth census are not really difficult to handle; furthermore, matches between "an old husband and a young wife," are now quite fashionable, and this leaves room to manage the problem of "single men."

Third, if the imbalance of the sex ratio at birth could not be corrected and was left to worsen, newborn boys would continue to outnumber newborn girls year after year, the problem would exacerbate, and a sex ratio crisis would eventually break out in the near future. Should it happen, the tens of millions of "single men" would really become a tough social challenge difficult to resolve. This situation would challenge marriages and families, law and order, ethics and values, social stability, and the progression of socialist spiritual civilization, and would eventually harm the healthy development of the economy and the society.

At the end of the discussion, I emphasized that the growing sex ratio at birth should be widely advertised for attention and needed effective measures. The key to solving the problem was to find the right way in and to bring down the human-assisted elevated sex ratio at birth as soon as possible by adjusting fertility policies, improving the policy environment, strengthening law enforcement, and intensifying social monitoring. If the sex ratio at birth could be lowered in a short period of time, then all the problems would be easy to handle; however, if the ratio could not be lowered for a long time, the excessive number of males would continue to grow and it would lead to ever-tougher problems; therefore, the sooner the measures were taken, the earlier the problems were solved with fewer efforts, while the later the measures were taken, the later the problems were solved with doubled efforts.

Now that more than a decade has passed, how has the increasing sex ratio at birth been handled? As mentioned earlier, the high sex ratio at birth has not been effectively managed for the past more than 20 years, and it fluctuated at a high level until recently, when it showed some evidence of decreases and reached 115.88 in 2014. Thus the seed planted by the long-term progressive increases in the already high sex ratio at birth sprouted with time and rang the alarm for rises in the sex ratio of those of marriageable age. In fact, a comparison of the sex ratios of those aged between 0 and 19 between the fourth census in 1990 and the sixth in 2010 would show the risk clearly (Table 5.3).

As shown in Table 5.3, between the two population censuses in 1990 and 2010, the sex ratio of the age group 0–19 increased by 7.23 from 107.61 to 114.84. There were 15,868,099 more males than females between 0 and 19 years of age in 1990, and the number increased to 22,186,941 in 2010, a net increase of 6,318,842. Among them, the age group of 0–4 had an increased

Table 5.3 Sex ratios of those aged between 0 and 19 in the 1990 and 2010 population censuses

Age	*Sex ratio, 1990*	*Sex ratio, 2010*
0–4	110.22	119.13
0	111.73	117.96
1	111.59	121.06
2	110.11	119.66
3	109.12	118.55
4	108.47	118.34
5–9	108.23	118.66
5	108.65	118.45
6	108.64	118.68
7	108.69	118.83
8	107.77	118.90
9	107.37	118.45
10–14	106.68	116.24
10	107.43	118.23
11	106.84	117.30
12	106.45	116.57
13	106.49	115.53
14	106.19	113.92
15–19	105.37	108.17
15	105.74	112.06
16	105.24	108.89
17	105.24	107.45
18	105.36	107.33
19	105.32	105.88

Sources: *1990 Population Census of China*, vol. 2, p. 2; *2000 Population Census of China*, vol. 1, p. 265.

sex ratio by 8.91, from 110.22 to 119.13; the sex ratio in the age group of 5–9 increased by 10.43, claiming the highest increase among all; the second highest increase in the sex ratio was in the age group of 10–14, which was 9.56; and the lowest increase in the sex ratio was observed in the age group of 15–19, which was only 2.80. The underlying reasons are as follows.

The compromised increase in the sex ratio of age group 0–4 was due to the decreased sex ratio at birth in recent years; the highest increase in the sex ratio of the age group 5–9 was the consequence of the acute increases in the sex ratio at birth during the first few years of the 21st century; and the lowest increase in the sex ratio of the age group 15–19 was due partly to the limited increases in the sex ratio at birth in the first half of the 1990s, which contained the ratio below 116.0, and partly to the slightly higher age-specific mortality rate of males under 20 than females, particularly the higher risk of accidental deaths and lower survival of males than females.

Apparently, there is a dynamic transmission process between the sex ratio at birth and the sex ratio at marriageable age, and the higher age-specific mortality rate of men lowers the latter. Therefore, a scientific evaluation should be performed to avoid simple equalization of increases in the sex ratio at birth to increases in the sex ratio at marriageable age.

Such increases in the sex ratio at birth have already delivered a blow to marriage and families. Marriage and families are the cells that constitute reproduction and are indispensable factors in the life cycle of the population. It is widely known that the basic marital status has four forms – single, married, divorced, and widowed – among which the married can be either married and not separated or separated, the divorced and the widowed can be either living alone or remarried, and the married could be in a first or subsequent marriage.

In addition, people may live together without having married, which does not belong to any of the aforementioned four forms and can be considered a supplementary status. The sex ratio at birth in any given year will be translated into a certain number of males and a certain number of females who are of reproductive age 14 years later, and into males and females of marriageable age after another 5 to 7 years. Therefore, the continuous rise in the sex ratio at birth since the 1980s in China has walked through 35 years now, and its impact on marriage and families has already manifested (Table 5.4).

As shown in Table 5.4, between the three population censuses in 1990, 2000, and 2010, the proportion of the unmarried decreased first and then increased, with similar changes in men and women; the proportion of the widowed, including men and women, first decreased slightly and then stabilized, while the proportion of men had similar changes and that of women showed evident increases and only somewhat stabilized after it reached 8.0%. In contrast, the proportion of the divorced kept increasing, from 0.6% in 1990 through 0.9% in 2000 to 1.4% in 2010, which were increases of 0.3 and 0.8 percentage points, respectively, and the proportions for both men and women kept increasing.

Table 5.4 Marital and family status in the 1990, 2000, and 2010 population censuses (%)

	1990			*2000*			*2010*		
	Total	*Males*	*Females*	*Total*	*Males*	*Females*	*Total*	*Males*	*Females*
Single	25.1	29.0	21.1	20.3	23.7	16.7	21.6	24.7	18.5
Married	68.2	66.4	70.0	73.3	71.8	74.8	71.3	70.4	72.3
Widowed	6.1	3.8	8.5	5.6	3.4	7.8	5.7	3.4	8.0
Divorced	0.6	0.8	0.3	0.9	1.1	0.7	1.4	1.5	1.2
No. per family	3.96			3.4			3.1		
Single-person families	6.27			8.7			14.5		

Sources: *1990 Population Census of China*, vol. 3, pp. 2–18 and 514–519; *2000 Population Census of China*, vol. 1, p. 643 and vol. 2, pp. 1586–1587; *2010 Population Census of China*, vol. 1, p. 345, and vol. 2, pp. 1850–1851; *China Statistics Yearbook 2013*, p. 101.

The most prominent change in marital status is the continuous shrinkage of the size of families. The average number of people per family shrank from 3.96 in 1990, to 3.4 in 2000, to 3.1 in 2010, while the proportion of single-person families saw marked increases, from 6.7% in 1990, to 8.7% in 2000, to 14.5% in 2010. The abrupt increases in single-person families reflected the accumulation of men of marriageable age due to the increases in the sex ratio at birth, which was sideline evidence of the progressive impact of the increases in the ratio.

The impact of the increases in the sex ratio at birth on marriage rates can be further analyzed from several perspectives. In fact, the following three marriage rates are deeply affected by the increases in the ratio, which deserves attention.

First, the crude (first) marriage rate is seriously affected. The crude (first) marriage rate is the number of marriages per 1,000 people in a given population in a given period of time (usually one year). The formula to get the rate is as follows:

> Crude (first) marriage rate = number of (first) marriages / average population per year x 1,000.

Second, the general (first) marriage rate is affected. The (first) marriage rate is the number of (first) marriages per 1,000 people above age 15 in a given period of time (usually one year). The formula to get the rate is as follows:

> (First) marriage rate = number of (first) marriages / average population above 15 per year x 1,000.

Third, the sex age-specific marriage rate is affected. The sex age-specific (first) marriage rate is the number of (first) marriages by sex and age per 1,000 people in a given time (usually one year). The formula to get the rate is as follows:

> Sex age-specific (first) marriage rate = number of (first) marriages per sex and age / average population per year x 1,000.

In addition, the total (first) marriage rate, i.e., the sum of all age-specific (first) marriage rates, is also affected. The increases in the sex ratio at birth may impact all (first) marriage rates to a certain degree. Year after year, the males who have reached marriageable age outnumber the females who have reached marriageable age and they pile up as the number grows of those males who have to postpone marriage because they cannot find a spouse or are unwilling to get married; therefore, the number cannot be added to the numerator (marriages) and cannot be counted as the number of marriages, but must be included in the denominator as the population of a given period of time, leading all the aforementioned marriage rates to continuously decline.

In fact, the situation is already clear in the changes in families. As shown in the comparison of the three censuses, the size of families has kept shrinking and now the majority of Chinese families have only three people; meanwhile, single-person families have grown rapidly, from 13,532,357 in 1990 to 28,273,351 in 2000, with the latter 1.09 times greater than the former, and to 58,396,327 in 2010, which was 1.07 times greater than 2000 and 3.32 times greater than 1990. The average annual growth rate of single-person families from 1990 to 2010 reached 7.58%, a speed rarely observed in history as the number essentially doubled less than every decade.

Indirect impact on social development

Sustained increases in the sex ratio at birth and decreases in the proportion of females both affect the economy, politics, the culture, and the society to a degree. Some are affected strongly, some to a lesser degree, and others negligibly. Under the current situation, the impact on women's rights, social order, and cultural traditions deserves special attention.

IMPACT ON WOMEN'S RIGHTS

The soaring sex ratio at birth results in more males compared to females, who then become scarcer, and it seems that this benefits women. However, with outnumbered men comes a growing number of males who refuse to stay single, and the imbalance in the sex ratio elevates the risk of women being violated, which will certainly harm women's rights. In addition, the imbalance of the sex ratio puts women at risk for falling into extramarital affairs and sexual relationships, leading all sorts of sexual harassment to become more frequent.

Crimes that violate women's rights, such as prostitution, have never been successfully eradicated, despite countless efforts, including actions to eliminate pornography, prostitution, and illegal publications. Like Chinese chives, which always grow back no matter how many times they are mowed, practices such as buying wives, bigamy, and women trafficking are all rooted in the vice left over from the old society. Some were not entirely wiped out after the new China was established, and others managed to revive under new conditions. Unfortunately, the mounting sex ratio at birth year after year has exacerbated the situation and created conditions for these vices to make a comeback.

Furthermore, the violation of women's rights is not only physical but also mental, and extends to economic and social aspects. According to the third survey on Chinese women's social status, a joint venture by the All-China Women's Federation and the National Bureau of Statistics, which provided data synchronized on December 1, 2010, a much higher proportion of rural women than men suffer from mental distress. While 36.7% of the women in the three cities of Beijing, Tianjin, and Shanghai suffer from mental distress, only 15.2% of the men do, a difference of 21.5 percentage points. In the mid-west area, where the majority of the left-over population in rural areas are women, 42.2% of the women and 33.8% of the men suffer from mental distress, a difference of 8.4 percentage points.

Meanwhile, the traditional concept that values boys over girls is still so powerful that females, despite continuous increases in the number of years they receive education, have received apparently less education than men; 60.8% of the urban women aged between 18 and 64 are employed, which is 19.7 percentage points lower than the employment rate for men, 80.5% of whom are employed, and women on average only have an annual income that is 67.3% of that of men.[5]

Furthermore, women lose lands easily, have to give up land benefits often, have limited access to decision-making, and are overburdened with domestic chores. All these problems show that women's lawful rights are violated and threatened, which demands proper solutions.

IMPACT ON THE SOCIAL ORDER

The normal progress of reproduction is necessary for social stability and development, which is preconditioned by whether the population's sex ratio can be maintained within the normal range. If the sex ratio of a population loses balance, the prerequisite of reproduction will be faulty, which will in turn impact the social order by transmitting negative energy to social stability and development. This is exactly why increases in the sex ratio at birth have a certain degree of impact on the social order, especially in the following aspects.

Impact on the marriage order. The present marriage order is founded on the marriage institution based on monogamy and family relationships centered on the core family. As described earlier, sustained increases in the sex ratio at birth and in the number of men who refuse to stay single boost extramarital affairs and sexual relationships and foster the pornography industry and sex trades, which definitely delivers blows to the current marriage institution and harms the stability of families. Such blows may be manifested as increases in divorce rates and sex crimes as well as difficulty in eliminating trafficking of women.

Impact on employment. Increases in the sex ratio at birth and progressive increases in the number of men lead to an imbalanced sex ratio of the adult population, which in turn results in an imbalanced sex ratio on the job market so that some males have to squeeze into branches and industries traditionally dominated by women. Although there is no clear-cut classification of industries for men and women, some industries have marked gender-affiliated characteristics and a preference for either gender has been naturally formed. For example, the heavy-chemical industries such as coal and charcoal, metallurgy, construction, and oil and petrochemistry mostly hire men, and industries such as textiles, nursing, and domestic services usually hire women.

Long-term increases in the sex ratio at birth and that of the working age have driven surplus male laborers to enter fields traditionally filled with women, breaking the old employment pattern. Some Western countries have concluded that the large-scale ground-breaking projects in China such as the construction of high-speed rail, highways, and urban infrastructure are the "male projects" purposed to absorb surplus male laborers. It is of course out of their prejudice, yet it also reflects how the international community is concerned about the impact on employment brought by imbalanced sex ratios, and we may get some inspiration from its comments.

Impact on education. The imbalanced sex ratio at birth mirrors how deeply people are affected even today by the tradition that values boys over girls. This idea of favoring boys has remained a strong presence in education, especially in the laid-back areas in the west where many girls still cannot enjoy the same right to education as boys. Some surveys have revealed that in several western rural areas, the school dropout and defection rates are much higher for girls than for boys and the imbalance of the sex ratio in school worsens with grades. In fact, average families in those areas do not expect girls to receive a high level of education and believe that girls need only to be literate to read newspapers and books, thus a much lower proportion of high school girls continues to college than that of high school boys.

IMPACT ON CULTURE

The word *culture* may be used in a broad sense, a narrow sense, or a general sense. Here the word is used in a general sense and denotes the culture of ideologies. Many social surveys have found that the sex ratio of first-order births is usually comparable to or slightly higher than the standard value while that of second- and higher-order births often shows abrupt increases, resulting in a distinct distribution of sex ratios at birth by birth order.

Why does the sex ratio at birth increase abruptly for second- and higher-order births? It is generally agreed that this increase results from sex-selective abortion. Unfortunately, the increases in the sex ratio at birth lead to increases in the number of men who have to stay single, which in turn affects divorce rates and extramarital affairs and sexual relationships, and eventually women are hurt. As a matter of fact, promotion of gender equality has made significant progress by advocating "a different era, the same for both sexes" since the new China was founded. Unfortunately, however, sex-selective abortion and various forms of sexual violation of women under the marriage squeeze have slapped the culture of gender equality.

Another kind of slap is social evils such as prostitution, which had been extinguished for decades but found their way back over the dignity of pursuit of gender equality. These phenomena devalue traditional Chinese morals such as affection, loyalty, and trust while holding above all the value of exchanges based on money, the negative impact of which has already shown up and cannot be overlooked.

Tracking back to the origin of the increases in the sex ratio at birth

There are currently consensuses among various social sectors about the manifestation and the consequences of the increases in the sex ratio at birth; however, when it comes to why the ratio has been climbing continuously and what is the reason, great disagreement arises with various views that cannot reach any consensus although hundreds of papers, reports, and books have been devoted to the question. In my opinion, it is important to first reduce things to the original form and to expound it from the surface to the core in a reasonable way with theories and practices combined.

The variously asserted "reason"

Since the sex ratio at birth started to rise in the 1980s, people from academies and various social sectors have discussed intensively the underlying reason, which has produced hundreds of papers and books with analyses made from various perspectives, as summarized in what follows.

From the economic perspective, differences between men and women in physical strength, education level, labor, employment, and income have been screened for the economic foundations of sex discrimination such as lower employment rates, limited job fields, lower positions, fewer technological challenges, earlier retirement ages, and lower incomes for women than for men. Under these circumstances, raising a daughter is certainly not cost-effective, and sometimes even considered "a business with deficit spending," which triggers a strong preference for people to have boys.

From the cultural perspective, China's thousands of years of a feudal society have been explored. This history produced a traditional culture, an important part of which was that men were superior to women. From Confucius's statement that "women and small men are difficult to nurture" and Mencius's that "there are three ways to be unfilial, the worst which is to produce no heir," to Sangang Wuchang (the three cardinal guides and the five constant virtues) of the school of Chengs and Zhu, one of which is that "husband guides wife," women became bound in ethical and moral values.

A woman could obtain an honorable seat in the society and the family only after she produced a son, and if she failed, which was considered the first among the "seven reasons to divorce a wife," she might be humiliated by divorce. After the new China was founded, the old rotten culture was intensively criticized for several reasons, which included the concept that men were superior to women, and things became quite different. However, changing people's minds is always arduous, and the transformation of the idea of having a son has been particularly difficult. Therefore, the concept that "there are three ways to be unfilial, the worst which is to produce no heir" is still influential and dominates people's reproduction behaviors.

From the political perspective, it has been emphasized that women were long excluded from the social political system as the old, iron-strong doctrine, "men outside, women inside," dictated that only a man could support a family and have a career. After the new China was established, such a rotten idea started to withdraw from history with changes in social politics, but it is not completely gone yet. Women still have fewer opportunities than men to participate in political decision-making and account for a smaller proportion and hold lower positions among decision makers, with decreasing proportions at higher positions. Therefore, the promotion of women's political and social status has been limited and women are still underprivileged to a degree.

From the policy and management perspectives, it has been argued that social supervision and management has not caught up with the 1980 CCCPC policy that each couple could have only one child, and thus many holes and blind spots have remained in the policy. Despite the government's repeated strict prohibition of nonmedical examination for fetus sex and sex-selective abortion, lack of supervision, management, and law enforcement has always compromised the effect of the government's statements. Particularly, lack of effective mechanisms to monitor sex-selective abortion has led to large numbers of such abortions, driving high the sex ratio at birth artificially.

The analyses, summarized earlier, have unanimously landed on the fertility policy in the end, i.e., whether the increases in the ratio are related to the current fertility policy and whether the former is decided by the latter. There are currently three views, as described in what follows.

First, there is the no-relation view, i.e., the increases in the sex ratio at birth in the past 30 years are not related to the fertility policy. Why? The fertility policy has never advocated for people to have boys; on the contrary, it prohibits nonmedical examination for fetus sex and sex-selective abortion. Although the policy advocating for one child per couple narrowed the fertility space, only increases, but not decreases, in the sex ratio at birth followed. Apparently, the increases are rooted deep in people's minds and in the reproduction concept with a preference for boys.

Second, there is the decision view, i.e., the increases in the sex ratio at birth in the past 30 years have resulted from the tightening fertility policy, especially the policy that advocates for one couple to have only one child. After all, the preference for boys has existed since ancient times, and it was there from the 1950s to the 1970s after the new China was established; however, there were never increases in the sex ratio at birth. Why? There was no one-child policy then. With wide fertility space and room to manage, a couple could always get a boy as long as they kept trying; thus reproduction could follow its own course and there was no need for sex selection. Therefore, the increases in the sex ratio at birth, following the tightening of the fertility policy, were caused by the one-child policy.

Third, there is the partial-relation view, i.e., the increases in the sex ratio at birth in the past 30 years are partially positively associated with the fertility policy. This view holds that the stricter the fertility policy is and the narrower the room for reproduction is, the more easily the sex ratio at birth increases. However, the fertility policy is not the only reason the ratio has increased, and other economic, cultural, and social factors combined have led to the increases in the ratio.

These three views are only roughly classified, and various opinions may be close to and can be grouped with one of the three. Apparently, all the views are reasonable while at the same time they all have their own problems. The first two emphasize different aspects and have opposite conclusions on the impact of the fertility policy on the sex ratio at birth, with one acknowledging and the other denying the impact.

The third view seems to have combined the first two and has included the opinions of many to various degrees. However, this view settles with the explanation that the one-child fertility policy has squeezed the space for reproduction and fails to dig deeper to identity which specific policy rule has the definitive role; meanwhile, it fits the relationship between the fertility policy and other factors into a general "symptom and root" analysis and concludes with a solution to tackle both the symptoms and the root. However, what are the symptoms and what is the root of the increases in the sex ratio at birth? Where should reforms and measures be focused, the symptoms or the root? The third view fails to provide clear descriptions and is thus confusing. Therefore, a more realistic and clearer explanation based on both theories and practices is needed.

Looking for a realistic explanation

In line with this train of thought, the following three questions that are logically tightly associated must be answered in turn. What is the concept or motive behind the increases in the sex ratio at birth? What is the foundation of the concept or motive? What was the key to or condition of the increases in the sex ratio at birth in the 1980s? Such an exploration from the surface to the core and from the concrete to the abstract may lead us to the exact reason that agrees with reality.

The domination of the reproduction culture of sex preference

No one would deny that the increases in the sex ratio at birth have been driven by the preference for boys in people's minds. After all, there would not have been any increase in the ratio had it not been for this preference, in which case the sex of newborns would have been entirely in the hand of natural laws. It is widely known that the human sex ratio has roughly stayed in balance through the more than 4 million years of human history as sex is determined by a natural law. Modern medical and genetic studies have already revealed the law.

In humans, each cell has 23 pairs of, or 46, chromosomes, among which, the 23rd is the pair of sex chromosomes. The sex chromosomes in males comprise one X chromosome and one Y chromosome, while those in females comprise two X chromosomes. When a sperm bearing an X chromosome fuses with an egg bearing an X chromosome at conception, the fertilized egg will develop into a female fetus. If the sperm bears a Y chromosome, the fertilized egg will develop into a male fetus.

Mutations on the 23rd pair of chromosomes may lead to aberrant forms of the chromosomes, e.g., addition or deletion of one chromosome, and abnormal sex forms may result, such as male-oriented sex (type I intersex), female-oriented sex (type II intersex), and dual-sex (type III intersex or hermaphrodite). Some even classify the intersex into seven types, but no matter how many types there are, intersex is rare and humans are basically male and female.

In summary, the sex determination of a fetus in the mother's womb is entirely a biological process and there is no room for intervention. The only way to intervene with the sex of babies is to abort the fetus of an undesirable sex. Therefore, sex-selective abortion is the direct and major cause of increases in the sex ratio at birth.

To learn about the preference for boys among the Chinese, one must first understand that the preference has long been internalized by the society as a culture: a culture with a preference for boys in reproduction. What is *culture*? I have seen various definitions, the total number of which easily exceeds 100. There are this many definitions because, one, the definition differs in various disciplines as a different definition will result if approached from history, philosophy, literature, arts, religion, economics, politics, or law; two, different applications, e.g., some focusing on the inside or mental aspects, others on the outside or generic aspects, result in different definitions; and, three, different temporal perspectives also give rise to different definitions as some examine the past and histories, some the present, and others the future. With all aspects combined, the definition of *culture* may be interpreted from the following three layers.

The first layer is the culture in a broad sense. Ancient Egyptians built pyramids, which highlighted the great achievements in construction of the ancient people, embodied the scientific and cultural development of ancient Egypt, and therefore represented the Nile culture. China's Great Wall, the Imperial Palace, and the Summer Palace have all been selected as World Heritage Sites by the United Nations Educational, Scientific and Cultural Organization (UNESCO) as these constructions represent the material and spiritual civilizations of their own historical eras.

Similarly, the large number of constructions from the 14th to the 16th centuries in Italy embody the Renaissance culture that is human oriented, against religion and medieval scholasticism, and for scientific spirits. Such broad-sensed cultures are the sums of the material and spiritual wealth of certain historical periods.

The second layer is the culture in a general sense. Greece has an ancient civilization that originated in Crete, an island in the Aegean Sea. The residents in Crete started to have commercial ties with the tribes around the Mediterranean Sea from a very early age, and their fair trades shaped a culture in the general sense of early times, i.e., social ideologies, or the concept of "equality" and the idea of "democracy," including thoughts, concepts, traditions, beliefs, religions, moral values, ethics, and conventions.

For China, it is a different story. China is surrounded by mountains on three sides and is obstructed by deserts. Such a closed environment, together with an inverted culture, was in dominance for a long time with the help of deeply rooted feudal thoughts despite the great accomplishments of the Silk Road and Zheng He's expeditionary voyages by sea that later became legendary. Over a long time, there formed a complete feudal value-specific culture on relations between monarch and minister and between father and son – i.e., "Xiao (filiality), Ti (brotherhood), Zhong (loyalty), Xin (trust), Li (rites), Yi (justice), Lian (honesty), and Chi (shame)" – which became the culture in the general sense in traditional China.

The third layer is the culture in a narrow sense, i.e., people's scientific knowledge and level of education. For example, when filling out forms, one always encounters a blank under "cultural degree" or "cultural level," meant to be filled with an educational level such as college, high school, primary school, half-illiterate, or illiterate.

The culture with preference for one sex in reproduction falls into the category of ideological cultures in the general sense. It describes the concepts, ethics, moral values, and behavioral codes associated with the preference for one sex formed during the evolution of reproduction, or the ideologies representing the development of the preference for either sex in reproduction together with the materialized forms of the changes in the ideologies. In fact, the preference for boys started fairly early in China.

As early as in the periods of Spring and Autumn and the Warring States (770–221 BC), Confucius (551–479 BC) linked pluralism, as in his remark "how populous it is!" to preference for boys. In fact, Confucius did not simply want a large population, but a high-quality large population that could only be reached when "populous-ness" was associated with "sons." He also said, "women and small men are difficult to nurture," which superimposed women and small men and categorically classified them as disposable, and it became part of his thought system and theories of governance.

Inheriting Confucius's thoughts, Mencius (372–289 BC) said, "there are three ways to be unfilial, the worst of which is to produce no heir." This famous line left a deep mark on history as it is still well known in China after more than 2,000 years. Women would lose their status in their families and society if they failed to produce heirs, which reduced them to a reproductive tool for men.

Such status as a tool was further confirmed during the Han Dynasty (206 BC–AD 220), when Emperor Wu (156–87 BC) adopted Dong Zhongshu's advice and established Ruism as the official state philosophy while providing favorable packages for Ruist scholars to take positions in the central university and schools across counties and towns. This act, named "expelling hundreds of schools, honoring only Ruism," started a long history of feudal China ideologically ruled by Ruism.

During the Northern Song Dynasty (AD 960–1127), Zhou Dunyi (1017–1073) started the school of Li (principle), and his disciples, Cheng Hao (1032–1085) and Cheng Yi (1033–1107), who were brothers, developed his ideas to use the eternal "Li" to explain the universe, which made the relations between monarch and minister and between father and son the "universal principle" that was to be unchanged and followed in all times and all dynasties.

Later, in the Southern Song Dynasty (1127–1279), Zhu Xi (1130–1200) studied and integrated all lines of the school of Li and established a fairly complete system of Li, which preached "following the universal Li, eliminating human lust." The moral values were subsequently intensified of "*san gang wuchang*," or Sangang (three cardinal guides, i.e., ruler guides minister, father guides son, and husband guides wife) and Wuchang (five constant virtues, i.e., benevolence, righteousness, propriety, wisdom, and faithfulness), and the feudalistic ethics of "Sancong Side" of women, or threefold obedience (obeying father as daughter, obeying husband as wife, and obeying son as widow) and four virtues (wifely virtue, wifely speech, wifely demeanor, and wifely work), which, all together, became overwhelming public opinions and moral codes and had far-reaching influences.

Particularly, these values associated "multiple sons" with "multitude of fortune" to explicitly show the aim of increasing the population, which then became the belief of the people in pursuit of a prosperous family with many members; reproduction was also included in the feudalistic moral codes and families without a son as an heir were chained with the shackles of "unfiliality," an intimidating charge to the public. Moreover, the association of multiple sons with multitude of fortune found its way to marriage, reproduction, families, clans, occupation, health, ethics, moral values, household registration, statistics, astronomy, geology, and taxation, and, combined with social policies of land, land tax, and poll tax, resulted in a complex web of formidable demographic policies that were either direct or indirect, which dominated people's reproductive behaviors.

Feudal landlords invested heavily in these values and promoted the concept of "multiple sons, multitude of fortune," binding and unifying people through writing family lines, building ancestral halls, and erecting chastity memorial arches together with novels and dramas. With time, the resulting reproduction culture became religious. Furthermore, "multiple sons, multitude of fortune" did not only cover the material benefits for the family and the parents, but also the honor one would enjoy – honor that could only be obtained through good deeds, charitable behaviors, and honorable acts, without which one would suffer a fate with no sons or heirs and become unfilial.

Such intangible cultural shackles shaped people's reproductive behaviors and, shapelessly, silently, and breathlessly, inspired them to desire as many sons as possible. As a result, people reproduced under these norms for thousands of years. This reproduction culture with preference for boys had its specific denotations and connotations and decided what ought or ought not be done, what was to be approved or opposed, and where the lines were between good and evil and between the beautiful and the ugly, and it was binding and intimidating.

In addition, one prominent feature of public opinions is its popularity, which forms an intangible web in people's minds and shapes people's behaviors, possessing the power to "crush down people with tongues." In the traditional reproduction culture, which was a set of public opinions, the women who became pregnant without having been married were considered unforgivable and harshly reproached for their immoral acts. Women also had to marry according to their parents' wills and stay loyal to their husbands because they must "devote to a chicken if marrying one and a dog if marrying one," had no right to divorce their husbands, and could only assume the role as the deserted.

Further, wives were denounced as "broom stars" who had not done anything good in their past lives if failing to give birth or having only daughters, and they might even be expelled. In fact, public opinions usually have overwhelming power in where to lead people when it comes to the spread of ideological cultures, and they play their monitoring role when society tries to stay away from the ideas that are in opposition to the dominant culture. Meanwhile, religion, as a form of ideologies, integrates the dominating ideas, ethics, and moral codes and deifies them into sacred values with mystic and justice covers to govern people's minds.

Fundamental effects of the cost–benefit ratio of having children

The reproduction culture with preference for boys, like all other superstructures, did not emerge from nowhere or result from individual wills, but was founded on a particular socioeconomic base. The cost–benefit theory of having children summarizes and describes the relationship between the particular socioeconomic base and reproduction.

THE COST–BENEFIT THEORY OF HAVING CHILDREN

It is generally agreed that the cost–benefit theory of having children was first proposed and described by Western demographic economist H. Leibenstein, and it was later developed, modified, and supplemented into a fairly complete system by G. S. Becker, R. A. Easterlin, and J. C. Caldwell.

Leibenstein's cost–benefit theory of having children. Leibenstein classified the cost of having children into two types: the direct type, i.e., the expense on clothing, food, shelter, transportation, health care, education, and marriage from conception to adulthood, which is the direct spending of money on the child, and the indirect type, i.e., the loss of income due to pregnancy and breastfeeding and because the parents, especially the mother, have to take care of the child and cannot obtain more education, better positions, or promotions, which is the loss of potential opportunities, also called the opportunity cost. The latter is different from the former in that the former is direct money spending and the latter is indirect time spending.

People are willing to pay the price for children because children will bring corresponding benefits to their parents and families after they grow up. However, the benefits are anticipated and futuristic at the time the parents make payments. These benefits are as follows.

One is the labor-economic benefit. Children will grow up into laborers and provide labor for their parents and families or direct economic incomes by taking on occupational labor.

A second one is the old-age security benefit. In less-developed countries, older people have to rely heavily on their children for economic security and other services due to underdeveloped social insurance systems, and thus raising children is essentially investment in old-age security.

A third one is the consumption-leisure benefit. Children, as "enduring consumer goods," may satisfy their parents emotionally and psychologically and bring them the happiness of family life.

A fourth one is the risk benefit associated with family prosperity. The labor-economic benefit anticipated of children is also closely associated with the future economic risk of families. Generally speaking, the higher the benefit anticipated of a child, the stronger the risk resistance of the family; on the contrary, the lower the benefit, the weaker the resistance.

A fifth one is the benefit to maintain family status. In many developing countries, parents associate family prosperity with reproduction, such as "multiple sons, multitude of fortune," and children may inherit their parents' wealth and continue and enlarge the business of the families as well as taking on the responsibilities of the families and to the societies, so that the social status of the families is maintained.

A sixth one is the benefit of family security. Among a forest of families, a family must possess a lot of members to prosper. A large number of members and children brings a high security coefficient to the family, while a low number brings a low security coefficient. Children continue and extend the security of a family, which, from a development perspective, certainly increases with increases in children and decreases with decreases in children.

Leibenstein has shown that the cost of having children is positively associated with income and the direct cost has apparent increases with increases in income while the indirect cost, or the opportunity cost, also increases with time. What about the benefits, then? Except for the consumption-leisure benefit that is not quite clear and has little correlation with socioeconomic development, all the benefits show decreases. Particularly, the marginal labor-economic benefit of having children shows marked decreases with economic development, increasing family income, continuous technological advancement, and improvement in child quality, especially the quality of education, which all bring significant increases in the marginal cost of additional children, particularly the cost of quality nurturing, while the marginal labor-economic benefit an additional child brings shows marked decreases.

The marginal old-age security benefit an additional child brings his parents also shows decreases: economic development and increased incomes result in growing social and family savings and society can afford more welfare schemes, including establishing a fairly complete security system of old-age insurance. Meanwhile, laborers can afford to set aside money from their incomes to pay for old-age insurance. In practice, the insurance provided by society is usually combined with the insurance provided by families, which forms an institution and system of old-age security with the society and families playing complementary roles, dwarfing the old-age security benefit of having children.

Other benefits, such as the risk benefit to carry on family businesses, the benefit to maintain family status, and the family security benefit, all show various degrees of decline. Leibenstein also investigated the impact on decreases in fertility rates of various social factors, including growing proportions of core families, population urbanization, decreases in mortality rates, improved educational levels of women, weaning interest in having boys from parents, withdrawal of traditional values, and promotion and employment of various contraceptive ways, and found that they overall assisted with the decreases and weakening of the benefits children would bring their parents. Yet the most fundamental basis and definitive factor of the decreases is economic development.

In addition, based on the socioeconomic stratifications he made according to average family incomes, Leibenstein's conclusion is that in developing countries transitioning from an agricultural to an industrial economy, the direct and indirect costs increase with the transition while the benefits, particularly the labor-economic and old-age security ones, decrease, with the only exception being the consumption-leisure benefit.

Becker's quantity–quality trade-off theory of children. Becker, a Nobel Laureate in economics and a professor at Chicago University, built upon Leibenstein's child cost–benefit theory, established the child quantity–quality trade-off theory, and described the trade-off model. He studied the demands of families for children by placing family laborers in markets and introducing the indifference curve of consumption demands, complementation, and replacement of commodities and the theory of equilibrium of the consumer; proposed the idea of net cost of children; and deducted the maximization of child benefits.

Becker argued that the net cost of having a child was the direct cost a family anticipated to pay for the child, plus the indirect time cost (through the shadow price) on the parents, minus the anticipated income in terms of cash and labor of the child. He set 18 as the age of a child at which his parents would stop raising him as he became independent, and the period before the child reached this age was the cost period and that after, the benefit period.

If a child's net cost is positive, the benefits the child brings his parents will be lower than the cost his parents have paid, which makes the child a kind of average enduring consumer good to his parents, who will only obtain mental benefits from him/her; if a child's net cost is negative, the benefits the child brings his parents will be large enough to cover the cost the parents have paid, which makes the child a kind of enduring production good that brings added value.

The maximization of child benefits and the child quantity–quality trade-off model are built upon these scenarios, which are innovations of Becker and the Chicago school of economics he belonged to. In contrast to Leibenstein, who focused on the marginal benefits of additional children, Becker further studied the maximization of benefits and showed that with a fixed family income, the quantity and the quality of children were negatively correlated. The family would naturally choose to trade quantity for quality of the children, resulting in large-scale reduction in fertility rates with economic development and increased incomes.

Easterlin's child supply–demand theory. Based on the studies of Leibenstein and Becker on people's reproductive behaviors and number of children through cost–benefit analyses from the perspective of families' demands for children, Easterlin, a professor at the University of Southern California, added two more variables, supply of children and cost of fertility control, and developed the supply–demand theory in reproductive decision-making. His definition of child demand has no peculiar point and it is the anticipated number of live children of a couple that is independent of other coefficients, and his definition of child supply is the number of children of a couple that is independent of other coefficients, which is decided by the natural fertility of the couple and the survival rate of their children.

The variable of cost of fertility control includes the economic cost of the control and the mental cost of releasing the emotional burdens brought by fertility control. When the cost of fertility control is excluded, there is no need for fertility control if the supply of child is below the demand, as in an agrarian society, and there is a need for fertility control if the supply exceeds the demand. When the cost of fertility control is included, Easterlin argued, the cost would be an important variable that deserved attention.

Since the cost is near zero in developed countries, as Easterlin noted, together with the considerable reduction in newborn and child mortalities, i.e., increased supply of children due to increased child survival, fertility control has become widespread and the fertility rates are kept low. In contrast, in developing countries, the cost of fertility control is usually high, with relatively high newborn and child mortalities, i.e., decreased child supply due to relatively low child survival, fertility control is not as widespread, and the fertility rates are kept high; the situation is particularly common in countries and areas with underdeveloped economies and cultures.

Caldwell's theory of intergenerational wealth flows. Caldwell, a demographer at Australian National University, built upon the child cost–benefit theory and formulated the intergenerational wealth flows theory by exploring the directions and amounts of wealth flow between parents and children in various societies.

Caldwell's wealth included not only money and assets but also labor and services, which are not to be neglected in intergenerational relations. His analyses have shown that in a traditional, preindustrial society, the net wealth flow is from children to parents as the cost of raising children is low but the labor-economic and old-age security benefits are apparent. In a modern society after industrialization, children must be brought up into laborers with certain cultural and professional abilities to find jobs, and parents have to invest additional wealth in the education of their children in anticipation of reasonable benefits; however, the development of commercial and market economies has resulted in elevated independence of children and continuous shrinkage in family sizes, and the net wealth flows from parents to children. Therefore, people pursue the quality rather than the quantity of children, which also brings reduction in fertility rates.

SEX DISPARITY IN THE CHILD COST–BENEFIT RATIO

Despite their various descriptions of the cost and benefits of raising children, these scholars all had the same framework, core task, and direction when describing marginal changes in the cost and benefits of children that shaped the fertility decisions of families. However, their theories did not differentiate between the two sexes and that has to be considered a pity.

After all, it is only meaningful in practice when the theories can be applied and combined with the sex of children. In the early 1990s, I, as principal investigator of a project supported by a UN population fund CRP/90P06, *Study on Family Economies and Fertility in China*, conducted a sampling survey, in collaboration with proper agencies in Hebei, Liaoning, Shanghai, Zhejiang, Shandong, Jiangxi, Guangdong, Shanxi, Sichuan, and Guizhou, on families' economic and fertility situations in 10 provinces in China in 1992 and obtained a complete set of field data.

The survey covered 12,200 families, which could be classified into the following groups according to the number and the sex of children: 2,228 single-boy families, accounting for 18.26% of all the families, 1,667 or 13.66% single-girl families, 1,133 or 9.29% two-boy families, 493 or 4.04% two-girl families, 2,696 or 22.1% one-boy-one-girl families, and 3,983 or 32.65% families with three or more children. The survey data showed distinct differences between the two sexes in the marginal child cost and benefits. Such sex-specific difference in the cost and benefits of raising children is the economic foundation for the preference for boys in China's reproductive culture, as well as the economic foundation for the increases in the sex ratio at birth.

Sex difference in the cost of raising children. With the indirect cost of mothers taking care of children excluded, the direct cost of raising children, as shown by the weighted data from the 1992 sampling survey, was on average 628.92 yuan per year for the first boy of a family paid in the monetary currency, and 576.89 yuan for the first girl, with the ratio of boy to girl being 1.0902. That is also to say, the monetary cost of supporting a first-order boy was 109.02% of that of a girl.[6] The costs of the second-, third-, and higher-order births were somewhat different, but they were all close to the same number. Therefore, 109% represents the difference in the cost between one family raising a boy and one a girl.

Sex difference in the benefits of raising children. Based on the six benefits of children posited by Leibenstein, together with China's conditions, the weighted data in the 1992 sampling survey listed the benefits of increasing family incomes and providing labor, old-age security, emotional comfort, and pleasure in family lives, continuing the family line, inheriting family businesses, and other benefits. The national average anticipated benefits showed considerable differences for boys and girls. The benefits of increasing family incomes and providing labor anticipated of boys accounted for 17.97% of all the benefits, slightly higher than the percentage of girls, 17.05%.

In terms of the old-age security benefit, what was anticipated of boys accounted for 23.01%, 31.64% higher than that of girls, 17.48%, with the ratio of boys to girls being 131.64:100.00. Yet when it came to the benefit of emotional comfort and pleasure in family lives, what was anticipated of boys accounted for 15.25%, and of girls 34.64%, a marked distinction between the two sexes. For the benefit of carrying on family lines, what was anticipated of boys accounted for 24.40%, the highest of all benefits among boys, and only 5.06% for girls, with boys 4.82 times that of girls and claiming the largest difference in benefits between boys and girls.

In terms of the benefit of inheriting family businesses, what was anticipated of boys accounted for 11.99%, 2.70 times that of girls, 4.44%, marking this item as the second largest difference between boys and girls. In the category of other benefits, what was anticipated of boys accounted for 7.38% and of girls 21.45%, also showing a large difference between the two, which was mostly because girls would provide more types of services than boys. Overall, boys mostly provided the benefits of carrying on the family line, providing old-age security, and inheriting family businesses, and girls showed significant impact on mental benefits as their largest benefit proportion was of emotional comfort and pleasure in family lives. Apparently, sons provide material benefits while daughters bring mental ones.

Now that China is transitioning from a country of low and medium incomes to one of high incomes, the benefits sons bring are of clear advantages and thus are more important than those provided by girls. This is why there is still a strong preference for boys in China, and it is the root of interventions into fetus sex and the continuous increases in the sex ratio at birth. Meanwhile, it also shows the direction for reforms of and management of the increased sex ratio at birth.

REPRODUCTIVE DESIRES MANIFESTING THE PREFERENCE FOR SONS

The objectively present differences in the cost and benefits between raising boys and girls, when reflected in reproductive desires, become the sex preference that is after sons in reproduction. The 1992 sampling survey showed that the sampled families differed greatly in their reproductive desires according to the sexes of the children they already had. Among them, the desires of the single-boy and single-girl families are shown in Tables 5.5 and 5.6.

The desires of the families that already had two boys or two girls are listed in Tables 5.7 and 5.8.

The desires of the families that already had one boy and one girl are listed in Table 5.9.

Table 5.5 Reproductive desires of urban and rural single-boy families, 1992 (%)

Respondents	*No more*	*1 more boy*	*1 more girl*	*1 more child*	*2 more children*	*3+ more children*
National						
Males	63.30	1.64	21.18	6.96	4.49	0.43
Females	69.11	0.59	21.47	6.04	2.74	0.04
Cities						
Males	72.16	1.48	18.36	5.72	2.12	0.17
Females	74.89	0.51	17.64	5.58	1.39	0.00
Towns						
Males	61.92	0.65	27.16	8.07	2.21	0.00
Females	63.33	0.50	28.35	6.11	1.72	0.00
Counties						
Males	60.81	1.89	20.85	10.86	5.71	0.60
Females	65.82	0.73	22.22	6.49	4.54	0.09

Source: Tian, Xueyuan, ed., Hu, Weilue and Liu, Qiming, sub. eds., *Materials of 1992 Sampling Survey on Family Economic and Fertility Situations in 10 Provinces and Municipalities in China*, China Economic Publishing House, 1995, pp. 85–88.

Table 5.6 Reproductive desires of urban and rural single-girl families, 1992 (%)

Respondents	*No more*	*1 more boy*	*1 more girl*	*1 more child*	*2 more children*	*3+ more children*
National						
Males	48.46	38.33	0.46	7.20	5.03	0.52
Females	61.12	24.80	1.07	9.75	3.26	0.00
Cities						
Males	72.66	18.24	0.21	6.68	1.38	0.83
Females	71.64	16.32	1.42	9.59	0.94	0.00
Towns						
Males	57.50	32.19	0.71	8.76	0.84	0.00
Females	56.52	30.81	1.34	10.11	1.21	0.00
Counties						
Males	36.94	47.60	0.50	7.07	7.38	0.50
Females	48.73	33.68	0.45	9.66	7.48	0.00

Source: Tian, Xueyuan, ed., Hu, Weilue and Liu, Qiming, sub. eds., *Materials of 1992 Sampling Survey on Family Economic and Fertility Situations in 10 Provinces and Municipalities in China*, China Economic Publishing House, 1995, pp. 85–88.

Table 5.7 Reproductive desires of urban and rural two-boy families, 1992 (%)

Respondents	*No more*	*1 more boy*	*1 more girl*	*1 more child*	*2 more children*	*3+ more children*
National						
Males	89.82	0.21	8.26	0.37	1.00	0.33
Females	93.42	0.33	5.54	0.13	0.00	0.59
Cities						
Males	94.06	0.00	5.04	0.90	0.00	0.00
Females	97.71	0.00	2.29	0.00	0.00	0.00
Towns						
Males	92.34	0.00	8.58	0.35	1.06	0.00
Females	92.60	0.00	5.84	1.56	0.00	0.00
Counties						
Males	89.40	0.24	8.58	0.35	1.06	0.37
Females	92.29	0.48	6.43	0.00	0.00	0.83

Source: Tian, Xueyuan, ed.; Hu, Weilue and Liu, Qiming, sub. eds., *Materials of 1992 Sampling Survey on Family Economic and Fertility Situations in 10 Provinces and municipalities in China*, China Economic Publishing House, 1995, pp. 89–92.

Table 5.8 Reproductive desires of urban and rural two-girl families, 1992 (%)

Respondents	*No more*	*1 more boy*	*1 more girl*	*1 more child*	*2 more children*	*3+ more children*
National						
Males	76.37	21.50	0.00	0.00	1.40	0.73
Females	86.48	9.61	0.00	0.00	3.91	0.00
Cities						
Males	95.94	4.06	0.00	0.00	0.00	0.00
Females	99.17	0.83	0.00	0.00	0.00	0.00
Towns						
Males	77.89	20.04	0.00	0.00	2.07	0.00
Females	89.70	10.30	0.00	0.00	0.00	0.00
Counties						
Males	72.83	24.66	0.00	0.00	1.59	0.91
Females	79.55	13.70	0.00	0.00	6.74	0.00

Source: Tian, Xueyuan, ed.; Hu, Weilue and Liu, Qiming, sub. eds., *Materials of 1992 Sampling Survey on Family Economic and Fertility Situations in 10 Provinces and municipalities in China*, China Economic Publishing House, 1995, pp. 89–92.

The reproductive desires of the families of various numbers of children and combinations of children's sexes in 1992, as shown in Tables 5.5–5.9, clearly illustrate the effects and impacts of the factors associated with sex ratio at birth.

First, people already had further understanding of fertility control after years of advocacy for one child per couple, and a considerable proportion of

Table 5.9 Reproductive desires of urban and rural one-boy-one-girl families, 1992 (%)

Respondents	*No more*	*1 more boy*	*1 more girl*	*1 more child*	*2 more children*	*3+ more children*
National						
Males	94.02	3.51	0.02	0.98	1.34	0.13
Females	91.82	5.46	0.00	0.20	2.20	0.31
Cities						
Males	98.38	0.00	0.45	0.44	0.74	0.00
Females	99.36	0.32	0.00	0.00	0.32	0.00
Towns						
Males	97.03	0.00	0.00	0.66	0.58	1.73
Females	98.73	1.27	0.00	0.00	0.00	0.00
Counties						
Males	93.63	3.87	0.00	1.03	1.41	0.07
Females	89.40	7.08	0.00	0.26	2.85	0.41

Source: Tian, Xueyuan, ed.; Hu, Weilue and Liu, Qiming, sub. eds., *Materials of 1992 Sampling Survey on Family Economic and Fertility Situations in 10 Provinces and Municipalities in China*, China Economic Publishing House, 1995, pp. 93–94.

the families that already had a child had no intention of having more children. The proportion of families with no intention of having more children grew with the number of children, and it was particularly high in families that had already one boy and one girl.

Second, the concept of having a perfect pair of a son and a daughter is deeply rooted in people's minds, which is also reflected in the desired sex of one more child. As shown in Table 5.5, among the families that already had a son, 21.18% desired to have a daughter, which was 57.71% of all those who wanted more children, and a slightly higher proportion of female respondents wanted a daughter than men, which was 21.47%, accounting for 69.5% of all those who wanted more children. The highest proportion, however, occurred in the families that already had a daughter, and 38.33% of the male respondents wanted a son, accounting for 73.37% of all those who wanted more children, while 24.80% of the female respondents wanted a son, accounting for 63.79% of all those who wanted more children. Apparently, most families were after both sons and daughters, as "a son and a daughter add up to a flower," which had the biggest impact on the increases in the sex ratio at birth.

Third, these observations were based on the national data, and when broken down into urban and rural data, the desire of having a son is stronger in rural than urban areas. Among the families with one girl that wanted more children, 66.72% of the urban male respondents wanted a son and so did 63.79% of the women while the two percentages were as high as 75.48% for men and 65.69% for women in rural areas, both of which were higher than the urban numbers by a large scale.

Fourth, the desire for another boy declines with the number of children in families. For example, 38.33% of the men in the families that already had a daughter wanted a son, and so did 24.8% of the women while only 21.50% of the men in the families that already had two daughters wanted a son, and only 9.61% of the women did; when it came to the families that already had a son and a daughter, only 3.51% of the men and 5.46% of the women wanted another son. These three types of families were most closely associated with the increases in the sex ratio at birth, especially the type with one daughter in pursuit of a son.

These observations, drawn from the 1992 sampling survey, were still true in the next 20 years. Several surveys conducted later showed that the highest proportion of people wanted two children, which was usually above 70%; the ideal was one boy and one girl, which was of an even higher proportion; and a considerable proportion of families with two daughters still wanted a son.

Apparently, although people no longer live in big families with four or even five generations under the same roof, the desire for a son has not really waned much for families of three or four members. The desire has waned more obviously in urban areas than in rural areas, and not at all in a considerable number of peasant families. All these situations have shown that the tradition of valuing boys over girls has not withdrawn with the closing gap of child cost and benefits between the two sexes that is caused by economic development, technological advancement, and social reformations; after all, changes in ideologies are always behind those in real life.

The key role of population policies

The foregoing description showed that the increases in China's sex ratio at birth since the 1980s were directly under the influence of the traditional reproductive culture with preference for boys while the differential child cost and benefits between daughters and sons added to the foundation of the culture with economic reinforcement. Both causes are fundamental: the preference for boys in the reproductive culture laid the conceptual foundation for the increases of the sex ratio at birth, and the boy-favoring child cost–benefit ratio laid the economic foundation.

However, it is certainly not sufficient to explain the increases with only these two causes – they had both been there for a long time, but the increases were not there during the first 30 years after the establishment of the new China, during which various degrees of decreases were actually observed, and suddenly showed up after 1980. After all, the cultural and economic foundations are only foundations just like one in construction; a building must be erected on a foundation, but when it is finally finished depends on whether the materials and the workers are ready and how fast it is built. The abrupt increases in the sex ratio at birth in the 1980s meant that the building of the increased ratio had been ready. What was the condition to make it ready? It was the newly issued demographic policy that aimed to tighten the fertility and birth rates.

Changes are based on intrinsic factors and conditioned by exterior ones, and this is a fundamental theory of dialectical materialism. However, it does not mean that the intrinsic factors are important while the exterior ones are not when it comes to the changes of real objects. For example, a chicken may break out of an egg when the temperature is right, but no matter how right the temperature is, a chicken may never come out of a rock; on the other hand, an egg will never hatch if put in a refrigerator or an oven no matter how long it is left there. Here, the exterior condition – temperature – is important because without the right condition, or the right temperature, the change will not occur. Likewise, the issuance of the policy that advocated for one child per couple with associated regulations in the 1980s enabled the increases in the sex ratio at birth to find the "right temperature" and they quickly sprouted and grew.

The government officially advocated for one child per couple in 1980. From late March to early May, the Secretariat of the CCCPC commissioned the General Office to hold five consecutive meetings on how to effectively control population growth, whether the one-child policy would be practical, and if yes, what challenges would face us and how to deal with them. Later a report was submitted to the Secretariat that resulted from these meetings and in the report, six potential problems of the one-child policy were described and analyzed, and trend prediction and solutions were also provided.

Increasing sex ratio at birth was one of the six problems, which was described in the report as such: "Some under the influence of the traditional ideas of having heirs may treasure sons more than daughters and may even commit crimes such as drowning and deserting newborn girls, which should be taken seriously and prohibited by law." To be fair, the report is honest and predictive.

In fact, if taken seriously and managed with effective measures from the beginning, the subsequent increases in the sex ratio at birth may not have happened, or may not have been as severe even if they did happen. Unfortunately, for a long time, the increases were not paid close attention to, neither was there any effective measure. Thus the problem aggregated and worsened. Therefore, there was indeed an impact on the increased sex ratio at birth by the tightened population policy; however, the situation worsened step by step because no measure had been taken from the beginning.

There have long been irreconcilable mismatches between people's reproductive desires and what is allowed in policies, and some attempts to reconcile them, e.g., the policy that allowed rural families with one daughter to have another child, only made things worse and fostered the increases in the sex ratio of second- and higher-order births.

Previous descriptions of the relationship between the population policy and the increases in the sex ratio at birth mostly focused on the point that the one-child policy squeezed out much space for fertility and people had only one chance to realize their pursuit for boys. It is no doubt a reasonable point.

After it was advocated that each couple ought to have only one child, people were left with minimal fertility space and the previously naturally occurring sex ratio at birth might have been artificially altered. In ages with high fertility rates, such as the aforementioned 1950s and 1960s with TFRs above 5.0 and the 1970s with TFRs above 4.0, people did not really care about the sex ratio at birth, which balanced itself under the influence of the natural law; even when there was an imbalance of sexes among the first two or three children, who were all boys or all girls, continuation of reproduction would normally remedy that, and there was usually no problem of getting a child of a desired sex.

Now that only one child per couple was advocated, the sex ratio at birth had no other choice but to be decided by the only children among all families; the preference for boys thus drove people to intervene with the sex of fetuses, resulting in the increases of the sex ratio at birth. The data of the fourth, fifth, and sixth censuses, for example, showed that the sex ratios of first-order births in 1990, 2000, and 2010 were 105.07, 107.12, and 113.73, respectively.[7]

Among these numbers, only the sex ratio of first-order births of the fourth census was within the normal range, and that of the fifth exceeded the upper limit of the normal range, 107, by a little bit, both of which were exceeded by the markedly high ratio of the sixth, 6.61 percentage points higher than the fifth and 8.66 percentage points higher than the fourth.

However, the limited increases in the sex ratio of first-order births were not enough to boost the overall sex ratio at birth fast or for long. The abrupt increases of the sex ratio of second- and higher-order births also helped greatly. As mentioned earlier, the birth-order-specific sex ratio at birth was the highest at third- or fourth-order births, but these two orders of births accounted for an extremely low percentage of all births, 5.30% and 0.98%, respectively, in the sixth census, for example, and together, they only accounted for 6.28% of all births.

In contrast, first-order births, with the sex ratio at birth being 113.73, accounted for 62.17% of all births, and second-order births, with the ratio being 130.29, accounted for 31.28% of all births.[8] Together, first- and second-order births accounted for 93.45% of all births, shaping the level of the overall sex ratio at birth fundamentally. Between the two birth orders, there was a great difference in their impacts on the sex ratio at birth: the ratio of first-order births was 113.73, 7.48 points lower than the overall ratio. Apparently, the ratio of first-order births was only high for a normal sex ratio at birth, but the lowest among the birth-order-specific sex ratios at birth in the sixth census, thus it actually pulled down instead of boosting the overall sex ratio of the census. It then put the sex ratio of second-order births, 130.29, a value 9.08 points higher than the overall ratio, at the center of the driving force to boost the overall ratio.

Compared to second-order births, third- and higher-order births only accounted for 6.55% of all births and had extremely limited impact on the overall sex ratio at birth despite a much higher sex ratio. Therefore, the increases in the sex ratio of second-order births, which accounted for nearly one-third of all births, were the decisive factor to boost the sex ratio at birth.

Then, what was the reason for the sex ratio of second-order births to jump all the way up to over 130.0? Was it related to policies? If yes, which ones? Previous studies have simply attributed the increases to the one-child policy and its impact on squeezing out the fertility space. As reasonable as it is, i.e., people were allowed only one child and could only manage to get the preferred sex of this child, it fails to explain why the sex ratio of first-order births was not very high, yet that of second-order births soared and decided the overall sex ratio at birth. Is any regulation in the population policy related to child sexes, especially the sex of second-order children? To answer the question, one must, and will benefit from doing so, look through all fertility-related policies issued after the one-child policy and make analyses and conclusions based on real situations. The major policies related to fertility since the 1980s are as follows.

From late March to early May, the Secretariat of the CCCPC commissioned the General Office to hold five consecutive meetings, and no sex-specific population policy resulted from these meetings, neither was there any in the report later submitted to the Secretariat. It was, however, proposed in the report that precautions should be taken by law to prevent crimes such as drowning and deserting newborn girls in order to maintain the balance of sexes, as already mentioned.

On September 10, 1981, the Secretariat of the CCCPC held a meeting to discuss how to draft a population policy that could fit the realities and be accepted by the people. It was reiterated during the meeting to "unswervingly continue to advocate for one child per couple in cities and towns and strengthen the work in rural areas based on the new situations after the responsibility system was implemented with moderate loosening up of the policy." Two proposals were made on how to moderately loosen up the policy in rural areas and then circulated among provinces, municipalities, and autonomous prefectures for feedback.

The feedback showed that six provinces (areas) were in favor of the first proposal and 15 (areas and cities) and the leader group of the national family planning commission supported the second; five wanted to keep the framework of the *Public Letter*; three did not provide any feedback. In fact, the second proposal was as follows: "It is generally advocated for one child per couple, but for those who have real difficulties with only one child, a second birth is allowed."

In February 1982, the CCCPC and the State Council issued the *Instruction on Further Carrying Out Family Planning* and stated:

> Late marriage, late reproduction, fewer children, and quality reproduction are to continue to be advocated for. The specific requirements are as follows: only one child is allowed for a couple who are cadres and employees of government agencies and urban residents except for those

> with approval due to exceptional conditions. One child is allowed for a couple in rural areas, and for those who have real difficulties and need a second child, due procedures for approval are to be run and a second child may be planned reasonably. Under no circumstances is a third child allowed.

The *Instruction* also specified the reward and regulatory articles to fine-tune the implementation of the policy.

In October 1982, the CCCPC and the State Council forwarded the *Minutes of the National Meeting on Family Planning* by the National Commission of Family Planning. The *Minutes* listed the three conditions for a second child in all provinces, municipalities, and autonomous prefectures before the issuance of the *Instruction*, which are couples with the first child having noninheritable disabilities and unable to grow up to a normal laborer, rearranged families with one party having only one child from the previous marriage and the other of first marriage, and couples who are sterile after having been married for many years and get pregnant after having adopted a child.

After the issuance of the *Instruction*, many provinces, municipalities, and autonomous prefectures added four to five and sometimes even six to seven conditions for rural residents to these three preexisting conditions, and these additions can be summarized into the following types: 1. families with only one son for two or three consecutive generations; 2. families with only one fertile son out of all sons; 3. couples with the husband registering to the wife's family while the wife is the only child of her family; 4. couples with both parties being the only children to their parents; 5. disabled military members; 6. couples with both parties having moved back from overseas; and 7. particularly desolate families in remote mountainous areas and along seaside fishing areas.

In 1984, the No. 7 file of the central government was issued, which was interpreted in various ways, with some taking it simply as a policy to loosen up control on second births, resulting in fluctuations in the birth and fertility rates. In March 1988, the Standing Committee of the Political Bureau of the CCCPC held a meeting to discuss the *Outline of the Report on Family Planning* and reiterated:

> The current policy on family planning is to advocate for late marriage, late reproduction, fewer children, and quality reproduction, and for one child per couple; cadres and employees of government agencies and urban residents, except for rare situations that may obtain approval, can only have one child per couple; some in rural areas with real difficulties, such as the families with only one female child, may be allowed to have a second child, but it must be approved first and the second birth must be a few years after the first; under no circumstances is a third birth allowed; and family planning should also be advocated for in minority-residing areas and specific policies may be drafted by the provincial or prefectural government based on the realities there.

The meeting took special care to state that these policies would be persisted with and carried out for a rather long term and they must remain stable to benefit population control.[9]

Among these policies that had various degrees of relevance to child sexes and real situations, the one that allows rural families with only one daughter to have another child is the most explicit policy that involves gender and thus played a key role in the increases of the sex ratio at birth. Although the proportion of second- and higher-order births stayed high in rural areas after the official implementation of the one-child policy, no policy had been officially issued concerning a second birth until 1988, when, in a rather complete description of population policies, it was explicitly stated that

> some in rural areas with real difficulties, such as the families with only one female child, may be allowed to have a second child, but it must be approved first and the second birth must be a few years after the first.

Thus second births were legalized, which immediately exerted its impact. In the fourth census in 1990, the sex ratio of second-order births went up to 121.52 and the number further climbed to 151.92 in the fifth census in 2000.

I have always opposed the policy that allows rural families with one daughter to have another child. Why is that? In the first place, regulation of child numbers allowed based on sex is itself sex discriminative. There was originally no differentiation in the one-child policy issued in the 1980s between urban and rural areas or between the two sexes. The subsequent policy that allowed another child for the rural families with only one daughter differentiated between urban and rural areas and between the two sexes.

Differentiation between urban and rural areas was the right thing to do since there was apparent disparity between urban and rural economies. However, differentiation between boys and girls was totally another issue. Why may a rural family with only a female child have a second child? Why can't a rural family with only a boy child have another one? Apparently, girls are inferior to boys. It has to do with the status of girls in families and society, as well as how to comprehend their status and roles, and it is highly inappropriate for a government policy to have this implication.

In the second place, the policy clearly favors the preference for boys in reproduction. When it was first issued, the policy did not intend to encourage people to pursue boys; however, it did not prohibit interventions to obtain boys, either; neither did it provide any associated mechanism and regulation. Only when it was later found out that the sex ratio of second-order births abnormally soared high did the government issue regulations to prohibit non-medical examinations for fetus sex. In fact, under the dominating boy preference in China, would rural families with one daughter already want another daughter? The answer is certainly negative. After all, as mentioned earlier, most people are affected by the deeply rooted ideology that values boys over girls and desire "one boy and one girl to make a flower." The ideology and the reproductive desire, once combined with the policy that allowed a second birth for rural families with only one daughter, quickly broke the balance of newborn sexes and lifted the sex ratio at birth.

In the third place, technological advancements have made fetus sex extremely easy to identify. A major breakthrough was the application of ultrasonic imaging. Before the technique, identification of fetus sex was difficult and not accurate at all, and after it, it is as easy as flipping a hand and is performed quickly. There has been some effect since nonmedical examinations for fetus sex were prohibited; however, the effect is limited as it is extremely hard to decide whether the procedure is for nonmedical reasons and patients need not mention "fetus sex" for it to be well identified.

I once performed a field survey on this topic and learned this lesson dearly. Let me provide an example with details. A pregnant woman comes to an obstetric hospital for a check-up and she tells the obstetrician that she went through the initial phase of pregnancy easily but she has recently experienced belly pains that have affected her appetite and sleep; she has heard that boys are restless in wombs, stretching arms and kicking legs, yet she is not sure that is what she's experienced and asks what it could be. She also asks the obstetrician to examine her thoroughly with ultrasound and she expresses her gratitude sincerely. The obstetrician understands immediately, gives her an ultrasound, and tells her that she is all right and the belly pain she's felt is most likely caused by the stretching and kicking of the fetus. The patient gets what it really means and leaves after thanking the doctor multiple times. A dialogue like this, even when recorded, is hardly evidence for "nonmedical examination for fetus sex" and escapes punishment of any sort.

This is by no means intended to deny the real difficulties rural families with only a daughter are faced with or the difference between males and females in reality. It is intended to figure out a population policy that has no, or as little as possible, negative effect with acknowledgment of the difficulties and the difference. The negative effect here means abnormal changes in the sex ratio at birth or increases in the ratio. Under China's dual economic and social structure between urban and rural areas, a differential population policy for urban and rural areas is reasonable and practical in that one child is allowed for urban residents and two for rural ones. Some may argue that such a "rural 2 and urban 1" policy does not meet the principle of the one-child policy. However, the discrepancy is only superficial. People who know the reality understand that since the implementation of the one-child policy, the real, nationwide number of the average children per couple has been 1.5, roughly fitting the pattern of "rural 2 and urban 1." In one of the previous sections, it was shown that the TFRs from 1980 to 1990 were from 2.24 to 2.31, and 2.31 to 1.72 from 1990 to 2000, and the numbers may be averaged down to a level slightly higher than the "rural 2 and urban 1." Therefore, such a differential policy between urban and rural areas, if implemented to replace the sex discriminative fertility policy, would not boost the fertility rates in rural areas or around the country, but would keep the rural sex ratio of second-order births at a natural state, which would effectively lower the rural and the nationwide sex ratios at birth.

Managing the high sex ratio at birth

The foregoing analyses highlighted two points. First, the policy that advocated one child per couple since 1980 and in particular, the one that allowed two children for rural families with only one daughter were the key to the increases of the sex ratio of second-order births and the overall sex ratio at birth. Second, failure to recognize the key and lack of effective measures that targeted it underlay the long-term high sex ratios at birth, which could not be lowered by the various measures that targeted both "the symptoms and the root." Therefore, it is imperative now to adjust population policies and wave goodbye to the sex-discriminating policy that allows two children for rural one-girl families in order to lower the high sex ratio at birth while at the same time, a strict and effective supervision system and mechanisms must be established to strengthen management of nonmedical examinations to identify fetus sex and sex-selective abortion.

Replacing two-children-for-one-girl-families with two-children-for-all in rural areas in combination with fertility policy adjustment

As described earlier, various reasons underlie the high sex ratio at birth, which can be categorized into the economic foundation, i.e., the child cost–benefit ratio that favors boys; and the cultural foundation, i.e., the traditional reproductive concept that values boys over girls. The two foundations both have their own economic, political, thought, ideological, cultural, legal, and institutional compositions.

There is no doubt that any reform that touches on these areas may have some impact on the high sex ratio at birth and is therefore indispensable. However, the problem can never be completely solved if the major contradiction is missed. The major contradiction of the high sex ratio at birth is the policy that allows two children for rural one-girl families, which must be abandoned in order to eliminate the increases. Reform to target this policy will involve changes in many areas and needs to be performed one step after another in coordination with adjustments to the population policies. Now the "two-children-for-all" policy has already been implemented, but the impact of policies on the sex ratio at birth still waits to be recognized and efforts are to be made to achieve the recognition.

The *Report* that the demographic meetings in 1980 submitted to the Secretariat highlighted the point that the policy that advocated one child per couple could not be taken as only temporary or permanent, but as a particular policy for a particular period. "A particular period" describes the time of one generation in the reproduction of population and is usually around 25 years, at the most 30 years. After one generation, timely adjustment would be made to the fertility policy based on the new situations. This point was not only highlighted in the *Report* but also reiterated in the *Public Letter by the CCCPC to All Members of CPC and the Communist Youth League on Controlling the Population Growth in Our Country*. "The currently intensive population growth will be alleviated after 30 years when a different population policy will be taken."[10]

Unfortunately, the due adjustment was not made 30 years later. As the one who drafted the *Report* to the Secretariat, I was terribly upset and published a signed article in *People's Daily* in 2009, "China's Population Policies in Retrospect and Prospect." In this article, I described how the population policies were formed, emphasized that the promise at the time of implementing the policies must now be delivered, and provided options for decision makers. Specifically, I proposed three suggestions to adjust the population policies: 1. "two-for-double-singles," i.e., couples who are both single children may have two children; 2. "two-for-one-single," i.e., couples with one party being a single child may have two children; and 3. "two-but-not-three", i.e., two children are allowed for all in the provinces, municipalities, and autonomous prefectures that may guarantee the prohibition of three children.

My calculations showed that none of these three options would bring any big fertility rebound, as the birth rates would only grow slightly and remain stable, or much effect on the zero population growth goal. Now, the "two-for-double-singles" policy has already been in effect for quite a while, and the "two-for-one-single" policy was also implemented after the issuance of the *Decision by the CCCPC on Several Major Issues about Comprehensively Deepening the Reform* in 2013, which was carried out following the requirement in the *Decision* to "persist with the basic state policy of family planning, initiate the policy to allow two children for the couples with one party being a single child, and to adjust and perfect the population policies stepwise."[11]

After the implementation of these two policies, there is now only a baby step and a short time away from the "two-but-not-three" policy. In fact, the "two-for-one-single" covers rural one-girl families and it has actually made the previous policy for those families to have another child after a few years exit on its own, and the increases in the second-order births resulting from the policy have good prospects to be resolved to a large degree. Nevertheless, the adjustment that would bring fundamental changes to the population polices is still the one to allow two children for all, which, once implemented in 2015, automatically annihilated the one that allowed two children for rural one-girl families, and the increases in the sex ratio at birth may be entirely resolved.

In addition, the interval between births deserves discussion. It was originally regulated that rural one-girl families must wait for four years to have second children, which was aimed to control the birth and growth rates of the population by a wide interval between births and a long reproductive cycle. However, the regulation provided enough time for people to select the sex of their second children and helped increase the sex ratio at birth. I have always opposed the regulation on birth intervals; after all, restriction on the number of children is quite enough and there is indeed no need to regulate the interval. Moreover, it is actually extremely difficult to manage the interval and it brings considerable mental effects to people.

Furthermore, it is also worth considering establishing a reward for girl births in rural areas, a market leverage to lower the long-term, high sex ratio at birth as soon as possible. As analyzed earlier, the cost–benefit ratio is quite different between raising boys and girls under the current social forces of production and reproduction culture, and it is also different between city- and countryside-born girls. It takes a lot of pressure resistance and a price to pay, economically and mentally, to give birth to a girl and bring her up safe and sound in rural areas, especially now that it is quite easy to identify the fetus sex with ultrasound and to perform sex-selective abortion.

Therefore, it may be quite effective if market leverage is employed to reward girl births with material and emotional prizes in rural areas in combination with strict law enforcement and management of fetus sex identification and sex-selective abortion. The reward may also help promote women's family and social status and gender equity as well as benefit the construction of spiritual civilization. Concrete measures may involve setting up a girl-birth reward fund and a foundation with corresponding regulations on how to award prizes.

The sources of the fund may come from the government's treasury and social endowment while the foundation may, following a well-defined procedure, attract donations from entrepreneurs and people from various social sectors. The government may also consider offering policy incentives such as tax exemption of the donations as well as girl-first guidelines in social welfare policies.

Prohibiting nonmedical fetus sex identification and extinguishing sex-selective abortion by law

If these measures, allowing two children for all and rewarding girl births in rural areas, are to guide people and to pave the way for girl births, the suggestions here are to eliminate all kinds of artificial intervention into newborn sex by strengthening supervision of illegal fetus sex identification and sex-selective abortion. In the past, the increases in the sex ratio at birth were definitively boosted by examinations for fetus sex out of nonmedical reasons and sex-selective abortion, which must be strictly prohibited. In practice, these behaviors are usually associated with professional and administrative corruption and should be on the anticorruption list.

In fact, the CCCPC and the State Council attach great importance to the increased sex ratio at birth and have held multiple meetings on how to manage the problem. A series of decisions, policies, and decrees was issued and many typical illegal cases were punished by pertinent government agencies. However, it is difficult to obtain evidence for such cases and is therefore hard for judges to make decisions on one hand, and, on the other hand, it is difficult to manage the situation as those behaviors are often interlocked with professional and administrative corruption.

In light of such a circumstance, I suggest the following measures. Nonmedical fetus sex identification and sex-selective abortion are to be listed as corrupt behaviors and as one of the major tasks in the anticorruption missions of related fields with determination and increased management strength. A law or regulations may be considered to cover nonmedical fetus sex identification and sex-selective abortion so that these behaviors are included in the national governance of rule of law. Articles related to these behaviors in the criminal law should be modified to hold accountable the parties involved. Pertinent agencies should take the responsibility of law enforcement and strictly manage those involved in these two kinds of illegal behaviors as well as strengthen law enforcement on crimes such as drowning and deserting baby girls to protect their right to survival. Laws and regulations must have strengthened respect for their solidity and authority and must be made public. Publicity is vitally important and experiences of successfully punishing certain corruptive behaviors and typical cases should be made public and shared through the power of news media, which may play their part in monitoring.

A specialized team may be established to investigate nonmedical fetus sex identification and sex-selective abortion cases, just like in child-trafficking cases. Those going through the illegal procedures, medical staff performing the procedures, and the government agencies in charge should be punished with loud voices to be effectively intimidating to people for a certain period of time. Meanwhile, arduous and in-depth advocacy should also be performed such as asking the punished to state their minds. The goal is to make everyone understand that a normal sex ratio at birth is protected by law and illegal behaviors are to be punished. Eventually, everyone respects and abides by law, has lawful reproductive ideologies, and behaves by law.

Notes

1 National Commission of Family Planning of the People's Republic of China, ed., *Chart for One per Thousand Population Fertility Sampling Survey in China*, Population and Economy, 1984, Special edition.
2 "Six Consecutive Decreases in Our Country's Sex Ratio at Birth," *Daily Post* of Xinhua Press, February 4, 2015.
3 *2000 Population Census of China*, vol. 1, Beijing, China Statistics Press, 2002, p. 570.
4 Ibid., p. 270.
5 All-China Women's Federation and the National Bureau of Statistics, *Major Data of the Third Survey on Chinese Women's Social Status*, October 2011, pp. 4–5, 16–17.
6 Tian, Xueyuan, ed., Hu, Weilue, and Liu, Qiming, sub. eds., *Materials of 1992 Sampling Survey on Family Economic and Fertility Situations in 10 Provinces and Municipalities in China*, Beijing, China Economic Publishing House, 1995, pp. 59–60.
7 Calculated based on the data of pages 536–537 of *1990 Population Census of China*, page 1681 of *2000 Population Census of China*, and page 2014 of *2010 Population Census of China*.

8 *2010 Population Census of China*, vol. 2, China Statistics Press, 2012, pp. 2024–2026.
9 National Population and Family Planning Commission, ed., *A History of China's Population and Family Planning*, Beijing, China Population Publishing House, 2007, pp. 125–129.
10 Peng, Peiyun, ed., *A Complete Book on China's Family Planning*, Beijing, China Population Publishing House, 1997, p. 16.
11 *An Assembly of Files of All the 3rd Plenary Sessions of All the Central Committees since the Reform and Opening-Up*, Beijing, People's Publishing House, 2013, pp. 211–212.

Bibliography

1990 Population Census of China, vol. 3, Beijing, China Statistics Press, 1993.
2000 Population Census of China, vol. 2, Beijing, China Statistics Press, 2002.
2010 Population Census of China, vol. 2, Beijing, China Statistics Press, 2012.
All-China Women's Federation and the National Bureau of Statistics, *Major Data of the Third Survey on Chinese Women's Social Status*, 2011.
Assembly of Files of the 3rd Plenary Session of the 18th Central Committee of the Communist Party of China, Beijing, People's Publishing House, 2013.
Chen, Xu, et al., ed. *Daughters May Also Carry Family Lines*, 1993.
National Population and Family Planning Commission, ed., *A History of China's Population and Family Planning*, Beijing, China Population Publishing House, 2007.
Peng, Peiyun, ed., *A Complete Book on China's Family Planning*, Beijing, China Population Publishing House, 1997.
Tian, Xueyuan, The Potential "Sex Crisis" Should Be Taken Seriously, Special Information Report, *Chinese Academy of Social Sciences*, vol. 29, 2001. (The article is collected in *Works by Tian Xueyuan*, vol. 3, Beijing, Social Sciences Academic Press (China), 2011.)
Tian, Xueyuan, ed., Hu, Weilue, sub. ed., *Studies on China's Family Economies and Procreation*, Beijing, China Economics Publishing House, 1997.
Xiang, Huali, and Li, Boping, Surveys on Current Procreative Preferences of Rural Women of Reproductive Age: Examples of Hubei Province, *Journal of Nanjing College for Population Programme Management*, October 2010.

6 The comprehensive-improvement trend in the health of the population

Exploring the path of innovation and reinvigoration with science and education

Accelerated increases in population health

People always forget about the large-scale improvement of the health of the population when talking about the great achievements since the Reform and Opening Up. A look into these reasons may identify an important one that resembles the situation that one cannot see the full picture of a mountain when climbing it: everyone is a member of the population and thus ignores the improvement of their own quality. Another reason is that the controversy about whether the younger generation really is healthful leads to lack of consensus and difficulty in evaluation. Therefore, how to comprehend the current state of population health and its progression since the Reform and Opening Up merits in-depth discussion. After all, only a clear understanding and precise positioning may lay a solid foundation for improving the health of the population, strengthening the aggregation of human capital, and reinvigorating China through science and education with development driven by innovation.

The concept of population health

What is the health of a population? There is no consensus on the answer among academic and social sectors. In general, health is the physical state, yet when combined with population, it makes up a new term that cannot be simply interpreted as the physical state of a population. In my opinion, the health of a population may be interpreted as a combination of the population's "self-cultivation and quality," which generates new denotations and connotations. *Self-cultivation* is one's daily practices in terms of mastery and application of pertinent knowledge and the resulting behavioral codes, and it covers physical and mental health as well as virtues, scientific and educational levels, cultural tastes, and civility. *Quality* describes the mass of an object and can be generalized to mean the degree of excellence of something. Therefore, the health of a population describes the physical strength and health of the individuals in the population, their intellectual and educational levels, and their degree of civility. In other words, the health of a population comprises three factors: physical health that measures physical strength and health, intellectual health that measures scientific and educational levels, and civil health that measures spiritual, moral, and cultural merits. Any discussion of population health must be grounded on the following three basic principles.

First, the health of a population describes the overall nature of the population. It is a collective concept that does not simply equal the sum of individuals, but carries the nature of the whole with all the individuals integrated. Therefore, one must first differentiate between the three concepts of human, mankind, and population in order to comprehend the concept of population health as a whole. The three concepts of human, mankind, and population are just as related as they are different. The *Modern Chinese Dictionary* defines *human* as "a higher animal that is able to produce tools and use the tools for labor"[1] and *mankind* as "the collective name of humans."[2] The specific denotations and connotations of the abstract concepts of human and mankind separate them from all other animals in the natural world and reveal the very nature of humans and mankind.

In fact, human and mankind are both abstract concepts and there is no room for counting; for example, we may say men, women, Asian people, American people, Mongolian people, and Indian people and these names do not differentiate between a small number of people and a large one. Population is different. In English, *population* bears the same wholesome concept as *universe*, and although *population* is often used to describe a specific group of people, such as a younger population, an elderly population, an urban population, or a migrant population, it usually represents the size or the number of individuals in a certain geographic area within a certain period of time. Population is a collective concept and by default it represents a people with a certain size when no other conditions are specified.

It is of great importance to highlight the collective feature of the concept of population health. In reality, two populations may always have quite different states of health even though they are quite similar in their average physical strength and health, intellectual level, and civilization level due to their different mechanisms and systems of population management, values, and bonds to hold people together. This is the difference between "1+1=2" and "1+1>2," and it is manifested as the difference of collective health of the populations.

Second, the composition of the health of a population needs to be specified. There is currently no consensus about the composition of the health of a population among academic fields and various social sectors. However, despite the lack of consensus, all descriptions are bound by the three frames of physical strength, intelligence, and mental health. As mentioned earlier, some summarize population health as the combination of physical, education, and political or ideological quality, while others think of it as the sum of natural (physical) and social quality. Apparently, different definitions of population health, especially whether a definition is focused on the population itself or on the "social nature" of humans, result in different views of its composition.

All of these views were compared and summarized by Mr. Li Jingneng, a pioneer of theoretical studies in demography, at the beginning of the 21st century. Li agreed that the health of a population was bound by the population's cognitive abilities and the conditions and the capacities it possessed to change the world, and at the very basis of this concept was the population's physical, ideological, and cultural and scientific strength. On this basis, he proposed to divide the concept into two layers: the base layer that comprises physical strength (which embodies the biological nature of the population) and cultural depth (which embodies the social nature of the population), and the superstructure layer that is on top of the base and that describes ideological strength (also embodying the social nature of the population), i.e., moral values and ethics, political ideas, and various ideologies. He further argued that population health could have a narrow sense and a broad sense. The former describes the physical strength and cultural depth of a population and the latter, ideological strength in the superstructure layer.[3] Other early demographers, such as Mr. Liu Hongkang and Mr. Wu Zhongguan, agreed on the idea of a narrow-sensed and a broad-sensed concept.

> In the broad sense, population health is the characteristics of the population in various social relationships, and the characteristics can be grouped into three big classes, i.e., ideological and moral strength, cultural and technological depth, and physical and intellectual abilities. The narrow sense of population health approaches population as a factor of the productive forces, and from this perspective, population health is composed of two aspects of the individuals' physical and intellectual strength and cultural and technological depth.[4]

In addition, several scholars, such as Zhang Chunyuan and Pan Jiyi, offered somewhat different descriptions of the concept, which are not detailed here. What needs to be detailed with clarity are the following two questions.

One question is whether the concept needs a narrow sense and a broad sense. Papers and books that favor this classification never answer the question, and they simply describe what each sense comprises. Most descriptions classify the "human nature" of a population, including physical strength and levels of education, science, and technology, to the narrow sense, and "social nature," including thought, morality, and cognitive abilities, to the broad sense.

Why has "nature" been used as the standard of classification? In order to answer this question, we have to track back to the 1980s and 1990s, when the concept of the human and social natures of population health was established. It is well known that demographic topics were once highly sensitive, as some were criticized for their publicly released views, with a few even labeled as rightists and dismissed from their jobs.

Later, the Reform and Opening Up restored fact-oriented practice, corrected many faulty theories, and achieved a great deal in many areas; however, during the whole course, especially in the early years of the Reform and

Opening Up, people often resorted to classic Marxist theories in order to clear themselves from concerns and to stand by victory all the time, which brought them to Marx's descriptions of the "social nature" and health of populations. They then began to argue that in contrast to Western scholars' focus on the physical nature of population, they put more emphasis on the social nature – the essential nature – of population.[5]

This is how demographic scholars came to emphasize those features of thinking, political, and moral values that could best represent social nature. It is entirely apprehensible and was even necessary at the time. Now, 35 years after the initiation of the Reform and Opening Up, we are in the new historical stage of the "Four-Pronged Comprehensive Strategy," and academic research should also catch up with the progress of time and the trend of innovative development. When it comes to the conceptual frame and composition of the health of a population, I propose that only when the "social nature" can represent the quality of population can there be reasonable understanding of the concept of population health. It is one thing to argue that population health has its "social nature" and completely another whether or to which degree "social nature" can represent the health of population. I believe that population health is what it is, representing the quality of the overall population, while "social nature" is not part of it, but only a factor impacting it. This is why there is really no need to give the concept both a narrow and a broad sense.

Another question is how to define the three factors of the health of a population. In line with the foregoing analysis, population health does not need to be described from natural and social natures or in a narrow and a broad sense; instead, it is composed of three factors: physical strength and health, intellectual ability and scientific and educational levels, and civility. These three factors are detailed next.

The physical strength and the health of a population

Physical strength and health, commonly called *physical quality*, describes the state of all organs and systems, including the neural, skeletal, vascular, respiratory, and digestive systems and limbs. It is reasonably described since it represents whether one is well developed in terms of height, weight, brain, organs, skeleton, muscles, limbs, and cardiovascular circulation. However, does it mean that the more developed these organs and systems are, the higher the quality of one's body is? I'm afraid we cannot draw a conclusion yet. After all, the physical quality of a population may only describe the physical aspects of the health of the population, but it falls short when its values and quantification are concerned.

In contrast, when the "physical strength" of a population is described, there is a clear value orientation for physical quality as well as an evaluation of the synergy of all organs and systems. The key to good or strong physical strength is that all organs and systems, the neural, skeletal, vascular, respiratory, and digestive systems and limbs, match, work with, and coordinate with each other. For example, an average, 1.70-meter-high person should have a moderate brain, skeleton, heart, lungs, limbs, muscles, and weight that match and coordinate with each other. These parts do not have to excessively develop, or some of them develop well while others do not. Only balanced development of all organs and systems may put one in the optimal state of physical strength.

However, it is not enough to have normally developed and coordinated organs and systems because there is another important indicator, health. After all, two populations with the same height, weight, and development of organs and systems may have vast differences in health and totally different qualities of physical strength and health. According to the World Health Organization (WHO), the health of a population includes physical health, mental health, and an intact social state, which is more complex than diseases. Of course, diseases have a great impact on the physical health of a population, but it is also important to understand the impact of mental health on physical health, especially on the physical health of the entire people that is defined by a population's physical strength and health. In addition, where a society stands in terms of health institutions, mechanisms, and structures is influential on the health of its population, and this is widely known. These social aspects are not population health themselves, but they guide, organize, and supervise it and therefore guarantee improvement in a population's physical strength and health.

Intellectual ability and scientific and educational levels

This is the core of a modern population, and it describes the educational level and the scientific and technological literacy of the population. Previous studies have usually included a factor of culture in this aspect, with some even calling it the *population cultural quality*.

However, I do not agree on this term. There are two reasons. First, what is culture? There are three types of culture. First, culture in a broad sense is the sum of all the material and spiritual civilizations a population creates in a specific historical period, such as the Renaissance culture in Europe, the culture of the glorious Tang Dynasty, and the ancient Egyptian culture. In fact, almost all the cultures on the world heritage list belong here as they represent the material and spiritual civilizations of specific historical periods.

Second, there are cultures in a general sense, which belong to the ideological paradigm, such as the Eastern culture, the Western culture, the feudal culture, and the modern culture. Third, there is also culture in a narrow sense, which describes one's educational level. For example, there is always a "cultural degree" blank to fill in on résumé forms, and one is expected to write down how many years of education he/she has received. Then, which sense of culture does the term *population cultural quality* refer to? How is the quality evaluated? In addition, the term does not cover what is taught or the intellectual ability of the educated.

The term also ignores the scientific and technological literacy of a population, and thus cannot reflect the knowledge, techniques, experiences, and problem-solving abilities the people of the population may acquire, master, and apply. Furthermore, intellectual capacity also includes the abilities to observe, think, make analogies with, deduce, judge, and experience the world, as well as to abstract the theories concluded from scientific experiments and social practices, all of which drive the loop of practice – theory – practice to go deeper. Therefore, the intellectual ability and scientific and educational levels of a population do not only include scientific and technological literacy, but also the intellectual capacity to apply scientific and technological knowledge and to solve real problems with it. The definition of *educational level* needs no more deliberation, and it is the education degree and level of a population and pertinent behavioral codes. Scientific capacity is associated with one's intellect, which represents the ability to apply what one has learned in practice.

Civility

Terms such as *political awareness* and *moral codes* have been used frequently in previous studies on similar topics, but no one has used the term *civility*. The Chinese term for civility is usually interpreted in two ways. One describes a fairly high level of mastery of theories, knowledge, thought, and art, which is interchangeable with terms such as *theoretical level* and *literary level*. The other describes one's well-educated attitude and ways to greet and interact with people; for example, someone who is said to have good civility is thought to be open-minded, forgiving, well-spoken, and polite. The second interpretation is used here, with particular emphasis on the word's connection to civilization to show the civilization characteristics of a population.

A third question is how to differentiate between *population health* and *population quality*. *Population quality* is often used in works on population health because, as related by many, everything has its quantity and quality and population, as no exception, should see the unity of its quantity and quality. In addition, population quality is thought to comprise physical health, scientific and educational levels, and ideological quality, the three of which define the overall quality of a population. Voices are also loud on the other side, which argue that population health, the quality sum of the physical health, scientific and educational levels, and ideologies of a population, comprises a wider range of concepts than population quality and highlights the quality of the population. It is therefore necessary to clarify the relationship between the health and the quality of a population as well as which one, health or quality, contrasts population quantity.

Quality has two meanings: one is physical and describes the mass of an object, which equals the ratio of the net force on it to its acceleration, while it sometimes also describes the quantity of a material; the other meaning is used in a general sense to describe the excellence of a product or work. The quality of a population is certainly meant in the second meaning. In contrast, *population health* is a somewhat different term. When broken down to the basics, the first character of the term (in Chinese, *suzhi*, or, 素质) means the original color and state that has always been so, which describes the fundamental character of an object, while the second character means nature, essence, and the real denotation of something.[6] Therefore, the health of a population describes the nature and character of the entire population and can be dissected as population civility and quality. *Civility* describes daily behavioral codes – i.e., one's understanding of morality, intellect, physical health, and anesthetics – and *quality* describes the degree of excellence of civility. Based on these analyses, I believe that *population health* is a better term than *population quality* to describe the nature and essence of the entirety of a population. It covers the reasonable denotations of population quality, and is therefore one-half of the whole concept that contrasts to the other half, population quantity.

Improvement in population health accelerated by the Reform and Opening Up

As the 20th century drew to a close, two articles were published in *Science Times*, one of which was " 'The Scientifically Illiterate' Dragged the Economy from Further Development." According to the 1998 *Survey on Public Scientific Literacy in China*, the basic scientific literacy of the Chinese people was 0.2%; in contrast, the basic scientific literacy of the European Union was 4.4% in 1990 and 6.9% in the United States, which were 22 and 34.5 times that of China, respectively. At the time, as many as 500 million people were scientifically illiterate, who indeed dragged the economy from further development. Another article was "Red Alarm, Urgent Situation: A Great Collapse of China's Talent Reservoir," which claimed that "there [was] a severe loss of talents from research institutes, universities, and colleges at the end of the century while foreign countries [were] embracing and even fighting for them with big smiles," and that "loss of talents [was] the biggest loss of national assets" with some survey data to show that the rate of lost talents, especially young talents, was more than 50.0%. The article concluded with a great anxiety over China's modernization under these circumstances.

However, 15 years later, statistical data showed that the number of those who had come back after having finished studies abroad increased 38.5 times, from 9,121 in 2000 to 360,000 in 2014, and the total number of returnees during the 15 years reached 1.8096 million, which was 74.5% of that of those who went overseas to study. Underlying these numbers were, one, the sustained rapid economic growth since the Reform and Opening Up boosted a high demand for various talents; two, state policies such as the national projects of "introduction of one thousand talents" had offered a wide stage for the returnees; and three, China's integration into the international community had started new trends, providing increased freedom for people to come and go and making it possible for "seagulls" and "dumbbells" to migrate between China and other countries.

What is the trend in the improving population health? Looking back at the past 65 years since the establishment of the new China, we see many obstacles as well as new hopes during the improvement in the health of the population. In fact, similar changes were present in all three aspects, i.e., physical strength and health, intellectual ability and scientific and educational levels, and civility, of population health.

Improvement in physical strength and health

Physical strength is the quality of a human body's stamina and health. Stamina is decided by the health of the brain, limbs, internal and other organs, and whether they are all normal, as well as the health of the supporting systems such as the neural, skeletal, respiratory, and vascular systems. All these organs and systems form a human body with a certain height, weight, and chest width, and with limbs, a skeleton, muscles, internal organs, and a nervous system, which, all integrated together, reaches a certain degree of strength.

Health, as defined by the WHO, does not merely describe whether one has diseases, but also covers the state of physical, mental, and social well-being; thus it is a state of complete physical, mental, and social well-being. Apparently, a series of indicators that cover various aspects is needed to evaluate the physical strength and health of a population. Of course, a population, covering all people living in a specific area, is best described by its infant mortality rate and the average life expectancy at birth, which may be called the chief indicators. That is because the two indicators combine and unite the majority of the factors comprised in physical health while embodying the importance of environmental factors. That is also why many authoritative institutes such as the World Bank have listed these two indicators as highly weighted ones to evaluate countries' human development index (HDI). When it comes to China, these two indicators are also very sensitive to and representative of the physical strength and health of the Chinese population.

STEPWISE DECREASES IN THE INFANT MORTALITY RATE

The infant mortality rate is the ratio of the number of deaths of infants under one year old to the number of live births in one year, and it is usually calculated for each year and represented as permillages. On the eve of the establishment of the new China in 1949, China had a fairly high infant mortality rate, which was estimated by both domestic and international sources to be near 200‰. In contrast, it is now below 10‰ according to pertinent agencies, which is a low level compared to global numbers.

However, there have been discrepancies among data from statistical studies, government agencies, and research institutes on the track of the decreases in the rate, and there is no consensus. The UN combined several statistical

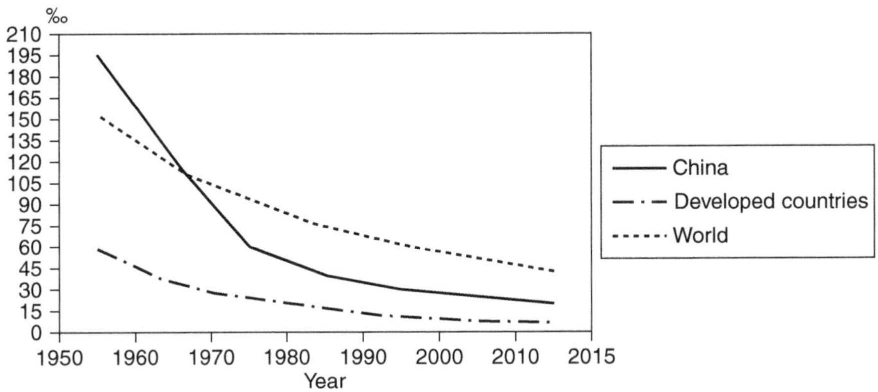

Figure 6.1 Trend in the infant mortality rates worldwide, in developed countries, and in China, 1950–2015.

materials from China and elsewhere and calculated the rates over the years with demographic statistical methods. Based on the UN's results and the worldwide data of the rate, Figure 6.1 was made to show the decreases in the infant mortality rates worldwide, in developed countries, and in China from 1950 to 2015 (Figure 6.1).

As shown in Figure 6.1, in the past 65 years, long-term and large-scale decreases were prevalent in the infant mortality rates worldwide, in developed countries, and in China except that the rate in China decreased by an even larger scale, which decreased from 195.0‰ during 1950–1955 to 20.0‰ during 2010–2015, a reduction of 175 permillage points. During the same period, the rate in developing countries decreased by 127 permillage points, from 174.0‰ to 47‰, a reduction lower than China's by 48 permillage points. The global rate decreased by 109 permillage points, from 152.0‰ to 43.0‰, lower than that of China by 66 permillage points.

Developed countries had a reduction of 53 permillage points, from 59.0‰ to 6.0‰, lower than that of China by 122 permillage points. Data from various surveys have shown that the current rate in China is at or below 10.0‰, only a few permillage points away from that of developed countries, marking China as one of the countries with extremely low levels of infant mortality.

Why did China succeed in lowering the infant mortality rate quickly and maintaining it at an extremely low level? One reason is long-term, sustained socioeconomic development, especially after the Reform and Opening Up, which has led to continuous improvement in people's lives and provided favorable nutritious conditions for pregnant women. As mentioned earlier, the GDP was 63,613.87 billion yuan in 2014 and the per capita GDP was 46,507.5 yuan, which laid a helpful material foundation for pregnancy and labor for women. Another reason is the sustained development of medical and health industries, which has continuously spread knowledge about genetics and contraception, significantly boosting the health levels of pregnancy and lowering the rate of genetic and other newborn diseases. A third reason is the implementation of the basic state policy of family planning. The advocacy for one child per couple has focused people's attention on procreation, and family-planning agencies of all levels have established specialized hospitals to provide obstetric services, which helps to ensure the health of newborns and improve the rate of live births. With better knowledge, measures, material lives, and medical services have certainly come decreases in the infant mortality rate.

SUSTAINED INCREASES IN THE LIFE EXPECTANCY

Life expectancy is the average time one is expected to live at birth, or the average life span of a cohort born in the same period given age-specific mortality rates. However, the mortality rate is not a constant, and the average life span of a cohort is actually a predicted number. What factors decide one's life span? Studies have shown that the most important factor is genetic. Then come environmental factors, some of which are direct, such as one's health, diseases, and how long one stays healthy, and some of which are indirect, such as economic conditions, medical services, supporting facilities that may decide one's health, diseases, and how long one stays healthy.

Therefore, different sexes, ages, races, living conditions, economic levels, medical services, health programs, and natural geographic conditions may all lead to different life expectancies. According to the UN, the global average life expectancy was 66.7 years for males, 71.1 years for females, and 68.9 years for all from 2010 to 2015; in developed countries, it was 74.7 years for males, 81.3 years for females, and 78.0 years for all; and in developing countries, it was 65.2 years for males, 68.8 years for females, and 67.0 for all.

Why do women always have longer life expectancies than men except in a few countries? The phenomenon is actually in total contrast to the gender inequality in many countries. Unfortunately, there is no authoritative answer yet, although most scholars favor genetic factors in that women have historically had a longer life expectancy; some also argue that women may have a stronger hematopoietic function and other related physiological functions due to periodic loss of blood in menstrual cycles, which helps with a longer life span. Figure 6.2 shows the average life expectancies in China, worldwide, in developing countries, and in developed countries projected from 1950 to 2050 based on the UN data.

As shown in Figure 6.2, both the speed and the scale of the increases in China's average life expectancy are faster and larger than those in the world and in developing and developed countries. From 1950 to 1955, the average life expectancy in China was 40.8 years, and it was as long as 72.0 years from 2000 to 2005, which will be further elongated to 79.3 years during 2045 and 2050; the increases in the two intervals were 31.2 and 7.3 years, respectively. During the same periods, the global average life expectancy increased by 19.8

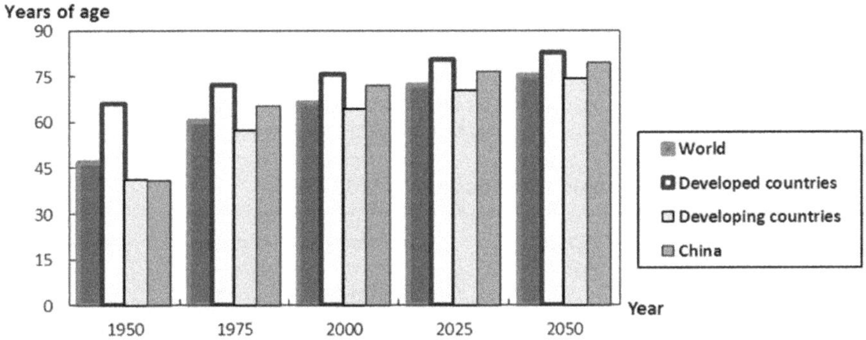

Figure 6.2 Projected average life expectancies in China, worldwide, in developing countries, and in developed countries in some years during 1950–2050.

and 9.1 years, from 46.6 to 66.4, and then to 75.5 years; that in developed countries, by 9.8 and 7.0 years, from 66.0 through 75.8 to 82.8 years; and that in developing countries, by 23.4 and 9.9 years, from 41.0 through 64.4 to 74.3 years. Between the periods of 1950–1955 and 2000–2005, the increase in China's life expectancy was 10 years more than the world average, 21.4 years more than that of developed countries, and 7.8 years more than that of developing countries. Between the periods of 2000–2005 and 2045–2050, the increase in China's life expectancy is expected to be 1.8 years fewer than the world average, 0.3 years more than that of developed countries, and 2.6 years fewer than that of developing countries.

Why is China expected to have fewer increases in the life expectancy from 2045 to 2050 compared to the world and developing countries? The prime reason is that China has already experienced fast increases in the life expectancy and it has slowed since the beginning of the 21st century. The real life expectancy in China now is actually higher than what the UN projected and is approaching that in developed countries. It will continue to near that of developed countries although further increases will show a downward trend due to inertia.

Improvement in the scientific and educational levels

The scientific and educational levels of a population are usually decided by the educational level and the scientific and technological literacy of the population. The improvement in both aspects as well as their characteristics are described next.

IMPROVEMENT IN THE EDUCATIONAL LEVEL

How well a population is educated is directly decided by the overall educational level of the population and is associated with the advancement of the education industry and the number of years people attend school. During the 65 years after the new China was established, the development of the education industry may be reflected by the increases in various schools as well as their numbers of teachers, enrollment, and graduates (Tables 6.1, 6.2, 6.3, 6.4, and 6.5).[7]

Table 6.1 Numbers of schools at various levels, 1952–2014

Year	*Higher education*	*Middle schools*	*Secondary vocational education*	*Primary schools*	*Preschools*
1952	201	4,298	1,761	526,964	6,531
1965	434	18,102	1,265	1,681,939	19,226
1978	598	162,345	2,760	949,323	163,952
2000	1,041	78,462	1,194	553,622	175,863
2010	2,358	68,948	13,939	257,410	150,420
2014	2,529	65,876	11,878	201,377	209,881

Note: Preschools offered kindergarten education before 1978 and preschool education after it.

Table 6.2 Full-time teachers in schools at various levels, 1952–2014 (10,000)

Year	*Higher education*	*Middle schools*	*Secondary vocational education*	*Primary schools*	*Preschools*
1952	2.7	9.4	3.5	143.5	1.4
1965	13.8	45.7	5.5	385.7	6.2
1978	20.5	318.2	9.9	522.6	27.7
2000	46.3	404.4	12.5	586.0	85.6
2010	134.3	504.3	87.4	561.7	114.4
2014	153.5	515.5	85.8	563.4	184.4

Note: Preschools offered kindergarten education before 1978 and preschool education after it.

Table 6.3 Enrollment in schools at various levels, 1952–2014 (10,000)

Year	*Higher education*	*Middle schools*	*Secondary vocational education*	*Primary schools*	*Preschools*
1952	7.9	138.3	35.1	1,149.3	
1965	16.4	673.0	20.8	345.7	
1978	40.1	2,743.6	44.7	3,206.4	
2000	220.6	2,768.3	81.0	1,946.5	1,531.1
2010	661.8	2,552.8	871.5	1,691.7	1,700.4
2014	721.4	2,244.4	620.0	1,658.4	1,987.8

Table 6.4 Students graduating from schools at various levels, 1952–2014 (10,000)

Year	*Higher education*	*Middle schools*	*Secondary vocational education*	*Primary schools*	*Preschools*
1952	3.2	22.1	6.8	149.0	
1965	18.6	209.8	9.1	667.6	
1978	16.5	2,375.3	23.2	2,287.9	
2000	95.0	1,935.0	26.4	2,419.2	
2010	575.4	2,544.8	667.1	1,739.6	1,057.6
2014	659.4	2,213.1	623.2	1,476.6	1,527.2

Table 6.5 Numbers of students in graduate schools and studying overseas, 1952–2014

Year	*Graduate schools*			*To study overseas*	*Overseas returnees*
	Graduating	*Enrollment*	*In school*		
1952	627	1,785	2,763		
1965	1,665	1,456	4,549		
1978	9	10,708	10,934	860	248
2000	58,767	128,484	301,239	38,989	9,121
2010	383,600	538,177	1,538,416	284,700	134,800
2014	535,863	621,323	1,847,689	459,800	364,800

These five tables capture the full course of education development after the new China was established, which went through three histological stages when the development was first rapid during 1949–1965, stopped and retrogressed for 10 years during the Cultural Revolution, and accelerated again after the Reform and Opening Up.

In the first stage between 1949 and 1965, education developed quickly. The establishment of the People's Republic of China in 1949 announced that the people became masters of their own country as well as masters of education. The education field started to prosper after the national economy took three years to recover. As shown in the tables, the number of higher education institutions increased 1.16 times from 201 to 434, that of ordinary middle schools increased 3.21 times from 4,298 to 18,102, that of ordinary primary schools increased 2.19 times from 526,964 to 1,681,939, and only secondary vocational schools saw a decrease of 28.17% in number, from 1,761 to 1,265. Overall, except for the adjusted decrease in secondary vocational schools, schools at all levels leapt in development at a fairly high speed.

Meanwhile, the proportion of students enrolled in schools at various levels out of the entire population increased by 8.62 percentage points, from 9.47% to 18.09%, with an average growth rate of 0.66 percentage points. The number of people with a college degree per 10,000 people increased by six, or 1.82 times, from 3.3 to 9.3, that with a high school certificate per 10,000 people, 191.5, or 34.82 times, from 5.5 to 197, and that with a primary school certificate per 10,000 people, 713, or 80.2%, from 889 to 1602. The distribution of students among various school levels also had marked changes: the proportion of college students of all the schooled increased from 0.4% to 0.5%, that of middle school students from 5.8% to 10.9%, and that of primary school students from 93.9% down to 88.6%. Apparently, with development in education, the proportion of those receiving higher education out of all students climbed while that of those receiving only primary education dropped. Such a change in the distribution of students among various educational levels marks the improvement in the educational level of the population and increases in those receiving more years of education.

The second phase, from 1966 to 1978, saw pauses and retrogression of education. The Cultural Revolution that broke out in 1966 delivered an unprecedented blow to the development of education and the population's educational level. From 1965 to 1978, the proportion of students in schools at various levels out of the total population increased slightly from 18.09% to 22.18%; however, the number of those with a college degree per 10,000 people actually decreased by 0.4 from 9.3 to 8.9, although there were fairly obvious increases in that of those with a middle school certificate, from 197 to 690, an increase of 2.5 times, and that of those with a primary school certificate decreased by 5.18%, from 1,602 to 1,519.

These numbers reflected an unfavorable shift in the distribution of students at various school levels: the proportion of college students out of the total population went down from 0.5% to 0.4%, while that of middle school students increased from 10.95% to 31.1% and that of primary school students decreased from 88.6% to 68.5%. On a side note, most of the college students during the Cultural Revolution were worker, peasant, and soldier students (WPSS), who gained very limited knowledge, and many of them had to go back to school later.[8]

In the third stage since the Reform and Opening Up, education has embraced rapid development. The Third Plenary Session of the 11th Central Committee of the CCCPC restored respect of facts to the Party's guiding principles and corrected many errors in all fields. In the education field, the legend of "Mr. Blank Paper" was clarified and the absurd logic that "the more knowledge, the more anti-people" was overthrown while the college entrance examination was restored and higher education institutions were allowed to enlarge enrollment; thus unprecedented development in education followed and the educational level of the population was greatly improved.

Based on the indicators listed earlier, we may safely conclude that the speed of development, the number of talents educated, and the contribution to socioeconomic development in this stage are all unparalleled. The development of higher education is particularly prominent. From 1978 to

2014, the number of higher education institutions increased 3.23 times, from 598 to 2,529; the number of full-time teachers 6.45 times, from 206,000 to 1.535 million; enrollment 16.95 times, from 402,000 to 7.214 million; the number of schooled students 18.76 times, from 856,000 to 25.477 million; and the number of college graduates 38.96 times, from 165,000 to 6.594 million.

In addition, enrollment in graduate-level institutions also increased from 10,708 to 621,323, a factor of 57.02, while the number of graduate students increased 158.0 times, from 10,934 to 1,847,689, and that of those graduating from graduate-level institutions 59,539.33 times, from 9 to 535,863. Also increased was the number of those going overseas for further study, which increased 533.65 times, from 860 to 459,800, among whom an increasing number eventually came back to work: in 1978, 248 came back from overseas and in 2014, 364,800 did, an increase of 1,469.97 times. In the history of China's education development, such scales of increases in higher education, overseas study, and overseas returnees have never been seen before and have set new records.

While higher education prospers, secondary education has shrunk in size. Various degrees of reduction have been observed in recent years in the number of secondary schools, full-time teachers, schooled students, enrollment, and graduating students. Even more obvious reduction was present in the number of primary schools, full-time teachers, schooled students, enrollment, and graduating students. The decreases in the number of schools, teachers, and students in primary and secondary education are rooted in the long-term, sustained decline in the birth rates of the population, which has led to continuously shrinking numbers of births and school-age children year after year. In 1987, the birth rate was 18.25‰ and there were 17.5673 million new births; in contrast, in 2014, the birth rate was only 12.37‰ and new births numbered 16.9199 million, fewer than 1978 births by 677,400.[9]

Reduction like this accumulated for more than 30 years and there has to be shrinkage in the size of primary and secondary education. Another less important reason is that in some places, local governments pushed for school mergers to get good sizes of schools during education reforms as a small-sized school would be disadvantageous for teachers to get promotions as well as for improvement in teaching quality and economic benefits of schools.

Therefore, middle schools in adjacent areas were merged in some regions, and so were primary schools, while some schools disappeared because of the mergers, which was reflected in statistics as reduction in the number of schools. On the other hand, it is worth noting that preschool education experienced rapid development. The number of children in preschools increased from 7.877 million in 1978 to 40.507 million in 2014, a 4.14-fold increase. It also reflected improved understanding of education among people. Call it improving the educational level of the population or parents anticipating children's success, what the numbers have told us is that people now understand that education needs to start early, as early as preschool.

IMPROVEMENT IN SCIENTIFIC AND TECHNOLOGICAL LITERACY

The descriptions of the improvement of the educational level of the population in the previous section has already touched on improvement in scientific and technological literacy. From example, from 1979 to 1985, the cumulative number of students graduating in the fields of science, engineering, agriculture, and medicine in higher education institutions were 975,700, with an average number of graduates of 162,600 per year. In 2015, the number grew to 1.721 million, an increase of 9.6 times, which showed obvious improvement in scientific and technological literacy.[10]

In addition, in 1980, the number of students in secondary vocational and technological schools was 761,000, including not only those in the fields of science, engineering, agriculture, and medicine but also those in finance, politics and law, and art. In 2016, the number grew to 13.352 million, among whom almost half were in the fields of science, engineering, agriculture, and medicine.[11] The number of full-time-equivalent (FTE) scientists and engineers (10,000 per year) was 752,000 in 1995, 822,000 in 1999, 2.554 million in 2010, and 3.759 million in 2015.[12] These numbers speak to the speed of improvement in the population's scientific and technological literacy.

Looking into the future, we may foresee sustained strong improvement in the scientific and technological literacy of the population. One of the reasons is that, as mentioned earlier, the new technological revolution pioneered by microelectronics and initiated after WWII is still prosperous, although it has progressed into a new phase dominated by life sciences. This background demands teams of specialists to continue innovations in research and development at the full front line of all fields on one hand, and on the other hand, it pushes for science education on a much larger scale so that further development of science and technology will be founded on sustained improvement in the scientific literacy of the public.

Another reason is that it has been decades since the strategy of reinvigorating China through science and education was implemented, and the idea has been deeply rooted in people's minds; meanwhile, the government has laid grand plans for carrying out the strategy, which covers all areas and fields. A third reason is that the current reform to transform the economic mode and adjust the economic structure is now deepened with the new economic normal showing itself all out, which necessitates that further socioeconomic development fundamentally relies on technological advancement and human capital, and this is the key to the comprehensive deepening of reforms and innovative development.

IMPROVEMENT IN CIVILITY

As already described, *civility* covers daily behavioral codes and civilization. Daily behavioral codes include one's understanding of politics, thoughts, morality, will, culture, literature, art, science, and technology, with pertinent behavioral codes and frames. *Civilization*, on the other hand, has multiple interpretations, and it is close to and has cross-overs with the concept of *culture*. In my opinion, civilization may be apprehended in three layers.

The first layer is civilization in a broad sense, i.e., the sum of all the material and spiritual civilizations mankind has created. Civilization in this sense is related to specific historical stages in that a civilization at the macroscopic level of a particular historical stage represents the achievements of science, technology, literature, and art during that stage and its associated behavioral codes. The English word *civilization* comes from Latin, *civis*, which means citizen, and describes the state and level of the people living in cities. Such a state and level of living is superior compared to previous social forms and represents the direction that a more advanced culture and society marches in; thus they become a civilization.

Such an interpretation of civilization from the perspective of historical progression is by all means helpful, but it has its own limitations. It has a hidden assumption that advanced forces of production as well as knowledge and technologies equal civilizations while less advanced forms may not be called so, wiping out that civilizations correspond to historical stages. In fact, the concept of civilization should be much broader than that. It is the sum of all the material and spiritual wealth created by mankind after our primitive, barbarous state, and it includes not only ancient and agricultural civilizations but also modern and industrial civilizations.

In the modern age, due to the imbalance of development of various races, ethnic groups, and nations during civilizations' history, four major civilizations characterize human society, the Western, Arabian, Eastern, and Indian civilizations, or, as favored by some, the three major civilizations of the West, Arabia, and the East, with sublevel civilizations that include the Baltic, Russian, Southeastern, and Oceanian civilizations.

The second layer of civilization describes various domains, i.e., material civilization, spiritual civilization, and ecological civilization. These three are as different from as they are related to each other.

The material civilization is the achievements humans have made through comprehending and transforming the material world. Mankind started from a primitive state, progressed to nomadic and agricultural societies, and then advanced to industrial and modern societies; the most important mark of each step is breakthrough in the means of production. Based on this standard, during the long human history of more than 4 million years, mankind has experienced, in ascending order, the age of handmade tools, the age of mechanical tools, and the age of intelligent tools, and has created and accumulated material wealth on enormous scales.

The spiritual civilization is the sum of all the spiritual achievements mankind has made during the course of comprehending and transforming both the objective and the subjective worlds. The material civilization is the foundation of the spiritual one while the latter is the manifestation of the former. The Industrial Revolution, initiated by the replacement of handmade grinders by steam engines and that of the hand-powered spinning wheel by spinning machinery, fostered the concepts of capital, exchange value, necessary labor time, average rate of profit, and industrial reserve army as well as the ideas of freedom, equality, and philanthropism.

In the modern age, the new technological revolution that is pioneered by microelectronics, together with the fast-progressing informatization, economic globalization, and "Internet plus," has catalyzed competitions of traditions, ethics, and morality with genetic engineering and cloning technologies while the concepts of tradition, ethics, equality, and justice have to be reshuffled. Therefore, the spiritual civilization has two sides: on one side is the spiritual production that includes the achievements of science, technology, education, and cultures and their levels, and on the other side lie ideologies, including achievements in politics, thoughts, concepts, ethics, morality, and values and their levels. The former is manifested by people's intellectual depth and the latter by moral integrity. The two sides are united into one by supporting and completing each other.

The ecological civilization, as far as I can find, has not been acknowledged by others as part of the concept of population health, yet I insist that it should. There are several reasons. First, today when humans are more capable than ever of "conquering" nature and can do almost as much as they want, whether individuals and mankind are aware of the ecological side of civilization can make a huge difference, and it is therefore reasonable to include one's ecological literacy as part of behavioral codes.

Second, the scarcity of resources and the deterioration of environmental health have become alarming now after more than 4 million years of human history, and the environment has become "underprivileged." Therefore, it is of high priority to raise awareness of ecological civilization to protect resources and the environment. It is one's social responsibility and has become an important indicator to evaluate one's public consciousness and morality.

Third, ecological civilization is also associated with the benefits of mankind, and any act that harms it by an individual will harm the population the individual belongs to, no matter whether he is aware of it or not; it is also associated with the population of a certain geographical area, even all of mankind, theoretically. Therefore, the quality of ecological civilization is an important part, with growing weight, of the morality of a population.

The third layer of civilization is in a narrow sense and it describes the degree of excellence of one's thought, concepts, morality, cultivation, etiquette, and awareness and associated behavioral codes. This layer overlaps with spiritual civilization, but it focuses more on the practical side such as how one presents oneself and effects, impacts, and behavioral codes. The aspect of civility of the health of a population should primarily be concerned with the civilization at the ideological level.

Having described the concept, we may now analyze the actual changes in the civility of the Chinese population during the 65 years after the new China was established. There are in fact many different views, some of which are in complete contrast.

Some argue that the civility of the Chinese population has declined. To them there are plenty of examples. No one dares to ask or give a hand to the elderly who trip out of fear of being held accountable; youngsters are seen to occupy the yellow, priority seats on buses to play with their phones while paying no attention to the elderly standing on the side or to the reminder of "yielding the seat to the elderly" by the bus staff, for whom and for the underprivileged, the sick, and the pregnant the seats are really set. No one steps up in department stores when seeing a thief stealing and everyone pretends that they never saw it because they are afraid of retaliation. Cases are on the rise in which aging parents are forced to sue their own flesh because their sons refuse to provide for them, with some even abusing them. Actions to eliminate pornography, prostitution, and illegal publications all have short-lived effects, as these problems persist, just like how Chinese chives always grow no matter how many times they are mowed and like what is described in an ancient poem, "wild fire cannot burn out grasses, they come back to life with a breeze of spring." Economic growth has offered people better lives and more and more people can afford to travel overseas, but reports have also increased of cases such as washing feet in the pond right outside the Louvre and carvings of Chinese characters of "I have been here" on ancient Egyptian pyramids and underneath the Sphinx. Aren't these examples enough to show that the civility of the Chinese population is declining?!

On the other hand, some do not agree that civility is declining because to them, these examples are isolated and cannot represent the mainstream of society, which is good and improving in civility. There are also some who do not have an opinion and who prefer to watch future development without judging whether there has been a decline or an improvement.

Why is there such a vast difference in people's opinions on civility? It is rooted in people's perspectives and how the issue is approached and evaluated. I have realized that those who believe in a "declining civility" usually come from a conventional perspective while those who see an "improving civility" come from the perspective of development. Apparently, the methodology one uses to approach the issue decides one's conclusions.

In other words, this subject becomes a battlefield of stands, views, and methodologies. One must choose either to take the traditional stand and use the unchanged standards or to take the stand of the changed present and the perspective of development for evaluation. When it comes to how to evaluate the civility of the Chinese population, we must first discern the marks of each historical stage on civility. After all, each stage has its own characteristic denotation of civilization.

In China, the feudal society lasted for thousands of years. What is the denotation of the feudal civilization, then? It is the morality and ethics based on *zhong* (loyalty), *xiao* (filiality), *ren* (humanness), *yi* (justice), *li* (rites), *zhi* (wisdom), and *xin* (trust). *Zhong* is loyalty to the monarch, e.g., "when a monarch orders his minister to die, the minister must obey or he is not *zhong*." *Xiao* is respect for parents and older generations in general, e.g., "when a father orders his son to die, the son must obey or he is not *xiao*." *Ren* is to refrain oneself and to honor rites, dealing with others with empathy and love. *Yi* shows fairness and justice, the courage to step up when seeing others in trouble. *Li* covers manners, etiquette, and respect for others. *Zhi* describes wisdom and knowledge and encourages people to improve themselves in wisdom. *Xin* shows honesty, trust, and the ability to keep promises.

As mentioned in the introduction, there were 100 schools of thought during the periods of Spring and Autumn and the Warring States (770–221 B.C.), with scholars such as Confucius, Mencius, Zhuang Zi, Lao Zi, Han Feizi, and Xun Zi, who all competed, with no single ideology or moral value and ethics dominating the others. During the reign of Emperor Wu (156–87 B.C.) in the Han Dynasty (202 B.C.–A.D. 220), however, the policy of "expelling the hundred schools, honoring only Ruism" was implemented, pushing Ruism to the top of all schools of thought and to become the dominating one in the whole nation.

By this time, a relatively complete system of ideologies and behavioral codes of a feudal society had been established. In the Song Dynasty (960–1279), Ruism was sublimated into the School of Chengs and Zhu, and a web of feudal moralities and ethics was later established that contained "Sangang Wuchang," or three cardinal guides (ruler guides ministers, father guides son, and husband guides wife) and five constant virtues (*ren*, *yi*, *li*, *zhi*, and *xin*), which set a high bar for civility and were deeply rooted in people's minds. Under such a circumstance, whoever behaved according to these values was by all means civil and whoever violated them was uncivilized and considered a rebel against feudal moralities and ethics.

Although these moralities and ethics were essentially shackles of people's minds, ideas such as "following the universal *li*, eliminating human lust," and "to be starved to death is unimportant, to lose one's pride is important" poisoned generations after generations and were sustained and even preached for a long time in the disguise of civilization. Things finally changed after the May 4th Movement, which popularized the slogan to "destroy the school of Confucius," and there is no doubt that the slogan marked an enormous step forward; however, the shackles on people's minds had been hammered and tempered for hundreds and thousands of times, and were so strong that some parts are still emitting energy now.

After the Industrial Revolution in the mid-18th century, capitalist revolutions prevailed, holding that feudal morality and ethics were ignorant, underdeveloped, rotten, and uncivilized, and that they must be abolished and replaced by freedom, equality, and consciousness. After the Industrial Revolution spread to China, the feudalist civilization represented by *zhong*, *xiao*, *ren*, *yi*, *li*, *zhi*, and *xin* was abandoned, and remarks and behaviors that were in line with the ideas of freedom, equality, and consciousness were taken as signs of civility. However, freedom, equality, and consciousness are not the destination of civilizations. There will always be new patterns of civility that highlight the ideologies of new ages, as irresistible as new waves pushing those ahead, with economic development, continuous upgrades of the means of production, social advancement, changes in people's ways of living, cultural development, and updates in ideologies, concepts, traditions, ethics, and morality. From such a perspective, the civility of today's Chinese population is experiencing violent transformations to let go of the old codes and to digest new ones. In other words, we are now in the middle of establishing a civilization that fits modern society with critical evaluation of our traditions to remove the dross and inherit the essence. This is an ongoing process, which is deepening day by day, and it certainly deserves some elaboration.

First, the concept "to stay loyal to the monarch" is exiting the historical stage. In the pyramid of the superstructure built by the ruling class in the feudal society, the monarch is on the top with absolute authority. Such a totalitarian rule stamps over freedom, equality, and human rights, focusing the power of all to the monarch. Fortunately, there came the democratic revolution led by Sun Yat-sen that overthrew the imperial rule of the Qing Dynasty and established the Republic, delivering a lethal blow to the imperial system and ringing the death knell for the ideology of "staying loyal to the monarch."

Unfortunately, however, traditions always bear great inertia. There went emperors, but the ideology of staying loyal to them stayed. As it turned out, Yuan Shikai, warlord of the Beiyang army, crowned himself as Emperor Hongxian and stayed emperor for 83 days; he was forced to abdicate and to abolish the imperial system after being criticized by the whole country. The subsequent May 4th Movement in 1919 held high the banner to oppose imperialism and feudalism with a loud voice of "destroying the school of Confucius," marking the accelerated decline of the ideology of Ruist "loyalty to the monarch." However, ideas that were born under its influence could not have possibly disappeared right away, and they were destined to experience repeated cycles of practice, acknowledgment, and then practice again.

In the history of the Communist Party of China (CPC), for example, Lin Biao once advocated for "one sentence as good as ten thousand" and "execution of orders with or without apprehension." His behavior opposed the red flag while carrying it right on his shoulders, and didn't he try to usurp the power of the Party and the government with the help of the loyalty ideology?

Another example is the lesson of "two whatevers," which is also worth summarizing. Fortunately, the CPC matured, saw through Lin Biao's conspiracy and smashed it, and then corrected the mistakes of the "two whatevers" and made several big decisions about some historical issues, with complete and accurate description of the scientific system of Mao Zedong's thoughts, i.e., the scientific system that had been tested and proved by China's revolution and construction.

The concepts and theories that had been proven wrong in practice, which belonged to Mao's personal thought, such as the continuation of fights between classes and the continuation of the revolution after the proletariat obtained power, were peeled off the scientific system of Mao's thought.

Next, the concept of *xiao* also needs discretion. *Xiao* is particularly influential in the traditional values in China and has been a symbol of civilization. Today, we should inherit and continue to carry out the good side of it by advocating respect and provision for parents so that all parents, as well as all the elderly in the society, are supported, helped, and pleased. However, at the same time, the bad side of it, i.e., the hierarchy between generations in the feudal society, must be eliminated, together with the belief that parents, or an older generation, may determine the lives of their children while children may only obey them. We need an updated civilization of generational relationship based on respect and equality that frees children from "listening to and obeying" their parents.

Third, a set of new morality and ethics is to be established. The feudalistic morality and ethics characterized by *ren*, *yi*, *li*, *zhi*, and *xin* are more oriented toward evaluation and comments, and they ask people to lower themselves in social relationships and in dealing with others by following the principle that "the world is bigger when you take one step back." With a positive attitude to discern the good side of things, these values are not completely malignant or useless; however, these ethics and behavioral guides were fundamentally coded out of the need to sustain the feudal patriarchal system, and they are in opposition to the modern concepts of freedom, equality, and honesty and thus must be abandoned.

On the present foundation of a socialist economy and within the framework of current institutions, values and ideologies must first be sorted out before the establishment of positions of individuals in society and inter-human relationships. The 24-word socialist core values, although controversial in a way as some find them to have an overly wide coverage and excessively long contents, hard to memorize and master, and necessary to be further discussed and modified, actually are rich.

These 24 words are firmly grounded on China's present conditions and deeply rooted in the traditions of the great Chinese civilization while having absorbed elements of modern civilizations around the world. They also embody the values and civilizations of this age and reflect the progress the civility of the population has made on its efforts to absorb the good part and get rid of the bad part as well as the orientation of the values at present and in the future. From the perspective of the state, "prosperity, democracy, civility, and harmony" are the major tasks and goals of China's modernization.

That "civility" is superimposed with prosperity, democracy, and harmony here demonstrates the importance of improving the civility of the population as it is one of the major objectives and a spiritual pillar. From the perspective of the society, "freedom, equality, justice, and rule of law" are the foothold of social constructions and ideals for the future. Of course, it was during the capitalist revolution when the slogans of freedom, equality, and consciousness were proposed, but these ideas do not only belong to the capitalist class, but are needed in socialist societies as well. Freedom, equality, and justice mirror people's possession of the power to be the masters of their own country and their longing for a wonderful life, and rule of law guarantees the possession while curbing with laws the governance of the state and the development of the civilization.

From the perspective of individuals, "patriotism, dedication, integrity, and friendship" are not only the moral codes for citizens but also the manifestation of civilization. Improvement in the population's civility needs patriotism and dedication from the people so that they may dedicate themselves to contributing to China's informatization, industrialization, urbanization, and agriculture modernization, as well as honesty, keeping promises, friendliness, and willingness to help each other so that a new, civilized, and modern interhuman relationship may be established.

These analyses have demonstrated that the civility of population is inheritable in that the present civility of the Chinese population has inherited the excellent traditions of historical civilizations while it also bears marks of each age, and comments and evaluation on it entail historical, development, and updated perspectives. Therefore, I believe that the core values need further discussion to be more concise. The 24 words touch on too many aspects and cover too many areas to be deemed a core. Of course, regardless of how to define the core values, I have always believed that the civility of the current Chinese population has not declined, but has improved instead. It has improved itself through efforts to abandon the bad part and pursuit of including new features and it is in transition from a traditional to a modern civilization.

While it is difficult to quantify the civility of the population and there is also lack of statistics, criminal cases tried in people's courts are used here to illustrate my points since those holding the view of "a declining civility" have primarily targeted the young generation. As shown in the numbers that follow, after the Reform and Opening Up, the number of youngsters convicted in criminal cases climbed to a degree and then decreased. For example, between 2008 and 2014, the total number of youngsters convicted in criminal cases reduced by 22.5%, from 322,061 to 249,576, among which the reduction in those under 18 was particularly remarkable, 38,476, or 43.3%, and the proportion of teens also decreased by 11.0 percentage points, hinting at improvement in the civility of the young generation (Table 6.6).

Table 6.6 Numbers of young criminals convicted in people's courts

Year	*Total*	*Under 18*	*18–25*	*% of all criminals convicted*
2000	220,981	41,709	179,272	34.5
2002	217,909	50,030	167,879	31.0
2004	248,834	70,086	178,748	32.6
2006	303,631	83,697	219,934	34.2
2008	322,061	88,891	233,170	32.0
2010	287,978	68,193	219,785	28.6
2012	282,990	63,782	219,208	24.1
2014	249,576	50,415	199,161	21.1

Source: *China Statistical Yearbook, 2015*, p. 819.

The new phase of overall improvement in population health

In November 2013, the *Decision by the CCCPC on Several Major Issues of Comprehensively Deepening the Reform* was passed by the Third Plenary Session of the 18th CCCPC and published. Later, in December 2014, General Secretary Xi Jinping emphasized on his research tour in Jiangsu Province that coordinated efforts were needed to build a moderately prosperous society, to deepen reform, to push for rule of law, and to strengthen the disciplining of CPC members, leaving the Reform and Opening Up with the task to enter the age of the "Four-Pronged Comprehensive Strategy." The population, as the propeller for the strategy, are now faced with the age of improvement of its health, which is the new focus of the strategic development of the population.

The age of improvement in population health is the historical stage during which a moderately prosperous society will be built, China will be a moderately advanced country by the mid-21st century, and the Chinese nation will see its great revival, and in this stage, the improvement of population health shall be comprehensive. The prospect for improvement in population health is based on the following foundations.

First, the health of the population shapes each development stage, and improvement in population health echoes the planning of the "Four-Pronged Comprehensive Strategy." The history of the 65-year-old new China has shown that various aspects of population civility were improved in different times with diverse impacts on socioeconomic development. Among the three stages of the development of population health described earlier, the first stage, from the establishment of the new China to the eve of the Cultural Revolution, saw rapid development of public health, medicine, and sports side by side while the wounds from the wars healed with speedy improvement of all indicators of the physical strength and health of the population until finally the hat of "Sick Men of East Asia" was tossed away.

At the same time, the scientific and educational levels of the population were also quickly elevated; colleges, middle schools, primary schools, and vocational schools all prospered; and science and technology stepped up the ladder of research despite foreign pressure. Also elevated apparently was the civility of the population in that new relationships between individuals, between superiors and subordinates, and between the exteriors and the interiors were established, and Lei Feng became the spiritual civilization model of the time. Exactly due to the large-scale improvement in population health, the comprehensive development of the economy, politics, and society was offered reliable human resources.

The national economy sped up steadily during the first Five-Year Plan, people enjoyed evidently better and improved lives, and society was filled with a vibe of integrity and honor never seen before. Such good population health was also the reason why the nation could pull through the subsequent three years of economic hardships. Even under the extreme scarcity of living materials in those three years, people still had confidence in the country, and, united to fight the ordains, eventually greeted a fundamentally better national economy.

The second stage, from the start of the Cultural Revolution to the eve of the Reform and Opening Up, saw colleges and universities, including medical schools, shut down because the students joined the revolution with slogans such as "take down anti-revolutionist academic authorities" and "more knowledge, more anti-people." The schools were occupied by workers, peasants, and soldiers after they were reopened. As a result, the physical strength and health, the scientific and educational levels, and especially the civility of the population that had been cultivated through countless efforts were disrupted ruthlessly and they retrogressed in a historic phenomenon.

We suffered greatly from the consequences of these events: the economy stayed put and was even at the brink of collapse; traditions, ethics, thoughts, moralities, cultures, and social orders were all upside down; and the only thing left was that "it [was] reasonable to revolt."

The end of the Cultural Revolution and the initiation of the Reform and Opening Up marked the starting point of the third stage. Errors in all areas were corrected in theory and what was right was restored; the national science conference specified science and technology as the primary productive force and the key to the modernization of China; the national education conference asked explicitly to restore the national college entrance examination to prepare endless supplies of talents for future socioeconomic development; the causes of public health, medicine, sports, and social welfare were vowed to be reformed and developed quickly while the spiritual civilization was strengthened; and once again, the health of the population was improved greatly.

However, in my opinion, the three aspects of population health were not improved equally, and that was associated with the imbalance in the reform and the development of industries. The reform and the development of education, science, and technology were indeed prominent, but they subconsciously tilted over the "exam-oriented" path and showed some sort of imbalance. While it must be fully acknowledged that the reform and the development of science and education systems provided abundant human resources for high-speed economic development and great leaps in the progress of traditional industrialization, which pushed China to become the world's second largest economy and first largest manufacturer in a short time, it cannot be ignored that the high-end talents with real experiences are not enough to support the reform to change the mode and adjust the structure of the economy to improve its quality; as a result, the quality of the economic development is not very high and the industrial structure is still behind.

In fact, it is widely known that it was proposed more than 20 years ago to change the mode of economic development and to make structural adjustments to the economy, but why was it never effective or making any real progress? Some of the reasons could be found in the economic institutions and system, but some are apparently lying in the "exam-oriented" education system that has failed to produce enough highly intelligent, high-end talents. It is probably exactly the situation in "the question by Qian Xuesen": schools have not operated in ways to educate innovative talents, and that is why we are short of extremely excellent scholars.

Therefore, the present proposal to improve the health of the population covers not only improvement in physical strength and health as well as scientific and educational levels and civility, with the weak side of civility climbing more quickly, but also improvement in the ability to apply the knowledge learned from books and people's intellect. It is also imperative for the education and science systems to walk out of the misleading zone with "exam orientation" and to strengthen the cultivation and training of the practical abilities of middle- and high-end talents.

Second, the goal to build a moderately prosperous society necessitates improvement in population health. In the *Suggestion by the CCCPC on the 13th Five-Year Plan of National Economic and Social Development* that was passed in the Fifth Plenary Session of the 18th CCCPC in October 2015 (referred to as the *Suggestion* hereafter), five development goals were depicted in order to achieve common prosperity by 2020: sustained economic development at a medium-high speed, an overall better life for the people, remarkably improved population health and social civility, an overall enhanced ecological environment, and mature, stable institutions in all areas.

Realization of any of these five goals needs help from improved population health, which was in fact listed as one of the goals. The first goal, for example, describes the objectives of economic development, which are, as detailed in the *Suggestion*:

> to keep the economic growth at a medium-high speed. Specifically, the GDP and the average income per capita in both rural and urban areas will double by 2020 compared to 2010 under the condition of improved balance in development, tolerance, and sustainability, with coordination and balance in all major economic indicators, optimized development space and structure, remarkable improvement in the efficiency of investment and enterprises, further advancement in the integration of industrialization and informatization, progression of all industries to the medium-high end, accelerated development of advanced manufacturing industries, sustained growth of innovative industries and industry clusters, increased proportion of services in the economy, remarkably increased contribution of consumption to the economic growth, speeding urbanization of the population with household registration, and considerable progression in agricultural modernization, all of which will bring China to the cohort of innovation countries with a strong talent pool.[13]

Economy is the foundation, and the ultimate goal to build a prosperous society must also be founded on economic development. To achieve the goal, economic growth must be sustained at a medium-high speed, i.e., a minimum of 6.5% growth rate in the next five years based on the rate during the 12th Five-Year Plan.

Now that the "three carriages" of investment, consumption, and exports have all lost the thrust to drive further economic growth and the extensive mode of growth can no longer be sustained, such a rate can only be realized if the mode of economic development is transitioned, the economic upgrade is boosted, and industries march to the medium-high end, all of which translates to the path of intensive economic development. There are actually only two ways that may lead us to the path from the perspective of production: one way is to increase labor, i.e., addition of investment in resources, laborers, and capital, and the other way is to increase efficiency, i.e., socioeconomic development through technological advancement and scientific governance. There may or may not be a third way, which is to increase both labor and efficiency. However, increasing both will see the cross-over of the two, and as a temporary state, the cross-over will lead us ultimately to improvement in efficiency.

Then how is efficiency improved? Well, there are also two ways, upgrading the facilities for laborers and equipping them with improved technologies, which are both rooted in improving laborers' level, particularly their intellectual ability and scientific and educational levels. Only when their intellectual ability and scientific and educational levels are improved can there be effective technological improvement and revolution, which will then bring improved informatization, automation, profession, serialization, and standardization, and ultimately remarkable improvement in efficiency.

It is noteworthy that there is a precondition of the goal of "dual doubling," i.e., increased development balance, tolerance, and sustainability. The "dual doubling" is important, but it is not so important as to pay any price. It must be founded on the increases in the aforementioned three features, which will by no means be sacrificed. Then how is development founded on the increases in the three features? The *Suggestion* already laid out a frame with five prospects, i.e., persistence with innovation of development while focusing on improving quality and benefits, persistence with coordinated development while focusing on a balanced structure of development, persistence with green development while focusing on improving the ecological environment, persistence with opening up while focusing on collaboration and creating win-win situations, and persistence with mutual development while focusing on bettering the welfare of the people.

In line with these five prospects, medium-high economic growth will be pushed for; the space and structure of development will be optimized; efficiency of investment and enterprises will be improved; industrialization and informatization will be further integrated; advanced industries, new industries and industry clusters, services, consumption, and agricultural modernization will all be accelerated; and the urbanization of the registered population will also be improved. Apparently, all these goals demand comprehensive improvement in the health of the population, as also recognized in the *Suggestion*, which concludes with "bringing China to the cohort of innovation countries with a strong talent pool."

Third, the key to realizing modernization by the mid-21st century is comprehensive improvement in population health. The goal to achieve common prosperity by the 100th anniversary of the establishment of the CPC is a milestone in the history of the Chinese nation. By then, we will be at a point as described in a couplet by the Middle Heaven Gate of Mount Taishan: "You are halfway through now; it's been a whole day since you started." When halfway through Mount Taishan, one must continue to pass the Slow Eighteens (stairs of eighteen levels), the Hard Eighteens, and through the Southern Heaven Gate before reaching the top; similarly, accomplishing the goal of the 100th anniversary is a historic achievement as well as the foundation for realizing the second 100th-year goal by the 100th anniversary of the establishment of the new China.

We are only 35 years away from the 100th anniversary, and how do we continue with development and what principles do we follow? It's fair to say that we have a clear idea now. Socioeconomic development has accomplished astonishing achievements since the Reform and Opening Up, and that has been well recognized around the world.

However, together with these achievements, a huge price has also been paid: immense consumption of natural resources, human resources, and wealth with alarming environmental pollution of land, seas, and air. Such an extensive mode of economic development, aside from being left behind the time and bound to be discarded to make way for a new mode, is no longer functional even though it is to be kept. Why is that?

Many conditions that once backed economic development have changed and are no longer there. Shortage of natural resources is increasing, fresh water and land are becoming scarce, and many mineral resources such as oil, iron, and copper have heavy reliance on imports. In addition, the proportion of the working age passed the Lewis turning point in 2010, marking the end of the age with an unlimited supply of laborers, and economic growth has become less and less dependent on investment due to declining marginal profit of investment. We are now at the point of mode transition regardless of our wills. As long as we want further development, including that at a medium-high or only medium speed, we must change the mode. What changes do we make? We are changing to an intensive mode of development to walk a walk of improving quality and benefits with innovations.

On the international market, products "made in China" are often cheaper than similar ones made elsewhere. There are various reasons such as poor quality or craft that compromises the value and the lifespan of the products, lack of diversity of product types or specifications that fail to meet various demands and restrict the sale within a small group of consumers, and unfashionable look or design that leaves the products in discount zones. For the past nearly 30 years, products "made in China" were everywhere around the world and the most important reason why they were this competitive was their low price.

However, with upgraded development and time, Chinese goods are losing their price advantage at a fairly high speed and the advantage in price is turning into a disadvantage. The challenge is going to be met with mode transition that transforms the competitiveness by price into competitiveness by quality, variety, and brand. As the old saying goes, villages may be situated on the western bank of the Yellow River for 30 years and on the eastern bank for another 30; great changes, even revolutionary ones, may occur between the first and the next 30 years during a 60-year period. Nothing stays the same forever.

During the 65 years after the new China was founded, the first 30 years was dominated by a command economy, and on this economic foundation stood an entire web of ideologies, including politics, laws, religions, arts, and philosophies as well as associated political and legal systems. During the next 30 years and more, the highly centralized command economy was disrupted and a market economy stepwise took root, bringing reforms of the superstructure, which led to social ideologies, politics, and the legal system that were coordinated with the market economy. The goal to build a prosperous society, especially that to reach the great revival of the Chinese nation by the second 100th year anniversary, can only be realized through summarizing the lessons from the two 30-year periods with an attitude that respects facts and science so that the experiences of successes may be borrowed and those of failures and outdated concepts may be discarded.

In this way, we may take on the historical task to continue the development and walk a walk that leads to the great revival of the Chinese nation. The path of the walk needs both positive and negative experiences from the international community, and the priority now is to learn the lessons from the countries that have skipped the middle-income trap and those that have failed, from around the world with experiences of dealing with financial and economic crises, and from those with experiences of sustainable development of populations, economies, societies, resources, and environments, as well as to persist with a development mode based on technological advancement and innovations.

It is also of particular importance that China's unique conditions must be fully considered while the experiences of the past 65 years must be studied thoroughly in order to go for comprehensive reforms, innovations, and scientific development. In fact, comprehensive development means to further push for the Reform and Opening Up and scientific development according to the "Four-Pronged Comprehensive Strategy."

In my opinion, the concept of innovative, coordinated, green, open, and sharing development proposed in the *Suggestion* may serve as the guideline not only for the 13th Five-Year Plan, but also for long-term development. In practice, this five-layered development concept will continue to be enriched and extended. The five layers of the concept are actually a unified organism with all layers completing, boosting, and developing each other; however, I still think that the layer of innovation is the most powerful engine of development.

In fact, shifts of the seat of the global economic center in recent history have already shown that economic development is always centered on science and technology while the context of the shifts is aggregation and convergence of human resources and the core is how fast and to what degree population health is improved. Science and technology are the most important forces of production. Only when great leaps are made in the population's physical strength and health, intellectual ability and scientific and educational levels, and civility can we truly reinvigorate China with talents, science, and education and realize the ambitious blueprint for the second 100th anniversary in the mid-21st century.

Fourth, the strategy of population development has shifted its focus, which demands comprehensive improvement in population health. In 2010, the proportion of the working age, from 15 to 64 years of age, reached its peak and population changes have since shown new characteristics, bringing a shift in the strategy of population development. I have always argued for taking the number, the health, and the structure of population into consideration all together when making strategies for population development, and my suggestion for the strategy is a three-step one to control the number, improve the health, and adjust the structure while watching the balance between the population and the economy.

In 1992, the TFR and the NRR of women both fell below the replacement level, marking the completion of the first step. The second step was to shift the focus of controlling the size of the population to improving its health and adjusting its structure while the size was also to be watched to coordinate with the sustainable development of the economy, society, resources, and environment. We are currently in the middle stage of this step, which will last until 2030, when the population reaches zero growth. The third step seeks a moderate size of the population from all angles based on the basic conditions of China at the time zero growth is reached.

A moderate size of the population from all angles means an appropriate size for the population with good health and a reasonable structure; meanwhile, the population is in concert with the economy, the society, the resources, and the environment in changes and development, which is also sustainable. Of course, a moderate size of the population is only an academic concept now, and it is not practical at all yet; however, it represents and summarizes the direction of future change and the development of the population and its coordination with the environment, it bears related demands, and it should be taken as the goal and value of the present strategy of population development.

We are now in the middle of the second step of the population strategy, and while still controlling the size of the population, we are now trying to shift the focus of population development from size control to health improvement and structural adjustment. To help with this shift, it is necessary to stabilize the fertility rate, which is already below the replacement level, and given the conditions of China, the policy of two children per couple is absolutely necessary since it will bring slight increases in the fertility rate while maintaining it at a relatively stable level and alleviating the pressure from population aging, supply of laborers, and the speed of the post-demographic transition.

On the other hand, population health has already improved since the Reform and Opening Up, which will help with the shift. The improvement in population health was described earlier, but how much improvement has there been? Well, the improvement is enough to help with population development, although it needs further improvement so that it is consolidated and strengthened. Consolidating and strengthening the improvement in population health should focus on improvement in population health.

To improve population health, when it comes to the intellectual ability and the scientific and educational levels of the population, which has already been improved greatly, the focus should be on "ability." If education and learning are ways to acquire "intellect" or knowledge, then knowledge from older generations and books is far from enough because it is "dead." Knowledge that is "alive," or "ability," is also important, which can only be acquired through extracting and applying the "dead" knowledge. From "ignorance" to "intellect," it is a journey of elevation that is knowing, and from "intellect" to "ability," it is another, more important journey of elevation that is accessing and applying what is known.

Current problems, as already mentioned, are almost all rooted in valuing "intellect" over "ability," and "factories for the college entrance examination" and "barracks of the college entrance examinations" are typical examples of "exam-oriented" education and research. To solve these problems, we must break the "exam-oriented" education and research system and find a development path with our own innovations. This point is further elaborated on in the next section.

The strategy to reinvigorate China through science and technology

Since the establishment of the new China, especially after the Reform and Opening Up, there has been remarkable improvement in all three aspects of population health, despite problems such as favoring "intellect" over "ability" during the improvement of the population's intellectual ability and scientific and educational levels, and less impressive progress in improving the physical strength and health and the civility of the population. Therefore, in order to improve population health, the problems should first be solved such that intellectual ability and scientific and educational levels are elevated and the physical strength and health and the civility of the population are also improved greatly.

As several previous sections have described how to improve the physical strength and health as well as the civility of the population with suggestions on reforms, development, and policies, these subjects are no longer touched here. In the following sections, deliberation is made on the association of improving intellectual ability and the scientific and educational levels with the strategy of reinvigorating China through science and education, and on why the foundation of the strategy is human capital.

Demographic demands in various development stages

The human history of more than 4 million years is, from a certain perspective, one of continuous advancement of science and technology. The staging of economic ages does not depend on what is produced, but how and with which tools production occurs. Observation on the economies until today would come up with roughly three basic eras or stages.

The first stage is the time of handmade tools, which spanned from the beginning of time until the end of agrarian society. This stage covers the primitive, slavery, and feudal societies and accounts for more than 99% of human history. Despite continuous advancement in science and technology that empowered mankind during the struggle against nature, all the means of production during this stage were handmade from the perspective of science and technology, and all the advancements did not really change the nature of handmade tools; meanwhile, production in this stage was mainly powered by humans and animals with a few cases of employing natural forces such as water and wind energy, and the basic mode of production was handmade tools.

In this stage, strategies aimed at building and strengthening a country ultimately focused on the population, which held the key to the forces of production. Only a prosperous population would bring prosperity to both the population and the society, and this concept, proven true by numerous cases in the history of China and around the globe, found its way through practice to become a belief, and even part of the ideology among the ruling class. For example, during the Spring and Autumn Period, Goujian, the duke of the Yue state, was defeated by the duke of the Wu state and forced to submit to Wu. He swallowed the shame and implemented a strategy of "ten years of reproduction and immigration and ten years of learning the lessons."

The "ten years of reproduction" concept aimed to encourage all residents of Yue to procreate. It was illegal for men to stay single after 20 and for women to stay single after 17. Those giving birth to children would be rewarded, and those with three children would get free nannies from the court. The "immigration" idea was meant to attract people to come and live in Yue, and together with the pro-reproduction policies, it would increase the population of Yue by both mechanical and natural growth. Through the policies of "reproduction and immigration" and the lessons learned in defeat, Yue became strong again and eventually defeated Wu, leaving behind legends of Xishi rinsing silk yarns, Wu Zixu crossing Shaoguan, and Goujian sleeping on firewood and licking a tiger gallbladder that have never faded.

During the periods of Spring and Autumn and the Warring States, Ruism was born and thrived. Confucius based his thought on *ren*, which he believed was the key to governance and a peaceful world. He also said, "it is the Junzi's shame if his land is too large for his people,"[14] and "the one who gets the people gets the state, and he loses the state if he loses the people."[15] Then the question became how to fill the land with people. The answer is in *Zilu* of *Analects of Confucius*: "The Lord of She asked about governance. The Master said, 'Those nearby are pleased, those far distant come.'" That means the people will not leave their land if the state gives them a good life while those living elsewhere, including various talents, will also be attracted to live there. The key to giving the people a good life is for the ruler to practice *ren*.

> If a ruler loved *li*, none among the people would dare be inattentive; if a ruler loved right, none would dare be unsubmissive; if a ruler loved trustworthiness, none would dare be insincere. The people of the four quarters would come to him with their children strapped on their backs.[16]

In summary, every agrarian society valued a prosperous population with stability and peace as the key to consolidating a state, and this is the only logical choice of strategies under the condition of handmade tools.

The second stage is the era of mechanical tools, and it covers the traditional industrialized societies. Machines are fundamentally different from handmade tools in that they are not driven by humans, animals, or, in a few cases, natural forces, but rely on steamers, internal combustion engines, and electronic engines for power while consuming large amounts of fossil energy. Machines are not only tools of transportation and operation. They have brought revolutionary changes to materials in their intensity, solidity, elasticity, resistance to erosion, and resistance to heat.

Strategies that accommodate to an industrialized society are often rooted in the search for a large market in pursuit of an engine to drive market economies. Another foothold of the strategies in this stage is to obtain abundant raw materials to ensure the continuation of production. A third foothold is to have enough cheap laborers to prevent the cost from climbing up quickly. Therefore, almost all the capitalist countries implemented a strategy to expand their markets and power overseas in the initial phase of industrialization, and to do so, they occupied lands of other countries with the help of cannons and fleets and founded for themselves one colony after another, which directly led to wars between invaders and defenders and between predators and those against them, with some of them even escalating to world wars.

Things changed greatly after WWII. On one side, peace with relative stability finally arrived, and on the other side, a new technological revolution was started. The revolution was pioneered by microelectronics and covered material, martial, astronautic, and biological technologies, bringing their development to break the bondage of previous machines, and science and technology became highly valued in socioeconomic development.

The foothold of strategy making also shifted. A typical example is Japan. With a "land not big enough," Japan stepped on a path of expansion by war after the Meiji Restoration. Japan walked to the highest point of the path during WWII, when it invaded China and Southeast Asia and then started the Pacific war to pursue its dream of establishing a "Greater East Asia Co-Prosperity Sphere." After it lost the wars, Japan transitioned from "wars" to "trade" and "technology" to strengthen itself, which helped Japan develop into a world-class economic giant in several decades.

However, it is noteworthy that Japan now seems to be inflated with its economic and military strength under Prime Minister Abe Shinzo as it has had increased friction with its neighbors while Abe has sent ritual offerings to the Yasukuni Shrine several times and vowed to modify Japan's constitution, showing an intent to go back to "wars to consolidate Japan." We must watch and be preventative.

Now we are in the third stage, when scientific and technological development is dominated by intelligent tools. In fact, both handmade tools and machines may be taken as extension and intensification of human arms, and they both amplify the physical strength of human beings to different degrees. Intelligent tools, in contrast, amplify, extend, materialize, and externalize human brains and intellect with informatization as the symbol of the third stage. In the second half of the 20th century, international academics presented with detailed arguments several major development trends of globalization, industrialization and post-industrialization, urbanization, informatization, and integration of regional economies, among which informatization and economic globalization were the most influential.

In fact, the concept of informatization was proposed as early as the 1960s, and it was explained in later discussions as the process through which information industries take hold of and dominate all industries during the transition from industrialization to an informatized society. With the development of practices, studies on informatization have become wider and deeper and it has been proposed to break through the limitation of computerization and to realize informatization that covers computerization, modernized communication, and Internet modernization, or the "triple c" (computer, communication, and control), as well as the "quadruple c" (with the addition of convergence) that integrates digitalization of information exchange and transmission, communication and Internet management, and the informatization that includes information environment and the transition from tangible to simulated products. Despite various definitions of informatization given by various disciplines and agencies, consensus has been formed on more and more details.

First, it is agreed that information technologies and industries have become increasingly influential in socioeconomic development. Informatization is a dynamic process with decreases in the proportion of traditional industries of material production and increases in that of information industries while the value of the sector in information production and services is elevated and consolidated, making these industries indispensable to socioeconomic development.

In fact, the information industry has created increasingly high value and has become a wealth-intensive field. Such a situation has been made clear by the Forbes World's Billionaires list of 2015. On March 2, 2015, Forbes published its 2015 list of global billionaires, who owned, either by themselves or with their families, a net asset worth at least $1 billion (USD) (approximately 6 billion RMB). The first three on the list were Bill Gates, Carlos Slim

Helu, and Warren Buffett, who were worth $79.2 billion, $22.1 billion, and $72.7 billion, respectively. Bill Gates came back to the top of the list in 2015 after having lost the position for four years, occupying the seat of the world's richest man for 15 years out of the past 21 with an ever-growing net worth.

Among the first 20 billionaires, 15 were American, 6 of whom were either founders or CEOs of high-tech companies in the United States, marking the impact and the power of informatization and the information industry. Compared to 2014, the 2015 list had more billionaires from China and the United States than anywhere else. More than 500 came from the United States and 300 came from China, among whom 213 were from mainland China, showing the rise of Chinese entrepreneurs from the mainland. Wang Jianlin, for example, ranked 29th with a net worth of $24.2 billion, Ma Yun ranked 33rd with $22.7 billion, and Li Hejun ranked 38th with $21.1 billion (Table 6.7).

Second, it is agreed that information has a growing value. Informatization translates into continuously decreasing consumption of material wealth during commodity production and labor with ever-growing labor on information. The market for information has continued to expand and has growing importance for the entire market, which will ultimately boost high the value of information resources.

Table 6.7 Forbes World's Billionaires 2015

Rank	*Name*	*Net worth (billion USD)*	*Age*	*Origin of wealth*
1	Bill Gates	79.2	59	Microsoft
2	Carlos Slim Helu	77.1	75	Telecom
3	Warren Buffett	72.7	84	Berkshire Hathaway
4	Amancio Ortega	64.5	78	Zara
5	Larry Ellison	54.3	70	Oracle
6	Charles Koch	42.9	79	Diversified
6	David Koch	42.9	74	Diversified
8	Christy Walton	41.7	60	Wal-Mart
9	Jim Walton	40.6	67	Wal-Mart
10	Liliane Bettencourt	40.1	92	L'Oréal
11	Alice Walton	39.4	65	Wal-Mart
12	S. Robson Walton	39.1	71	Wal-Mart
13	Bernard Arnault	37.2	65	LVMH
14	Michael Bloomberg	35.5	73	Bloomberg LP
15	Jeff Bezos	34.8	51	Amazon.com
16	Mark Zuckerberg	33.4	30	Facebook
17	Li Ka-shing	33.3	86	Diversified
18	Sheldon Adelson	31.4	81	Casinos
19	Larry Page	29.7	41	Google
20	Sergey Brin	29.2	41	Google

Sources: *Bill Gates Topped the Forbes Billionaire List Again*, China news web, March 3, 2015; MBA Think Tank Encyclopedia, http://wiki.mbalib.com/, November 23, 2015.

Informatization has greatly reduced spatial and temporal distances; for example, a computer with Internet connection enables one to track index changes in multiple financial markets in New York, London, Tokyo, and Hong Kong, China; the future price of a certain product; and the dynamics of economic, technological, cultural, and social development in major countries around the world, thus providing all kinds of necessary dynamic data for economic and social development. Of course the value of information keeps growing. With ever-deepening informatization, it is now inevitable to employ modern digital and microelectronic technologies to mine data and share the information to improve the intellectual ability and potential of society.

Third, it is agreed that informatization has quickly improved the efficiency and the effect of the agricultural and industrial production and service industries. While the information industry is progressing rapidly, all the sectors of the national economy and social development, including agricultural and industrial material production, nonmaterial services, labor, and management, have all benefited from advanced information technologies and achieved overall improvement in production efficiency, social efficiency, and benefits. Meanwhile, economic growth has also transitioned to rely on investment in human intellect and aggregation of human capital while the favored industries are closely associated with information and with those industries that have low consumption but high efficiency. The mode of economic growth has changed fundamentally.

With such a trend of informatization and the series of revolutionary changes it brings to socioeconomic development, a country or a region may not go anywhere without a set of strategies consciously accommodated to them. In China, reinvigoration with science and education is such a strategy at the national level. In fact, as early as the eve of the success of China's democratic revolution, Comrade Mao Zedong already proposed at the Second Plenary Session of the Seventh CCCPC to transform China from an underdeveloped agricultural country to a modern industrial one.

He later mentioned modernization of industry, agriculture, science and technology, and national defense many times in his speeches and articles. In 1964, Zhou Enlai, following Mao's suggestion, solemnly vowed in the *Report on the Work of the Government* at the first meeting of the Third National People's Congress to build China into a socialist power with modern agriculture, modern industry, modern defense, and modern science and technology within the 20th century. To achieve this goal, he also proposed a two-step plan. The first step was to build an independent and fairly complete industrial system and a national economy within 15 years, which would bring China's industry near the world's leading ones.

The second step was to bring China's industry to the first tier of the world with completely modernized agriculture, industry, defense, and science and technology by the end of the 20th century. These goals were subsequently quantified by Deng Xiaoping, the master designer of the Reform and Opening Up, to be a per capita GDP of $1,000 by the end of the 20th century, the level of "a prosperous society." The report of the 18th CCCPC in 2012 summarized industrialization, informatization, urbanization, and agricultural modernization as the "new four modernizations" and called for promoting their integrated development. However, in my opinion, modernization should be oriented toward people, shaped by a scientific scope of development, and associated with "mode transformation and structural adjustment." In summary, the strategy of reinvigorating China through science and education unifies goals and means and is the most vital pillar to consolidate and revitalize the country.

Key: improving accumulation of human capital

Sustained accumulation of human capital is the key to reinvigorating China through science and education. Human capital is the value of one's knowledge, techniques, experiences, and health. From the historical perspective, it is now the best time for China to start accumulating human capital. Economically, the GDP reached 63.61387 trillion yuan in 2014 with a per capita GDP of 46,507.5 yuan, $10.3601 trillion and $7,574, respectively, if calculated according to the median exchange rate between the renminbi and the U.S. dollar, just enough to be grouped as a country with medium-high incomes according to the standards of the World Bank.

Under such a circumstance, it is of particular importance to transform the mode of economic development and to adjust the economic structure, and it is also possible to do so now. The ultimate goal of mode transformation and structural adjustment is to improve production efficiency and the technological depth of enterprises, both of which rely on improvement in human capital.

From the perspective of structural demographic changes, China's post-demographic age before 2030 offers two favorable conditions for accumulating human capital.

One is the favorable condition for implementing the strategy to replace the pursuit of population size with the pursuit of quality now that both the absolute number and the proportion of the working-age population have started to decline. As already detailed, the Chinese economy has grown at an amazingly high speed since the Reform and Opening Up was initiated 35 years ago, and the economy is now strong and people are living a remarkably better life than before.

However, the high speed of economic growth is impossible to sustain for long, and the economy is bound to land on a track of a medium-high speed. I have projected that it would be a fairly good rate if the average annual growth rate of the GDP from 2015 to 2030 were to be maintained around 5% to 7%. At a rate in this range, China's GDP in 2030 will reach 138.8611–187.7986 trillion yuan, which is 1.18–1.95 times more than that in 2014. Apparently, if the national economy is to be doubled in the next 16 years while the number and the proportion of the working-age population are declining, it is only possible if production efficiency is to be increased through technological advancements, human capital accumulation, and innovations.

The other condition is disparity of changes in the proportion of the aged and that of children among the dependent population as the child population will grow by a small scale and then decrease until stabilizing. The population aging in China is characterized by a high speed, progressive growth, and by disparate distribution of the elderly between urban and rural areas. Overall, the elderly dependency ratio grows faster and may reach a higher level compared to the child dependency ratio. In particular, new changes will occur to the child population before the mid-21st century, when the population will have aged seriously.

In 2013, the *Decision* by the CCCPC announced at the Third Plenary Session of the 18th CCCPC the policy to allow two children for couples with one party being a single child. In 2015, the *Suggestion by the CCCPC on the 13th Five-Year Plan of the National Economic and Social Development* further announced that all couples were allowed to have two children. It has been commonly forecast that the next decade or two will see a rise in the fertility and birth rates.

Accordingly, the proportion of the child population will increase first, then decrease, and eventually stabilize with some fluctuations. It has been projected that the absolute number of the population aged 0–14 will increase by 48.33 million, or 21.4%, from 225.58 million in 2014 to 273.91 million in 2020 at an average annual growth rate of 3.29%. Meanwhile, the total population will grow from 1.36782 billion to 1.44427 billion, an increase of 5.59% at an average annual rate of 0.91%. These numbers demonstrate that the added child population will outgrow that of the total population by 2.38 percentage points.

However, the child population will subsequently decrease slowly during 2020–2040 until 219.80 million in 2040, at which time its proportion will be about the same as now. In fact, from 2040 to 2050, both the number and the proportion of the child population will not change much: the number will grow to 220.68 million in 2050, only 880,000 more than that in 2040, while the proportion will increase to 15.74%, higher than that in 2040 by only 0.59 percentage points (Figure 6.3).

Therefore, the first half of the 21st century is the best window both to replace the pursuit of population size with the pursuit of quality and from the perspective of changes in the child population. After the midterm of the 21st century, the reduction of the working-age population will accelerate in both number and proportion while the aged dependency ratio will be fairly high, creating a much more adverse environment for human capital accumulation compared to the first half of the century.

In fact, from the perspective of economic development, it was proposed long ago, in the 20th century, to transform the mode and adjust the structure of the economy; however, it has been difficult to do so due to the changes in the working-age population and the pressure to stabilize unemployment rates and the job market. Now that the post-demographic transition is upon us and the working-age population has passed the Lewis turning point, we are now in the post-golden age of the population structure. The first half of the 21st

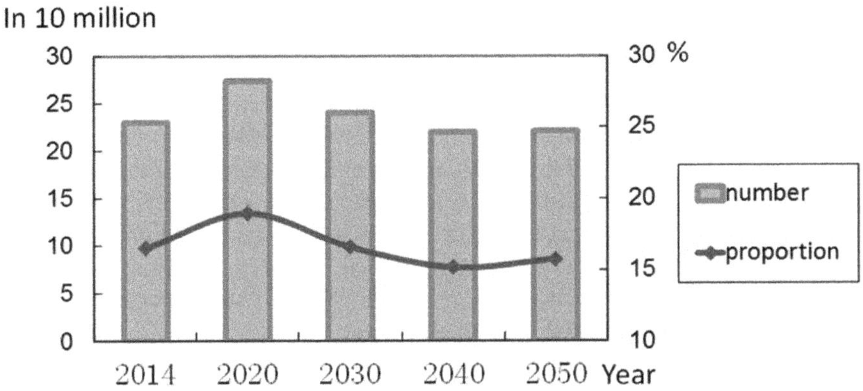

Figure 6.3 Projections of the population aged 0–14, 2014–2050.

century is a valuable strategic window. We must not miss the window; meanwhile, we must hold high the banner of reinvigorating China through science and education, improve the intellectual ability and the science and educational levels of the population, and sustain the growth of human capital.

Persisting with reform and innovation

The foregoing analyses have shown that the great achievements in education and science since the new China was established 65 years ago are mostly expanding numbers, but the quality and the structure have not improved as much. Therefore, it is necessary to push for reforms of the education and science systems with great efforts and to persist with reforms and innovation in order to reinvigorate China through science and education, to reach common prosperity, and to realize the modernization goals by the mid-21st century.

Innovative reforms of education

Since the establishment of the new China, especially since the Reform and Opening Up, education reforms have been constantly updated and remarkable achievements have been widely acknowledged. Arguments in what follows are based on real problems. To highlight the motives for studies and reforms of the education system, I start with the problems in the current education system and then move on to discussions of reforms.

Tactics of education

Education tactics are the guidelines and principles for education, and they therefore form the soul of the education system and the prime issue for all educators to understand in the first place. In fact, no matter whether people are aware or not, every country has its own education tactics in every stage, which are not only founded on a certain social economy but are also integrated with the consciousness, thoughts, traditions, and cultures of the society. Education tactics are particularly closely associated with cultures, and the two are often mixed to give rise to terms like *cultural education* and *cultural level*. Leaving aside the broad- and the narrow-sensed cultures, culture in the general sense is divided into three lineages: the Western culture, the Ruist culture, and the Islamic culture. The Islamic culture, somewhere in between the Western and Ruist cultures and under obvious religious influence, has its own unique education tactics and is not discussed here. Only the education systems and tactics closely associated with the Western and Ruist cultures are compared and analyzed briefly in what follows.

The Western culture, represented by the United States and including the major economies in Europe, the Americas, and Oceania, values the abstract concepts of freedom, equality, and consciousness, and thus has education tactics accommodated to these concepts. For example, curriculums, teacher recruitment, and requirements of school enrollment are usually decided and managed by schools on their own; public and private schools both have room to develop freely, and many schools of philosophy, academic factions, and philosophical thoughts coexist and develop and run their courses under market rules.

Guided by such tactics, the education system is generally laid out as schools founded by society with good ones surviving and bad ones eliminated based on free competition, and education is thus pushed forward. Further observations reveal that teaching of the concepts of freedom, equality, and independent thinking actually starts in preschool and family education. Parents teach children these ideas by following them in everyday lives themselves; for example, parents always knock at the door to obtain permission before entering their children's rooms, and they never touch their children's personal belongs or read their letters to show their respect for the children as an equal party and for their privacy. As a result, everyone is born to enjoy freedom and equality, learns to respect his parents and others, and is open-minded with a relatively outgoing personality.

The Ruist culture and its education are different from the West. It is founded on Confucianism and values traditional ethics between generations. Analyzed with formal logic, the Western culture is one from small to big in that the culture emphasizes that a group is made up of individuals, that the group can survive only when the individuals do, and that the small (individuals) decide the big (group).The Ruist culture is one from big to small in that it has an entire set of paradigms that defines the relations between monarch and minister and between father and son in traditional society while placing country before families and group before individuals. Maybe the paradigms are not really written, but they have become customary and everyone is used to the unification culture that the small obey the big.

Let us take an example from daily life to illustrate the difference. One of my children is now studying in the University of California at Los Angeles.

Each time I write to him from Beijing, I write down my given name, family name, and address on the upper left corner and his in the middle of the envelope while the order of the address lines is of particular interest: salutation (Ms./Mr.), given name, and family name on the first line and the address on the second. Below appear the department, college/school, university, street number, street, city, postal code, and country in descending order. The whole sequence is from small to big: from the given name to the surname, from department and college to university, and from street to city and finally to country.

In contrast, it is entirely different when a letter is sent to China: China first, then the province (autonomous prefecture or municipality), district, street, number, and finally the surname and the given name of the recipient. The whole sequence goes from big to small. Whether it is a mind-set from the microscopic to the macroscopic or from the macroscopic to the microscopic reflects the fundamental difference between the two cultures. It is not at all a surprise that some call the Western culture a microscopic one and the Ruist culture a macroscopic one.

When the education system is immersed in the Ruist culture, education tactics and concepts arise such as "those good in school become government officials" and "those who labor with their minds govern others and those who labor with their strength are governed by others." Such education prospects and tactics are undoubtedly aimed to educate people suited for maintaining the rule of the feudalist ruling class. Let us take a look at the Qing Dynasty. Students studied only classic books of Ruism, and Emperor Qianlong assigned Fang Bao to compile *The Four Books Reckoned Royally* as the official textbooks. Students needed to first pass a junior examination to obtain the title of Xiucai as the qualification to take further exams at the county, provincial, and central court levels to be granted the titles of Juren, Gongshi, and Jinshi at each level while some had to be tested for an extra time. Eventually, those who passed the final exam would be assigned official positions according to their performance.

Meanwhile, the teacher–student relationship emphasized obedience as depicted in the old saying, "taught by a teacher for one day, treat him as father all life long." Nevertheless, only a small fraction of the students educated under such tactics managed to climb to the top rungs of the social ladder and become part of the ruling class. Most stayed in the countryside performing agrarian labor while hoping for their children to walk the walk of studying, taking exams, and assuming official positions, only to witness the majority of another generation to be shut out of the ruling class once again, although the next cycle of hopes would begin soon. Such a system of official selection based on examinations was sustained for more than 1,000 years and eventually walked to its tomb at the end of the Qing Dynasty when it completely disappeared from the historical stage in 1905.

The establishment of the People's Republic of China in 1949 initiated a new chapter in the education history of China while new education tactics were also born. How to evaluate the education tactics and reforms in the new China? In my opinion, the key is a clear answer to the following three basic questions: Who is the education system for? Which path does it take? What kinds of people does education produce? Only when these three basic questions are answered satisfactorily can we offer objective evaluation of the evolution of education tactics in the past 65 years and identify the right direction and track for deepening reforms.

What is education? In Chinese, *education* is a compound word made up of *teaching* and *nurturing*. *Teaching* is to pass on knowledge and implies imperatives; *nurturing* promotes growth, development, and thriving and implies receiving of imperatives. With the two combined, education provides teaching and passing on of knowledge to help the educated grow and thrive. The connotations of education are primarily embodied in formal education, which may be taken as education in a narrow sense.

Education in a broad sense involves social and family education of various scales and types. Denoted in the narrow or broad sense, education cannot avoid the aforementioned three basic questions, and education tactics are practically the answers to these questions with an abstractive summary as concise as possible based on the state requirements for the education system. From this perspective, a basic understanding of the education tactics since the establishment of the new China 65 years ago is as follows: the foundation of all education tactics is what Comrade Mao Zedong described in *On How to Correctly Handle the Internal Contradictions of the People* in 1957, and every modification of the tactics based on the shifted focus of the work of the Party in each historical stage is revision and complementation of the foundation.

In fact, Comrade Mao Zedong had long paid attention to cultures and education since leading the revolution and the construction of China. As early as 1934, when he presented his report to the Second National Congress of Soviet Delegates, Mao proposed Soviet cultural education: "the tactic is to educate the people who labor in poverty with the communist spirit, to subject cultural education to the service of revolutionary wars and battles between classes, and to associate education with labor."[17] After the success of the revolution, Mao specified in 1957, "our education tactic ought to offer the educated the development in morality, intellect, and physical strength and to transform them into cultured laborers with socialist consciousness."[18]

It is fair to say that Mao's statement laid the foundation and set the tone for the education cause in China, and has had far-reaching impact until now. Although short and addressed to the educated, the statement actually demonstrated the guidelines and principles for education and educators through the requirements for the educated and practically answered the three basic questions of education. It answered the question of who the education system served by saying that education must be provided with the communist concept so that students could have socialist consciousness; in order to produce "cultured laborers," the statement emphasized combining education and production and labor so that education was to be immersed in practice, which stood in contrast to the 1,000-year-long doctrine that "those who study well should take office." It also answered the question of what kind of people education should produce by saying that the educated should develop in morality, intellect, and physical strength, demonstrating that the goal of education was to provide a new type of people with all-around development.

Following these tactics, further modification and complementation were made in the *Temporary Working Regulations on Schools of Higher Education Directly Affiliated with the Education Ministry (Draft)* (60 rules of higher education) in 1961: that education must serve proletariat politics; be combined with labor and production; bring development for the educated in morality, intellect, and physical health; and transform the educated into cultured laborers with socialist consciousness. Here the answers to which path and what kinds of people the education system was intended to take and produce were the same as Mao's 1957 statement. The only difference was in the "two musts": education must serve proletariat politics and must be combined with labor and production, which provided an even more specific answer to the question of who the education system was for.

Unfortunately, however, the education field later became a battleground during several waves of extreme "leftist" movements. From criticisms of the "plainly professional path" through the anti-right movement to the unprecedented Cultural Revolution, political issues were highlighted and class wars were taken to the extreme, which later led to the examination system overthrown by "Mr. Blank Paper" and the slogan "the more knowledge, the more anti-people."

Meanwhile, higher education institutions were filled with worker, peasant, and soldier students nationwide, and the education tactics of the Party were completely damaged and ruined. Fortunately, things were corrected at the Third Plenary Session of the 11th CCCPC with the restoration of the theoretical principle to respect facts and establishment of economic development as the core task of the country, and a new historical stage began with the Reform and Opening Up. The education tactics also welcomed additions to accommodate to the shift of the core tasks of the country and the Party as well as to the Reform and Opening Up.

Deng Xiaoping, master designer of the Reform and Opening Up, proposed that education must face modernization, the world, and the future. The "three faces" brought new spirits to and invigorated the education tactics and were written into the *Decision by the CCCPC on Systematic Reforms of Education* in 1985. It was proposed in the *Decision* that education must serve the socialist cause and that the socialist cause must rely on education, which marked a transition of the goal of education from "serving proletariat politics" to "serving the socialist cause" and the integration of education with the Reform and Opening Up and modernization.

The ideals of the education system were later modified progressively in the planning of the Eighth Five-Year Plan of national economic and social development, the *Outline of Reforms and Development of China's Education*, the *Education Law of the People's Republic of China*, and the *Decision by the CCCPC and the State Council on Comprehensively Deepening Educational Reforms and Pushing for Education of Population Health* so that "aesthetic taste" was added to the list of intended talents and the term *socialist successors* was added to the goals of education.

Education tactics thus evolved to include the insistence that education must serve the socialist cause and the people and that education must be combined with social practices, the fundamental principle of improving the health of the population, the focus on nurturing students' innovative capacities and practical skills, and the goal of training socialist builders and successors who have all-around attainments in moral, intellectual, physical, and aesthetic education. The addition that education must serve the people and be combined with social practices is the update in the new era.

Furthermore, the report of the 17th CCCPC stated that the education tactics must be implemented entirely, that the priority of education must be moral education and oriented toward people, that education must aim to improve the health of the population, and that education must be modernized in order to train socialist builders and successors who have all-around attainments in moral, intellectual, physical, and aesthetic education.

The *Decision* passed at the Third Plenary Session of the 18th CCCPC to deepen the Reform provided new descriptions of the education tactics under the current conditions:

> The Party's education tactics must be fully implemented, moral education and personality training must be persisted with, the teaching of the socialist core values must be strengthened, the fine traditional Chinese culture must be well conveyed, and an effective pattern and a mechanism with long-lasting impact must be established to train students to love study, labor, and the country and to boost their senses of social responsibilities, innovative capacity, and practical skills; meanwhile, physical education and extracurricular activities must be strengthened to promote the physical and mental health of the young generation so that they would be strong; and aesthetic education must be revised to improvement students' aesthetic taste and humanity depth.

Apparently, the *Decision* offered innovative descriptions of the education tactics: "moral education and personality training" was placed first to give it a leading role and it actually comprised the all-around interpretation of the three basic questions of "for whom, which path, and what people." Then "moral education" and "personality" were described in detail in subsequent lines.

In fact, "moral education and personality training" were still about the question of "for whom," and the subsequent descriptions combined "which path" and "what people" and specified that through the "two teachings" of socialist core values and the fine traditional Chinse culture an effective pattern and a mechanism with long-lasting impact should be established to train students to love study, labor, and the country and to boost their senses of social responsibility, innovative capacity, and practical skills; that through strengthening physical education and extracurricular activities, the young generation would have boosted physical and mental health; and that through revising aesthetic education students' aesthetic taste and humanity would be improved.

These tactics may seem perfect to some, but in my opinion, there is room for further discussion to make it more compact. My own experience tells me that the tactics in the 1950s–1960s, such as that "education serves proletariat politics and is combined with production and labor," that "education trains cultured laborers with socialist consciousness," and "all-around development of students with moral, intellectual, physical, and aesthetic education," were all deeply rooted in people's minds, easy to recite, and convenient for teachers and students alike to follow.

Therefore, I figure that modern-day education tactics may be summarized with "moral education and personality training," and its further explanation is all-around development of students with moral, intellectual, physical, and aesthetic education. A brief term and four aspects of education in fact include the essence of the descriptions of education in the *Decision* and should be proposed and promoted with some effort. Of course, more additions to the explanation pertaining to modern civilization are also useful to elucidate the education tactics, but these shall be included in the descriptions to provide further details. We do not need a complete and complex description of the tactic now. We need something concise that highlights the most important points and that is easy to remember and recite so that it may be integrated in the behaviors of all teachers and students.

"De-administratization"

Discussions have been made of the issue of simplifying administrative procedures and a certain degree of consensus has been reached. Many believe that there has been too much administrative interference in colleges and universities and "de-administratization" is needed; meanwhile, some hold somewhat different views because they think that *de-administratization* is a term too absolute to be helpful as some administrative management cannot be eliminated. Apparently, the difference lies in how to interpret and define *de-administratization*.

Administratization comes from a Chinese term that adds *hua* to the end of *administration*. In Chinese, a noun is transformed into a gerund with the suffix *-hua* to describe the process of reaching the state or character of the meaning of the noun, e.g., "green-*hua*" (landscaping), "water conservancy-*hua*" (the state of water conservation), "machine-*hua*" (mechanization), "standard-*hua*" (standardization), "city-*hua*" (urbanization), and "old age-*hua*" (aging). "Administratization" of colleges and universities is a progress of higher education institutes toward administrative establishment with institutions and management converging to standardized protocols so that colleges and universities are in a state with marked administrative characteristics. "De-administratization," therefore, aims to get rid of the state or to reverse the progress, but not to discard all administrative institutions or management. Some even use the term *de-over-administratization* to avoid confusion, which, in my opinion, is a bit overstretched. "Administratization" of colleges and universities is already wrong, and "over-administratization" is of course worse; thus the addition of "over" is rather confusing. In addition, "de-over-administratization" may lead people to think that only "over-administratization" is to be discarded, but not "administratization."

During the first 30 years and more after the establishment of the new China, the highly centralized command economy led China's economic development to a dead end and at the same time built an extremely powerful image of the government. Such a powerful government infiltrated all the political, economic, cultural, and social areas and instilled the official rank standard into people's minds in that everything was oriented toward it. Such an ideology has dominated people's behaviors subconsciously and there is no exception in colleges and universities in the education field. As a matter of fact, schools are and should be places for people to study, and teachers, staff, and students are all equal; there is no space for official rankings.

However, all schools in the command economy age were established and run by the government and all school leaders were designated by the government, some of whom had been government officials and thus brought their official ranks and associated salary packages to the schools. In addition, the state initially designated a group of schools to be key schools, and added some to the list at a later time, which gained a higher rank compared to those not on the list.

After the 21st century, the Ministry of Education gained the authority to designate each college and university directly affiliated with the ministry one party committee secretary of sub-ministerial rank and one president, which marked these schools with evident administrative characteristics and pushed for their "administratization." Specifically, the relationship between the government and the universities and colleges has become such that the government interferes excessively with school matters, and the planning, allocation, and management of schools' human and wealth resources must be approved and decided by the government, leaving limited or even no autonomy to the schools. Inside colleges and universities, the governance structure, cadre and teacher placement, ranks and salaries, and major decision-making are all dominated by administrative leaders, who also implement and execute the decisions.

Under such circumstances, a university is a small-scale society with its gates shut. A set of mechanisms of administrative management runs through everything, from department structure to assignment of cadres at all levels, from cadre and teacher hiring to awarding of administrative and academic ranks, from student enrollment to job hunting after graduation. In fact, since the market economy, universities and colleges, as relatively independent mainstays, have established close bonds with various market mainstays and become indispensable to socioeconomic development by providing services needed and pushing mutual prosperity and development of education and the social economy.

However, the administrative management described earlier, with increasing interference from the government, has inhibited the capacities and spirits as well as innovation of universities and colleges. Some surveys have shown that many higher education institutions have established bonds with domestic and international institutes, and some have built bases to integrate production, learning, and research, which have all made irreplaceable contributions to the nation and its socioeconomic development. For them to further contribute, universities and colleges must be granted a certain degree of autonomy in decision-making and management so that teaching and research may be more efficient and effective and administratization is reversed or at least decreased.

Mechanisms of research management

This issue is related to "de-administratization." Universities are important bases for scientific research and technological innovation, yet the mechanism of research management and the system of study evaluation have a lot of room for reforms. The Ministry of Education has set uniform standards for evaluation of higher education institutions, which, particularly the key indicators among them, decide the placements of schools at various strategic levels such as key schools, Project 211, and major bases, and consequently their rankings.

Universities and colleges, in an attempt to climb the ranking ladder, pass the standards down to schools, departments, and institutes of graduate study to use them as a whole set of quantitative indicators to evaluate and manage research. Teachers in universities are thus faced with these indicators in their efforts to get promotions, academic advancement, and salary increases. As a result, many, if not all or the majority, of university teachers devote themselves to grant applications and paper writing and try their best to get their papers published in SCI, authoritative, national-level, and core journals. Some universities have specific rules on academic promotion; for example, one may be promoted to the rank of professor if he has obtained a national-level grant and published a certain number of papers in SCI or core journals, and to the rank of associate professor for provincial-level grants or above and a certain number of papers in national-level or core journals.

Some universities have even promised to match national-level grants at ratios of 1.0:1.0, 1.0:2.0, and more and to award publications in SCI, core, and national-level journals with prizes from a few thousand yuan to tens of thousands. Not surprisingly, we find university teachers extremely busy. They are busy with grant applications, research projects, literature reviews, and paper writing. After all, they see no hope of getting promoted if they fail to meet the "hard standards."

What's worse is that some, in attempts to get promoted as soon as possible and attracted by short-term benefits, dare to mass-produce low-quality research and papers, and some even try all that is possible to get what they want, including resorting to means such as plagiarizing others' works or hiring people to do their own part. The consequences are grave. First, quantity is valued over quality and many research projects are just repetitions at low levels; second, theories are valued over practices and research projects have difficulty being transformed into production and are thus of low effects and benefits; third, short-term benefits are valued over long-term ones and people aim to get grants, patents, and publications in high-level journals while ignoring consolidation of fundamental theories; and fourth, academic misconduct becomes difficult to correct.

In fact, although these behaviors are primarily caused by people's low moral values and behavioral codes, the entire system of evaluation also contributes, which we cannot afford to ignore. Some hold the view that "the good are forced to turn bad," but I do not agree as academic misconduct, like everything else, is fundamentally caused by those who attempt misconduct. However, I agree that a flawed system or mechanism may induce these behaviors, and that deserves attention and must be reformed and corrected.

Direction of reforms of the exam-oriented education system

In the previous sections, education tactics, "de-administratization," and the system of research management were described and an umbrella analysis was made of the current problems and the orientation of reforms. The key conclusions are as follows: education tactics must be constantly updated to accommodate to time and specify reasonable denotations and connotations of the three basic questions of "whom for, which path, and what talents to be obtained."

I also proposed to simplify the current education tactic as "moral education and personality training" while the tactics should be supported by the four pillars of all-around development with moral, intellectual, physical, and aesthetic education. "De-administratization" of universities and colleges targets the relationship between the government and schools and aims to reduce inappropriate administrative interference from the government and to gain autonomy for schools while schools should be off the hook of administrative levels and decide standards of academic and occupational promotions based on teaching and research effects.

In addition, the "de-administratization" inside universities should respect the natural laws of education development and reform the mechanisms and management institutions based on administrative levels by handing the management of teaching and research to agencies with academic authority and by modifying the system of academic evaluation to improve efficiency, benefits, and the capacity to transform research results to production.

Fortunately, the *Decision* demonstrated the goals, the path, and the basic policies for future reforms, and no more discussion is made here. Instead, discussion is made from one perspective, i.e., the exam orientation that seems capable of explaining many problems in education, to expound the necessity, possibilities, and policy suggestions of further education reforms.

HISTORICAL LESSONS

Multiple rounds of reforms have been made to entrance exams of big, medium, and small schools, among which two were most comprehensive and influential: the restoration of the national college entrance examination in 1977 and the enlarged enrollment of higher education institutes in 1999.

The national college entrance examination was restored in 1977 after having been suspended for 10 years during the Cultural Revolution. At the time, all fresh high school graduates, educated youths who had worked in the mountainous and rural areas and who had returned home, demobilized soldiers, cadres, workers, and peasants could take the uniform exam and those with the best scores would be admitted to colleges and universities.

The act restored respect for knowledge and talents and was a great achievement with far-reaching impacts that corrected the mistakes in the education field. It reunited all factions in the education system that had resulted from the Cultural Revolution, called back professors, teachers, cadres, and staff from all around the country, and picked up and reorganized all textbooks, teaching props, and laboratory practices that had been long deserted, setting the stage for reinvigorating China through science and education.

Now, 37 years later, we have advanced on the road initiated by the restoration, and millions of talented people in all fields and areas have been trained along the way, marking the advantage of a country rich in human resources. According to statistical data, the total enrollment in undergraduate colleges and colleges for professional training ranged from 281,000 to 609,000 each year in the 1980s, 609,000 to 2.206 million in the 1990s, and 2.206 million to 7.214 million during the first 14 years of the 21st century.

Between 1980 and 2014, the total enrollment increased 24.7 times, the number of graduates from undergraduate colleges and colleges for professional training increased by a factor of 39, from 165,000 to 6.594 million, the number of students in graduate schools increased 168 times from 10,934 to 1,847,689, and the numbers of students studying overseas and of those who returned after overseas study increased 534.7 times and 1,047.3 times, from 860 to 459,800 and from 348 to 364,800, respectively.[19]

The educated, including those with specialties in math, physics, chemistry, biology, and geology; those in literature, history, philosophy, economics, and law; and those in industry, agriculture, medicine, water conservation, and forestry, trained and supplied in large and continuous numbers, have supported China's informatization, industrialization, urbanization, and agricultural modernization as well as its innovative development of natural and social sciences.

Of course, we must pay attention to potential negative impacts of the restoration of the national college entrance examination while acknowledging its great achievements. The most prominent negative impact was that the restoration set alight people's hope for pushing their children to success by taking the exam, which later led education to orient toward exams.

The demographic factor was also involved. Shortly after the restoration, the CCCPC officially advocated for one child per couple in 1980. Since then the number of children in each family has downsized to one and parents' hopes for their children can only land on their single children; hence they try everything possible to find paths for their children to become "dragons."

Starting from preschool, parents pick the best schools without calculating the cost: in Beijing, some are even willing to pay a huge amount of money for their children to go to famous preschools such as Blue Sky and North Sea. On entering junior and high schools, key schools, such as the middle school affiliated with Peking University, the middle school affiliated with Renmin University, the fourth school, and the eighth school, are certainly priorities. Even after their children have enrolled in these schools, parents still want them to be picked by key classes, Olympic math classes, and experimental classes so that the children will have a better chance to enter prestigious universities such as Peking University and Tsinghua University. With time an education paradigm has formed that is oriented toward exams.

The other significant education reform was the expansion in the enrollment in higher education institutes in 1999. In fact, the immense increases in the numbers of higher education institutes, graduate students, and college graduates described earlier are all directly related to the expansion. A review of the international history of higher education would give us few precedents of the rapid development in China after the expansion.

From 2000 to 2012, ordinary higher education institutes saw a 1.35-fold increase in number at an average annual rate of 7.36%, from 1,041 to 2,442; the number of full-time teachers increased 2.11 times at an average annual rate of 9.92%, from 463,000 to 1.440 million; and the number of students in colleges and universities, 3.3 times at a rate of 12.92%, from 5.561 to 23.913 million.[20]

Expansion on such a scale greatly boosted the proportion of high school graduates enrolled in colleges and universities. In 1978, the total enrollment of all undergraduate colleges and colleges for professional training was 402,000 while 6.827 million students graduated from high schools, resulting in a ratio of college enrollment to high school graduates of 402:6827, or 1.00:16.98. The ratio was reduced to 220.6:301.5, or 1.00:1.37, in 2000 and further to 688.8:791.5, or 1.00:1.15 in 2012.[21]

In other words, the proportion of high school graduates who were able to go to college increased from 5.89% in 1978 to 73.17% in 2000 and 87.02% in 2012.[22] It is noteworthy that the college enrollments also included a small number of non-high school graduates, and the actual proportions of high school students who were able to go to college were slightly lower than the previously cited numbers; however, the non-high school graduates were of a very limited number and more than 95% of those taking the national college examination each year were still high school graduates.

Nonetheless, it is true and a certainty that the rapid increases in the proportion of high school graduates enrolled in colleges reflect how the expansion of college enrollment has boosted the proportion. Now people no longer worry about going to college; instead, people worry about whether they can go to prestigious ones. Furthermore, the expansion has also stimulated investment in education, which has already overtaken the mid- to long-term goal of education planning that investment in education would account for 4% of the GDP.

In addition, the expansion has elongated the term of people in school and postponed the age at which people become *homo economicus*, which thus has alleviated the pressure on the job market caused by considerable increases in the working-age population. The most far-reaching impact of the expansion is that it has improved the educational level of the entire population greatly. Let us take a look at some data from three national population censuses, the second (1964), the fourth (1990), and the sixth (2010). The proportion of those with professional college education or higher increased from 0.42% through 1.42% to 8.93%, that with high school or secondary vocational education from 1.32% through 8.04% to 14.03%, that with middle school education from 4.68% through 23.34% to 38.79%, and that with primary school education from 28.33% to 37.06% but then decreased to 26.78% in 2010, which was due to the 67.53 million reduction in the juvenile population aged 0–14, or a 6.3 percentage point reduction in its proportion.

Meanwhile, the illiterate and the half-illiterate quickly disappeared. Per the three censuses in 1964, 1990, and 2010, the number of the illiterate and the half-illiterate decreased from 233.6058 to 180.1888 and to 54.7008 million while their proportion of the entire population decreased from 33.63% to 15.89% and to 4.08%.[23] Overall, between 1964 and 2010, the proportion of those with professional college or higher education increased by 8.51 percentage points, that with high school and secondary vocational education 12.71 percentage points, and that with middle school education 34.11 percentage points, while the proportion of those with primary education decreased by 1.55 percentage points and that of the illiterate and the half-illiterate, 29.55 percentage points.

In fact, 61.75% of the population had at least finished middle school as shown by the sixth census in 2010 and this number would be much higher if children and extremely old people were removed from the denominator. The proportion has actually been climbing in recent years, and the working-age population has all had at least middle school education while the proportion of those with at least professional college education has soared the fastest. All these numbers have shown that the expansion of college enrollment has exerted a powerful impact on educating the public.

However, the expansion has also led to many problems, among which three are most prominent. First, the scale of expansion exceeded the capacity of the colleges and universities at the time, leading to various degrees of decline in the quality of education that could be offered. Some schools admitted hundreds, even thousands, of extra students, and they immediately saw a sharp shortage of teachers, classrooms, laboratories, dorms, dining halls, and other facilities.

According to some statistics, the ratio of students to teachers in ordinary higher education institutes was 8.00 in 1993, and it was elevated to 11.62 in 1998 on the eve of the expansion; after the expansion in 1999 and up until 2002, the ratio increased by two percentage points every year and it reached 19.00 in 2002, which was an increase of 137.5% compared to 1993.

It is true that the number of teachers also increased at the same time; however, the increase was much slower than that of the number of students. In fact, the expansion was aimed to have more students and teachers alike, but while it was quite easy to get more students, it was much more difficult to have more teachers since not many were available on the job market. The "three shortages" of college teachers, classrooms and laboratories, and living facilities were integrated with and impacted each other, directly leading to a marked decline in the quality of college education, which is also a serious defect in the expansion.

Second, one of the consequences of the expansion is that it has become difficult for college students to find jobs. Ordinary higher education institutes are four-year schools now, and those who enrolled in colleges and universities at the beginning of the expansion in 1999 mostly graduated in 2003, when the difficulty in finding a job immediately showed itself. In 1999, 848,000 students graduated from colleges, and so did 1.877 million in 2003, marking a 1.4-fold increase over four years.

This has posed a great challenge; after all, now that the number and the proportion of the working-age population have already exceeded peaks, the supply of college graduates has exploded. Why is it challenging? It is challenging because, one, college students are enormous in number and have become the majority of newcomers on the job market, and, two, these job seekers with higher education are not well suited to the current economic development level and economic structure, leading to a mismatch between supply and demand.

This is exactly why the expansion has led to difficulty for college graduates to find jobs, i.e., the expansion has created a new type of imbalance between supply and demand, which definitely affects the wage rate of college graduates. Decreases in the wage rate then become a negative factor that compromises people's intention to go to college. To eradicate the root of the difficulty, reforms must be performed of the higher education system and the structure of the job market and industries.

Third, colleges and universities had to spend immense amounts of money on school expansion and are now in enormous debt. The expansion led to an imbalance between students and teachers, staff, classroom buildings, laboratories, dorms, dining halls, libraries, gyms, and shower facilities, and the immediate response to that was to erect more buildings and other kinds of constructions.

Where did colleges and universities get land? Fortunately, they had a strong case for land expropriation: to satisfy the demands of enrollment expansion. Where did they get money? Aside from administrative allocation of funds by the government and donations from domestic and international celebrities and enterprises, the most important channel was to get loans from banks. As a result, 10 years from the beginning of the expansion, the total loans of all higher education institutes nationwide exceeded 200 billion yuan, leaving the institutes deeply in debt. I once asked the presidents of a few universities that were in debt about how they planned to repay the loans. To my surprise, none of them were worried. Some answered that the loans could be paid slowly by increasingly expanding enrollment, which was actually the only thing universities could do.

After all, as long as enrollment keeps growing, the number of students will grow, bringing increased revenue to the schools and enabling them to pay their debts. However, all those schools that spent a lot of money on new constructions suffered decreasing revenue from expanded enrollment, and the best of them could only manage to pay the interest while paying back the loans of billions of yuan seemed a dream too sweet to be realized.

Some universities pursued a large size and a Western style and expropriated excessive land; unfortunately, however, subsequent breaks on their capital chain forced them to suspend the constructions and large areas of land have since been idling. Overall, expanded enrollment year after year has led the imbalance that was already there to further increase, and schools' promise to improve education quality cannot be kept. It seems that the series of problems, including the huge debts, caused by the expansion have to wait for solutions that can only rely on education reforms.

REFORMING THE EXAM-ORIENTED EDUCATION SYSTEM

The *Decision* on deepening the reform devoted a fairly long paragraph to the descriptions of the tactics, the direction, the idea, the key, and the policies of education reforms.

> Great efforts are to be made to push for education equality, complete the system to support the students from poor families, establish a mechanism to employ information technologies to enlarge the coverage of high-quality education, close the gaps between different regions, urban and rural areas, and different schools; allocation of education resources is to be coordinated between urban and rural areas; public schools are to be run with a standardized mechanism and a rotation mechanism for principals and teachers; key schools and key classes are no longer allowed; difficulty in choosing schools is to be solved; students are to have lesser pressure from school work with measures touching on the surface level as well as the root; establishment of a modern system of vocational education is to be accelerated; education is to be deeply integrated with production with schools collaborating with enterprises to train high-quality laborers and technical talents; the mechanism of student training in higher education institutes is to be innovated; higher education institutes are encouraged

> to find their own characteristics; and preschool, special-need, and continuing education is to be reformed and developed.[24]

This narrative has pointed to a clear direction to restart education reforms and the reforms should follow these guidelines.

The *Decision* also specified how to reform the exam-oriented education system:

> Reforms [of] the mechanisms of college admission are to be pushed for, and in order to eradicate the detriment from the root of the mechanism that a single exam decides one's future, investigation should be made to establish a new system in that admission and entrance examinations are moderately detached, students have multiple choices of exams, colleges and universities may have their own admission procedures, professional agencies organize admissions, the government offers macroscopic supervision, and the society is included in the monitoring.[25]

The most important point here is to reform the "detriment" of the "mechanism that a single exam decides one's future." We may not deny the great accomplishments of the national college entrance examination or its contributions in the past 37 years after its restoration; however, problems have also emerged and built up, which are mostly caused by the exam-oriented nature of the education system.

Now all the teachers and students are very busy in school. What are they busy with? Teachers are busy with teaching, but how well they teach depends on how well students do on their exams and, in particular, the proportion of those admitted by colleges and by good ones. Students are busy with study, but how well they study is evaluated by almost nothing else but grades and, in particular, the proportions of those admitted by colleges and by good ones. In a nutshell, all teachers and students are busy with taking exams and strive to get into colleges, particularly key ones.

Similarly, leaders and executives of schools such as secretaries of school Party committees and principals are all busy with and work around the central theme of various exams. As a result, students advance in learning from and reciting books with possibly good grades and a satisfying proportion of those admitted by colleges including good ones; however, their ability to think independently and to solve problems on their own by applying the knowledge from textbooks, their innovative thinking, and their creative ability are not satisfying, and perhaps are even seriously lacking. In my opinion, this is why Chinese students are better in knowledge storage but worse in problem solving when compared to foreign students, as mentioned earlier in this book, and it is also a logical answer to the "question by Qian Xuesen."

My inspiration to answer the "question by Qian Xuesen" came from the article "Interpreting the 'Question by Qian Xuesen' Correctly," by Comrade Zhang Yu. The article explained that:

> The commonly referenced "question by Qian Xuesen" was in fact not asked by Qian Xuesen, but summarized by others. The term first appeared on November 11, 2009, 12 days after Mr. Qian Xuesen died, [in] the newspaper *Xin'an Evening* of Anhui Province. The newspaper published *An Open Letter to Call for Frank Confrontation of the "Question by Qian Xuesen"* to the Ministry of Education and the entire education field coauthored by 11 scholars including Shen Zhengbin. In that letter, a question was asked, "why can't our schools nurture outstanding talents?" based on summarization of Qian's remarks about which kind of mechanisms enabled universities to train innovative, scientific, and technological talents, and the question was labeled as the "question by Qian Xuesen." On the next day of the publication of the letter [in]*Xin'an Evening*, i.e., November 12, 2009, a reporter from the Renmin web interviewed Tu Yuanji, who had been Qian's personal assistant and rephrased the question in the interview, i.e., "why do our schools have difficulty in nurturing outstanding talents?" which was later published [in]*People's Daily* on November 13, 2009.

Apparently, the question was first phrased as "inability to nurture" and then modified as "difficulty in nurturing outstanding talents."

In Zhang's article, the details of the "question by Qian Xuesen" were also revealed. On July 29, 2005, Wen Jiabao, then premier of the State Council, visited Qian in the Chinese PLA General Hospital. When talking about scientific and technological innovation, major breakthroughs, development support, and future directions in the next 15 years, Qian concurred on all the points by Wen and added,

> I must add the issue of education. One of the important reasons why China has not completely developed is that there is no university that runs in a mode to train innovative scientists with its own unique characteristics. Outstanding talents always fail to stand out. That is a big problem.

Comrade Zhang Yu argued that "Qian pointed out that universities were defective in nurturing innovative scientists and in the operation modes," and that "it was not accurate to summarize Qian's point with the question 'why [can't] our university … nurture outstanding talents?'"[26] For quite a while, the "question by Qian Xuesen" had been hotly discussed; some were for it, some agreed on the basics but found the question exaggerating; others were against it and called it a "false question." Therefore, Zhang's digging and interpreting of the evolution of the "question by Qian Xuesen" was quite helpful to clarify some misunderstandings.

Based on her article, I think that the "question by Qian Xuesen" was actually there, and it was valuable as the last contribution Qian had made to the cause of education and science in China. The question cuts precisely to the biggest problem in college education in China, i.e., "there is no university that runs in a mode to train innovative scientists," which is the original and essential value of the "question by Qian Xuesen."

After all, different modes of running universities produce different results. When running in a mode that is not streamlined to nurture innovative scientists, a university has no unique characteristics and outstanding talents will never stand out. How to run a university is the cause and the root, and talents are the consequence and the tip. The commonly referenced "question by Qian Xuesen," "why can't our universities nurture outstanding talents," only talks about one consequence and does not touch on the root cause. It therefore falls short of representing the full meaning of the "question by Qian Xuesen" and is not accurate. In fact, when problems of education are dug from the mode of running universities, we are reaching to the root, and that is the key to nurturing talent. Therefore, education reforms should start from it.

How much do grades mean and how valuable are good grades if they are earned only by reading textbooks, let alone the fact that the textbooks are preached somewhat forcibly to students? What is worse is the system that one single exam decides one's future. How can such an education system be expected to meet the challenges of improving the health of the population and of modernization?

Therefore, the exam-oriented education must be reformed. The orientation of the reform is to cut admission to the institutions, and that is why the *Decision* called for explorations of three channels of moderate separation of admission from the examination, multiple choices of exams for students, and colleges to decide their own ways of admission as permitted by law while the operation of all these are subject to three mechanisms of organization by professional agencies, macroscopic supervision by the government, and monitoring by the society. The *Decision* also specified that:

> Students should enroll in nearby schools for compulsory education with no exam administered, and trials should be tested on the mechanisms of school districts and nine-year education schools. Exams on academic proficiency should be combined with evaluation [of] overall literacy in junior and senior middle schools. Differentiated admission to vocational colleges and schools based on exams or registration should be accelerated to be established. Steps should be taken to finalize the mechanism of higher-education qualification based on the national college entrance examination combined with senior middle school overall evaluation [of] academic proficiency. Exploration should be made to reduce the number of disciplines in the national college entrance examination while abolishing the stratification of science and humanity students and offering multiple exams per year for certain disciplines such as foreign languages. Life-long study should be encouraged and facilitated by enabling credit transfer between ordinary higher education institutes, vocational colleges, and colleges for general study.[27]

Following the "three channels" under the "three mechanisms," the *Decision* made clear how to reform the education system oriented toward the college entrance examination with specific goals and requirements, i.e., students should enroll in nearby schools for compulsory education with no exam administered, higher-education qualification should be based on the national college entrance examination combined with senior and middle school overall evaluation of academic proficiency, the number of disciplines in the national college entrance examination should be reduced while abolishing the stratification of science and humanity students and offering credit transfer between colleges, and lifelong study should be encouraged and facilitated. In other words, the direction is shown, the road is paved, and it now boils down to how the reform will be practiced.

In order to push for the reform of the exam-oriented education system and to change the mode of university operation, the tactics of moral education and personality training must be thoroughly studied and widely publicized. The concept that education is oriented toward people must be digested by people as well as a clear understanding of the fundamental objective of education, i.e., to meet people's demands for all-around development, including physical, mental, social, and cultural education.

Further economic and social advancement relies on human capital, which is best strengthened by education. Establishing a source-efficient and environmentally friendly society relies on scientific and technological advancement, which is based on education. As the old saying goes, it takes 10 years to grow a tree, 100 to grow a population. The quality education embodied in moral education and personality training isn't aimed at the present, but at hundreds and thousands of years; it is therefore a must to modernize and empower our socialist country as well as the foundation of realizing the dream of the great revival of the Chinese nation.

Of course, various exams, including entrance exams, are detectors of textbook knowledge, and they are necessary because they can detect how much students have learned, which will be used to plan for the next phase. Students must take make-up classes if they have missed some parts of the knowledge already taught. After all, learning is progressive in that further learning is always based on what has been learned in the previous phase. However, detectors are means and cannot and should not be taken as goals. The goal of education must be shifted completely and wholeheartedly to quality education and improvement in people's abilities. In this way, multilayered laborers, such as elites and talents, and ordinary laborers can all be nurtured who may support and advance various causes in our country.

An adamant will, as strong and as brave as that of a valiant man who breaks his own arm, is needed to push for an innovative education reform in order to change the way schools are run, to transform the exam-oriented education system in which "one single exam decides one's future," to persist with moral education and personality training, and to nurture talents and laborers with all-around development in moral, intellectual, physical, and aesthetic training. To this end, I was personally inspired by a few reports in the *Whenhui* newspaper.[28]

On October 25, 2012, a long report was published in *Whenhui* with the title "Conditions to Become Elites: Empathy and Compassion – Experiencing Rural China by a Group of Shanghai Middle School Students." Jiang Peng, lead reporter of this article, wrote in the introduction:

> Middle school students in metropolitans, especially those from prestigious schools, usually live around study, with various decorative social activities, which are labeled to reach "overall self-improvement" of course. In their minds, they will go overseas for school trips, academic exchanges, or school competitions, participate in charity activities, enroll in a good university, or study abroad if everything goes well. However, as sharply pointed out by Guo Fangxian, principal of the affiliated middle school of Shanghai Fudan University, "middle school students in Shanghai know much more about the U.S. and European countries than inland China," and that is the "small problem" of middle school students in the "big Shanghai." That is also why the affiliated middle school of Shanghai Fudan University initiated an "elite program" last year, which provided students two choices: one, living and studying for one week in Wujiang Fudan Middle School in Xifeng County, Guizhou Province or Xituo Middle School in the autonomous region of Tujiazu in Shizhu, Chongqing, and two, social practice for one week in Jinze town, Qingpu or Street Yinhang, Yangpu. This October, another 169 students who enrolled in the "elite program" started their journey and 60 of them went to Guizhou and Chongqing. The two schools they were going to arrive at are both located in the nationally recognized destitute counties. Although only a three-hour ride from Guiyang and Chongqing, a distance that can hardly put the two counties in remote mountainous or wooden areas, the students, despite their "preparedness for hardships," were still shocked at the daily lives of the middle school students in the two schools.

The report then went on to describe experiences shared by the students from Shanghai. "I thought for many times about what it would be like, whether it would be a place with nothing growing and full of shabby things. I was wrong. The school here is actually quite modern."

> There are differences in the environment, but what struck us the most was the difference in their lives and attitudes towards life. We take the college entrance examination because we have dreams to realize while they do that to change the fate of their families, and that is the real difference.
>
> Many born in the 1990s like to say 'it doesn't matter' all the time. For them, nothing really matters except for exams and getting admitted by universities. With such an attitude, they left home and were greeted by many surprises, especially boys.

A year and a half later, journalist Tang Wenjia wrote two reports, *Bizarre Principal Chen Guohua Led 25 Children to Jiangxi for Complementary Study: A Rural "Study Tour" for the Shanghai Teens* and *"Villain Principal" and 25 Shanghai Teens Adventured to Jiangxi*. These two in-depth reports focused on a bold form of education favored by some parents whose children were in prestigious primary and middle schools in Shanghai: a week of study and life in a destitute mountainous region in Shangrao, Jiangxi for 25 students led by the principal of Violet Primary School who was nicknamed "Captain Demon."

The students refused the services of others, worked on their own to cut firewood, light stoves, boil water, cook, and dig out bamboo shoots and fresh leaves to have "more dishes for a better life," and employed what they had learned to heat up water by solar energy in order to take a shower and to connect the classroom to the only power outlet in the place. The students also volunteered to teach the rural kids. They ate and lived in the school, sat in on each other's classes and gave comments, distributed the books they had brought to the kids in the village, and put up with the enormous disparity between the rural life and their home life.

For a week, they were away from computers, TV, telephones, air conditioners, and even lightbulbs and were thus away from their habitual life full of services provided by others; however, they applied what they had learned and tasted the hardships and joys from it. Through experiencing the contrasting lives in Shanghai and the remote mountainous village, and through the help they gave, they felt the responsibilities on their shoulders and saw another facade of the real society.

In fact, such a form of "demon education," or "rural study trips" and "dream troupes," as it is called by some, is not a modern invention. There were plenty of precedents in history. In the 1950s and 1960s, many schools led teachers and students to factories and villages to work, eat, and live with workers and peasants to be educated while providing services with what they had learned as a way to implement the education tactic at the time of "combination of education with production and labor."

Even the movement to encourage the educated youth to go to mountainous areas and the countryside during the Cultural Revolution had its positive impact if evaluated from the perspective of training the young generation. Of course, the movement severely interfered with the normal progress of schools and harmed the healthy development of the education cause because it made no discretion and was pushed with haste in the entire country.

In addition, such "dream troupes" have also long been present in other countries. For example, the U.S. book *There Are No Shortcuts* recapitulates the story of a primary school in Los Angeles. Teacher Rafe Esquith organizes the poor immigrant students in the school to stage Shakespearean plays as a way to teach the importance of good virtues, and encourages them to aim high and to work hard and read passionately. Eventually, his class scores in the 95th percentile and many are admitted by famous universities such as Stanford and Yale.

Inspired by the story of this classroom, a "dream troupe" was founded and it prospered. Therefore, education reforms may also borrow useful experiences from international society. In the United States, for example, John Dewey challenged German education specialist Johann Friedrich Herbart and proposed to reform the education system to center it on teachers, textbooks, and classrooms. The U.S. government also passed the National Defense Education Act (NDEA) in 1958 in order to take the lead in space technology, authorizing the government to fund education at all levels in order to train high-quality technological workers to meet the demand for national defense.

Another example is Japan, where education reforms were initiated during the Meiji Restoration and continued with two big acts after WWII and in the 1990s. The three reforms enabled Japan to make three big leaps in education, supporting its postwar economy to sustain a "golden era" for 30 to 40 years.

South Korea also takes education seriously in its governmental strategy for national development. Education is a priority, with the introduction of modern school systems, calls for equality in education and fairness for all, and a goal of basic education for all. Multiple education reforms in South Korea have also effectively improved its population quality, facilitated the rapid growth of its national economy, and strengthened its social stability.

At least two points are noteworthy for us from the experiences of the education reforms in these countries. First, education reforms must favor quality education. In the aforementioned reforms, while classroom teaching was given attention, quality education, especially ways to train students to think and solve problems independently, was particularly emphasized. In our reforms of the education system, we must let go the evaluation standards and education concepts that "heroes are those who do well in exams," "hero schools are those that have high ratios of college admission," and "heroes are those who are admitted by key schools" and place in top priority the real quality education mechanism that may improve people's intellectual and physical strength and that value moral education and personality training.

Second, the relationships between the government and schools and between centralization and localization must be well handled. In the reforms described earlier, the governments were all dominant; meanwhile, the relationships between the government and schools and between centralization and localization were handled quite well and schools were treated as the mainstays in their education systems.

In our education reforms, we should, on one side, employ the government and specify its responsibilities, i.e., lawmaking, planning, designing, organizing, supervising, and providing services, while helping the government to transition its roles and to exit from the functions that it should not serve, and, on the other side, help schools to exert their functions as the mainstays of the education system and offer them greater autonomy in school operation and admission examination. Meanwhile, the responsibilities and the rights of schools should be specified in admissions exams, discipline planning, teacher hiring, academic promotion, and fund uses, so that schools may be transformed into true legal persons with autonomy in running themselves.

Innovative reforms of science and technology management

The *Decision* by the CCCPC in the 13th Five-Year Plan proposed to "deepen the reforms [of] the scientific and technological management system, construct innovative associations that pioneer industrial technologies, facilitate interdisciplinary innovation collaborations, and boost in-depth integration of science and technology in the economy." It also vowed to build platforms for strengthening exchanges between technologies and intellectual properties; to establish an innovative financing pattern that covers the whole process from the lab through trials to production; to formulate a universal system of policies to support innovations, increase financial support, and tax incentives; to deepen the reform and strengthen the protection of intellectual properties; to enhance the autonomy of higher education and research institutes; to grant more autonomy to principal scientists in grant management and decisions of technological routes; to implement policies that base distribution on intellectual value; to increase the proportion of benefits of translational production that goes to researchers; and to encourage people to devote themselves.

To realize these reform goals, we must find the direction and ideas of reforms from dissections into the managing system of science and technology and the current situations as well as by connecting the five development principles of deepening the reform and the goals of the two centennial anniversaries.

The current system of science and technology management

In my opinion, the current system of science and technology management has problems that are the same as those in the education system, i.e., orientation toward exams, and reforms are thus needed to change the orientation.

A LOOKBACK IN HISTORY

The Chinese nation is a great one and its people are diligent, brave, and wise. The Four Great Inventions of the compass, gunpowder, papermaking, and printing made outstanding contributions to the advancement of human civilizations. Confucianism has a far-reaching impact and natural and social scientists such as Sunzi, Zu Chongzhi, Zhang Heng, and Li Shizhen all shone brightly in history.

However, we fell far behind in recent history, and when steamers and weaving machines were made to drive the Industrial Revolution, we were still in the age of human-powered grinders and spinning wheels. When imperialist powers bombed open the doors that had been shut tightly by the Qing Dynasty with strong fleets and powerful cannons and invaded us with massive killings, we were defending ourselves with long spears and heavy knives. When the West was busy with education and scientific and technological revolutions, we were lingering around formatted articles and official-selecting exams with our science and technology staying at the level of craftsman techniques.

Under such circumstances, how could we resist invasion and prevent China from becoming a half-colonized and half-feudal country? Apparently, even for a country with as large a population, as immense a land, and as rich a supply of resources as China, it is inevitable to be left behind and bullied if its scientific and technological level drags behind that of other countries by a large distance.

The next question is how we got behind, from the leading seat with the Four Great Inventions to the position where we were forced to fight pistols and cannons with spears and knives. The answer is the feudal rule that lasted for a long time and grew rotten with all its associated ideologies, moralities, ethics, and education systems and methods. We had been self-righteous, stubborn to hold on to the old ways, and adamant in refusing to move on, and all these faults led to the disastrous consequences that made up China's 100-year history of being bullied and insulted since the Opium War in 1840. That history ended in 1949, when the People's Republic of China was founded, which opened a new chapter in China's scientific and technological development.

When the new China was first established, political, economic, scientific, technological, and social institutions and mechanisms were all copied from the Soviet Union, which were characterized by a high degree of centralization. A specific agency was set up to manage scientific and technological development and research institutes were also founded at the national level by the CCCPC and the State Council as well as at the levels of provinces, autonomous prefectures, and municipalities.

Some higher education institutes also set up research institutes within their own strong disciplines. Research projects, researchers, and management of research institutes were all included in national and regional plans, which were carried out, supervised, and tested by research managing agencies and the executives of the institutes. I'm sure all who have watched the documentary *Two Bombs and One Satellite* were touched by how the researchers devoted themselves to the research of atomic bombs, hydrogen bombs, and artificial satellites with independent work, great hardships, and sustained efforts in an age with extremely scarce references, people, facilities, and materials.

In November 2010, supercomputer Tianhe-I set a new world record for the fastest computer with a peak computing rate of 4.7 petaFLOPS. I once had a chance to visit the supercomputing center where Tianhe-I was located and listened to an introduction given by the staff there. Such a super-scaled integrated circuit computer was really astonishing. However, it was not long before Japan and the United States produced even faster supercomputers, overtaking Tianhe-I.

Fortunately, good news came again, in November 2013, that Tianhe-II, developed by the National University of Defense Technology, won the world record again with its superb double-precision, floating-point calculations with a peak rate of 5.49 petaFLOPS and a continuous computing rate of 3.39 petaFLOPS. In fact, Tianhe-II headed the newest list of the global top 500 supercomputers and it is almost one fold faster than the U.S. Titan, second on the list. "It is a booster to realize the 'Chinese Dream,'" remarked Yang Xuejun, president of the Chinese University of Science and Technology, "but speed isn't the only thing we are after. We are in pursuit of a 'supercomputing dream' that contributes to the building of an innovative country and to advancements in the human civilization with better and faster supercomputers."[29]

Scientific development and research have their own patterns, and ways that are suitable for administration do not usually work on science, or they do with compromised quality and benefits. Fortunately, the Third Plenary Session of the 11th CCCPC blew the charging horn for the Reform and Opening Up and brought scientific development and research to spring. In fact, on the eve of the session in March 1978, Comrade Deng Xiaoping had already asserted that science and technology were the primary force of production on the opening ceremony of the national convention of science and technology, which drew the curtain on structural reform of the system of science and technology management. There are now multiple views on how to stage the reforms. I agree with the one arguing that the reform should be divided into four stages, but disagree with its starting point in that I think it should start from the national convention of science and technology. The four stages are as follows.

The first stage, from 1978 to 1995, is the initiation phase of the reform. The *Decision by the CCCPC on Reforming the Science and Technology System* in 1985 and the *Decision on Several Issues about Deepening the Reform of the Science and Technology System* in 1988 conveyed a crucial message about the reform, which is to bring structural reform to the battlefield of economic construction. The decisions called for application of scientific achievements to production and for the reform to fully liberate researchers and the scientific and technological force of production and encouraged research institutes to introduce competition mechanisms, implement various forms of the contracted responsibility system, separate the right of management from the right of possession, lift restraints from institutes and researchers, and march onto the battlefield of economic construction and the Reform and Opening Up.

The second stage, from 1995 to 2006, is the reform phase of research institutes in systematic transformation. The national convention of science and technology in 1995 proposed a strategy with far-reaching impacts, to reinvigorate China through science and education, made the *Decision to Accelerate Scientific and Technologic Advancement*, and specified the direction, tactics, and tasks for the reform. In 1999, the CCCPC and the State Council issued the *Decision on Strengthening Technological Innovations, Developing High-Tech Industries, and Industrializing Innovation and High-Tech*, which stated that the structural reform of the science and technology system should go side by side with that of the economic system. Implementation of the two decisions initiated structural transitions and mechanism reformations in research institutes.

The third stage, from 2006 to 2012, is the phase of reforming the system of science and technology management. The national convention of science and technology in 2006 published the *Decision on Implementing Science and Technology Planning to Improve the Capacity of Autonomous Innovation*, in which a 16-word tactic for the scientific and technological development in the new age was proposed, i.e., "autonomous innovation, major leap, supporting development, leading future."

The State Council also pointed out, in *Mid- to Long-Term Planning of National Development of Science and Technology*, that an innovation system should be established centered on enterprises and that integrated production, education, and research should push for all-around completion of the national innovation system, to bring new changes to the managing system of science and technology, and to create a multilayered mode of management.

The fourth stage, starting in 2012, is the phase of deepening of the reform. In *Suggestions on Deepening the Reform of the Science and Technology System and Accelerating the Construction of the National Innovation System*, promoting the integration of science and technology into economic development was assigned as the central task of the deepening of the reform. The 18th CCCPC proposed in 2012 to implement the "strategy of development driven by innovations," which placed scientific and technological innovation at the central stage of the state's innovation development.

In 2013, the *Decision* by the CCCPC on deepening the Reform listed "deepening the reform of the science and technology system" as an independent item and proposed to:

> establish a healthy and complete system that [encouraged] original innovation, integrated innovation, and innovation based on learning and mastering advanced technologies, [to] perfect the system of innovation that [was] market oriented, and to allow the market to play its role in choosing technologic directions and routes, factor prices, and allocation of various innovation factors, explore a mechanism that [coordinated] production, education, and research, strengthen the role of enterprises as mainstays in technologic innovation, facilitate big-sized enterprises to take on the major responsibility of innovation, stimulate middle- and small-sized ones to participate in innovation, advance the reform to transform applied research institutes to orient with the market and run as enterprises, and to build a national innovation system.[30]

In 2015, the *Suggestion* by the CCCPC on the 13th Five-Year Plan showed that the reform of the science and technology system stepped into a phase with a comprehensive system of innovation as the planning combined the

"Four-Pronged Development Strategy," the five development prospects, and the strategic goal to realize the great revival of the Chinese nation with specific tasks, a direction, and key areas of the reform, and it was a top-down design.

CURRENT PROBLEMS

While the great accomplishments made since the new China was founded, especially since the Reform and Opening Up, are reckoned, problems and gaps in the current stage are also to be confronted. Overall, the intellectual ability and scientific and educational levels of the population are still low, the return on investment in science and technology is low, the capacity to transform technologies and patents into real forces of production is low, and the quality of research is not very high.

What do the three "low" and the one "not very high" aspects tell us? In my opinion, they tell us that our mode of scientific and technological development is similar to that of economic development in that they both favor expansion in numbers but not improvement in quality. It is true that we have made a series of major breakthroughs in advanced scientific and technological research and applications in computer science, astronautics, marine science, biology, new materials, and high-speed rail aside from the "two bombs and one satellite," many of which are leading the studies in these fields. After all, many studies are following an intensive mode of development, which values improvement in quality.

The question is whether the overall development mode of scientific research in China is intensive or extensive, and that is a question that demands an answer. Even if both modes are present, it is necessary to find out which is dominant. In my opinion, our mode is more extensive than intensive. Some have argued that we have unsatisfactory research achievements and outstanding researchers because there has only been one Nobel Prize laureate from the mainland under the condition that the new China has existed for 65 years, the Reform and Opening Up has been around for 35 years, we have the largest population in the world and the most specialists and technological workers, and our economy has risen to the second place in the world with relatively rapid growth.

However, I do not agree that the Nobel Prize should be used to evaluate research or research quality, let alone be the only standard, as the rules, the culture, and the languages behind the prize are not in our favor, although it may be used as one of the standards, but only one of many, for it does reflect research consequences from one aspect. What I think is more indicative of the lack of our current research strength is that we have not nurtured any scientist as achieved as Ding Zhaozhong, Yang Zhenning, and Li Zhengdao, who have been well recognized globally. The lack is also relevant to the "question by Qian Xuesen": no school is run in such a way as to train scientific and technological inventors but they are all run in an exam-oriented way.

Looking back helps with learning the present, and learning the past and the present helps with finding reasons for what has happened and solutions to problems. Why are there the "three low" and "one not very high" aspects in the development of science and technology? There may be many reasons, but they can all be attributed to the system and development mode, where the reform should begin. Since the Reform and Opening Up, the economy has grown rapidly and the strength of the country has improved quickly while a large-scale increase in research funding has been provided by the government. Recently funding has been guaranteed and it is no longer a "bottleneck" factor that holds studies in government-affiliated research agencies or research sectors in higher education institutes. Between 2000 and 2014, for example, the expenditure on research and experiments increased from 89.57 billion all the way up to 1.3015 trillion yuan, a 13.5-fold increase calculated by the prices then while the proportion of the expenditure of the GDP also increased by a large scale, to 2.05% in 2014.[31]

With the large-scale increases in research funds has come continuous growth of research projects, research institutes, and results. However, the quality and benefits of research have not grown accordingly. For example, a total of 171,928 scientific and technological papers was published by research and development institutes in 2014, a number that can hardly be ignored by anyone; however, only 47,032 of these papers, or 27.36%, were published in international journals; meanwhile, 24,870 applications were filed for patents, among which 15,786, or 63.47%, were inventions.[32]

In addition, despite the large number, the publications were not all of high quality: not very many papers were truly innovative, valuable in theory or practice, or cited frequently by international studies, and even fewer cast a significant impact on their fields. Similarly, the number of patent applications was large, but inventions did not make up for a high proportion and many inventions were not important ones that involved core and innovative technologies. We must reflect on these phenomena. Now that research funding is abundant, research teams are stronger than ever, and facilities and laboratory conditions keep being improved, innovative and significant creations are still taking time. Are there problems in the system of managing science and technology development? That is a question that reforms must answer.

Comments on the current system of science and technology management in China do not agree with each other, but there is one clear consensus: that multiple channels, multiple leaders, and multiple managing modes coexist. In the government, the Ministry of Science and Technology of the People's Republic of China is in charge of all things related to science and technology in the country under the State Council. It came from the National Science and Technology Commission that was founded in May 1956. Off the government, the Chinese Association for Science and Technology was founded in 1958.

In addition, the National Natural Science Foundation was established in 1986 with approval from the CCCPC and the State Council, and the committee of the foundation is directly affiliated with the State Council.

In the same year, the National Social Science Foundation was established together with a committee to lead the planning for national philosophical and social scientific studies. Among the government-affiliated research entities are four research institutes: the Chinese Academy of Sciences, the Chinese Academy of Social Sciences, the Chinese Academy of Engineering, and the Development Research Center of the State Council.

In addition, many government sectors have their own research divisions, and so do higher education institutes, Party schools, and administrative schools. Furthermore, a considerable number of research institutes are affiliated with all provinces, autonomous regions, and municipalities. Apparently, there are a large number of research institutes at various administrative levels such as national, government agency, and regional levels, and they have various sources of funding, modes of management, evaluation standards, and mechanisms of research translation. It is therefore quite challenging to integrate all of them.

The Ministry of Science and Technology is the government sector in charge of all scientific and technological studies, but it is only a ministry of the State Council and it has difficulty to supervise and coordinate all the research institutes in the country. In addition, the ministry does not have all of the money since quite a proportion of research funds is allocated directly to various research institutes. The National Natural Science Foundation and the National Social Science Foundation are growing quickly in terms of the funding they get, but they distribute grants to all based on research topics; thus they can only guide studies by deciding which topics get funded and fall short of overall planning and coordination.

Research institutes in government agencies, provinces, districts, and cities are clearly marked with agency and regional characteristics and they are managed by governments in terms of the direction of research, topics studied, evaluation, and translational work. All these factors have led to the current situation of fragmented research as well as certain chaos, as described in what follows.

Chaotic management of research grants. Various institutes at different levels make every effort to advance their research plans, projects, and topics of importance in order to get funded, which leads to redundant applications such that the same proposal is submitted year after year or to multiple departments or foundations with minimal revision at each submission. National foundations have issued strict regulations to prevent such repeated and multiple applications and have made reforms of the existing mechanisms, which has had some effect. However, these measures are met with great difficulties due to the fragmented management system.

Chaotic management of research topics. Grants are usually sent to the research unit of the principal investigator whose proposal is funded and that is where the money is managed. Despite specific articles on usage of grants, many do not follow the rules carefully, and some money is even spent in a pepper-sprinkling way of "feast finance." Furthermore, management of the progression of research projects is not strict enough in that many studies are rushed to make deadlines, which often fails, since they have been used to apply for grants multiple times; more importantly, the quality of the studies is seriously compromised.

Chaotic research results. Repeated applications for research grants directly lead to a large amount of repetition of studies at an average, and even low, level. Sometimes, people produce coarse studies in order to make deadlines, and only a small proportion of studies has been carefully carried out. Some even resort to plagiarism and arbitrarily include others' results in their own works, typical of academic misconduct. Unfortunately, many such results have been happily taken with very few negated due to a variety of reasons such as loose supervision of the research system, evaluation reports in the hands of institute leaders, traditional favor of the beginning to the end, and social connections that force only good words, but not bad ones, out of people's mouths.

The chaotic funding, management, and results of research coexist to a certain degree, reflecting the "exam-oriented" type of problems in the research system. Many research institute leaders find all ways possible to conceive and set up projects to apply for grants while researchers try their best to apply for projects with sometimes even repeated applications for the same proposals. Once money is obtained, studies are divided up between groups and in the end compiled to form a book, which is then used as the announcement that the project has been concluded.

During the whole process, everyone, from leader to group member, is busy. They are busy with grant and reimbursement applications, research, and evaluation of the studies. After the conclusion of one project, they move on to apply for the next, leading the cycle to repeat itself over and over again. This is why the enormous number of papers, books, and research reports mentioned earlier has been published while the contribution, value, and impact of these publications are on the minds of very few. Researchers who follow such a path of research may, given time, all be promoted to associate professors and then professors without bumps along the way. When further generalized, such a mode of research management becomes routine for all research and higher education institutes, Party schools, and administration schools with the "quantification management" employed in both research and education, which then becomes the "exam-oriented" kind of research system like what it is in education.

"Quantification management" evaluates performance based on the number of publications and the level of the journals of the publications while promotion is made based on the same standards. For example, it is set as the "hard standard" for academic promotion whether one has obtained national-level research projects and whether one has publications in recognized journals in some research and higher education institutes.

They classify the journals as authoritative, level 1, core, and average, and the requirement for promotion to professorship is to have taken on national-level projects with one or more publications in authoritative journals, two or more in level 1 journals, or three or more in core journals. For associate professorship, the requirement is team membership of national-level projects with one or more publications in level 1 journals, two or more in core journals, or three or more in others.

With these requirements, researchers and teachers have specific goals to pursue, which must be strived for and realized. They therefore make every effort to apply for national-level projects and get their papers published in recognized journals. What if they cannot get the grants or publications? Some have come up with ideas such as obtaining project funds and publications through "back doors," which has led to malpractices such as paying to get published and thus to decreases in the quality of journals and papers. It is now high time to reform such an "exam-oriented" research management system. No quality research may result without reforms, neither will scientific and technological innovation be there, and straightening up academic ethos will be just vain words.

Reforming the "exam-oriented" science and technology management system

To reform the "exam-oriented" science and technology management system demands accurate steering of the reform. Apparently, all of the problems described earlier are closely related to the government and the market, or specifically, they result from a strong government combined with a weak market. For example, research projects are usually proposed by pertinent government agencies at both the central and regional levels and decided in corresponding government meetings. Some high-quality projects proposed by national foundations usually seek opinions from specialists and agencies in the fields while the projects are being conceived. The leading group for national planning of social sciences recently set up a consultant committee made up of philosophical and social science scholars to provide suggestions that help the research projects to line up with the very frontlines of disciplines.

When projects are concluded, evaluation is usually needed from specialists, who in general give high-quality comments. However, some projects funded by regional agencies are often inspected and evaluated by leaders of pertinent agencies, which echoes the saying "you are good if I say so; you are not if I say so," while most may pass the inspection. Of course, inspection and evaluation of research projects centered on leaders deserve more than just denials as high-quality inspection with respect for the truth has been observed in some cases; however, in general, such practices are more about what the superior officials think than what the science dictates, which is a basic fact that cannot be denied. Therefore, reasonable placement of the government and the market and "de-administratization" are where reforms should be.

The *Decision* by the CCCPC on deepening the reform stated that:

> The reform [of] the economic system is the most important part of the mission of comprehensively deepening the Reform and its core task is to

> straighten up the relationship between the government and the market so that the latter may play a decisive role in resource allocation and the former may also play its role well. It is a general law of a market economy that the market decides resource allocation, and perfecting the socialist market economy must follow this law and efforts must be made to solve the problems of the incomplete system of our market economy, excessive interference by the government, and lack of supervision.[33]

This principle in the *Decision* also applies to the reform of the science and technology management system as the reform must also focus on straightening up the relationship between the government and the market by sorting out the roles for both the market and the government.

Then what should the government do in the systematic reform of science and technology management? The government should fill in support for the studies that are fundamental, strategic, and pioneering as well as those that are universal, that integrate scientific and technological plans and resources, and that build a moderate support mechanism – these are the most fundamental and important positions of the government in the *Decision*. Here the government's role in directing the four kinds of studies and in setting up a supporting mechanism actually marks its biggest difference from the market.

Fundamental studies are the precondition for the development of all sciences and disciplines, without which they are like water with no source and trees with no root and will never thrive. Strategic studies are characterized with long-term, wholesome, and macroscopic perspectives, important to the overall situation of scientific and technological development, and of course to be taken on by the government, especially the central government. These roles can never rely on a market since the market does not have the capacity or mechanism. A market may only take on partial responsibilities to support pioneering studies, while strategic studies that have wholesome value may only fall on the shoulders of the government to be carried out with real progression. Studies with universal traits are somewhat beneficial to the public and do not seek profit, which is entirely opposite to the nature of a market, and must be assumed by the government.

In addition, the *Decision* also listed two important reforms. One is to "establish an innovative survey and an innovative report institution to lay out an open and transparent system to manage and evaluate the national scientific and technologic research." This reform is a requirement of the government's role to support fundamental, strategic, pioneering, and universal studies and to integrate science and technology plans and resources, which do need innovative survey and report institutions as well as an open and transparent system for management and evaluation.

The other is to "reform the system of how academic members are selected and managed, optimize discipline lay-out, increase the proportion of middle-age and young scholars, and implement regulations for academic members to retire from and exit the system."[34] This is a reform to keep up with the time and it is aimed to innovate the system of academic members and increase fresh blood so that the system is vigorous with the entrance and the exit both wide open.

What should the market do, and how does it do it? Well, except for the reforms on the government side, everything else should be included in the market-oriented reform progression. The *Decision* proposed specific tasks for the reform of the science and technology management system given the overall goal to establish an innovative system for scientific and technological research. The tasks are as follows.

First, the mechanism of market-oriented technological innovations should be perfected. The *Decision* sought to "perfect the mechanism of market-oriented technologic innovations, allow the market to play its role in directing the orientation of technologic development, path selection, factor prices, and allocation of various factors of innovation."[35] It is noteworthy that "perfecting" but not "establishing" is used here, which means that the mechanism has already been established but it is not good yet, and that the mechanism that may orient innovations is to be perfected, not any mechanism in the general sense. That is also to say that an accurate judgment is needed of the science and technology market, and that further perfection is needed of a market mechanism that has already been or is being established.

Second, an innovative mechanism should be established to coordinate production, education, and research. This is an important part of the national innovative system. First, enterprises must be strengthened as mainstays of technological innovations, which is very specific. Many enterprises in fact lack the awareness of innovation. They only care about production and refuse to invest in research and development, leading to "all-through" products for several, even tens of years that eventually fall far behind the time and drive the enterprises to the brink of bankruptcy. Some, in contrast, are willing to invest in research and development, which forms bases for production, education, and research to collaborate; technological innovation keeps growing, and so does their innovative capacities; thus the enterprises keep going up steps and win many competitions. The *Decision* has left no room for ambiguity about enterprises being the mainstay of technological innovation, which must be fortified. Next, each type of enterprise has specific responsibilities in technological innovation. Big-sized enterprises are the backbone and should play their part in technological innovation, while medium- and small-sized ones are flexible and should be stimulated and energized to play their part. Then, applied technologies should be pushed forward to orient toward the market and managed like enterprises, which is a requirement of the innovative system integrating production, education, and research. Applied technologies, when released on the market, may meet the market demand for new technologies, on one hand, and, on the other hand, may obtain reasonable return from the market with patents of new technologies, which will stimulate and encourage innovation and advancement of science and technology.

Third, the incentive mechanism for technological innovations must be perfected. The following measures are to be taken.

First, intellectual property should have stronger function and protection. On one hand, advocacy, exhibition, and introduction meetings may raise awareness in the society of intellectual property and allow it to exert its function; on the other hand, strengthening protection of intellectual property entails administrative, economic, and legal measures while it has also been proposed to explore the establishment of intellectual property courts.

Second, a management mechanism should be established that the market is decisive. The previous practice that administration dominates everything and the government is fragmented into agencies must be abolished, and the new mechanism should seek resource allocation decided by the market and everything else should also be left to the market as much as possible.

Third, the mechanism for technology transfer must be perfected. The technology market must be advanced greatly, technology transfer and the platform for transfers standardized, law enforcement strengthened, and the lawful rights of both parties of any intellectual property exchange well protected.

Fourth, the mechanism of managing venture capital must be perfected. The conditions for medium- and small-sized scientific and technological companies to finance should be bettered to solve the problems caused by small scales and lack of capital. A new system should be established that the market decides which technological innovation is invested in, how to allocate funds, and how to evaluate results so that the innovations may meet the demand of the market, funds are properly used, and the scientific and application value is increased. In order to do so, perfection of the investment mechanism is needed to obtain stronger resistance to risks.

Notes

1 Office of Dictionary Compiling, Institute of Languages, Chinese Academy of Social Sciences, *A Modern Chinese Dictionary*, Beijing, Commercial Press, 1997, p. 1061.
2 Ibid., p. 1063.
3 Li, Jingneng, *New Demographic Theories*, Beijing, China Population Publishing House, 2001, pp. 100–101.
4 Liu, Hongkang, and Wu, Zhongguan, *A Handbook of Population*, Chengdu, Southwestern University of Finance and Economics Press, 1988, p. 403.
5 Li, Jingneng, *New Demographic Theories*, Beijing, China Population Publishing House, 2001, p. 100.
6 *A Modern Chinese Dictionary*, 5th edition, Beijing, Commercial Press, 2010, pp. 1301–1302, 1757.
7 *China Statistical Yearbook 1987*, Beijing, China Statistical Press, 1987, pp. 749–754; *China Statistical Yearbook 2015*, Beijing, China Statistics Press, pp. 700–702.
8 *China Statistical Yearbook 2000*, Beijing, China Statistics Press, p. 656.

9 *China Statistical Yearbook 2015*, pp. 700–702.
10 *China Statistical Yearbook 1986*, China Statistics Press, p. 733; *China Statistical Yearbook 2016*, Beijing, China Statistics Press, p. 686.
11 *China Statistical Yearbook 1986*, p. 734; *China Statistical Yearbook 2016*, Beijing, China Statistics Press, p. 696.
12 *China Statistical Yearbook 2000*, p. 681; *China Statistical Yearbook 2015*, p. 653; *China Statistical Yearbook 2016*, p. 638.
13 "Suggestion by CCCPC on the 13th Five-Year Plan of National Economic and Social Development," *People's Daily*, November 4, 2015.
14 Confucius, *On Relatives*, vol. 2, *Liji.*
15 Confucius, *University*, *Lijin.*
16 *Zilu*, *Analects of Confucius.*
17 The Central Archives, ed., *Selected Topics of Works by Mao Zedong*, Beijing, Central Party Literature Press, 2003, p. 1631.
18 Ibid., p. 1633.
19 *China Statistical Yearbook 2015*, pp. 701–702.
20 *China Statistical Yearbook 2013*, Beijing, China Statistics Press, pp. 683–685.
21 Ibid., pp. 684–685.
22 Calculated based on the data from *China Statistical Yearbook 2013*, pp. 683–685.
23 *China Statistical Yearbook 2013*, pp. 95, 101, 683–685.
24 *Decision by the CCCPC on Several Major Issues about Comprehensively Deepening the Reform: An Assembly of Files of All the 3rd Plenary Sessions of All the Central Committees since the Reform and Opening-Up*, Beijing, People's Publishing House, 2013, p. 207.
25 Ibid., p. 207.
26 Zhang, Yu, "Interpreting the 'Question by Qian Xuesen' Correctly," *Hongqi Essays*, vol. 3, 2013.
27 *Assembly of Files of All the 3rd Plenary Sessions of All the Central Committees since the Reform and Opening-Up*, pp. 207–208.
28 Reports on *Wenhui* on October 25, 2012, May 8, 2014, and May 9, 2014.
29 "Supercomputers in China Accelerated 5,000 Times in 10 Years," *Wenhui*, June 18, 2013.
30 *Assembly of Files of All the 3rd Plenary Sessions of All the Central Committees since the Reform and Opening-Up*, pp. 185–186.
31 *China Statistical Yearbook 2015*, pp. 10–11.
32 Ibid., pp. 652–653.
33 *Assembly of Files of All the 3rd Plenary Sessions of All the Central Committees since the Reform and Opening-Up*, p. 178.
34 Ibid., p. 186.
35 Ibid., p. 185.

Bibliography

Chen, Xi, "Accelerating the Construction of a Strong Country with Talents," *People's Daily*, November 11, 2015.

Decision by the CCCPC on Several Major Issues about Comprehensively Deepening the Reform: an Assembly of Files of All the 3rd Plenary Sessions of All the Central Committees since the Reform and Opening-Up, Beijing, People's Publishing House, 2013.

"Outline of Mid- to Long-Term Development Planning of National Education (2010–2020)," *Postdoctoral Communication*, vol. 3, 2010.

Ouyang, Song, and Gao, Yongzhong, eds., *An Oral History of the Reform and Opening-Up*, Beijing, China Renmin University Press, 2014.

"Suggestion by CCCPC on the 13th Five-Year Plan of National Economic and Social Development," People's Daily, November 4, 2015.

Tang, Junchao, "Increased Education Inequality at School Enrolment," *Sociological Study*, vol. 3, 2015.

Tian, Xueyuan, *Hardships of a Big Country: A Macroscopic View of China's Population in the 20th Century*, Beijing, China Social Sciences Press, 2013.

Tian, Xueyuan, ed., *Population Aging and the Middle Income Trap*, Beijing, Social Sciences Academic Press (China), 2013.

Xi, Jinping, "Explanations of the 'Suggestion by CCCPC on the 13th Five-Year Plan of National Economic and Social Development'," People's Daily, November 4, 2015.

Zhang, Yu, "Interpreting the 'Question by Qian Xuesen' Correctly," *Hongqi Essays*, vol. 4, 2013.

7 The stepwise-loosening trend in fertility policies

Exploring the path of "family planning" with Chinese characteristics

A major change was made to the fertility policy in 2013 that two children were allowed for each couple as long as one party was an only child when the CCCPC issued the *Decision by the CCCPC on Several Major Problems of Comprehensively Deepening the Reform*, which came 33 years after the policy of one child per couple was officially advocated for by the CCCPC in 1980. In 2015, change was once more made with the issuance of the *Suggestion by the CCCPC on the 13th Five-Year Planning of National Socioeconomic Development* and two children were allowed for every couple. The curtain of comprehensive adjustment to and stepwise loosening of fertility policies was thus drawn.

Tracking back the origin of fertility policies

Reproduction is bound by people's concepts of it, which is ultimately decided by the level of productive forces and the nature of productive relations in a society. Therefore, to track the evolution of fertility policies, one must dig deeply into history to learn the mode of production in each stage and the resulting reproductive culture.

A peek at historical fertility policies

Fertility worship

As one of the ancient civilizations, China was not an exception in the prehistoric world where fertility rites were common. As suggested by the name, fertility worship originated in prehistory when mankind worshipped reproduction out of ignorance, which was associated with the extremely low level of the forces of production at the time. I visited many sites in Western Europe, Northern Europe, Japan, and Thailand and saw paintings, sculptures, and stone carvings of fertility rites when I went abroad on scholarly activities.

China has its own culture of fertility worship. The exact time when fertility worship began in China cannot be determined now, but we are sure that it went back to at least the era of the Three Sovereigns and the Five Emperors in the Neolithic Age. We usually talk about "the five thousand years" because the history of China is generally believed to date back 5,000 years. However, *Addition to the History of the Three Sovereigns*, written by Sima Zhen, pushed back the history recorded in Sima Qian's *Records of the Grand Historian* by 2,000 to 3,000 years.

In fact, there have been conflicts in historical records of the Three Sovereigns and the Five Emperors. As many as six figures were mentioned as the Three Sovereigns in history books such as *Lu's History*, *Biography of Qin's First Emperor* in *Records of the Grand Historian*, *Latitude of History*, *Baihu Tong*, *Complementary Records of Tongjian*, and *Han Wen Jia* in *Li Wei*, and they were Sui Ren, Fu Xi, Shen Nong, Nv Wa, Gong, and Zhu Rong. Among these figures, Fu Xi and Shen Nong were mentioned in every book while each of the other four was mentioned in one.

The current consensus is as follows: Sui Ren, Sovereign of Heaven, was the first to make fire by rubbing two stones (or two sticks in some accounts). Fu Xi, Sovereign of Humans, studied the relation between heaven, the land, and mankind, created and made Bagua trigrams, invented signs to note down events, started authentication of marriage with deer pelt halves, defined units of measurement, and set up the solar terms, which were all important to humans' lives. Shen Nong, Sovereign of the Land, invented cultivation and taught it to people and thus became the deity of the land.

There are also various editions of the Five Emperors, but those recorded in *Biographies of the Five Emperors* in *Records of the Grand Historian* are widely accepted: Huang Di, Zhuan Yu, Di Ku, Tang Yao, and Yu Shun. The consensus is that the Five Emperors lived 4,300 to 5,000 years ago while the Three Sovereigns lived 5,000 to 8,000 years ago. Sui Ren, Sovereign of Heaven, and Shen Nong, Sovereign of the Land, did not leave behind many things for study, yet Fu Xi, Sovereign of Humans, did. Thus Fu Xi has had the greatest impact among the three and is the most worthy to study.

A few years ago, I learned quite a lot when I conducted a field study in Tianshui, Gansu, where I visited the Dadiwan cultural site, which was the hometown of Fuxi, Guatai Mountain, where Fuxi invented the Bagua trigrams, and the hometown of Nv Wa. I came to realize that Fu Xi made the following two distinguished contributions to fertility worship and reproductive culture.

His first contribution was to include fertility worship in the Bagua trigrams he created. As recorded in *Yijing* (*The Book of Changes*), in the ancient time when he was the sovereign of the land, Baoxi (another name of Fuxi) looked up to observe the universe, down to observe the land, around to observe birds and beasts to learn their connections with the land, near to learn about himself, and afar to learn about things; then he created Bagua to relate to deities and to represent the whole world. Therefore, Fuxi created Bagua in order to reveal the relation between the universe, the land, and humans, which were dependent upon each other, and the laws of nature, with the emphasis on the law that underlay human activities and the changing courses of nature and humans.

The law was first decided by the reproduction of humankind, and that was why Fuxi placed fertility worship in the middle of Bagua. Professor Guo Moruo has argued that the permutations and combinations of the signs of *yin* (--) and *yang* (—) in Bagua trigrams symbolized coitus between a man and a woman, and was therefore fertility worship. I applaud his opinion, and to add to it, I believe that the fertility worship in Bagua is highly abstract and seemingly simple but with deep denotation.

Isn't there a pair of *yin* and *yang* fish in the middle of every Bagua trigram that represents fertility worship? The *yin* fish and the *yang* fish are connected head to tail and are positioned in the middle of each Bagua trigram. The endless changes of Bagua, including the 24 changes according to the permutations of *qian*, *dui*, *kun*, *li*, *kan*, *gen*, *zhen*, and *xun*, and those based on the 24 changes such as 64 changes, Wuxing Bagua, Yin Yang Bagua, Taiji Bagua, Xiantian Bagua and Houtian Bagua, are all derived from the motions of the *yin* fish and the *yang* fish in the middle and are permutations and combinations of *yin* and *yang*. Compared to the sculptures, carvings, and paintings depicting reproductive organs and behaviors, which are simple and direct representations of fertility worship, Bagua is original and raw, can be generalized, and controls the core of fertility worship. It fuses implicativeness, depth, and comprehensiveness with science and is therefore a higher form of fertility worship that was distilled and abstracted from concrete objects.

The second contribution by Fuxi was to the institution of marriage, i.e., authentication of marriage by deer pelt halves, and it was the origin of China's quality reproduction. Fuxi lived during a time when China was transitioning from a matriarchal to a patriarchal society. At the time, communal marriage was predominant among tribes and incest and cousin marriage halted human reproduction and impaired people's health greatly. Thus Fuxi decided to reform.

According to studies, the tribe of Fuxi resided in the area of Tianshui, where there were sparse forests and abundant deer. Fuxi then set a rule of deer pelt halves: upon the birth of a child, the pelt of a deer was cut into halves, with one half staying in the tribe and the other half given to the child. When two people wished to get married, both needed to show their pelt halves. If both halves could be matched to two halves possessed by the tribe, then they were actually members of the same tribe and thus could not marry each other. Only those who didn't have a matching half-pelt or none at all could be married.

With time, the rule of deer pelt halves ensured that one could only marry someone from another tribe, which later laid foundations for marriage between tribes. Although still a polygamous society, Fuxi's tribe benefited from the new marriage tradition and its members quickly multiplied, which enabled them to defeat and merge the neighboring tribes. The core tribe of Fuxi fought its way eastward from the west up to Henan, where Fuxi himself was buried. Fuxi was a proponent of the argument that "no live birth would result from a marriage of the same surname," and his tribe became a strong power because of fertility worship and quality reproduction.

As he lived in a society that was transitioning from matriarchy to patriarchy, Fuxi later was transformed into a symbol of masculine fertility worship. The transformation had vital impacts on marriage, fertility, and changes of the entire population in feudal China. There have been increasing discoveries of sculptures, carvings, and paintings depicting masculine fertility worship in many places and excavations, as well as scripts and astronomical and calendrical materials with implicative worship of masculine fertility.

For example, the Chinese character *zu* (祖) originally lacked the left part and its right part was actually an image of a male reproductive organ. In contrast to the West, where many cultures embraced the concept that God created mankind, China shut women out of the mainstream of society little by little after entering the patriarchy, and fertility worship evolved stepwise into worship of male ancestors. Therefore, a male-centered reproductive culture that believed "the more children, the better" was formed in the feudal society.

Concept of reproduction: the more, the better

The passing down of fertility worship and its impact on reproduction concepts and behaviors in the later societies can be attributed at least partially to Confucius (551–479 B.C.), the founder of Ruism (Confucianism). Confucius's teachings on population, history, social affairs, and economics have been extensively described and studied, and it is also generally agreed that he passed down fertility worship from ancient times, advocated for large populations, actively sought to attract immigration from other feudal states, and was therefore a pioneer of preaching a large population.

However, little has been said about the status of Confucius's teachings of population in Ruism or how it was incorporated into Ruist philosophy. I argue here that his thought on population is indispensable to Ruist doctrines, and it was a premise and foothold of his teachings when he travelled around the feudal states to educate the public and to promote his political beliefs.

At the core of Ruism is *ren* (humanness). How is it linked to humans and populations? Where is Confucius's population thought positioned on the checkerboard of *ren*? Let us first take a look at *Analects of Confucius* (*Lun Yu*). Yan Yuan asked about *ren*, and Confucius answered, "*ren* is to discipline self to fulfill *li* (rites), and the day when self-discipline fulfills *li*, *ren* is upon all." He also added:

> Do not look at what is not in accordance with *li*, do not listen to what is not in accordance with *li*, do not speak what is not in accordance with *li*, and do not act when it is not in accordance with *li*.[1]

Then what is *li*? *Analects of Confucius* also has the answer. Duke Jing of Qi asked Confucius about ruling, and Confucius answered, "let the ruler be ruler, ministers ministers, fathers fathers, and sons sons."[2] That is also to say that self-discipline must be conducted in accordance to the relations between lords and subjects and between fathers and sons to complete the rites. Furthermore, *li* comprises those before and after death: "serve your parents during their lives according to *li*; when they die, bury them according to *li* and make sacrificial offerings according to *li*."[3]

Apparently, Confucius valued *li* during one's life as well as during events after death such as burials and sacrifice; they both had temporal connotations of his concept of *xiao* (filiality). Then how did people continue *li* to honor their ancestors and to keep incense burning on their ancestral altars? The only way was to reproduce so that the incense could be lit up through generations. Confucius lived 2,500 years ago, which was a time with high birth rates, high mortalities, and low population growth. In addition, his time was in the Spring and Autumn and Warring States Periods (770–221 B.C.) of Chinese history, when wars were fought year after year, and that added considerably to the mortality rates. It was therefore even more important to have high rates of births. After all, only a high number of births would make it possible to have a lot of offspring, who could then carry on the rites to honor the ancestors.

Now it is clear what Confucius held as his population thought: "How populous indeed!"[4] The Chinese character for populous, *shu*, has another meaning in the traditional patriarchal family system that denotes someone or a line of a family that is different from the "legitimate" one. Thus a concubine is called with the addition of this character, and so is her son. When he said "how populous indeed," Confucius was praising a large population. Although we cannot assert it, is it possible that he was also trying to encourage "illegitimate" descendants?

Confucius also advocated for implementation of *ren* rulings so that "those who are near are pleased and those far away long to come."[5] He argued that a *ren* monarch would please the subjects in the state and facilitate population growth, while at the same time, people from other states would be attracted and the population would further grow. Although there was no such thing as demography, Confucius was actually teaching a school of thought that matched the "push-pull" theory in demography some 2,000 years later. His line of thought on population can be summarized with the following formula:

ren — *li* — *xiao* — *shu* — *ren*

Here *ren* is the start as well as the end, and it is also the core of Ruism. To implement and realize *ren*, one must act and only act according to *li*, which is embodied in one's *xiao* during one's parents' lives and after their deaths. In order for *xiao* to be passed down through generations, *shu*, or population growth, must be ensured. *Shu* is also the result of ethics and *ren*, which thus brings us back to the start, *ren*.

After Confucius, Mencius (372–289 B.C.) further developed his thought on population in two aspects. One of them is the well-known saying that "there are three ways to be unfilial (not *xiao*), the worst of which is to produce no heir." Confucius only talked about serving, burying, and making sacrificial offerings to parents during their lives and after their deaths as his definition of *xiao*, but in order for *xiao* to be passed on, everyone must reproduce. Thus Mencius ranked reproduction as the top deed of *xiao*, and took failure to marry or to reproduce after marriage to be the worst against *xiao* as it would eventually put an end to the family rite to honor the ancestors.

Later, failure to produce a son after marriage was considered one of the seven reasons to divorce one's wife (*qichu*), and individuals were then immersed in the ethics of families and became enactors of *xiao* and tools of reproduction. The saying by Mencius had a deep impact on people as it inspired each family to recall their ancestors and everyone now tried to find a position for himself in the genealogy while trying to keep the family tree growing. It also stirred up people's desire to have a son and made them proud of their marriage that would result in sons.

In contrast, one who failed to have a son was condemned as a "family killer" (*juehu*) and was considered to have suffered from his own malicious deeds. The impact has lasted until now even with today's restrictive fertility policy. Various data and surveys have shown that a considerable proportion of those who want another child want a boy and an even higher proportion of those who already have a daughter want a boy.

The other aspect is also a well-known saying, i.e., the unity and morale of people (*renhe*) are more important than advantages in the terrain (*dili*), which are more important than the timing (*tianshi*). Building upon the teachings of Confucius, who, out of his thought of *ren*, hoped for a densely populated state through rulings that made "those who [were] near pleased and those far away long to come," Mencius further pointed out that of the three factors of timing, terrain, and people, the factor of people was the most important.

Seeing acres and acres of land uncultivated, he explained that large lands with few people were easy to snatch and that a *ren* monarch could attract people to settle down with intellectuals to help build the state, farmers to cultivate the lands, and merchants to energize the market. Therefore, the unity and morale of people were the most important factor that decided and represented the strength of a state. This thought of Mencius also had a deep impact, and in particular, some of his points to realize *renhe* are still talked about, passed around, and applied.

A few other figures during the time of Confucius and Mencius in the Spring and Autumn and Warring States Periods also touched on topics of population and they were Guan Zhong (?–645 B.C.), Mo Di (480–420 B.C.), Shang Yang (390–338 B.C.), and Han Fei (233–208 B.C.). Some of them echoed the large-population view held by Confucius and Mencius. For example, Mo Di argued that only population growth would ensure abundance in wealth and also called for marriage at young ages, simple burial rites, and abolition of the traditions that impaired population growth such as excessive possession of concubines. Some had their own opinions. For example, Han Fei, a master in *fa* (law, measurement, and statistics), wrote in his essay *Wu Du*:

> In the ancient times, no man cultivated and there were enough plants to feed everyone; no woman wove and there were enough animal furs to warm everyone. A small population possessed overabundant wealth, thus no one fought for it. People were able to manage themselves at the time and there was no need for laws of generous rewards or cruel punishment. Now one may have five sons and does not think of it as a large number, while the five sons each have five sons. He, now a grandfather, is alive with 25 grandchildren already. Therefore, a large population leads to inadequacy of wealth, and although people work very hard, they don't get enough payment. How can they not fight for more wealth? Under this circumstance, there will be no rest in the society even though the rewards and punishment are both doubled.

It seemed to Han Fei that "inadequacy of wealth," "not enough payment," and "unrest" were all rooted in the large size of a population.

Still others held views that were in between these two. Guan Zi (Guan Zhong) worried about three problems: a huge land that was not properly managed, a large population that was overcrowded, and a strong army that did not know how to stop a war. Guan Zi also proposed that the way to manage a large population was not through reducing its size, but through setting up officials to manage childcare and media. In summary, all these people had valuable thoughts on the subject of population, but they had little impact during their times and were barely comparable to Confucius and Mencius.

The more children, the better fortune

The 2,000 years after the Spring and Autumn and Warring States Periods, from the Western Han Dynasty until the Opium War during the reign of Emperor Dao Guang in the Qing Dynasty (206 B.C.–A.D. 1840), covered Imperial China. No matter how historians variously stage and date this period, the ideologies during these 2,000 years were the most representative of Imperial China, and there is no question about it.

Similarly, no matter how many times concepts and thoughts on population were tried and tested dynasty after dynasty, they only became clustered around the core: the more children one had, the better fortune he would get.

The most influential scholars in demography during this period were Jia Yi (200–168 B.C.), Chao Cuo (200–154 B.C.), and Dong Zhongshu (179–104 B.C.) in the Western Han Dynasty (202 B.C.–A.D. 8); Xun Yue (148–209) and Xu Gan (170–217) in the Eastern Han Dynasty (25–220); Liu Yan (715–780) and Du You (735–812) in the Tang Dynasty (618–907); Su Shi (1036–1101) in the Northern Song Dynasty (960–1127); Ye Shi (1150–1223) in the Southern

Song (1127–1279) and Jin (1115–1234) Dynasties; Ma Dunlin (1228–1322) during the Southern Song, Jin, and early Yuan (1271–1368) Dynasties; Xu Guangqi (1562–1633) at the end of the Ming Dynasty (1368–1644); Feng Menglong (1574–1646) at the turn of the Ming and Qing (1636–1912) Dynasties; and Hong Liangji (1746–1809) and Wang Shiduo (1802–1899) in the Qing Dynasty.

They all inherited various lines of population thought in the Spring and Autumn and Warring States Periods, and, according to their respective historical environment, made multi-angled, multidisciplinary, and multilayered exploration and description. Their views covered large and small populations, population size and distribution, population migration and flow, supply of laborers and soldiers, population quality and education, demographic statistics and taxation, management of household registration and agricultural land taxation, and fertility and sex.

They also conducted empirical studies on the contemporarily demanding issues of population. However, only a handful of books was dedicated to population study during these 2,000 years. Most scholars' efforts were scattered around their works when they talked about how to build a wealthy country, how to make a strong people, how to collect taxes on agricultural lands and from individuals, how to build roads and facilitate commerce, and how to reform. Among the views of these people, what was considered the most orthodox view was to describe and further develop the thought of Confucius and Mencius, which was well represented by the movement of "honoring Ruismonly," led by Dong Zhongshu in the Western Han Dynasty, and the school of Chengs and Zhu in the Song Dynasty.

After Emperor Wu (140–87 B.C.) ascended the throne in the Western Han Dynasty, the social economy leapt in development after long terms of social rest and stability, national defense was strengthened, and the dynasty reached its peak. However, local lords were still powerful in their own realms, great landowners and merchants kept annexing farmers' lands, and Xiongnu (a confederation of nomadic peoples) never stopped invading the border areas, all of which made a strong central government imminent.

Under this circumstance, Dong Zhongshu put forth the argument that the Hundred Schools of Thought did not agree with and sometimes contradicted each other and thus impaired the implementation of bills and orders from the central government as well as the strength of the nation. He therefore proposed to honor the appropriate rites between the emperor and lords and between fathers and sons to uphold the imperial authority, to replace the Hundred Schools with a unified school of Ruism, and to select government officials only among scholars of Ruism.

Emperor Wu took his advice and assigned Ruism in the government academy where only five classic works of *Shi, Shu, Yi, Li, Chunqiu* were taught. Subsequently, the scholars of Daoism who honored effortless actions and managing selves were all excluded from government schools to make space for Ruist scholars, and those who did not study Ruism were removed from the government positions of Taichang Boshi. This was the famous movement of "Expelling the Hundred Schools, Honoring Ruism Only." From then on, Ruism was officially acknowledged as the orthodox school in China, and it dominated Chinese history for the subsequent 2,000 years.

After Dong Zhongshu, Ruism was once more distilled in the Song Dynasty by the Lixue (study of *li*) School of Chengs and Zhu. It is generally agreed that Zhou Dunyi (1017–1073) in the Northern Song Dynasty was the first to conceptualize Lixue, and his two students, Cheng Hao (1032–1085) and Cheng Yi (1033–1107), further developed his thought and became the founders of the school of Lixue. They started from the eternal *li*, or the universe forces, and attempted to explain everything with it. They argued that the natural world and human society both ran on their respective tracks of *li*, and the proper rites between emperors and lords and between fathers and sons were the "*li* of the universe" manifested in human society, which would never change.

Zhu Xi (1130–1200) in the Southern Song Dynasty studied the thoughts of all the branches of Lixue and fused them to build a theoretical framework of Lixue. He believed that all the changes and development of the universe, the land, and human society were dominated by *tianli* (universal forces) that had existed since the beginning of time and would never change, and the task of mankind was to "get rid of human lust to conform to Tianli." He gave an example to explain this idea: it is *tianli* that one wants to eat when hungry, but it is human lust when he wants to eat things delicious.

In other words, Zhu's thought was to persuade people to let go of their own lust to meet the demands of *tianli* that was the rule of nature and the human world. Later *tianli* was thought in human society to be manifested by the moral values of "Sangang Wuchang," or three cardinal guides (ruler guides subjects, father guides son, and husband guides wife) and five constant virtues (benevolence, righteousness, propriety, wisdom, and faithfulness). These values and those of the "Sancong Side" of women, or threefold obedience (obeying father as a daughter, obeying husband as a wife and obeying son in widowhood) and four virtues (wifely virtue, wifely speech, wifely demeanor, and wifely work), which showed up later in history, became powerfully binding in public opinion and society, although the values were themselves intangible.

They did not only carve social, political, and cultural China deeply but they also shaped China's population in size, sex ratio, education, and policy orientation. After the "Expelling the Hundred Schools, Honoring Ruism Only" movement and the establishment of Lixue by Chengs and Zhu as the dominant ideology in Imperial China, the population concept also went from the large-population concept by Confucius and Mencius to the one that more children equaled better fortune. Both concepts wanted a large population, and in this aspect, they were not different. However, going through the feudal society for 2,000 years, the latter was continuously deepened, perfected, and spread, and was rooted deeply in people's minds to become a pillar of their reproductive belief. The development and escalation of the concept can be summarized as follows.

First, the number of children was associated with fortune, and reproduction thus had an objective. Why did people want to have a lot of children? It was because they wanted good fortune. The causal relation of the two was gradually rooted in society. Actually, this idea was widely accepted by society because there had been an economic base to it. It is widely known that staging of economies is not based on the products, but on the means and tools of production. As Karl Marx remarked, manual mills set forth a society dominated by feudal lords and steamer mills a society dominated by capitalists.

Imperial China was founded on agrarian economies. During the long history of the 2,000 years, advancement in productive tools certainly brought many inventions, but they were all manual tools, not machines. All the tools were driven by forces of humans, animals, and sometimes natural forces such as water and wind. These manual tools were essentially externalized and materialized extension of human stamina, and laborers were always the primary factor and in the dominant position among the productive factors, including laborers and means of labor.

The agrarian economies in Imperial China based on family-sized cultivation and weaving made certain that the number and quality of laborers, especially male laborers, were the determinant of how wealthy a family could be. Similarly, the strength of the feudal empire that was founded on these agrarian economies was dependent on the quantity and quality of its laborers. Therefore, vigorous reproduction and education and a large, prosperous population were the most important for both the micro-unit of families and the macro-level of a nation's strength and wealth.

Second, the concept of "the more children, the better fortune," once incorporated in the value system in Imperial China, became a shocking part of the culture. Confucius and Mencius placed the idea of a large population (*shu*) in the thought system centered on *ren*, and the line of their logic was clear: *ren* — *li* — *xiao* — *shu* — *ren*. Confucianism and Mencianism, after being combed, completed, and systemized by scholars, including Dong Zhongshu, Cheng Hao, Cheng Yi, and Zhu Xi, became the orthodoxy of feudal society, and the concept of "the more children, the better fortune" was also replaced by moral doctrines such as Sangang Wuchang and Sancong Side.

The class of feudal landowners worked hard to spread these doctrines. They wrote genealogies, built ancestral temples, erected chastity arches (*zhen jie pai fang*), and patronized many novels, poems, and plays, which all imprinted the concept in people's minds. The concept, binding and converging people with time, eventually became a demographic culture like a religion. The better fortune rewarded people not only with material benefits but also with pride. After all, only someone who did many good deeds could be rewarded with the good fortune of many children, and on the contrary, if one had a bad reputation or did bad deeds, he would not be able to have a son and had to become someone without *xiao*. Once imprinted in people's minds, the concept effortlessly triggered a strong desire to reproduce, especially to get boys.

Third, a wide range of aspects were touched on to address the population issue. Compared to Confucius and Mencius, who focused their arguments on the size, sex, education, and migration of population, the concept of "the more children, the better fortune" covered a much larger range of areas such as marriage, reproduction, families, clans, occupation, health, ethics, moral values, household registration, statistics, astronomy, geology, land, and poll taxes. Some works, such as *Three Generals* (*General Classics*, *General Ruling*, and *General Bibliography*), made the list of classic demography works with their passages on population.

Some, although not dedicated to population studies, discussed extensively some of the toughest population issues at the time, making the issue of population indispensable to socioeconomic development by revealing that the population study was on the edge of and at the same time covering several disciplines. After all, woven with fundamental social problems in Imperial China, especially with land, agricultural land taxes, poll taxes, and wars, issues of population were always among the most pressing problems during the transitional times between dynasties.

However, in recent history, the concept of "the more children, the better fortune" was under attack and started to change. Yan Fu (1854–1921), an intellectual of enlightenment in China, was inspired by Darwin's theory of evolution, that the fittest survive in nature, and stated, in his books *On Strength* and *Additional Comments on Survival*, that, despite its large size, the population of China was not well educated, that it was of low quality with a high birth rate, and that it was a problem that demanded a solution.

To solve this problem, he proposed to educate the public, restrain marriage, and select for quality reproduction, which had been already practiced in the West. Similarly, Liang Qichao included population in his views on reforms, and expounded his opinions in supporting late marriage in his books *On Inhibiting Early Marriage* and *Collections of Yinbing Study*. He pointed out five harmful aspects of an early marriage: 1. It's harmful to parents' health. 2. It's harmful to reproduction and the growth of children. 3. It's harmful to the education of children. 4. It's harmful to the schooling of children. 5. It's harmful to the whole nation.

He further compared China to the West and concluded that people usually married early in underdeveloped areas, and in contrast, people married late in civilized areas. Based on this conclusion, he advocated for late marriage to improve the quality of the population. However, he opposed Malthus's theories, and argued that the idea that population would grow exponentially was false, and that what Malthus proposed to prevent the growth, actively or inactively, was just not practical.

Sun Yat-sen (1866–1925), the pioneer of China's democratic revolution, also paid close attention to China's population trend. He believed that the reason why Western colonialists failed to annex China was exactly because of the population:

> Compared to China, their population sizes are too small. However, 100 years from now on when their populations will have grown significantly while ours have stopped growing, they will outnumber us by a great margin and will definitely seize all our land. When that happens, we will not only lose sovereignty, but also the whole country. In addition, the Chinese people will be reduced by them, and perhaps even extinguished.[6]

Nevertheless, Sun did not want a growing population. On the contrary, he sometimes showed great anxiety over the large size of China's population.

Chen Duxiu (1879–1942) and Li Dazhao (1889–1927), founders of the CPC, also contemplated problems of population. Both published works to illustrate their views, Chen with *Demographic Theories of Malthus and China's Population Problem* and Li with *War and Population*, and both argued against Malthus's points pertaining to population by listing many facts of population growth in China and other countries.

They pointed out that the problem with China's population was rooted in the social system that had been rotten in that the means of livelihood, although enough for the population, had not been distributed evenly and the landowners occupied lands and capitalists had the productive means, and that the only way to solve the problem was through revolution. They attacked Malthus because he only called for restricting population growth without trying to increase employment opportunities, which was clumsy as if he tried to "flatten camel humps with stone bars."

However, their views were opposed by many from a school of social studies that preached abstinence that raised its voice in the 1920s and 1930s. It started in 1918 when Chen Changheng published *On China's Population*, followed by *Three Principles of the People and Population Policies*. This was followed by Xu Shilian, who published *Problems of China's Population* and *Outlines of Demography*; Chen Da, who started *Population Supplement* in the *Morning Post of Peking* and subsequently published his book *Population*; and many others such as Wu Jingchao and Li Jinghan, who also published their own works.

Their basic views can be summarized as follows. First, they agreed with Malthus that the population had outgrown the means of livelihood and that China's population had exceeded a "moderate population density" and had perhaps even reached "a full house."[7] Second, they advocated for restraining population growth and improving its quality and argued that "just as competition for survival contradicts competition in academics, the quantity of a population contradicts its quality"[8] so that an excessively growing population would invariably lead to decreases in its quality. They thus proposed small-numbered and quality reproduction, developing education and science, and "one flower," or at the most "two flowers," for a man and a woman.

Third, they advocated for restraining fertility. To them, there were two ways to solve China's population problems with one providing only temporary solutions and the other eradicating them. Development of agriculture, immigration, and public health was the former, and delaying marriage and restraining fertility, the latter. Apparently, the school of social studies for abstinence was deeply impacted by Malthus, and its publications helped spread its views. At the same time, some of their points, such as moderate population density, restraining the population size, and improving the population quality, had their own value in science. However, these views were restricted to academics and did not arouse much public interest. After all, the concept of "the more children, the better fortune" and its resulting demographic culture had been predominant in China for a long time, and they directly bore population policies that encouraged reproduction.

Population policies that interfered with fertility directly or indirectly

Much space earlier in this chapter was given to historical views of population because every social policy in history was the reflection of the contemporary dominant view by the people. In order to understand the pulse of historical population policies, we must first understand how the concept of "the more children, the better fortune" was formed, how it was imprinted in people's minds, and how it was supported and followed by people.

Although many "heretic" views of population had been outspoken since the Warring States Period by Han Fei and others, their view of "a small state with a small population," from Han Fei, through Hong Liangji and Wang Shiduo in the Qing Dynasty to the social school of abstinence in the early 20th century, never made its way to the mainstream and only caused a few splashes. The rise of reformists and revolutionists in recent history brought new insight into demography. They rode the tide of their time and became influential. They essentially made modifications to the traditional values in their efforts to learn from the West in search for remedies to save China and the people after China was forced open with cannons and guns by the West. Despite their efforts, they did not completely break away from the traditional values that honored a large population and multiple children; instead, these values survived tenaciously and even made their way into their ideals and books.

In fact, the Ruist thought of a large population and the concepts of "the more children, the better fortune" and male supremacy that were later normalized were all the mainstream ideologies in Imperial China and thus dominated population policies, and the policies, no matter whether they affected populations directly or indirectly, were always formed and implemented based on them. This book was not intended to evaluate the policies through dynasties. That has already been done by scholars such as Mr. Wu Xiyong with his book *A History of Population Thought.*

This book is aimed at expounding population policies in the current stage, and as anything current is actually based on history, it cannot ignore ancient and recent histories when talking about the present. Therefore, outlines of the population policies in the past 2,000 years must be given first to discern the track of the policies, their basic points, and what they were really intended for.

POLICIES THAT INTERFERED WITH POPULATION DIRECTLY

These policies can be further classified as those that interfered directly with the natural changes of population and those with the mechanical changes of population.

Policies that interfered directly with the natural changes of population. These policies aimed at interfering with natural changes such as births and deaths, and took multiple measures such as encouraging reproduction and rewarding births of boys.

A. Encouraging reproduction. Reproduction encouragement was the theme of various population policies in ancient and recent histories. It never changed during the long period of more than 2,000 years with its impact spilling through every aspect in that other policies all eventually came back to it in order to increase the population. As early as the Spring and Autumn Period, Duke Goujian of Yue, while sleeping on sticks and tasting a gall, issued a policy of "ten years of reproduction and immigration and ten years of learning the lessons" after he came back to Yue following his defeat by Duke Fuchai of Wu.

   The policy was in fact one that encouraged reproduction more than 2,000 years ago. The first half of the policy included two aspects: encouraging the natural growth of population and attracting people to settle down in Yue. To encourage reproduction, Goujian had three regulations: 1. A young man could not marry an old woman, or an old man a young woman, as a marriage must facilitate reproduction. 2. If a man failed to marry by the time he turned 20, or a woman failed to marry by age 17, their parents would be held accountable. 3. The birth of one boy was rewarded with two bottles of wine and a dog, the birth of a girl merited two bottles of wine and a pig, two births had prizes, and three were given extra care. Yue's policy, which encouraged reproduction and restricted age at marriage, late marriage, and refusal to marry, was very fruitful and eventually Yue saw its strength in a prosperous population and had its revenge when defeating Duke Fuchai of Wu.

In the Han Dynasties, new rules were issued with both rewards and punishment to encourage reproduction. For rewards, a man received two years of corvée exemption when he had a newborn child during the reign of Emperor Gaozu,[9] and in A.D. 85, Emperor Zhang of the Eastern Han Dynasty issued an order that a man would receive a three-year exemption from the poll tax if he had a newborn boy and that a pregnant woman would receive three *hu* of rice while her husband was exempted from the poll tax for a year.[10]

For punishment, Emperor Hui ordered in 189 B.C. that any woman who failed to marry from age 15 to 30 would turn in a poll tax five times the normal amount.[11] It was probably the first time in history when a poll tax was to be collected from unmarried women, but if we look at it from the perspective of demography, the order targeted women of reproductive age, thus it was vitally important to improve fertility rates. A woman had to pay a poll tax if unmarried, but was exempted as soon as she became pregnant until after she gave birth, when she would receive additional rewards. The population policies with both rewards and punishment must have played important roles in increasing population. In fact, starting with Emperor Zhang, the poll tax became institutionalized, and how to collect this tax also became a flexible measure to adjust population policies.

After the poll tax became the major revenue of the ruling class, population growth automatically translated into increases in tax revenue, and the government certainly would want the population to grow fast. However, it also halted population growth at the same time and underreporting was also common. In the Qing Dynasty, reforms were finally made to the laws of land and taxation because the rulers saw the danger to the throne and the country that was inflicted by excessive land annexing at the end of the Ming Dynasty.

During the reign of Emperor Kangxi of the Qing Dynasty, a bill was issued to lighten the burden of the people in that the total amount of taxes of a family was set at a constant and new births would never bring any extra tax. However, local officials often took advantage of population migration and found ways to increase people's taxes. Therefore, the poll tax had to be reformed.

After years of trials and studies, Emperor Yongzheng issued a bill of "Tan Ding Ru Mu" in 1723. The bill abolished the poll tax and divided the total amount of taxes due in each county to all the lands in the county to be collected as land taxes. This policy was a key reform of the taxation system in China. It put an end to the poll tax that had been in use for more than 1,500 years, and set free new births from the fear of tax increases, thus playing an important role in the doubling of the population during the three reigns of Kangxi, Yongzheng, and Qianlong, as well as in the subsequent population growth.

B. Encouraging the birth of boys. The aforementioned policies in the Han Dynasty that encouraged reproduction did not reward any birth, but only that of boys. Such sex discrimination has come a long way. It is widely known that Confucius once said, "women and small men are difficult to nurture," and Mencius once said, "there are three ways to be unfilial, the worst of which is to produce no heir," where only a son was considered an heir. When it came to the period of the Northern and Southern Dynasties (420–589), Emperor Ming of the Qi Dynasty announced that the parents of those who birthed a son would be exempted from taxes and corvée for a year.[12] Now the rewards for births of sons were expanded to the parents of both the husband and the wife, and the exemption was given both in taxes and in corvée. In addition, there were material rewards in the form of 10 *hu* of rice.

When it came to the Tang Dynasty, Emperor Taizong ordered after his coronation that the women who gave birth to sons since January would be rewarded with one *hu* of millet,[13] which reflected the pride and the good fortune people thought having son would bring. In some dynasties, underprivileged families with sons received living stipends, and those with triplet boys received special rewards. For example, in the Yuan Dynasty, families with triplet boys were exempted from taxes for three years, and in the Ming Dynasty, such families received rice until the boys reached eight years of age.

In the Qing Dynasty, rules had it that families with live births of triplet boys received 10 *pi* of cloth and five *dan* of rice, which would not apply to those who gave birth to both girls and boys at the same time or triplet girls.[14] Therefore, emperors explicitly encouraged reproduction because they wanted more boys, not girls. Such sex discrimination went way back and was firmly formed.

C. Advocating for early marriage and reproduction. Age at marriage was first recorded in *Situ, Office of the Land*, in *Zhou Li*: "Let men marry at 30 and women, 20." There have been various explanations of this account. Some hold that the ages mentioned were the youngest ages at which men and women should be married, which then would be proof of a tradition of late marriage and would be in direct contrast to the social norms at the time. Others hold that they were the oldest ages, and this view has been taken by most people since Confucius. However, there is no explicit note to this account in *Zhou Li*, and we do not know for sure now. However, there is no question that early marriage and reproduction were advocated for in Imperial China.

For example, the essay *On Great Emperors* in *Mozi* has the following statement: "In the past, the great emperors ordered that a man at 20 must marry and a woman at 15 must marry. This was the order from the great emperors." The ages mentioned here were undoubtedly the oldest ages at which men and women should be married, and "must" suggests that there were rules to regulate the behavior. Similarly, the aforementioned strategy of "ten years of reproduction and immigration and ten years of learning the lessons," proposed by Duke Goujian of the Yue State, also specified that "the parents of a woman who does not marry by 17 will be held accountable and those of a man who does not marry by 20 will be held accountable." Apparently, there were rules then to make sure that all women married by 17 and men by 20.

Similar rules and regulations were in effect until the early Tang Dynasty, when in year 22 of the Kaiyuan Calendar (A.D. 743), the ages at which people were allowed to marry were set at 13 for girls and 15 for boys.[15] The ages were further adjusted in the Ming Dynasty that "all men above 16 years of age and all women above 14 years of age may be married."[16] Apparently, early marriage and reproduction were reasonable in Imperial China since the ruling class wanted a large population as a sign of national strength and the public wanted a lot of children in their pursuit of better fortune. Then the only question was how early one could be married, and it was up to the practical situations.

The determinant in practice is always the maturity in sexual development of boys and girls, and in this aspect, our ancestors decided that "men mature at 16 and women at 14," which, actually quite scientific, then served as the starting ages for people to get married. In addition, as pregnancy takes approximately 10 months, it was certainly reasonable for men to start having children at 17 and women at 15. Of course, this was only the general case, and in reality, a lot of other factors were common in feudal society such as matching the backgrounds of families of both parties, obedience of children to their parents about the matter of marriage, the need to have a medium in marriage, childhood marriage, baby marriage, and engagement in pregnancy, which all brought varieties to the phenomenon of early marriage and reproduction.

D. Advocating for large families. Families were the cells of society and the principal units of economies and population reproduction in the feudal age of agriculture and handcrafting. Therefore, the type, the size, and the structure of families and how well families might function became a facade of population policies and were constantly watched by the whole society. In accordance with policies encouraging population growth and reproduction in Imperial China, the concept of a big family with generations living prosperously together was also welcome. After all, only big families were full of opportunities to practice *xiao*, preached by Confucius and Mencius, to maintain the ethics of "letting fathers be fathers and sons be sons," and to experience the joy of a prosperous population.

As the old saying goes, a country has its laws and a family has its rules. Let us not forget that the laws of a country and the rules of the families are associated, and as a matter of fact, family rules in feudal society were often dependent on laws. As mentioned earlier, Ruism valued *xiao* and with this value, the concept of self was buried in ethics and moralities, and individuals became existent as sons and daughters of their parents. When this value was transcended in families, the authority of parents must be maintained and children and grandchildren were gathered around them to practice *xiao* to establish large-sized families with parents being the core and possessing absolute power.

Confucius once said, "make no long trips when parents are alive." It sounds as if one could only be in accordance with *xiao* if he stayed at his parents' side, and to stay at his parents' side he would have to live with his parents under the same roof. Such a concept was further strengthened by the ruling class who wrote it into law. For example, Emperor Xuanzong of the Tang Dynasty wrote in A.D. 742:

> Local officials need to communicate with the families that have split into smaller ones due to a large number of people and persuade them to move back together to set examples for the whole society. If there are more than 10 adult men in one family, two are exempted from corvée and taxes. For a family of more than 5 adult men, one is exempted.[17]

Here the rewards were proportionate to the size of the family, and in modern terms of statistics, it was a progressive system of rewards. The purpose here was to "set an example for the whole society" so that the feudal family ethics were maintained. At the same time, it was also implicative that big families were beneficial to population growth. In addition to rewards, there was also punishment: "those who register their households and start new families somewhere else when their parents are still alive are to be jailed for three years," and "adopted sons who desert their son-less foster parents are to be jailed for two years."[18] Similar rules were kept in effect in the subsequent dynasties, with more or less modification. With time, large families with four and even five generations living together became more and more common, resulting in increases in the power of these big families.

E. Inhibiting deserting and drowning babies. Policies were made in almost all the feudal dynasties that inhibited deserting and drowning babies and supported adoption by the government and people in order to foster population growth and to guard the ethics and moralities at the time. In the provinces of Zhejiang, Fujian, Guangdong, Jiangxi, Jiangsu, and Shanxi, which were all historically densely populated and economically prosperous, desertion and drowning of babies were quite common. The root of the phenomenon was poverty. At the same time, these babies were also the victims of traditional sex discrimination, and most of the babies deserted or drowned were girls.

   Getting rid of a baby girl forced the mother to wean, and the next pregnancy, in hope of a boy, would happen earlier. In addition, getting rid of a girl saved the family a large amount of potential expense, including the future dowry. In attempts to stamp out baby desertion and drowning, the local governments of these provinces all issued orders to punish people committing the crime. Such orders were mostly restricted to local areas before the Song Dynasty, and in 1205, during the Southern Song Dynasty, "deserting and killing babies [was] strictly prohibited," with, unfortunately, no specifications noted down.[19]

Specific and strict orders were implemented in the Yuan Dynasty:

half of the family wealth is to be given to the army from those who have drowned their baby girls; a slave is to be freed from the status if he reports such a crime, and an official is to be held accountable for his failure to cope with a situation involving such a crime.[20]

To add to these already strict rules, one more item of punishment, "punishment to be generalized to the five families related," was in effect in the Ming Dynasty.

As for adoption, an official institute was set up under Emperor Li in the Southern Song Dynasty to manage the issues related to adopting deserted babies. Emperor Kangxi in the Qing Dynasty, aside from "demanding the law enforcement officials to strictly prohibit killing babies and to be thorough in arresting and conducting trials of those having committed the crime," established orphanages so that "those of the Man ethnic group may send their babies in to be raised there if they cannot afford it."[21]

According to historical books such as *Comprehensive Research on Books and Historical Accounts*, the orphanage in Guangqumen in Beijing was operated very well and its experience was introduced nationwide, and the Jiangxi orphanage took in baby girls with the annual numbers ranging from a few hundred to more than 1,000, considerably contributing to population growth.

Policies that interfered directly with the mechanical changes of population. Changes in population are caused by births, deaths, and migration; the first two are natural changes and the last is mechanical. Population policies, which are direct mirrors of the traditional values of a large population and "the more children, the better fortune," can directly affect population from both the natural and mechanical sides. From the mechanical side, encouraging migration and floating of the population to facilitate its growth was an indispensable part of population policies throughout the dynasties.

Despite various measures, all the policies were aimed at producing more people and both natural and mechanical growth were encouraged side by side. For example, the aforementioned policy of "ten years of reproduction and immigration," by Duke Goujian of Yue, had its focus on attracting immigrants from other states to increase the population in Yue in order to strengthen the power and armies of the state. Another successful example was Shang Yang (approximately 395–338 B.C.), who, appointed by Duke Xiao of the Qin State, enabled the state of Qin to become one of the strongest powers among the states through establishing household registration, abolishing salaries through inheritance, rewarding military contributions, setting up counties and towns, encouraging cultivation and weaving, and unifying units of measurement. In terms of immigration, Shang Yang realized that Qin had a small population for its land while the surrounding states were all densely populated with smaller lands. He then decided to attract immigrants from these states, especially from the Three-Jin area of Han, Zhao, and Wei. According to him, there were at least two benefits to doing so: one was to bring more people to cultivate the land and develop the agriculture of Qin so that its army would have abundant supplies to fight wars, and the other was that enemies were harmed in that the population in Three-Jin would be reduced if its people emigrated to Qin.

These measures were thus as effective as if Qin had won battles. Then how did he attract people to move over for cultivation? The reform of "abolishing the system of Jingtian and cultivating more lands" did it. With the old land restrictions abolished, calls for more and more farmers to cultivate the uncultivated lands, benefits promised to farmers, and lands allowed for sales, many people were attracted. Meanwhile, Shang Yang also ordered that whoever produced above-average crops or cloth would be exempted from corvée and taxes while those who stopped cultivating to run businesses and those who fell into poverty due to failures to do his own work would be reduced to government slaves. With carrot and stick, Shang Yang successfully motivated local residents and immigrants to carry on agricultural activities, which laid the foundation for Qin to defeat the other six and to eventually unify China.

After the Qin Dynasty, with the exception of the chaotic times of separatist regimes, the policies to attract immigration in the dynasties such as Han, Tang, Song, Ming, and Qing with strong, centralized governments were mostly applied in local regions. For example, after the Eastern Han Dynasty, the northern areas were subjected to long terms of wars and unrest through the ages of Wei, Jin, the Northern and Southern Dynasties, the Revolt by An and Shi, and the wars during the Five Dynasties and Ten Kingdoms. As a result, people lost their homes, many moved to the south, and the Yellow River basin was in serious desolation.

Emperor Zhu Yuanzhang, after he established the Ming Dynasty, called in the north for "farmers to cultivate the lands with each person receiving 15 *mu* of land, two *mu* of land for growing vegetables and tax exemption for 3 years" in addition to "permanent exemption of taxes on the additionally cultivated lands."[22] The policy attracted people to move back to the north from Jiangsu, Zhejiang, Anhui, and Jiangxi, and helped proper distribution of the population. A more typical example of the policies to encourage immigration in Imperial China was to deploy armies on the borders to cultivate the lands.

In fact, cultivation activities by the production-and-construction armies in today's Xinjiang, Inner Mongolia, and Heilongjiang have been practiced for eras and carried on mostly by armies. The policy to cultivate the borderlands also offered benefits to attract people from the inner land to move there, resulting in a growing population at the borders to help stabilize the areas.

POLICIES THAT INTERFERED WITH POPULATION INDIRECTLY

The policies that directly target the natural and mechanical changes of the population are the direct population policies while the indirect ones are the economic and social policies that also have an impact on population growth. During the long history of China, the effect of the indirect policies could not be undervalued because they included population changes in the development of economies and societies and their effects were therefore long-lasting, stable, and accumulative, especially the policies for people to rest and those of lands and taxation.

Policies for people to rest. These policies are usually implemented after a long term of wars and social unrest, and are essentially a compromise in exchange for the society to recover, agriculture to develop, the people to be released from heavy burdens, and the social institutions to stabilize. The 2,000 to 3,000 years of China's history with one dynasty after another has a common pattern of three periods.

The initial phase of a dynasty experiences the transition from unrest to stability, i.e., a new dynasty is established as a result of ending wars, and, in pursuit of a strong country and a happy people, the monarch makes compromises to inflict small amount of taxes and corvée duties so that farmers are not heavily burdened and development and production are resumed. The middle phase experiences the transition from ascending to descending, typically reflected by continuous increases in land annexing, farmers' burdens, social unrest, and conflicts inside the ruling class. The late phase sees the end of the dynasty: more and more farmers lose their lands, heavier and heavier taxes are demanded, larger and larger deficits grow in government budgets, and tides of wars and revolts by the people rise, all of which eventually leads to collapse of the dynasty.

With this recurring pattern come periodic changes in population: increases during the initial phase, reaching peak during the middle phase, and decreases during the late phase. Generally, population grows slowly with rising and resting waves that follow the upward and downward trends of each dynasty. This is an important point because the population increases in China usually happen during the initial and middle phases of each dynasty, which is the result of the policies for people to rest, and the decreases in the late phase, which are caused by corruption of the ruling class and nonstop wars.

After the Qin Dynasty, the first emperors in many dynasties, such as Liu Bang, Emperor Gaozu of the Han Dynasty, Li Yuan, Emperor Gaozu of the Tang Dynasty, Zhao Kuangyin, Emperor Taizu of the Song Dynasty, and Zhu Yuanzhang, Emperor Taizu of the Ming Dynasty, were either leaders themselves or closely associated with leaders of farmer revolts, and thus understood deeply why farmers had revolted in the first place. They therefore all implemented various policies for people to rest and recover after they ascended the throne.

For example, Emperor Gaozu of the Han Dynasty, after he was in power, issued a series of regulations, based on modifications of Qin laws, for the society and the people to rest so that people could have a good life after long terms of wars. He recruited talents widely so that able people could be properly employed, collected only small amounts of taxes and corvée in that the tax rate of crops was only 1/15 with exemption for the first few years in cultivation, called for migrants to go back home to cultivate the lands, and assigned lands and houses to veterans according to their contributions in the army, among which the veterans from Guandong who stayed in Guanzhong were exempted from taxes and corvée for 12 years and those who went back to Guandong were exempted for 6 years. All these policies relieved farmers from heavy burdens, motivated them to work and cultivate their lands, bridged the conflicting classes of farmers and landowners, and facilitated population growth.

Land policies. Land is the root of agriculture and the lifeline of farmers, thus land policies impact many social aspects, including population changes. According to the three-phase pattern of all dynasties mentioned earlier, the primary task of each dynasty when it was first established was to solve the land problems left from the last dynasty. The major solutions were land averaging from the Northern Wei to Song Dynasties and sales of lands after the Song Dynasty.

In A.D. 485, Emperor Xiaowen of the Northern Wei Dynasty (386–534) decided to classify all lands into the two categories of *sang* and *lu*. The *sang* land could be passed down and inherited through generations and thus could not be sold while the *lu* land was given by the government to one when he/she matured and would be turned back upon death. The *lu* land could be bought and sold, and those who were already at a senior age at the time the law was announced could not obtain a *lu* land. A man received 40 *mu* of *lu* land when he turned 15 and a woman received 20 *mu*.

Servants were also considered good citizens and could receive lands and cows. A similar law was used in the Tang Dynasty, called the law of Zu Yong Diao. The law was enacted in A.D. 624 when Emperor Gaozu of Tang announced it. A man would receive one *qing* of land when he reached 18, among which 20 *mu* were considered “permanent land” and the remaining 80 *mu* was an “individual share.”

However, only permanent residents in a village with sufficient lands for all would get the entire 100 *mu* of land, and those in a village with limited lands would only get half, i.e., 50 *mu*, and people in a village with sufficient lands and a large proportion of the population in business would also get only half while those in a village with limited lands and a large proportion in business would not get any land at all.

There were also specific rules on how migrants could receive lands. In return for the land obtained, everyone having received land must turn in the following every year as taxes: two *dan* of millet, which was called Zu, and two *zhang* of each of the three forms of silk product (*juan*, *ling*, and *zeng*) and two *liang* of silk floss, or alternatively two *zhang* and four *chi* of cloth and three *jin* of linen, whichever applied to the local products, and these were called Diao.

People with land endowment also had to pay their corvée, which was 20 days of labor every year and 22 if there was a leap month, and it was called Yong. The implementation of the laws to average lands to people from the Northern Wei to Tang Dynasties met the demands of farmers for lands to a degree, especially during the initial phase of each dynasty, when there were usually large lands uncultivated and a population reduced by wars.

Such land policies, when implemented in the initial phase, were usually quite effective. However, with the development of society and population growth, land annexing also became more and more common, and when the dynasty entered the late phase, the class of landowners came to possess a high proportion, if not all, of the country's lands and the achievements of the land policies were finally consumed completely.

The law of Zu Yong Diao in the Tang Dynasty was completely abolished first by the rebels of An and Shi and then by a great revolt of farmers. After the Song Dynasty, the scale of land sales kept increasing and finally became institutionalized. On one hand, land sales made it convenient for the class of landowners to annex more lands and therefore strengthened their status, and on the other hand, farmers had opportunities to break away from the land and had the liberty to move to other places to work, either cultivating uncultivated land or renting land to grow crops.

Both the laws of land averaging and the system of land sales were beneficial to population reproduction and growth. The former enabled farmers to obtain new lands after losing their old ones at the establishment of a new dynasty, which gave them stability and opportunity to cultivate and possibly later reproduce. The latter enabled farmers who had lost their lands to explore new opportunities such as cultivating a new, uncultivated land in a remote area or starting a small business, which pushed the society to transition to one based on owner-peasants and built up agrarian families based on them. As the old saying goes, a self-sufficient family had "30 *mu* of land and a cow with a wife, children, and a warm bed." Such families were the best examples of why people wanted to have more children for better fortune, and were the hotbed of population growth in Imperial China.

Taxation policies. The taxation policies that directly affected the natural and mechanical changes of the population have been summarized. The focus here is on those that did not touch on population changes, especially the ones that were made after reforms.

Historically in China, the taxation policies did not consider population changes. Before the Han Dynasty, taxes were collected only from lands and through corvée. Tax revenue at the time did not change according to population growth. Neither did it impair population growth. Starting from the Western Han Dynasty, poll taxes were collected at the same time with land taxes, and the rewards for births of sons and the punishment of those who failed to marry were both essentially forms of the poll tax.

The most key change to the taxation policy in the Han Dynasty was that there were several categories of the poll tax, e.g., childhood taxes collected from those aged 7 through 14, adult taxes from 15 to 56, and male adult corvée from 20 to 56. The amount of taxes due for the first two categories, as well as the specific age ranges, changed with time, but they were always much higher than land taxes and accounted for a major proportion of government revenue. The situation continued for as long as 1,900 years, until Emperor Kangxi of the Qing Dynasty, who put an end to the endless increases in the poll tax in 1712: "a new birth will never inflict a higher tax."

In fact, poll taxes had many problems. One example is that when people ran away from their residence, the local official would not report it in order to continue to demand the same amount of taxes. Problems like this seriously impaired population growth as well as government tax revenue. Therefore, the poll tax was officially ended in 1723 when Emperor Yongzheng of the Qing Dynasty announced a new taxation policy of "Tan Ding Ru Mu." The policy, although not a population one, set free families with new births from fears of increased taxes, and thus had a far greater impact on reproduction and population growth than any population policy. The population doubled twice during the 150 years from the reign of Emperor Kangxi to that of Emperor Daoguang in the Qing Dynasty, a perfect example of the impact of the policy.

Evolution of fertility policies in the new China

Various standards exist among academics and related fields to stage the evolution of fertility policies after the establishment of the new China. My opinion is that population is indispensable to socioeconomic development, and it is perhaps a good choice to fit it in with the practical and historical course and describe its changes by the stages of socioeconomic development. My descriptions are detailed next.

Three-year recovery phase (1949–1952)

The three years of economic recovery from 1949 to 1952 largely saw policies that restricted birth control. The major task at the establishment of the PRC in 1949 was to stabilize society, carry on the democratic reform, develop production, and improve people's lives so that the economy would equal the highest level before the wars as soon as possible. As far as population was concerned, the whole nation was under the impact of Comrade Mao Zedong's criticism of Acheson, and the pessimistic views on China's large population were swept all off. In just three short years, China transitioned from high births, high mortalities, and low population growth to high births, low mortalities, and high growth, which was more or less associated with the policies that restricted birth control at the time.

On April 20, 1950, the Department of Hygiene of the People's Central Government and the Division of Hygiene of the Committee of Revolution Militaries of the Chinese People, with the issuance of *Restrictive Rules on Abortion for Woman Cadres in Government and Armies*, ordered that "signed consent of both the husband and the wife must be obtained," authentication from an obstetrician of a public hospital must be offered, and approval from an authoritative office must be given before an abortion could be performed, and that "both the surgeon and the patient must be punished for an abortion performed without the due procedure."

On December 31, 1952, the Committee of Culture and Education in the Department of Political Affairs of the Government of the Chinese People gave consent to the Department of Hygiene on the drafts of two laws, *Temporary Regulations on Restricting Birth Control and Abortion* and *Trial Regulations on Prenuptial Physical Examination*. The former mandated that

> any violator who performs or is performed surgical sterilization or abortion is to be held accountable for illegal abortion, both the patient and the surgeon are to be sued in People's Court ... and the surgeon is subject to administrative penalties.

In addition, pharmacies must first obtain approval from the local authoritative department of hygiene before providing birth-control items, and all birth-control items are strictly prohibited on the shelf and from street vendors without approval.[23]

Regulations with policy connotations like these covered primarily surgeries of abortion and sterilization on woman cadres and illegal sales of birth-control items. For the general public, these regulations were not very binding, yet few women had desires for birth control anyway. In addition, there was a worldwide baby boom after WWII with a loud cry for prohibition of abortion, and many countries issued regulations to meet the demand, the influence of which could also be felt in China.

The First Five-Year Plan (1953–1957)

The First Five-Year Plan on large-scale development of the economy was implemented from 1953 to 1957 in China. However, the policies that restricted birth control were still in effect, and there was need for someone to turn the tide. At this time, Comrade Deng Xiaoping, then vice prime minister in the Division of Political Affairs, stepped up. In August 1953, he demanded the Department of Hygiene modify the current regulations on restricting birth control and prohibiting contraceptive pills and imports of birth-control tools, and pushed for the formation of *Regulations on Contraception and Abortion*. On May 27, 1954, Vice President of National Democracy and the Women's Federation Deng Yingchao wrote Deng about the demands for birth control by woman cadres, and he replied quickly on the next day:

> I believe that contraception is entirely necessary and beneficial. However, the comrades in the hygiene department seem reluctant to touch on this issue. I hereby ask the comrades from the committee of culture to communicate with them and ask for their opinions. With their consent, we should be able to come up with some effective measures.

In fact, Prime Minister Zhou Enlai once said, "we should advocate for birth control, and the inventor of this advocacy is Comrade Deng Xiaoping."[24] Later, in February 1955, the CPC committee in the Department of Hygiene sent a report to the CCCPC, in which they reflected on their previous attitude concerning birth control:

> We failed to value this issue in our heart, nor did we study it carefully, and we recklessly decided on the regulations to restrict birth control ... We lacked careful research and failed to send feedback to or consult and seek advice from the central committee, thus we have made grave mistakes of divisionism by overlooking the leadership of the party and making decisions on our own. We have learned the lesson.

Their report also proposed that: "According to the CCCPC, we believe it is optimal to have moderate birth control in today's situations in China. In the future, the voluntary contraceptive behaviors of the public should not be prohibited, either." With the proposal, they made specific corresponding rules and management regulations.

On March 1, the CCCPC replied,

> our party is in favor of moderate birth control. The local party committees should properly publicize the policy to cadres and the general public (excluding the areas of ethnic minorities) so that the people will have correct understanding of birth control.[25]

In 1956, Prime Minister Zhou Enlai reiterated, "we are in favor of moderate birth control," in the *Report of Suggestions on the 2nd Five-Year Planning of the National Economy*. It was then proposed in *Outlines of the Development of National Agriculture from 1956 to 1967 (Modified Draft)* that "planned births should be advocated for";[26] and finally, the policy was specified to "advocate for birth control and planned births"[27] by Comrade Mao Zedong in his speech to the Eleventh Top-Level Conference on National Affairs (Extended) on March 1, 1957. By this time, there had been a fundamental turn in the understanding of birth control from the central government to the local CPC committees in that most were now in favor of birth control compared to their previous unfavorable attitude. In addition, the idea of family planning was proposed for the first time – "planned births."

However, it was only a preliminary idea of contraception and planned births during the First Five-Year Plan, and it was also tentatively and cautiously mentioned. The CPC committee in the Department of Hygiene used the word "moderate" several times in their report to the central committee: 1. "Moderate birth control is to be practiced." 2. "No string is to be attached to birth control, which should be moderately publicized." 3. "Moderate publicizing and guidance, but not wide-range propaganda, should be provided to the public so that people have correct understanding of birth control to prevent potential problems."

The central committee also used the word "moderate" twice in their reply: 1. "We in the party are in favor of moderate birth control." 2. "The policy should be moderately publicized."[28] The reasons behind birth control were also detailed in the aforementioned report:

> There are more than 600 million people in China now, with addition of 12 to 15 million every year. ... Excessive growth of the population will add greatly to the burden of both the country and families at least temporarily. The burden on the country is caused by lack of childcare, schools, and living resources while the burden on families is primarily on the parents who, with a lot of children, will have difficulty in carrying out their own work, study, and lives as well as in child education.[29]

Meanwhile, the reply from the central committee mentioned that birth control should be approached from the angle of "the interest of the nation, families, and the new generation," a big step forward from what had been said such as the aspects of health for mothers and babies and of parents' work and study. However, nothing was said about the potential problem of population surplus. Not only that, the report by the CPC committee in the Department of Hygiene took special care to mention that their proposal for birth control was "entirely different" from Malthusian demography or Neo-Malthusianism out of fears that they would be labeled Malthusian or Neo-Malthusian.

The Great Leap Forward and the three years of hardships (1958–1961)

Just as moderate birth control was started to be favored, advocated for, and publicized, the movement of the "Great Leap Forward" was also started with full vigor and vitality in the young republic, which was accompanied by calls for building a socialist country through full confidence, hard work, and smart measures as well as by the fast-paced establishment of people's communes. The movement was, unfortunately, a blow to the newly formed policy of birth control.

In the beginning of 1958, Comrade Mao Zedong said in his speech at the Top-Level Conference on National Affairs on January 8, "which is better, a large population or a small one? I say it's better to have more people now and we need more than what we have now." He also said,

> we cannot ignore the grave problems brought by a large population with a lot of potentials; however, we should not be afraid, either. I'm not afraid.

> In fact, I believe the problems will be solved if we have 200 million more people.[30]

On May 5, Comrade Liu Shaoqi, when making a report to the Second Plenary Session of the Eighth National People's Congress (NPC) on behalf of the CCCPC committee, criticized without mentioning any name the views on restricting population sizes led by Ma Yichu:

> Some scholars even asserted that the agriculture development would not be in pace with the population growth. They believe that a growing population will bring increased consumption and decreased accumulation. … They only see consumers in people, but not producers. Actually, with a growing population comes a growing force of laborers with increased production and accumulation. Apparently, their views are against Marxianism and Leninism.

Again on December 10, a similar statement was made at the Sixth Plenary Session of the Eighth National Congress of the Communist Party, and in the *Resolution on Several Problems of People's Communes* that was passed in the meeting, the future prospects were described as follows:

> People used to worry about our large population and small arable lands; however, the harvest in 1958 negated the worries decisively. In fact, as long as we spread our experience of deep and fine cultivation, layered fertilization, and reasonable planting, which led to high yields, we will find out that our lands are not insufficient, but are sufficient, and that what we have is not an excessively large population, but a shortage of laborers. It will be a striking change. We should make every effort to reduce the current cultivated lands by perhaps 2/3 according to local conditions, grow crops on the reduced lands and dedicate part of the freed lands to growing pasture grass and field grass and the other part, growing trees to make forests and digging to make lakes. Meanwhile, we can grow various landscape plants on the land, mountains, and water surface to transform our land into gardens of thousands of colors.[31]

The speech by a central government official and the document from the central committee both set the tone to be "benefits of a large population" and "potential shortage of laborers," and at the same time criticized without mentioning names the views that "only saw mouths but not hands." At this time, how could anyone talk about birth control or implement family planning? Just like this, the calls for birth control were devoured by the waves of the Great Leap Forward.

The subsequent three years of hardships from 1959 to 1961 saw sudden deceases in births and population growth rates and increases in mortalities, and the population showed negative growth in 1960 for the first time after the establishment of the PRC. Therefore, all the work on publicizing and implementing birth control paused. No new policy was issued; neither was any present policy stopped during the period. Thus everything essentially followed the policies in the past, yet an excessively low birth rate resulted from the extremely difficult economy.

On April 12, 1960, *Outlines of National Development of Agriculture from 1956 to 1967*, made by the CCCPC, was passed on the Second Plenary Session of the Second NPC. The second item of the document reiterated the basic consensus of birth control:

> With the only exception in areas of ethnic minorities, birth control should be publicized and spread in all the densely populated regions and planned births advocated for so that the families will not suffer from heavy burdens and the children will be able to receive quality education with plenty [of] employment opportunities.[32]

Comprehensive adjustment to the national economy (1962–1965)

Faced with the hardships of the previous three years, the CCCPC announced an eight-character policy of adjustment, consolidation, completion, and improvement in September 1960. By 1962, the adjustment had preliminary results, yet there was still space for further efforts. In May 1962, the CCCPC called for a working meeting to discuss and then pass the *Report on Discussions of the Adjustment Plans in 1962* submitted by the financial and economic group of the CCCPC, and reached a uniform decision to make comprehensive adjustment to the national economy based on the consensus that further development could only be obtained after we took a few steps back. The comprehensive adjustment to the national economy here was actually a further deepened plan based on what had already been achieved through the adjustment made in 1962, and it would cover the next three years, from 1962 to 1965.

The low fertility rates during the three-year hardships could have never been achieved by any policy that tried to control fertility and population growth; however, it was not what we had expected. Not surprising, fertility and population growth rates showed great leaps upward right after the end of the hardships as if people were trying to compensate for those three years, which resulted in a second baby boom of an additional population of more than 300 million.

These 300 million people became a huge bulk in the population structure, and were to exert far-reaching effects on population development. Meanwhile, the population policies concerning birth control that had been in effect were mostly about attitude: policy makers showed favor to birth control and planned births, gave permission for moderate advocacy to explain why birth control and planned births were favored, called for people to follow suit, and spread some simple knowledge on contraceptive measures.

To some degree, these policies stayed with top officials for discussion, and some made it to a few trial sites, mostly big cities and a few densely populated villages. Just as people were still wavering about the question "which is better, a large or a small population?" the national population reached 672.95 million in 1962, a net increase of 131.28 million from the establishment of the PRC in 1949, and at the time China had just walked out of the three-year hardships and was yet to step into the next baby boom.

No one could afford to ignore the population reality now. Under the circumstances, in December 1962, the CCCPC and the State Council issued guidance to seriously advocate for family planning, then in 1963, approved and publicized a report by the CPC committee of the Department of Hygiene on the meeting of the department officials and approved what was issued from the second meeting on city work. Finally in 1965, they approved and publicized the report on family planning by the CPC committee and Population Committee of Shanghai, which detailed the population situation at the time and policies on family planning, as summarized in what follows.[33]

Family planning is an indispensable policy to build socialist China. The term *family planning* was first used by the CCCPC in central files in the *Instruction by the CCCPC and the State Council on Advocating Family Planning* (Zhongfa [62] No. 698), distributed on December 18, 1962. As stated in the *Instruction*, family planning is

> indispensable to the policies for building the socialist China; carrying out the policy carefully for long terms is beneficial to the health of mothers and children, to child education, to both men and women while exerting their potentials to the fullest in production, work, and study, and to the health and prosperity of our nation. Therefore, advocacy for birth control and family planning meets the demands not only of the people, but also of the plan to develop our socialist country; however, the call for birth control in our country is not to be confused with the anti-revolutionary Malthusian demography. The CCCPC and the State Council, in light of the situation in the recent years that the work on birth control and family planning was loosened up, have decided to reiterate to the party committees and governments at all levels that the work needs more attention and [to] be strengthened.[34]

This statement at the beginning of the *Instruction* is particularly important.

First, it specified the position of family planning, which is "indispensable to policies" and must be "carried out carefully for long terms." Second, it explained why family planning was important and the objectives and meanings of its implementation. Four "benefits" were listed in the explanation, which were not only restrained concerning mothers, children, and families, as had always been the case, but also talked about "the health and prosperity of our nation."

The benefits were later expanded to six aspects in the *Minutes of the Second Meeting on Cities* approved for issuance by the CCCPC and the State Council in 1963, i.e., family planning

> benefits the planning for the socialist construction, benefits the control of the population growth in cities, the lightening of agricultural burdens, and the alleviation of the pressure on living supplies in cities and other facilities such as residential and school housing, benefits the increase in the strength of the country and the consumption level of the people, benefits laborers in production, work, life, and study, benefits the health of mothers and children, and benefits the education of the next generation.[35]

In fact, the association of family planning in the document from the central government with macroscopic perspectives on the national and state levels and the descriptions of its relationships with economic planning, national strength, consumption, and population marked a great leap in the understanding of policies, a leap that had important implications for theories and practices. At the end of the *Instruction*, it was pointed out that the work on birth control and family planning had been loosened up in recent years and it was demanded that Party committees and governments at all levels "pay more attention to and strengthen the work" and "include it in their working agenda" so that the implementation of the policy could be supported.

The major objective of family planning was to lower the birth and natural growth rates of the population. It was specifically stated in the *Instruction* by the CCCPC and the State Council in 1962 to "moderately control the natural growth rate of the population." It was later proposed in the *Minutes of the Second Meeting on Cities* approved for issuance by the CCCPC and the State Council in 1963 that "every city should make an effort to lower its birth rate" with specific goals that "the urban natural growth rate should be decreased below 20‰ in the three years of adjustment, below 15‰ during the 3rd Five-Year Plan, and below 10‰ during the 4th."[36] It was the first time when concrete goals of birth rate control were proposed in the files approved by the CCCPC, which in fact highlighted a position on the government agenda for family planning.

The implementation of family planning was first targeted at cities and densely populated villages. China has vast lands with immensely different natural conditions and regional differences such as imbalanced economic, scientific and technological, cultural, and social development and great disparities in population density, health, structure, and racial and ethnic composition. In the early 1960s, when transport means were limited and communication was restricted, differential measures had to be taken to implement family planning in various regions with different conditions as "one clear-cut" measure was destined to fail, and that required differential policies.

The *Instruction* and the several documents by the CCCPC mentioned earlier all specified to "advocate for birth control in cities and densely populated villages" or "for family planning." It is thus fair to say that family planning was carried out only in some areas, where it was meant to be tested and then generalized if successful, but not in the entire country without discrimination.

Publicity and education were important to carry out family planning while technical support was also provided for birth control. The *Instruction* listed specific regulations on how to educate people about family planning: in terms of what was to be taught, the benefits of family planning on the health of mothers and children as well as on individuals and families were to be explained. In terms of who was to be taught, family planning was to be advocated for young, married employees of both sexes, members of communes, and urban residents while young, unmarried laborers of both sexes, art apprentices, students in higher education institutes, and members of communes should also be talked to about prohibition of early marriage and encouragement of moderately late marriage.

Education was to be strengthened in higher education institutes to encourage students to focus on study and to help them stay away from premature love affairs and marriage, which may interfere with their study and add to their burden. In terms of principles of publicizing family planning, it emphasized that various traditions, habits, and ideologies should be respected and practical, differential measures taken while educating people, vulgarization should be avoided, blind proposals of slogans, rations, and competitions should be prohibited strictly, wide-range advocacy should be avoided in areas inhabited mostly by minority groups, sparsely populated, rich in natural disasters, or prevalent with gynecologic diseases, and technical support should be provided to individuals of both sexes who have birthed multiple children and are amenable to future conception. In terms of means of education, small-scale oral communication was the first priority to educate people on contraception with the help of brochures made by public health agencies when necessary and publicity in newspapers and magazines should be avoided.

Implementation of family planning focused on contraception and production and the supply of contraceptive drugs and tools was valued. The *Instruction* specified that it was most effective to apply contraceptive measures for birth control and it must be explained clearly to the people that abortion would harm women's health. Given that contraceptive knowledge had not been well mastered by people and the supply of contraceptive drugs could not meet the demand at the time, the *Instruction* also required public health agencies to make concrete plans and create positive conditions for abortion and sterilization so that people would not be harmed, disabled, or even killed by undergoing illegal abortion because they did not have access to scientific surgeries. In addition, the *Instruction* reiterated that the supply of contraceptive drugs and tools must be guaranteed; quality, variety, and specification improved; supply means revised; and sites increased so that it would be easy for people to get them, while it ruled that the prices of the drugs and tools might not rise.

These five aspects showed that the population polices in the stage of comprehensive adjustment of the national economy from 1962 to 1965, mostly the family planning policy, were maturing from all angles. Family planning was affirmed as an indispensable policy that needed to be carried out for long terms, its goals and importance specified, and basic principles, concrete contents and measures, publicity and education means, and focus on contraception with technical support all regulated. Although demographic theories were still in a "forbidden stage" at the time with no academic publications, our understanding of demography actually leapt far forward since in the *Instruction* and other documents from the CCCPC, a clear breakthrough was made that the benefits of birth control were no longer restricted within the range of women's health and families, but elevated to be superimposed with economic planning and the health and prosperity of our nation.

The leap was also manifested in the establishment of family planning committees at various levels. Before 1962, family planning was under the hand of the Ministry of Hygiene, which set up a department of family planning under the division of women and children in the same year; in 1963, it was required in the *Minutes of the First Meeting on Cities*, approved for issuance by the CCCPC and the State Council, that family planning committees be established in central and regional governments to see to the work of family planning.

According to the requirement, the Family Planning Commission under the State Council was established in January 1964, headed by Zhou Rongxin, then secretary-general of the State Council. Level 1 commissions of family planning were subsequently established in 25 provinces, autonomous regions, and the municipalities of Beijing, Tianjin, Hebei, Shanxi, Liaoning, Jilin, Heilongjiang, Shanghai, Jiangsu, Zhejiang, Anhui, Fujian, Shandong, Henan, Hubei, Hunan, Guangdong, Guangxi, Sichuan, Guizhou, Yunnan, Shaanxi, Gansu, Qinghai, and Xinjiang, while in those provinces and autonomous regions with no commissions, a committee of technical support was also established to strengthen family planning.

With better understanding and more mature policies, government agencies at various levels gradually landed the work of family planning, and many provinces, autonomous regions, and municipalities came up with their own, more detailed fertility policies, which bore the prototypes of later policies of population and fertility.

The eve of the Cultural Revolution (1966–1970)

The unprecedented Cultural Revolution, initiated in 1966, delivered a heavy blow to all causes in China and led the national economy to the brink of collapse and social orders to the edge of anarchism. Of course, the blow was felt differently by different causes and by the same cause at different times.

The cause of population development and family planning, for example, felt the blow more strongly and saw more serious consequences in the early than in the late phase of the 10 years of the Cultural Revolution. Therefore, description of the population and fertility policies during the 10 years does not have to follow the contour of the Cultural Revolution, but can be divided up based on the policies and their effects into the early (1966–1970) and the late (1971–1978) phases.

Fertility policies in the early phase of the Cultural Revolution (1966–1970) more or less inherited what had been practiced before, which can be proved by the remarks by the CCCPC on the January 1966 report by Comrade Qian Xinzhong, *Several Problems of Family Planning*.

> Family planning is vitally important. The CCCPC instructed party committees at various levels in 1962 to strengthen their hold on the implementation of family planning. Experiences in the recent years [have] shown that it meets the demands of not only the people, but also the plans of all socialist causes in our country. Meanwhile, good methods and a willing people can always generate good results. Comrade Qian Xinzhong provided very good materials on problems in implementing family planning, which should be read by party committees in all regions at the beginning of implementing the 3rd Five-Year Plan, who, following the instructions by the CCCPC and the State Council in December 1962, are to summarize lessons and generalize them while actively carrying out family planning in cities and densely populated villages to further bring down the population growth rate and to accommodate to the demands of economic development and for a better life for the people.[37]

Unfortunately, however, the Cultural Revolution, particularly the prevalent anarchism in its early phase, struck the Party and government agencies unprecedentedly and paralyzed or nearly paralyzed them, leaving many tasks, including family planning, unattended to, and with the seriously compromised implementation of family planning during this period, reproduction was met with a second baby boom.

From the late phase of the Cultural Revolution to the eve of the Third Plenary Session of the 11th CCCPC (1971–1978)

The worldwide baby boom after WWII marked a new peak in population history. During the 1970s, the world had a population of 3.69699 billion, which grew from 1.17752 billion 20 years before, an increase of 46.7% at an annual rate of 1.94%, marking the period as one with the fastest population growth the world had ever seen.

Such a rapid growth of population attracted much attention from the wise around the world. In fact, two influential incidences took place in 1972. One was the publication of *The Limits to Growth* by Donella H. Meadows et al., commissioned by the Club of Rome, and it shocked the world upon its publication in the spring. The report performed computer simulations with population, food production, natural resources, industrialization, and pollution data from the prior 70 years and concluded that the limits to growth would be reached within 100 years.

> The world will be as such that industrial production shrinks to zero, population decreases dramatically, pollution of the seas, land, and air cannot be remedied, and civilizations are long lost memories. ... What is more shocking is that the collapse will not arrive step by step, but all of sudden like mountains dumping and oceans pouring, leaving humans no means of defense.[38]

The report was immediately translated into multiple languages and aroused strong responses to its unique analyses and answers to several major problems concerning the future and the fate of mankind such as the dilemma we were faced with, the contrast between the finite world and infinite human demands, and rejection of blind objection to development with objection to blind development.

The responses varied from different sectors, and in general, economists were mostly against it, ecologists were for it, and others were divided. As for demographers, some were for it and some against and the majority agreed partially with it. Nevertheless, the report offered unique views on population growth, and linked it with changes in and development of natural resources, food production, industrialization, and pollution. It was generally agreed that the report helped improve people's comprehension of the consequences of population growth.

The other influential incidence was the UN Conference on the Human Environment in Stockholm, Sweden, in June 1972. The conference agreed upon the *Declaration of the United Nations Conference on the Human Environment*, which emphasized that humans were produced by the environment while also shaping it and thus were responsible to inspect the impacts on the environment when planning for any action. Concepts such as "development accommodated to the environment," "development with no damage," and "sustained and sustainable development" were proposed in the declaration. It was the first meeting of countries around the world on environmental problems and seeking global environmental protection. It associated population changes with environmental changes and placed in front of everyone the question of how to realize sustainable development of humans and the environment.

The two incidences actually had little impact on China because we were still locking ourselves up in the early 1970s. However, history is full of coincidences as the old saying goes, "no story is made without any coincidence." As mentioned earlier, 800 million is a number people always watched for on population growth as well as a milestone of China's population development. As it happened, just at the crossing of the 1960s and 1970s, the Chinese population exceeded 800 million, which exposed many population problems and brought a serious population pattern upon us, echoing the two influential events in the world.

Meanwhile, as the Cultural Revolution was still going on at the time, with cadres receiving labor education on the "May 7th" path and educated youths working in mountainous and rural areas, the pressure of urban population growth was alleviated to a degree. However, policies that went against the trend of urbanization could not last, and they could only buffer, but not solve, any population problem. When the milestone of 800 million people was reached in the early 1970s, people were worried from the government to the public and it became imperative to release policies that could effectively check population growth. Therefore, the anarchic family planning in the early phase of the Cultural Revolution was swept away and new signals were observed of upcoming policies of birth control.

The first signal is to make indicators of population policies concrete. The population and fertility policies in the 1950s and 1960s were mostly advocacies in a general sense, with reiteration that Party committees and governments at all levels should strengthen their work on pushing for family planning and include it in their agendas, and only in a few cases were indicators ever mentioned in the planning for the national economy, e.g., Qian Xinzhong's report *Several Problems of Family Planning*, approved for distribution by the CCCPC in 1966, proposed to contain the national population within 800 million by 1970 in the part about the draft of the Third Five-Year Plan with specific goals for Shanghai, Tianjin, Hebei, Shandong, and Sichuan.

After 1970, in contrast, specific goals were constantly stated for population growth. In June 1973, for example, the NPC proposed in the *Report on National Economic Planning* to "manage to bring the net growth rate of the urban population within 10‰ and that of the rural population within 15‰ by 1975." In February 1978, the State Council approved the distribution of the *Report on the National Family Planning Conference*, in which it was proposed to lower the natural growth rate of the national population to 10‰ in three years; the goal was announced to the public in the *Report on the Work of the Government* in the First Plenary Session of the Fifth CCCPC, and it was reiterated in 1978 when the CCCPC approved for distribution the *Report on the First Meeting of the Family Planning Leader Group under the State Council.*

In the report, it was further proposed to lower the natural growth rate of the national population to 9‰ by 1985.[39] Apparently, not only were goals for fertility and growth rates proposed but the proposals also became stringent with time. Meanwhile, goals for controlling the number of births for each couple also became clear gradually. As mentioned earlier, as early as the early and mid-1960s, many regions already proposed various goals for controlling the number of children for each couple, such as "ideally two, and not exceeding three" children, "procreating later with a longer interval between childbirths and a fewer number of children," and that "one child is not too few, two children are the best, and three would be too many."

In the 1970s, the number became nationally unified. In October 1978, the *Report on the First Meeting of the Family Planning Leader Group under the State Council*, approved by the CCCPC for distribution, stated to "advocate for one child, at the most two, per couple with at least three years between childbirths, and allow flexible regulations on later reproduction and longer intervals in each region with specific conditions." As for late marriage, the *Report* defined it as "23 years of age for women and 25 for men in rural areas and slightly higher ages in urban areas."[40]

This was the first time that "one child for the best and two children at the most" for each couple had appeared in a document by the central government, which was in fact only one step away from the subsequent policy of advocating for one child per couple. It is well known that in the age of a command economy, a prominent feature of planning for economic and social development was to specify quantitative goals. In the 1970s, China's population policy that had been centered on birth control eventually stepped on the same path with quantitative goals.

The second signal was to include the goals for population control in the national economic planning. In the age of a command economy, the quantitative goals for economic and social development distributed by the central government were legally binding. To ensure control over population growth and realization of the goal of births, the quantitative goals of population control have been included in the indicator system of the national economic planning since 1973. The aforementioned goals in the *Report on the National Economic Planning* in June 1973, i.e., to "push for family planning with great efforts, lower birth rates of the population, and manage to bring the net growth rate of the urban population within 10‰ and that of the rural population within 15‰ by 1975," were the first population growth goals included in national economic planning.

As ruled in article 7 of the *Report on the National Economic Planning 1975*, drafted by the NPC and approved by the CCCPC for distribution:

> Family planning was first proposed by Chairman Mao, and the population must be controlled. Following the instructions of the CCCPC, party committees at all levels must include family planning in their agendas and have one comrade assigned to be in charge of the work on it. All forces from various sectors should be mobilized to educate people so that they would volunteer to marry late and plan for their families in terms of having children.

It was vital to include the population goals in the national economic planning under the command economy because only when it was included in the system of economic goals could family planning be on the agenda of all Party committees and governments.

The third signal was the 36-word tactic of population policies. In 1973, when the goals of population growth control were included in the national economic planning, the State Council restored the leader group of family planning and its office with Comrade Hua Guofeng, a member of the affair group in the State Council, as group head to take charge of family planning; in 1976, Wu Guixian, vice-premiere of the State Council, succeeded to be the group head, and in June 1978, the State Council issued the *Notification on Adjusting and Complementing the Family Planning Leader Group under the State Council* ([1987] file No. 117) and appointed vice-premiere Chen Muhua to succeed as the group head and Wang Shoudao, Jiang Yizhen, Su Jing, and Li Xiu as vice-heads.

After taking office, Chen Muhua immediately held a meeting of the group to summarize lessons from the work of family planning in various regions and proposed a tactic of 36 words: "headed by General Secretary, participated in by all party members, publicity in combination with education, guided by typical examples, strengthening scientific research, improving technologies, landing all measures, mobilizing the people, persisting with the work for long." The 36-word tactic first highlighted the nature of the Chinese society, i.e., led by the CPC, the cause of population and family planning was integrated in various tasks of the Party and put on the agendas.

Why has China succeeded in controlling population growth and in family planning? I have talked with many people from various sectors in different countries and have discovered a consensus that China is a society with organization. What is hidden behind the line is that the leadership of the Party ensures top-down organization. Several other countries have tried their own family planning policies; for example, India implemented strict policies to control population growth under the rule of Mrs. Gandhi, but the policies failed and Gandhi left office.

Second, the tactic emphasized publicity and education in implementing family planning, which was intended to explain to people why population growth was to be controlled and family planning's benefits to the country and to individual families; meanwhile, powerful examples were to be found and publicized to guide the people, especially peasants, to volunteer to participate in family planning. Third, technical support was valued on birth control and a supply of contraceptive drugs and tools that were safely produced, highly effective, and convenient to use would be welcomed by people as well as showing responsibilities. Fourth, persistent efforts should be made with attention to details to educate, mobilize, and organize people. At the time, the 36-word tactic was influential because it defined not only how to carry out family planning but also implementation tactics, principles, and attitudes that embodied the basic requirements of the policies of population and family planning.

The key decision in 1980

The Third Plenary Session of the 11th CCCPC with restoration of the line of thought that respected facts and concentration on economic development, like thunder on the ground, brought all sciences, including demography, to spring. Correcting theoretical errors and restoring the right paved the way for policies, among which population policies were at a new crossroad.

Correcting errors of demographic theories

Development of many social science disciplines, including demography, is often affected by social changes in China, and it was particularly so before the 1980s. On May 10, 1978, "Practice Is the Only Standard to Test Theories" was published in the 60th issue of *Trends in Theories*, which started a series of discussions on standards of truth. The rigid line of thought such as the "two whatevers" was criticized, and demographic studies saw a dim light.

These discussions were also heard at the National Conference of Demographic Theories and Sciences in November 1978. More than 30 papers poured into the conference. They were all centered on demographic patterns in a socialist society and the relationship between population and the four modernizations. In terms of demographic patterns in a socialist society, many agreed with what was in the *Demographic Theory*, i.e., "planned growth of the population is the objective law of population reproduction in a socialist society," while some made more or less different arguments or complementary points on the nature, expression, contents, and mechanism of the demographic pattern in a socialist society.

Apparently, the doctrine in the Soviet Union's *Textbook on Political Economics* – that "continuously rapid growth of population [was] the socialist demographic law" – had been broken through and it was now "planned growth." However, the papers at the conference still followed the theory that socialist economies should be planned and proportional, and so must population reproduction; in addition, it seemed to many that as long as references could be made from the works of Marx, Engels, Lenin, Stalin, or Mao Zedong, what they proposed would automatically prove true. In terms of the relationship between the population and the four modernizations, discussions at the conference were made with more depth than those on the socialist demographic pattern.

It was first acknowledged that the population growth in our country had been quite fast. It was then concluded that a well-planned low level of population growth would benefit proper employment of laborers, social aggregation, improvement in the scientific, educational, and cultural level of the entire nation, improvement in the efficiency of labor, provision of a better life for the people, and liberation of women; control of population growth was necessary to realize the four modernizations. The conference was approved by Comrade Chen Muhua, alternate member of the CCCPC, vice-premier of the State Council, and head of the Leader Group of Family Planning under the State Council. She participated in the conference and listened to some participants' discussions and gave a long speech on the relationship between theories and practices, current issues that needed to be studied, and how to advocate for theories. Some of the key points of Chen's speech are shown next.[41]

Theories come from practices and then guide practices. When studying theories, we should first look at practices, both in China and elsewhere. According to statistics, the population growth rate in the U.S. is not high, it has stayed around 50 million in France for years, the populations in both Germanys are decreasing, and there are some countries with fairly high growth rates of population. Of course, there are also countries with high birth rates but low growth rates. Then the question is why these situations occurred in those countries. What characteristics are there in their respective economies? What policies have they adopted? How are these policies manifested on populations? These are all questions we need to answer. I have been to Czechoslovakia. The women there did not want to have children, so the government encouraged women to give birth by giving them a pretty stroller once their children were born, a long maternity leave, and stipends. The situation there is that procreation is encouraged but people are not willing to have children. In contrast, we have family planning but people are not willing to have fewer children. Why is that? We may compare the situations in China and other countries in our study.

We have criticized the Malthusian demography; however, how popular is the theory in the capitalist world? Is the Malthusian theory followed in capitalist countries, or are there other patterns that have functioned? Which theories are adopted? We have always said that humans are the most valuable wealth because humans create wealth, are capable of laboring, and all wealth is created by humans, without whom nothing is possible. After all, no matter how automated production is, a person is needed to at least push the button to start the automation. Meanwhile, humans have dual roles as producers and consumers. When the labor efficiency is extremely low, humans' role as consumers becomes prominent because a large population will be a heavy burden for a society. Therefore, the population policy of each country must accommodate to the country's conditions.

Theoretical studies must be combined with practices. Theories come from practices and must go back to guide practices so that our behaviors are more conscious. We have implemented family planning for more than 20 years, but we are still weak in demographic theories. Therefore, research on this aspect must be strengthened so that the family planning can be carried out with more consciousness. Whether or not our views are correct must be tested in practices. After all, practice is the only standard to test truth, and wrong views need corrections while correct ones need to be persisted with. We need to bring our practices to the height of theories and bring our theories back to practices, and practices to theories again. A few rounds of cycling may improve our understanding. We need to be more open-minded and break out of "forbidden zones." In fact, we should follow the "three negatives" in academic discussions and follow whoever is right. In the past, we were intimidated

> by economic calculations because once such calculations were made, we were Malthusian. Now we are doing economic calculations, and no one is labeled with Malthusianism. That is because the economic consequences are there and will not go anywhere just because people turn a blind eye to them. In summary, theories must be combined with practices and knowledge needs to be tested in practices. We will persist with and publicize whatever is right and correct whatever is wrong.

Comrade Chen Muhua also proposed topics that needed to be studied based on the conditions at the time, among which the following were of particular importance.

> What is good for the development of the Chinese population, a still state, a slow growth, or a slightly slower growth than what it was? Alternatively, is it good to have a still population for a while, followed by shrinkages in size for a period of time and then by moderate growth for a while?
>
> Now the material life has been improved, medical services advanced, and life expectancies increased. Our ancestors said that there were very few who could live to their seventies, but now it is quite common to live to one's seventies. Some say that the population will thus age, i.e., the proportion of the elderly increases while that of the young decreases. Others argue that the quality of laborers will decline. These are the questions that are worth studying.
>
> There are now 18 million new births and 6 million deaths every year in our country, with a net increase of 12 million people. If the population is to reach the still state, i.e., it does not grow or reduce in size, will it be beneficial to production? After a few years of the population staying still, will there be need for it to start growing again? Is it better for production if the population grows by a small scale? If growth is needed, how much is the best, 7–8‰, 10‰, or 5‰? Arguments are needed for an answer. We should be more open minded, assume as many situations as possible, and provide as many theoretical references as possible for the national leaders to make population policies.
>
> Quantitative goals for the population started to be listed in the national plans in 1973, and the current goal was set by Chairman Hua in the *Report on the Work of the Government* on the 5th People's Congress. Is this goal scientific or not? It is open for study. After all, goals may be changed. It is all right to have immature opinions, and inside discussions should be made frank for the reference of leaders. I sincerely encourage everyone to perform more theoretical study and give us more suggestions – only the arguments must be logical and well structured.

Comrade Chen also commented that not only should theoretical problems be studied but the real questions that troubled the people should be taken seriously and solved through education and advocacy.

For example, the concept is prevalent in our society that people bring up their children so that they can be taken care of when aged. Why is that? In capitalist countries, children do not necessarily take care of their aging parents. People usually move out to live on their own when reaching adulthood, and pay for their food when going back to their parents' homes and vice versa. Everyone is on their own. Why do they behave like that and why do we believe that children are to care for their aged parents? It is possible that we are under the influence of Confucius and Mencius, and it is also possible that social policies have made us so. A clear answer needs study and education. Another example is the concept that daughters cannot take care of their aged parents after being married while men, if married into the wives' families, are despised, gossiped, and discriminated against even in production teams where they always get assigned jobs that are dirty, exhausting, and poorly paid. These ideas and behaviors are certainly wrong and need to be corrected by writing articles; however, when educating people with these ideas, differentiation must be made between various situations and no single line of advocacy should be expected to work for all. For example, do daughters always have to be married into men's families? Does everyone want to have a son? The answers are not always positive. In fact, many urban residents want daughters because girls are said to be "fitting padded jackets" and mothers like to live with daughters. Apparently, various situations exist between rural and urban areas in the same China, and these need careful and arduous work to sort out in theoretical studies as well as practical services. Articles are needed to address problems on people's minds for education and advocacy. In fact, a large range of aspects are involved in carrying out family planning, such as medical care, hygiene, health of women and infants, and education. Education must be valued. We need to educate our children and train them into high-quality individuals. Modernized production needs high-quality workers and we must offer full-coverage education of science and culture to improve the scientific and cultural literacy of the entire population. Meanwhile, scientific and technological advancement is also helpful to the cause of family planning. In fact, blind reproduction also embodies a low level of scientific and cultural literacy of our population to a certain degree. With family planning well carried out, people will have improved health and a better life, much fewer worries, and significantly boosted motivation.

Comrade Chen Muhua also encouraged all to persist with what had been done correctly in educating people on policies and to modify what had not been well done.

In fact, there were concerns over family planning in that many thought that it was not something proud to advocate for it. These concerns are not

> well founded. Family planning is a great cause and advocacy for it should be made loudly and proudly. Studies are to be conducted, books written, and logics clearly sorted out.[42]

Chen's speech called for liberation of people's minds and a combination of theories and practices. It also called for studies with theoretical and practical explorations integrated, actively sought ideas to solve the population problems in China, initiated demographic studies untouched for years, and delivered a powerful push to the development of demography. In fact, in the 17 years when theoretical demographers were still, leaders in the central government never stopped talking about demographic problems, which were also frequently mentioned in central government documents, with progressive updates on their understanding of the problems.

For example, Mao Zedong emphasized that "the large population of China [was] a great thing" and "no miracle [was] impossible as long as there [were] people" when he criticized Acheson right before the establishment of the new China. He also agreed with the view of population control with planned reproduction that Ma Yinchu and Shao Lizi held, but went back to the point that "a large population [was] good indeed" when the wave of the Great Leap Forward rose.

Mao once planned for 700 million and 800 million for the Chinese population. These two milestones were reached in 1964 and 1969, respectively, and the national population soon marched over 900 million in 1974, at the end of which year he eventually admitted that "the population must be brought under control" when giving instructions on the *Report on the National Economic Planning of 1975* made by the NPC. This was the last instruction concerning the population Mao made in his life.

In my opinion, Comrade Mao Zedong held in his heart that "the large population in our country [was] a good thing although it [brought] difficulties as well." Of course, his demographic thought developed with time. From 1947 to 1976, his thought went from "a large population [was] great," to "planned reproduction," to "a large population [was] good indeed," and finally to "the population must be brought under control," with apparent emphasis in different years and landing on the need to control the population.

Other leaders in the central government such as Zhou Enlai and Deng Xiaoping reiterated the importance of controlling population growth and implementing family planning and actually carried them out while doing their jobs. In December 1974, the CCCPC approved the distribution of the *Report by the Shanghai Revolutionary Committee on Carrying Out Family Planning and Advocating for Late Marriage* and the *Report by the CPC Committee in Hebei Province and the Revolutionary Committee in Hebei Province on Holding a Province-Wide Meeting on Family Planning* and stated in the *Notification*, "implementing family planning is a deep reformation of people's minds that breaks the old thoughts and establishes the new." The CCCPC required that the Party committees at all levels include family planning in their agendas and get down to details of strengthening their roles in family planning.

In October 1978, the CCCPC stated in the notification of distributing the *Report on the 1st Meeting by the Leader Group of Family Planning under the State Council,*

> family planning is a great cause that has been called for by Chairman Mao for years. How well family planning is carried out directly affects the health of the Chinese nation, the improvement of our scientific and cultural literacy, and the prosperity of our country. All the party members should have thorough understanding of its strategic importance and volunteer to do well on this cause.[43]

Now population control and family planning were upgraded from the health of mothers and children and alleviation of family burdens to the level that it affected the national economy, the four modernizations, development of science and culture, and the prosperity of the entire nation, demonstrating new, deepened understanding of population issues. It was also implied that the population was already in surplus although it was not stated explicitly. The gradual deepening of the understanding of population issues from the top down and the stepwise stricter policies of population control laid the necessary theoretic foundation and prepared people mentally for the next phase of population policies in the 1980s.

The Third Plenary Session of the 11th CCCPC at the end of 1978 woke China up from an unusually dull state although it had been seemingly noisy and delivered vigor to all front lines and causes. The Party committee in Xiaogang Village, Fengyang County, Anhui Province took the lead and held high the banner of the agricultural system of household contract responsibility and quickly started a big wave of reforms in the countryside that then encircled cities. The initiation of the trial in the first group of enterprises to increase their management autonomy drew the curtain for the reform on separation of politics and business. The national science and education conferences were held, science and technology were confirmed as the primary force of production, and the national college entrance examination was restored, all of which signaled the coming development of human resources and the construction of a country with strong talents.

Now the development of objective situations challenged demography: are there population problems in China, and if any, what is the nature of the problems? How would we study and solve them? These challenges placed in front of us the task of correcting demographic theories.

An important feature of the correction of errors in all aspects that was initiated at the Third Plenary Session of the 11th CCCPC was that it was accompanied by fixing wrongly and arbitrarily convicted cases. The demographic field was faced with the same situation. In fact, one such wrongly convicted case in the field was Mr. Ma Yinchu's *New Population Theory* that had been criticized twice in the late 1950s and the early 1960s. If the name of Ma's theory could not be cleared, the shackles on people's minds would not be broken, and people would still have doubts in their demographic studies out of fear of becoming another Ma Yinchu.

In addition, if the name of Ma's theory could not be cleared, the very nature of the problems with the Chinese population would not be recognized, and correcting the errors in demographic theories would be just vain words; the principle of respecting the truth would not be able to land in the demographic field, and the new prosperous academic pattern required by the "two hundred" tactic would be found nowhere. Therefore, after the Third Plenary Session of the 11th CCCPC, proper and objective reevaluation of Ma's new population theory became the key to the correction of demographic errors and the restoration of science in demography as well as a new departure for the demographic science to further develop and thrive after the Reform and Opening Up.

When it comes to reevaluating Ma's theories, one article cannot be missed, i.e., "Proper and Objective Reevaluation of Mr. Ma Yinchu's New Population Theory," written by me and published in *Guangming Daily* on August 5, 1979. In fact, an academic colleague showed great dismay at this article and my work to edit Ma's *New Population Theory* for publication. He once made a guess on the Internet and said that:

> At the time the central government wished to clear Ma's name and the task was assigned to the Economic Research Institute of the Chinese Academy of Social Sciences [where I worked at the time]. Maybe Tian Xueyuan used to work in an education agency and graduated from Peking University; maybe he also had some unique and sharp comprehension of demography. It was thus eventually assigned to him to clear Ma's name.[44]

When I read this, I understood why my colleague felt so and how he made his guess; unfortunately, however, he did not get it right. In fact, it was not a task for me to clear Ma's name.

The truth is it was something that had been on my mind for a long time and that was finally released. In 1959, I joined Peking University (PKU) as a student and was met with the second wave of criticisms of Ma's new population theory upon entrance. I was naïve and knew little then, but I was eager to learn, so I went to the fifth library of PKU, which was a periodical reading room, and found and read several articles Ma had published in journals such as *New Suggestions* and newspapers and magazines such as *Guangming Daily*.

As I proceeded, I became convinced by Ma's theory as well as attracted by his spirit that never bowed before those who tried to persuade him only through power but not reason. I also read the criticisms, which, in contrast to Ma's, were all similar to each other and were all written by excerpting a few lines of Ma's, criticizing them harshly, making references to relevant lines from Marx's, Engels's, and Mao Zedong's analects, and concluding with an umbrella conviction that Ma had attacked the Party using demographic problems as China's Malthusianism.

Such criticisms were not convincing at all, and I felt angry to a degree. Ma later "disappeared" with no reason and was displaced from his positions as PKU president and a member of the Standing Committee of the NPC. I felt even angrier. I started to collect relevant materials, and as I read them from time to time I grew a wish to clear Ma's name. However, the wish could never be realized in the Cultural Revolution, when right and wrong were upset.

Fortunately, the day eventually came for me to clear Ma's name when the Third Plenary Session of the 11th CCCPC was held that restored the principle of respecting the truth and the discussion of practice as the only standard to test truth and that started to correct the wrong in the past. I immediately picked up my pen and wrote diligently. After a few rounds of modification, I submitted my article, at the time named "Clearing the Name of Mr. Ma Yichu's New Population Theory," to *Guangming Daily*.

Why did I choose *Guangming Daily*? One reason was that it was the most prominent newspaper in the field of science and education, and it was a proper platform of media to publish such theoretical articles. Another reason was that *Guangming Daily* was at the forefront of the battle of criticizing Ma Yichu's theory, and it had a responsibility to clear its own past. My article was treated with great attention and I was told that it would be used as "an article of prime importance." In fact, two short articles had already been published that repined at the criticisms of Ma, but they were, as related by a leader of *Guangming Daily*, only drizzling while mine was going to be a definitive publication for the newspaper to correct its wrongs, which was also expressed in the editor's comments on the article when it was eventually published.

Therefore, the article that spoke out for Ma's new population theory was not an "assigned job," but something I had planned for long – as long as 20 years. On a side note, although I had planned it for 20 years, the article was not published as the very first one aimed to clear Ma's name out of concerns of the newspaper mentioned earlier. Some colleagues labeled it as "the first article that cleared Ma Yinchu's name," but that was not true. It was only long, written from all angles, and had a fairly large impact.

Reevaluating Ma's population theory opened a new chapter of correcting errors in demographic theories and offered theoretical support and necessary public opinions for population policy in the new era. The new theoretical support and necessary public opinions may be comprehended from the following aspects.

First, the relationship between "mouths" and "hands" of a population is sorted out. As mentioned earlier, a theoretical foothold on which criticisms of Ma's and others' theories that argued for population control were founded was "speaking of mouths but not hands," which was meant to criticize that those advocating population control only saw mouths of people to eat, but not their hands capable of all sorts of work. Some even took it so far as to propose replacement of "study of human mouths" (literally *demography* in Chinese) with "study of human hands."

It is of course widely known that the mouth and hands of a person are not separable and it is therefore absurd to talk about someone's mouth separately from his hands. Of course, the criticizers who emphasized the "study of human hands" meant to direct people's attention to the value of a human as a laborer while belittling his role as a consumer. Based on their logic, since everyone has a pair of hands capable of all sorts of work, people may generate endless wealth; therefore, the more people there are, the more wealth they create, leading to the conclusion that a larger population is always better.

Reevaluation of Ma's theory first corrected the situation that "only hands but not mouths were emphasized" that had resulted from the criticisms of "speaking of mouths but not hands," which not only swept off the impact of such a metaphysical theory, but restored humans to be unification of laborers and consumers as well. From the theoretical perspective, if the changes in a population are in concert with economic and social development and with resources and the environment, then a stable population is appropriate no matter whether the people are considered laborers or consumers; if a population and the laborers it may provide are not enough, then an increase in the population is appropriate and beneficial no matter whether the people are considered laborers or consumers; and if a population and the laborers it may provide are in surplus, then an increase in the laborers or consumers will have an adverse impact on economic and social development and on the coordinated development of the population and the resources and the environment.

Given that the Chinese population was in surplus at the time, further increases in the population would lead to increases in consumption, although people were also the most active factor of the forces of production, and with the underdeveloped forces of production at the time, addition to the social burden would lead to adverse effects. Population reproduction is characterized by a long period of stable increases in that it takes one to two decades from birth to becoming a laborer; therefore, increases in a population will first boost consumption, and that must be recognized clearly. In addition, people as laborers need proper means of production and proper positions, without which no one can be a real laborer. Given that China had a surplus of people and laborers, it was inappropriate to only address the side that people were laborers while ignoring the side that people were also consumers.

Second, the relationship between population and the four modernizations was clarified. It has been the dream of all ethnic groups in China since the Opium War to realize the four modernizations of industry, agriculture, science and technology, and defense. What is the four modernizations' relationship with the population? Following the labor-deficient theory of the Great Leap Forward, one would come to the conclusion that continuous increases in the population and laborers were required to speed to the goal of the four modernizations.

Reevaluation of Ma's new population theory put the upside-down theory upright. It helped people understand that there were different requirements of the size and the quality of a population in different historical stages and under different levels of the forces of production. To strive for socialist modernization, we must adopt advanced technologies as much as possible, equip laborers with improved technologies and improve the organic composition of production, realize mechanical production, automation, and electric production, and elevate production efficiency by a large scale – all of which would lead to a decreasing demand for laborers.

Some sectors such as services might have an increased demand for laborers, which would add to the overall demand for laborers, but many other sectors, especially those of direct production of material means, would have a decreased demand for laborers, which actually showed a nonreversible trend. At the end of the 1970s, the total number of laborers in China equaled the sum of those in the first and second worlds, with a much less developed modernization level. Therefore, the modernization of China posed a basic requirement for the population, which was to control the growth of the population and its laborers while at the same time improving their quality by all means possible, particularly effective improvement of the population's scientific and educational level.

Third, the "two types of production" of population and material means were differentiated. Right after Ma's name was cleared, people were still haunted by past shadows and had to frequent the theories of classic Marxian authors for inspiration on theoretical studies of demography. Thus *The German Ideology* and *Origin of the Family, Private Property and the State*, two books by Marx and Engels, were often used for theoretical notes, and the following statement by Engels was cited particularly frequently:

> The determining factor in history is, in the final instance, the production and reproduction of immediate life. This, again, is of a twofold character: on the one side, the production of the means of existence, of food, clothing, and shelter and the tools necessary for that production; on the other side, the production of human beings themselves, the propagation of the species.[45]

Based on this, it was proposed and argued during the reevaluation that the production of the material means was the foundation, with which the production of people must be in concert while the production of people was not useless as it could boost or prolong the production of the material means.

Given China's conditions, it was also proposed and argued that there was inconsistency between the total population and the means of existence, between the population of working age and means of production, demography, education, cultural level, economic level, and technological advancement, and between the urban–rural distribution of the population and the industrial composition of the "twofold production." It was proposed to make every effort to control the size, improve the quality, and adjust the structure of the population while developing the production of material means by all means so that the production of population could match the production of material means.

Fourth, the theory of optimum population was discussed in detail. Optimum population was first proposed by British economist Edwin Cannan in the late 19th century. It describes a moderate population that may produce the largest income per capita given a certain degree of production level; any size that is larger or smaller than the optimum will lead to reduction in the income per capita. Based on this idea, Hugh Dalton proposed a formula, $M = (A - O) \div O$, where O was the optimum population, A the actual size of the population, and M how much the population was out of control. When M is positive, the population is in surplus; when M is negative, the population is in deficit; and when M equals 0, there is optimum population.

The theory of optimum population was later further developed by a French demographer, A. Sauvy, who proposed and described two concepts of economic optimum and power optimum in that economic optimum was the size of a population that would generate the maximal economic benefit while power optimum was the size of a population that would empower the country with maximal strength, which was therefore a higher level of optimum population. Although there have been various opinions on optimum population, the theory has occupied a seat in demography that could not be ignored.

In China, the theory of optimum population had been treated as capitalist. The reevaluation of Ma's theory echoed some of the points in the theory of optimum population and pushed for studies in this line. In fact, in the early 1980s, optimum population was a hot topic in academics, which resulted in quite a few achievements from several disciplines.

Fifth, the socialist demographic pattern was explored. After Ma's new population theory was criticized, the doctrine in the Soviet Union's *Textbook of Political Economics* that "continuously rapid growth of population [was] the socialist demographic pattern" ruled the theoretical field in demography for one to two decades in China. The doctrine was modified somewhat after the downfall of the "Gang of Four" and it was changed to "planned growth of population [was] the socialist demographic pattern" where the term "continuously rapid growth" was changed to "planned growth."

Nevertheless, socialism was interlocked with "population growth" and the development of the socialist cause would always be accompanied by population growth. However, reevaluation of Ma's theory helped people regain understanding of the theory of demographic transition and begin studies on general population reproduction patterns from high births, high deaths, and low growth to high births, low deaths, and high growth, and finally to low births, low deaths, and low growth, which broke the shackles that a socialist population could only grow.

It was also proposed that changes in and development of a population were subject not only to the forces of production and social institutions but also to biological laws of nature, the development level of the social forces of production, scarcity of resources, supply of food, and environmental conditions. Therefore, the nature of the socialist demographic pattern is coordination between population changes and socioeconomic development to boost the advancement and development of society. The coordination is mainly embodied in the coordination between the entire population and the means of existence, between the population of working age and the means of existence, between population aging and social security, between population quality and the advancement of science and technology, between population urbanization and changes in the industrial structure, and between regional distribution of the population and the planned distribution of the productive forces.

An account of the birth of the policy to advocate for one child per couple

Correcting the errors in demographic theories raised fundamental consensuses about the population problems in China, which prepared people for the upcoming policies aimed at further control of population growth. From late March to early May 1980, the Secretariat of the CCCPC commissioned the General Office to hold five consecutive meetings on population issues.

The meetings were first held in the conference room in the West Wing of Zhongnanhai. Among the 63 official attendees were 25 comrades from the NPC, the State Nationalities Affairs Commission, the Ministries of Hygiene, Civil Affairs, Public Security, and Agriculture, the State Labor Bureau, the Central Committee of the Communist Youth League, and the All China Women's Federation; 19 scientists from the fields of neuroscience, gynecology and obstetrics, urology, genetics, contraception, and cybernetics; and 19 social sciences scholars in the fields of demography, economics, and sociology from the Chinese Academy of Social Sciences, higher education institutions, and government research agencies.

The meetings were chaired by Comrade Feng Wenbin, the deputy director of the General Office of the Central Committee. Feng specified the purpose of the meetings at the beginning and said that the CCCPC planned to study population issues and the Secretariat of the CCCPC had commissioned the General Office to hold meetings with specialists in various fields and comrades in charge of pertinent issues to collect opinions and suggestions on population policies for the next 20 years or even longer. He briefly summarized the history of the population and family planning, which experienced changes in policies from "late, sparse, and few" births, through "one is not too few, two are just good, and three are too many," to that "one is the best and two are the most," and it was now proposed to allow one child per couple.

He asked what kind of population policies we really needed and in particular what would become of the policy of one child per couple, problems that might arise, and how to handle them. He invited all to speak out. In April, the meetings continued in the Great Hall of People, but fewer attendees came, with only a few comrades in the social sciences and half the original number in the natural sciences, although department heads from the CCCPC and the State Council were still almost all there with perhaps a few additions.

The meeting in the Great Hall of People was more focused, in-depth, and professional compared to the previous one. The fourth meeting was moved back to Zhongnanhai in the second conference room with a decreased number of attendees that was slightly more than 20, and focused on summaries of what consensuses had been reached so far, the core contents and expression of the due population policy, potential problems, and policies to handle the problems.

I was assigned to draft the report to the Secretariat. At that time, writing a report was different from what it is now when a whole team works on it together. I had to write it on my own and asked people to discuss and modify it. The last meeting was held in the Hall of Qinzhengdian, and more than 20 leaders of pertinent departments and committees of the CCCPC and the State Council showed up to discuss the report draft to the Secretariat. Based on the suggestions and comments in the meeting held in the office of the Secretariat, I made a last round of revision on the report, which concluded the *Report on the Demographic Meetings* that included the main parts and five appendices.

There has been questioning of the demographic meetings for a while and some even refused to believe that these meetings had ever been held, calling it "a colossal lie" and "extremely misleading." I do not believe that "a lie becomes truth after being told for a thousand times" because of the principle of mass conservation. Many proofs are still there about the meetings, including the *Report on the Demographic Meetings* and its five appendices, the *Outline of the Report on Population Issues*, the minutes of the group discussions of the second meeting on April 9, 1980 (with the first group in the

Guangxi room), the meeting in the fourth conference room in Zhongnanhai on April 25, 1980, the meeting in the Hall of Qinzhengdian on the afternoon of April 25, 1980, and the meeting by the Leader Group of Family Planning under the State Council to discuss the report to the Secretariat on April 26, 1980, the report on the discussion meeting held by the deputy director of the General Office of the CCCPC, Feng Wenbin on April 30, 1980, and some of the original records of the field studies in various places at the time.

How can all these perish or be destroyed no matter how many labels of crimes have been put up? Some questioned why there was no report on the list of all attendees, names of those who spoke at the meetings, titles of the report appendices, etc. These were not entirely decided by me, and some of the information questioned was, in my opinion, not necessary to be released to the public or at least not by me. As for the conclusion that the meetings and the *Report* were both "articulately fabricated lies" reached by some who claimed to have found no information on them in the materials and references they searched for, isn't that amusing? Why can the materials and references they used be standards for conclusions and why is nothing existent as long as it is not listed in those materials?

To those who could shamelessly use the "proofs" and "reasoning" and insult formal logic to that degree, what can be said? The only thing that can be said to them is the following. History is history and what has happened cannot be undone just because some don't believe it or claim that it never happened. What is there is there, and any attempt, including insults with various "reasons," to deny its existence will eventually prove futile.

I will waste no more space on the subject as I have said my basic points clearly. Now let us get back to the population polices and the issues discussed at the meetings in 1980. I actually believe that it would be helpful for people to understand how and why the policies were made 35 years ago if the *Report on the Demographic Meetings (First Discussion)*, its appendices, and other materials such as meeting minutes were released to the public; after all, it's been 35 years and there is nothing secretive about it any longer.

However, I, as the writer who drafted it, have no right to publicize the *Report*, especially in its entirety, since it was prepared for the Secretariat, and all I am entitled to is to provide some explanations of the important points as accurately as possible and to cite a few lines when necessary. This is why I never agreed to publish my draft when asked by some research institutes and news media. If it ever becomes necessary to publish it, I still think it must be published by proper government agencies or approved by them for publication. Proper procedure should be followed.

The full title of the report is *Report on the Demographic Meetings (First Discussion)* (*Report* hereafter). The opening statement of the *Report* is as follows.

> To the Secretariat: According to the instruction of the Secretariat, the General Office of the CCCPC recently held meetings on demographic

> issues. A total of 63 people attended the meetings, among whom 25 were from pertinent departments and committees of the CCCPC and the State Council, 19 were scholars in the social science fields related to demography, and 19 were scholars in natural sciences and medicine. The meetings hosted discussions on the potential policy of one child per couple and problems it would generate from various perspectives. The account of the meetings and the major problems proposed are reported below.

The *Report* has three parts. The first is on the point that energetically advocating for one child per couple is the key to solving the population problems at the time in China. As stated in the *Report*, the attendees of the meetings believed that the population problems in our country at the time must be fully attended to due to the following reasons.

> First, the population growth is fast. Since family planning was implemented in the 1970s, the natural growth rate of the population has rapidly decreased … by about 55 million births during 10 years. However, if calculated for the 30 years since the liberation, the natural growth rate of the population would be as high as 20‰, twice as much as the 10‰ rate in the old China. The national population increased from 540 million in 1949 to 970 million in 1979 (excluding Taiwan province, same below), and that was a net increase of 430 million people, illustrating a speedy growth.
>
> Second, the baseline population is large. When the base is large, the annual net increase of births will be nonetheless a huge number even when the natural growth rate has decreased significantly. In fact, the birth rate in 1979 was lowered to 17.9‰, 14.7‰ lower than that of 1955, but there were still 17.27 million births in that year.
>
> Third, the population has a young age structure. According to sampling surveys, there were 343 million juveniles below 14 in 1978, accounting for 35.8% of the total population, 264 million between 15 and 29, accounting for 27.6% of the total population … 4.6 million at 65 or higher, accounting for only 4.8% of the total population. … Such a young age structure has a definitive impact on the future development of the population.

The *Report* stated that:

> Given the discord between increases in the population and those in the means of existence in our country, between those in the working-age population and those in the means of production, and between population development and the development in public services such as science, education, public health, shelter, and transport, there exist serious population problems (appendix table [appendix table should be corrected to "appendix," author's note] 1), and it is high time to control the population growth with a strong hand, lower the birth and natural growth

> rates of the population by large scales, and increase the proportion of one-child families.[46]

The title for Appendix 1 is "Current population problems in our country," and the major problems are described in three aspects. First, the increases in the means of existence failed to match those in the total population. From 1950 to 1976, the residential income in our country saw a 10.6-fold increase, and when it comes to the per capita income, a 4.6-fold increase, while the population grew by 69.1% during the same period. Production of some goods in our country, such as coal and charcoal, iron and steel, and cloth, ranks high among the world, but it drops to the bottom when per capita production is counted. The national income per capita in China is still among the lowest, 129th among the 160 countries and regions in the world.

Second, the increases in the means of production failed to match those in the working-age population.

> Now an industrial worker is equipped with technologies worth 10 thousand yuan approximately while the average annual increase in fixed assets from 1952 to 1957 was only two million yuan, which, if all spent on creating jobs, would absorb an extra two million workers. In contrast, however, the average annual increase in laborers after 1966 (who were born after the liberation) was approximately 17 million, five million more than the 12 million annual increase before 1966 (those who were born before the liberation), leading to increased numbers of people looking for jobs. ... In 1979, the state managed to create jobs for eight million people, which softened the contradiction on the urban employment market; however, if the population is not effectively controlled, the contradiction will sharpen. In the countryside, the contradiction between a large population and limited lands will grow tense. The area of arable lands per capita in the country has decreased from 2.71 *mu* upon the liberation to 1.57 *mu* now, with some provinces by the southeast coast possessing only several tenths of one *mu* land per capita. In contrast, the world average area of arable lands per capita is 5.5 *mu*, and we are only 28.5% of this average, marking us as a country with insufficient arable lands. Meanwhile, the average area of arable lands cultivated by each rural laborer has also decreased quickly, which was 9.3 *mu* in 1952 and 5.1 *mu* in 1977.

Third, the development of public services such as education, housing, public health care, and transport failed to match population development.

> There are now approximately 5.20 million people with a college or higher degree nationwide, accounting for 0.5% of the national population, 210 million with middle school certificates, accounting for 22% of the national population. ... Currently, only 5% of high middle school graduates may continue to higher education institutes, 41% of junior

> middle school graduates may continue to study in schools at a higher level; despite these low percentages, there is an intense demand for teachers, school constructions, and teaching props. Since the establishment of the new China, the area of urban residential constructions has increased by 49.3 million square meters; however, due to a fast growing population, the average area of housing per person decreased by 0.9 square meters (m^2), from 4.5m^2 upon the liberation to 3.6m^2 in 1977. In addition, there was one hospital bed per 132 urban residents in 1977 and people had to bear with a crowded environment and difficulty to get a bed in hospital, and there were three public transportation buses per 10 thousand people. The supply of water, coal, and gas is also very tense.

The *Report* stated that these problems had been caused partially by economic reasons in that accumulation over the years took up an excessively high proportion and consumption a low proportion; meanwhile, investment in production construction during accumulation was of an excessively large proportion, and investment in nonproduction construction such as culture, education, public health care, employee housing, and public transport was of a small proportion. Therefore, a big debt was owed.

In addition, such a rapid growth of the population after the liberation could not be ignored as a contributor to the problems, and that was the very nature of the population problems in our country.[47]

Given the population problems that were actually there, the *Report* made a clear statement at the end of the first part. "In order to resolve the contradiction between the population development and the four modernizations well, the tactic of advocating for and encouraging only one child per couple must be persisted with for quite some time." The *Report* not only proposed that it was a must to advocate for one child per couple in order to solve the population problems, but specified that "the tactic must be persisted with for quite some time."[48]

The second part of the *Report* described the discussions from six aspects on the policy of one child per couple and its potential problems.

One aspect is laborers and the dependent population.

> Some worry that the potential population aging in the future will result in a shortage of laborers and army forces and that increases in the dependent population will force two laborers to support four aged parents and one child, i.e., the issue of the 4:2:1 ratio.

To address the concerns, the *Report* explained, "even the policy to advocate for one child per couple can be successfully carried out, the total number of laborers in the next half century will not be fewer than the current number," "the dependency index (the number of the dependent supported by each laborer) will keep declining in the next 25 years," and "the 4:2:1 ratio will not be possible from the perspective of the entire society."

The *Report* also pointed out that "population development is a long, progressive, and stably growing process, and planning and policy-making for population should aim far to prevent problems in advance." Furthermore,

> some comrades have suggested to land the policy to advocate for one child per couple completely down to every couple in 1985 and then to continue to carry it out for another cycle of population reproduction, i.e., until 2010, or to 2015 at the most (Appendix 2).[49]

The title of Appendix 2 is "Suggestions on the policy of one child per couple," and it is divided in three parts. "First, it is imperative to advocate for one child per couple," the *Report* said. "The strategic task can only be completed if the birth rate is lowered significantly now, steps are taken so that every couple has only one child by 1985, and the policy enforcement is kept for a fairly long term."

"Second, the project that each couple has only one child may be carried out until around 2010," the appendix said.

> It is imperative to implement the policy to advocate for one child per couple, but what is the appropriate period of time to enforce it for? That is a problem people all care about. At present, some of the concerns people have towards the policy are actually out of misunderstanding; for example, some think that the policy will be carried out forever, which has triggered all sorts of wild imaginations of unbearable consequences. Therefore, it is important to tell the people clearly that the policy will not be permanent. It will only be carried out for a period of time. I think we can start counting from 1985 when the policy will be successfully carried out throughout the country, and continue with the policy for another cycle of population reproduction, i.e., until around 2010.

The appendix also emphasized that

> it [was] entirely necessary to carry out the policy to advocate for one child per couple until 2010 in order to solve the population problems in our country one step at a time, when the total population, working-age population, dependency index, and population aging [would] not become big problems.

"Third, the average fertility rate should be adjusted moderately after 2010," the appendix pointed out.

> There will be a larger population and a larger working-age population in 2010 than now, and it will seem that the policy to advocate for one child per couple can be sustained. However, population reproduction differs greatly from material reproduction in that the former is a long-term,

> progressive, and stably growing process. Therefore, implementation of a population policy should take into account the consequences of at least the next 25 years, and the longer the better. According to the plan of the policy to advocate for one child per couple, the following scenarios will emerge after 2010: one, the population growth will decline quickly despite its larger total size than now; two, the growth of the working-age population will also quickly decline although its size then will be larger than what it is now; and three, although the dependency index will be lower than the current one for a long time, the dependent will be fundamentally different then.

The major difference here is that there would be a decrease in the proportion of the young and an increase in the proportion of the elderly. Based on these scenarios, it was proposed that "the policy to advocate for one child per couple could only be carried out until 2010 if counting from 1985, or to 2015 at the most."[50]

The second aspect is population quality. The *Report* said that:

> Implementation of the policy to advocate for one child per couple should pay special attention to improving the population quality. For a long time, interferences from leftists have made it a taboo to talk about "population quality" and "quality reproduction" and to study genetics, resulting in a considerable proportion of the retarded and people with hereditary diseases. Therefore, sex education must be strengthened among teenagers, prenuptial medical examination must be performed with proper regulations, and those with hereditary diseases may be allowed to marry, but not procreate. These should all be specified in the law of family planning or marriage.

It also emphasized that "scientific study on genetics and eugenics should be strengthened to effectively improve the quality of the population and the health of the Chinese nation."[51]

The third aspect is social insurance for the elderly. The *Report* argued that:

> This will be an imperative issue once the policy to advocate for one child per couple is implemented. At present, employees in state-owned units are covered by a retirement plan, which is still not applicable on most employees in collectively owned units and members of rural people's communes. They have to reply on their children in their twilight years. After the policy to advocate for one child per couple is implemented, the parents of either party of a couple will be left careless. Under such a circumstance, not only retirement pensions, but also housing, life service facilities, and medical services are all to be managed. All pertinent agencies should study the issues carefully and make plans to handle them … so that the concerns of the masses are eradicated from the root.[52]

The fourth aspect is child education.

> "Single children are always the pearls in their families, enjoying intensive attention and love from their parents, and may easily get spoiled. According to the survey of an institute in Shanghai, a fairly large proportion of single children are picky with food and wearing and are self-willed … which deserves attention.

However, "these problems can be solved through strengthening education in the society and at home." "As for whether [the] crime rate will be high among single children, there has been no sufficient evidence. … We should stay alert to this issue; however, it is fundamentally an education problem and will not necessarily happen."

The fifth aspect is contraceptive means.

> It is important to strengthen studies on contraceptive means and tools in order to promote the policy to advocate for one child per couple. At present, abortion and midterm induced labor account for a large proportion … The family planning agency should come up with medications and tools that are safer, more reliable, more convenient, and more effective and promote male sterilization.

The sixth aspect is sex ratio of the population. The *Report* deliberated:

> After implementation of the policy to advocate for one child per couple, will there be human-assisted imbalance of the sex ratio? For example, some under the influence of traditional ideologies of heirs that value boys over girls may deliberately drown or abandon their girl infants, and that deserves serious attention and must be prohibited by law.[53]

The third part of the *Report* contains seven suggestions, summarized next.

> First, the public should be exposed intensively to and educated on the policy. Advocating for and encouraging couples to have only one child is a revolution of reproduction concept. Intensively publicizing the policy is the prime task to prepare the public. … Continued advocacy is needed for population control is important to the realization of the four modernizations as well as a vital strategic task. … Knowledge of genetics, eugenics, and ecology should also be intensively publicized to improve the quality of the population.

It was also suggested that columns be dedicated to demographic theories and family planning in newspapers such as *People's Daily* and *Guangming Daily*; that an Institute of Population be founded in the Chinese Academy of Social Sciences and a journal of demography be established to strengthen the study of demographic topics; that a course of physiological health, sex education, and population control be offered in middle schools and courses of demographic theories and demography be added to the curriculum of college political economics; and that the Office of Family Planning under the State Council recruit research staff to study policies and perform surveys and field studies to steer the work of family planning to science.

Second, the law of family planning should be made as soon as possible. "All regulations lack legal annotation and are thus difficult to enforce ... or to be carefully implemented. Therefore, the comrades at the meetings aspire to a law that can be enforced across the country."

Third, a population commission should be established. "At present, the leader group offices of family planning at various levels are still temporary and are restricted to family planning. ... This is in discord with the developing situation." "Many comrades suggest that the state set up a population commission to take charge of all population issues."

Fourth, social insurance for the elderly should be established stepwise.

> While encouraging couples to have only one child each, we should also start dealing with social insurance for the elderly now. First, in the collectively owned units that do not have a retirement plan, it is perhaps reasonable to set aside as insurance fund a small portion of the incomes of the individuals and the collectives. The fund, together with a certain amount of subsidy provided by the state, may be used as retirement pensions and distributed to the elderly in installments. Insurance companies have come up with three plans to tackle the insurance issue for reference (Appendix 5). ... Second, life facilities should be planned as a whole to offer accessibility for the elderly who are not taken care of by children.

Fifth, indicators should be properly set for population control.

> The Standing Committee of the People's Congress has recently discussed the draft of the Law of Marriage, in which it is regulated that the legal age of marriage is 22 for men and 20 for women, which is three to four years younger that the ages that are currently promoted as the standards for late marriage and late reproduction. ... Birth and natural growth rates will thus rebound by a large scale. ... The strategic goal that the natural growth rate is to be lowered below 5‰ will not be realized ... how old the legal marriage ages should be needs to be deliberated by the central government.

Sixth, women's health and child education must be well managed if one child per couple is to be advocated for. The *Report* listed all relevant areas, i.e., perinatal care and maternal health, new technologies of delivery, baby nursing, psychological development, child health, and construction of daycare centers, preschools, and kindergartens, and the goal was for children to "have a low number, all thrive, and become capable."

Seventh, couples who have only one child may get rewarded.

> There are now 28 provinces, cities, and autonomous regions that have constituted their own rules of one-child reward and temporary rules to inflict economic restrictions on those with three or more children. The reward money may come from welfare funds for urban employees and for peasants. The reward may be offered as work points from the welfare fund of rural people's communes. … We suggest that the government subsidize the units and regions that are struggling economically through central and regional treasuries.[54]

What has been described are the major points in the *Report on the Demographic Meetings (First Discussion)*,which were held in 1980 and submitted to the Secretariat. To be fair, the *Report* recast the meetings reliably, including the consensuses reached, the basic views the attendees held, and the controversies. Revisiting the *Report* 35 years later, we may conclude that the studies then on the potential problems of the policy to advocate for one child per couple were fairly comprehensive and the problems listed have already been proved in practice to be rather precise.

Perspectives on the problems, including opinions, trends, and conclusions, are all basically correct, which made the *Report* a fairly good prediction. The suggestions given there were made with prospective angles and were largely practical and operational. History is a mirror of the present and time is the most impartial referee. The *Report* has withstood history.

Unfortunately, however, some stepped up to question it, denying even the very fact that the meetings had ever been held. They questioned loudly and called facts "lies" with arbitrary labels, sticks, bad mouths, insults to dignity, and all means possible. In the beginning, I thought they might have misunderstood something since they were not at the meetings, or maybe they felt a grudge and needed to let it out, and all these were understandable; however, my understanding and tolerance were ruthlessly stamped on and the denial and distortion of the facts went even farther, so far as to violate my right of reputation, and that was not to be tolerated. This book was first and foremost aimed to clarify the facts so that the readers could understand what had happened; therefore, let us get back to population and fertility policies.

A few months after the *Report* was submitted to the Secretariat, on September 25, 1980, the *Open Letter by the CCCPC to All Members of the Communist Party and the Youth League about Controlling the Population Growth in Our Country* was published and it was in line with what was in the *Report*, marking the official implementation of the population and fertility policy that was dominated by the policy to advocate for one child per couple and a new stage of strict control of population growth.

Adjusting the fertility policy timely

The birth of the policy that advocates for one child per couple, described above, illustrates that population and fertility policies, like all other policies, are both relatively stable to fully exert their power and functions and phased to demand timely adjustments when the demographic transition enters a new stage.

Updating the policy with adjustments

The fertility policy gradually stabilized

After the issuance of the policy that advocated for one child per couple, the rate of single children became a fashion chased by many for a while and some advocacies simplified the policy as the "one-child policy" or "one-birth policy." However, "advocating for one child per couple" does not equal "one-child policy" or "one-birth policy." In fact, the *Public Letter* stated that:

> Some may have real difficulties that are acknowledged in the policy and they can be allowed to have two children although three is strictly prohibited. For minority groups, looser regulations may apply following the policy instructions. Birth control should be performed primarily through contraception, and the means should be offered to the masses for them to choose freely.[55]

Apparently, when one child was advocated for in the beginning, it was never a "one-cut" or "one-birth" policy, and it was clearly specified that those with real difficulties should be taken care of, minority groups should have looser regulations, and contraception should be the major way to control birth with people freely choosing the means.

In September 1981, the Secretariat of the CCCPC held a meeting to clarify the principles of the population and fertility policy, and it was proposed that the concrete rules of the population and fertility policy for rural areas should be drafted after careful surveys and studies. It was demanded that "the tactic and policy of family planning must be further studied according to the new situations and practical experiences so that they would be applied on real situations, accepted by the people, and realized through efforts." Apparently, the meeting emphasized that the population and fertility policy must fit the reality and be practical.

> One child per couple should continue to be advocated for in cities unswervingly and in rural areas, strengthened and loosened at the same time according to the new situations after the implementation of the responsibility system. How loosened the policy should be in rural areas may follow two plans. First, one child per couple is advocated for while

> two are allowed and three prohibited. Second, one child per couple is advocated for while two are allowed for those with real difficulties.

It was also decided to "follow the party's mass line and discuss the issue with specialists in pertinent fields and comrades at grassroots and seek opinions from secretaries of party committees in all provinces, municipalities, and autonomous regions."[56]

After the meeting, the Secretariat sent the relevant materials and documents to all provinces, municipalities, and autonomous regions for opinions. The feedback was as follows: 6 provinces and autonomous regions were for the first plan, 15 were in general agreement with the tone of the *Public Letter*, and 3 autonomous regions did not respond. Based on the feedback, the CCCPC held a meeting in December 1981, with first secretaries of all provinces, municipalities, and autonomous regions, and through many rounds of discussions the second plan won the majority support at the meeting.

Subsequently, on February 9, 1982, the CCCPC and the State Council jointly issued the *Instruction on Further Carrying out the Work of Family Planning*, and it specified that:

> Late marriage, late reproduction, reduced births, and quality births should continue to be promoted. The specific requirements are the following. Cadres and employees of government agencies and urban residents are allowed one child per couple with the exception of those in exceptional situations. One child per couple is to be promoted across all rural areas while those with real difficulties can be allowed to have a second child with good planning after their applications are approved. In no circumstances are third-order births allowed. For minority groups, family planning is also to be promoted, and moderate loosening of the regulations may apply. Specific rules may be drafted by ethnic group autonomous areas, relevant provinces, and autonomous regions according to their respective conditions and implemented after approved by the Standing Committee of the People's Congress or the People's Government at the next higher level.

The *Instruction* also specified rules of rewards and restrictions. Among the rewards and the care offered to single children and their families were "health fees for single children" and "moderately extended maternity leave with full payments of salaries and no impact on their future qualifications for salary rises or promotions." In the rural areas and units where the responsibility system had been implemented, "lower quota of production or larger areas of contracted lands" were offered to single-child families.

Among the residents who failed to follow family planning,

> cadres and employees of government agencies and urban residents who had second births without approval of family planning authorities should

> be stripped of their medical and welfare benefits attached with family planning births with potential punishment of salary withholding at a moderate proportion or deprivation of hardship or daycare subsidies,

and "rural members of people's communes should not be allocated responsibility lands or private plots to the extra children; alternatively, the commune member who had extra children should be given fewer contract responsibility lands or higher quota of production."[57]

While the population and fertility policy was being implemented, the conditions for allowing a second birth were acknowledged quite differently in different areas. In August 1982, the National Family Planning Commission (NFPC) held a nationwide meeting of family planning to study and implement the No. 11 file from the CCCPC. After the meeting, the commission submitted the *Minutes of the National Family Planning Working Meeting* to the CCCPC and the State Council.

On October 20, the General Office of the CCCPC and the General Office of the State Council distributed the *Minutes*. It was emphasized in the *Minutes* that the efforts to realize the goal of family planning should be combined with helping people in real difficulties to place the policy on a more solid foundation that agreed with the reality. In the *Minutes*, how the family planning policy had been implemented in all regions was summarized as follows.

> Before the receipt of the *Instruction* [the *Instruction on Further Carrying out the Work of Family Planning* by the CCCPC and the State Council in 1981], three conditions were acknowledged in all provinces, municipalities, and autonomous regions to allow for a second child: 1, that the first births had non-hereditary disabilities and could not become a normal laborer, 2, recombination families with one party having a child and the other in first marriage, and 3, pregnant couples with an adopted child due to sterilization for many years after marriage. Later, during implementation of the *Instruction*, many provinces, municipalities, and autonomous regions added four to five or six to seven conditions to the above three in rural areas, which are 1, couples with the husband family having only one son for consecutively two or three generations, 2, couples with the husband's brothers all sterile, 3, couples with the husband having married into the wife's family in which the wife is the only child, 4, couples with both parties being single children, 5, disabled veterans, 6, couples with both parties being returning emigrants, and 7, families with exceptional difficulties in remote mountainous and coastal areas.[58]

Based on these situations, the CCCPC pointed out the symbol for successful work in the future was to "advance with achievements, overcome shortcomings, and solve problems" while acknowledging the great achievements in family planning in the past few years on April 13, 1984, in the *Approval for Distribution on the "Report on the Work of Family Planning" by the National Family Planning Commission* ([1984] No. 7 CCCPC file). It also emphasized that "the work of family planning should be based on reasonable conditions, approval by the people, and the good performance of cadres."

> One child per couple should continue to be promoted while specific rules and regulations should be further perfected in the work of family planning. Currently, the followings need perfection: 1, further loosening up of the policy is to be made moderately in rural areas with good control, i.e., second births are approved as long as they meet the requirements and gain approval; 2, wild loosening up is strictly prohibited, i.e., second births not allowed by family planning rules and higher-order births; 3, corruption is strictly prohibited and all cadres who open the door for corruptive behaviors are to be punished strictly; 4, moderate policies should be made for the family planning of minority groups, *e.g.*, the minority groups with a less than 100 million population may be allowed two children per couple while three are allowed in exceptional cases and four are strictly prohibited. Specific regulations may be made by the People's Congress and the People's Government in ethnic group autonomous areas, relevant provinces, and autonomous regions according to their respective conditions and implemented after approved by the Standing Committee of the People's Congress or the People's Government at the next higher level.

Comments and opinions were also offered in the No. 7 file on promoting eugenics, strengthening scientific and technological instructions, use and management of funds, and bettering cadres' attitudes during the work of family planning.[59]

The CCCPC's No. 7 file cast a considerable impact on the work of family planning and the birth rate went back up by a small scale under the guidelines of "moderate loosening up" and "prohibiting wild loosening up." After several years of practice, the Standing Committee of the Political Bureau of the CCCPC held a meeting on March 31, 1988, to discuss the *Outline of the Report on the Work of Family Planning* by the NFPC. The policy of family planning was reviewed and its issuance course was summarized as follows.

The CCCPC published the *Public Letter* in 1980 to advocate for one child per couple while stating, "some who have real difficulties should be allowed to have two children although three are strictly prohibited." During the subsequent several years, cadres made arduous efforts to land the policy and achieved significantly although there were problems at the same time. Under the circumstances, Shandong Province proposed "moderate loosening up and prohibition of wild loosening up" to solve practical problems and their trials concluded with good results, which the CCCPC acknowledged. The following was reiterated at the meeting:

> The current family planning policy is such that late marriage and reproduction and reduced and quality births are promoted, as well as one child

> per couple. Cadres and employees of government agencies and urban residents are allowed one child per couple except for those in exceptional situations. Those in rural areas with real difficulties, including the family with only one daughter child, may be allowed for a second birth after approved with a few years of birth interval. Under no circumstances are third births allowed. Family planning is also to be promoted in minority groups and specific methods and regulations may be made by relevant provinces and autonomous regions based on their unique conditions.[60]

As far as I can tell, this was the first time the CCCPC specified that rural families with only one daughter were allowed a second birth, and the policy had a deep impact on subsequent population changes. It was also specified at the meeting that the policy as stated earlier would be persisted with and followed through for a long term. The stability of the policy must be ensured to facilitate population control.

Following the policy by the CCCPC, Comrade Peng Peiyun, the director of the NFPC, stated in her speech at the meeting with nationwide directors of family planning commissions in 1989:

> The current family planning policy made by the CCCPC must be fully implemented continuously with strict control in all regions. It is absolutely forbidden to follow policies of other authorities or to make one's own. If loosened implementation is carried out in a region, an official application must be submitted to the central government. Continued promotion must be made of late marriage and reproduction and reduced and quality births as well as one child per couple. In cities, suburbs, and economically advanced villages, what has already been achieved must be consolidated to contribute more to the state control of the population growth. In other villages, while one child per couple is being advocated for, the policy that a second birth with a few-year interval is allowed for families with only one daughter child and that must be followed through.[61]

By then, the population and fertility policy was finally stabilized after practices, discussions, and revisions for as long as 10 years.

All provinces, municipalities, and autonomous regions made their own specific rules following the policy of the central government. According to the *Chinese Population and History of Family Planning*, edited and published by the NFPC, the 31 provinces, municipalities, and autonomous regions may be divided into five groups based on their family planning rules.

The first group allows one child per couple except for those with exceptional situations (approximately 10 situations acknowledged in the regions in the group) who may have a second birth. In this group are the provinces and municipalities of Beijing, Tianjin, Shanghai, and Jiangsu.

The second group has differentiated instructions in that the policy that rural one-daughter families may have second births is implemented. In this group, Chongqing Municipality and Sichuan Province have geographically differentiated implementation and the provinces of Zhejiang and Fujian have implementation that is differentiated based on the level of the work of family planning. In the mountainous areas of Chongqing and Sichuan, peasants are allowed two children.

The third group allows rural one-daughter families to have two children. In this group are the provinces and autonomous regions of Hebei, Shanxi, Inner Mongolia (only applicable to the Han people), Liaoning, Jilin, Heilongjiang, Anhui, Jiangxi, Shandong, Henan, Hubei, Hunan, Guangxi, Guizhou, Shaanxi, and Gansu.

The fourth group allows two children for all rural families. In this group are the provinces of Guangdong (before 1998), Hainan, and Yunnan, as well as some regional areas, such as the mountainous area, dam regions, and the coastal fishing area in Hebei, the border area in Heilongjiang, the mountainous area in Anhui, the sparsely populated areas in Fujian, the border area of the Guangxi Zhuangzu autonomous region, some mountainous areas in Chongqing, the mountainous area in Sichuan, and the trial sites of family planning such as Yicheng, Shanxi and Jiuquan, Gansu.

The fifth group contains ethnic autonomous regions that have made their own family planning policies for minority groups. In this group are the Inner Mongolia Autonomous Region (where two children are allowed for all minority groups except that couples with both parties in husbandry are allowed three and those of the minority groups of Dawoer, Ekewen, and Elunchun are offered technical services for family planning), the Guangxi Zhuang Autonomous Region (where the minority groups with less than 100 million in population are allowed two children), the Xizang Autonomous Region (where the urban residents such as cadres and employees of the Zang ethnic group are allowed two children, among whom those with exceptional situations are allowed three, voluntary family planning is encouraged in the central husbandry area and no more than three children is promoted, and only advocacy is made in the border area of husbandry and to the minority groups of Menba, Luoba, Xiaerba, and Deng), Qinghai Province (where all peasants are allowed two children and herdsmen of any minority group in the pasturing area are allowed three), the Ningxia Hui Autonomous Region (where all couples with either party or both being peasants are allowed two children while peasants of minority groups in the eight counties of Guyuan, Haiyuan, Xiji, Longde, Jingyuan, Pengyang, Yanchi, and Tongxin are allowed three), and the Xijiang Weiwuer Autonomous Region (where peasants and herdsmen are allowed two children, peasants and herdsmen of minority groups are allowed three, and those with exceptional situations are allowed four).[62]

Adjustments to the fertility policy updated with time

The report on the demographic meetings in 1980 submitted to the Secretariat of the CCCPC was focused on the point that the advocacy for one child per couple would be neither temporary nor permanent, but a unique policy aimed to control the birth rates of one generation, i.e., 25 years or 30 at the most, and that after one generation, things would be different and the population and fertility policy should also be adjusted accordingly.

When it drew close to the end of the 25-year period, the expected time for policy adjustment, there was no sign of any adjustment. I could not sit back and wait, so I published a signed article in *People's Daily* when it was close to the end of the 30-year period, "A Look Back at the Population Policies of the New China and Future Prospects," as well as a book, *Sixty Years of China's Population Policies*, which was later included in the series *A Glorious Course: Celebrating the 60th Year Anniversary of the Establishment of the New China* by the Department of Publicity of the CCCPC and the General Administration of Press and Publication.

In the article and the book, I expounded on how the population and fertility policies were formed in the new China, discussed the current population situation, and presented the necessity of adjusting the current fertility policy with specific suggestions based on theories and practices as well as my own experiences. I proposed several suggestions: two for double singles, i.e., couples with both parties being single children may have two children in the whole country with no strings attached; two for one single, i.e., couples with either party being a single child may have two children, which should be implemented in rural areas immediately and two years later in urban areas; and two but not three, e.g., all are allowed two in the provinces, municipalities, and autonomous regions that may guarantee the absence of third- or higher-order births except for minority groups.

After all, in the current frame of family planning implementation, the specific rules of family planning are actually in the hands of the People's Congress or its Standing Committee in each province, municipality, and autonomous region. I argued that if these suggestions were to be adopted, small scales of rebound in the birth and fertility rates might be observed, but there would be no large-scale rebound, and the goal of population development would not be greatly affected and the strategy of population development could still be advanced with the previously made "three-step" plan.

In fact, there was a fairly loud voice in the demographic field to adjust the fertility policy. People might have different projections and different suggestions on how much adjustment should be made, but they all agreed on the direction and how to adjust the policy. However, adjustment took a long time to come. Until November 2013, the Third Plenary Session of the 18th CCCPC was held and the *Decision by the CCCPC on Several Major Issues about Comprehensively Deepening the Reform* was passed, which marked the initiation of another round of reforms. About the population and family planning, the *Decision* said that:

> The basic state policy of family planning should be persisted with, the policy of two children for the couples with either party being a single

> child should be initiated, and steps should be taken to perfect the fertility policy in order to promote the long-term, balanced development of the population.[63]

To this point, the "two for one single" policy was finally landed, marking a big step in the timely adjustments to policies.

After that, the adjustment to the population and fertility policy was accelerated to a degree. Two years later, the *Suggestion by the CCCPC on the 13th Five-Year Planning of the National Economic and Social Development* in 2015 proposed to persist with the basic state policy of family planning and to perfect the strategy of population growth while implementing the policy of two children for all, improving reproduction health care and the health of women and children, and public services such as daycare centers, offering help to families with real difficulties with family planning, and paying attention to family development.

Implementing the "two-for-one-single" and "two-for-all" policies was a fundamental turn from the policy that advocated for one child per couple, and it was a strategic adjustment. It marked the end of the fertility policy that was centered on one child and the start of the era of "two children for all." Will it bring rebound and increases in the birth and fertility rates? In my opinion, it surely will, but the real question is the height of the rebound and the scale of the increases. A rough estimation is that 2 million to 3 million more births will result every year in the near future. By the end of 2015, the total population in the mainland of China was 1.37462 billion with 16.55 million new births, leading the birth rate to be 12.07‰; 9.75 million deaths, leading the death rate to be 7.11‰; and 6.8181 million added population, leading the natural growth rate to be 4.96‰. If there are 2 million to 3 million more births, the annual births will be 18.55 million to 19.55 million, setting the birth rate at 13.49–14.22‰.

If the death rate stays put at 7.11‰, the natural growth rate will be 6.38–7.11‰, 1.42–2.15 permillage points higher than that of 2015. Of course, birth rates are subject to many factors. For example, 2016 was the year of monkey. Some believe that people born in monkey years are clever and may rush to have children for auspiciousness, leading to a possibly higher birth rate that year. However, the "two-for-all" policy has not been implemented for long, and it takes "ten months of pregnancy to give birth on one day," and many may not be able to make a monkey baby even if they rush.

I predict that the rebound and the increase in the birth rates will more or less rest in five to six years when those who want a second child wave goodbye to their reproduction peak and the birth and growth rates will meet a new normal and stabilize. Therefore, after the policy adjustments of "two for one single" and "two for all," the rebound of the birth and natural growth rates will not be high, it will not affect the realization of the zero growth goal of the national population, and it should be part of the three-step strategy of population development.

Exploring the path of family planning with Chinese characteristics

Family planning is an organizational form of international reproduction services, and it aims at the economy, the health of the wife, and the reproductive behaviors from the perspective of a family. It is widely known that the world population grew like a fairy tale after the Industrial Revolution in the mid-18th century, which attracted wide attention and fostered various theories of population control.

Particularly, Thomas Robert Malthus published anonymously *An Essay on the Principle of Population as It Affects the Future Improvement of Society with Remarks on the Speculations of Mr. Godwin, M. Condorcet, and Other Writers* in 1798, which was in fact the original draft of Malthus's *An Essay on the Principle of Population.* In 1803, Malthus published *An Essay on the Principle of Population*, which was actually the second edition, and it soon became a hot topic of how to handle the population in surplus.

However, the proposals by Malthus to check population growth, be it "preventative checks" such as celibacy and birth control or "active checks" such as war and plague, were all violently opposed by public opinion. Under such a circumstance, birth control and contraception became popular and spread widely in the West, which later became neo-Malthusianism. Among the activists, one American, Mrs. M. Sanger, was quite prominent. She founded a federation of birth control in New York, published *Debate on Birth Control*, later went on birth control campaigns in Japan and India, and established the world's first clinic to provide birth control instructions in New York in 1923 – the Clinical Research Bureau. Under her advocacy, the first conference on world population was held in Geneva, Switzerland in 1927, and birth control was the theme of the conference. In the 1930s, family planning was first coined and used in the United Kingdom, which spread quickly and cast far-reaching impact on birth control and planned births.

After WWII, Mrs. Sanger collaborated with many females in multiple countries who worked on family planning and established the International Planned Parenthood Federation (IPPF) in 1952. The federation was aimed to promote family plans in all countries, protect the health of parents and children both physically and mentally, offer population education to the world, facilitate research on human reproduction and regulation of human reproduction, and generalize the research results. After the establishment of the IPPF, national family planning organizations from more than 120 countries and regions joined the federation. It has played its due role as an international organization and been rated positively across the world.

The IPPF and family planning organizations in various countries all aim to promote family-planned births, protect the health of women and children, and advance policies, measures, and actions that are in line with that aim. However, countries vary in their domestic conditions, economies, science and technology, cultures, and social development, and the focus and the orientation of family planning in each country is also different. In Western advanced countries, it is emphasized to respect and protect human rights, and housewives have autonomy in family planning. In many developing countries, in contrast, birth rates are generally high due to less-developed economies, cultures, and social development, and the goals of family planning are usually landed on the number of births, some of which are essentially the same as birth control.

China, as the largest developing country in the world, owns an association of family planning which talks directly to the IPPF, and possesses similar situations to most developing countries. However, the real leader of the work of family planning in China is the NFPC with subordinate family planning commissions in each province, municipality, and autonomous region (which has been renamed twice as the National Population and Family Planning Commission and the NHFPC) under the State Council and regional governments, respectively. This is completely different from other countries, where social organizations take charge of family planning, which, including the organizations in some developing countries in charge of family planning for the countries, are all nongovernmental organizations (NGOs) or nonprofit organizations (NPOs) that do not belong to government.

Since the implementation of the "two-for-all" policy, people have already started to discuss what will become of the government family planning commissions and various views have emerged. Some hold the "no-change" view that argues for the continuation of the commissions at all levels with the same institutions, features, and functions. Some hold the "cancellation" view and call for the restoration of the right of reproduction to the people since population growth will need encouragement instead of control just like some countries in the West.

In my opinion, the "no-change" view fails to recognize the pattern that the demographic transition in China has made a fundamental transformation and is now in the middle phase of the post-demographic transition and that the population will reach zero growth in about 15 years, which will be followed by negative growth. It also fails to recognize the current overall social background with the "Four-Pronged Comprehensive Strategy" of comprehensive prosperity, comprehensive deepening of the Reform, comprehensive rule of law, and comprehensive strictness in Party governance, or how population management shall adapt to it. Particularly in the background of comprehensive rule of law, the institutions, mechanisms, and policies of population management will eventually be steered to the track of rule of law and the right of reproduction will also be restored to individuals and families.

On the other hand, the "cancellation" view, despite its grip on the overall background, still needs detailed analysis and in-depth discussion when it comes to specific issues. For example, what is the nature of the population in China? Are we at the turning point from population growth suppressing the forces of production to the forces of production suppressing population growth? In my opinion, now and in the fairly long-term future, the nature of the population is still that the forces of production are suppressed by population growth, or the population in surplus. Therefore, there will be no need for large-scale increases in the population; instead, moderate control is still needed. In fact, realizing zero growth and then negative growth to a degree of the population is part of the terminal goal of the three-step strategy of population development and is part of the demand for sustainable development of the population, the resources, the environment, the economy, and the society.

However, it is a long progress to carry out the strategy of sustainable development of the population, the resources, the environment, the economy, and the society, and there may emerge a structural shortage of laborers when the population is at zero or negative growth to a degree, a fairly serious situation of population aging, and a heavy burden on the society, which will bring both positive and negative impacts to socioeconomic development. Our task is to advance the positive impacts and lessen the negative and make every effort to promote the good side and avoid the bad and to orient with benefits and avoid harms.

According to the *Decision by the CCCPC on Several Major Issues about Comprehensively Deepening the Reform* passed at the Third Plenary Session of the 18th CCCPC and the themes of several subsequent meetings, the task and the direction of the reforms of population management shall be to reform the management institutions and mechanisms of the government population agencies, proactively absorb the reasonable parts of international family planning organizations, and establish a family planned reproduction institute with Chinese characteristics.

To advance the reform of the government family planning commissions we must first study the conditions of China and learn our own lessons. During the 65 years after the establishment of the new China, the population and family planning cause went through multiple bumps and gained abundant experiences, and it has not been easy for us to be where we are now.

As described earlier, the population is now in the middle phase of the post-demographic transition and the intrinsic natural growth rate of the population has been negative for more than 20 years. Zero growth is not far away from us and conditions are now favorable for policy adjustment aimed to increase the birth rates moderately. The economy is now at a new normal and "population bonuses" and "population benefits" have been declining, both of which demand a moderately higher birth rate so that the economy will sustain its development in the mid- to long term. The society is walking toward comprehensive prosperity and harmonious development, which requires good coordination between population policies and population aging, changes in the working-age population, changes in the population sex structure, and changes in the population distribution between urban and rural areas, so that health, coordination, and sustainable development are facilitated and the government transitions to a service provider.

In fact, it is not difficult for family planning commissions to transition to providing services. It is actually easier than other sectors such as economic and social departments. Why is that? Family planning concerns families, and if the government agency is transitioning to services, people will approve and there will not be much obstruction from them. The real obstruction comes from the system. After all, when the functions of the commissions change, many things will also change accordingly, such as the feature and the structure of the commissions, the personnel structure, and the salaries and the benefits, all of which need comprehensive planning, coordinated management, and reasonable transition.

Next, the experiences from the family planning activities in the international community should be reasonably borrowed. Although "family planning" is interpreted variously in different countries, consensus has been reached about its basic meaning, features, and operational mechanisms. Despite controversies on NGOs and NPOs, they are both independent of the government and do not seek profit, and that is also a consensus. The two consensuses shall be borrowed while the Chinese family planning commissions transition from administrative to nongovernmental, nonprofit social organizations and become a strong hand to help family reproduction, survival, and livelihood while providing economic and technical support as well as social services.

However, one point must be clarified. Family planning has been implemented in China for decades, and it was also issued as the first basic state policy more than 30 years ago; therefore, it is rooted in numerous families and known by everyone, and, together with the "one veto vote," it mirrors the strong image of the government; thus the administrative roles of the commissions will not cease to exist immediately. Meanwhile, we are still far away from the ultimate goal of the "three-step" strategy of population development, which will need some of the government's administrative functions, and the Western type of family planning that is totally independent of the government will not be able to assume these functions. The direction of the reform and development to "family-planned reproduction" should be acknowledged while the speed and the rhythm of the reform and the transition shall be well controlled based on the practical conditions in China. We should explore a path of family planning with Chinese characteristics during the reform that reduces administrative interference and highlights family decisions.

Notes

1 Confucius, *Analects of Confucius*, p. 94.
2 Ibid., p. 99.
3 Ibid., p. 10.
4 Ibid., p. 107.
5 Confucius, *Lun Yu*, p. 109.
6 *Selected Works of Sun Yat-sen*, vol. 2, p. 610.
7 Chen, Changheng, *On China's Population*, Beijing, Commercial Press, 1918, p. 54.
8 Chen, Da, *Population*, Beijing, Commercial Press, 1934, pp. 307–308.
9 *History of Han, Biography of Emperor Gaozu.*

10 *Additional History of Han, Biography of Emperor Zhang.*
11 *History of Han, Biography of Emperor Hui.*
12 *History of the Southern Dynasties*, vol. 6, *Biographies of Emperors of Liang Dynasty.*
13 *A New History of Tang Dynasty*, vol. 2, *Biography of Taizong.*
14 Xiao, Shuang, *Accounts in the Reign of Long-Lived Emperor Yongzheng*, vol. 1.
15 Wang, Pu, *Marriage, Accounts of Tang Dynasty.*
16 *Accounts of Ming Dynasty* in the Wanli Calendar.
17 Du, You, *Tong Dian*, vol. 6, *Food and Goods*, item 6.
18 *Comments on Laws of Tang Dynasty*, vol. 12.
19 Ji, Huang, *Addition to Bibliography Book*, vol. 12.
20 *Tong Zhi Tiao Ge*, in *Yuan Dynasty*, vol. 2.
21 *Cases of Law Enforcement in Qing Dynasty*, vol. 1036.
22 *History of Ming Dynasty, Accounts of Food and Goods.*
23 National Commission of Population and Family Planning, *History of China's Population and Family Planning*, Beijing, China Population Publishing House,, 2007, pp. 17–18.
24 Ibid., p. 20.
25 Peng, Peiyun, ed., *Encyclopedia of Family Planning in China*, Beijing, China Population Publishing House, 1997, pp. 1–2.
26 Ibid., p. 3.
27 National Commission of Population and Family Planning, *History of China's Population and Family Planning*, pp. 24–25.
28 Peng, *Encyclopedia of Family Planning in China*, pp. 1–3.
29 Ibid., pp. 1–2.
30 National Commission of Population and Family Planning, *History of China's Population and Family Planning*, p. 44.
31 Peng, *Encyclopedia of Family Planning in China*, p. 4.
32 Yang, Kuifu, Liang, Jimin, and Zhang, Fan, *An Outline of Major Events in China's History of Population and Family Planning*, Beijing, China Population Publishing House, 2001, p. 26.
33 Peng, *Encyclopedia of Family Planning in China*, pp. 4–6.
34 Ibid., p. 4.
35 Ibid., pp. 5–6.
36 Ibid., p. 6.
37 Ibid., p. 8.
38 Meadows, Donella H., et al., *The Limits to Growth*, translated by Zhu, Cenlou, and Hu, Weili, Taibei, Blue Ocean Publishing House, 1974, p. 2.
39 National Commission of Population and Family Planning, *Chinese Population and History of Family Planning*, pp. 86–87.
40 Peng, *Encyclopedia of Family Planning in China*, p. 14.
41 *Proceeding of the First National Conference on Demographic Theories and Science*, November 1978, pp. 2–4.
42 Ibid.
43 Peng, *Encyclopedia of Family Planning in China*, pp. 10, 12.
44 The World Forum, www.creaders.org/, October 24, 2006.
45 *Selected Works of Marx and Engels*, vol. 4, Beijing, People's Publishing House, 2012, p. 13.
46 *Report on the Demographic Meetings (First Discussion)*, original draft, pp. 1–3.

47 *Appendix 1, Current Population Problems in Our Country*, original draft, pp. 1–5.
48 *Appendix 2, Suggestions on the Proposal of One Child per Couple*, original draft, p. 4.
49 *Report on the Demographic Meetings (First Discussion)*, original draft, pp. 4–6.
50 *Appendix 2, Suggestions on the Proposal of One Child per Couple*, original draft, pp. 2–6.
51 *Report on the Demographic Meetings (First Discussion)*, original draft, p. 6.
52 Ibid., pp. 6–7.
53 Ibid., pp. 7–8.
54 Ibid., pp. 8–12.
55 Peng, *Encyclopedia of Family Planning in China*, pp. 16–17.
56 National Population and Family Planning Commission, *Chinese Population and History of Family Planning*, pp. 125–126.
57 Ibid., pp. 126–127.
58 Ibid., p. 127.
59 Ibid., pp. 127–128.
60 Ibid., pp. 128–129.
61 Ibid., p. 129.
62 Ibid., pp. 129–130.
63 *Assembly of Files of the 3rd Plenary Session of the 18th CCCPC*, Beijing, People's Publishing House, 2013, p. 69.

Bibliography

Beinhauer, Hagan H., and Schmacke, Ernst, *World in Prospect in 2000 A.D.*, translated from German by Zheng, Muqi, Xu, Xinmin, and Gong, Guangyu, Beijing, Beijing People's Publishing House, 1978.

Division of Population, National Bureau of Statistics, *Data Compilation of the Second National Population Census of the People's Republic of China*, 1986 (reprint).

Keyfitz, Nathan, and Flieger, Wilhelm, *World Population*, Chicago, University of Chicago Press, 1968.

National Population and Family Planning Commission, ed., *Chinese Population and History of Family Planning*, Beijing, China Population Publishing House, 2007.

Office of Population Census under the State Council & Division of Population, National Bureau of Statistics, eds., *Materials of the 1982 Population Census in China*, Beijing, China Statistics Press, 1985.

Peng, Peiyun, ed., *Encyclopedia of Family Planning in China*, Beijing, China Population Publishing House, 1997.

Population and Employment in China in 2000, from *China in 2000* by Research Institute of Technology Economics of the State Council, 1984.

Shelby, Philip, and Schechter, Mal, *Aging 2000*, translated by Xin, Wei, and Huang, Yufu, Beijing, SDX Joint Publishing, 1987.

Song, Jian, Tian, Xueyuan, Yu, Jingyuan, and Li, Guangyuan, *Population Forecast and Control*, Beijing, People's Publishing House, 1981.

Works by Tian Xueyuan, Beijing, China Economic Publishing House, 1991.

Yang, Kuifu, Liang, Jimin, and Zhang, Fan, *An Outline of Major Events in China's History of Population and Family Planning*, Beijing, China Population Publishing House, 2001.

Yu, Wang, *Practices and Theoretical Explorations of the 30 Years of Family Planning*, Beijing, China Population Publishing House, 2007.

Zhang, Weiqing, ed., *Encyclopedia of the Chinese Population and Family Planning (1997–2007)*, Beijing, China Population Publishing House, 2013.

8 The development trend in ecologic civilization

Exploring the path of population and sustainable development

In Chapter 6, the concept of civilization and the classification of civilization types have already been described, which is not be repeated here. The focus of this chapter is to take a further step to make in-depth analysis from the standpoint of people orientation and the perspective of the combination of human development and civilization advancement, particularly the perspective of the game between the human-controlled and nature-controlled systems that bears phase-specific characteristics.

During the more than 4 million years from the birth of mankind through development until now, civilization is the outcome of the development as well as the goal of humans. Civilization advances continuously with new types constantly emerging. Each historical stage has its own socioeconomic, political, scientific, technologic, and cultural characteristics with phased changes in the size, the quality, and the structure of population, resulting in multiple stages of human civilization. It is generally agreed that there are "four civilizations" of human society, and my interpretation of them is as follows.

The primitive civilization is a historical stage when the nature-controlled system is in entire dominance over the human-controlled system and human activities can only reach the products of nature. It is therefore a civilization with passive acceptance of what nature has to offer. The agricultural civilization is a historical stage when the nature-controlled system is handing over dominance to the human-controlled system. Production means such as iron tools help mankind to obtain the products of human labor and activities start to break some of the limitations of the nature-controlled system. The industrial civilization is a historical stage when the human-controlled system tries to master the nature-controlled system. Scientific and technological advancements become a powerful weapon to facilitate the shift of power, but population, resource, and environmental crises force people to reflect on their own activities. The modern ecologic civilization is a historical stage when the human- and nature-controlled systems seek coordinated development while development at the cost of resources and the environment is discarded and sustainability of population and development is chosen as the final goal. At present, the population, resources, environment, and development are all at a crossroad: are they coordinated or separated in further progression? The two choices represent two ideas, two thoughts, and two futures, and every country, nation, and ethnic group, as well as the entire human race, must make a clear choice.

The development trend in human civilization

Tracks of human civilization

What is *civilization*? Various definitions are available in different disciplines and fields, among which several are representative. One definition is the sum of all the material and spiritual wealth produced by mankind that has reached a fairly high level, which is actually similar to the definition of *civilization* in the broad sense except for its emphasis on the fairly high level and on representativeness. Another definition only describes spiritual wealth and equates civilization to milestone achievements in thought, ethics, literature, art, education, science, technology, and religion, which is similar to the definition of *civilization* in the general sense except for its emphasis on the fairly high level and on representativeness. A third definition looks at the relationships between people, between people and society, and between people and nature and describes civilization as a harmonious and respectful state among them. Civilization in this sense includes ethics and morality, ideologies that maintain the public interest and order, and ideas to protect the ecologic environment and to adapt to the laws of nature in development.

A fourth definition describes specific civilizations formed when all things described earlier were met with the development of a country or a race and major historical events, such as the ancient Roman civilization and the Renaissance civilization in Europe and the prosperous Tang civilization in China. Apparently, to discern the historical tracks of civilization development, we must first straighten out the course of the birth and development of mankind so that we may recognize that civilization emerges, grows, and replenishes itself with the birth and development of mankind.

The origin of the human race

When it comes to the question of when and where humans originated, there are still several different views. The most popular one holds that humans diverged from hominids and evolved into modern mankind through labor. Some disagree with the hominid view and argue that all primates, including monkeys and apes but excluding humans, make vocalizations, but not tears, when crying because none of them has a lacrimal gland. If humans had evolved from hominids, how did human lacrimal glands emerge? This is one powerful line of evidence against the view that humans evolved from hominids.

We often read about how people frequently see and watch tigers and wolves and hear tigers roar and apes gibber in novels, poems, movies, and plays that describe ancient societies with sparse populations. In fact, almost all who have heard tigers roar and apes gibber are filled with awe and fear toward the tiger roar that penetrates deep into vast mountains and woods while they are annoyed by the unpleasant, tearless, dry gibbering of apes that sound like something in between an animal and a bird. Humans are the same: everyone sounds unpleasant if they fake a cry without showing any real emotions.

However, if humans did not evolve from hominids, then where did we come from? The answer is the fish. Look, isn't he just like a happily moving fish when someone swims in the water? During the evolution from fish to human, the two cheeks evolved into ears and the tail split and became two legs. In fact, however, evidence for human evolution from the fish is far from sufficient; therefore, the view can only be taken as a view, and we cannot yet conclude that human beings came from fish. As a result, we have to come back to the theory that humans diverged from hominids as defined by Darwinian evolution and Huxley's description of the human position in nature.

Every school of history is founded on explorations of historical events and extant documents. A theory of the birth and the development of mankind also keeps revising itself with new discoveries. In the West, the story of Adam and Eve spreads wide and far, and they are taken as the ancestors of humankind. In China, the most popular tale concerning the origin of humans is that "Pangu created heaven, Nvwa created humans." In Chinese mythology, Pangu died after he separated the land from the sky and his body gave rise to everything between the sky and the land. Goddess Nvwa scooped mud from the Yellow River and shaped it into individual humans who came to life.

However, a myth is just a myth and cannot be taken as evidence. According to the books *Sapiens: A Brief History of Humankind* by Yuval Noah Harari, *A Global History: From Prehistory to the 21st Century* by Stavrianos, and *Our Eastern Inheritance: The Story of Civilization* by Will Durant, consensuses have formed, although arguments differ on the origin and the development history of mankind, and the following few points are particularly agreed upon.

It is agreed that scientific studies on the origin of mankind started in the 19th century. In 1809, French scholar Lamarck proposed in his book *Philosophie Zoologique* that higher animals originated from lower ones and concluded that humans originated from hominids. However, his view passed without notice.

The most prominent figure who delivered the decisive influence on the exploration of human descent was British scholar Charles Darwin. In 1859, he published *On the Origin of Species*, in which he proposed and explained that animals and plants alike evolved from simple to complex and from lower to higher forms. In 1871, he published another book, *The Descent of Man*, in which he proposed that humans originated from animals and evolved from an ancient species of ape. He also hypothesized that the earliest humans emerged in Africa.

Darwin's conclusions were entirely based on his observations of animals and plants. Right around the same period when Darwin proposed his theories, fossils of ancient humans were discovered for the first time. In 1859, a piece of skull and skeletons of Neanderthals were found in the Neander Valley of Duesseldorf, Germany. Scientists suggested Neanderthals lived approximately 40,000 to 70,000 years ago. In 1868, skeletons of Cro-Magnons, together with stone tools, perforated seashells, and reindeer bones, were found in a rock shelter in southern France. The remains were dated to approximately 40,000 to 100,000 years ago.

A series of archaeological findings at the end of the 19th century and the beginning of the 20th tracked ancient humans back even earlier. In 1891, a skullcap and a thighbone of an early human, later named Java Man, were found in Java, Indonesia, and the remains were estimated to belong to humans living 800,000 years ago. In 1929, the first skull of Peking Man was uncovered in Zhoukoudian, Beijing, China, which was followed by the discovery of 5 more pieces of skull, 11 mandibles, 7 thighbones, 2 humerus bones, 147 teeth, and skeletal fragments. Studies concluded that Peking Man lived approximately 500,000 years ago.

Unfortunately, however, these fossils were all lost during the anti-Japanese war. Rumor had it that they were onboard a ship that sank somewhere between the Bohai and Yellow Seas while some claimed that the Japanese invaders snatched the remains. Exactly what happened to them or where they were last seen needs further investigation. What is noteworthy to mention here is that the discoveries of the Java Man and the Peking Man provided some evidence for the Asian origin of mankind.

In 1961, a professor at Yale University published a scientific paper arguing that *Rampithecus*, living about 15 to 30 million years ago, was the earliest known species of the *Homo* genus. Now the time when humans emerged was pushed way back, from tens of thousands to 15 million years ago. Such a big push with little evidence led to much argument. In the late 1960s, Allan Wilson and Vincent Sarich from the University of California at Berkeley compared the structures of proteins drawn from blood samples of modern humans and African apes and concluded that the *Homo* genus first appeared about 5 million years ago, which negated the claim that *Rampithecus* was an ancestor of modern humans. Subsequent studies further narrowed human origin to 5–4 million years ago, which is widely accepted now.

Although there are still various viewpoints about the origin of human civilization and how to stage it, there are overall three types of descriptions of civilization: vertical, horizontal, and vertical and horizontal combined. The vertical description divides human civilization into several development stages along the timeline. The horizontal description differentiates between civilizations that are formed in particular historical stages, regions, and conditions and finds the particular pattern in each of them. Studies of the development courses of populations, resources, environments, and civilizations and their relationships and interactions usually rely on the vertical analysis while vertical comparisons through various historical stages may tell us the dynamic changes in the human- and nature-controlled systems, which may further lead to the course and patterns we need to realize sustainable development.

Changes in the means of production and civilizations

The economy is the base of the superstructure that includes ideologies, science, technology, education, culture, and politics, as well as the base for the birth and development of a civilization. Classification of economic stages is not based on what is produced, but on tools used and the means of production. The human history of more than 4 million years may be therefore classified into the three major eras of handmade tools, mechanical tools, and intelligent tools. The era of handmade tools corresponds to the primitive and agricultural civilizations, the era of mechanical tools to industrial civilization, and the era of intelligent tools to modern ecologic civilization.

THE ERA OF HANDMADE TOOLS CORRESPONDS TO PRIMITIVE AND AGRICULTURAL CIVILIZATIONS

Two standards are available with which to evaluate the nature of production tools and their level, one of which is the engine of the tools or how they are driven and the other of which is the materials, techniques, structural features, and production efficiency of the tools or the nature of the tools in terms of technology, function, and efficiency. Based on these two standards, the production tools used in primitive and agricultural civilizations are all handmade tools.

Handmade tools and primitive civilization. Immediately after men started to walk upright, which distinguished them from the kingdom of animals, and lived in a society of primitive communism, humankind embarked on a difficult and winding journey of evolution. This journey accounts for more than 99% of human history, and many think that this prolonged period was just the barbarian stage of human history with nothing even close to a civilization. Another view differs considerably and holds that human activities in the late phase of the primitive stage of human history actually left behind the earliest human culture and civilization while labor was the key to evolution from primate to human, which created tools and helped with the last leap that resulted in the emergence of humans.

Primitive civilization, although extremely simple and perhaps negligible in the eyes of modern people, claimed many revolutionary creations that were comparable to any great invention in subsequent human history as they were the achievements of humans after they outgrew the most primitive state with bare hands by using the simplest tools when they stood up and took a walk for the first time, used a stick or stone as a tool or weapon for the first time, and started a fire by using sparks from lightning, especially by rubbing stones or drilling wood, for the first time, and it thus deserves a seat in the history of human development.

After all, the time needed for the birth and the application of such a civilization and the hardships along the way are far more immense than any other later civilization could even imagine. Just think about this: when early humans tried to stand up and walk, to use a stick or stone as a tool or weapon, and to start fires by rubbing stones and drilling wood, they had to endure many trials, failures, injuries, and even deaths in order to consciously complete such primitive labor with their brain that had been preoccupied by the animal instinct of food hunting. From picking up a stone to attack beasts to sharpening stones to make cutting tools and weapons and particularly from using sparks to make a fire to cook food, keep themselves warm, and protect themselves from beasts, the early humans walked through incredible hardships while their brains made a fundamental transformation along the way from instinctive thinking to cognition and consciousness. Owing to this, all the subsequent civilizations could emerge, develop, and advance. Therefore, we must keep in mind that the origin of all human civilizations is here. No matter how glorious and magnificent later human civilizations are, nothing is possible without the creations in the primitive stage.

Handmade tools and agricultural civilization. It is generally agreed that primitive civilization was approximately 10,000 years ago, after which humans entered the agrarian age and started a new era of agricultural civilization. Agricultural civilization experienced three stages: primitive agriculture, conventional agriculture, and modern agriculture, during which tools and means of production were revised and upgraded step by step.

Primitive agriculture emerged approximately 10,000 years ago when mankind was in a period, which was at least 5,000 years long, between the late phase of the Paleolithic and the early phase of the Neolithic. The majority of the tools for agricultural production were sharpened stones with some made from wood and bones, all of which were very primitive and handmade. The means of production were mostly centered on cultivation, harvesting, and pastoral activities, and everything was powered by men.

Conventional agriculture emerged approximately 5,000 years ago. The tools of production transitioned from stones and sometimes wood to metal, especially iron, and the forces of production of human society were significantly improved. The earliest known smelted iron artifact in the world was a dagger with a bronze handle and an iron blade uncovered from a Hittite tomb in northern Turkey (Anatolia) that was 4,500 years old (2,500 B.C.). The earliest in China were two iron rods uncovered from a burial site of the Mogousiwa culture in Lintan County, Gansu Province and dated 3,310–3,510 years old (1510–1310 B.C.), the discovery of which took the title of China's oldest iron artifact from an iron-bladed bronze *yue*, uncovered in Pinggu, Beijing, and the title of China's oldest smelted iron artifact from an iron sword with a jade handle from the Guo state of the Western Zhou Dynasty (1046–771 B.C.).[1]

Studies show that many tools of agrarian production emerged as early as the late phase of the primitive society in China, such as *si*, shovels, hoes, *jue*, ploughs, and *hua*, which were mostly made of stones and sometimes wood. Bronze artifacts prospered quickly in the Western Zhou Dynasty, while iron ploughs, *hua*, and hoes emerged in the Spring and Autumn (770–476 B.C.) and Warring States (476–221 B.C.) Periods. In the Han Dynasty (202 B.C.–A.D. 220), iron ploughs, *hua*, and chariots were quite popular; rakes and rollers emerged in the period of the Wei, Jin, and Southern and Northern Dynasties (A.D. 220–579).In the Sui (A.D. 581–618) and Tang (A.D. 618–907) Dynasties, curved-ridge ploughs, scoop wheels, and vertical shaft waterwheels emerged; in the Song (A.D. 960–1279) and Yuan (A.D. 1271–1368) Dynasties, ploughs with a foot pedal, *lidao*, *tuilian* (a kind of sickle), *dunche* (wheeled rollers), *yangma*, and *yuntang* emerged; and in the Ming (A.D. 1368–1644) and Qing (A.D. 1636–1912) Dynasties, ploughing frames and windmills were used.

All these advancements in cultivating tools were closely associated with the application of iron tools, which made various tools to be used interchangeably, in combination with each other, and for multiple purposes, as well as laid the foundation for deep ploughing and fine cultivation in agriculture. More important, the convenience of iron tools made it much easier for people to enlist the help of domesticated animals and cow-powered cultivation quickly spread and developed.

Meanwhile, ploughs, moldboard ploughs, spades, and picks made of iron offered new possibilities for building water irrigation systems and water irrigation became popular. Therefore, a general paradigm was formed for agricultural production, in which the conventional agricultural civilization was born that was characterized by iron ploughs, cow-powered cultivation, and water irrigation. With this paradigm, agricultural production kept developing in depth and width and China led the world with many achievements in terms of water- and wind-powered transport, irrigation, and grinding, making significant contributions to agricultural civilization.

Modern agriculture emerged after the Industrial Revolution and, equipped with industrial technologies and guided by scientific experiments, it relied on markets and modern logistics for circulation. With the Industrial Revolution came new technologies, new production, and new circulation channels, and modern agriculture also kept changing. The most modern agriculture is represented in the countries with high levels of industrialization whereas amazing production that is hundreds and thousands of times more efficient than conventional agricultural is realized with modern, advanced technologies in post-industrialization countries.

In terms of the accommodation agricultural civilization made to each historical stage, conventional agriculture is the most typical. How advanced conventional agriculture is varies greatly across times and areas, but all agriculture forms in this type are powered by handmade tools. To accommodate to handmade tools, small-scale farming based on individual families prevailed everywhere, which also decided the foundation of the human-controlled system in agricultural society. Such a control system was undoubtedly a significant advancement from primitive civilization, where the human-controlled system was practically nonexistent; however, the system was still weak and could not break the confinement of the nature-controlled system.

Agricultural society thus showed a transition of dominance from the nature-controlled to the human-controlled system. Under such a circumstance, the nature-controlled system was fairly stable. Damages to nature were of course there; for example, slash-and-burn cultivation and arbitrary lumbering harmed the natural ecologic system to a degree. However, human activities had limited effect on nature in the age of agricultural civilization because the world population was sparse compared to the land as its limited scale only reached 1.65 billion people in 1910 with a population density of 12.3 people per square kilometer; on the other hand, restricted by handmade tools, humans were not able to really devastate land, mountains, rivers, or air or to form a lethal menace to the entire ecologic environment. Therefore, the nature-controlled system could regenerate on its own and repair itself to recover from the damages quickly.

In addition, the damages in the age of agricultural civilization were mostly physical in nature with limited power and impact; in comparison, the damages in the age of industrialization that is chemical in nature are far deeper and more serious with the use of pesticides and fertilizers and the generation of carbon dioxide, poisonous liquids, and gases.

THE ERA OF MECHANICAL TOOLS CORRESPONDS TO INDUSTRIAL CIVILIZATION

The Industrial Revolution first broke out in the United Kingdom in the mid-18th century and quickly spread to major countries on the European continent. Although the revolution was not restricted to the forces of production alone and covered certain social and cultural aspects, the change in the tools of production, as the initiation of the revolution and its symbol, was still decisive.

The change was first in the nature of the tools – spinning machines replaced hand-powered spinning wheels, starting the age of machine industries – and then in their power – steam engines replaced hand-driven grinders, which initiated the age of engines powered by fossil materials such as coal, charcoal, and oil.

It was an influential revolution from handmade to mechanical tools. Compared to the agricultural age, when handmade tools were prevalent, labor was isolated, and technology had no advancement for long terms, production efficiency was improved 100 and 1,000 fold with machines in the industrial age. Together with this, large-scale production was a demand and the means of labor, laborers, technologies, and techniques all showed a trend of convergence. Industrial civilization formed, or, the second wave as it was called by futurist Toffler, i.e., modern civilization based on industrialization and steered by mechanical mass production whereas laborers and resource allocation are optimized by the market, labor division is finely furthered, production scale is extended, economic rights are centralized, and enterprise profits are maximized.

New development trends have also emerged: the industrialization trend, more and more classifications of industries with finer and finer divisions claiming higher and higher proportions of the national economy, showing the sole importance of industry; the urbanization trend, acceleration of the transformation of agricultural population to industrial population with an increasingly higher proportion of the urban population and cities as the center of economies, politics, science and technology, and cultures; the trend of rule of law, protection of legal persons such as enterprises as mainstays of the market in an industrialized society based on a market economic system with proper systems of law and democracy in the economic, political, and social aspects; and the trend of increasing mobility, inevitable, reasonable increases in the mobility of people, wealth, and things with continuous improvement in production efficiency and increases in the economy. Particularly today with prosperous new technologies pioneered by microelectronics, informatization and economic globalization have reached out to every corner of the world, and unprecedented speed and mobility have significantly shortened geographical and temporal distances.

However, the industrial civilization based on industrialization and steered by mechanical mass production has led to risks and crises that have built up day after day while greatly improving the forces of production, creating wealth increments that are hundreds and thousands of times compared to those of the previous eras, and facilitating breakthroughs in science, technology, cultures, and democratic and legal advancement. The most prominent risks and crises are the following three.

The first risk and crisis is in resources. From the perspective centered on humans, all production tools are just extensions and externalizations of human physical and intellectual strength. From this perspective, industrial civilization has reached unprecedented achievements, perhaps to the extreme of what is reachable. Spacecraft have helped people realize the dream of space travel, high-speed rail and highways have made true people's wish to travel 1,000 kilometers per day and to cross mountains, carriers and luxury cruisers cut open the waves and speed proudly in wide seas and oceans, dams stop big rivers, nuclear plants send light to millions of families, and a computer with Internet connection enables people to access the world on the screen.

However, all these – aircraft, trains, automobiles, ships, nuclear plants, and computers – are products made through material exchange by human labor, which consumes considerable amounts of natural resources. With continuous advance of industrialization, the human capacity to produce and consume natural resources has grown miraculously and industrial civilization is now on the eve of complete exhaustion of most natural resources, spotting yellow signs of warning one after another. It is true that astronautic technologies have made great progress; in fact, the latest news said that there might be other planets in the universe suitable for humans to live on, making possible human migration to other planets; however, Earth is still the only practical place for mankind to live and interstellar migration is still a hypothesis and dream. We cannot build our future on a hypothesis or a dream, but only solidly on practical foundations. Important resources of the earth are faced with the risk of exhaustion, shaking the foundation of human livelihood and development, and this issue must be met with solutions.

The second risk and crisis is in the environment. Environmental pollution comes side by side with excessive consumption of resources. Excessive emission of carbon dioxide, sulfur dioxide, nitrogen dioxide, and other poisonous and harmful gases has led to increasingly severe air pollution, acid rain, and widening of ozone holes and has caused a greenhouse effect. Large discharges of wastewater, solid waste, and poisonous objects from industries, especially the conventional heavy chemical industry, together with excessive use of fertilizers and pesticides in agriculture and excessive excavation of underground water, have compromised the water quality of rivers, lakes, and oceans, polluted underground water, and caused the water table to decrease significantly, with some regions even faced with the menace of underground water exhaustion.

Meanwhile, soil has been polluted to various degrees in different regions, threatening the safety of food grown in it. At present, many developed countries, having endured the pain of managing the environment after it had been polluted by human development, have made great efforts in pollution management and made temporary successes; however, many developing countries have not realized the challenge of pollution or been restricted by their economic capacity to do anything and are, unfortunately, forced to walk the walk developed countries once walked, allowing the environmental risk and crisis to build up, barring sustainable development.

The third risk and crisis is in cultures. In agrarian society, when the human-controlled system had to rely on the nature-controlled system to a large degree, the economy was dominated by a self-sufficient, natural form based on cultivation by men and weaving by women. Commercial economies were underdeveloped and exchange was just a supplementary economic activity to the self-sufficient economy; in accordance, thoughts, concepts, and ideologies were all conserved and isolated.

Under such circumstances, a traditional culture formed in China centered on *zhong* (loyalty), *xiao* (filiality), *jie* (chastity), and *yi* (justice) with the behavior codes of *xiao*, *ti* (brotherhood), *zhong*, *xin* (trust), *li* (rites), *yi*, *lian* (honesty), and *chi* (shame), and these codes were used as the standards of civilization. Industrial civilization, on the contrary, was based on industrialization and steered by mechanical mass production. In the industrial age, the natural, self-sufficient economy gave way to a market economy with free competition and fair exchange, feudal institutions and ethics gave way to capital-serving concepts of rule of law and democracy, and a culture centered on people formed.

The ideals, thoughts, and way of thinking that came with the people-centered culture were certainly a big step forward in human history; however, as there are two sides to everything, risks and crises came side by side with this step forward. People always put themselves above nature and overestimate their ability to control it, believing that they can develop, use, change, and master nature at will. So they greedily take from nature like reaching for things in a pocket, leading to exhaustion of resources, exacerbation of the ecologic environment, and eventually threat to the survival, safety, and development of mankind. In fact, the madness of some human activities in industrial civilization was partly due to the explosive achievements in scientific and technological development. The madness toward nature was backed by the explosive advancements in productive tools, and the madness toward the underdeveloped was founded on the explosive power of weapons.

Any technological advancement in the eras of primitive and agricultural civilizations, no matter how small, was always first applied to production, but in the age of industrial civilization, it was first and foremost applied to the production of weapons. The reason many breakthroughs were made in nuclear technology during WWII was exactly the intent to find a decisive weapon with which to win the war. As it turned out, the very first application of nuclear technologies was the two atomic bombs dropped on Hiroshima and Nagasaki, which expedited the surrender of the Japanese invaders like a catalyzer. Now the nuclear weapons in the world are enough to destroy earth and humankind many times over. Are we to die together or to live in peace with them? This is a game beyond the competition between the human- and nature-controlled systems, one that may destroy both systems at the same time.

THE ERA OF INTELLIGENT TOOLS CORRESPONDS TO MODERN ECOLOGIC CIVILIZATION

After WWII, a new technological revolution took place pioneered by microelectronic technologies, which was later followed by even newer technologies pioneered by life sciences, including typically biological technologies, genetic engineering, cloning technologies, and nanotechnologies.

The pioneering microelectronic technologies have proven in the development of modern sciences to be indispensable to any new technology. Supercomputers, big data, and cloud calculation have now been widely applied in many areas and they have been shown to possess certain traits of the human brain such as storage, memory, analysis, decision, and prediction, and their performance is several times more efficient than that of the human brain. Sometimes the tasks they perform cannot even be assumed by humans.

For example, from March 9 to March 15, 2016, a five-game Go match was played between Li Se-dol, a South Korean professional Go player of 9 dan rank, and AlphaGo, an artificial intelligent computer program of Go and AlphaGo beat Li in four out of the five games. Perhaps AlphaGo may be deemed an intelligent tool, one that possesses the intelligence and the capacity of many human Go masters and that has finally defeated a human. Meanwhile, AlphaGo is also a robot. In fact, robots are now widely applied not only in production fields but also in many aspects of daily lives, including keeping company and taking care of people and conducting simple interactions that involve emotions; moreover, robots are used in transport such as auto-piloted cars and airplanes as well as in military fields such as mature technologies in auto-piloted airplanes and spaceships.

Ecologic civilization is a modern civilization that emerged after industrial civilization. It breaks the limitations of the linear development of industrial civilization and aims to build a system that unifies and coordinates the human- and nature-controlled systems. Ecologic civilization is a higher-level civilization that pushes mutual evolution and coordination of human society and its surrounding environment. Thus advancing ecologic civilization enlists further study of the changes in the human- and nature-controlled systems in primitive, agricultural, and, more important, industrial civilizations and requires summarizing the lessons from the changes in the human-controlled system, especially those learned when it tried to override the nature-controlled system. To do this, more advanced technologies are needed, e.g., intelligent tools.

For example, weather satellites can monitor Earth's atmosphere with their cameras to learn the pattern of its changes to offer accurate weather forecasts by obtaining accurate information on sudden rain, flood, drought, snowstorms, and typhoons; the development of diving, sonar, and material technologies has enabled humans to see the very bottom of oceans thousands of meters deep to observe, study, and reveal deep-sea secrets and to master the ocean's motions; and transgenic and cloning technologies have directly linked human activities to changes in external creatures.

Ecologic civilization takes into account the human race, the environment, and their relationship and seeks to handle the changes and development of the two while managing the changes and development of humans. To build a unified system that integrates the nature- and human-controlled systems, ecologic civilization demands not only wisdom but also superior technological tools, intelligent ones that surpass the capacity of handmade and mechanical tools.

The ultimate significance of ecologic civilization

Along the footsteps of human history, ecologic civilization covers and summarizes primitive, agricultural, and, in particular, industrial civilizations while bearing the information of a future civilization's direction, trend, and characteristics. It therefore concludes the past and initiates the future, which speaks for its ultimate significance.

The orientation of values: from unilateral to coordinated development

Every civilization has its own orientation of values. Primitive civilization was founded on the direct procurement of useful materials from the natural world as the means of livelihood, and it was thus first oriented toward satisfaction of human demands for survival; therefore, almost anything that benefited it was civilized. Stone artifacts, bows and arrows, and fire were the earliest primitive tools. They helped humans in hunting and picking food and improved the chance of humans to obtain food and other useful materials from the natural world. They were therefore major symbols of civilization in the primitive age.

In the agrarian age, people did not rely on the natural world to offer food that was ready to eat. People started to cultivate food, which continued to grow in variety, improving the human capacity to supply food. Humans also became more capable of employing the renewable energies in nature – animals, wind, and water – while production tools and weapons advanced to the stage that all were primarily made of iron. Cultivation and ranching were the main activities of production. The inventions of scripts, black powder, paper, printing, and pottery, as well as continuous advancements in production tools and weapons empowered the human-controlled system, and the value orientation started show signs of shifting to honoring development.

Industrial civilization has recorded the advancements of the human-controlled system and humans' growing lust for controlling the nature-controlled system. It is therefore expected to override and conquer nature. What is the civilization oriented toward in value, then? It is oriented toward increments of capital. Maximization of profits is the central axis that controls the economic operation as well as the central nervous system that adjusts the allocation of resources. However, each force has an equal and opposite reaction and this is a universal law in nature and in the human world. Therefore, every time the human-controlled system is reinforced with a victory, nature reacts by exerting a reaction to us as retaliation. After having paid a high price, the proud industrial civilization has finally woken up and reflected on its grave consequences while looking for a new orientation of values.

Therefore, primitive, agricultural, and industrial civilizations all have something in common as well as differences in terms of value orientation. They differ in their value orientations in that primitive civilization was mostly oriented toward the demands of human survival; agricultural civilization was first oriented toward the demands of human survival with class-specific orientations such that peasants were after survival and the landlord class was after survival, leisure, and development at the same time; and industrial civilization is after maximization of profits, which has driven a sort of unilateral, one-sided development with crises in various areas including resources, the environment, and cultures.

Meanwhile, these civilizations also have something in common in that all are oriented toward development. Some may disagree that there was any "development" in primitive civilization; after all, it was a historical period that started 10,000 years ago, when humans were passively attached to the nature-controlled system and had no "development." However, it was not the whole story. Primitive civilization is the longest stage in the history of human civilizations with the slowest progresses; however, the first stone tool, the first arrow, and the spark saved to make a fire all bore clear objectives when humans used them, and these actions were thus intentional human labor, showing the transition from instinctive behaviors such as fruit picking and fish hunting to intentional labor.

Such intentional or semi-intentional labor facilitated early humans to be distinguished from other animals and was thus the key to evolution from primates to humans. Is that development or evolutionary development? It is true that such development differed fundamentally from today's development in terms of its objectives, means, and ways; after all, the development in primitive civilization was perhaps just picking up a stone and using it as a tool or making an arrow while people's intention was probably just to get a fish or a bird. Nevertheless, what is *development*?

Development is a process of material exchange when something goes big from small and upgrades from a less-developed form. When early humans succeeded in catching a fish or a bird with the simplest tools possible and completed a process of the simplest material exchange through labor, it was a kind of tremendous development at the time, perhaps a milestone for human development no matter how trivial it may seem now.

As for agricultural and industrial civilizations, the goals of development were quite clear. Although the modes of development are quite different in the two civilizations, the tools used are all progressively revised and there is no doubt that both achieved more in development with time. The problem is, industrial civilization has overdeveloped in that countries are rated for their strength based on the development scale, societies are classified based on their level of development, and people are evaluated for their abilities based on personal development achievements and sometimes even on GDP.

Driven by such a development concept, production value, production, and maximization of profits have become the common goals of industrial civilization and humans have put themselves above the natural ecologic system by calling out slogans such as "people capable of conquering nature" and "beating nature." Unfortunately, however, things have not gone quite as intended. Such a mode of development has brought severe consequences, especially exhaustion of resources and exacerbation of environmental pollution. Only by this time have people realized that the development mode based on unilateral pursuit of production value, production, and maximization of profits is a dead end.

In contrast, the concept of development in ecologic civilization seeks coordinated development of populations, resources, environments, economies, and societies, and its value is oriented toward harmony between humans and nature, between humans and society, and between humans. The concept of development that seeks maximization of production and measures everything based on GDP is discarded; also discarded is the concept of development that wastes resources, pollutes the environment, harms the health of this generation, and compromises the development of the next. After all, when air is heavily polluted, PM 2.5 reaches level 4 or 5, and people are deprived of the freedom to breathe fresh air, what can we do with GDP? What is the use of a maximized profit? When values are oriented differently, the making of ecologic civilization becomes promising.

Positioning of ecologic civilization: higher and more comprehensive

People always look at the economic side when observing a civilization. It is not wrong as the economy is the base of all, but at the same time, observation of a civilization cannot always stay on the economic side and must touch on many other aspects, including ideologies, concepts, ethics, moralities, legal systems, politics, cultures, and institutions, which combined may give a comprehensive evaluation of a civilization. Observation of primitive civilization looks at the relationship between humans and nature and evaluates civilized behaviors of humans dominated by the nature-controlled system. Observation of agricultural civilization looks at a much wider range. Agricultural cultivation, irrigation, seed selection, and fertilization all progressed significantly in technology to meet the growing demands of humans; in particular, the revolutionary development of agrarian tools led to the plough, *hua*, shovels, and picks all being made of iron.

In addition, with agricultural development, literature, arts, operas and plays, music, and dance all prospered while the superstructures of societies such as politics found their unique shapes to generate civilizations that combined cultivation and feudal caste systems. Industrial civilization has based its economies on the market frame and boasted its ideologies as freedom, equality, and consciousness while putting the human-controlled system on top of the nature-controlled one, leading to confusing and upside-down positions of humans and nature with growing risks and crises.

In contrast to these three, ecologic civilization captures the reasonable cores of all of these civilizations – the respect of primitive civilization for the nature-controlled system, the achievements of the advancing agrarian tools in agricultural civilization, including those of positive ideologies, and the explosive forces of production in industrial civilization that have led to unprecedented scientific, technologic, and cultural accomplishments – and at the same time discards their negative effects, especially those in industrial civilization that have brought risks and damages to resources, environments, and cultures, in order to establish a whole new civilization that is superior to and more comprehensive than the previous three with their advantages integrated and disadvantages discarded. This is the original goal of ecologic civilization and its proper positioning among the four civilizations.

Choice of strategy: sustainable development

A later section in this book is devoted to sustainable development and the focus here is that ecologic civilization needs the awareness of sustainable development and a proper strategy. As already analyzed, before the emergence of mankind, a good ecologic system ran well on Earth, which repaired itself and evolved into new stages on its own after the movement of tectonic plates, eruption of volcanoes, and major earthquakes, and maintained the ecologic balance.

During the 5,000 years of agricultural civilization, the ecologic balance was more or less maintained while the natural, objective laws of evolution, transformation, absorption, cleanse, and material circulation were by and large kept, and humans lived in harmony with nature. There were of course small-scale damages. For example, people cut down trees and destroyed woods excessively to make way for cultivation, which led to damages to primary forests; however, these damages were only to a degree and were far away from ripping off the entire ecologic system. Why did primitive and agricultural civilizations manage to maintain a fairly good ecologic environment? There are two reasons from the perspective of society-controlling systems.

One reason is a small population. When humans distinguished themselves from other animals by completing the transformation from primates to humans, there were approximately 50 million humans on the earth, which translates into a population density of 0.4 per square kilometer (km^2). The world population did not reach 1.56000 billion until the end of the 19th century and the start of the 20th, when the population density was only 11.6 per km^2. With such small populations, together with the slow growth at the time, primitive civilization only saw simple reproduction and population growth increased in agricultural civilization with extremely limited scales. Therefore, humans were restricted to where they could reach and there were immense areas on the earth never touched by humans; of course the natural ecologic system could be preserved by and large. This, without question, fits with the codependent, changing relationship between the two systems of nature and humans.

The other reason is the underdevelopment of productive tools. In the age of primitive civilization, the major productive tools and weapons were fire, stone tools, and bows and arrows, which were already great achievements in human history. However, inventions and applications like these took so long as to make human progression seem trapped in stagnation or semi-stagnation.

In the age of agricultural civilization, iron tools such as spades, hoes, ploughs, and *hua* and black powder, printing, and scripts were invented, which also resulted in big leaps forward in the functions of productive tools and weapons. However, the leaps were also restricted to things that could be produced by hand. That is also to say, productive tools were principally manual workshops and labor was mostly conducted by individuals while humans and animals drove the operation of all tools with simple employment of some wind- and hydropower. Before monstrous nature, humankind seemed small, capable of producing limited products as well as damages; therefore, the pattern that the natural ecologic system had the say in everything was fundamentally in place.

Fundamental changes to this pattern came from the Industrial Revolution and industrial civilization. On one hand, the Industrial Revolution called out a large size of populations from nowhere miraculously, and the world had 7.30219 billion people in 2015 at a density of 54.4 per km^2. From the 115 years between 1900 and 2015, the world population saw a 2.68-fold net increase of 5.74219 billion, at an annual growth rate of 1.35%. The population density increased 135.0 fold at an annual growth rate of 4.4%.

The 20th century was unarguably the century with the largest scale and the fastest speed of population growth and the most rapid increase in population density, which altogether sent the world population to a record high.[2] Industrial civilization brought people to many places that had never been reached by primitive and agricultural civilizations and the world's untouched areas were acutely reduced; at the same time, humans' ability to interfere with the natural ecologic system grew miraculously and the chain that maintained the self-repair and self-reproduction of the natural ecologic balance was broken. The nature-controlled system thus malfunctioned and was subject to the human-controlled system to a degree.

Why are humans now so powerful in damaging and destroying nature? The answer is that humans now own powerful tools and weapons. As described earlier, mechanical tools have extended human bones, muscles, and limbs to reach considerably far and wide and significantly empowered humans. All of sudden, mankind became upright and grew big before nature. The increasingly empowered and strengthened humankind who happened to see nature as a resource reservoir that would never go exhausted began to dig it freely, and just like looting valuables, people from everywhere have made every effort to dig and develop the earth madly and to produce and consume endlessly. Eventually, when a large amount of wealth has been generated, all major resources seem near exhaustion, water, air, and soil are heavily polluted, and various harmful waste solids have piled up. Now people are forced to look back at their own behaviors and the paths they have taken and come to a reluctant conclusion that industrial civilization cannot sustain itself.

Ecologic civilization is based on industrial civilization and is the reasoned choice after the latter is faced with a dead end. Ecologic civilization highlights the importance of the ecologic environment, and emphasizes that humans and nature are codependent and inter-functional and live together. However, ecologic civilization is not only about the relationship between humans and nature. It is also about the relationships between humans and between humans and societies and encompasses all relationships between the nature- and human-controlled systems.

To realize ecologic civilization we must straighten out the relationships between humans and nature, between humans and societies, and between humans and find a path of coordinated development of populations, resources, environments, economies, and societies, a path of sustainable development. From the perspective of people-oriented development, sustainability must meet the demands of the current generation while bringing no harm to how the demands of future generations are met. Therefore, it must meet the demands of people for civilization development as well as a good ecologic environment to realize peace, harmony, and mutual development of humans and nature. To reach this goal, human development needs to be steered comprehensively from its continuity and sustainability. In general, development is in line with ecologic civilization as long as it is continuous and sustainable. In summary, to push for the realization of ecologic civilization, we must master the overall direction of sustainable development and raise awareness and understanding among people of its values, ideals, and strategies.

Choosing the strategy of sustainable development

Theories and practices of the strategy of sustainable development

Up until now, sustainable development has stayed only a proposed strategy because it has been advanced, discussed, and agreed upon with certain consensus in a series of international conferences. Many countries then followed suit and wrote their own action plans for sustainable development, which were meant to be implemented as national policies. Moreover, with heated attention on sustainable development from all social sectors, many theoretical studies have reached new accomplishments and studies with theories and practices combined have also made new conclusions. Now further, in-depth research on the theory of sustainable development has become possible and necessary.

Early ideas of sustainable development

Philosophers, politicians, and military strategists have long studied the relationships between a population and the economy and social development, which could be tracked back to ancient times. Ancient Greek philosopher Plato (427–347 B.C.) once stated in his book *On Politics* the following: a country cannot have too large a population for its area or too small. Another ancient Greek philosopher, Aristotle (384–322 B.C.), also expressed similar ideas in *Politics*: the ideal country is one with a proper population size. They both included population size as part of their ideal country, and from this perspective, they planted the seed of the theory of a moderate population.

In 1662, John Graunt, honored as the father of demography, published *Natural and Political Observations Made upon the Bills of Mortality*, in which he treated demography as an independent subject. After that, studies on population and its development progressed quickly. In 1798, Thomas Robert Malthus published *An Essay on the Principle of Population*, which had six editions in 28 years and exerted considerable impact. Whether Malthus was right or wrong with his points is a separate issue, but his work lit heated discussions that pushed the development of demography and economics. By the mid-19th century, British economist Edwin Cannan had put forward the theory of optimum population, which was later interpreted by H. Dalton, who also provided a formula to give the theory multilayered definitions.

Later, French demographer A. Sawvy differentiated between an economically moderate population, i.e., the size of the population that could gain the biggest profits or welfare for an economy, and a moderate population for power, i.e., the size of the population that best empowers a country. In 1972, a report from the Rome Club, *The Limits to Growth*, by Donella H. Meadows et al., was published in which it was argued that if the world population, industrialization, pollution, food production, and resource consumption maintained the same growth, the limits of the earth would be reached within 100 years and thus "zero growth" must be found. In the same year, "sustainable development" was first put forward at an international environmental conference held in Stockholm.

China boasts one of the world's ancient civilizations and there were arguments on whether a large or a small population was good as early as the Spring and Autumn and Warring States Periods in the 6th century B.C.. The subsequent dynasties observed populism, i.e., a large population was desired, although views kept emerging that argued for a moderate population. For example, Hong Liangji in the Qing Dynasty concluded that the growth of the means of livelihood was behind that of the population and his conclusion came earlier than Malthus's.

In the 1920s and 1930s, the school of sociology that favored population control introduced Western demography into China by writing books centered on "a moderate population." In the mid- to late 1950s, Ma Yichu published *A New Population Theory*, which was also centered on the point that population growth should accommodate to economic development as excessive population growth would hold back economic growth.

In the late 1970s, discussion arose of "two productions" when some scholars performed studies of what was the moderate population for China from multiple perspectives, which touched on aspects of sustainable development in attempt to seek a kind of development that might coordinate population and resources as well as population and economic growth.

The formation and the development of the strategy of sustainable development

The foregoing description has shown that more and more attention has been attracted to the contradiction between population growth and sustainability of resources and the environment since WWII. Sustainability, as a remarkable concept, was first put forward at an international conference. It later gained wide recognition in a series of international meetings with its meaning deepened, and eventually became a strategic goal for the international community.

In June 1972, the UN Conference on the Human Environment was held in Stockholm, the capital of Sweden, at which the *Declaration of the United Nations Conference on the Human Environment* was agreed upon. The principles of the declaration are that humans are produced by the environment while shaping it at the same time and that humans must inspect the impact of their actions on the environment. Also in the meeting, ideals such as "development that agrees with environmental demands," "development without damages," and "continuous and sustainable development" were proposed. This was the first time governments around the world gathered to discuss environmental problems in attempts to figure out how to safeguard the global environment, which also presented the concept of sustainable development before the world.

In 1987, *Our Common Future*, a report published by the UN's World Commission on Environment and Development (WCED), chaired by Gro Harlem Brundland, then the Norwegian prime minister, described sustainable development definitively from the three principles of fairness, sustainability, and commonness and explained that sustainable development would meet the needs of the present generation without compromising the ability of later generations to meet their own needs. This interpretation of the concept of sustainable development was widely accepted and had significant, long-lasting impact.

In June 1992, 183 countries and regions and 102 government heads participated in the UN Conference on Environment and Development in Rio de Janeiro, Brazil. The conference resulted in a series of important documents, including the *Rio Declaration on Environment and Development*, *Agenda 21*, *Framework Convention on Climate Change*, *Convention on Biological Diversity*, and *Forest Principles*, which negated the conventional development mode with high input, high output, high consumption, and high pollution prevalent since the Industrial Revolution and called for a new global "partnership" to maintain the environment, and sustainable development was affirmed through a declaration of the participants.

In September 1994, 182 countries participated in the International Conference on Population and Development (ICPD) in Cairo, Egypt, and the central topic of the conference was sustainable development. The *ICPD Program of Action* adopted at the conference stated that "human beings [were] at the center of sustainable development," which was an important complement to the *Rio Declaration* and *Agenda 21*. The large-scale growth of the world population was recognized, and the role of the population in sustainable development was emphasized.

In March 1995, the World Summit of Social Development was held in Copenhagen, Denmark. Many issues about sustainable development were discussed from the perspective of social development while social justice and international partnership were emphasized. Sustainable development was then extended from the environment, resources, populations, and economies to social aspects and became a systematic project for the whole society.

Many more international conferences were held subsequently and sustainability was further strengthened as a common, major problem facing humankind in the 21st century while the importance was underscored of controlling global population growth, saving up on energy and resources, and reducing environmental pollution. It's noteworthy that the UN Climate Change Conference held in Bali, Indonesia, in December 2007, discussed how to further reduce the emission of greenhouse gases after the *Kyoto Protocol* ended in 2012 with the reiteration that no one in the whole world could escape the influence of climate change. The conference agreed upon the *Bali Road Map* that aimed for advanced countries to take on their responsibilities and help developing countries reduce their emission of greenhouse gases. In 2009, the first negotiating meeting on climate change was held in Bonn, Germany in attempt to land the *Bali Road Map*.

From November 30 to December 11, 2015, the 21st UN Climate Change Conference was held in the Le Bourget exhibition center in the northern suburb of Paris, France. It was the 21st yearly session of the Conference of the Parties to the 1992 *UN Framework Convention on Climate Change* and the 11th session of the Meeting of the Parties to the 1997 *Kyoto Protocol*. One hundred and eighty-four countries submitted their *Intended Nationally Determined Contributions* that drafted their plans in response to climate change and covered 97.9% of global carbon emission. More than 150 national leaders and government heads attended the opening ceremony of the conference.

The nearly 200 parties to the *UN Framework Convention on Climate Change* agreed unanimously on the *Paris Agreement*, which specified the responsibilities among the international community to tackle climate change after the second term of the *Kyoto Protocol* ended in 2020, thus a new global agreement on emission reduction was reached under the framework of the *Convention* that was "binding and suitable to all parties."

The goal was set to maintain the average global temperature within 2 Celsius degrees higher than that before the Industrial Revolution and hopefully within 1.5 Celsius degrees. The *Paris Agreement* and other documents signed at the Paris climate change conference marked an important step forward in the international community's efforts to check climate change. The conference was a milestone as it preluded that the global climate management would enter a new, much stricter phase after 2020.

Ever since it was proposed, the strategy of sustainable development has been valued as an international guideline and a national-level development strategy and has been implemented after consensus was raised. Meanwhile, theoretical studies have also deepened and made several breakthroughs. Particularly, after the 1994 Cairo *ICPD Program of Action* stated that "human beings [were] at the center of sustainable development," studies of the status and function of human beings in sustainable development made substantial progresses. In my opinion, all development is physical transformation of resources, including natural and social resources. From this perspective, that "human beings are at the center of sustainable development" translates into the people-oriented ideal and strategy of sustainable development and it has the following six-fold meanings.

THE GOAL OF SUSTAINABLE DEVELOPMENT IS TO MEET THE NEEDS OF ALL-AROUND DEVELOPMENT OF PEOPLE

Development is supposed to meet people's needs, but with the advancement of the forces of social production, especially after the Industrial Revolution, when competitions grew increasingly intense and unprecedentedly large capital showed a strong tendency to augment its own value, countries and enterprises alike all started to chase the speed and scale of development, which has often derailed development from the track of meeting people's needs and sometimes onto the track of development for the sake of development.

Such a conventional mode of equating economic growth with development can only meet certain needs even if the development is not derailed from the people-oriented track, and many other needs are rarely or never met. In contrast, when the all-around development of humans is considered, needs from all aspects, including physical, mental, social, and cultural demands, are addressed. Among all these needs, the most basic is physical needs, and only when people's physical needs are met can reproduction of population be conducted continuously and production and reproduction of material means be operated normally.

The mental needs of people come next and they have become more and more important in the modern age because with society increasingly moving fast, people are heavily burdened mentally and mental health has become a social issue of common concern. In addition, according to the World Health Organization, being healthy does not only mean being disease free but also being physically and mentally healthy and socially well. Therefore, intensified social interaction is also characteristic of modern society; in addition, informatization and economic globalization have substantially augmented social interaction, modernization has shortened the temporal and spatial distances between people, and the demand for social communication has grown rapidly. As for cultural needs, they are particularly attended to in the modern age.

From the perspective of the entire history of human development, economic growth is a matter of time: it comes sometimes early and sometimes late and goes advanced or stays behind, yet it always comes. It is just like a marathon race where different people lead the race in different segments. In contrast, cultures descend through history and are relatively stable; thus different cultures are usually extremely hard to integrate fundamentally and cultural clashes are common. Therefore, to meet people's cultural needs, especially advanced cultural needs, we must look at even higher levels. Furthermore, it is worth reiterating that it is the all-around needs that are to be met and satisfaction of one need may not come at the cost of others. For example, in order to meet the demand for food, people have destroyed woods for cultivation and transformed pastoral lands into agricultural lands, which has led to loss of soil and water and a dryer and harsher climate. Another example is in agriculture. In order to increase the production per unit of land, people have expanded the use of fertilizers and pesticides, which has led to serious pollution of water and soil. Such production of grains and development of the chemical industry have, on one hand, met people's demand for food and maintained the reproduction of population, and on the other hand, damaged the environment humans relied on for survival, compromised human health, and hindered the pursuit of people's all-around development.

Sustainable development is targeted at creating a natural and social environment that benefits people's all-around development and discards the way that meets one need at the cost of others. From this perspective, the statement that "humans are at the center of sustainable development" in the 1994 Cairo *IPCD Program of Action* uses humans to describe people's all-around development and thus development is to meet the demands of people's all-around development.

SUSTAINABLE DEVELOPMENT FIRST CONSIDERS THE NEEDS OF THE PRESENT GENERATION

A review of sustainable development practices since the 1970s showed that the idea was first proposed by political leaders and scholars in advanced countries, a few of whom had a hidden agenda to use it to restrain and limit developing countries from advancing. Fortunately, however, multiple rounds of discussions and arguments helped people reach a consensus little by little: developed countries, with their endless efforts to push for industrialization, especially traditional industrialization, should be held accountable for the deteriorating global environment that hampers sustainable development of the world. That is why an act was passed at the 1992 UN Conference on Environment and Development in Rio de Janeiro that developed countries would spend 0.7% of their gross domestic national product annually as an official development assistance (ODA) fund to help developing countries eradicate poverty and manage the environment.

For more than a decade, only a few countries in Northern Europe actually kept their promise and many did not. One thing is for sure: sustainable development does not negate development; instead, developing countries should speed up their development to meet the needs of the present generation and to eliminate poverty. If the demand of the present generation for means of livelihood cannot be met, crimes may result from poverty and social orders may be lost. If the demand of the present working-age population for natural and production capital in employment cannot be met, a large number of unemployed will result who may have nothing good to do but to make trouble, society will lose stability, and normal development will be hampered, let alone sustainable development. Therefore, development is the precondition of sustainable development and it aims to first meet the demands of the present generation. Particularly, developing countries should position their development to center on economic growth and stay away from the misconception that sustainable development means reduced development or none at all.

SUSTAINABLE DEVELOPMENT DOES NOT COMPROMISE THE ABILITY OF FUTURE GENERATIONS TO MEET THEIR NEEDS

Sustainable development emphasizes the continuity of development, and the continuity is not reflected by one or a few economic indicators, but by the generational equality of population, economies, and social development, which fully embodies the development ideal that is oriented toward people, a basic point of the interpretation of sustainable development in Brundland's report, *Our Common Future*.

Conventional development equates development with economic growth, which leads to pursuit of economic growth in every way possible, and the resulting increasing pollution of the environment, waste of resources, and even exhaustion of some resources have hampered the ability of future generations to meet their own development needs. Therefore, sustainable development is based on generational equality, a fundamental principle of the concept. After all, if the development of the present generation comes at the cost of the benefits of future generations, leaving many hurdles for the offspring to pursue further development, the principle of generational equality is then destroyed and there will be no sustainable development.

THE ULTIMATE ENGINE THAT DRIVES DEVELOPMENT IS HUMAN CAPITAL

Throughout human history, natural capital, output or production capital, human capital, and social capital have taken turns to dominate human development. Overall, in agrarian society and all types of societies before that, economic and social development was dominated by natural capital. After the Industrial Revolution in the mid-18th century, output or production capital became increasingly powerful in that the primary accumulation of capital first laid the foundation for industrialization and traditional industrialization then expanded consecutively with the continuous accumulation of output capital. Unfortunately, economic and social development that relied primarily on natural and output capital, especially traditional industrialization, was usually accompanied by predatory exploitation of resources, leading to serious damages to the resources and to environmental pollution. After WWII, the new technological revolution pioneered by microelectronic technologies upgraded the traditional industrialization and laid the foundation for the next technological revolution.

At present, the modern technological revolution, marked by genetic technologies, life sciences, and nanotechnology, has already been initiated. The human genomic mapping was finished ahead of schedule and it will reveal the secrets of life for us, and the new development of genetic and cloning technologies with life sciences taking the lead will create a whole new era of science and technology. Given these circumstances, the value of the knowledge, techniques, experiences, and health possessed by humans, i.e., the role of human capital and all human capital-associated social capital such as organization, management, and marketing, will be fully exerted to determine how development takes the next step.

Therefore, from the perspective of sustainable development, the reliance on natural and output capital must be shifted to human capital and its associated social capital in order to fully explore natural resources, improve the efficiency of resource use, and effectively save on resources and protect the environment. To push for human capital as the major engine to drive development is a fundamental transformation of development ideals that touches the very original driver of human development.

HARMONIOUS DEVELOPMENT OF HUMANS AND NATURE

Advancement in sustainable development is primarily reflected in a better ecologic environment, remarkable improvement in the efficiency of resource employment, and harmony of humans and nature. To realize this harmonious, all-around development we must raise awareness of coordinated economic growth, including intensive growth of the economy on its own development and coordination between economic and social development. Raising awareness of all-around social development, aside from solving the problems left behind in the social realities, fundamentally requires understanding the necessity of coordination between population, resources, and the environment and the harmony of humans and nature. We emphasize the coordinated development of economies and the all-around advancement of human society because our ultimate goal is to better solve the problems of population, resources, and the environment and to promote the harmony of the three and the harmony of humans and nature, i.e., to position humankind properly in nature. After all, humans come from nature and will eventually go back to nature; thus any viewpoint that despises nature and any action that treats nature arbitrarily, including those inappropriate slogans such as "conquering nature," are wrong and harmful.

HARMONIOUS DEVELOPMENT OF HUMANS AND SOCIETIES

A society is the sum of the economic base and superstructures and reflects the relations between humans who are linked to each other with mutual material conditions. Therefore, a society is first grounded on the economic base that comprises population reproduction, natural resources, labor and jobs, social security, science and education, public hygiene and health care, and infrastructure, and then formed with ideologies, including politics, laws, religions, arts, and philosophical thoughts, and the state apparatus, including politics, laws, and military power that support the ideologies.

The basic theory of sustainable development of societies touches the very base of societies in that an economic base that can facilitate the all-around development of humans is to be established through proper social causes with the advance of the forces of social production and the change in the relations of production. As a result, the superstructures will change and advanced ideologies and government organization will emerge, pushing societies to march forward.

The coordinated development of humans and societies is integrative as populations, economies, resources, and the environment are an integrated whole to develop in coordination, and its goal is social harmony, which will be realized by properly solving the reoccurring problems of population, unemployment, education, environment, poverty, and safety.

The theoretical framework of sustainable development

The strategy system of sustainable development

Population, resources, environment, economic development, and social development are five factors that make up the framework of the strategy of sustainable development. There is no consensus on their relationships. Some put ecologic relationships at the center of the framework and believe that sustainable development should move around ecologic balance. Some put population at the center and argue that sustainable development is dominated by humans. Some hold that economies are the base of all development, including sustainable development, and that economies are decisive.

In my opinion, the theoretical framework of sustainable development can only be decided through theoretical and practical exploration that may clarify the relationships between the five factors. My basic points are the following.

Resources – the starting point and condition of sustainable development. Looking at development, all sorts of development, including sustainable development, from the perspective of resources, we may say that development is an exchange of substances: exchange of substances of natural resources, of social resources, and more often, of natural and social resources combined. Therefore, no development is possible without any exchange of resources and resources are the starting point and the condition of sustainable development.

Population – the key to overall sustainable development. The exchange of substances of natural resources without humans involved is evolution of the natural world, and what is called development and sustainable development must involve humans in exchanges and the exchanges must be made by the human will. According to the UN's WCED report in 1987, *Our Common Future*, sustainable development "meets the needs of the present generation without compromising the ability of later generations to meet their own needs." Such a definition of sustainable development from the perspective of generational relationship has raised consensus among many and the principle of sustainable development is thus agreed upon to orient toward people. Whether a kind of development is sustainable largely depends on changes in the population, including its size, quality, and structure. Human productive and social activities, or economic and social development, shape resources and the environment, which becomes a development mode in a particular historical stage.

Environment – the destination and goal of sustainable development. With explosive growth of the world population and the increasing ability of humankind to make exchanges of substances, particularly the fast-paced industrialization after WWII, the environment has been seriously damaged. People have started to reflect on their conventional mode of development. What will become of us if such development is continued? What are the destination and the goal of development? The reflection has led to a series of international environmental conferences since the 1970s at which environmental issues and sustainable development were brought up and discussed. In fact, the idea of sustainable development originally occurred to people in response to environmental problems. The environment is the alarm of every mode of development and sustainable development is ultimately aimed to create an environment that benefits the all-around development of humans.

Economic and social development – the channel and the regulator of sustainable development. Sustainable development requires the coordination of population, resources, and the environment. How are they coordinated? They are coordinated through economic and social development. On one hand, the present ability of people to make exchanges of substances and the environmental conditions are the consequences of past economic and social development. After all, environmental situations are always associated with a certain degree of economic and social development. On the other hand, resource exchanges and the environmental quality may be modified to facilitate sustainable development through adjusting the mode of economic growth and social development and through structural adjustments to economies and societies.

Based on the five factors of population, resources, environment, economy, and society in sustainable development, the theoretical pillars of the framework of the strategy of sustainable development may be described as follows.

The first pillar is the all-around moderate population theory. As described earlier, the conventional "moderate population" theory is restricted to the size of a population and describes whether a population is too large or too small and seeks its moderate size by examining changes in the number of people in the population and its relationship with resources and development. In contrast, the strategy of sustainable development not only looks at the number of people and its changes but also is fairly demanding for population health in physical strength, education, and civility, the age and sex structures of the population, and the urban and rural distribution and geographic distribution of the population in order to find the optimal combination of population size, quality, and structure and of the population with the resources, the environment, the economy, and social development. That is also to say, the strategy of sustainable development requires an all-around moderate population.

The second pillar is the scarce resources theory. By the definition that development, including sustainable development, is essentially exchange of substances of natural resources, a scientific view of resources and development is needed. A view of resources and development comprises basic points of how to interpret the status and the function of resources in development, which is preconditioned by the understanding that resources, mainly natural resources, are limited. The issue of natural resources is like a truth both absolute and relative in that resources are absolute and unlimited while at the same time relative and limited. They are absolute and unlimited because humans have growing potential and increasing capacity to learn, explore, and employ resources and the availability of resources also grows as previously unusable resources keep becoming usable and sometimes even highly valuable new resources emerge with continuous advances in science and technology.

For example, nuclear fission was only discovered 70 years ago, but we've witnessed the explosion of the first nuclear bomb and construction of large-scale nuclear plants and we all believe now that nuclear energy is an importance resource and can initiate a new era of energy. Meanwhile, under any given economic and technological level, the amount of any resource is limited, and so is the degree by which people learn, explore, and employ it; therefore, resources are also relative and limited and they cannot be forever available for us to take and use. A right view of resources and development must then be based on the unification of the absoluteness and relativity and of the limitedness and unlimitedness. For sustainable development, what is the most important is to raise the awareness of development with scarce resources, i.e., resources, especially natural resources, are always scarce for human society in a certain development stage and development can only be sought after it is based on economical and reasonable exploration and employment of resources.

The aforementioned report *The Limits to Growth* has a far too grim conclusion, which the authors also admitted when they later made modifications. However, the warning in the report, like a yellow card on consumption, has attracted intense attention that the growing population with people's pursuit of high-quality lives boosts economic growth, which accelerates exploration and employment of resources, which in turn leads the consumption of resources to exceed the growth of the population. Sustainable development is inevitably faced with progressive consumption of resources, and the awareness of development with scarce resources must be raised.

The third pillar is the ecologic system theory. The idea of sustainable development was first put forward at an international environmental conference. Discussions about it have been kept heating up due to people's close attention to environmental issues for the next more than 40 years. Developed countries have called out in surprise: the global environment has been severely damaged and conventional industrialization can no longer be continued. Developing countries are also concerned with environmental damages despite their focus on economic development and that is why many consensuses about resource protection and environmental issues have been reached around the world. A series of international conferences on sustainable development have been held and announcements, conventions, statements, and action plans have been issued focused on environmental issues.

Some environmental scholars of international organizations interpret sustainable development from the perspective of the environment and ecologic balance and define it as protection and intensification of the productive and renewal ability of the environmental system (the International Association for Ecology [INTECOL] and International Union of Biological Sciences [IUBS], 1991) while others describe sustainable development as an optimal ecologic system to support the ecologic entirety and the realization of humans' desire for survival and livelihood and to sustain the environment on which humans rely (Forman, R. T. T., 1991). Maintaining a good environment and ecologic balance is the ultimate goal of sustainable development, and approaches to population, resources, economic development, and social development from this perspective help us understand development based on the ecologic system.

The fourth pillar is the overall economic benefits theory. Conventional economic development is after the maximization of production amount and value, through which profit is maximized and enterprises obtain clear benefits and interests. After Keynesianism started to be popular in the 1930s, many countries took turns to use gross national product (GNP) as the major, and sometimes even the only, indicator to measure their economic development, and the mode of industrialization with scale economies has since become the only choice for development. The idea of sustainable development targets exactly at the mode by arguing that development could look after not only the benefits of enterprises but also the benefits of the entire society and that development could protect not only the benefits of the present generation but also the benefits of future generations, setting forth the view of development with overall economic benefits. If profit maximization was the principal guideline and theory to guide the previous economic operation, maximization of overall benefits is the goal of economies in sustainable development and the new concept and theory to guide economic development. The new concept and theory of economic development has a three-layered meaning.

The first layer is the development concept of quality and benefits. The conventional economic development is simply after the growth in production amount, production value, and profits and equates development with economic growth and economic growth with growing numbers, which is therefore a mode of extensive expansion and reproduction. Such a mode of industrialization has already been at a dead end; after all, economic development is dependent not only on the amount of products but increasingly on the quality. Given the various sorts of "industrial syndrome" that have emerged since the beginning of industrialization, between the growing numbers and the quality of economic growth, sustainable economic development values benefits and quality and seeks survival and development based on improvement in quality.

The second layer is the development concept of spatial benefits in a broad sense. It aims to get out of the sphere of an enterprise or a region and to cover all exterior effects, including resources, the environment, and social development, when evaluating economic benefits so that the benefits may be objectively evaluated and development taken from economic growth and from both the interior and exterior effects combined. Thus two types of input–output ratios are formed: one is in the narrow economic sense and is the ratio of investment in production or operation to output benefits, and the other is in the broad spatial sense and is the ratio of societal investment in production or operation to output benefits. The conventional concept of economic development only values the former ratio while that of sustainable development values both.

In addition, design of the development indicator system should also look at a wider range than a single indicator of GDP and choose those that are more representative of the broad spatial sense. For example, an evaluation system including indicators of economic, social, environmental, cultural, and life quality has been in effect in the United States since the 1960s; the World Bank has adopted a variety of indicators, including per capita GNP, average annual inflation rate, life expectancy at birth, and adult literacy rate, to evaluate development for years; and the United Nations Development Program (UNDP) uses a human development index (HDI) and a physical quality of life index (PQLI).

The third layer is the development concept of long-term benefits. Of course, economic development values the current economic benefits; after all, any goal of economic development is and should be concrete with clear, short-term effects. Sustainable development values long-term benefits while taking care of the short-term at the same time and negates any practice that seeks short-term benefits at the cost of long-term ones. In fact, when Mrs. Brundland defined sustainable development as something that "[would] not compromise the ability of future generations to meet their needs," both generational relations of population reproduction and the relation of short-term and long-term benefits were taken into account. In this sense, the focus of sustainable development on long-term benefits is a definitive marker that differentiates it from the conventional development concept of industrialization.

In addition, exactly because it is focused on long-term benefits, sustainable development evaluates the accumulation of economic growth as well as the impact the growth has on its own, i.e., whether the growth strengthens or compromises further development. The latter is of course unsustainable. The focus of the development concept of overall economic benefits is on the nurturing of sustainability so that development potential is guaranteed to emerge continuously and development continuity is warranted.

The fifth pillar is the social coordinated development theory. Exchange of substances of natural and social resources in a society is completed through production of material means, population reproduction, and environmental production, which becomes the economic base of the society. Meanwhile, a superstructure, i.e., political, legal, religious, art, and philosophical ideologies in a particular historical stage and the state apparatus that sustains the dominating ideologies, is also formed that accommodates to the forces of production and the changes and development in the relations of production.

As a result, the movement of the contradictory economic base and the superstructure is also formed. The basic theory of social sustainable development is to advance social causes with the development of social forces of production and the changes in the relations of production to establish an economic base that may promote the all-around development of humans. Accordingly, the superstructure also changes with the emergence of advanced ideologies and government management agencies and organizations that push the society to march forward. Coordinated development of a society is integrative in that it integrates the development of the population, the economy, the resources, and the environment and emphasizes hot social issues such as population, unemployment, environment, education, poverty, and security.

The demographic view of the strategy of sustainable development

The strategy of sustainable development that is oriented toward people needs to integrate the sustainable development of population into itself to persist with the all-around development of people as principle and human capital as the major engine to drive development and to seek coordinated development of population with resources, the environment, the economy and the society and their sustainable development. To land such a strategy of sustainable development, we must first reveal the proper position of population in the strategy as well as its relationship with resources, the environment, the economy, and social development so that the direction, strategic key points, and decisions may be specified.

SUSTAINABLE DEVELOPMENT OF POPULATION AND RESOURCES

The idea of sustainable development holds that resources, especially natural resources, are scarce and the scarcity is closely associated with demographic changes and development. China is a typical example. By population, China is the largest country in the world, and China has fairly copious resources with complete variety so that an independent system of the national economy has been established based on domestic resources. However, there is significant lack and absolute shortages of some important natural resources such as arable lands, fresh water, and minerals that are all directly associated with the survival and development of the population. There is also a structural shortage of resources in that some highly demanded, important resources such as oil, natural gas, iron, manganese, bronze, aluminum, gold, and silver are not abundant while some in low demand are, such as tungsten, antimony, molybdenum, and rare-earth mineral.

In addition, there is an application shortage in that some minerals are deeply buried or coexistent with others, which makes it highly difficult, expensive, and technologically challenging to dig for and use the minerals and their exploration and employment are therefore limited. What deserves the most attention is that the large population in China, 1.375 billion now, leads the per capita possession of natural resources to fall to an extremely low level.

The issue was given special attention in *Readings for Cadres on the Sustainable Development of Population, Resources, and the Environment*, for which I was the liaison with three pertinent ministers as editors. In the book, great efforts are made to coordinate the data from various sources that are often contradictory to one another and to offer pictures as accurate as possible through organizing the data from authorities. The amount of the major resources and their per capita possession in China at the turn of the 21st century provided in the book are listed next.[3]

In 2000, the world per capita area of land was 2.259 hectares and that of arable land was 0.230 hectares. The two numbers were 0.784 and 0.077 hectares in China, which were 34.7% and 33.5% of the world averages, respectively. The per capita area of woodland in China was 20% of the world average, and that of grassland was 50%. A low proportion of the land resource might be developed and employed and only 24.6% of the undeveloped land resource had potential for development, but these lands were all of low quality, had a fragile ecologic system, and were hard to develop.

China is rich in mineral resources. Among the 171 mineral reserves and the 156 minerals with known reserves, the mineral resources in China accounted for 12% of the world total in 2000, ranking third in the world following the United States and Russia. The per capita amount of mineral resources was 58% of the world average, ranking 53rd.

As of 2000, the global average annual renewable water resources were 41,022 cubic kilometers (km^3) and it was 2,812.4 km^3 in China, only 6.9% of the world resources. The per capita resources were 7,176 cubic meters (m^3) in the world and 2,292 m^3 in China, or 31.9% of the world resources. In addition, the water resource is unevenly distributed in China in that the per capita possession of water in the north is only 5% of that in the south. It is also unevenly distributed by season in that rainfall is concentrated in summer and autumn, especially during the transition of the two seasons.

When it comes to the area of territorial sea, China is also a large country. However, the per capita area was only 0.0027 km^3 in 2000, one-tenth of the world average. Ocean resources, including biological, nonbiological, and spatial resources, are poor with an excessively low per capita amount.

In terms of biological resources, we only possess 4% of the world's forest area and 3% of the world's growing stock. The per capita area of woodland was 0.11 hectares in China in 2000 with the growing stock being 8.6 m^3, accounting for 12.5% and 14.2% of the world numbers, respectively. In terms of grassland, China possessed 400 million hectares in 2000, ranking second in the world and the per capita area of grassland also reached about half of the world average. However, the ratio of high-, medium-, and low-quality grassland is around 2:4:4, showing a sharp problem of grassland quality.

Other resources such as air and natural sceneries all have similar situations to these. In terms of development, with socioeconomic development during the more than 60 years since the establishment of the new China, especially the recent 30 years with consecutive, rapid development, consumption of resources showed sudden increases under the extensive growth that was dominated by investment in fixed assets. The "capital of coal," the "capital of bronze," and the "capital of oil" that once prospered have all become cities with exhausted resources. Important resources have shown apparent reduction, and land area has decreased with worsening quality. Water resources are not sufficient to meet demands, rivers stop flowing, underground water has a decreasing water table, and the quality of water is also decreasing, and all of these have shown an increase trend. The crisis of mineral resource shortage is emerging with decreasing reserves-to-production ratios. Biological resources have been affected by damages to wood, retraction of grassland, desertification of land, shrinkage of water areas, and frequent natural disasters, biodiversity is threatened, and it is particularly worrisome that species have shown a decrease trend.

In addition, there is a remarkable weighted effect of population on the consumption of resources. Resource consumption does not linearly increase with population. It increases by a factor of a coefficient, i.e., exponentially. As people have unlimited lust for high-quality lives, socioeconomic development is certainly fueled by that lust, which is then needed for development; however, the lust also adds an exponential coefficient to resource consumption, which cannot be overlooked.

For example, in 1949, when the People's Republic of China was founded, only 158,000 tons of steel and 130,000 tons of steel products could be produced by the entire country. Let us suppose that all could be consumed by production and daily lives, then every person consumed 0.29 kg steel and 0.24 kg steel products. In 2015, 803.825 million tons of crude steel and 1.123496 billion tons of steel products were produced by the entire country with per capita production of 584.5 kg and 817.3 kg, respectively, which were also 2015.5 and 2818.3 times more than those in 1949.[4] Apparently, the addition of steel and steel product consumption for every added person in 2015 was astonishingly higher than those in 1949. In fact, the weight population growth brings to resource consumption is still on the rise.

SUSTAINABLE DEVELOPMENT OF POPULATION AND ENVIRONMENT

The history of environmental evolution has shown that it is closely associated with changes and development of population while witnessing population growth and increasing domination of human activities. The impact that changes in and development of population have on the environment may be summarized in the following three aspects.

First, a simple arithmetic calculation will tell that metabolic excretes increase with population growth, which will certainly impact the environment and its quality.

Second, population has a weighted effect on resource consumption, as already described, and the weighted growth of consumption also means weighted growth of wastewater, waste gases, and solid waste, i.e., the weighted effect is also on the relationship between changes in population and the environment.

Third, unprecedented pressure has been felt by the environment with accelerating industrialization, urbanization, and the urban–rural distribution of population. Not only have solid waste and water pollution been growing with the population, but climate change is also closely associated with changes in population.

Most participants in the UN's climate change conference in Bali, Indonesia in December 2007 agreed that global warming had mainly been caused by population growth and strengthened human activities, which had led to large-scale increases in the emission of carbon dioxide, methane, and nitrous oxide and remarkably concentrated greenhouse gases. The view has been widely accepted. In the fifth assessment report on climate change from 2013 to 2014 issued by the UN, the degree by which human activities had impacted global warming was adjusted from "very high" – over 90% probability – to "extremely high" – over 95% probability.

At the 21st UN Climate Change Conference held in Paris, France in 2015, the nearly 200 parties of the *UN Framework Convention on Climate Change* passed the *Paris Agreement* smoothly and called for a swift arrival at the emission peak of greenhouse gases so that "zero emission" would be realized in the second half of the 21st century. Also at the conference, a meaningful transition was made in how to implement the emission reduction agreed among the international community, i.e., from mandatory implementation demanded from the top down to the bottomup and voluntary implementation "decided by countries to choose their own contributions to the reduction," and the transition was also attached with much expectation.

Developed countries promised to continue to take the lead on emission reduction and to strengthen help to developing countries in funds and technologies. For example, the United States proposed to reduce 28% of the emission of greenhouse gases in 2025 compared to 2005. China promised, in its "country voluntary contribution" document, to reach the emission peak of carbon dioxide by 2030 while trying to peak as early as possible, to decrease the carbon dioxide emission per GDP unit by 60–65% compared to 2005, to make nonfossil energy account for approximately 20% of all primary energy consumption, and to increase the forest growing stock by 4.5 billion m^3. During the Paris conference, China was making the 13th Five-Year Plan for economic and social development and the aforementioned goals concerning the emission of carbon dioxide were included in the plan and thus warranted.[5]

SUSTAINABLE DEVELOPMENT OF POPULATION AND ECONOMY

The descriptions of the theory of sustainable development have illustrated that a population's accommodation to and coordination with economic development is basic to the realization of the population's accommodation to and coordination with resources, the environment, and social development. Later, another perspective is taken to describe a population's accommodation to and coordination with economic development in a macroscopic and a microscopic frame.

First, to illustrate the relationship between population and economic development in the macroscopic frame, there are two views that are different from and even completely contrasting to each other.

One is a pessimistic view. The most representative of those holding the view are Malthus and the subsequent Malthusians. From Malthus's *An Essay on the Principle of Population* to *The Limits to Growth* by the Rome Club, worries concerning population growth were prevalent from arguments on how population growth exceeded the growth of the means of livelihood to descriptions of industrialization, resource exhaustion, and worsening pollution, among which lines such as "population explosion" and "the end of the world" were most striking. To check population growth, Malthus proposed in the first edition of *An Essay on the Principle of Population* to use two measures – wars and plague as "positive checks" and celibacy and birth control as "preventative checks" – and he later softened his position on how to resolve surplus population for the "positive checks" were rarely mentioned in the later editions of the *Essay*. Neo-Malthusian scholars such as F. A. Pearson and W. Vogt do not agree on the "positive checks" and called for birth control so that zero and negative population growth would be realized through long-term, consecutive decreases in fertility rates and there would be no surplus population.

The other view is optimistic. Those holding this view are not concerned with the pressure on economic growth brought by population growth. On the contrary, they believe that the latter brings demands and engines to economic development, which is necessary for the former. John Maynard Keynes examined the world economic crisis from 1929 to 1933 and published his influential work, *The General Theory of Employment, Interest, and Money*, in 1936, in which he described that population, level of life, and capital coefficient were the three basic elements of economic development and that the major cause of the Great Depression was "insufficient effective demand." Insufficient effective demand results from decreases in fertility rates, and elevating fertility rates to ensure a stable growth of population is important to escape the crisis and to promote economic growth.

Later, American economist A. H. Hansen and British economist R. F. Harrod built upon and further developed Keynes's theories and attributed long-term economic stagflation to decreases in fertility rates and the low and zero growth of the changing population. It is also worthwhile to mention that some later influential figures in development and institutional economics never called themselves holders of the optimistic view, but they almost never showed any mark of Malthusianism or neo-Malthusianism in their works; instead, they elaborated on some aspects of the relationship between population and economies and made certain breakthroughs, such as the theoretical work by Lewis in his dual-sector model and that by Kuznets in his study of population and economic growth.

Second, there is also the microscopic frame. People holding this frame have proposed and elaborated on the cost-benefit theory of raising children and discussed reproduction decisions of individuals and families based primarily on the consumption demand theory that takes children as enduring consumer goods. As described earlier, the prominent holders of this view are Leibenstein, Easterlin, Becker, and Caldwell, whose arguments are not repeated here. What is worth noting is that studies of the microscopic relationship between population and economic development have made some progress while stimulating studies of the scale, structure, function, and life cycle of families, which is important to adjustment to family economies and reproductive behaviors to make them coordinate with and accommodate to each other.

These theories and practices of accommodating and coordinating population and economic development from both the macroscopic and microscopic frames are not only concerned with the number of people in a population but also with a population's quality and structure. Most of the proposed theories are concerned with the number of people in a population; after all, changes in the number are given more attention in practice to their coordination with and accommodation to economic development and more actions are taken against them. However, since the new technological revolution was taken to a whole new stage dominated by life sciences after the beginning of the 21st century with new levels of informatization and economic globalization, the impact of population health has become more and more remarkable and human capital has shown strengthening effect on economic development. A fairly lengthy analysis has been made on this point in the section of population health and economic and technological advancement in this book, while at the same time, considerable space was devoted to population structure, especially the paired analysis of the changes in the working-age population and economic development, population aging and social security, population urbanization as part of population distribution structure and structural adjustment of industries, and population geographic distribution and layout of the forces of production. In fact, all these aspects must be taken into account when whether population and economic development are coordinated with and accommodated to each other is considered.

SUSTAINABLE DEVELOPMENT OF POPULATION AND SOCIETY

In the strategy of sustainable development between population and resources, environment, economy, and society, the accommodation and coordination of a population and society are integrative. The factors of population, resources, environment, and economy are all confined in a given social background, and how they are coordinated and accommodated depends on how integrated they are in the society. Improving the integrating ability of a society cannot ignore the impact of population size and quality while it is closely associated with population structure. When it comes to China, the following three types of integration should be paid particular attention to.

The first is the integration of economic and social development. The history of developed countries and some developing countries has already shown that it is not a good practice to advance the economy first and develop the society next. That is because economic development usually leads to population problems, unemployment, pollution, serious waste of resources, and a widening gap between the rich and the poor, and these social problems are not only totally against the ideal of all-round development of people but also will hinder further economic development when left unsolved to a degree. The idea of sustainable development argues for timely intervention in social problems while developing the economy so that the economy and the society may be synchronized and coordinated in development. This will not only benefit the construction of a harmonious and advanced society, but it is also necessary for smooth development of the economy.

The second is the integration of the development of the thrice industries. The structure between the primary, secondary, and tertiary industries reflects the economic structure in a given development stage and the population structure of employment while at the same time showing a certain social structure and how advanced the society is. In fact, many industries, such as medical services, public health, insurance, environmental protection, commerce, food and drinks, and services, are all closely associated with social development, and the proportion of the tertiary sector of the GDP mirrors the development of social causes and whether social development is coordinated with economic development. In theory, there is an appropriate proportion of the tertiary industry for countries at every development stage. After all, an excessively high proportion traps a country in burdens of social welfare and hinders its economic development and social advancement and an excessively low proportion may hold its economic development and reforms, which also hinders its economic development and social advancement.

The third is the integration of domestic and foreign affairs. With economic development and advances in science and technology, the distances between countries and regions have been shortened and connections increased; meanwhile, how a country is doing economically may affect development in the surrounding regions, sometimes even countries and regions far away, in ways that cannot be overlooked. For example, the emission of carbon dioxide and sulfur dioxide of a country or region may affect the air quality of neighboring countries and regions, coastal pollution may spread to international waters, and the spread of acid rain may be closely watched by many countries and regions for its remarkable harms.

At present, the idea of sustainable development has already been deeply rooted in people's minds and a series of international contracts have been publicized, while the economic development of a country with its air, river, and sea quality is closely watched by all other countries, regions, and pertinent international organizations. The social issues that are inseparable from sustainable development, such as poverty, intelligence property, and environmental laws, are also valued by countries and international organizations around the world.

Due to controversy on the nature of human rights, more and more consensuses have been reached about maintaining people's basic rights such as right of survival and right of development, although a few still use human rights as an excuse to advance their political agendas, and the true situations of human rights are on the hot spot of the international community. Now that sustainable development has walked to today, every country is trying to shape its own image, an image that integrates economic development, environmental situations, and social advancements. Countries and regions are also evaluated by their images on where they are on the path to sustainable development and the progression of their development.

Exploring the path of sustainable development for the population

This book is devoted to the search for an optimal path for China's development. Where is the path? Ultimately, the path leads the population to sustainable development. That is because China, with the largest population in the world as of now, is considerably affected and influenced by the situation of its population while at the same time, the Chinese people share a common dream, one aspired to for a century, of socioeconomic development toward the great revival of the Chinese nation. The key here is persistence with a scientific concept of development in today's practices to advance development, i.e., what we want is sustainable but not unsustainable development. If we can find the path of sustainable development for the population with clear visions for the future to carry on all of our past glories and to further advance, not only will the great revival of the Chinese nation be realized, but the ideal of "integration of *tian*[universe, nature] and mankind," proposed by Ruists more than 2,000 years ago, will emerge on the eastern horizon of the earth, shining on the healthy progress of the human race in the 21st century.

The "three-step" strategy of China's population development

To find a path of sustainable development for the population, we must consider various aspects of the population, the resources, the environment, the economy, and the society and find corresponding development strategies with tactics and policies. This book is focused on population and associated demographic issues and therefore offers particular description of the strategy of population development.

The basic foothold of population strategy

For quite a while, the word *strategy* has become immensely popular around the globe and numerous strategies took turns to pop up and many have been overwhelmed by them. Therefore, before any discussion of the strategy of population development, a certain degree of clarification must be made to the definition of *strategy*. *Strategy* was originally used as a military term. In the West, *strategy* came from the Greek word *strategos*, which means a military general or a regional leader, and it was later developed as a military term to mean the overall plans and schemes in military operations.

In China, strategic thoughts can be tracked back to *The Art of War* (*Sunzi Bingfa*, also called *Sunwu Bingfa* or *Sunzi Bingshu*) written by Sun Wu more than 2,500 years ago. The book is a treatise of war tactics, plans, and schemes that are generally applicable, and it comprises great wisdom and planning on how to dwarf enemies and win wars; therefore, it is a military treatise of strategies. From these origins, strategies that were originally used in wars were generalized and applied to many economic and social areas in the subsequent thousands of years, resulting in today's development strategies in all areas, including industry, agriculture, science and technology, education, culture, population, resource, environment, and national defense. However, no matter how many strategies there are, they must follow certain physical rules, which are the common nature of all strategies.

First, strategies cover long terms. The primary goal of having a strategy is to achieve the ultimate victory; therefore, everything goes with the point that "whoever laughs last, laughs best" and a single loss or a temporary failure is not taken with much weight. A good example is the contention between Chu and Han more than 2,000 years ago. The Han leader, Liu Bang, was defeated many times, yet after each defeat, he always got back on his feet and made statements to comfort the people following him and won their support. He thus managed to rise stronger after each defeat until winning the ultimate victory and the whole country.

In contrast, the Chu leader, Xiang Yu, achieved many victories initially, but each victory came at the cost of certain sacrifices and a certain degree of loosening up of his alertness. He thus became a little weaker after every battle until his final collapse when he cut his own throat by the Wujiang River after leaving his suiciding concubine, leaving behind only a famous historical legend of *Bawang Bieji*. Therefore, small victories in a short term, despite their importance as they may culminate in a big victory, do not automatically translate into big ones and the final result is only achieved with big and complete victories. Development strategies aim at ultimate victories and involve a series of progression from time to space. That is why development strategies all cover long terms.

Second, strategies are comprehensive. It is another important feature of development strategies in that they aim at ultimate, comprehensive but not local victories. Although a comprehensive victory is achieved by local wins and thus local victories cannot be overlooked, local wins may not replace a comprehensive one and only the one who achieves the comprehensive victory is the real victor. Therefore, when striding down the path to a comprehensive victory, we must be prepared for bumps and defeats and carefully learn the lesson when bumped and defeated with the attitude that "failures are the mother of successes" in order to fight again until the comprehensive victory.

Third, strategies cover multiple phases. In general, big strategies are usually divided into several phases with specific plans for each phase. No strategy aims to achieve the ultimate victory by one strike. For example, the strategy for our war against the Japanese invasion was divided into three phases of strategic defense, strategic stalemate, and strategic strike back. In each phase, a specific set of tactics and plans was adopted, e.g., we withdraw when the enemy advances, attack when he is weary, and pursue him when he withdraws, and the comprehensive victory was achieved ultimately. Now that we are implementing the strategy of sustainable development and that of reinvigorating China with science and education, several phases may also be introduced into the strategies so that we may make differential plans, goals, and means and paths for implementation in each phase.

I spent some time to explain the common features of strategies here because these features are also present in the strategy of population development, which should be evaluated by these three basic features. Of course, aside from these three, particular attention should also be given to population-specific features such as the size, the health, and the structure of a population and the relationships among them as well as between the population and the economy, social development, resources, and the environment. These all have close association with population, and thus restrain the strategy of population development. "One always loses something when gaining something." We should keep this in mind when making the strategy of population development. Our goal is to make and follow a development strategy that gains us the most and costs us the least.

If the strategy of population development is made according to the criteria and guidelines presented earlier, a good strategy may be decided on once the trend in future population changes is figured out. In fact, the trend in future changes of the Chinese population has already been detailed in a previous section on population policies, and three possible scenarios, the "hard landing" brought by the low projection, the "soft landing" brought by the medium projection, and the "slow landing" brought by the high projection, have been analyzed. Since development strategies are particularly concerned with long terms, comprehensive situations, and stage characteristics, the three projections should also be evaluated on how well they cover long terms, comprehensive situations, and stage characteristics.

The biggest advantage of the "hard landing" in the low projection is the remarkable effect of population control in that zero growth of the population would come a few years earlier than in the other projections, by which time the total population would be fewer by 70–80 million; meanwhile, remarkable progress would also be made on improvement in population health and the adjustment to the population structure. The biggest disadvantage is the excessively rapid changes in the population structure, especially the age structure, which would lead to growing social problems. Therefore, the "hard landing" of the low projection is too challenging for the society as it would bring strong negative effects on the normal progress of demographic, economic, and social development, and in particular, sustainable development.

In contrast to the "hard landing" brought by the low projection, the "slow landing" of the high projection is the most advantageous in terms of the slow, soft changes it would bring to the population age structure and the slow aging of the population. As a result, the "golden age" with a relatively high proportion of the working-age population and the associated "population benefits" and "population bonuses" would stay longer and help China maintain the advantage of low-cost laborers. The most prominent disadvantage, however, is poor population control in that the projected population is larger than the medium and low projections by 46 million and 105 million in 2020, respectively, and by 197 million and 407 million in 2050, respectively. For China's large population issue, this projection brings no fundamental changes, which thus is its fundamental problem, and cannot be adopted.

Compared to these two, the "soft landing" brought by the medium projection has both the advantage of effective population control in the "hard landing" of the low projection and the advantage of reasonable population structure, especially the age structure, in the "slow landing" of the high projection while at the same time avoiding the problems of the unreasonable population structure in the low projection and the poor population control in the high projection. As projected by the medium variant, the total population would reach 1.465 billion in 2030 and at the same time achieve zero growth, after which it would slowly decrease. The population would age at a medium speed in that 23.07% of the population would be 65 or above in 2050, after which the proportion would be stabilized with a slight reduction trend. In addition, as it already reached the peak of 74.5% in 2010 and has since been decreasing, the proportion of the working-age population of 15–54 would arrive at 67.42% in 2030 and 61.18% in 2050, at an annual reduction rate of 0.33 percentage points, which is in an acceptable range. Therefore, this scenario is the most appropriate for China's current population pattern and future changes in the population size toward a reasonable population structure, and it benefits the coordinated development between the population and the economy, the society, the resources, and the environment. To aim at the strategic goal of sustainable development for the population, the development strategy of the population should be based on the "soft landing" medium projection.

In summary, the guideline and the basic points of the development strategy of the Chinese population are as follows: guided by a scientific development concept that values comprehensiveness, coordination, and sustainability and through reasonable changes in the size, the health, and the structure of the population, the harmonious development of the population with the economy and the society is to be promoted, the relationships of the population with the resources and the environment are to be revised and optimized, and sustainable development for the population will eventually be realized. Such a guideline and basic points are similar to and show historical continuity from the population development strategy made in the early 1980s, i.e., "combining size control, health improvement, and structural adjustment of the population with the focus on the size control," since the new strategy is still concerned with size control while at the same time it shows a completely different picture that embodies the new characteristics of the present population changes. The first difference is in the guidelines: the most imperative task in the 1980s was to lower the high speed of population growth as soon as possible to alleviate and gradually eliminate the pressure of the population and laborers in surplus; in contrast, it is now imperative to include population control in the vision of scientific development to push the implementation of sustainable development for the population.

The second difference is that it used to "focus on size control" while it is now important to balance many other aspects, especially the population age structure with continued size control so that population development will transition step by step to improvement in the population health and structural adjustment. The third difference is in the strategic goals: we were at the "first step" of the population development strategy in the 1980s, when the primary task was to bring the fertility rate below the replacement level; we are now at the "second step" aimed at zero growth while concerned with the long-term, actually centennial, goal of an all-around moderate population. Therefore, the entire population strategy may be implemented according to the "three steps" while each step is connected to the next so that the strategic goals, focuses, and measures taken in all the steps are associated as well as differentiated, making each step a continuous yet integrative part to the whole strategy.

THE "THREE STEPS" OF THE POPULATION DEVELOPMENT STRATEGY

Since the 1970s, the global birth and growth rates have shown a slow decrease trend which has continued well into the 21st century. The decrease is particularly severe in the post-industrialization countries and all the concerns about excessively low fertility rates, insufficient supplies of laborers, and serious population aging have been validated. Therefore, voices on elevating fertility and birth rates and increasing population are raised from time to time and echoed by some. Of course, more are opposed to the suggestions mostly out of the following reasons.

First, most countries with below-replacement fertility rates and negative population growth are developed ones. In 2010, 1.237 billion people lived in developed countries, accounting for only 17.90% of the world's 6.909 billion people then, and changes to these countries would have very limited effect on the world population. In contrast, as many as 5.671 billion people lived in developing countries, accounting for 82.10% of the world population, and thus the trend in the world population would be primarily decided by developing countries.

Second, there is still a strong growth of population in developing countries. From 2010 to 2015, the birth rate of developing countries was 21.2‰, the death rate 7.9‰, and the growth rate 1.28‰. Although somewhat lower than before, the numbers still show characteristics of the population type of high birth, low death, and high growth and bear strong energy for growth.

Third, the growth trend in the world population in the long run is still to be continued. It has been projected that the TFR of the world population, 2.62 from 2010 to 2015, will decrease to 2.28 from 2025 to 2030 and to 2.05, which is below the replacement level, from 2045 to 2050. The total population, 6.115 billion in 2000, will increase to 7.675 billion in 2020 and 9.150 billion in 2050 accordingly, and it will reach zero growth and be stabilized in 2100 when approaching 10 billion.[6] Therefore, controlling the size of the world population remains a common problem for humankind, which may not be overlooked when sustainable development is boosted globally.

Compared to the world population, the Chinese population has similarities as well as differences. China has the largest population in the world and will pass on the seat of the "largest country by population" around 2030. The population problems in China are essentially a surplus in population and of laborers, i.e., the problem of the population oppressing the forces of production. Through the efforts of controlling the population in the past 30 to 40 years while the economy was fast growing, the problem has been bettered and solved to a degree. However, it has not been solved completely as China is still a country of medium incomes. Although it has passed the threshold of the medium-high level and is slightly higher than most developing countries, the income in China is still some distance away from the world average, $10,000, and it will take a considerable period of time for China to walk out of the medium-income trap. It will also take some time for China to reach zero growth and even longer to realize an all-around moderate population. Therefore, I have always persisted with the following points: great efforts are still needed to control the size of the Chinese population in order to solve the population problem while at the same time improvement in the population health and structural adjustment should be pushed for with the tactic of a combination of "control," "improvement," and "adjustment"; however, the focus may differ in different stages and eventually the population size, health, and structure will all be reasonable while the population is coordinated with socioeconomic development and with the resources and the environment, transmitting positive energies from the population side to the effective implementation of the strategies of reinvigorating China with science and education and sustainable development.

Based on these points, three steps may be taken to implement a population development strategy that covers a long term, all-around development, and multiple stages. At the first step, tactics and policies aim at controlling the size, improving the health, and adjusting the structure of the population while size control is the most important. The goal is to lower the high fertility rate until it is below the replacement level so that the population reproduction transitions from high births, low deaths, and high growth to low births, low deaths, and low growth. At the second step, after the fertility rate is below the replacement level and before the population reaches zero growth, i.e., during the post-demographic transition, tactics that combine the "control," the "improvement," and the "adjustment" are continued so that population development transitions from size control to health improvement and especially to structural adjustment step by step; meanwhile, the relationships of population changes with socioeconomic development and with resources and the environment are coordinated to push for sustainable development.

At the third step, the population reaches zero growth and after that, it will show a decrease trend due to momentum; then a strategic decision is to be made for an all-around moderate population according to the economic, social, resource, and environmental conditions at the time. An all-around moderate population does not only mean a moderate number of people, but also good health, a reasonable structure of age, sex, and urban–rural and geographic distribution, coordination with resource, environmental, economic, and social development, and support for the country's strategy of sustainable development.

The first step of the "three-step" strategy of population development has already been finished, which was marked by the entrance of the post-demographic transition when China's TFR descended to 1.98, a below-replacement level, in 1991; by that time, the population reproduction had transitioned from high births, low deaths, and high growth to low births, low deaths, and low growth. We are now halfway through the second step, which is predicted to be finished around 2030 when we will march to the third step. We must understand that the "three-step" strategy of population development is closely associated with the Chinese dream of realizing the great revival of the Chinese nation, with the current mode transformation, structural adjustment, and reform promotion, and with the development goal of informatization, industrialization, urbanization, and agricultural modernization – the new four modernizations – and must be advanced without reserve.

The current vital "second step"

We are currently at the second step of the "three-step" strategy of population development and in the middle phase of the post-demographic transition. It is a key step that continues what has been achieved before and starts what is to be done in the future. To continue what has been achieved, the implementation of the policies, which experienced the course that the strategy became gradually clear and went from the advocacy of one child per couple to two children for all, is vital. To start what is to be done in the future, it decides whether we will glide through the post-demographic transition safely, whether the adjustment to the population policies will be thorough and complete, and whether the goal of an all-around moderate population will be realized. Therefore, the second step is the key to the overall "three-step" strategy, and we must deepen our understanding, position to the right direction and goals, and master the speed and rhythm of the progress to walk through the entire second step with resolution.

Position to the right direction and goals

The temporal coverage of the strategy of sustainable development is as long as the unlimited "time series" and its spatial coverage is as wide as the unlimited "universe space"; therefore, it is a must to associate the second step of the population development strategy with the post-demographic transition and to include them in the concept of sustainable development. A safe walk through the second step and completion of the post-demographic transition will lead the population development to shift from population control to health improvement and particularly to structural adjustment while size control is also taken into account, which will then lay a solid foundation for realizing the all-around moderate population that is agreeable with the sustainability of the population, the resources, the environment, the economy, and the society, showing the features of long-term coverage, all-around development, and multiple phases.

That is also to say, the direction and the goals of the second step should be that zero growth of the population is reached, the health greatly improved, and the structure more and more reasonable, and a solid foundation is laid for the third step, which will lead to an all-around moderate population. In fact, improving population health is an eternal theme and is reasonable and clear at any time and in any stage. Therefore, the task at the second step is really to push the strategic focus to transition from size control to health improvement, and it emphasizes the shift of the strategic focus, which is to add weight to population health, science and education, and the construction and development of the population's civility. However, the most important shift in the post-demographic transition at the second step is to the focus on structural adjustment, the shift from focusing on size control to structural adjustment.

Why is that? It is because the focus was on controlling population size at the first step of the population development strategy, which has resulted in long-term decreases in birth and growth rates, an increasingly aging structure of the population, a transition from increases to decreases in the supply of laborers, and considerable impact on the population structure, including the sex structure, the employment structure, the urban–rural distribution, and the geographic distribution. It is now imperative to face and solve these problems with great care and effort, and the strategic focus of the second step must target them.

However, when the strategic focus is on improving population health and in particular the structural adjustment, it does not mean that population size is not important any more. On the contrary, size control needs continued attention so that zero growth will eventually be reached in 2030. At present, with the changing climate in the demographic policies, voices have been raised to cool down the heat of population control. Some believe that the fertility rate in China is already extremely low and cannot be any lower, and it is therefore imperative to put a stop to the policy that controls population growth until the basic state policy of family planning is completely abandoned to keep our top rank by population. They argue that population is a country's basic strength and bears creators of wealth and that the advantage of having the largest population must be kept. Some are so progressive as to deny and sometimes even defy all theories and opinions on population control, the basic state policy of family planning, and the demographic policies. It is therefore not surprising when people say it is now time again to discuss whether China has too large or too small a population.

Then does China have a too large or too small population? What tactics and policies are needed? It now seems that we have to get back to demography 101 and answer these questions from theoretical and practical levels.

THEORETICAL ANSWERS

From the theoretical perspective, it is essentially the fundamental difference between populism and abstinence. The present debate on too large or too small a population is to some degree a recapitulation of the debate on and criticism of Ma Yinchu's new population theory in the late 1950s. At the center of the theoretical analysis is whether humans – and humankind for that matter – are producers or consumers. Some take the former as more basic to humankind and some the latter; thus the two sides cannot be reconciled. In fact, it is already clearly sorted out in demographic economics: humans, when analyzed as a whole in economic activities, are not solely consumers or solely producers, but both consumers and producers. However, they are consumers unconditionally and all are consumers in that no matter whether they are young, adults, or elderly and whether healthy or disabled, everyone is a consumer. In contrast, one must meet a certain condition to be a producer, and the condition is set in demographic economics as being 15–59 or 15–64. People of these age groups are of the working-age population and also laborers. Except for a few who are disabled and cannot work, all may grow up into a normal laborer and become a real one. Therefore, the new births each year are first additions to consumers and they will only be transformed into members of the working-age population after 14 years.

In this sense, analyses of increases and decreases in population shall take the perspectives of unification, differentiation, and association of people as producers and consumers without unilateral focus on either side. What is pivotal is to make concrete, layered, and stage-specific analyses based on appropriate socioeconomic situations and then an answer may be made to whether the population is too large or too small. Of course, once the answer is found, demographic policies, including fertility policies, must also be adjusted accordingly to orient toward encouragement or control of population reproduction.

PRACTICAL ANSWERS

The answers may also be found from the 1.375 billion population in China now and the economic, social, resource, and environmental situations. In fact, the earlier section on population policies has already offered a full account of the situation. What needs reiteration is that a decision should be made based on practical situations by the goal of sustainable development for the population. According to statistics and relevant data, the population density in China was 145 per square kilometers (km^2) in 2014, 258.9% of the world average, the GDP per capita (USD per person) 70.3%, the per capita area of arable lands 33.5%, the per capita possession of fresh water 31.9%, the per capita area of territorial seas 10.0%, the per capita area of forest 13.0%, and the per capita area of grassland 50.0%.

As for fossil energy resources such as oil and natural gas and mineral resources such as iron, manganese, and copper, the total amounts and per capita amounts have decreased by a large scale and a severe shortage of these resources made us dependent on imports; meanwhile, pollution of air, water, soil, and noise is still increasing, approaching the limit of what the ecosystem can take. In fact, the reforms to change the economic mode and make structural adjustment have been extremely difficult because, aside from problems in the economic system, there is a large population in China and the population with its laborers has levied a lot of pressure on the forces of production.[7]

For example, after the financial crisis broke out in the United States in 2008, the Chinese government sought to maintain the economic growth rate at about 8.0% for consecutive years, which was jokingly called the "old Eighth Route Army" in pertinent fields. What lies behind the joke is that "maintaining economic growth is to maintain employment rate." That is because it has been shown by analyses that with every 1.0 percentage point decrease in the economic growth rate comes a 0.5 percentage point increase in the unemployment rate; therefore, to maintain stability and contain unemployment, economic growth must be maintained.

In 2015, the national birth rate was 12.07‰ with 16.55 million new births; this cohort would become part of the working-age population 14 years later except for those deceased prematurely and shape the employment rate at the time from the supply side. If the largest country by population rank is to be kept and we have really too small a population, reproduction-encouraging policies may even be released and the pressure on the job market will continue with possible increases, setting more barriers to the economic mode transition, structural adjustment, and improvement in the labor efficiency, which will negatively impact the healthy development of the economy.

The logic here is straightforward. Labor efficiency is the most important and the primary weapon with which a new institution defeats an old one and is thus the touchstone to test institutions. Meanwhile, it is common sense that labor efficiency is positively proportional to the technological equipment of laborers and inversely to the number of laborers. In fact, modern economies have long abandoned the development mode that relies on the number of laborers and now rely on improvement in labor efficiency for development. Although China has made proud accomplishments with a consecutively speeding economy, the mode of economic development is still far behind with low labor efficiency, and that is a major setback. It is true that fairly fast progress has been made on the improvement in labor efficiency for the past 30 to 40 years, which deserves positive comments; however, the efficiency is still low and has not been fundamentally revised, and that is also true.

At present, the labor efficiency in China is lower than one-tenth of that in the United States and Japan, lower by a considerable scale than other post-industrial countries, and even lower than some developing countries in Asia and South America. There are many reasons behind the low efficiency. On one side, science and technology have not been widely applied in labor, laborers do not master all techniques, management is underdeveloped, and raw materials as the subjects of labor and their quality are questionable. On the other side, there are the problems of how many laborers are available, how technically trained they are, and how good the industry reservoirs are.

Both sides work on efficiency while the number of laborers, their techniques, and the industry reservoirs are more basic than others. In the past, there were almost unlimited supplies of laborers in China, which in effect greatly inhibited advancement in technology and improvement in labor efficiency. In 2010, the working-age population passed the Lewis turning point, and its number and proportion both declined. However, due to a large baseline number of people and that of women of reproductive age, more than 15 million births occur every year and an additional 3 million every year now as two children are allowed for each couple; therefore, employment pressure will be present for a long time. Some may present the phenomenon of the "shortage of peasant workers," which has always been used as a powerful line of evidence for a shortage of laborers and a population that is too small. Following the evidence, they then advocate for abolishment of the basic state policy of family planning and issuance of reproduction-encouraging policies. However, let us not forget that the "shortage of peasant workers" showed up at the same time with difficulty in finding jobs for college graduates and the latter has become even more serious. This proves that the "shortage of peasant workers" is due to a structural shortage of laborers, not a shortage of their total number.

For quite some time, the happiness index has become popular, which spills on the objective of the population production and reproduction from a certain side. On November 15, 2012, Xi Jinping, recently elected secretary-general, together with the other newly elected members of the Standing Committee of the Central Political Bureau of the CCCPC on the First Plenary Session of the 18th CCCPC, held a press conference with domestic and foreign journalists. At the conference, Xi Jinping said, "people's pursuit of a happy life is what we struggle for," and it was enthusiastically applauded. People's pursuit of a happy life touches on a variety of material, mental, environmental, and social aspects, and each aspect includes several layers; therefore, each aspect and each layer are associated with population size, health, and structure to a certain degree and have a certain degree of impact on the happiness index. Dominant indicators show the close association between the happiness index and the population situation, e.g., per capita income, possession of enduring consumer goods, and pollution index of the living environment, where the number of people of the population usually assumes the role of a denominator, while there are also recessive, emotion indicators that are not quantifiable, for which reason they are often ignored, but they are influential on the changes in the happiness index as people are always surrounded by them. Therefore, studies of the relationship between population and environment and between population and sustainable development should perhaps spend some time on the emotion indicators by examining the happiness index that can be actually felt by people.

Allow me to give you an example from my own experiences. Between the United States that is vast in land and sparse in population and Japan that is narrow in land and crowded in population, the happiness indices measured by the recessive, emotion indicators are completely different, actually as different as ice and fire. In 2012, the land area of the United States was 983.2 km^2, accounting for 7.32% of the world's land, the population was 332 million, accounting for 4.61% of the world population, and the GDP was $15.6848 trillion, accounting for 21.87% of the global GDP. In contrast, Japan had 37.8 km^2 land area, accounting for 0.28% of the world's land, 128 million people, accounting for 1.78% of the global population, and $5.9640 trillion GDP, accounting for 8.32% of the world's GDP.[8]

The economic density per population (GDP per person) was $47,243.37 in the United States and $46,593.75 in Japan, which were quite similar; however, the geo-economic density (GDP per 10,000 km^2) was $15.953 billion in the United States and $157.778 billion in Japan, the latter being 9.89 times as much as the former. Apparently, Japan has a very high geo-economic density. Based on such a high density, clusters after clusters of cities, rows after rows of factories, webs of railways, roads, air routes, and highly intensive industrialization, informatization, and economic globalization all together resulted in the per capita GDP and the income that were similar to that of the United States.

What is not similar is that the United States has more countryside-associated cities that are dispersed from one another despite Tokyo-like high-rise city clusters such as New York. For example, the city clusters centered on Chicago and Los Angeles are typical of the dispersed city groups. In these cities, there are rarely the narrow, noisy, and crowded subways that are common in Japanese cities or living environments that lack leisure space and that are thus suffocating; instead, spacious houses in the countryside and sufficient leisure space such as parks and lakes are everywhere, and people drive in most places except for in extremely large cities, winning the residents the title of people living on automobile wheels in an automobile kingdom.

Not surprising, many Japanese complain about inability to buy bigger houses, wider roads, and more comfortable living environments no matter how much money one possesses unless he lives in the northernmost and southernmost parts of the four main islands of Japan – Kyushu and Hokkaido – where he may enjoy slightly more space. However, it is always difficult to leave your hometown, and with increasing population migration and flow, the slightly bigger space is also changing.

Americans are different in that they are confident that as long as they have the money, everyone may obtain houses as large and as luxurious as they want where they may play tennis, swim, and hold masquerade parties. Further, many like to integrate a modern lifestyle into the primitive ecosystem to enjoy a free life that has no restraints and is close to nature.

China's current GDP per capital is about one-sixth of those in the United States and Japan, and China is expected to become an advanced country to a medium degree, with a further goal to reach the level of highly advanced countries. No one has cast doubt on the goal that sets us on the path to become richer and richer when we move on to every next stage. However, which kind of rich lives do we choose, the American or the Japanese? Which kind is the real pursuit of ours for a happy life? I'm afraid the American style of rich lives is not possible for we have a land similar in area to the United States but the population ratio of China to the United States is 1.37462 billion:332.33 million, or 4.1:1.0. Therefore, the kind of urbanization, i.e., what has resulted in the city circles centered on Chicago and Los Angeles with free access to natural resources such as land, forest, and grassland, is not possible for China, where industrialization and urbanization may not touch natural resources arbitrarily because economical energy use and environmental protection have become China's basic state policy.

In principle, industrialization, urbanization, informatization, and agricultural modernization must all be conducted in an intensive way and saving on natural resources such as land and in particular arable lands is a basic state policy that no one can be waved from. In fact, Japan is rich in experiences in this aspect for us to borrow, and China actually has a slightly more favorable condition than Japan in that the densities of factories, mines, and transport webs are lower. Nonetheless, an intensive mode of development is a must when sustainable development is considered that takes into account all aspects and every choice must be made within the frame. To realize sustainable development, controlling the population growth and family planning must be persisted with as basic state policies, as well as the "three-step" strategy of population development and the strategy of sustainable development for the population, the resources, the environment, the economy, and the society. Therefore, the seat of the largest country by population should not be occupied forever by us and the basic state policy of family planning may not be abandoned; neither should any policy be issued to encourage reproduction.

Mastering the speed and the rhythm of walking the second step

The speed and the rhythm by which the second step is being taken, especially of the progress to zero population growth and the structural adjustment, must be well controlled and mastered in order to realize the goals of the step, i.e., the strategy of population development transitions from the phase of size control to that of health improvement and in particular structural adjustment, revise and optimize the relationships of the population with the resources, the environment, the economy, and the society, and to lay a solid foundation for the transition to the third step when an all-around moderate population is met.

THE SPEED AND THE RHYTHM OF WALKING TO ZERO GROWTH OF THE POPULATION

As I am writing this, it happens to be the long weekend of May 1. News of how a variety of attraction sites have been packed with visitors frequents the reports by central and regional television stations as the holiday unfolds. On Tian'anmen Square, jostling crowds stand shoulder to shoulder and toe to heel and it is almost impossible to take a snap with the Tian'anmen Gate and without anyone else. People reluctantly have their photos taken with strangers, who are also having their photos taken with other strangers. After passing the Tian'anmen Gate and walking to the little square before the Wumen Gate, one has to wait in a long line in order to enter the Palace Museum which has a limit of the maximum number of visitors allowed. In fact, such a practice is quite common in many famous attractions in Shanghai, Jinan, Nanjing, Hangzhou, Wuhan, Guangzhou, Chongqing, Kunming, and Xi'an as it is a dear lesson learned from previous stampede accidents, and it has to be adopted for safety reasons in spite of reduction in the revenue from admissions. In addition, in those famous attractions such as Qiao's Grand Courtyard in Shanxi, the Qinhuai River in Nanjing, the Broken Bridge in West Lake of Hangzhou, the Shaolin Monastery in Songshan Mountain of Henan, the Pavilion of Prince Teng in Nanchang, Jiangxi, the Yellow Crane Tower in Wuhuan, the Huangshi Village in Zhangjiajie, Hunan, the Jiuzhaigou National Park in Sichuan, the Terracotta Army of the First Emperor of China in Xi'an, and the Old Town of Lijiang in Yunnan, there are so many visitors as to form mountains and seas of people and everyone has to only move slowly following the crowd ahead.

On the Great Wall, visitors build a new wall of people. The Huangshan Mountain and the Crucian Carp Back of the Emeishan Mountain are filled with people who tremble and arch their backs while trying to climb up. On the steep and slow Shibapans of the Taishan Mountain, people move up like worms and stay back to rib with complaints from the young and the elderly alike. When all these things happen, can anyone feel the relief and pleasure as described by Ouyang Xiu (1007–1072) in *On the Zuiweng Pavilion*? Also a visitor, Ouyang Xiu wrote in *On the Zuiweng Pavilion* that

> those carrying heavy loads on their backs sang while walking, and those hiking up rested by trees; someone called from ahead and someone echoed from behind; people arched their backs and held on to each other. Visitors came group after group, and they were all from Chu to come for a visit.
>
> When the sun rises, the mist in the wood disperses; when the clouds come back, the rocky caves in the mountain look dim; from brightness

> to darkness there goes a day from morning to evening in the mountain. Wild flowers blossom with fragrance, fine trees stand beautiful and cast thick shades; white and clear frost comes with wind; when water subsides, rocks emerge, and there go the four seasons in the mountain … the drunk old man is not drunk of liquor, but of the scenes among the mountain and the water.

Now every place is packed with tourists, and how complicated it feels when one recites the descriptions of a relieved, pleased mind of a tourist written by an ancient intellectual. Then a question, which has haunted me for a long time, occurs to me again: is the unlimited growth of the population in line with or opposite the pursuit of a happy life? Shall we help populism take an exit off the historical stage or shall we reinvigorate people's desire for reproduction?

My conclusion is this: it is difficult for populism to exit the historical stage since the traditional concept that equates multiple sons with a multitude of fortunes needs a prolonged time to wean, and it is unwise to reinvigorate people's desire for reproduction since it is against the pursuit of a happy life. The intuitive feelings are from all the scenes described earlier, which tell us that we should follow a path that leads to coexistence, co-survival, and coordinated development of the population and nature, that we should follow but not violate the objective rules of nature, and that this should be a mark and a reasonable choice for modern human civilization.

For China at the second step of the strategy of population development, the most important is to follow the direction and objectives of what has been set for the step and to find a good speed and rhythm to walk in the direction with determination. With a clear direction and objectives, how good the speed and the rhythm are is pivotal to the consequences of the strategy implementation. The 1.375 billion people is too large a population for China, but it by no means requires a population as small as possible or a decrease in the growth rate as fast as possible. In fact, it is one thing that the population is too large, and it is entirely another when it comes to how to control population growth, how much reduction is needed, and which tactics, policies, and plans are needed.

When a population is too large, control and reduction are needed; however, as changes in the number of people are correlated to those in the population age structure, the reduction must meet the demand for a reasonable age structure and be affordable for socioeconomic development. The reduction in the birth rates, births, and natural growth rates must be controlled within a reasonable range while a fast linear drop in these indicators should be avoided to stay away from unnecessary negative impacts. To reach the goal that the natural growth rate of the population should be lowered to zero by 2030, the following scheme may be adopted while the reduction in the natural changes of the population is brought about.

The birth rate may be lowered to 11.96‰ in 2020, which will be 0.11 permillage points lower than that in 2015, 12.07‰, at an average annual rate of 0.02 permillage points. The death rate may increase to 8.18‰, higher by 1.07 permillage points than that in 2015, 7.11‰, at an average annual rate of 0.21 permillage points. The natural growth rate may be reduced to 3.78‰, lower by 1.18 permillage points than that in 2015, 4.96‰, at an average annual rate of 0.24 permillage points. The faster increase in the death rate is primarily due to the fast aging of the population and that the elderly population has a higher death rate than other cohorts.

In 2025, the birth rate may be lowered to 10.41‰, which will be 1.55 permillage points lower than that in 2020 at an average annual rate of 0.31 permillage points. The death rate may increase to 9.08‰, higher by 0.9 permillage points than that in 2020 at an average annual rate of 0.18 permillage points. The natural growth rate may be reduced to 1.33‰, lower by 2.45 permillage points than that in 2020 at an average annual rate of 0.49 permillage points.

In 2030, the birth rate may be lowered to 9.89‰, which will be 0.52 permillage points lower than that in 2025 at an average annual rate of 0.10 permillage points. The death rate may increase to 10.07‰, higher by 0.98 permillage points than that in 2025 at an average annual rate of 0.20 permillage points. The natural growth rate may be reduced to −1.09‰, lower by 2.42 permillage points than that in 2025 at an average annual rate of 0.48 permillage points.

This scheme divides the 15 years between 2015 and 2030 into three five-year periods. During each five-year period, the natural changes in the population walk down a step so that the birth rates, death rates, and the natural growth rates do not change drastically while there are remarkable changes when all are added up. In this way, the zero growth of the population will be realized in 2030 when the population will negatively grow.[9]

THE SPEED AND THE RHYTHM OF THE POPULATION STRUCTURAL CHANGES

The speed and the rhythm need to be kept in control to bring about the changes in the population age structure, sex ratio, urban and rural distribution, and geographic distribution. The high sex ratio at birth is a prominent problem of the population's sex structure. Many measures have been taken over the years in attempts to contain the high ratio, but they have not been effective.

Now that the "two-but-not-three" adjustment has been made to the fertility policy, the probability for people to have both a boy and a girl, as dictated by the natural laws of reproduction, is considerably elevated, and the sex ratio at birth is expected to drop to a level that is slightly higher than the normal value with a somewhat speedy rhythm. The geographic distribution of the population is going through a profound change with the implementation of the strategy to develop the west, reinvigorate the northeast, and boost the middle area in that the old distribution pattern is broken and a new one is being formed. It is noteworthy that the new pattern is dominated by the market and that it thus has a solid foundation. However, the changes in the geographic distribution of the population are overall limited, and except for some special

Table 8.1 Projections of the population age structure, 2015–2030 (%)

s	*0–14*	*15–64*	*65+*
2015	17.60	71.90	10.50*
2020	18.97	69.00	12.04
2025	18.01	68.30	13.69
2030	16.35	67.42	16.23

Note: *The 2015 data are from the communiqué of the National Bureau of Statistics and the first two cohorts are in fact aged 0–15 and 16–64.

cases – the emigration of the residents in the Three Gauges Dam area, for example – that need direct mediation of society, the speed and the rhythm of most changes are dominated by market rules and need no further artificial mediation. Next are some supplementary discussions on the adjustments to the age and urban–rural structures of the population.

First, the speed and the rhythm of the population age structure are described here. According to my predictions, the approximate speed and rhythm of the changes in the age structure of the population at the second step are as follows (Table 8.1).[10]

As shown in Table 8.1, from 2015 to 2030, among the cohorts of those aged 0–14, 15–64, and 65 and higher, the first two show overall declines in their proportions while the elderly at 65 and higher show increases with rather smooth changes in all the three cohorts of the young, adults, and the elderly. However, the changes are in smaller scales in the first few years compared to the last and they are most evident after 2025. If the changes in the age structure of the population may be maintained within the predictions here, there will be no big problems and they are also acceptable to the population as well as to socioeconomic development.

Second, the speed and the rhythm of the urban–rural distribution of the population needs attention. In fact, many descriptions were already made previously in this book and three points are reiterated here.

In the first place, the speed and the rhythm of urbanization must be overall in good control. At present, moderate speeding of the population urbanization is actually necessary, but the speed and the rhythm must be well controlled. Both the horizontal expansion of cities like "spreading the dough to make a big pita" and the vertical expansion that blindly fosters high-rise buildings are to be contained.

In the second place, the speed and the rhythm of transforming agricultural population into urban residents must be well controlled. While improving the level of the population urbanization with differential guidelines according to different conditions, the barriers for the peasant workers to become equal urban residents must be removed one by one so that the urbanization is oriented toward people and both human development and socioeconomic development are synchronized.

In the third place, the speed and the rhythm of the changes in the scales of small-, medium-, and large-sized cities must be well controlled. We are currently at the second phase of urbanization and the population is flowing from small- and medium-sized cities to large-sized ones, which is in line with natural principles. However, the migration and the transfer of the population should be based on the upgrade and adjustments of urban economic structures, but not on arbitrary upgrades or administrative orders of population migration and transfer. We must recognize the objective pattern of the current direction of population migration at the second phase of urbanization while at the same time mastering the problems and harms of the current arbitrary upgrade of urbanization and population transfer in order to maintain the right speed and rhythm of the upgrade and the transfer.

Third, the speed and the rhythm of the sustainable development for the population, the environment, the resources, the economy, and the society must be well controlled. To walk through the second step of sustainable development for the population, we need to maintain the right speed and rhythm of our own development and changes while mastering the speed and the rhythm of the progression of the sustainable development for the population, the environment, the resources, the economy, and the society. Based on practical conditions, on one hand, we need to acknowledge the great achievements since the implementation of the basic state policies of saving on resources and protecting the environment and the elevation of the status of sustainable development in people's minds, and on the other hand, we must face the many problems that are fundamental to the incoordination and unsustainability of the development of the population, the resources, the environment, the economy, and the society and thus there is a long way to go for sustainable development. However, as long as we persist with the strategy of sustainable development for the population and make scientific and reasonable policies timely that will be strictly enforced, the road of a big country will emerge before us and the great revival of the Chinese nation will one day become true.

Notes

1 Age of Iron (Human Historical Ages), Baidu Encyclopedia, http://baike.baidu.com, May 2016.
2 United Nations, *World Population Prospects: The 2008 Revision*, New York, 2009, p. 48.
3 Zhang, Weiqing, Sun, Wensheng, and Xie, Zhenhua, eds., *Readings for Cadres on the Sustainable Development of Population, Resources, and the Environment*, Hangzhou, Zhejiang People's Publishing House, 2004, pp. 171–187.
4 *China Statistical Yearbook 1986*, China Statistics Press, 1986, pp. 91, 296; National Bureau of Statistics, *Statistical Communiqué 2015*.
5 www.baidu.com, May 2016.
6 United Nations, *World Population Prospects*, pp. 48–52.
7 *China Statistical Yearbook 2015*, China Statistics Press, pp. 961–966; Zhang, Sun, and Xie, *Readings for Cadres*, pp. 171–187.

8 *China Statistical Yearbook 2013*, China Statistics Press, pp. 953–956; United Nations, *World Population Prospects*, pp. 48, 292, 494.
9 Tian, Xueyuan, et al., *A Study on the Strategy of China's Population Development in the 21st Century*, Beijing, Social Sciences Academic Press (China), pp. 451–452.
10 Ibid., p. 451.

Bibliography

Agenda 21, United Nations Environment and Development Conference 1992, translated by National Environmental Protection Bureau, Beijing, China Environmental Science Press, 1993.

Brown, Lester R., *Plan B: Rescuing a Planet under Stress and a Civilization in Trouble*, translated by Lin, Zixin, et al., Beijing, Oriental Publishing House, 2003.

Chen, Jian, ed., *Report on China's Reform 2013*, Law Press, 2013.

China's Agenda 21: White Paper on China's Population, Environment and Development in the 21st Century, Beijing, China Environmental Science Press, 1994.

Decision by the Central Committee of the Communist Party of China on Several Major Issues about Comprehensively Deepening the Reform: From Assembly of Files of the 3rd Plenary Sessions of CCCPC since the Reform and Opening-Up, Beijing, People's Publishing House, 2013.

Durant, Will, *The Story of Civilization: Our Oriental Heritage*, Beijing, Huaxia Publishing House, 2010.

Engels, Friedrich, *Origin of the Family, Private Property, and the State: From Selected Works of Marx and Engels*, vol. 4, Beijing, People's Publishing House, 2012.

Fridtjof Nansen Institute, ed., *Green Global Yearbook 2001/2002*, translated by the Department of International Collaboration, National Environmental Protection Bureau, Beijing, China Environmental Science Press, 2002.

Gerontology Society of China, *Gerontology and Gerontic Problems in the 21st Century*, Beijing, China Labor and Social Security Publishing House, 2000.

Harari, Noah Yuval, *Sapiens: A Brief History of Humankind*, translated by Lin, Junhong, Beijing, Critic Press Group, 2014.

He, Chuanqi, *Modern Science: The Scientific Principle of an Advanced Country*, Beijing, Science Press, 2010.

National Population and Family Planning Commission, ed., *China's Population and History of Family Planning*, Beijing, China Population Publishing House, 2007.

Ouyang, Song, and Gao, Yongzhong, eds., *An Oral History of the Reform and Opening-Up*, Beijing, China Renmin University Press, 2007.

Pan, Jiahua, and Wei, Houkai, eds., *Report on China's Urban Development No. 6*, Beijing, Social Sciences Academic Press (China), 2013.

Selected Edition of Xi Jinping's Remarks on the Chinese Dream of Realizing the Great Revival of the Chinese Nation, Beijing, Central Party Literature Press, 2013.

Szombatfalvy, Laszlo, *The Greatest Challenges of Our Time*, translated by Zhou, Yamin, et al., Beijing, Central Compilation & Translation Bureau, 2012.

Stavrianos, Leften Stavros, *A Global History: From Prehistory to the 21st Century*, translated by Wu, Xiangying, et al., Beijing, Peking University Press, 2014.

Sun, Lujun, ed., *An Assembly of China's Policy Documents Concerning the Elderly*, Beijing, China Social Publishing House, 2009.

Thomas Henry Huxley, *Humanity's Place in Nature*, translated by Cai, Chongyang, et al., Beijing, Peking University Press, 2010.

Tian, Xueyua, et al., *A Study on the Strategy of China's Population Development in the 21st Century*, Beijing, Social Sciences Academic Press (China), 2007.
Tian, Xueyuan, ed., *Population Aging and the "Middle Income Trap,"* Beijing, Social Sciences Academic Press (China), 2013.
United Nations, *Long-Range World Population Projections: Based on the 1998 Revision*, New York, 2000.
United Nations, *Population and Development*, New York, 2001.
United Nations, *World Population Prospects: The 2008 Revision*, New York, 2009.
United Nations, *World Population Projections: Two Centuries of Population Growth 1950–2150*, New York, 1998.
Wang, Xiaolu, "The Route of China's Urbanization and Economic Analysis on City Scales," *Economic Research Journal*, vol. 10, 2010.
Wang, Yiming, "Adjustment and Transition: China's Economic Development in the Post-Financial Crisis Age," *Macroeconomics*, vol. 12, 2009.
Zhang, Kaidi, ed., *A Study on the Social Activities and Mental Conditions of China's Urban and Rural Elderly Population*, Beijing, China Social Publishing House, 2009.
Zhang, Weiqing, Sun, Wensheng, and Xie, Zhenhua, eds., *Readings for Cadres on the Sustainable Development of Population, Resources, and the Environment*, Hangzhou, Zhejiang People's Publishing House, 2004.
Zheng, Bingwen, and Sun, Yongyong, "Half Provinces Fail to Make Ends Meet of the Old-Age Insurance for Urban Employees," *Journal of Shanghai University*, vol. 3, 2012.

Index

Note: The page numbers in **bold** refer to tables and the page numbers in *italics* refer to figures.

For Product Safety Concerns and Information please contact our EU representative GPSR@taylorandfrancis.com
Taylor & Francis Verlag GmbH, Kaufingerstraße 24, 80331 München, Germany

www.ingramcontent.com/pod-product-compliance
Ingram Content Group UK Ltd.
Pitfield, Milton Keynes, MK11 3LW, UK
UKHW022006180926
475701UK00003B/221

* 9 7 8 0 3 6 7 7 2 7 8 8 8 *